COGNITIVE PSYCHOLOGY

SECOND EDITION

ADVANCED PSYCHOLOGY TEXTS

Lyle E. Bourne, Jr.
Series Editor

Advanced Psychology Texts (APT) is a series of intermediate but highly readable textbooks and monographs in the core areas of psychology. The primary objective of the series is to give undergraduate student majors and beginning graduate students in psychology a basis for evaluating the state of the science and a springboard into further guided or independent scholarship in a particular area. Each volume will center on the current issues and the basic concepts of a core content area of psychology. Students who use these books are expected to have some general background in the field. The textbooks take advantage of that background, building it into a sophisticated contemporary understanding of the facts and of the important yet-to-be answered questions. Each text focuses on recent developments and the implications of those developments for future research. Although the emphasis is on psychology as an evolving systematic scientific discipline, applications of basic research findings are also included. Authors have been asked to present clearly and thoughtfully what it is that each sub-area of psychology has to contribute to human knowledge and welfare.

Volume 1 *Skill Acquisition and Human Performance*
Robert W. Proctor and Addie Dutta

Volume 2 *Cognitive Psychology* (2nd edition)
Ronald T. Kellogg

Volume 3 *Motivation and Emotion*
David C. Edwards

Volume 4 *Human Genetics for the Social Sciences*
Gregory Carey

COGNITIVE PSYCHOLOGY
SECOND EDITION

RONALD T. KELLOGG
Saint Louis University

SAGE Publications
International Educational and Professional Publisher
Thousand Oaks ▪ London ▪ New Delhi

For information:

Sage Publications, Inc.
2455 Teller Road
Thousand Oaks, California 91320
E-mail: order@sagepub.com

Sage Publications Ltd.
6 Bonhill Street
London EC2A 4PU
United Kingdom

Sage Publications India Pvt. Ltd.
M-32 Market
Greater Kailash I
New Delhi 110 048 India

Printed in the United States of America

Library of Congress Cataloging-in-Publication Data

Kellogg, Ronald Thomas.
Cognitive psychology / Ronald T. Kellogg.— 2nd ed.
    p. cm. — (Advanced psychology texts; v. 2)
Includes bibliographical references and index.
ISBN 0-7619-2130-3 (alk. paper)
  1. Cognitive psychology. I. Title. II. Series.
BF201 .K45 2002
153—dc21

                        2002007104

This book is printed on acid-free paper.

03 04 05 06 10 9 8 7 6 5 4 3 2 1

Acquisitions Editor:	Jim Brace-Thompson
Editorial Assistant:	Karen Ehrmann
Production Editor:	Sanford Robinson
Copy Editor:	D. J. Peck
Interior Art:	Barry Burns and Nicholas Alexander
Typesetter:	C&M Digitals (P) Ltd., Chennai, India
Indexer:	Karen McKenzie
Cover Designer:	Michelle Lee

To Alicia and Kristin

BRIEF CONTENTS

CONTENTS

to serve as a core text in a graduate course in cognition. For advanced undergraduate or graduate courses, additional readings from the primary literature or specialized books could then supplement the book appropriate to the instructor's plans.

As in the first edition, I sought to provide a synthesis of cognitive psychology at its best rather than a chronicle of its arguments and conflicts. Certainly, the difficult struggle of cognitive approaches in psychology during the past 100 years deserves coverage, as do the many disagreements in contemporary theories and findings. But controversy can easily be overdone to the point of befuddling students. More advanced courses can dig deeper into the many controversies in the field by consulting the primary sources cited throughout the text or through supplemental readings assigned by the instructor.

For similar reasons, I avoided extensive discussions of the experimental methods on which findings are based. Although the methods are vitally important for researchers, too much focus on how an experiment was conducted can obscure the main point for students. Upper level undergraduates, and certainly graduate students, should supplement this text with readings in the primary literature. The original journal articles detail experimental designs, procedures, and materials.

I again sought to encapsulate the relevant background, theory, and research within each chapter. For example, details about the development of language, memory, and perception are covered in their respective chapters rather than being culled and packaged as cognitive development. Similarly, findings from cognitive neuroscience are frequently cited throughout the book. A significant change from the first edition, however, is an introduction to cognitive neuroscience in Chapter 2. The methods of cognitive neuroscience, particularly neuroimaging of the brain as a person perceives, attends, learns, remembers, and thinks, are far more prevalent and influential than they were in 1995. Understanding cognitive psychology and, more broadly, cognitive science now requires a deeper understanding of the brain than was the case in the past. Investigations of cognitive processes now routinely include or are based on studies of their neural correlates. The approach taken here is that cognition cannot be understood without reference to both its development and its biological bodily substrate.

Besides the addition of many new references, the second edition includes a new chapter on distortions of memory (Chapter 7). A substantial body of work has been done since 1995 on the encoding and retrieval processes involved in false memories, including applications of this basic research in police and court proceedings. Another new feature of this edition is to incorporate the applications previously discussed in boxes into the

PREFACE

Cognitive psychology has evolved over the past half century to become the dominant approach to virtually all aspects of human psychology. Its influence is strong in clinical, assessment, developmental, social, comparative, and physiological psychology, among other areas. Alternative approaches such as psychoanalysis, behaviorism, and humanistic psychology carry less force not only in psychology but in related fields as well. Linguistics, computer science, philosophy, anthropology, and the other sister disciplines of cognitive psychology are part of a remarkably encompassing and exciting enterprise known as cognitive science. The cognitive approach is now beginning, during the early years of the 21st century, to become so integrated into psychology as to be invisible and taken for granted.

It is important, therefore, for students of psychology as a whole to receive a solid introduction to the concepts of cognitive psychology. The aim of this book is to present a readable survey of the discipline. It is designed to meet the needs of instructors and students in introductory and advanced-level courses. It can be used as a primary text in lower division undergraduate courses in cognition, presenting the scope and methods of cognitive psychology in Part I and its foundational concepts in Part II. Selecting chapters from the subsequent sections to cover core concepts in long-term memory (Chapters 6 and 7), language (Chapter 10), and thinking (Chapters 13 or 14) might complete an introductory survey.

As a text for an advanced course in the field, instructors can add chapters as desired. For example, concept learning and the development of skills and expertise (Chapter 9) can be explored in addition to the basics of how concepts are represented in semantic memory (Chapter 8). Language comprehension (Chapter 12) can be studied by itself or in conjunction with a full treatment of speaking and writing (Chapter 11) in addition to listening and reading. The book concludes with an integrative chapter on intelligence (Chapter 15), showing the centrality of the discipline to a highly visible, important arena of psychology as a whole. The book as a whole is designed narrative of the text itself. Too often, students ignore the boxed material or regard it as unnecessary detail. Therefore, I selected the most important material and worked it into the story line of each chapter. Another important pedagogical feature of the second edition is the inclusion of margin notes. These notes summarize important concepts and ought to be of benefit in previewing and reviewing each chapter.

The book is divided into five sections. Part I introduces the discipline of cognitive psychology and cognitive neuroscience. I turn to the basic cognitive operations of perception, attention, and memory in Part II. Part III addresses acquiring and using knowledge and skill. Part IV covers language, its nature, and its use. Part V explores thinking skills and intelligence.

ACKNOWLEDGMENTS

No author composes a book alone. Many individuals helped with the first edition, and the list has now grown substantially longer with the second edition. Above all, I wish to thank Jim Brace-Thompson, senior editor at Sage Publications, who provided invaluable assistance and advice in planning the new edition and waited patiently for it to be born. Lyle E. Bourne, Jr., the series editor, critiqued the entire draft of the second edition and provided the encouragement to write the first edition.

The new edition continues to benefit from the many useful suggestions on the first edition provided by James Chumbley and Ira Fischler. I thank Michael E. J. Masson and James Chumbley for their careful critical reading of the entire manuscript for the second edition.

In addition to their contributions, numerous useful suggestions and criticisms on individual chapters were provided by Michael Anch, Terry Au, Russell Buhite, Thomas H. Carr, David C. Geary, Lewis O. Harvey, Paula Hertel, Donald Homa, Ken McRae, Akira Miyake, Lance Rips, Steven Sloman, John E. Taplin, and a few anonymous reviewers. I am indebted to their efforts to improve the book but take full responsibility for the final product.

The graphics in the new edition are a major addition to the book. Barry Burns crafted many informative and artful drawings to illustrate the ideas of the text. Barry's drawings are complemented by the skillful line drawings, graphs, and tables of Nicholas Alexander. Their images enhanced my words greatly. I thank them both for creating the essential visual communications of the text from my crude sketches.

The words as they appear here benefited from the careful copyediting of D. J. Peck. His dedicated attention to detail, consistency, and clarity is very much appreciated. I thank him for taking the student's perspective to improve the readability of the text.

Karen Ehrmann, Anna Howland, and Karen Wiley at Sage assisted with this edition. Special thanks are due to Karen Ehrmann, who worked hard at making sense of my minimal notations regarding graphics and permissions.

I also thank Darlene Turner, Alicia Kellogg, Kristin Kellogg, Adam Pollard, Kevin Kelley, Bridget Gregg, and Nancy Holt for their assistance in obtaining permissions and preparing the glossary and test bank questions.

Lastly, I thank my wife, Carol, for once again tolerating the long hours and frustrations involved in writing a book. Her steadfast support and encouragement throughout both editions made it all possible.

PREFACE

Cognitive psychology has evolved over the past half century to become the dominant approach to virtually all aspects of human psychology. Its influence is strong in clinical, assessment, developmental, social, comparative, and physiological psychology, among other areas. Alternative approaches such as psychoanalysis, behaviorism, and humanistic psychology carry less force not only in psychology but in related fields as well. Linguistics, computer science, philosophy, anthropology, and the other sister disciplines of cognitive psychology are part of a remarkably encompassing and exciting enterprise known as cognitive science. The cognitive approach is now beginning, during the early years of the 21st century, to become so integrated into psychology as to be invisible and taken for granted.

It is important, therefore, for students of psychology as a whole to receive a solid introduction to the concepts of cognitive psychology. The aim of this book is to present a readable survey of the discipline. It is designed to meet the needs of instructors and students in introductory and advanced-level courses. It can be used as a primary text in lower division undergraduate courses in cognition, presenting the scope and methods of cognitive psychology in Part I and its foundational concepts in Part II. Selecting chapters from the subsequent sections to cover core concepts in long-term memory (Chapters 6 and 7), language (Chapter 10), and thinking (Chapters 13 or 14) might complete an introductory survey.

As a text for an advanced course in the field, instructors can add chapters as desired. For example, concept learning and the development of skills and expertise (Chapter 9) can be explored in addition to the basics of how concepts are represented in semantic memory (Chapter 8). Language comprehension (Chapter 12) can be studied by itself or in conjunction with a full treatment of speaking and writing (Chapter 11) in addition to listening and reading. The book concludes with an integrative chapter on intelligence (Chapter 15), showing the centrality of the discipline to a highly visible, important arena of psychology as a whole. The book as a whole is designed to serve as a core text in a graduate course in cognition. For advanced undergraduate or graduate courses, additional readings from the primary literature or specialized books could then supplement the book appropriate to the instructor's plans.

As in the first edition, I sought to provide a synthesis of cognitive psychology at its best rather than a chronicle of its arguments and conflicts. Certainly, the difficult struggle of cognitive approaches in psychology during the past 100 years deserves coverage, as do the many disagreements in contemporary theories and findings. But controversy can easily be overdone to the point of befuddling students. More advanced courses can dig deeper into the many controversies in the field by consulting the primary sources cited throughout the text or through supplemental readings assigned by the instructor.

For similar reasons, I avoided extensive discussions of the experimental methods on which findings are based. Although the methods are vitally important for researchers, too much focus on how an experiment was conducted can obscure the main point for students. Upper level undergraduates, and certainly graduate students, should supplement this text with readings in the primary literature. The original journal articles detail experimental designs, procedures, and materials.

I again sought to encapsulate the relevant background, theory, and research within each chapter. For example, details about the development of language, memory, and perception are covered in their respective chapters rather than being culled and packaged as cognitive development. Similarly, findings from cognitive neuroscience are frequently cited throughout the book. A significant change from the first edition, however, is an introduction to cognitive neuroscience in Chapter 2. The methods of cognitive neuroscience, particularly neuroimaging of the brain as a person perceives, attends, learns, remembers, and thinks, are far more prevalent and influential than they were in 1995. Understanding cognitive psychology and, more broadly, cognitive science now requires a deeper understanding of the brain than was the case in the past. Investigations of cognitive processes now routinely include or are based on studies of their neural correlates. The approach taken here is that cognition cannot be understood without reference to both its development and its biological bodily substrate.

Besides the addition of many new references, the second edition includes a new chapter on distortions of memory (Chapter 7). A substantial body of work has been done since 1995 on the encoding and retrieval processes involved in false memories, including applications of this basic research in police and court proceedings. Another new feature of this edition is to incorporate the applications previously discussed in boxes into the narrative of the text itself. Too often, students ignore the boxed material or regard it as unnecessary detail. Therefore, I selected the most important material and worked it into the story line of each chapter. Another important pedagogical feature of the second edition is the inclusion of margin notes. These notes summarize important concepts and ought to be of benefit in previewing and reviewing each chapter.

The book is divided into five sections. Part I introduces the discipline of cognitive psychology and cognitive neuroscience. I turn to the basic cognitive operations of perception, attention, and memory in Part II. Part III addresses acquiring and using knowledge and skill. Part IV covers language, its nature, and its use. Part V explores thinking skills and intelligence.

ACKNOWLEDGMENTS

No author composes a book alone. Many individuals helped with the first edition, and the list has now grown substantially longer with the second edition. Above all, I wish to thank Jim Brace-Thompson, senior editor at Sage Publications, who provided invaluable assistance and advice in planning the new edition and waited patiently for it to be born. Lyle E. Bourne, Jr., the series editor, critiqued the entire draft of the second edition and provided the encouragement to write the first edition.

The new edition continues to benefit from the many useful suggestions on the first edition provided by James Chumbley and Ira Fischler. I thank Michael E. J. Masson and James Chumbley for their careful critical reading of the entire manuscript for the second edition.

In addition to their contributions, numerous useful suggestions and criticisms on individual chapters were provided by Michael Anch, Terry Au, Russell Buhite, Thomas H. Carr, David C. Geary, Lewis O. Harvey, Paula Hertel, Donald Homa, Ken McRae, Akira Miyake, Lance Rips, Steven Sloman, John E. Taplin, and a few anonymous reviewers. I am indebted to their efforts to improve the book but take full responsibility for the final product.

The graphics in the new edition are a major addition to the book. Barry Burns crafted many informative and artful drawings to illustrate the ideas of the text. Barry's drawings are complemented by the skillful line drawings, graphs, and tables of Nicholas Alexander. Their images enhanced my words greatly. I thank them both for creating the essential visual communications of the text from my crude sketches.

The words as they appear here benefited from the careful copyediting of D. J. Peck. His dedicated attention to detail, consistency, and clarity is very much appreciated. I thank him for taking the student's perspective to improve the readability of the text.

Karen Ehrmann, Anna Howland, and Karen Wiley at Sage assisted with this edition. Special thanks are due to Karen Ehrmann, who worked hard at making sense of my minimal notations regarding graphics and permissions.

I also thank Darlene Turner, Alicia Kellogg, Kristin Kellogg, Adam Pollard, Kevin Kelley, Bridget Gregg, and Nancy Holt for their assistance in obtaining permissions and preparing the glossary and test bank questions.

Lastly, I thank my wife, Carol, for once again tolerating the long hours and frustrations involved in writing a book. Her steadfast support and encouragement throughout both editions made it all possible.

PART I

SCOPE AND METHODS

Cognitive psychology is part of an interdisciplinary field known as cognitive science. Other disciplines represented in cognitive science include computer science, linguistics, philosophy, and cognitive neuroscience. The cognitive or mental functions of perception, attention, memory, language, and thinking are studied by cognitive scientists. The disciplines of cognitive science differ in their approaches to this work. Cognitive psychologists chiefly study cognitive functioning in laboratory settings using behavioral measurements such as error rates and response times in experimental tasks. Cognitive neuroscientists attempt to image the living brain as these laboratory tasks are performed in an effort to relate neuroimaging and behavioral evidence.

CHAPTER 1

INTRODUCTION

Cognitive psychology and its more inclusive partner, cognitive science, have come of age. They have come to exert a strong influence on psychology as a whole and promise a scientific understanding of the human mind in all its complexity and significance. The discipline that you will study in this book concerns itself with the science of mental life, as defined by contemporary research methods, theories, and findings. Although the questions raised by cognitive psychology typically have ancient roots, the answers provided by the discipline are recent and undergoing continual refinement. Here you will learn how far we have come in one of science's grandest quests: the mind seeking to understand itself.

The time and place of cognitive psychology today both contribute to its vibrancy. The 1990s were declared as the "Decade of the Brain" by the U.S. Congress. Cognitive psychology, neuroscience, developmental psychology, evolutionary biology, anthropology, linguistics, philosophy, computer science, and other research programs that together make up the broad interdisciplinary field of cognitive science are thriving. The congressional declarations symbolize the hope that the mysteries of brain, mind, and behavior are within our grasp. Discoveries beckon in understanding how humans perceive, remember, imagine, think, and create. The despair of a child who struggles with reading because of dyslexia and the anguish of family members who lose a parent to the confusion and memory loss of Alzheimer's disease may one day find relief through applications of these basic discoveries.

The place as well as the time of cognitive psychology attracts students of both the sciences and the humanities. If you were to imagine a map of psychology and related fields, you would find cognitive psychology centrally located and bordering numerous neighbors. The shortest path from, say, evolutionary biology to linguistics, or from computer science to neuroscience, cuts through the territory of cognitive psychology. The discipline you will find in this book has been crossed by many students of human nature and circumvented only by those pursuing the long way around.

● DEFINING COGNITIVE PSYCHOLOGY

Cognitive psychology refers to the study of human mental processes and their role in thinking, feeling, and behaving. Perception, memory, acquisition of knowledge and expertise, comprehension and production of language, problem solving, creativity, decision making, and reasoning are some of the broad categories of such study. Experimentation lies at the heart of cognitive psychology, but as we will see, mathematical models and computer simulations also play a role. Cognitive psychologists measure behavior in laboratory tasks so as to reach conclusions about covert mental processes. As we will also see, the related discipline of cognitive neuroscience uses neuroimaging methods that try to relate activity in the brain to the behavioral measurements.

The discipline often portrays the human mind as, first, a processor of information; it computes answers to problems in a manner analogous to the software of a computer. A digital computer represents an arithmetic problem, such as $21 + 14$, in a symbolic code of zeros and ones according to an agreed-on convention. Specifically, each digit is represented by eight bits of information, where each bit takes the value of either zero or one. Then, a software program processes those symbols according to the rules of addition, yielding the correct answer, 35. Similarly, as you read this problem and verified the answer, your mind represented the numbers and processed the information. The analogy between mental processes and computation has proved fruitful and provides what is called the information processing approach to cognitive psychology.

But the human mind does more than process information the way a computer would. Information technically refers to a reduction in uncertainty about events. For instance, consider the toss of coin as an event with an uncertain outcome. If it comes up heads, then the uncertainty about the

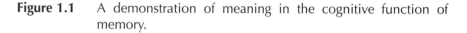

Trigram	Word
WAQ	PIG
BEC	LIP
LOK	CUP
RIZ	BAT
TUZ	MAP
LUT	CAP
DOX	TAG
PEM	RIB
GAX	CAT
MIB	LOG

Figure 1.1   A demonstration of meaning in the cognitive function of memory.

event has been reduced (one bit of information has been transmitted to be mathematically precise). Information is transmitted in this example, but the event is meaningless. Now, suppose that the coin is tossed again, but this time heads means you lose $500 and tails means you win $500. Are you ready for the toss? The outcome again reduces uncertainty by one bit, but more important, the toss now has meaning. It refers to other events that are significant to you as a human. Meaning, not information in the mathematical sense, provides the focus of human mental life (Bruner, 1990).

Throughout your study in this book, the fundamental importance of meaningfulness will be plain. A simple illustration concerns your ability to remember the items from two different lists. The first list in Figure 1.1 contains meaningless trigrams; each set of three letters carries few natural associations (unless your initials are there by accident). The second list contains three-letter words, each of which refers to an object that you have experienced in the world and know well. Study the trigram list for 30 seconds and then try to recall the items without looking. Then, do the same with the word list. Undoubtedly, you will find the meaningful list much easier to memorize.

The mind lives and breathes through meaning. Our use of symbols to refer to objects, events, and other experiences; our efforts to understand why experiences occur as they do; and ultimately our hope to understand the purpose of our own existence all reflect the human need for meaning.

Finally, the discipline of cognitive psychology assumes that the mind and brain are systems that emerged through evolution. They have adaptive functions that enable us to succeed as reproducing organisms. The structures of mind and brain must be related to these adaptive functions, just as the opposable thumb of primates is related to their ability to grasp objects.

Systems for perceiving, remembering, and thinking have evolved in a manner that allows us to adapt to our environment. Understanding these systems in the context of neurophysiology and evolutionary biology provides another driving force in the discipline. The human mind did not emerge from the spotless laboratory of a computer scientist; rather, it emerged from the messy forces of biological development and survival. Adaptations to the environment persisted in future generations through natural selection.

To understand the mind from an evolutionary perspective, psychologists make comparisons of, say, memory functioning across different species. Another useful method is to study the cognitive development of memory in a single species, from infancy through old age. Functions that develop rapidly early in life are assumed to be genetically specified predispositions that were naturally selected in the past history of the species. For instance, a predisposition to learn and use spoken language seems to be coded in the human genome, whereas the use of written language is not. Speaking is learned early and rapidly during the first few years of childhood, whereas reading and writing are learned later and more slowly.

Cognitive science may be defined as the study of the relationships among and integration of cognitive psychology, biology, anthropology, computer science, linguistics, and philosophy (Hunt, 1989). It represents an interdisciplinary effort to address basically the same issues that confront cognitive psychology. How is knowledge represented? How does an individual acquire new knowledge? How does the visual system organize sensory experiences into meaningful objects and events? How does memory work? As shown in Figure 1.2, these are among the problems that cognitive science attempts to understand in terms that make sense to scholars from diverse backgrounds.

Cognitive psychology is only one of the cognitive sciences. Others include behavioral and cognitive neuroscience, cognitive anthropology, and computer science.

Cognitive science is not a coherent discipline in and of itself but rather a perspective on several disciplines and their associated questions (Hunt, 1989). Researchers who regard themselves as cognitive scientists typically have educational backgrounds in at most one or two of the contributing disciplines. Furthermore, they approach the issues of mind and brain with research methods unique to their disciplines. Stillings and colleagues (1987), an interdisciplinary team of co-authors, explained in their pioneering text in cognitive science:

> Psychologists emphasize controlled laboratory experiments and detailed, systematic observations of naturally occurring behaviors. Linguists test hypotheses about grammatical structure by analyzing speakers' intuitions about grammatical and ungrammatical sentences or

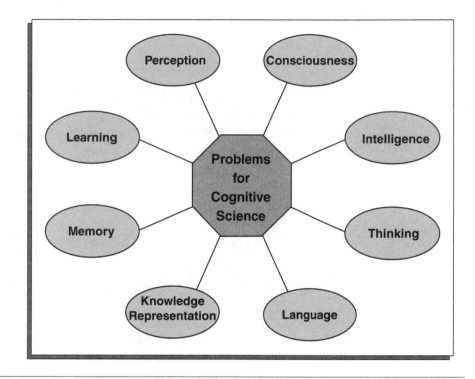

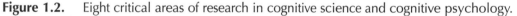

Figure 1.2.   Eight critical areas of research in cognitive science and cognitive psychology.

by observing children's errors in speech. Researchers in AI [artificial intelligence] test their theories by writing programs that exhibit intelligent behavior and observing where they break down. Philosophers probe the conceptual coherence of cognitive scientific theories and formulate general constraints that good theories must satisfy. Neuroscientists study the physiological basis of information processing in the brain. (p. 13)

The current textbook focuses on the theories, methods, and results of cognitive psychology. On occasion, we encounter in passing arguments and evidence that might constitute an entire section or chapter in a text of another branch of cognitive science. The book tries to provide you with enough context to grasp the matter at hand without assuming that you have had a course in, say, neuroscience and without elaborating to the point of distraction.

● CORE CONCEPTS

Mental Representations

The information processing approach is built on the assumption that an organism's ability to perceive, comprehend, learn, decide, and act depends on mental representations. A **mental representation** is an unobservable internal code for information. It is helpful to contrast a mental representation of an object with a physical external representation. Take a robin, for example. Your mental representation of a robin codes information about the bird's shape, size, colorings, and perhaps even its distinctive song. An artist's drawing of a robin is an external representation of the real thing. It too may convey properly the bird's shape, size, and colorings, but it would certainly lack its song.

Now, close your eyes and imagine viewing a robin. You are using your mental representations of birds to create an image that only you can experience. Some mental representations can be consciously experienced as images that are similar to visual, aural, and other kinds of perceptions. Unlike the artist's sketch, they cannot be observed by anyone else but you. Mental representations are private and are perceived, if at all, only by their owners. Not all mental representations are perceived as images, and they remain unconscious even to their owners. Even with the new technologies for examining the brain, scientists cannot read your thoughts because they cannot process your conscious or unconscious mental representations. Observing patterns of neural activity is not the same as experiencing mental representations. Look again in your mind's eye at the robin. Can you hear its song? Perhaps, but you will hear the real song of a robin only if you have acquired a mental representation of how a robin sounds. If you confuse it with the song of a cardinal or sparrow, that is because your mental representation is in error.

All perceptions, memories, flights of imagination, and dreams occur because of mental representations that code information.

Mental representations, then, provide the basis for all cognitive abilities. To perceive your environment, you must compute mental representations of the objects around you and the events that are taking place. To comprehend and learn from this text, you must mentally represent the information that is conveyed through language. All that you know about the world and your only basis for acting on the world is found in your mental representations.

Stages of Processing

Another basic concept of cognitive psychology is that processes modify mental representations in a series of stages (Massaro & Cowan, 1993). To see this point, it is easiest to consider a specific task such as the memory task presented earlier. To remember the trigrams, you needed to first perceive or encode them, meaning you had to read the letter combinations on the page. The encoding stage could be made harder by dimming the lights in the room so that the letters are not as legible. Next, you needed to store the encoded items in memory. The words were much easier to store than the meaningless letter combinations. Next, the items needed to be retrieved from memory, which was also easier for the meaningful material. Finally, the retrieved items needed to be spoken or written during the output stage of processing. So, to be able to recall WZT, you had to compute a mental representation during encoding, store this representation as an item on the list, retrieve the representation when trying to remember, and then convert the representation to a spoken or written word. **Stages of processing,** then, refers to the steps required to form, modify, and use mental representations in a cognitive task.

Serial Versus Parallel Processing

A fundamental question is whether cognitive processes occur one at a time or simultaneously during a given stage of processing. To illustrate, consider the encoding stage of the memory task. Is each item in the list encoded one at a time, or are all of them encoded simultaneously? **Serial processing** refers to cases in which cognitive operations occur one at a time in series. Are the letters P . . . I . . . G perceived one at a time or simultaneously? **Parallel processing** refers to cases in which cognitive operations occur simultaneously in parallel.

Multiple cognitive operations occur at once in parallel processing, or they occur one at a time in serial processing.

Hierarchical Systems

In biology, the body is divided into systems composed of many component parts. These parts are arranged hierarchically. The respiratory system, the muscular system, the cardiovascular system, and the nervous system all are organized this way. For example, the nervous system divides into the peripheral branch and the central branch. The peripheral branch further divides into sensory versus autonomic components. As you know, the autonomic branch must be further divided into the components of the sympathetic system, on the one hand, and the parasympathetic system, on the other.

In cognitive psychology, the mind is also viewed as a hierarchical system composed of many component functions. For example, the mind can be divided into branches of perception, memory, and motor output. Memory is further divided into a working or short-term system and a long-term system. The long-term system appears to be composed of further subsystems, an issue that we examine in Chapter 5. The mind can be best described as a hierarchical arrangement of functional components that can be analyzed and studied in isolation (Simon, 1969). A core task of cognitive psychology is to determine the number and organization of these functional systems. The related field of cognitive neuroscience attempts to specify the brain structures that support each functional system, as is discussed in Chapter 2.

Cognitive Architecture

The design or organization of the mind's information processing components and systems is referred to as its **cognitive architecture.** The distinction between a working memory system and a long-term memory system is an architectural distinction. Another such distinction is the organization of components or subsystems of, say, long-term memory. As a third example, some theorists contend that the mind is built from independent processing modules, with each module specialized for a particular function such as perceiving faces or recognizing speech. An alternative point of view is that building blocks of the mind are flexible, general-purpose mechanisms that perform many diverse functions. Long-term memory is one general purpose mechanism in that it stores representations of both faces and speech sounds from the past to enable perception in the present and future.

Symbolic models explain cognition in terms of simulations that operate like a computer program that encodes, stores, and manipulates symbols.

A fourth and final example is the distinction between symbolic and connectionist architectures. **Symbolic models** assume that the mind is built like a digital computer. Pioneering work on computers by von Neumann (1958) provided the foundation for such models. They assume that mental representations are symbols that are serially processed by a set of rules, just as the data in a computer are processed according to the rules of a program. Simon (1990) argued that "a system will be capable of intelligent behavior if and only if it is a physical symbol system . . . capable of inputting, outputting, storing, and modifying symbol structures, and of carrying out some of these actions in response to the symbols themselves" (p. 3). This class of architecture posits a centralized control over the flow of information from sensory input, through memory, to motor output. Shown in Figure 1.3 is Atkinson and Shiffrin's (1971) influential model of the control of short-term memory; it employs a symbolic architecture. Control processes such as rehearsal transfer information from a short-term memory store to a long-term store.

Connectionist models comprise an alternative class of cognitive architectures. Instead of looking to the digital computer, connectionist architectures try to use the structure of the brain itself as a model of the mind's

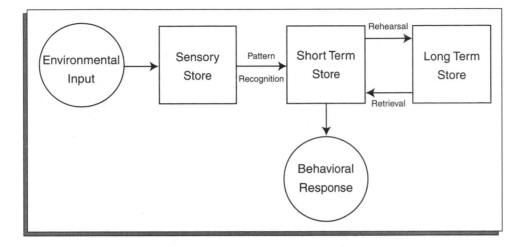

Figure 1.3. Cognitive architectures: Example of a symbolic model.
SOURCE: Adapted from Atkinson and Shiffrin (1971).

structure. Instead of a set of rules for operating on symbols, connectionist models are based on associations among numerous simple units called neurons. These are highly simplified units that bear scant resemblance to real neurons. However, the assumption is that a population of simple artificial neurons carries out computations that enable intelligent behaviors. Early connectionist models were proposed by McCulloch and Pitts (1943) and Hebb (1949). In connectionist architectures, there are no localized symbols to be processed. Instead, a mental representation is distributed over a population of neurons. Shown in Figure 1.4 is McClelland and Rumelhart's (1981) influential model of word recognition that uses a connectionist architecture. It employs three layers of units. The first layer represents visual features, the second represents letters, and the third represents words. Excitatory connections, shown by arrows, increases activation at a unit, whereas inhibitory connections, shown by dots, decreases it. Connectionist architectures are based on the spread of activation through local excitation and inhibition. Control of the flow of information is not centralized as it is in symbolic architectures.

> Connectionist models explain cognition in terms of simulations of simple neuron-like units arranged in complex networks.

Memory Stores

Atkinson and Shiffrin (1971) described a short-term store that retains information just attended to for several seconds (see Figure 1.3). They distinguished this kind of memory from a long-term store that retains information over intervals of several minutes, hours, days, weeks, months, or

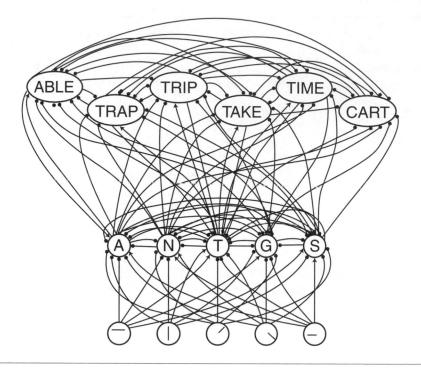

Figure 1.4   Cognitive architectures: Example of a connectionist model.

SOURCE: McClelland and Rumelhart (1981).

years. Furthermore, additional distinctions may be drawn. For example, very brief storage of information during perceptual processing takes place in the visual or auditory registers in Atkinson and Shiffrin's model—what is called sensory memory. Over the past 30 years, it has become clear that sensory, short-term, and long-term memory are by themselves insufficient to describe the complexity of memory stores. Long-term memory, for instance, is further divided into subsystems, as is described later in the book.

Consciousness

Consciousness is certainly a core concept in cognitive psychology. But it has been a difficult one to investigate for many reasons, and progress has been slow in coming. One major problem in studying consciousness is that the concept is not well-defined. People mean different things when they talk about consciousness, including the scientists who try to study it. Pinker (1999) explained that cognitive scientists sometimes talk about consciousness as

self-knowledge. An intelligent being can possess knowledge about many objects, events, and ideas. Included among these many kinds of knowledge is knowledge about the self. Humans can look in a mirror and recognize that they are viewing themselves precisely because they are conscious in the sense of self-awareness.

A second meaning of consciousness is **informational access,** the capacity to become aware of and able to report on mental representations and the processes that operate on them. Access-consciousness includes the end products of our perceptual systems, allowing us to see, hear, smell, and touch the world around us and to feel the positions and tensions of our bodies. Some of these mental representations are attended to and maintained in short-term memory for several seconds. We seem to also have access to our emotional states and to our self-concept—an awareness of an executive, I, who interprets why things happen the way they do and makes decisions about how to behave in response. At the same time, many mental representations and the processes that operate on them are unconscious and unavailable for verbal report. Just as you do not have conscious access to workings of the cardiovascular system or the autonomic nervous system, you also do not have access to the processes that create vision or audition. For example, all of the processes that detect the lines that make up a single letter on this page, match the letter shape to a representation in memory, and specify where on the page the letter appears are unconscious. You have awareness only of the product—the perceived letters and words.

Finally, there is the meaning of consciousness as **sentience,** the basic capacity for raw sensations, feelings, or subjective experience of any kind. How is it that a material object, the brain, can give rise to subjective experience? Trying to understand the relationship between consciousness as sentience and the brain has bedeviled philosophers and psychologists in what is known as the mind-body problem. A great deal is known about consciousness as self-knowledge and informational access. Despite mountains of books and articles on the problem, little if any progress has been made in understanding how, or even whether, the brain causes sentience. Although the core positions of the mind-body debates are reviewed in Chapter 2, most of what you will learn about consciousness in this book concerns findings about self-knowledge and informational access.

In cognitive psychology, the term *consciousness* can refer to self-knowledge, informational access, or sentience.

RESEARCH METHODS •

Laboratory experiments that measure behavior form the methodological backbone of cognitive psychology. The neuroimaging methods of cognitive neuroscience are increasingly being used in experiments and case studies to understand brain structures that support a particular cognitive function. Cognitive psychologists typically try to isolate a particular component of cognitive functioning such as working memory. They design a laboratory task that allows them to study the characteristics of this component by manipulating independent variables. For example, the digit span task calls for a research participant to recall a list of digits, such as 1-6-4-8-3-9-2, immediately after their presentation. The number of digits presented is an independent variable.

The independent variable causes changes in a dependent variable or measurement of performance in the chosen task. By manipulating the independent variable and measuring its effects, clear causal relationships may be established. In our example, the percentage of digits correctly recalled is the dependent variable. The percentage correctly recalled decreases once the number of digits exceeds about seven. Studies of this type are considered in Chapter 5 on working memory. Researchers commonly manipulate more than one independent variable at a time. For example, a researcher might vary both the number of digits presented and whether they are heard or seen by the participant.

Behavioral Measures

Typical dependent variables in cognitive psychology measure the speed and accuracy of human performance. Some tasks are so easy and automatic that few errors occur. For example, are these letter strings the same or different: WAQ, WAO? Now, try again with this pair: WAQ, BEC. **Reaction time,** the number of milliseconds to perform a task, provides a sensitive measure of the cognitive processes required. The participant is provided with two buttons and presses the one on the right for a same judgment and the one on the left for a different judgment. The first pair of letter strings requires identifying a single distinctive feature to make the correct "different" response, and the additional search time for this feature is easily detectable in reaction times measured with millisecond accuracy. Reaction times might range from 400 to 500 milliseconds in same-different judgment tasks, depending on the stimuli compared. Such times are much larger than the neural transmission time for inputting information from the eye to the brain and for outputting a motor response from the brain to skeletal muscles. Furthermore, reaction times vary in systematic ways as stages of processing are added or subtracted from tasks (Sternberg, 1995).

The proportion of correct responding, or conversely the **proportion of errors,** provides another widely employed measure. For example, in a memory experiment such as the one demonstrated in Figure 1.1, the researcher might measure only the proportion of errors made in recalling the words or nonsense syllables. Suppose that instead of recalling the words, a recognition test was given. Which of these two words appeared in Figure 1.1: PIG, DOG? Here, the researcher could readily measure not only the errors but also the time taken to reach a decision. Typically, the faster the reaction time in a task, the higher the proportion of errors. This relationship is called a speed-accuracy trade-off.

Lastly, **verbal protocols** or tape-recordings of people thinking aloud while they carry out a task provide a rich record of conscious processing. For example, suppose that you are presented with an arithmetic problem to solve. As you solve the problem, verbalize aloud your thinking. Remember to vocalize each thought you have as you solve the problem: $482 + 341 = ?$

Ideally, the research participant introspects and reports all that passes through consciousness without omitting any thoughts. Equally important, the process of thinking aloud ought not change the processes used to perform the task. If providing verbal protocols distorts the processes normally used when thinking silently, then the validity of the method is compromised. Problem solving, reasoning, writing, and related tasks have been investigated extensively using verbal protocols. In such tasks, it is possible to identify many of the steps individuals work through in arriving at final solutions. The use of verbal protocols is justified so long as the processes required by a task are mentally represented in a verbal format or can be readily translated into words, phrases, or sentences (Ericsson & Simon, 1980). It is also necessary to demonstrate that thinking aloud is inert and does not react with and alter the processes that the researcher is trying to reveal (Russo, Johnson, & Stephens, 1989).

Physiological Measures

Besides behavioral measures, physiological measurements of bodily systems, including the brain, are also collected in experiments. These include continuous monitoring of eye movements and other muscular activity or changes in the autonomic nervous system such as heart rate, blood pressure, respiration rate, and skin conductance. Direct measurements of brain activity are also examined. The electroencephalogram (EEG) is a multichannel recording of the continuous electrical activity of the brain. It is measured with a multichannel recorder that detects voltage changes generated by large numbers of neurons below each of many electrodes placed on the scalp. The frequency and amplitude of these voltage fluctuations depend on whether the brain is awake and alert, drowsy and relaxed, or at various stages of sleep, including the well-known phase of rapid eye movement sleep. Positron emission tomography (PET) is an example of how activity in a specific region of the brain can be measured as a task is performed. More is said about both of these techniques in Chapter 2 on cognitive neuroscience, but they can be introduced here to illustrate the methods of research.

For example, event-related potentials are EEG changes in response to a specific stimulus. Neurometric profiles can be developed that show how various stimuli and tasks evoke activities in different regions of the brain. Posner and his colleagues have developed a geodesic sensor net containing 64 electrodes for obtaining such profiles, as shown in Figure 1.5 (Posner & Raichle, 1994). Each electrode, in the form of a tube containing saline solution, rests on a small sponge that makes contact with a carefully calibrated spot on the person's head. By averaging together the voltage changes that occur following the presentation of a stimulus, a waveform can be plotted at each of the locations. Illustrated in Figure 1.6 are the waveforms obtained at the sites activated by the visual presentation of a meaningful word.

Experimental Design

Cognitive psychologists design tasks so that the pattern of outcomes on dependent measures reveals properties about the components, stages, and other features of mental processing. Designing an experiment in a way that leads to clear conclusions calls for ingenuity; it is the art embedded at the core of all science. Some of the methods used by cognitive psychologists are explained in the context of presenting the key concepts of the field in later chapters. For the moment, it will suffice to present one method of general importance that illustrates the logic of cognitive research.

The **method of subtraction** is used by cognitive psychologists to isolate the properties of a single stage of processing. Although the method can be used with behavioral dependent measures, here it is illustrated using neuroimaging data. To isolate the properties of a single stage, the method assumes that stages of processing used in a simple task are not modified in some way when a choice is added to the task. This is called the assumption of pure insertion. If a control task requires Stages 1 and 2 of processing and an experimental task requires Stages 1, 2, and 3, then pure insertion holds when the experimental task does not in any way alter the processes and time needed for Stages 1 and 2. In this way, the extra time required by the experimental task can be assigned to the demands of Stage 3 (Sternberg, 1969, 1995).

For example, suppose that researchers design two tasks for the participants that, in theory, demand exactly the same cognitive processes but for a single process of interest. The researcher then obtains neuroimages during

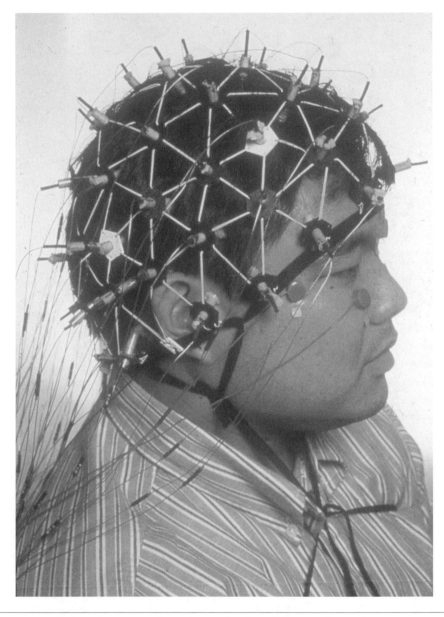

Figure 1.5 A geodesic sensor net of 64 electrodes for EEG recordings.
SOURCE: Posner and Raichle (1994).

both tasks and subtracts one from the other, leaving only the brain activity related to the process under study. A classic PET study on how word names are retrieved from long-term memory illustrates the method of subtraction (Posner, Peterson, Fox, & Raichle, 1988).

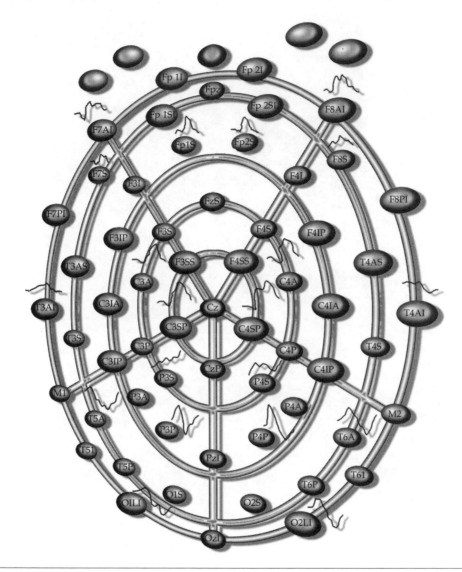

Figure 1.6. The average waveform recorded at selected electrode sites following the presentation of a visual word.

SOURCE: Adapted from Posner and Raichle (1994).

Participants in the study were presented with familiar nouns one at a time (e.g., *bottle*). The way the words were presented and the instructions regarding how to process the words were varied at different points during the experiment. The experiment was designed hierarchically, so that the processes engaged by one set of instructions provide a control condition for

Control	Experimental	Experimental-Control
Perceive Fixation	Perceive Word	Word Recognition
Perceive Word	Repeat Word	Speech Production
Repeat Word	Generate Use	Semantic Processing

Figure 1.7　The method of subtraction used in neuroimaging studies of cognitive processes.

examining the brain regions activated by a condition higher in the hierarchy. The design is shown in Figure 1.7. In the fixation point only or control condition, brain activity associated with focusing attention on the task is measured. The activation pattern obtained in this perceive fixation condition is then subtracted from the activation levels found when words are perceived as the experimental condition. This subtraction isolates the processes involved in word recognition. In the next experimental condition, participants repeated each word aloud. Now, the perceive word condition is used as a control, and its activation is subtracted from the repeat word activation. In so doing, the activation associated with speech production is isolated. Finally, the repeat word or experimental condition serves as the control for the task of generating functional uses of the words. For example, if presented with the word *bottle,* the participant might respond with *drink*. The use generation task requires that the meaning or semantic features of each word be processed, and the activation associated with this semantic processing is thus isolated.

The results are shown in Color Plate 1 in the section of color plates. Following convention, the relative degree of blood flow in a region is depicted in a different color. The highest to lowest levels of activation are coded by white, red, orange, green, blue, and purple, respectively. These show activation patterns resulting after subtracting the appropriate control activation patterns for each of the four tasks in the left hemisphere only. In the upper left scan, participants visually perceived each word. As shown, regions in the occipital cortex at the rear of the brain were activated in this condition. In the upper right scan, a similar passive perception condition is shown, except in this case the words were heard rather than seen. As a result, the auditory cortex in the temporal lobe was recruited into action. When participants repeated the words, PET revealed activation in the frontal motor areas of both hemispheres. Finally, generating a verb related to each word recruited extensive regions in the left prefrontal cortex, including Broca's area. This semantic processing also recruited regions in the temporal cortex that other research has suggested to be involved in representing meaningful categories.

Ecological Validity

Ecological validity refers to the degree to which laboratory tasks accurately measure cognitive phenomena that occur in real-world, everyday settings.

One problem with laboratory experiments is that they may lack **ecological validity.** This means that the task designed to study, say, working memory fails to reflect the way this component is used in everyday activities. Researchers design laboratory experiments precisely so that they can carefully control influences on their measurements and establish causal relations between independent and dependent variables. These requirements can rarely be met outside of the laboratory in real-world situations. On the one hand, the control of the laboratory is needed to establish a truly generalizable scientific effect (Banaji & Crowder, 1989). On the other hand, the laboratory may be so artificial that the essential characteristics of interest are lost (Neisser, 1976).

To ensure ecological validity, researchers may select tasks that model the essential characteristics of everyday cognition. For example, researchers could experimentally study in the laboratory an employee carrying out a task done on the job every day that demands the use of working memory (e.g., an air traffic controller remembering aircraft positions when the computer system fails momentarily). Researchers may also turn to naturalistic studies based on field observations, interviews, and other assessment methods that are not experimentally based. For example, a case study of a controller actually on the job directing air traffic could point to the importance of working memory. Similarly, correlational studies based on psychological tests, questionnaires, and field observations are useful. For example, air traffic controllers might be tested for their span of working memory and observed on the job. A correlation between span size and success on the job would be an ecologically valid finding about working memory. The naturalistic observations can highlight interesting relationships for experimental psychologists to bring under laboratory control (Roediger, 1991).

Experiments are designed to test theories regarding how the mind is organized and how it functions. Theories aim to explain a large number of phenomena discovered through laboratory experimentation with the fewest number of principles or assumptions. Theories account for the detailed pattern of reaction times, errors, or statements made in verbal protocols in a particular cognitive task. The more of these patterns accounted for, the better. Theories in cognitive psychology, like those in psychology and biology in general, are often stated in verbal form. A well-known example is the theory that memory is divided into a short-term store and a long-term store that differ in characteristics such as capacity and the means of retrieval. This principle accounts for a number of findings in the literature, as is shown in Chapter 5. A good theory must be stated clearly and make specific predictions that can be proven wrong by the outcomes of experiments. Progress is made in science when the prediction of a theory is falsified by an experimental result, leading to changes in the assumptions of the theory (Popper, 1974).

Theories sometimes take the form of a computer simulation that aims to duplicate the pattern of errors and correct responses made by a human in a particular information processing task. Because a program must be written, the assumptions of the theory must by definition be clearly stated. If the simulation produces results comparable to the person, then we infer that the processes used by the computer program provide a potentially valid model of human cognition. Such simulations may be based on either symbolic or connectionist models of cognition.

Closely related to simulations is the use of mathematical models of any kind. Again, correct responses, errors, and reaction times are predicted by a mathematical model in a particular task. As with simulations, a mathematical model states the assumptions of a theory in a specific clear manner. The data produced by humans are then fit to the predictions to test the assumptions of the model. When simulations or mathematical models are successful in fitting the observed data, one gains confidence that the theory is correct.

However, it is possible that simulations or mathematical models generate the "right answers" but do so with the "wrong methods," meaning that they make assumptions that do not match how the human mind actually works. It is possible, for example, to piece together many assumptions so as to account for the data from one task. One way to detect this problem is to ask whether the simulations or models can account for a wide range of experimental findings and not just fit the data generated by a single task. The more findings a theory can explain across different task domains with relatively few assumptions, the more likely it is on the right track.

> Good theories, whether expressed verbally, mathematically, or in computer software, should be able to explain a large number of phenomena in the simplest possible way.

OVERVIEW OF THE TEXT •

Chapter 2 provides an overview of cognitive neuroscience, a close neighbor that is having a profound impact on the field of cognitive psychology. The new neuroimaging technologies, combined with the experimental methods and theories of cognitive psychology, are advancing the science at an astonishing clip. It is increasingly essential for students of cognitive psychology to have a grasp of functional neuroanatomy and the meaning of neuroimaging data.

Following the first two introductory chapters, the basic cognitive operations are examined in the second section of the book. Perception, attention, and memory are covered in Chapters 3, 4, and 5, respectively. The third section of the book addresses the fundamental issues of learning and memory. Examples include how knowledge is represented and used in tasks such as learning a series of events, remembering events learned in the past, acquiring concepts, answering factual questions, and learning and performing a complex skill. Episodic memory, distortions of memory, semantic memory, and the acquisition of skills and expertise are covered in Chapters 6, 7, 8, and 9, respectively.

The fourth section presents research on the means by which humans use symbols to refer to abstract ideas such as in the case of language. Art, dance, music, architecture, software design, and many other creative endeavors all depend on creating and using symbolic representations that exist outside of the mind. A painting in a museum, a melody playing on the radio, the images on your favorite web page, and the text you are now reading all are symbolic representations that refer to abstract ideas about which we think and dream. The focus here is solely on language, perhaps the most intricate form of symbol use and certainly the most studied. Covered in Chapter 10 is the nature of language and its role in human thought. Then, in Chapters 11 and 12, the production and comprehension processes used in speaking, writing, listening, and reading are detailed.

Finally, the applications of language, memory, and other cognitive components to thinking skills are addressed in the last section of the book. In Chapter 13, the classic thinking task of problem solving is covered, with reasoning and decision making covered in Chapter 14. Along with language, human thinking skills have long been thought of as distinguishing features of our species. Moreover, there are often striking cultural and individual differences in performance on such tasks. When a person fails to respond in accordance with the answers dictated by the logic of Western philosophy and mathematics, just what does this imply? Is human reasoning flawed, or is the standard by which it is judged inappropriate? In the concluding Chapter 15, all of the material covered in the book is drawn together in the pursuit of measuring and explaining the nature of human intelligence. IQ testing, neurobiological indices of intelligence, and differences between men and women in intelligence are among the topics considered.

SUMMARY

1. The beginnings of a scientific understanding of the human mind are taking shape in the fields of cognitive psychology and cognitive science. These fields connect with numerous areas of inquiry, as one would expect of a science of mental life. Cognitive psychology is the study of human mental processes and their role in thinking, feeling, and behaving. Cognitive science takes a mathematical perspective of the mind or brain as a computational device and draws insights and methods from psychology, biology, anthropology, linguistics, philosophy, and computer science.

2. Information must be mentally represented so as to be involved in perception, memory, or any other cognitive activity. It is through our mental representations that we know anything and everything. Mental representations are processed in stages such as encoding the information, storing it in memory, retrieving it when needed, and manipulating the information to arrive at a decision. Cognitive operations needed to, say, retrieve an item from memory may in theory occur in a series of steps or in parallel. Symbolic models and connectionist models are two alternative ways to describe the architecture of the information processing system.

3. Consciousness is another core concept of cognitive psychology that does not stem from information processing theory. It is necessary to distinguish between unconscious cognitive operations and those that give rise to the subjective qualities of consciousness. There are three senses in which the term *consciousness* is used in cognitive psychology. Self-knowledge means being aware of the fact that we are aware—a form of what we discuss as metacognition later in the book. Information access means being aware of and able to report on mental representations and cognitive processes. Finally, sentience means the capacity for feelings and other subjective experiences.

4. The primary method of research is laboratory experimentation because it allows one to establish causal relationships between independent and dependent variables. However, concerns about the ecological validity of laboratory experiments prompts the use of other standard psychological research methods such as surveys, field observations, and case studies. In laboratory experiments, efforts are made to isolate one or more cognitive functions and investigate their properties. Dependent measures typically include the behavioral measures of reaction time and error rates. Verbal protocols might also be obtained by having an individual think aloud. Physiological measures such as electroencephalogram (EEG) recordings of brain wave activities and more recent neuroimaging techniques complement

behavioral measures. Theories in cognitive psychology must be clearly stated so as to make predictions that can be proven wrong in the outcomes of experiments. Simulations of performance using computer programs and mathematical models are sometimes used to state theoretical assumptions unambiguously.

● KEY TERMS

cognitive science	self-knowledge
mental representation	informational access
stages of processing	sentience
serial processing	reaction time
parallel processing	proportion of errors
cognitive architecture	verbal protocols
symbolic models	method of subtraction
connectionist models	ecological validity

CHAPTER 2

COGNITIVE NEUROSCIENCE

The field of cognitive neuroscience addresses how mental functions are supported by the brain. This close relative of cognitive psychology is exploding with new findings as a result of the discovery of methods for imaging the workings of the living brain. Neuroimaging technologies have revolutionized the study of the brain, but as will be seen in this chapter, their effective use requires the behavioral measures, research strategies, and theories of cognitive psychology. It is also important to understand that the core questions of cognitive psychology cannot be answered just by viewing the brain in action. One must first know which cognitive functions, such as short-term memory, to look for in a highly complex organ. In other words, cognitive psychology provides the theories that guide the search into the structures and activities of the brain.

The chapter begins with an introduction to the problem of how the mind and brain are related to each other. Next, a brief tour of functional neuroanatomy is provided, followed by a discussion of the methods used in cognitive neuroscience. Lastly, the fundamental properties of connectionist models are presented. As noted in Chapter 1, these are highly simplified models of the brain using artificial neurons that mimic some of the basic properties of real neurons. Connectionist models are now a central tool in cognitive neuroscience and the broader field of cognitive psychology.

● MIND AND BRAIN

Cognitive neuroscience confronts us with one of the most challenging, if not *the* most challenging, philosophical and scientific questions. What exactly is the relation between the mind and the body? Put differently, how is consciousness produced by the brain? Is a mental state reducible to a physical state of the brain, or are they separate phenomena?

One view of the relation between the brain and the mind is that they are one and the same. **Materialism** regards the mind as the product of the brain and its physiological processes. The mind does not exist independently of the nervous system, according to materialism. One version of materialism contends that it is possible in theory to reduce all cognitive processes to descriptions of neural events (Crick, 1994). The reductionistic point of view was well-expressed by Dennett (1991) in these words:

> The prevailing wisdom, variously expressed and argued for, is *materialism:* there is only one sort of stuff, namely *matter*—the physical stuff of physics, chemistry, and physiology—and the mind is somehow nothing but a physical phenomenon. In short, the mind is the brain. According to the materialists, we can (in principle!) account for every mental phenomenon using the same physical principles, laws, and raw materials that suffice to explain radioactivity, continental drift, photosynthesis, reproduction, nutrition, and growth. (p. 33)

Not all versions of materialism contend that the mind can be reduced to a description of brain states. An alternative version regards mental states as emergent properties of neural functioning (Scott, 1995). An **emergent property** implies that the whole is greater than the sum of its parts. It is not possible to predict the behavior of the whole just from knowing the behavior of the parts. In addition, it is necessary to understand how all of the parts interact with one another to produce the whole. A mental state can be viewed, then, as a whole that is more than the sum of the individual neurons firing. Regarding the mind as an emergent property is mentalistic but stays within the confines of materialism. Mental experience depends on, and is a functional property of, an active living brain. Sperry (1980) explained the mentalistic approach to materialism in the following passage:

Once generated from neural events, the higher order mental patterns and programs have their own subjective qualities and progress, operate, and interact by their own causal laws and principles which are different from and cannot be reduced to those of neurophysiology. (p. 201)

An alternative to materialism contends that attempts to connect mental states with brain states are mistaken. **Dualism** holds that the mind is an immaterial entity that exists independently of the brain and other bodily organs. This idea can be traced at least as far back as the French philosopher René Descartes. For a dualist, the attempt to reduce mental states to brain states is mistaken because it misinterprets correlation as causation. The dualist account recognizes that a subjective experience is correlated with activities in the brain. But as all students of psychology are aware, correlation does not prove causation. Perhaps mind and brain are correlated and have no influence on each other, or perhaps the mind actually causes brain activity rather than vice versa. Descartes assumed, as do contemporary dualists, that the immaterial mind interacts with the brain through a flow of information in ways not yet understood (Eccles, 1966, 1994; Popper & Eccles, 1977).

> For materialists, mental experiences can be reduced to states of the brain, or they may be an emergent property, meaning that the mind is different from the sum of the activity of neurons. For dualists, mental states are correlated with brain states and may even interact with neural processes, but the mind is not seen as rooted in matter.

Clearly, these deep fundamental questions will not soon be resolved. But progress in cognitive psychology and cognitive neuroscience does not depend on resolving them, and measurements at different levels of analysis are appropriate and necessary. Measurements of brain activity can be useful, but they are not sufficient by themselves. Behavioral measurements such as verbally reporting a memory, describing thoughts leading to the solution of a problem, and making a decision and rapidly pressing a button reveal the mind in a way that brain activity cannot. Cognitive psychologists, then, often adopt dualism as a methodological approach to research, as Hilgard (1980) observed:

My reaction is that psychologists and physiologists have to be modest in the face of this problem (consciousness) that has baffled the best philosophical minds for centuries. I do not see that our methods give us any advantage at the ultimate level of metaphysical analysis. A heuristic solution seems to me to be quite appropriate. . . . That is, there are conscious facts and events that can be shared through communication with others like ourselves, and there are physical events that can be observed or recorded on instruments, and the records then observed and reflected upon. Neither of these sets of facts produces infallible data. . . . It is the task of the scientist to use the most available techniques for verification of the database and for validation of the inferences from these data. (p. 15)

> The cognitive sciences today recognize that behavioral techniques are needed to measure mental states at the same time as neural techniques are needed to measure brain states. Neither replaces the other.

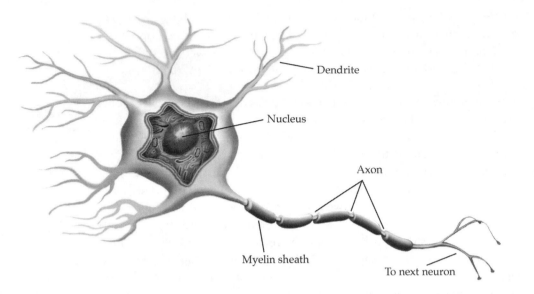

Figure 2.1. The basic components of a neuron.

● FUNCTIONAL NEUROANATOMY

The human brain may well be the most complex structure in the known universe. Consider just a few of the brain's properties to understand this point (Sejnowski & Churchland, 1989). A neuron is 1 of about 200 different types of cells that make up the 100 trillion (10^{14}) cells of the human body. As shown in Figure 2.1, a neuron includes dendrites for receiving signals from other neurons, a cell body, and an axon for transmitting a signal to other neurons via a synaptic connection. This is an idealized illustration of one of several classes of neurons that vary in the size, shape, number, and arrangements of their dendrites and axons. The dendrites of a single neuron may receive as many as 10,000 synaptic connections from other neurons. The central nervous system is comprised of 1 trillion (10^{12}) neurons of all kinds and about 1,000 trillion (10^{15}) synaptic connections among these neurons (see Figure 2.1).

At a larger scale, the brain is organized into major structures such as the lobes of the cerebral cortex. Shown in Figure 2.2 are the four lobes from a lateral view (a), a medial view (b), a dorsal view (c), and a ventral view (d). These regions are separated in part by anatomical markers called the central sulcus, lateral fissure, and longitudinal fissure. The lobes of the neocortex are divided into a left and right hemisphere by the longitudinal fissure. Large folds in the cortex identify the boundaries among four lobes of

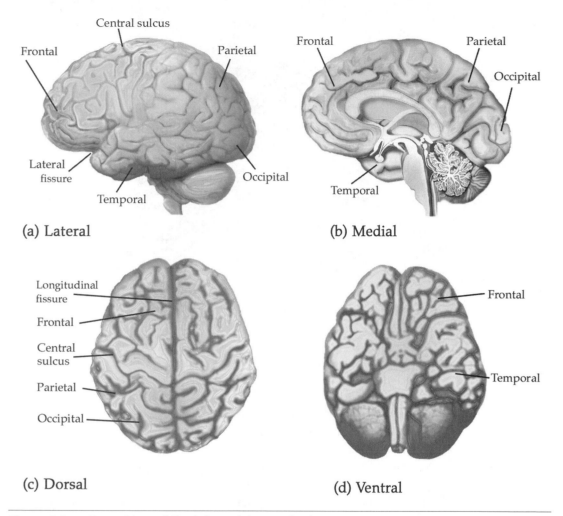

Figure 2.2. Four views of the lobes of the cerebral cortex.

the brain. The **frontal lobe** extends from the anterior of the brain back to the central sulcus. The **temporal lobe** lies on the side of the brain, beginning below the lateral fissure. The **parietal lobe** extends toward the rear of the brain, beginning at the central sulcus. The **occipital lobe** lies at the rear base of the brain.

Parallel Processing

Another complexity of the brain is its dependence on parallel processing. Many separate streams of data are processed to support a single cognitive

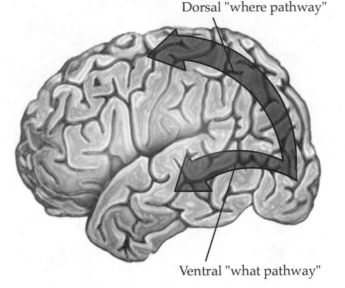

Dorsal "where pathway"

Ventral "what pathway"

Figure 2.3. The ventral "what" pathway versus the dorsal "where" pathway.

function. Each parallel stream involves a series of stages of processing. Consequently, it is misleading to think of a cognitive function, such as recognizing your friend across a crowded room, as dependent on just one cortical region. Although it is known that certain regions in the temporal cortex of the brain are necessary for face and other object recognition, in a parallel data stream in the parietal lobe, the location of your friend in the room is computed simultaneously (Gazzaniga, Ivry, & Mangun, 1998). As shown in Figure 2.3, a ventral or side pathway projects from the occipital lobe to the temporal lobe—the so-called "what pathway." The dorsal or top pathway projects from the occipital lobe to the parietal lobe—the "where pathway."

Shown in Color Plate 2 in the section of color plates are the results of a functional magnetic resonance imaging study in which the participants attended to the identity of a face (by matching it to another face) or attended to its location in a different matching condition. The red arrow marks the ventral pathway, and the green arrow marks the dorsal pathway. As may be seen, there was greater activation in the ventral pathway in the face matching condition and greater dorsal activation in the location matching condition (Haxby, Clark, & Courtney, 1997).

Although the brain uses parallel processing extensively, serial processing is also involved. For example, the streams of data corresponding to facial recognition and to identifying location both depend on an earlier serial stage of processing in the visual cortex of the occipital lobe. The occipital, parietal, and temporal lobes all are necessary for seeing your friend. No one region is sufficient by itself, and both parallel and serial processing are necessary.

If the brain is so complex, then why bother trying to understand its structure and function when the goal is to understand cognition? One answer is that neuroscience provides converging evidence for the theories of cognitive psychology. A cognitive theory is best supported if both behavioral data and neurobiological data lead one to exactly the same conclusion. Going still further, it is possible that the results of neuroscience can point theorists in the right direction so as to avoid blind alleys. As Sejnowski and Churchland (1989) phrased this point, "Neurobiological data . . . provide essential constraints on computational theories. . . . Equally important, the data are also richly suggestive of hints concerning what might really be going on and what computational strategies evolution might have chanced upon" (p. 343). As may be seen throughout this book, there are already a number of examples in which the theories of cognitive psychology can be supported by both behavioral and neurobiological data.

Brain Structures and Functions

As shown in Figure 2.4, the cerebellum and brainstem lie at the base of the brain. These are very old parts of the brain that are found in species that evolved long before mammals and primates. The **cerebellum** is a large structure that lies over the brainstem at the rear of the head. The best-known function of the cerebellum is its role in coordinating complex motor skills. Signals are sent to the cerebellum regarding the position of the body and the output of the motor system. It uses this information to maintain posture and coordinate movements, enabling complex motor skills such as walking, swimming, and skiing.

Brainstem and Forebrain. The **brainstem** consists of the hindbrain—the medulla oblongata and pons—and the midbrain. These are identified as separate structures because they represent anatomically distinct collections of neural cell bodies or nuclei. Lying above and around the midbrain are structures of the forebrain called the diencephalon, which links the cerebral cortex with the brainstem. This includes two major structures: the thalamus and the hypothalamus. The **thalamus** is extensively interconnected with numerous regions of the cerebral cortex including, but not limited to, specific sensory areas such as vision and hearing.

The **hypothalamus** controls internal organs, the autonomic nervous system, and the endocrine system to regulate functions such as emotion, sex, hunger, and thirst (Beatty, 2001). For example, it oversees the output of the

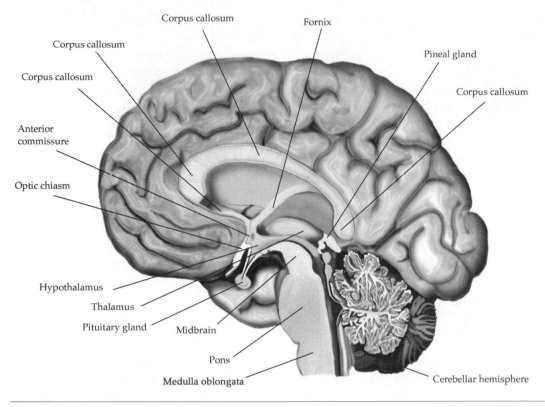

Corpus callosum

Corpus callosum

Corpus callosum

Anterior
commissure

Optic chiasm

Corpus callosum

Fornix

Pineal gland

Corpus callosum

Hypothalamus

Thalamus

Pituitary gland

Midbrain

Pons

Medulla oblongata

Cerebellar hemisphere

Figure 2.4. A view of the human brain showing the hindbrain and forebrain structures.

pituitary gland in emotional regulation. Endocrine glands secrete hormones into the bloodstream as a result of signals from the pituitary, the master gland. These hormones affect the emotional expression of internal feelings such as anxiety, relaxation, anger, pleasure, happiness, surprise, fight-or-flight reactions, and sexual responses. For example, the adrenal medulla is an endocrine gland that releases adrenalin (also called epinephrine). This hormone acts to increase the rate and force of the heart beat, constricts the small arteries of the skin and internal organs, dilates the small arteries of the skeletal muscles, and elevates the levels of glucose in the blood. All of these prepare the body for the expenditure of energy—fight-or-flight reactions. The hormones released by the endocrine glands then provides feedback to the pituitary gland, the hypothalamus, or both so as to regulate their output.

It has long been known that the brainstem, basal forebrain, and diencephalon are essential for maintaining the basic life support mechanisms of the body. The alertness cycle of waking and sleeping as well as the sensory and motor signals for the respiratory system, the heart, the mouth, and the throat are controlled here, for example. Signals are brought to these brain regions via nerve pathways or the bloodstream (e.g., pH, hormone, and glucose levels) to determine the state of body organs such as the heart, blood vessels, muscles, and skin. The function of these brain structures is to maintain, in a dynamic way, a condition of homeostasis in which bodily variables are kept within optimal ranges for the support of life. **Homeostasis** refers to a state of equilibrium of the internal environment of the body. When there is insufficient rest, food, water, or heat, for example, these brain structures initiate behaviors that change the internal state so that it falls back within an optimal range.

A useful metaphor for homeostasis is to compare these life support systems to a thermostat used to control an air conditioner during the summer. Temperature readings that exceed the set point used to keep the environment comfortable set off a response in the air conditioner. Other temperature readings have no effect at all. Homeostasis is thus achieved by maintaining room temperatures around the desired levels, even though it varies from moment to moment. The brainstem, basal forebrain, and diencephalon act essentially as a massive array of detectors whose values represent the state of the body from moment to moment (Damasio, 1999).

> The brainstem, basal forebrain, and diencephalon are essential for maintaining the basic life support mechanisms of the body. They provide homeostatic control over variables such as internal temperature, pH, hormone, and glucose levels.

Limbic System. The **corpus callosum** is the next structure identified in Figure 2.4. This is the large band of fibers that connects the right and left cerebral hemispheres together. Surrounding the corpus callosum, there is a layer collectively known as the limbic lobe, shown in Figure 2.5. In ancient primitive species such as the crocodile, most of the forebrain consists of the limbic lobe (Thompson, 2000). Above the corpus callosum lies the cingulate gyrus, a band of cortex that runs from the front or anterior portion of the brain to the back or posterior portion. The fornix extends from the cerebral cortex to the hypothalamus. The cingulate gyrus, fornix, hippocampus, and other related structures form a larger functional unit called the **limbic system.**

The limbic system is characteristic of the mammalian brain. In more primitive species, such as the crocodile, the limbic forebrain is devoted to analyzing the smells in the environment and to preparing approach, attack, mate, or flee responses. Although emotional responses are still among the functions of the limbic system, in mammals there is less reliance on the olfactory sense of smell. Of even greater interest, some of the structures of the limbic system have taken on the cognitive functions of learning and memory. For example, the **hippocampus** is involved in the learning and storage of new events in long-term memory.

> The limbic system consists of the limbic lobe and subcortical structures such as the hippocampus. Its functions include emotion, learning, and memory.

Cerebral Cortex. The remaining aspect of the forebrain is the cerebral cortex. The deep nuclei of the diencephalon and basil ganglia are surrounded by fatty myelinated fibers that appear white in color. The cerebral cortex, on the other hand, is called gray matter because of the grayish appearance of its

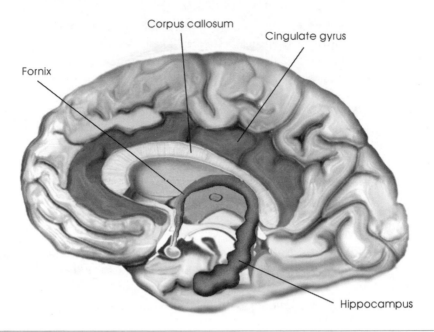

Fornix

Corpus callosum

Cingulate gyrus

Hippocampus

Figure 2.5. A view of some of the structures constituting the limbic system as seen in the right hemisphere with the left hemisphere removed.

unmyelinated, densely interconnected neurons. The overall thickness of the cerebral cortex averages only about 3 millimeters, arranged in layers parallel to each other and the surface of the brain (Gazzaniga et al., 1998).

The most recently evolved parts of the cerebral cortex, which is well-developed only in mammals, is called the **neocortex.** In humans, this comprises most of the cerebral cortex. The total surface area of the human cerebral cortex is 2,200 to 2,400 square centimeters, but most of this is buried in the depths of the sulci (Gazzaniga et al., 1998). To pack that much neural tissue in the small space of the human cranium is no small challenge. The evolutionary solution to this problem was to fold the cortex, creating the convoluted surface seen clearly in Figure 2.2 presented earlier. Each enfolded region is a sulcus. Cortical regions within these lobes have been mapped extensively based on how the neurons in those regions appear in structure and on how they are arranged with respect to each other.

Nearly half a century ago, brain surgeons began using direct electrical stimulation of the cortex to identify the regions that needed to be carefully spared during surgery to control epileptic seizures that failed to respond to drug treatments. The surgeons needed to remove the tissue causing the seizures while sparing the tissue that supported cognitive and behavioral functions such as perception, motor skills, and language. Because the central nervous system contains no pain receptors, patients remained awake during the surgery and reported their subjective experiences. A small electrical current applied to the cortex during surgery caused no discomfort, but it did activate motor responses and sensations (Penfield, 1959).

The motor cortex, lying just ahead of the central sulcus, and the sensory cortex, lying just behind it, were mapped region by region. For example, the regions of the motor cortex were systematically stimulated, and the hand, arm, leg, or other movement produced in the patient was recorded. The same was done for the somatosensory cortex, with the patient verbally reporting the sensation experienced by each stimulation. In a similar fashion, the cortical regions that control speech production and comprehension were identified. Through this research, Penfield (1959) was able to preserve the regions of the brain that serve spoken language, sensation and perception, and motor behaviors.

Electrical stimulation of some regions elicited what seemed to be recollections of past experiences. Penfield (1959) found, for example, that stimulating the temporal lobes produced an auditory memory of a song playing in the patient's mind, a song heard many years before. However, the interpretation of these observations is unclear. The experiences were rare and not easy to replicate in the patient. Repeating exactly the same stimulation did not produce exactly the same memory of the past. Furthermore, how can the neurosurgeon verify that the experience reported by the individual was in fact a true memory? It is possible that the stimulation created a false memory, an experience that only seemed as though it happened in the past but was actually a new event (Loftus & Loftus, 1980).

The portions of the cortex that do not elicit a sensory or motor response when stimulated are called association areas (Gazzaniga et al., 1998). For example, there are association areas in the temporal and parietal cortex that receive inputs from the primary visual cortex of the occipital lobe. These regions, as noted earlier, process visual inputs so as to recognize objects and specify their locations. Recall that multiple regions of the brain are required for complex cognitive functions such as memory, perception, and language. Even a sensorimotor skill such as riding a bicycle depends on more than just the somatosensory and motor cortical regions. Many regions of the brain are recruited to maintain balance, to navigate, and to attend to traffic on the road. Indeed, even seeing the road and the locations of cars, buses, and pedestrians involves multiple cortical regions in the occipital, parietal, and temporal lobes.

The two hemispheres look like similar structures, but they do not perform the same functions in exactly the same way. Instead, the left and right hemispheres have evolved to specialize to a degree in particular cognitive functions (Ornstein, 1997). For example, the left hemisphere specializes in producing and comprehending language. For its part, the right hemisphere specializes in recognizing faces and processing the spatial relationships among objects.

Some functions are known to be localized in the regions of the neocortex such as the sensory and motor regions on either side of the central sulcus in the parietal and frontal lobes, respectively. Regions critical for language are located in the left hemisphere, whereas facial recognition and spatial processing depend on regions in the right hemisphere.

● METHODS OF COGNITIVE NEUROSCIENCE

The focus here is on three of the most widely used methods of studying the functions of brain structures. These are the lesion, electrophysiology, and neuroimaging methods. A treatment of all methods of cognitive neuro-science is beyond our scope here. Moreover, behavioral neuroscience studies using animals in learning tasks and recordings of single neurons in the brain, plus studies in which lesions are created in the brains of animals, fall beyond the scope of this chapter but are fundamental to the scientific understanding of cognition and the brain. For example, the model of long-term memory that is introduced in Chapter 5 rests as much on animal research as it does on human research.

Lesions

The oldest method of studying the function of the brain is to examine individuals who have suffered damage to brain tissue through accidents, strokes, and diseases of the brain such as Alzheimer's and Parkinson's disease. For example, in the 19th century, Paul Broca reported a case study of "Tan," a man whose speech ability was reduced to saying the word "tan" repeatedly as a result of brain damage. Such tragic circumstances have provided the data for the field of clinical neuropsychology, which seeks to correlate specific lesions in the brain with specific kinds of behavioral and cognitive deficits. Lesions have also been experimentally created in rats, rabbits, monkeys and other mammals to determine the function of the damaged area. With the exception of psychosurgery performed on psychiatric patients, lesions have not been created in humans for ethical reasons. Indeed, many have questioned the ethics of treating even severely disturbed psychiatric patients with lesions in the frontal lobe and limbic system.

Until recently, clinical neuropsychology was limited to verifying the exact location of a lesion only after the death of a patient through postmortem examination of the brain. For example, Broca discovered that Tan's brain was damaged in the left frontal lobe. This became known as Broca's area when additional patients with speech disorders turned out to also suffer from lesions there. Today, the development of neuroimaging methods has allowed one to detect which regions of the brain have been damaged as the result of a stroke. This has hastened progress in using lesion case studies to understand how the brain supports cognition.

Lesion research is often based on individual case studies rather than on group results. Although most research in cognitive psychology is based on experiments in which the results for a group of people are averaged together, this approach can cause problems in cognitive neuroscience. For example, in a group of stroke victims, the exact locations and extent of the damage vary from one individual to the next. These anatomical differences may be important for the conclusions that are reached. Consequently, it has been argued that studying the behavior and cortical damage of one individual is the best approach (Caramazza, 1992). On the other hand, the group studies support conclusions about the functions of broad areas of the brain that are likely to generalize to everyone; they are not unique to one case.

In using single cases or group studies, the investigator attempts to find two tasks that discriminate between the performance of normal controls and patients with lesions in a particular region of the brain (Gazzaniga et al., 1998). The objective is to find evidence that one cognitive function is served by one brain region, whereas a different function is served by another brain region. To reach this conclusion, the investigator seeks to find double dissociations in which the specific type of brain injury affects performance in two tasks in different ways.

In general terms, a **double dissociation** refers to situations in which an independent variable affects Task A but not Task B, and a different variable affects Task B but not Task A. One independent variable might be a lesion in the parietal cortex as compared with normal controls. A second independent variable might be a lesion in the frontal lobe as compared with normal controls. To illustrate, suppose that Task A measures planning in problem solving and Task B measures locating objects in space. If it can be shown that frontal lobe damage disrupts planning performance relative to normal controls but has no effect on locating objects in space, then a single dissociation has been demonstrated (see Figure 2.6). If, in addition, it can be shown that the parietal damage affects locating objects in space but not planning in problem solving, then a double dissociation has been established. The double dissociation isolates planning as a function of the frontal lobe and locating objects in space in the parietal lobe.

The case study method of research is a valuable tool in cognitive neuroscience. The behavior of a patient is related to the specific areas of the brain known to be damaged by a tumor, accident, or stroke.

Electrophysiology

Electrophysiology reveals the activity of the brain by measuring the electric and magnetic fields that are generated by neuronal networks in the brain. As noted in Chapter 1, the electroencephalogram (EEG) is a record of the voltage changes created by the large populations of neurons activated within specific cortical regions. These brain waves can be measured with electrodes positioned on the scalp because the skull and scalp passively conduct the

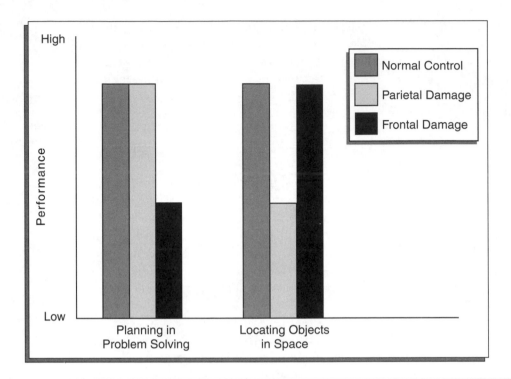

Figure 2.6. Hypothetical results of studies illustrating a single dissociation and a double dissociation.

electrical currents generated by the brain. The EEG led to the discovery that different brain wave patterns are correlated with different states of consciousness such as wakefulness, deep sleep, and dreaming.

The EEG provides a continuous measure of global changes in brain activity as a person carries out cognitive tasks. It permits one to study brain activity even in long and complex tasks. However, one drawback to the method is that changes in EEG activity caused by a particular stimulus are difficult to observe. Many responses are occurring simultaneously that have nothing to do with the particular stimulus of interest. Often times, investigators would like to know how a cortical region responds to the presentation of single stimulus such as a flash of light or the presentation of a word or picture. To this end, it is necessary to present the stimulus of interest on numerous trials. The EEG records from the trials are averaged together, making certain they are aligned with respect to the exact moment of stimulus presentation. All brain responses that are irrelevant to the stimulus are washed out of the picture through this averaging process, leaving only the response that the

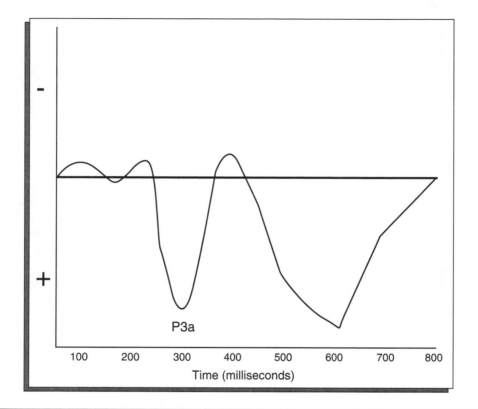

Figure 2.7. An idealized P3a ERP elicited 300 milliseconds after the presentation of a novel unexpected visual event. By convention, positive voltage changes are plotted below the *x* axis.

investigator is seeking. An EEG signal that reflects the brain's response to the onset of a specific stimulus is called an **event-related potential** (**ERP**) or simply an evoked potential.

To illustrate ERPs, consider the response of the brain to the presentation of a novel stimulus. An ERP called the P300 component (also known as the P3a) is the positive peak in the EEG signal that occurs 300 milliseconds after onset of an attention-getting stimulus, as shown in Figure 2.7. This component arises from an individual orienting to a novel stimulus and can be readily observed when recording from regions in the frontal lobe (Knight, 1996). Researchers use an "odd ball" task in which participants attend and count to an infrequent stimulus (e.g., red dot) while ignoring the frequent occurrences of another stimulus (e.g., green dot). In normal individuals, a novel

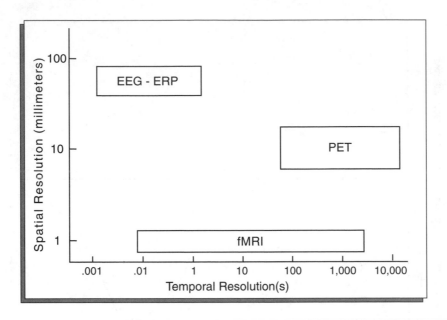

Figure 2.8. The spatial (y axis) and temporal (x axis) sensitivity of different neuroimaging techniques.

red dot elicits a P3 ERP associated with detecting and remembering its occurrence. It turns out that this response is absent in alcoholics, however, even when they have quit drinking. Abstinent alcoholics display a diminished or delayed ERP in the odd ball task, reflecting a long-term impairment in the processing of novel information (Rodriquez, Porjesz, Chorlian, Polich, & Begleiter, 1999). The effect does not reflect alcohol intoxication per se because the participant is sober when tested.

Moreover, the novelty deficit indexed by a P300 response might not even be related to the effects of chronic alcohol consumption per se. The children of alcoholics who have not yet consumed alcohol also show the same deficit in the odd ball task. Thus, this cognitive deficit may reflect a genetic predisposition to ignore novel stimuli rather than an alcohol-produced deficit. Of great importance, the ERP deficit can, in theory, be used as a marker of the genetic disorder. Children and adolescents who display this ERP deficit are vulnerable to alcohol dependence and should avoid ever starting to drink.

EEG and ERP provide information about the temporal dynamics of neural activation in the millisecond range. Such electrophysiological measures of brain activity show excellent temporal resolution (see Figure 2.8). But it is not possible to identify the specific location, within a few millimeters, of the neuronal networks that generate the evoked potentials and fields. To pinpoint the location of neuronal activity, other methods are required.

An ERP measures the activation of large numbers of neurons in a cortical region by detecting positive and negative voltage fluctuations on the scalp in response to a stimulus event. Multiple ERPs occur as time passes after the event is first registered.

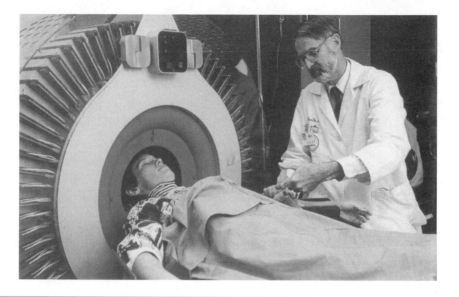

Figure 2.9.   A PET scanner at the Washington University laboratory in St. Louis, Missouri.
SOURCE: Posner and Raichle (1994).

Neuroimaging

Neuroimaging provides a measure of the location of neural activation generated during a cognitive task to within 3 to 10 millimeters. Two techniques now in wide use provide an indirect measure of more localized brain activity as compared with electrical scalp recordings. The first of these is **positron emission tomography (PET).** PET uses injections of radioactively labeled water (hydrogen and oxygen 15) to detect areas of high metabolic activity in the brain before the radioactive substance decays completely and is no longer radioactive (about 10 minutes). A person undergoing a PET scan is shown in Figure 2.9. PET images require multiple scans and allow the reconstruction of a three-dimensional picture of activated regions.

The second technique is called **functional magnetic resonance imaging (fMRI).** With fMRI, a powerful magnetic field is passed through the head to reveal detailed images of neuronal tissue and metabolic changes. Both PET and fMRI are based on the principle that as areas of brain increase their activity, a series of local physiological changes accompanies the activity and provides a way to measure it (Buckner & Petersen, 2000). PET works by detecting increases in blood flow in the vascular network that supplies a population of neurons. fMRI works by detecting changes in the concentration of oxygen in the blood. Thus, both methods reveal how the brain

PET and fMRI provide neuroimages of the living brain as it processes information in a cognitive task. An increase in brain activity in a region is detected by increases in blood flow with PET and by increases in blood oxygenation with fMRI.

supports behavior in a cognitive task by measuring local changes in blood properties. Because changes in blood flow and oxygenation take a few seconds to occur, the neuroimaging methods do not provide the temporal resolution found with evoked potentials (see Figure 2.8). The color plate section of the book includes several examples of PET and fMRI images.

Interpreting Neuroimages. A high degree of neural activation in one region in the brain provides evidence that it is necessary for the cognitive function under investigation. It does not mean that the region is sufficient, all by itself, for the function in question. The brain processes multiple streams of data in parallel, and multiple structures are typically activated in any task. Whether all of the necessary regions turn up in a neuroimaging study depends on the control task used in the subtraction method introduced in Chapter 1. If the control task used to subtract out the "irrelevant" activation happens to tap the other supporting areas, then the very design of the study prevents them from showing up in the final results. Determining the right control task is not a trivial concern.

Once the functionality of a given brain region is known, it is possible to use neuroimaging to identify which processes are invoked by a given task (Smith, 1997). For example, it has now been established by converging evidence from lesion data, direct electrical stimulation of the cortex, and neuroimaging findings that Broca's area mediates speech. If a task shows a 10% increase in blood flow in this left frontal area, then one can conclude that speech was produced even if it was subvocal without the participant uttering a single word. Such implicit speech might well occur, for example, when a participant silently rehearses a list of words or silently plans a solution to a problem. Changes in blood flow can detect this cognitive activity without requiring the participant to think aloud as in verbal protocols.

● CONNECTIONIST MODELS

As explained in Chapter 1, the digital computer provided a convenient analogy for understanding the architecture of the mind. Symbolic models were developed that shared key features in common with digital computers. Computations on information received by the senses were carried out in discrete serial steps such as encoding, memory storage, decision making, and response selection. A central processor used rules to process symbols similar to the rules used in computer software to process numbers and words. The digital computer helped to legitimize the study of the mind by providing an explicit model of the hidden operations of cognition that behaviorists viewed as inherently unavailable to scientists.

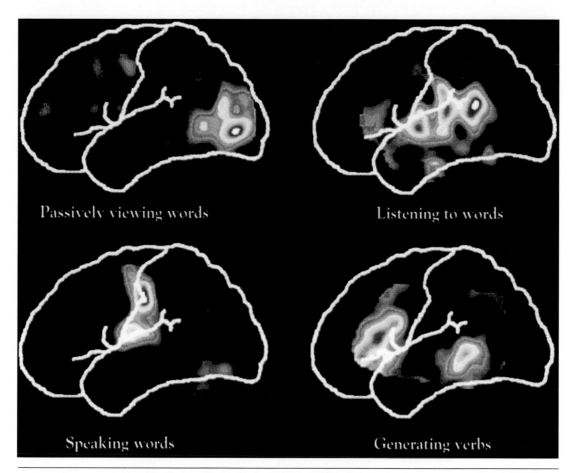

Color Plate 1. Different language tasks activate different brain regions, as isolated by using the method of subtraction in positron emission tomography (PET) neuroimaging. For example, the processes involved in, say, actively generating and speaking verbs aloud are isolated as compared with simply speaking words heard by the participant. Neural activation is inferred from blood flow detected by PET and is coded from high to low by white, red, orange, green, blue, and purple.

SOURCE: Posner, Peterson, Fox, and Raichle (1988).

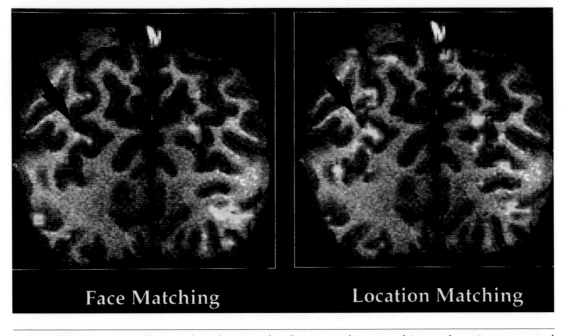

Color Plate 2. Attending to the identity of a face in a face-matching task activates ventral pathway regions (red arrow) in the temporal lobe, as revealed by functional magnetic resonance imaging (fMRI). By contrast, attending to the location of a face in a location-matching task activates dorsal pathway regions in the parietal lobe (green arrow).

SOURCE: Haxby, Clark, and Courtney (1997).

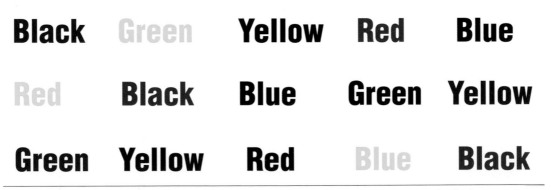

Color Plate 3. Stimuli for the Stroop task. Name the color of the ink in which the words are printed as rapidly as possible.

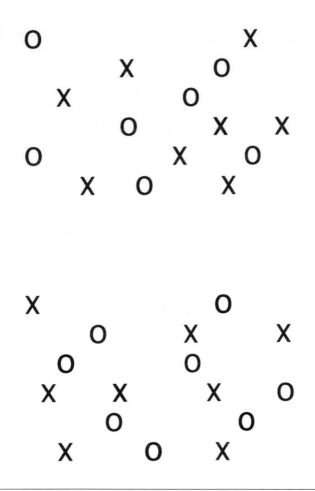

Color Plate 4. Stimuli used in the pop-out (a) and conjunctive (b) search tasks. Try to find a red X in each panel.

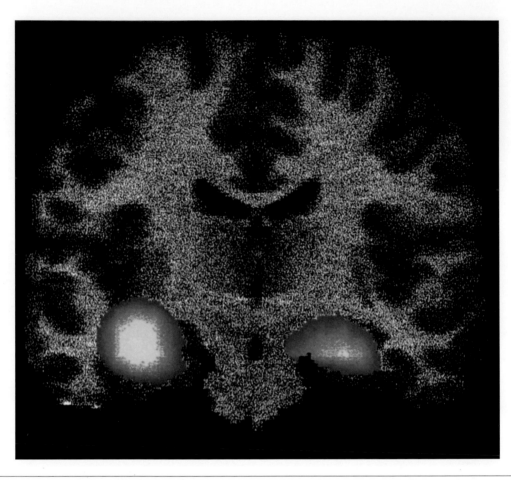

Color Plate 5. The temporal medial lobe, including the hippocampus, is activated by encoding pictures into memory. Shown here is bilateral activation of the hippocampus using functional magnetic resonance imaging (fMRI).

SOURCE: Martin, Wiggs, and Weisberg (1997).

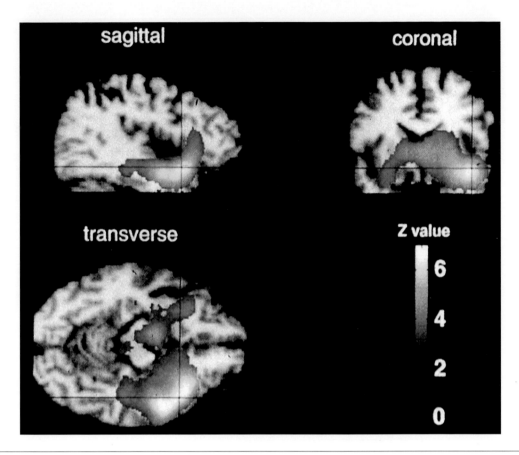

Color Plate 6. Retrieving an emotionally laden event from episodic memory activates regions in the right frontal and temporal lobes. Shown here are positron emission tomography (PET) results when an individual recollected a highly emotional episode that had occurred more than a year before.

SOURCE: Fink et al. (1996).

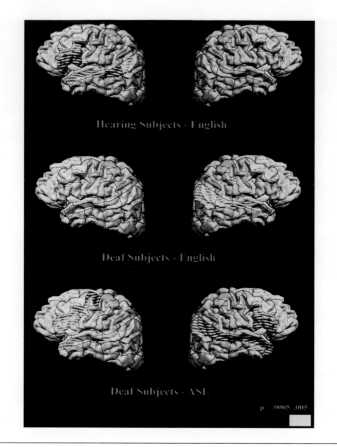

Color Plate 7.   Left hemisphere activation is revealed by functional magnetic resonance imaging (fMRI) both in hearing participants reading English and in congenitally deaf participants viewing signs in their native American Sign Language (ASL). When congenitally deaf native signers read English (their second language), activation is seen primarily in the right rather than the left hemisphere.

SOURCE: Neville and Bavelier (2000).

Example of the Four Types of Visual Stimuli

Words	Pseudowords	Letterstrings	False Fonts
ANT	GEEL	VSFFHT	ᴚᴚƎ
RAZOR	IOB	TBBL	ᒐԳᒐᴚ
DUST	RELD	TSTFS	ᴚOˀᴚ
FURNACE	BLERCE	JBTT	⊦ᒐⴖ
MOTHER	CHELDINABE	STB	ᴚᴚƎᒐᎮ
FARM	ALDOBER	FFPW	ᴚⴕOᴚ

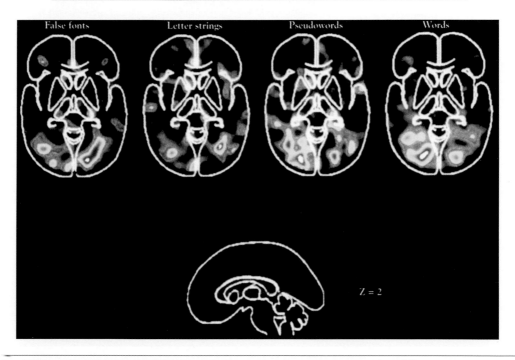

Color Plate 8. All four kinds of stimuli shown in the accompanying table activate regions in the visual cortex. Words and pseudowords that follow the orthographic rules of English activate additional language regions in the posterior left hemisphere.

SOURCE: Petersen Fox, Snyder, and Raichle (1990).

On the other hand, there are potentially important differences between the brain and a digital computer. As discussed earlier in the chapter, the brain performs computations in parallel and not in series. A single cognitive function is supported by parallel processing of multiple streams of data. Furthermore, it is not entirely clear whether the brain represents and processes symbols in the same way as a computer does. Although it makes sense for a computer to represent, say, a word as a unitary symbol, the brain may use a distributed representation. Recall from Chapter 1 that a connectionist representation of a word is distributed over multiple units, each of which codes one feature relevant to the word's meaning. Connectionist models are also called **parallel distributed processing (PDP)** models to emphasize these biologically inspired features that mimic the brain.

For example, consider how "coffee" could be represented in a connectionist model (Smolensky, 1988). It might include a node that codes "brown liquid" and another for "burnt odor." It would also include units that code features for different scenarios in which coffee appears. For example, nodes for "cup of coffee" would code for "upright container," "hot temperature," and "brown liquid contacting porcelain" as well as those already noted. Still other nodes would code features needed for a different scenario such as "can of coffee" (e.g., a node for "granules contacting tin"). Where in such a distributed representation is the symbol for "coffee"? It is everywhere and nowhere at the same time. All of the nodes that participate in coding the features of coffee together constitute the representation. Yet nowhere can one point to a specific node and say that this node, and not that one, is the symbol for coffee.

Neural networks are biologically inspired in the sense that they mimic the parallel computations of the brain and the use of distributed representations of knowledge. At the same time, neural networks are highly artificial because they are blatant but intentional simplifications of the brain. Each node is like an idealized neuron, and each connection is like an idealized synapse. They display none of the complexities of real neurons and synapses. The neural network operates with a very small number of nodes as compared with the billions found in a real brain. Finally, the network is designed to model a single function of the brain at a time. It is not intended as a complete replication of the brain, nor would this be of much value, for then the model would be so complicated that scientists would not understand it any better than the brain itself.

Basics of Neural Networks

Components of Neural Networks. Connectionist models attempt to understand the architecture of human cognition by using highly simplified, idealized

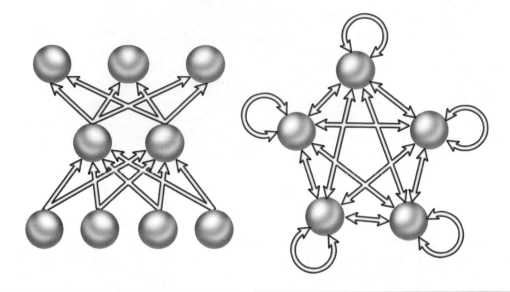

Figure 2.10. Two types of connectionist neural networks: a three-layer feedforward network (left) and a fully recurrent network (right).

models of the brain itself. Such models are composed of many nodes or nodes that behave in ways that mimic neurons. As with neurons, the nodes gather input from other nodes. Not all nodes are connected to all other nodes. In a typical model, there is a layer of input nodes that mimic sensory receptors, receiving information from the environment (see the left side of Figure 2.10). Another layer of nodes mimic motor neurons and provide a response from the network. Sandwiched in between is a **hidden layer** that receives information from the input layer and sends forward information to the output layer.

The connection between two nodes mimics a synapse between two neurons. In some networks, the connections between nodes are unidirectional. In other cases, the connections are bidirectional, meaning that feedback is provided to the node that sends forward information. A node can also be connected to itself, providing what is called recurrent feedback. A fully recurrent network with bidirectional connections is shown on the right in Figure 2.10.

Just as some synaptic connections are excitatory and some are inhibitory, positive or negative weights are associated with each artificial synapse in the neural network. The weight for a given connection between two nodes changes in value as the network processes inputs, gives outputs, and provides feedback. Each **connection weight** represents the knowledge state of the network; mathematically, the weight is a multiplier of the output value of the sending node.

The net input to node *i* is given by this equation:

$$= \text{net}_i = \sum_j w_{ij} a_j$$

The weight between node *i* and node *j* is given by w_{ij}, and the activation level of node *j* is given by a_j. To calculate the net input to node *i*, one sums the product of weight times activation for all node sources *j*.

Thus, if node *i* receives input from only one node whose output equals +1 and whose weight equals 0.5 (an excitatory connection), then its net activation equals 0.5. But if node *i* also receives input from an inhibitory node whose output equals +1 and whose weight equals –1.0 (an inhibitory connection), then its net activation would equal –0.5. In terms of the formula,

$$= [(+1 * 0.5) + (+1 * -1.0)] = -0.5.$$

Dynamics of Neural Networks. Each node responds to its summed input based on an activation function. The response of the neuron is given on the *y* axis for different input values, ranging from negative values to positive values. A linear function, for example, would gain strength in direct proportion to the strength of the inputs. This would mean that the response is always graded, gaining strength in direct relation to the strength of the inputs. Instead, neural networks typically use a nonlinear activation function such as is provided by the sigmoid function shown in Figure 2.11. Note that it mimics the all-or-none response of real neurons for any input value less than zero and for large positive inputs. That is, for negative inputs the response is 0.0, and for large positive inputs the response is 1.0. However, graded responses, falling between 0.0 and 1.0 in value, are obtained when the inputs are small positive values, between 0 and +5. The nonlinear response of this activation function is a crucial feature of how connectionist models achieve interesting behaviors (Elman et al., 1996). Each node behaves in a categorical all-or-none fashion under certain circumstances and in a sensitive graded fashion in others.

The connection weights in a neural network represent its current state of knowledge; mathematically, the weights are multipliers of the output values of all nodes sending information. Some weights are excitatory (positive values), and some are inhibitory (negative values). The net input to a given node is the sum of all excitatory and inhibitory input connections.

Logical Rules. To grasp how neural networks behave, it is useful to consider how simplified networks implement logical rules. Suppose that there are two input nodes and a single output node, as shown in the first two cases in Figure 2.12. This is a two-layer network with no hidden nodes. Suppose further that the activation function is strictly all-or-none, assuming output values of only 0 or 1. If input activation is less than or equal to 1, then node output is "off," taking a value of 0. If input activation exceeds 1 by any amount, then the node output is "on," taking a value of +1.

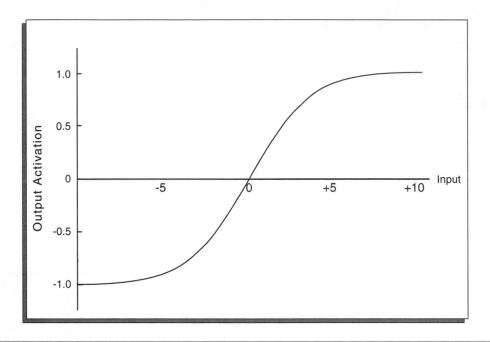

Figure 2.11. The sigmoid activation function typically used to relate inputs to output activation in each node of a neural network.

In the first case in Figure 2.12, the input patterns presented to the two nodes are shown below the two-layer network. Each input node sends an activation level to the output node equal to +1. The weight of each connection is 0.5. The net activation in this case is equal to 1.0, which triggers an "on" response from the output node. If the input from either node A or node B is less than +1, then the output is necessarily less than +1. This network models the logical AND relation. Its output is "on" if the input node on the left is +1 AND the input node on the right is +1; if one input or the other is 0 or if both inputs are 0, then the output is "off." In the next case, the weight for each node is changed to 1.0, and now a new logical rule is implemented. The OR rule stipulates an "on" output if one input or the other is +1 or if both inputs assume a value of +1. In all three situations, the net activation of the output node will equal or exceed 1.0.

The AND and OR rules are easily modeled with two-layer networks. Input patterns that are highly similar to one another give rise to the same output in both of these rules. They differ only in whether a single input node with 0 activation is grouped with the case of both nodes being 0 (OR), on the one hand, or whether a single input node with +1 activation is grouped with the case of both nodes being +1 (AND). A much more difficult logical rule is represented in the third case in Figure 2.12. This is called the Exclusive OR

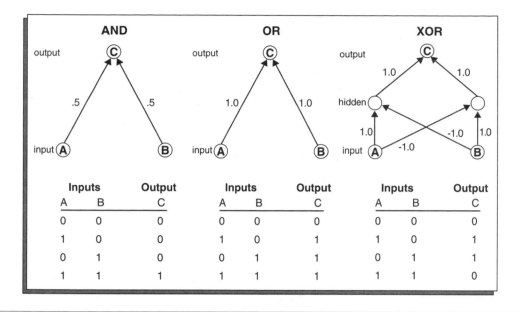

Inputs		Output	Inputs		Output	Inputs		Output
A	B	C	A	B	C	A	B	C
0	0	0	0	0	0	0	0	0
1	0	0	1	0	1	1	0	1
0	1	0	0	1	1	0	1	1
1	1	1	1	1	1	1	1	0

Figure 2.12. Two-layer neural networks can compute conjunction (AND) and inclusive disjunction (OR) logical rules. A hidden layer must be added to compute the exclusive disjunction (XOR) rule.

or the XOR rule. Now, similar inputs are not treated similarly at the output level. If one input or the other input, but not both, is +1, then the output is "on." If neither input is 0 or if both inputs are 0, then the output is "off." Here, then, highly dissimilar patterns must be categorized together. Take a few moments with assigning weights to the two-layer network to satisfy yourself that it fails to solve the XOR problem.

As you can verify, it is easy to get the network to produce an "off" or 0 output when the input patterns are (0, 0) and (1, 1). This can be achieved by setting the weights for each connection to 0. But this causes major problems in achieving the desired result for patterns (0, 1) and (1, 0). In these cases, we need a weight large enough so that the net activation reaches +1 when only one of the input nodes equals +1. By setting the weight at, say, +1, we solve our problem with these two patterns but foul up the results for the (0, 0) and (1, 1) cases.

The solution to the XOR problem illustrates how hidden layers can cause neural networks to behave in counterintuitive ways that are not based on similarity (Elman et al., 1996). In the third case in Figure 2.12, one hidden node is added to the network used to solve the AND problem. The connection weight between each input node and the hidden node above it is set at +1. However, the opposite hidden node is given an inhibitory connection with a weight equal to −1. The connection weights from the hidden nodes to the output nodes are excitatory with weights equal to +1. Running the test patterns (0, 1) and (1, 0) now yields outputs of +1, as required by the XOR rule. For example, an input of 1 to either one node or the other results in an "on" response from the output node. Note what happens to this network when both inputs are +1, however. In this case, the inhibitory connections to the hidden layer effectively cancel the input values in computing net activation. The net of the nodes in the hidden layer is 0, resulting in an "off" response at the output node.

The hidden layer in a neural network provides abstract internal representation of the inputs. By using inhibitory connections to the hidden layer, the network treats dissimilar inputs (0, 0) and (1, 1) as alike and similar inputs (0, 0) and (0, 1) as different. The central point is that adding a hidden layer augments the power of neural networks to produce complex and often counterintuitive behaviors.

> The hidden layer allows neural networks to solve the XOR problem, responding to similar inputs in different ways. It is akin to an abstract internal representation of information.

Back-propagation of Error. The XOR problem illustrates that, with the right architecture and weights assigned, a difficult logical rule can be modeled with a neural network. With these simplified networks, the modeler can determine the correct combination of weights that should be used to produce the desired output. As more and more nodes are added to the network and as more complex relationships between the inputs and outputs are needed, the number of computations needed for finding the right weights is too great. What is needed is a way for the neural network to learn on its own, slowly over long periods of time if necessary, a good combination of weights. So, how can neural networks learn through experience which weights should be adjusted to achieve a particular result?

A common algorithm or rule for teaching a neural network is called **back-propagation of error.** It is an illustration of supervised learning in which the specific outputs desired are known and serve as teaching values that provide feedback. Unsupervised learning can also occur in neural networks, but they fall outside the scope of this brief introduction. Another limitation of this discussion is that it illustrates only Hebbian learning. Hebb (1949) posited the following:

> When an axon of cell A is near enough to excite a cell B and repeatedly or persistently takes part in firing it, some growth process or metabolic change takes place in one of both cells such that A's efficiency, as one of the cells firing B, is increased. (p. 62)

Learning in neural networks is Hebbian when it takes place by altering the synaptic weights between A and B such that a future activation of A increases the probability of activating B.

The back-propagation algorithm is a procedure for training neural networks by returning an error signal from the output layer backward through hidden layers to the input layer. It aims to find the combination of weights that minimizes the error function. Back-propagation starts with the idea of comparing the weights from input nodes to those from output nodes so as to reduce the difference between the target output and the actual output (Elman et al., 1996). Because a target for the output layer is known, it is straightforward to evaluate the weights leading to these nodes and calculate how they should be changed. For the hidden layer, there is no specified target. How can one decide how much error is arising from a node weight at the hidden level if the desired output from that level is unknown? The answer is back-propagation.

The error is first calculated at the output level; the activation of an output node is subtracted from the desired output activation, called the target or teacher value. Next, the weights leading into that node are adjusted so that in future steps it is more or less activated, depending on the direction needed to reduce the error. This is done for all weights leading to the output node. If more than one output node is in the network, then these steps are repeated for each one. Finally, the "blame" for these output errors is assigned backward one level to the weights from the input layer to the hidden layer. This blame is apportioned based on (a) the errors observed on the output nodes to which a given hidden node is connected and (b) the strength of the connection between the hidden node and an output node. Thus, the error signal is propagated backward through the network to adjust the weights at the hidden layer. Although back-propagation is a useful technique, there is no guarantee that the optimal set of weights will be learned. However, a satisfactory, if not perfect, set of weights can often be found if learning takes place slowly by making only small changes to the weights with each error.

Back-propagation of error is a kind of supervised learning in which the specific outputs desired are known and serve as teaching values that provide feedback to the hidden layer and input layer.

Modeling English Verb Acquisition

Armed with the basic concepts of neural networks, it is helpful to examine how a connectionist model explains real findings on a problem of central importance in the field, namely, language acquisition in children. It is well-known that children move through three stages in learning the correct way to produce the past tense of English verbs. Some English verbs are regular, meaning that a suffix -ed is simply added to the verb stem to produce the past tense (e.g., show/showed). Other English verbs are irregular in various ways. In some cases the past tense form is similar to the present tense (e.g., grow/grew), and in some cases it is even identical (hit/hit). In other cases, the past tense bears no obvious sound or spelling relation to the present tense (e.g., go/went). Early in language acquisition, children begin to produce some irregular past tense forms correctly, saying "went" instead of "goed." However, as children learn more and more verbs and discover that regular verbs follow a simple rule of adding -ed, overgeneralization errors begin to intrude. That is, the -ed rule is overgeneralized to the irregular verbs already learned. It is as though children unlearn the correct forms of the irregular verbs and mistakenly learn, for example, goed. Finally, with additional exposure to the language, the overgeneralization errors drop out and children produce both regular and irregular verbs with few if any errors.

Rumelhart and McClelland (1986) examined how a two-layer network learned the past tense. A set of input nodes are connected directly to a set of output nodes with no hidden layer. The input is a phonological or sound representation of the verb stem, and the output is the phonological representation of the corresponding past tense of the verb. Each node represented a specific aspect of the sound representation in both the input and output layers. So, various clusters of these nodes were able to represent the different sound patterns needed to produce the verbs and their past tenses (e.g., /g/, /o/ and /w/, /e/, /n/, /t/). For example, some output nodes represented the -ed suffix used for regular verbs. Rumelhart and McClelland used back-propagation of error to teach the network the correct English past tense for all of the verbs.

Connectionist or PDP models of the brain are implemented as neural networks where each node acts as a simplified neuron. Knowledge representations are distributed across multiple nodes, and information is processed in parallel—two features that seem to be true of the brain.

More than 400 verbs typical of daily English usage (i.e., mostly regular with some irregular) were used to train the network. The results showed that the percentage of correct past tense verbs output by the model increased rapidly for regular verb forms early in training and then leveled off. Although it continued to improve with extensive training, the gains were quite small. Because most of the verbs were regular, the network quickly settled into adding the -ed suffix. Although this was beneficial for learning the regular verbs, it caused problems for learning the irregular verbs. Early on, performance improved rapidly for the irregular verbs also but then showed a sharp reduction in the percentage of correct forms. The point where this occurred coincided with the point where the network was nearly always correct with the regular verb forms. In other words, the network was likely to produce "goed" or "hitted" by mistake, showing overgeneralization errors. These mistakes generated large error signals that decreased the likelihood of turning on the -ed output nodes the next time. So, learning the irregular verbs interfered with learning the regulars and vice versa. Slowly, and only after extensive additional training, the network also was able to learn the correct forms for irregular verbs as well as for regular verbs. Thus, the well-established phenomenon of overgeneralization of regular verb forms was duplicated in a simple neural network using a single learning process.

SUMMARY

1. The relation of brain states to conscious states is an unsolved philosophical and scientific problem. The working assumption of many cognitive neuroscientists is materialism, which reduces mental states to brain states or regards mental states as emergent properties of the brain. Dualism is an alternative point of view that regards brain states and mental states as different entities altogether, although they may interact with one another. For example, a mental state might cause a change in the state of the brain or vice versa. To conduct research successfully in cognitive neuroscience, behavioral techniques are needed to measure mental activities (e.g., verbal reports), and neural recording techniques measure states of the brain. The aim is to relate these two parallel sets of data and not to replace behavioral measures with neurological measures. In other words, cognitive scientists adopt a methodological dualism to make progress in the field.

2. The human brain may well be the most complex structure in the known universe. The central nervous system contains on the order of 1 trillion neurons and about 1,000 trillion synaptic connections among these neurons. The organization of the brain is highly parallel, with many separate streams of data being processed to support a single function such as face recognition. Despite the complexity of interconnections, it is not the case that every neuron is connected to every other neuron through one pathway or another. Synaptic connections are either excitatory or inhibitory in their effect on the next neuron. The goal of cognitive neuroscience is to use data about the brain to help decide among alternative theories of perception, attention, memory, language, and other cognitive functions.

3. The cerebellum and brainstem are ancient structures and evolved long before mammals and primates. Lying above and surrounding the brainstem are the diencephalon and basal forebrain. These structures provide the basic life support functions of the body such as respiration and heart rate. They maintain a state of equilibrium in the internal environment of the body, called homeostasis. The limbic system lies in the next layer of neural structures and is similar in all mammals. The hippocampus is part of the limbic system and plays a critical role in emotion, learning, and memory. Surrounding the limbic system is the cerebral cortex. It appears gray in color, is arranged in layers, and averages only about 3 millimeters in thickness. Within the most recently evolved layer, the neocortex, enormous numbers of neurons are densely packed and folded, giving the brain its convoluted appearance on the surface. About 75% of the trillion neurons in the central nervous system are neocortical.

4. The neocortex is symmetrically divided into two hemispheres. Within each hemisphere, the frontal, temporal, parietal, and occipital lobes are distinguished. Some regions serve specific sensory and motor functions, whereas others—the association areas—play a role in numerous cognitive functions. Some functions are lateralized, meaning that one hemisphere plays a special role. For example, regions critical for language are located in the left hemisphere, whereas those involved in facial recognition and spatial processing depend on regions in the right hemisphere. It is incorrect to think of a cognitive function as completely lateralized, however. The right temporal lobe is necessary for the recognition of faces, but the visual processing of the faces in the left and right occipital lobes is also necessary.

5. Lesions or damage to cortical regions provide one way to study the cognitive functions served by the brain. Cognitive neuroscientists seek double dissociations in which one kind of lesion disrupts performance on Task A but spares performance on Task B, whereas a different kind of lesion disrupts Task B but spares Task A. Double dissociations suggest that the two brain regions damaged by the lesions support different cognitive functions, as measured by Tasks A and B. Electroencephalograms (EEGs) provide continuous recordings of the voltage changes created by large populations of neurons within a specific cortical region. An EEG signal that reflects the brain's response to a specific stimulus is called an event-related potential (ERP). Neuroimaging methods work by detecting changes in the blood supply serving the metabolic needs of activated neurons. Positron emission tomography (PET) measures blood flow and functional magnetic resonance imaging (fMRI). Using the method of subtraction, cognitive neuroscientists attempt to isolate the neural activation caused by a particular cognitive function.

6. Connectionist or parallel distributed processing (PDP) models are computer simulations that mimic basic features of the brain. The nodes of a PDP model can be activated in an all-or-none manner, and connections to other neurons can be either excitatory or inhibitory, as in real neurons. The representation of knowledge is distributed over many neurons. The connectionist architecture may include an input layer, an output layer, and a hidden layer that generates counterintuitive behaviors from the network. Neural networks can learn to provide the correct output from input received by modifying the strength of the connections among nodes. A typical way of learning relies on back-propagation of error signals from the output layer to earlier layers. Over time, the system adjusts connection weights to minimize the amount of error.

KEY TERMS ●

materialism
emergent property
dualism
frontal lobe
temporal lobe
parietal lobe
occipital lobe
cerebellum
brainstem
thalamus
hypothalamus
homeostasis
corpus callosum

limbic system
hippocampus
neocortex
double dissociation
event-related potential (ERP)
positron emission tomography (PET)
functional magnetic resonance
imaging (fMRI)
parallel distributed processing (PDP)
hidden layer
connection weight
back-propagation of error

PART II

FUNDAMENTALS OF COGNITION

Perception, attention, and memory are fundamental cognitive functions. Perception is needed to detect and recognize objects and events in the environment. Perceiving an event as it unfolds in the immediate environment is a here-and-now phenomenon. Yet even perception cannot take place without a variety of kinds of memory. For example, to recognize the book you are holding, it is necessary to have stored away in memory some representation of the concept "book." Memory involves mental representations of objects and events from the past. Yet these past experiences play a role in our perceptions of the moment as well as in our fantasies about the future. Of the tens, hundreds, and thousands of perceptions and thoughts about the past and future that we might dwell on at any one moment, only one is picked at any given instant in time. Attention is the means by which the mind focuses on one stream of thought to the exclusion of others. Attention works together with perception and memory to create a workable adaptive mind. All three are fundamental cognitive functions on which rests all higher order levels of thought such as language and reasoning.

CHAPTER 3

PERCEPTION

The mind comes to know the world through sensing and perceiving the environment. As the three-store model of information processing showed in Chapter 1 (Figure 1.3), input from the environment first enters sensory memory, where it is held briefly. Sensation refers to the transduction of physical energy, such as sound waves or electromagnetic radiation, into an initial mental representation that can be further processed and transformed over time. Transduction means the conversion of one kind of energy into another kind. For example, in vision, electromagnetic energy is converted into an electrical signal in neurons. As a result of this processing, the objects and events that are present in the environment are perceived in the sense of being detected. With still more processing, the objects and events are recognized in the sense of being categorized as meaningful. Even to recognize your own mother involves a sequence of processing stages that is complex and can take as long as a half second.

It is difficult to grasp that a process as rapid and effortless as perception involves multiple stages and transformations of mental representations. This point can be understood most easily when an illusion is perceived, that is, when perceptual processes construct a mental representation that does not accurately mirror the object in the environment. For example, examine the two creatures in Figure 3.1. The upper right creature appears larger than the

Figure 3.1. An illustration of the constructive nature of perception.
SOURCE: Shepard (1990).

lower left creature. Yet if you take a moment to measure them, you will find them to be equal in size. This is an example of an illusion related to depth perception. Cues in the drawing, such as the background lines converging from the bottom to the top of the picture, contribute to a perception of distance. Normally, an object at a distance is perceived as small relative to an object identical in size viewed from close-up. In Figure 3.1, the creature higher in the picture is inferred to be farther away, and yet it is not smaller as

is usually the case in the real world. As a consequence, the size of the upper right creature is transformed, and the end result of this constructive activity is an illusory perception of a large creature in the distance chasing a small creature in the front.

Perception, then, is the result of processes that construct mental representations of the information available in the environment. Such representations draw on information stored in memory as well as present in the environment. The knowledge that a familiar object is supposed to appear smaller at a distance affects our perception of the creatures in Figure 3.1. As further examples will demonstrate in this chapter, perception is always driven in part by expectations of how the world ought to look or sound based on knowledge stored in long-term memory. In a nightly dream or in the waking hallucinations of a psychotic individual, bizarre perceptions may be fabricated out of whole cloth, secreted from memory alone.

Perception is a large subject that lies well beyond the scope of a chapter in a book on cognitive psychology. To focus the discussion, four related problems in perception are addressed. Why is it that you can see anything at all, regardless of its identity? Given that you can see something, how do you recognize it as a person instead of, say, a hat rack? Even more specifically, how do you recognize that you are perceiving the face of a person rather than the back or side of the person's head? Finally, how do you recognize what the person is saying to you as the person moves his or her lips, uttering familiar sounds? Visual sensation, object recognition, face recognition, and speech recognition will illustrate important concepts in perception that lay the foundation of cognitive psychology as a whole.

VISUAL CONSCIOUSNESS ●

Visible light is a narrow band of electromagnetic energy. The wavelengths of light that may be sensed by the human visual system range from 400 to 700 nanometers, where 1 nanometer = 10^{-9} meters. As shown in Figure 3.2, the full spectrum of electromagnetic energy dwarfs this tiny band of visible light. Ultraviolet rays, X rays, and gamma rays are progressively shorter in wavelength and are not sensed by the visual system. The longer wavelengths of infrared rays, radar, radio waves, and AC circuits also go undetected. The visual system cannot construct a mental representation of an object without first transducing electromagnetic energy into a neural signal. It is sensitive only to wavelengths within the visible spectrum.

Visible light from the sun or other light sources, such as an indoor table lamp, is reflected off the objects in the environment. This light in what is called the visual field is structured in accordance with the structures of the

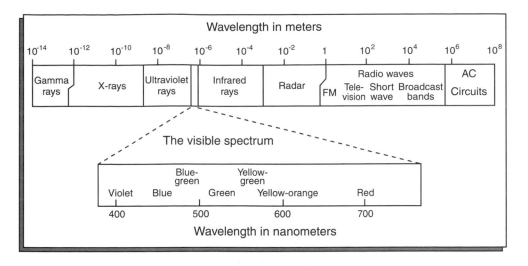

Figure 3.2. The spectrum of electromagnetic radiation includes a narrow band of visible light.

objects themselves. Without structured patterns of light in the visual field, it would be impossible to see in the sense of both detecting a stimulus and recognizing its identity. The detection process begins with the transduction of electromagnetic energy by photoreceptors in the retina of the eye. Photoreceptors are neurons specialized to convert visible light into electrical signals that may be propagated by the neurons of the visual system.

Visual Pathways

The cornea and the lens within the eye work together to bring the light reflected from an object into focus on the retina, the structure containing the photoreceptors. Failure to achieve a focused image is the cause of vision problems such as an inability to see a focused image of a close object (far-sightedness) or of a distant object (nearsightedness). The neural signals generated in the retina are sent via the optic nerve to a portion of the thalamus called the lateral geniculate nucleus, lying deep in the brain, as shown in Figure 3.3. The thalamus receives inputs from auditory and other sensory channels in addition to vision. The pathway continues onto the primary visual cortex in the occipital lobe.

The pathway from the optic nerve exiting the left eye projects to both the left and right hemispheres of the occipital lobe. Similarly, inputs to the

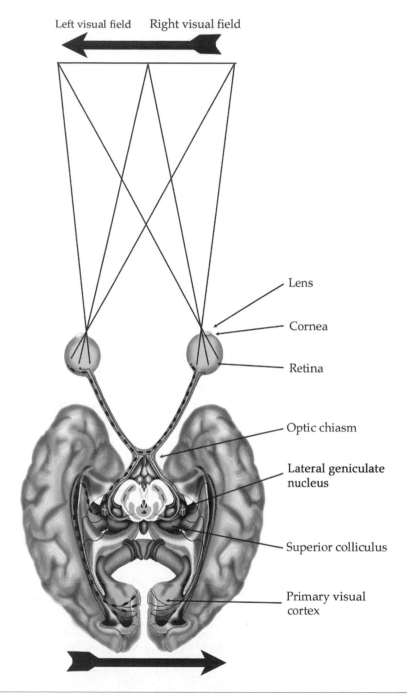

Figure 3.3. The visual pathways result in the representations of stimuli from the left visual field projecting to the right visual cortex and vice versa.

Representations of stimuli presented to the left visual field project to the right visual cortex, whereas those to the right visual field project to the left visual cortex.

right eye are also sent to and processed by both hemispheres. As shown in Figure 3.3, the axons of the optic nerve cross over to the opposite side of the brain at the optic chiasm. Here, the axons of the optic nerve from the inner or nasal half of each retina cross over to the opposite side of the brain. Those from the outer or temporal half remain on the same side of the brain. This arrangement results in a division of labor in vision such that the objects in the left visual field are processed by the right hemisphere and those in the right visual field are processed by the left hemisphere.

Although most signals follow the pathways just described, about 20% of the signals leaving the retina are projected to another structure lying at the top of the midbrain called the superior colliculus (Schiffman, 2000). This region controls eye movements. Importantly, then, there are signals from the retina processed by regions that do not terminate in the primary visual cortex. The significance of this pathway will soon become clear.

Visual Cortex

Seeing something rather than nothing depends on the processes that occur in the primary visual cortex (Crick, 1994). Visual consciousness hinges on more than a functional retina, an optic nerve, and a lateral geniculate nucleus. The occipital cortex must also function properly for one to be aware of an object in the visual environment. Two findings strongly support this conclusion.

Experiments on the development of the neurons in the visual cortex have shown that there are critical periods during which stimulation must be received for normal development. In cats, the critical period begins during the first few weeks of life and lasts about 3 or 4 months. In humans, the critical period may extend much longer to 4 or 5 years (Schiffman, 2000). To illustrate, Blakemore and Cooper (1970) raised kittens in an environment that restricted the kind of visual stimulation received. The kittens were kept in darkness for all but about 5 hours a day. During this time, they lived in a restricted environment consisting only of horizontal lines for one group of kittens and vertical lines for another group. After about 5 months of this selective exposure, the kittens were tested for their visual awareness of horizontal and vertical lines.

Some tests used single-cell recordings from the primary visual cortex. The cortical cells responded to the orientation of lines received early in life. Having been exposed only to horizontal lines, for example, the cells of the primary visual cortex fired at above baseline rates only to horizontal stimuli. Of critical importance, when a black bar was held horizontally, the kittens initially exposed to horizontal lines batted at the bar in play. Their behavior suggested that they could see the bar. By stark contrast, the kittens raised in the vertical line environment ignored the horizontal bar, implying that the cortical cells were needed for visual awareness.

A second result from a neuropsychological case study confirms the conclusion that the cortex is necessary for visual consciousness. The patient known as "D. B." was a 34-year-old male who suffered from severe migraine headaches. All treatments failed, and the migraines became so severe that surgeons took the extreme step of removing part of his occipital cortex. The surgery was successful in reducing the intensity of the migraines, but it left D. B. blind in about a quarter of his visual field, specifically objects presented to his left. A test light was presented on a screen situated in front of D. B. The location of the target was varied from trial to trial in a random way, and D. B. was asked to point to its location.

As shown in Figure 3.4, when the target was presented to his normal sighted visual field to the right, D. B.'s pointing responses tracked the actual location of the target, producing a straight line for sight with awareness. Astonishingly, D. B. performed nearly as well when the target was presented to his blind left visual field. Although D. B. reported no visual awareness of seeing anything on these trials, his pointing responses closely (but not perfectly) tracked the target (Weiskrantz, 1986). Despite his lack of conscious perception in these regions, when D. B. was encouraged to guess where the test light had occurred, he was remarkably accurate.

Vision without awareness as a result of lesions in the occipital cortex is called **blindsight.** It demonstrates the dependence of intact cortical regions for visual consciousness. Apparently, D. B. succeeded in the location task even in his blind field of vision by using information processed in the superior colliculus. This structure deep in the midbrain controls eye movements and seems to have allowed D. B. to identify the location of an object not consciously seen.

> Blindsight is vision without awareness that can be observed in patients with lesions in the occipital cortex.

PATTERN RECOGNITION ●

The term **pattern recognition** refers to the step between the transduction and perception of a stimulus in the environment and its categorization as a meaningful object. There is more to seeing or hearing than simply perceiving the patterns of light or sound available in the environment. It is necessary to categorize the object on the basis of its perceived features. Look at the drawings in Figure 3.5. Each drawing shows the same object from a different point of view. Although the visual information received by the retina in each case is

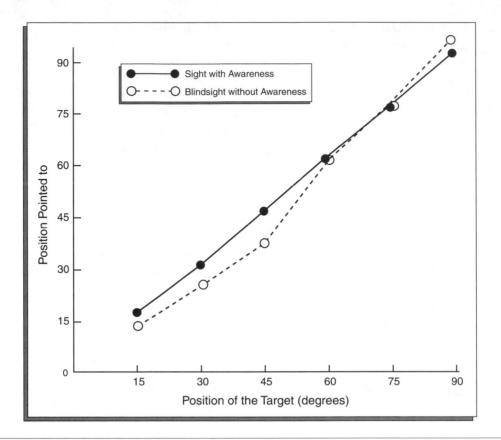

Figure 3.4. Blindsight enabled a patient to point to the location of a target unaccompanied by any visual awareness of seeing it.

The ability to perceive depends on pattern recognition— categorizing objects and events detected in the environment by matching their preliminary representations with patterns stored in long-term memory.

quite different, the same object is easily recognized. The visual features are perceived and then used to categorize the object as a dog. The mental representation of dogs, their appearance in particular, must be retrieved and matched against the visual features that are perceived in the drawing for recognition to succeed.

Agnosia

A stimulus can be perceived and understood in terms of its properties but not recognized as a meaningful object, a neuropsychological condition called agnosia. Patients suffering from lesions in certain regions of the brain can see objects but not recognize them at all. Such individuals are not blind;

Figure 3.5. An example of pattern recognition in which different features in each drawing are categorized as a dog.

nonetheless, they fail to see in the fullest sense because for them pattern recognition has failed.

For example, Sacks (1970) described a man identified as "Dr. P" who suffered from a massive brain tumor or degenerative disease that destroyed portions of his occipital cortex. Dr. P taught music at a local school and appeared to Sacks as a cultivated man with great charm, humor, and imagination—certainly not someone suffering terribly from a serious brain disorder. However, on closer examination, it became clear that Dr. P suffered from a form of visual agnosia, specifically an inability to recognize objects clearly from their shapes. For example, during a neurological examination, Dr. P had removed his shoe as part of a reflex test. When asked to put his shoe back on, Dr. P seemed baffled as he stared intently at his foot, put his hand to it, and said, "This is my shoe, no?" Stunned, Sacks replied, "No, it is not. That is your foot. There is your shoe." "Ah!," exclaimed Dr. P, "I thought that was my foot" (p. 9). The damage to Dr. P's brain had impaired his ability to pick up the concrete textures and other details of visual experience. Because the outline of his foot matched the outline of his shoe, he could not distinguish between the two. As Dr. P prepared to leave the examining room, he "reached out his hand and took hold of his wife's head, tried to lift it off, to put it on. . . . He had apparently mistaken his wife for a hat! His wife looked as if she was used to such things" (p. 10).

Two kinds of visual agnosia have been documented, depending on whether the right or left hemisphere had sustained damage (Gazzaniga, Ivry, & Mangun, 1998). In both cases, the primary visual cortex is intact and supports the ability to see objects in the visual field, but the objects cannot be recognized. Normally, humans can recognize an object despite wide variations in the details of how the object looks. A dog is a dog, no matter its distance, its orientation, or the angle of viewing. In the case of **apperceptive agnosia,** such ready object recognition fails of difficulties in identifying the visual features that define a perceptual category.

Warrington (1982) discovered that patients with damage to the rear or posterior region of their right hemispheres made frequent errors in recognizing objects presented at unusual angles. In the example given earlier, a picture of a dog from the front, showing its head in relation to its body, was easily recognizable by all patients in the study. Yet when the picture was taken from behind, without the dog's face or feet in the picture, patients with posterior right hemisphere damage often made mistakes, as shown in Figure 3.6. By contrast, other patients with posterior damage in the left hemisphere were able to succeed on this test with a high level of accuracy. Other data showed that damage to the anterior regions of either hemisphere did not cause a problem on the unusual views test, leading to the conclusion that the right posterior hemisphere is critical for successful perceptual categorization.

In the case of **associative agnosia,** object recognition fails because of difficulties in identifying the functional features that define a semantic category. The problem is not at all perceptual in nature. Instead, the sufferer of associative agnosia cannot categorize objects successfully at an abstract level of meaning. The unusual views test that trips up patients with apperceptive

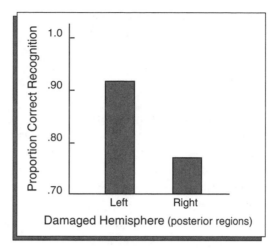

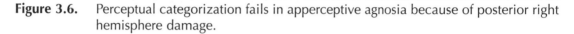

Figure 3.6. Perceptual categorization fails in apperceptive agnosia because of posterior right hemisphere damage.

agnosia fails to bother those with associative agnosia. By contrast, a test that requires matching objects in terms of semantic categories while ignoring their visual appearance causes problems for individuals with associative agnosia. For example, suppose that an individual is shown a cane, a closed umbrella, and an open umbrella and is asked to identify which two objects have the same function. An individual with perceptual agnosia has no difficulty in seeing the open and closed umbrella as representing the same semantic category. Individuals with associative agnosia often fail to do so; they cannot see beyond the perceptual similarities of the cane and the closed umbrella.

These two kinds of agnosia demonstrate that the pattern recognition process involves two separate levels of categorization. The visual features of an object must first be matched against representations in long-term memory that identify perceptual categories. Variations in how an object looks (e.g., its orientation, the angle of viewing) must be ignored, whereas features that do matter (e.g., eyes, ears, fur, tail) are heeded. This perceptual level of categorization appears to be mediated by posterior regions in the right hemisphere and occurs prior to semantic categorization (Warrington, 1985). As can be seen in patients with associative agnosia, it is possible to see two objects as alike perceptually (e.g., a cane and a closed umbrella) and to fail to see that they belong to different semantic categories and have different names. The functional features of an object must also be matched against representations stored in long-term memory to identify semantic categories and names.

Apperceptive agnosia refers to a failure of pattern recognition caused by an inability to categorize objects at a perceptual level of analysis. Associative agnosia, by contrast, is caused by an inability to categorize objects at a functional semantic level of analysis.

Warrington (1985) contended that this second stage is dependent on processes supported by the left hemisphere.

Top-Down Versus Bottom-Up Processes

Organized knowledge representations or schemas direct exploration of the environment to sample features of the objects and events to be perceived.

A **schema** is a mental representation that organizes knowledge about related concepts. Imagine for a moment the classroom that you attend for cognitive psychology. In forming a mental picture of this particular environment, you activate a schema that represents what you know about classrooms in general and their relations to other types of rooms. The schema involves many concepts such as those of a room, a desk, a table, a computer, an overhead projector, a projection screen, and a video recorder. In imagining each of these objects, you activate their conceptual representations, which represents what you know about the general characteristics of a category of objects, say, tables.

As you walk into the building on campus containing your classroom, your mind unconsciously begins to anticipate the objects and events that will soon be seen and heard. These anticipations play a vital role in directing exploration of the environment (Neisser, 1976). The steps you take, the way you turn your head, the objects you reach for and grasp, and the eye movements you make are directed by your expectations. For example, the eye movements made to explore the environment are guided by your immediate goals (Yarbus, 1967). If you anticipate seeing a particular friend in the classroom, for example, then your eyes will quickly scan the faces of people to confirm your expectation. If expectations are violated by novel surprising events, then these are explored extensively. For example, suppose that a student brings his pet boa constrictor to class one day. People, desks, and books are expected in a classroom—but not snakes. The surprising object would be scrutinized immediately.

Top-down or **conceptually driven processes** reduce the need to sample all of the information available in the environment by providing the perceiver with expectations. Simultaneously, bottom-up or **data-driven processes** analyze the edges, lines, areas of light and dark, colors, sounds, and other physical features available briefly in sensory memory. These processes pick up the features needed to confirm or refute expectations. Through such simultaneous processing from both the bottom up and the top down, people can perceive the features of the environment with remarkable quickness and accuracy.

The contribution of each type of process depends on the perceptual circumstances (Shepard, 1984). Strong bottom-up activation occurs when perceiving under good viewing conditions. In poor ambiguous viewing conditions, accurate perception depends more strongly on top-down than on bottom-up activation. Very strong top-down activation is responsible for the hallucinations experienced nightly in dreams. The lack of any significant external input during dreaming might be why it is experienced as real (Antrobus, 1991). Daydreaming, or imagining an event while awake and concurrently processing some external events, also depends on top-down activation, but it is less intense and is not experienced as real.

In the laboratory, several experiments have shown that the speed as well as the accuracy with which a person can identify an object depends on the context in which the process occurs (Biederman, Glass, & Stacy, 1973; Palmer, 1975; Friedman, 1979). One expects to see a cow in a farm scene or a fireplug in a city street scene. Putting the cow and the fireplug in the wrong scene measurably slows their recognition by pitting top-down processes against bottom-up processes. Preventing the activation of a schema or frame—by removing or scrambling the context so that it looks incoherent—also hinders pattern recognition by requiring that all of the work be done from the bottom up.

Perceiving each word on this page as you read is conceptually driven in part. Reicher (1969) presented a word (WORK), a nonword (ORWK), or a single letter (K) as a stimulus to participants. A mask (####) then appeared that stopped the processing of the original stimulus by filling the contents of iconic memory with irrelevant visual elements. Probe letters also appeared above (D) and below (K) the fourth element of the mask. The observers then guessed which of these had occurred earlier. Surprisingly, the letter K was correctly identified more often when it appeared in the word than when it appeared in isolation. The **word superiority effect** refers to a single letter being recognized faster in the context of a whole word than when presented as an isolated letter. The word activates conceptually driven processes that ease the recognition of each individual letter. The nonword stimulus fails to activate these processes and so supports the same level of identification accuracy as does the single letter.

Tulving, Mandler, and Baumal (1964) showed how varying amounts of context provided in reading speeds word recognition. They presented a target word either with no context (0 words), as the last word of a phrase (4 words), or as the last word of a sentence (8 words). The more context provided, the more conceptually driven processes should aid recognition of the target. As shown in what follows, the participant first read the context, if given, and then briefly viewed a target word such as "opponent":

opponent

challenged by a dangerous opponent

The political leader was challenged by a dangerous opponent

Paradoxically, a single letter is identified faster when in the context of an entire word than when isolated. This word superiority effect is caused by top-down or conceptually driven expectations activated by the word.

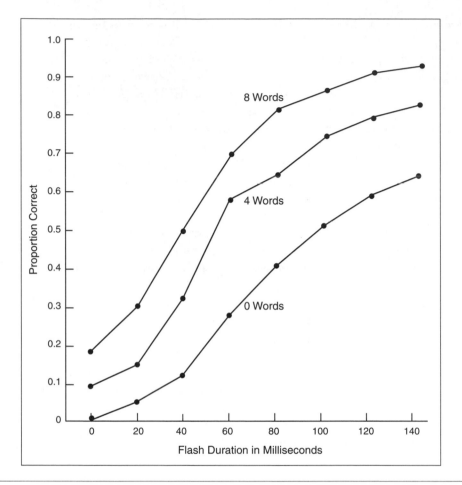

Figure 3.7. Word recognition varies with the amount of context provided.
SOURCE: Tulving et al. (1964).

Conceptually driven processes operate from the top down—from long-term memory to sensory memory—to identify the stimulus. Data-driven processes operate from the bottom up—from sensory memory to long-term memory—to achieve the same goal.

Tulving et al. also varied the exposure duration of the final word, "opponent," from 0 to 140 milliseconds. The longer the exposure, the more data-driven processes should aid recognition. Note that in the zero condition, only conceptually driven processes are at work, allowing perhaps a correct guess about the target word. As can be seen in Figure 3.7, with eight words of context, the proportion of correct recognition averaged nearly .20. The systematic increases with longer exposure durations show the role of making more data available from the bottom up. The differences among the eight, four, and zero word curves show the role of more precise expectations from the top down.

Object Representations

If pattern recognition requires matching perceived information against perceptual representations stored in long-term memory, then what is the nature of these representations? Research into this question has examined several possibilities, but a firm answer to the question remains elusive. One possible solution is that perceptual concepts are stored as lists of distinctive features. For example, the distinctive features of block letters can be specified readily. Some features are straight lines at particular angles (e.g., E, M) and others are curved (e.g., O, C). A list of a relatively small number of **distinctive features** allows a complete specification of the printed alphabet (Gibson, 1969).

Feature Detectors. There is powerful evidence that the visual cortex of mammals is organized to detect the presence or absence of simple features. Hubel and Wiesel (1959, 1963) presented an edge, a slit of light, or a darkened bar at different orientations to the eyes of a cat or a monkey. At the same time, they recorded the neural activity in single nerve cells in the occipital lobe of the lightly anesthetized animal. Hubel and Wiesel discovered that the cells were tuned to respond maximally to bars of a particular orientation. For instance, some cells fired rapidly to a vertical bar, whereas others preferred a horizontal bar.

In human vision, evidence for feature detection can be seen in visual search tasks. Neisser (1963) asked for the participant to search for a particular letter among a long list of lines of printed letters. In one condition, the letter shared many features with the distractors such as searching for Z among T, L, K, M, V, and other letters with straight lines. In another condition, the target letter, say Z, stood out clearly from the distracters such as O, Q, P, B, D, and other rounded letters. The more rapid search times obtained by Neisser in the second condition, in which the target stood out, suggests that the human visual cortex analyzes stimuli in terms of simple component features. Note that if people compared each letter to a unique template in memory, then their search time ought to be the same for the straight and rounded distracters. This is one of several experimental results at odds with the view that patterns are stored as templates (Hummel & Biederman, 1992).

The problem of how objects are recognized based on feature detection is more complex than the example considered so far. The distinctive features of printed text are easier to analyze than the features of real-world objects in general (Pinker, 1984). Although it is theoretically possible to describe objects in terms of line segments, widths, lengths, line crossings, rectangles, and other basic visual features (Julesz, 1986), it is unclear exactly how the

Distinctive features differentiate objects during pattern recognition. Neural cells in the occipital cortex are tuned to fire when stimulated by simple lines presented at a particular orientation.

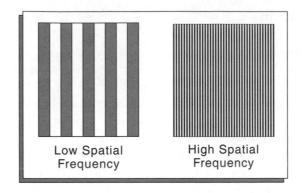

Low Spatial
Frequency

High Spatial
Frequency

Figure 3.8. The visual cortex includes channels selectively tuned to high and low spatial frequencies.

brain performs this analysis (Banks & Krajicek, 1991). Furthermore, it is known that the visual cortex responds to more than localized geometric features. Spatial frequencies refer to how rapidly a stimulus changes in light intensity as a function of space, a distributed stimulus property. For example, closely spaced alternations in light and dark bars illustrate a high spatial frequency, as shown on the right in Figure 3.8. A low spatial frequency is illustrated on the left. Some simple cells in the visual cortex respond best to gratings of a specific high, medium, or low spatial frequency (Maffei & Fiorentini, 1973).

Structural Descriptions. Other researchers have explored an additional problem with the feature detection theory of pattern recognition. Specifically, they have shown that the relations among features are as important to recognition as the features themselves. A letter Z is not simply three independent lines at certain angles. The lines must be structured in accordance with the rules for constructing the letter Z. A face, for instance, is not simply a collection of features positioned haphazardly—an eye here, a nose there, a mouth over there. The relations among features must conform to the rules that define the structure of the face. In other words, the whole object is not simply a list of independent features. The relations among features are equally important. One also needs a grammar or set of rules for how to put the features together properly (Reed, 1973; Sutherland, 1968).

Structural descriptions consider not just features, but also the relations among features, to facilitate pattern recognition.

The importance of such relations to perception can be seen in Figure 3.9. Notice that the objects labeled (a) and (b) contain the same features. But the structural relations among these features differ, and our perception differs accordingly. In the same way, the objects labeled (c) and (d) are seen as a cup and as a pail only by virtue of their structural relations among the same features (Biederman, 1985). Several other studies have shown that people

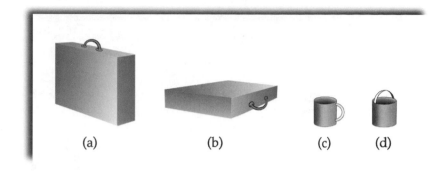

(a)   (b)   (c)   (d)

Figure 3.9. A demonstration of the importance of structural relations.
SOURCE: Biederman (1985).

process the relations among features in perception (Hummel & Biederman, 1992; Reed, 1974; Reed & Johnson, 1975).

Biederman (1987) proposed a set of 26 basic geometric features (geons) that, when put into proper structural relationships, constitute all visual objects. A sample of these is presented in Figure 3.10. A simple object such as a cup is comprised of the geons numbered 3 and 5. The telephone involves these geons and more that are related very differently compared with the cup.

An interesting prediction of Biederman's theory is that not only is relational information needed, but it may be more critical to perception than the features themselves. Biederman (1985) deleted 65% of the contours (features) from drawings of common objects, as illustrated in Figure 3.11. For example, the cup in the middle retains the vertices so that an observer can pick up the relations among the remaining contours. The cup on the right destroys this relational information by removing contours from the vertices. Biederman found that observers, after a brief 100-millisecond exposure, could accurately identify the middle cup 70% of the time as compared with only 50% for the right-hand cup. The color, texture, and other details that add such richness to our perceptual experience are less relevant to recognition than are the vertices. In support of this, Biederman and Ju (1988) found that schematic line drawings are indeed recognized as quickly as color photographs of objects.

FACE PERCEPTION ●

Thus far, it is clear that explaining how one is able to see and recognize a familiar object is a nontrivial problem. The visual system constructs a mental

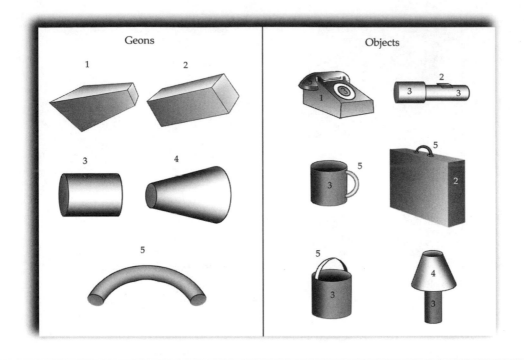

Figure 3.10. Examples of geons or basic subobjects involved in scene perception.
SOURCE: Biederman (1985).

representation that allows the object in the environment to be both seen and understood as meaningful. In the final two sections of this chapter, it is shown that particular kinds of pattern recognition invoke specialized processes. The evidence to date suggests that the perception of faces and speech each draws on processes that have evolved to cope with the particular demands of the task.

Because social interactions depend on the ability to recognize faces and speech, it is perhaps not surprising that the cognitive system is specialized in this manner. Obviously, speech is central to communication between two or more humans. Less obviously, facial expressions provide a key means for communicating emotional states. Through body language and particularly facial expressions, humans communicate whether they feel happiness, sadness, or anger, for example. The role of holistic processing and modularity in face processing is presented next, and then the chapter concludes with a consideration of speech perception.

Figure 3.11. Perception of the object depends on the availability of structural relations at the vertices.

SOURCE: Biederman (1985).

Holistic Versus Analytic Processing

Although the theorist can identify the features or parts that comprise a whole object, an observer may perceive only the meaningful object. Several factors control the extent to which perception is dominated by the whole versus the parts, including the type of stimuli presented to the observer and the task required of the observer (Treisman, 1987). **Holistic processing** refers to perceiving the whole object; **analytic processing** refers to perceiving the features that comprise the whole. Holistic processing, then, involves the spatial-relational aspects of the features of the whole face. Analytic processing targets the nose, the eyes, the lips, and other specific features instead of their relations. Faces, perhaps more than any other object, are perceived holistically rather than analytically. An intriguing demonstration of this fact comes from an illusion that occurs when the normal orientation of facial features is inverted (Thompson, 1980).

First, study the pair of faces in Figure 3.12 in the normal orientation. In the face on the left, the eyes and mouth have been turned upside down. As you can see, the face takes on a grotesque appearance as a consequence. Now, turn the book upside down and study the two faces again. Notice that when viewing the faces in an unusual orientation, the grotesqueness disappears. Both faces take on a normal appearance. This demonstrates that in the normal orientation, holistic processing heavily influences face perception. The individual features are encoded, but so too are their spatial relations that together comprise the whole face. By rearranging the normal relations among the eyes, nose, mouth, and eyebrows, the face looks grotesque. But the holistic processing of the face can be disrupted by inverting the face 180 degrees, a position that we rarely encounter in everyday perception. The face as a whole no longer dominates perception; the individual parts of the face are taken on their own terms and appear perfectly normal to the eye.

Faces are unique in that holistic processing is much stronger than analytic processing for them as compared with other objects.

Several studies have shown that face perception is more vulnerable to inversion than are other kinds of objects (Searcy & Bartlett, 1996; Valentine, 1988). Recently, Murray, Yong, and Rhodes (2000) found that as a face is rotated from 0 to 180 degrees, there is a discontinuity in how it appears. Up to rotations of 90 degrees, a normal face looks increasingly bizarre, whereas the distorted face looks less and less bizarre. Between 90 and 120 degrees of rotation, the distorted face begins to look fine and continues to do so on up to a complete, 180-degree inversion. This is not so with the normal face, which continues to look more bizarre as it is rotated on up to 180 degrees. Try rotating the page of this book and notice what happens to the distorted face somewhere between 90 and 120 degrees. Inversion disrupts the holistic processing of spatial-relational information more than it disrupts the analytic processing of features.

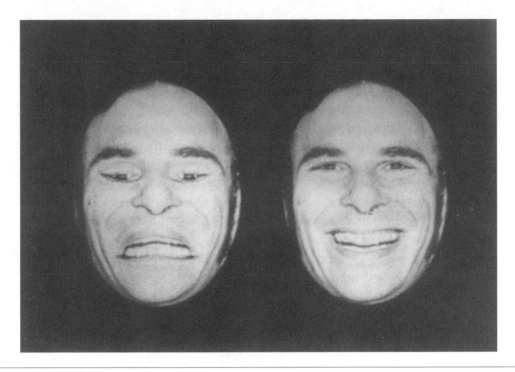

Figure 3.12. A demonstration of holistic processing of faces.
SOURCE: Bartlett and Searcy (1993).

Modularity

Why is it that upright faces should be perceived more holistically than analytically? Farah (1990, 1998) presented several lines of converging evidence pointing to the existence of a specialized module for face recognition. A **module** refers to a set of processes that are automatic, fast, encapsulated apart from other cognitive systems, and instantiated in a localized area of the brain (Fodor, 1983). There may be several modules, each dedicated to the perception of an important class of stimuli such as faces or speech.

Prosopagnosia is a selective inability to recognize faces that does not involve other kinds of vision difficulties. A prosopagnosic patient cannot recognize the photographs of famous individuals, but when the patient is tested on other kinds of complex visual discrimination tasks, no deficit is found (MacNeil & Warrington, 1993). For example, a sheep farmer had no problem in distinguishing photographs of his own sheep from pictures of other sheep despite their close similarity in appearance. Yet his recognition of human faces was profoundly impaired.

Inverted faces are not, therefore, processed holistically the way normally oriented faces are. If the holistic processing of spatial relations in faces is driven by a specialized module, then what would happen if this module were damaged as in prosopagnosia? Normal controls have more difficulty in recognizing inverted faces as compared with upright faces because the module constructs an accurate representation of the test face. If damaged, the module would provide inaccurate information and disrupt performance. Farah (1990) discovered that a prosopagnosic patient actually correctly identified more faces when they were inverted (72%) than when they were upright (58%). Normal controls showed the expected pattern of more correct identifications with upright faces (94%) than with inverted faces (82%). By inverting the face, the damaged module in the prosopagnosic was removed from play, thus improving performance.

Farah (1990) also discovered that damage to the occipital and temporal cortices, usually bilateral damage in both hemispheres, was correlated with prosopagnosia. A localized region of the temporal lobe seems to be crucial for face recognition. One way to demonstrate this localization is to examine other neurological disorders and compare their effects on different kinds of tests. Reading and face recognition tests both are complex visual tasks that reveal a double dissociation. There are a variety of kinds of lesions in the brain caused by head injuries or strokes that are collectively called acquired dyslexia. Relative to normal controls, dyslexic patients perform poorly on a reading test but show no impairment on a test of face recognition. By contrast, prosopagnosic patients show deficits on the face recognition test but not on the reading test, relative to normal controls. Because brain damage can be extensive, some of these patients had trouble in recognizing objects of any kind. That is, they suffered agnosia in addition to prosopagnosia or dyslexia. However, patients rarely suffered from a combination of dyslexia and prosopagnosia. In short, prosopagnosia was uncorrelated with acquired alexia, suggesting that they are handled by different structures in the brain and can be selectively damaged.

Another source of evidence in favor of a face recognition module comes from normal college students in an object versus part recognition task. Participants learned the names of normal upright faces and objects during the first phase of the experiment. Next, they were asked to recognize the faces or objects in the whole condition. For example, they either were shown a face and asked "Is this Jim's face?" or were shown a house in the object condition and asked "Is this Jim's house?" In the part condition, they were tested on particular features of the studied faces or objects. For example, they might be shown a nose in isolation and asked "Is this Jim's nose?" or might be shown a door and asked "Is this Jim's door?" Recognition was just as good for the parts of houses as for whole houses. However, recognition was substantially less

A specialized module is responsible for face perception. Other modules may exist for specific kinds of perception such as speech recognition.

accurate in the part condition than in the whole condition for faces. The participants had difficulty in processing the faces in an analytic manner—zeroing in on, say, the nose by itself—during study or test. This outcome is understandable if faces are processed holistically by a specialized module.

SPEECH RECOGNITION ●

The final example of pattern recognition may well be the most remarkable perceptual feat performed by humans. Having recognized the face of a person standing before you, the challenge remains to decipher the sounds being emitted by the person's vocal tract. Spoken language and its comprehension is a vast subject to which several chapters are devoted later in the book. The issue at hand here is how the complex, information-packed auditory signals of spoken language are perceptually recognized at an extraordinarily rapid rate, enabling you to hear the words spoken to you.

Consider that language uses basic speech sounds to distinguish words with different meanings. A speech sound or phonological segment that makes a difference in meaning is called a **phoneme.** Each phoneme is pronounced in a distinctly different manner from all others, and this difference in pronunciation signals a difference in the meaning. For example, pill and kill differ with respect to the initial phoneme, and this signals a difference in the meaning of the two words. Now, consider that normal speech unfolds at a rate of about 12 phonological segments per second. The speech perception system handles this rate with ease and can in fact cope very well with speech artificially accelerated to 50 phonological segments per second (Foulke & Sticht, 1969). A listener can even understand a speaker who whispers a sentence despite the fact that whispering alters not only the intensity of the acoustic signal but also its frequency. It has been estimated that the brain must process 40,000 bits of information per second to recognize the phonemes that are the building blocks of spoken language (Fodor, 1983). The fast automatic extraction of speech signals suggests that it is the work of a module dedicated to the task.

That everyday speech is riddled with noise and indeterminacy makes the task of speech perception all the more daunting (McClelland & Elman, 1986). Unless the speaker formulates complete sentences and articulates them clearly and slowly in a quiet setting, the speech signal is fragmentary. Yet somehow listeners manage to understand speakers who rapidly utter incomplete sentences and even distorted words in noisy environments. A speaker might not articulate clearly, but the listener uses top-down recognition processes to fill in the gaps. For example, Warren (1970) presented listeners with tape-recordings of a sentence with a single phoneme deleted, for example, "The state governors met with respective legi*latures convening in the capital city." The asterisk marked the spot where the /s/ was removed and replaced with a cough lasting 0.12 seconds. Warren presented the recording to 20 listeners and asked them if any sounds were missing. Only one individual heard a missing sound, and that person selected the wrong sound as missing. Clearly, the listeners had restored the missing phoneme. Even when the missing phoneme comes at the beginning of the word (e.g., *eel) and is disambiguated by a later word in the sentence (shoe), listeners rarely report any perception of a gap.

The primary reason for the intense computational requirements of speech recognition is that the acoustic signals arriving at the ear do not map in a one-to-one fashion to the critical speech sounds. A **speech spectrogram** represents the physical acoustic energy of an utterance by plotting frequency in hertz or cycles per second on the y axis and time in milliseconds on the x axis. Examples are shown in Figure 3.13 for "bab," "dad," and "gag" spoken with a British accent (Ladefoged, 1975). The darker the band of energy at a particular frequency, the greater its amplitude. Notice that the energy clusters at low-, medium-, and high-level frequencies. These bands are called **formants.** The first formant is the lowest frequency band, the second formant is at the next higher frequency band, and so on. One might expect that the spectrum for, say, "gag" could be neatly divided into three time segments, with the early segment providing an invariant feature for the phoneme /g/ followed by one for /a/ and then returning to the one for /g/. It turns out that the three time segments of the speech spectrogram do not match up with the three phonemes /g/, /a/, and /g/.

Coarticulation

First, each segment of the acoustic signal provides clues about the identity of more than one phoneme (Liberman, Cooper, Shankweiler, & Studdert-Kennedy, 1967). This is called **coarticulation.** As shown in Figure 3.14, each of the three phonemes of "beg" are being transmitted simultaneously. They are not separated in time, with /b/ followed by /ae/ and then /g/. Instead, the acoustic energy corresponding to the phonetic segment of /b/ overlaps that of the other phonemes.

Phrased differently, before you have articulated /b/, the vocal track already takes shape to articulate /ae/. Notice, too, from Figure 3.14 that you begin to articulate /g/ even before finishing the articulation of /b/. The key point about coarticulation is that multiple phonetic segments are being articulated in parallel at each point in time.

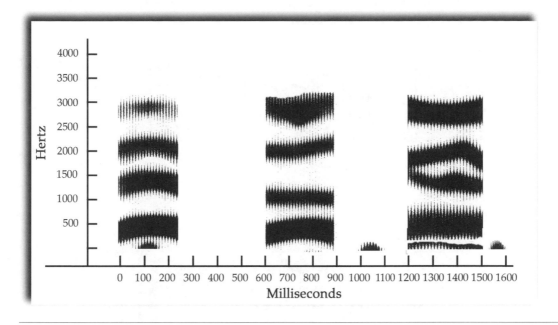

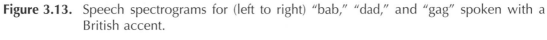

Figure 3.13. Speech spectrograms for (left to right) "bab," "dad," and "gag" spoken with a British accent.

SOURCE: Ladefoged (1975).

Lack of Invariance

Second, the acoustic spectrum fails to reveal a distinctive invariant feature for a particular phoneme that stays the same in all contexts (Liberman et al., 1967). Phonemes lack invariant distinctive features. As illustrated in Figure 3.15, the spectrogram for /di/ versus /du/ reveals different formants for the phoneme /d/ depending on whether it is followed by the phoneme /i/ versus /u/. The first formant is the same in each case. But look at the second formant containing the higher frequencies. As the speaker enunciates the /d/ phoneme, a remarkable change occurs at about 200 milliseconds; the formant turns to higher frequencies when followed by /i/ and to lower frequencies when followed by /u/. Consequently, a listener could not zero in on the acoustic spectrum and identify the phonetic segment of /d/ by matching it with a distinctive feature that remains the same in all contexts.

Both coarticulation and the lack of invariance imply that listeners must process the context in which a given acoustic signal occurs. The relations among features are just as critical as the features themselves. Recall that the same is true in understanding the recognition of visual objects; only a

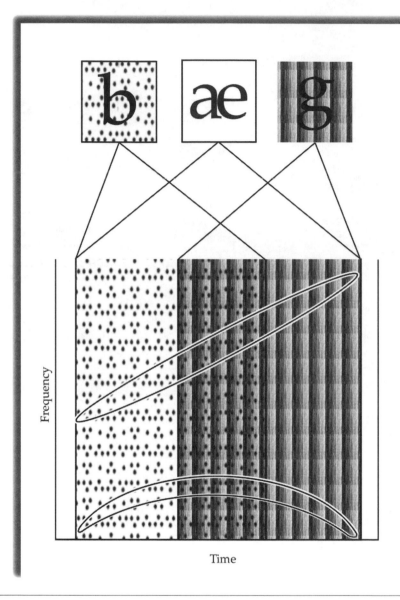

Figure 3.14. Coarticulation as parallel transmission of phonemes.

SOURCE: Liberman, Cooper, Shankweiler, and Studdert-Kennedy (1967).

structural theory that specifies both features and their relations is adequate. In speech recognition, a remarkably large number of features and relations must be processed in a fraction of a second simply to identify a single phoneme. Furthermore, unlike the recognition of static visual objects,

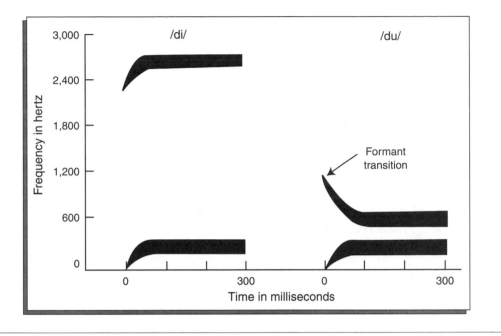

Figure 3.15. Spectrograms for /di/ and /du/.

SOURCE: Liberman, Cooper, Shankweiler, and Studdert-Kennedy (1967).

speech must be recognized over time. Both the sounds that precede a given phonetic segment and those that follow it influence perception (Salasoo & Pisoni, 1985). The contextual nature of the acoustic speech signal enormously complicates the job of the listener. To illustrate, a speaker can produce the phonemes /b/ and /p/ by changing only one feature during articulation. For the /p/ phoneme, the vocal cords do not vibrate, whereas for the /b/ phoneme, they do. The listener must detect this difference in discriminating words such as "pad" versus "bad." To do so, the listener must process 16 acoustic features that bear on the correct identification of /p/ versus /b/ (Lisker, 1986).

Phonemes are coarticulated, meaning that each segment of the acoustic signal provides clues about the identity of more than one phoneme. As a consequence, the signal lacks an invariant feature for a particular phoneme that stays the same in all contexts.

Continuous Speech Stream

Third, the acoustic signals comprising the speech stream are virtually continuous throughout a sentence (Foss & Hakes, 1978). Few pauses occur, and astonishingly, the pauses that do occur generally fall in the middle of words, not between words. Pauses mark boundaries between words less than 40% of the time (Cole & Jakimik, 1980). This phenomenon is illustrated with

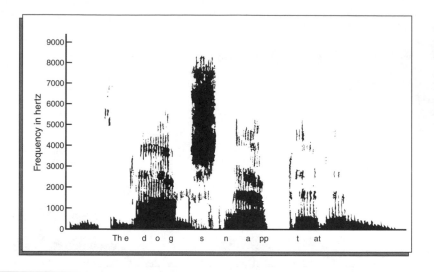

Figure 3.16. Portion of the speech spectrogram for "John said that the dog snapped at him."
SOURCE: Foss and Hakes (1978).

a portion of the speech spectrogram for the sentence "John said that the dog snapped at him" shown in Figure 3.16.

Notice the pauses in acoustic energy between the /s/ and the /n/ and between the /p/ and the /t/. The listener hears pauses between the words and phrases of the sentence, but the acoustic energy fails to provide them. Instead, they are inserted by the speech recognition processes that categorize the acoustic input; they divide the sounds into the words, phrases, clauses, and sentences through top-down or conceptually driven recognition processes. Conversely, the pauses in acoustic energy that do not signal an important linguistic unit, such as those in the word "snapped," are not perceived by listener.

It is easier to appreciate the role of conceptually driven processes in speech perception when listening to a foreign language. The continuous nature of the acoustic speech stream is perceived as it really is. The pauses that occur in the middle of a word are heard correctly. One word streams into another. The coarticulation effect discussed earlier applies across word boundaries as well as within word boundaries. Thus, the speaker is sending acoustic clues at any given moment about the identity of phonemes that belong to adjacent words. The true complexity of the stream, if analyzed solely from bottom-up or data-driven processes, can be readily heard in listening to a native speaker of a language that is foreign to us. But in listening to our own first language, the speech stream is heard as a sequence of neat and tidy packages of sound that specify meaning.

Categorical Perception

The categorization of speech input at the phonemic level is called **categorical perception.** Subtle variations in the acoustic signal are ignored unless they mark a boundary between one phoneme and another. For example, /b/ and /p/ differ in terms of the amount of time that elapses between the release of the lips and the onset of voicing. The voice onset time for /b/ is immediate (0 seconds). For /p/, the voice onset time is 0.06 seconds. Within this narrow window of time lies the boundary between hearing one phoneme versus another.

Lisker and Abramson (1970) demonstrated the phenomenon of categorical perception by continuously varying voice onset time from –0.15 to +0.15 using computer-synthesized speech. For the 31 stimuli, the acoustic signal differed by 0.01 seconds in voice onset time. Yet only two phonemes were heard. Listeners identified all sounds as /b/ over a large range of variation in the acoustic signal, from –0.15 seconds up to just over 0 seconds. As soon as the voice onset time slightly exceeded 0 seconds, the listeners began to hear /p/ instead of /b/ and continued to do so for all remaining stimuli. What matters, then, is not the degree of change in voice onset time; all variations of 0.15 seconds are heard as the same phoneme. Instead, what matters is whether the change in acoustic signal crosses a sharply defined boundary. There is, therefore, a sharp decision boundary that distinguishes the perception of one phoneme from the perception of another related one.

Although speech phonemes exhibit well-defined categorical boundaries, it is mistaken to conclude that the auditory system cannot sense the gradual transitions in voice onset time. Data-driven sensory processes plainly pick up these differences (Massaro, 1994). The sensory system detects continuous changes in the speech signal, but a decision process assigns the signal to one phonemic category or another. Repp and Liberman (1987) found that the boundary between two phonetic categories is flexible to a degree. Precisely where a given listener locates the boundary depends on the context provided by other stimuli.

> Speech signals are assigned to phonemes on the basis of well-defined categorical boundaries. The continuous speech stream is heard as separate words and phrases as a result of conceptually driven recognition processes.

Despite the complexity involved in extracting phonetic segments from the speech stream, infants between the ages of 1 and 4 months can detect the acoustic features that distinguish one phoneme from another. Indeed, it appears that at this age infants are prepared to identify not only the phonemes of their native language but virtually all possible phonetic segments used in human languages (Eimas, Miller, & Jusczyk, 1987). Such evidence is consistent with the idea that speech is perceived by a special processing module (Eimas & Miller, 1992).

Infants cannot, of course, report what they hear. Yet by ingeniously monitoring the rate of sucking on a pacifier, developmental psychologists can infer changes in attention to a stimulus. The sucking schema is well-established in a 1-month-old infant. In fact, sucking is one of a small number of reflexes present at birth. With experience in nursing, this basic sensorimotor schema develops and displaces the reflex. It turns out that infants suck faster when attending to a novel stimulus. With repeated presentations of the stimulus, the sucking rate slows down as the infant habituates to the stimulus. If the stimulus is abruptly changed in a way that is noticed by the infant, then dishabituation occurs (i.e., the sucking rate suddenly increases). Noticing the difference between preshift stimuli and postshift stimuli can be measured by the difference in rates of sucking.

Using this method, Eimas (1974) found categorical perception of speech by infants. The infants dishabituated when a change in the acoustic signal crossed a phonetic boundary. Subsequent research has shown that infants can in fact discriminate among the stimuli that fall within a phonemic boundary (Miller & Eimas, 1983). Like adults, however, infants appear tuned to pick up the critical differences that separate one phoneme from another and to process the context in which the acoustic signals occur.

Furthermore, infants are not born with full capabilities in categorizing speech. Newborns can detect differences among syllables that contain different phonemes, but their representations at this early stage of development might not be full-fledged phonetic segments (cf. Eimas & Miller, 1992). Instead, over the first 1 or 2 months of life, the infant may progress from a global representation of the syllable to the specific phonemic level representations (Bertoncini, Bijeljac-Babic, Jusczyk, Kennedy, & Mehler, 1988).

SUMMARY

1. Perception begins with the transduction of the physical energy of a stimulus into an initial neural representation of the stimulus. As a result, the objects and events that are present in the environment are perceived in the sense of being detected. With still more processing, the objects and events are recognized in the sense of being categorized as meaningful. Visual consciousness depends on representations being processed in the visual cortex. Patients with blindsight lack any visual awareness but are able to guess accurately about the actual locations of objects in space.

2. The ability to perceive depends on pattern recognition, that is, categorizing objects and events detected in the environment by matching their preliminary representations with patterns stored in long-term memory. A stimulus can be perceived and understood in terms of its properties but not recognized as a meaningful object—a neuropsychological condition called agnosia. Patients suffering from lesions in certain regions of the brain can

see objects but not recognize them at all. Apperceptive agnosia refers to a failure of pattern recognition caused by an inability to categorize objects at a perceptual level of analysis. Associative agnosia, by contrast, is caused by an inability to categorize objects at a functional semantic level of analysis.

3. Schemas generate expectations about the objects and events that will be encountered. These expectations direct exploration of the environment in the form of eye movements and other bodily movements that pick up the information available. The sampled information either confirms or modifies the original expectations, which in turn leads to renewed exploration. Top-down or conceptually driven pattern recognition refers to the use of expectations to ease the process of finding a match between incoming stimuli and schemas that store our knowledge about the world in long-term memory. Bottom-up or data-driven pattern recognition refers to the use of the features picked up from the environment. Both the data and the expectations play a critical role in rapid, accurate, and adaptive perception.

4. The representation of objects in long-term memory has been viewed theoretically as feature lists and as structural descriptions. An object can be represented in terms of a list of distinctive features that discriminate it from other objects. The problem with this view is that two objects might include the same features but differ in terms of their relationships. A structural description takes into account both the distinctive features and their relations.

5. Holistic processing refers to perceiving the whole object; analytic processing refers to perceiving the features that comprise the whole. Faces are unique in that holistic processing is much stronger than analytic processing for them as compared with other objects. A specialized module is responsible for face perception. Face perception is automatic, fast, encapsulated from other cognitive systems, and instantiated in a localized area of the brain. Prosopagnosic patients suffering from damage to the module are unable to recognize faces despite intact object recognition in general.

6. Speech perception is challenging because the acoustic signal for the basic sounds of speech that communicate meaning—phonemes—is highly complex. Phonemes are coarticulated, meaning that each segment of the acoustic signal provides clues about the identity of more than one phoneme. As a consequence, the signal lacks an invariant feature for a particular phoneme that stays the same in all contexts. Speech signals are assigned to phonemes on the basis of well-defined categorical boundaries. Gradual variations in the acoustic signal are perceived categorically. Finally, the acoustic energy in speech is often continuous across word boundaries. The continuous speech stream is heard as separate words and phrases as a result of conceptually driven recognition processes.

● KEY TERMS

blindsight
pattern recognition
apperceptive agnosia
associative agnosia
schema
conceptually driven processes
data-driven processes
word superiority effect
distinctive features

holistic processing
analytic processing
module
prosopagnosia
phoneme
speech spectrogram
formants
coarticulation
categorical perception

CHAPTER 4

ATTENTION

Our sensory systems are continually bombarded by sights, sounds, smells, and other signals from the external environment. At the same time, mental representations of events that just occurred seconds ago, to events from the distant past, to events only imagined in the present or future are also active. From moment to moment, one possible train of thought is taken to the exclusion of many others. Some internal or external events dominate consciousness, and others are barely noticed or not noticed at all. Attention refers to selecting certain stimuli from among many and focusing cognitive resources on those selected. William James described attention as "the taking possession by the mind, in clear and vivid form, of one out of what seem several simultaneously possible trains of thought. . . . Focalization, concentration, of consciousness are of its essence" (James, 1890, pp. 403-404). Attention allows us to focus on what is important at the moment and to ignore the rest. Without attention, the external world would overwhelm us with sensory information and our internal world would overwhelm us with memories or fantasies. When attention fails, we are left scatterbrained and unable to function.

Consider some everyday situations in which attention is important. In carrying on a conversation with someone, there are numerous irrelevant background stimuli. The sights and sounds of a nearby television, the distant roar of a commercial jet overhead, the songs of birds outside the window, the pressure of clothing on the skin, and the pain of a recently jammed finger all compete for your attention. The irrelevant thoughts must be ignored so that the demanding task of speech recognition takes precedence. In conversations, it is further necessary to divide attention or shift attention from listening, on the one hand, to speaking, on the other.

Now, consider carrying on your conversation on a cell phone while driving a car. Once again, it is necessary to ignore some distractions, such as the car radio and the sounds of traffic, so as to focus on speech production and comprehension. Yet at the same time, the task of driving is also attention demanding. Perceiving the road, other cars, and pedestrians is just part of what the task demands. Steering and braking can also demand attention, particularly when traffic is heavy. Thus, to drive a car and carry on a telephone conversation at the same time requires that attention be divided among multiple tasks, each of which can be highly demanding at a given moment in time. Not surprisingly, inattention is a leading cause of traffic accidents (Evans, 1991). If one gives too much attention to listening and speaking on a cell phone, then there is a risk of inattention to driving, even when both hands are on the wheel and one's eyes are on the road. The limits and workings of attention are vitally important for human performance.

When attention malfunctions, its importance to normal cognition and behavior is apparent. Attention deficit/hyperactivity disorder (ADHD) is a commonly diagnosed psychiatric disorder that usually occurs before 7 years of age. Children with ADHD are easily distracted and excessively restless and impulsive. This malfunction of attention disrupts children's ability to fit into social and academic environments and, later in life, into occupational settings. Behavioral symptoms of the disorder include making excessive careless mistakes, not following instructions or failing to finish tasks, avoiding tasks that require sustained effort, and showing signs of hyperactive fidgeting, talking, and impulsive behavior. ADHD is diagnosed when inattention, hyperactivity, and impulsivity are frequent and severe, beyond the range of normal behavior in young children (Shaywitz, Fletcher, & Shaywitz, 1995).

Theoretical accounts of attention are presented at the outset of this chapter. These theories are divided into two major camps. The first assumes that attention operates as a filter that blocks the processing of some stimuli and allows the processing of others. This camp addresses at what point in the processing of information selection takes place. The second assumes that the person actively chooses stimuli for further processing by allocating a portion of one or more limited pools of attentional capacity. This camp addresses how the concentration of cognitive processes on particular stimuli takes place. Filter theories and capacity theories have spawned impressive research on the nature of attention, and each class is considered in turn. Next, the

distinction between automatic processes, which proceed without attention, and controlled processes, which require attention, is illuminated. The chapter then concludes with a discussion of visual attention in selection, effort, and perception.

FILTER THEORIES ●

Selective attention refers to the ability to perceive a particular stimulus of interest while ignoring numerous other stimuli. It is contrasted with **divided attention,** in which two or more stimuli share cognitive resources. For example, at a noisy party, you can carry on a conversation with one person while other people are carrying on conversations all around you. With selective attention, you focus on your conversation with the person in front of you and ignore the rest. With divided attention, you attempt to listen to an adjacent conversation while maintaining limited involvement in responding to the person before you.

An extraordinary example of selective attention can be found in the use of hypnosis to control pain. If one selectively attends to other stimuli and ignores pain signals, it is possible to experience analgesia, that is, relief from the pain. This phenomenon has long been investigated with highly hypnotizable individuals who experience a form of dissociated consciousness (Hilgard, 1986). Some individuals are able to carry out suggestions to feel no pain in a portion of the body so that normally painful procedures can be performed in dentistry and medicine without the administration of anesthetics. They selectively attend to pleasant thoughts and filter out the pain signals. Hilgard (1986) used the cold pressor method to induce pain by asking a person to leave his or her arm in a bucket of ice water for as long as the person could tolerate. After the arm is in the ice water for 20 to 30 seconds, the pain is immense. But under deep hypnosis, the same individuals can tolerate the pain without difficulty.

Filter theories were designed to explain how selective attention operates. The classic laboratory task for studying selective attention, called dichotic listening, simulated the party situation just described. In dichotic listening, both ears receive stimuli in synchrony and participants are asked to attend to only one ear or channel. This is enforced by using what is called **shadowing,** in which the participant repeats aloud the stimuli presented to the attended channel and ignores the stimuli presented in the unattended ignored channel. This is illustrated in Figure 4.1.

In a pioneering study with shadowing, Cherry (1953) found that people noticed and remembered little about the second unattended series. Specifically, they seemed oblivious to the meanings of unattended words,

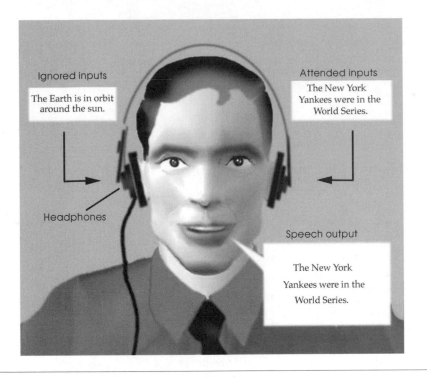

Figure 4.1. The shadowing task used to study selective attention.

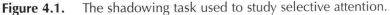

failing even to notice that on occasion the material shifted from English to German. In contrast to missing the meaningful or semantic features, they did notice changes in physical or sensory features such as when a low-pitched male voice changed to a higher pitched female voice. Thus, the first key finding to explain was that selective attention resulted in little if any processing of the semantic features of the unattended channel but did permit the processing of sensory features.

Early Selection

Broadbent (1958) proposed a model to account for the findings with the shadowing task (see Figure 4.2). It postulated two stages of information processing to explain the phenomenon of selective attention. In the first stage, all information from the senses are processed but only partially. Today, this stage is referred to as sensory memory. A selective filter then winnows the information to only the stimuli of interest, and these few items are fully processed in the limited capacity channel. **Early selection** refers to an

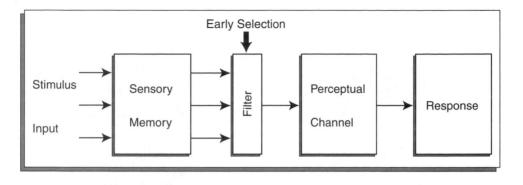

Figure 4.2. The early selection model of attention.

SOURCE: Adapted from Broadbent (1958).

attentional filter that operates after sensory processing but prior to meaningful semantic processing. The model also included a store of conditional probabilities about past events, what today is called long-term memory. Furthermore, a system for controlling behavioral output was described by Broadbent.

Broadbent (1957) examined how well a series of digits could be recalled under dichotic listening conditions. For example, suppose that the series 7-3-5 arrived at the left ear perfectly synchronized with the series 1-6-2 at the right ear, as shown in Panel (a) of Figure 4.3. Each pair was separated by only 500 milliseconds. When allowed to recall the digits in any order, the participants successfully recalled nearly two thirds of the digits. Interestingly, their successes came when they first reported from one ear and then the other (e.g.,7-3-5-1-6-2). However, when instructed to recall the digits in the order of their arrival (e.g., 7-1-3-6-5-2), they correctly reported less than a fifth of the digits on average.

Broadbent (1957) proposed a mechanical analogy to explain how an early selective filter might work to produce these findings, as shown in Panel (b) of Figure 4.3. The digits were briefly held in a sensory memory store specific to each ear. The perceptual analysis channel was limited in capacity relative to the sensory memory; thus, multiple stimuli had to be selectively filtered prior to perception. It was assumed that the limited-capacity perceptual channel could process only a single stimulus at a time. The selective filter precluded the passage of a stimulus from sensory memory into the perceptual channel. The filter could be switched so that it allowed passage from the left ear and then the right ear, or it could be held in place so that all digits were perceived first from, say, the left ear. Switching the position of the filter back and forth between ears was more difficult, and fewer digits were successfully remembered. Because the digits could be retained briefly in sensory memory, filtering

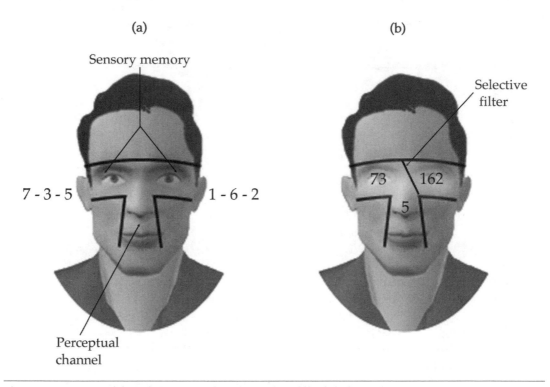

Figure 4.3. An early selection explanation of recall of dichotic input.
SOURCE: Adapted from Broadbent (1957).

first all digits from the right ear while the left ear digits were perceived and then allowing the right ear digits to pass led to the best recall.

Broadbent's model captured Cherry's findings in that only the shadowed channel benefited from full perceptual analysis at the deep level of semantic features. Shifts in languages should go unnoticed despite the fact that German was unintelligible to the English-speaking participants in the experiments. However, a sensory feature such as pitch should be identifiable at a very early stage of processing, the echoic store, even on the unattended channel. Identifying the pitch and storing it in echoic memory should occur simultaneously in both channels before the selective filter operates. Similarly, the model explained Broadbent's findings by assuming that with only 500 milliseconds between each dichotic pair of digits, the gate cannot be swung back and forth quickly enough to allow a correct report of digits in their order of arrival. Successful recall should occur only by leaving the gate in one position until all three digits from one ear move through the perceptual channel, followed by those from the other ear.

Shadowing or repeating a message heard in an attended ear or channel results in selective attention; the meaning of a messages heard at the same time in the other ear is ignored.

Attenuation

Other results showed that the early selection model oversimplified human attention. It turned out that if the participant's name occurred on the unattended channel, it sometimes received semantic processing and was reported (Moray, 1959). The participant did not divide attention between the two channels because the shadowing task is too demanding to allow a division. Nonetheless, even without attempting to divide attention between the two conversations, highly pertinent words such as one's name can still slip through the processes of selective attention. Moray's finding can readily be observed firsthand in any crowded, conversation-filled room. When you are engaged fully in one conversation, the words of an adjacent conversation are ignored—unless your name gets mentioned and then attention shifts to the previously ignored conversation.

This phenomenon suggests that the semantic content of items in the ignored channel must be processed to at least some degree. Otherwise, how would one recognize a name in an ignored conversation? Other experiments explored the idea of unattended semantic analysis further in the following task. Treisman (1960) presented a sentence to the left ear to be shadowed and a different sentence to the right ear to be ignored. However, one word in the right ear sentence fit the context of the shadowed sentence. To illustrate, the italicized words were those actually reported by the individual in the following sentences. Notice that the semantically appropriate "table" was perceived instead of the correct response of "three." The word from the unattended right channel, which fit nicely the meaning of the sentence being shadowed in the left channel, was perceived and repeated by mistake. An error in shadowing occurred because of a failure in selective attention.

Left: . . . *sitting at the mahogany* three *possibilities* . . .

Right: . . . let us look at these *table* with her head . . .

Such findings violated the assumptions of the early selection model. Processing the meaning of any item on the nonshadowed material should not occur if the filter selects only the shadowed items for complete pattern recognition. Perceiving "table" in Treisman's (1960) experiment or one's name in Moray's (1959) experiment refutes this claim. Clearly, an alternative theory is needed to explain such results.

One alternative to Broadbent's model again placed a filter early in the sequence of information processing, before pattern recognition. Instead of an all-or-none filter that allows only a single channel to undergo pattern recognition at a time, Treisman (1970) suggested a filter that attenuates the

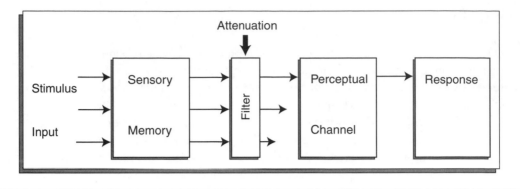

Figure 4.4.   The attenuation model of selective attention.

unattended channel, making its inputs less likely to be heard. **Attenuation** refers to an attentional filter that lowers the strength of the sensory signal on the unattended channel. Treisman's attenuation model is illustrated in Figure 4.4. The degree of perceptual analysis received by an item depends only in part on its signal intensity. The intensity threshold required for recognition also plays a part. A word is perceived if its stimulus intensity remains sufficiently high after the filter to exceed its recognition threshold; this is denoted by the long arrow reaching the perceptual channel in Figure 4.4. Other stimuli are attenuated too much to reach their recognition thresholds.

A word's recognition threshold depends on how important the word is or on how expected it is in a particular context. Thus, a weak signal intensity for one's name could exceed the threshold required and be responded to as the most pertinent stimulus. Similarly, because of top-down pattern recognition processes, there is an expectation and temporary low threshold for the word "table" right after the word "mahogany" in Treisman's experiment. As a consequence, the expected word was perceived and remembered rather than the next word in the sequence presented to the attended ear.

Late Selection

Another alternative to Broadbent's model moves the position of the filter. Instead of assuming that selection takes place prior to perception, the late selection model holds that all stimuli are recognized but are narrowed to the most pertinent ones during response preparation. In other words, the late selection model designed by Deutsch and Deutsch (1963) and refined by Norman (1968) placed the filter after pattern recognition. Late selection refers to an attentional filter that operates after meaningful semantic processing

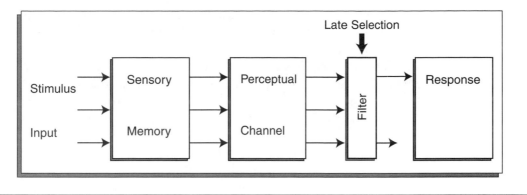

Figure 4.5. The late selection model of attention.

but prior to response preparation. The words are fully perceived, but then the perceiver responds only to the most pertinent item (see Figure 4.5). According to late selection theory, then, a process similar to the one envisioned by Treisman during perceptual analysis occurs later but prior to response preparation. There is a bias to respond to the most pertinent word, such as one's name, because of conceptually driven processes activating the name in long-term memory. Despite the fact that inputs receive the same full semantic data analysis from the bottom up, only the most pertinent word is selected at the time of responding.

The late selection model accounts for the same findings as does Treisman's attenuation model. Perceiving one's name and repeating an anticipated word from the unattended channel occur because of their high pertinence values, not because only they received full semantic analysis owing to their low thresholds. The only way to distinguish which model best explains attention is to try to tell whether stimuli that are unattended and unselected for further processing actually receive full semantic analysis. Some experiments suggest that they do.

For example, MacKay (1973) had the person shadow a sentence in one ear such as "They were standing near the bank." In the other ear, MacKay presented either the word "river" or the word "money" at the same time. The results showed that the unattended and unselected word successfully biased the individual's interpretation of the sentence as referring to a "river bank" or a "financial bank."

Marcel (1983) adopted a very different methodology, backward masking, but reached the same conclusion. If a word is presented very briefly and is quickly followed by another visual stimulus, then the original word is masked backward in time such that the observer fails to perceive it consciously. Thus, the word is both unattended and unselected for further processing. Even so,

Marcel found that the word primes the observer in a way that confirms the word had undergone semantic analysis. **Priming** refers to the presentation of a stimulus biasing how a subsequent stimulus is processed. Specifically, the time it takes to decide whether a subsequent string of letters is a word or not is speeded reliably if the original masked item is related in meaning. Lexical decision time, as it is called, is faster for, say, the word "ship" if the masked prime is "boat" as compared with "book." Remember that the observer claims no awareness of the prime itself, whether it is "boat" or "book." It seems as if the prime is perceived unconsciously.

Selective attention may result from filtering of the unattended channel. The filter could occur at an early stage, just after sensory processing, or at a late stage, after semantic processing. A third possibility is that the unattended channel is attenuated rather than filtered entirely.

Results of the type reported by MacKay (1973) and Marcel (1983) hardly settled the matter in favor of a late selection model. First, some questioned whether the unreportable words fell totally outside the scope of attention and awareness (Cheesman & Merikle, 1984; Holender, 1986). Second, compelling evidence could be marshaled for either an early or a late location of the filter or bottleneck in information processing (Johnston & Heinz, 1978). It was as if the filter could move depending on the task at hand. Third, an alternative theoretical approach took hold that showed that filter theories of any sort fail to capture the full complexity of human attention.

● CAPACITY THEORIES

Kahneman (1973) proposed that attention is limited in overall capacity and that our ability to carry out simultaneous tasks depends in part on how much capacity the tasks require (see Figure 4.6). For example, in the dichotic listening task presented earlier, the degree to which the secondary unattended channel is processed will depend on how much of the limited supply of attention is required by shadowing the primary channel. Because the shadowing task is highly demanding for most people, little if any capacity is left. If more capacity were available for allocation to the secondary channel, then the results would show a greater degree of processing. In principle, then, the results that seemed to support early or late selection could reflect the degree of capacity allocated to the secondary channel in shadowing tasks.

Mental Effort

The capacity approach conceives of attention as mental effort. The more a task required of a limited pool of available capacity, the more mental effort the person exerted. For instance, try these two mental arithmetic problems:

(a) $6 \times 6 = ?$ versus (b) $32 \times 12 = ?$.

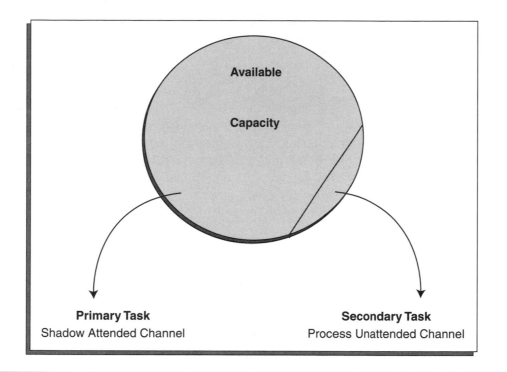

Figure 4.6. The capacity model of attention.

Clearly, Problem (b) demands more **mental effort,** that is, more of the capacity you have available for carrying out the task.

The central idea can be readily grasped by considering the dual task method of measuring mental effort. Suppose that while you carry out a series of either easy [Problem (a)] or hard [Problem (b)] mental multiplication problems presented over headphones, you are given a secondary task of detecting the random appearance of a light on a panel in front of you. Your instructions emphasize focusing attention on the primary multiplication task but to respond to the light with, say, a button press as rapidly as you can without disrupting primary task performance. The more effortful the primary task, the less capacity you will have available for rapidly detecting the light. The researcher can then compare your dual task reaction times with a simple reaction time, when light detection is the only demand on your limited attentional capacity. The more dual task reaction time increases over simple reaction time, the more effortful the primary task must be. In this case, the hard problems should slow you down markedly more than would the easy problems in detecting the lights.

Mental effort increases as the proportion of available attentional capacity increases. One way to measure mental effort is through increases in reaction time to a secondary task that competes for limited attentional capacity with a primary task.

Enduring dispositions, momentary intentions, and evaluation of current demands on capacity shape the allocation policy. For example, in navigating a car on an interstate highway at, say, 65 miles per hour, the driver may be attending to music on the radio, reducing slightly the capacity available for driving. Far worse, the driver may dial a number on his or her cell phone and carry on a highly attention-demanding conversation, markedly reducing the capacity available for driving. If something unexpected happens on the road ahead—a tractor-trailer begins to swerve into the driver's lane—then a quick evaluation of the demands may, if all goes well, rapidly force all available capacity to steering and braking. If this shift to full attention to driving occurs too late or incompletely, then an accident is in the making. Fatigue or intoxication reduces the amount of attentional capacity available to the driver in the first place.

Johnston and Heinz (1978) extended capacity theory to account for the conflicting conclusions about whether the structural filter comes early or late in information processing. They proposed that, depending on the demands of the task, a person can flexibly employ either early or late selection, although the semantic processing of late selection comes at the cost of greater capacity use. The researchers studied dichotic listening in which the shadowed message could be identified by a sensory feature of pitch (male vs. female voice) or only by a semantic analysis (same voice but different categories such as cities vs. occupations). They measured secondary task reaction times to detect a light during shadowing.

It took about 120 milliseconds longer to respond to the light while simultaneously shadowing using an early selection mode based on pitch relative to simply detecting the light alone. Yet it took more than 170 milliseconds longer when shadowing required a late selection mode based on meaning. It would surely have taken even longer if the participants had managed to maintain accurate performance in the late selection case. As it happened, their error rate quadrupled when semantic analysis was needed. Thus, a capacity theory can subsume the findings of filter theories and explain further the nuances of human attention.

Multiple Resources

Further research has shown that a full accounting of the complexities of human attention requires that still finer distinctions be drawn than those seen in Kahneman's capacity theory (Navon & Gopher, 1979). Multiple resource theories account for how two simultaneous tasks will interfere with each other depending on the kind and level of resources they require. For example, Wickens (1980) proposed three dimensions of resources. First, he

---

Capacity theory assumes that attention is limited in overall capacity and that our ability to carry out simultaneous tasks depends in part on how much capacity the tasks require. Selective attention occurs because shadowing demands most of the capacity, leaving little if any for the unattended channel.

distinguished auditory versus visual perceptual modalities. Second, he distinguished perceptual-cognitive resources (consumed by the demands of tasks such as reading and mentally calculating) versus response resources (consumed by the demands of tasks such as speaking and moving one's hand). Third, he distinguished verbal versus spatial processing codes; speech and text illustrate verbal codes, whereas pictures and diagrams illustrate spatial codes.

Multiple resource theories attempt to explain how well two tasks can be done concurrently by specifying the capacity or effort demands, on the one hand, and the types of resources needed, on the other. For instance, attending simultaneously to speech and pictures should be and is more manageable than processing two channels of speech (Allport, Antonis, & Reynolds, 1972). Similarly, attending to two channels of speech is easier when the capacity demands of the task are low, as when the shadowed message can be identified by pitch, than when the demands are high, as in semantic analysis (Johnston & Heinz, 1978).

> Multiple resource theories elaborate Kahneman's approach. The ability to perform two tasks concurrently depends not just on their respective demands on capacity but also on the specific kinds of resources required (e.g., perceptual vs. cognitive).

Conclusion

To summarize, filter theories evolved to explain the selective nature of attention. Experiments designed to test these theories showed the validity of assuming structural bottlenecks in the flow of information processing. However, they also showed the difficulty of specifying the exact location of these bottlenecks. Capacity theories built on the idea of bottlenecks but recognized that the location of the bottlenecks from early to late stages in perception and cognition can vary. Specifically, an individual can adopt either mode of selectivity in response to the demands of the current situation. Capacity theories also recognized that various dimensions of structural interference exist, such as the distinction between structures that use verbal versus spatial information. Lastly, and most important, capacity theories recognized the mental effort aspect of attention as well as the selective aspect. The degree of attentional resources demanded by a task became one focal point of further research, as explained in the next section.

AUTOMATIC PROCESSES ●

It has long been known that perceptual, cognitive, and motor processes may unfold automatically, without effortful control. Stroop (1935) devised an ingenious and somewhat diabolical test to study automatic reading (see Color Plate 3 in the section of color plates). The color terms register automatically and effortlessly. But the color terms (e.g., RED, GREEN, BLUE, YELLOW) are printed in an incompatible color of ink. The word RED appears in *green* ink, the word GREEN appears in *yellow* ink, and so on. The task is to say aloud the color of the ink while ignoring the meaning of the word itself.

Word recognition—one aspect of fluent reading—occurs automatically. That is, it is exceedingly difficult to ignore the meaning of the word RED when it appears in green ink. The correct response of GREEN competes with the habitual response of RED. Errors and delays in responding are the usual result. For more than 50 years now, the **Stroop effect** and variations on it have challenged theorists to account for the detailed patterns of errors and delays observed in experiments (MacLeod, 1991).

Word recognition illustrates one of many processes that have become automatic because of extensive practice, maturation, and skill development. Walking, running, riding a bicycle, and typing on a keyboard are among the many motor skills that people automatize. Perceptual and cognitive skills also become automatic. Depth and object perception, as seen in Chapter 3, occur effortlessly despite the intensive computations that they require. Speech recognition, as will be seen later in the book, is one of the most complex perceptual tasks that we undertake. Yet by 5 years of age, a child effortlessly deciphers and comprehends spoken language.

Criteria of Automaticity

Posner and Snyder (1974, 1975) categorized a process as automatic if it met three criteria. First, an automatic process occurs unintentionally. Second, the process occurs unconsciously, outside the scope of even peripheral awareness. Third, the process operates without depleting attentional resources. The automatic process can carry on without interfering with processes that demand limited attentional resources. Put differently, automatic processes are often called preattentive. Whereas **automatic processes** are unintentional, unconscious, and undemanding of attention, **controlled processes** are intentional, conscious, and demanding of attention. This distinction is critical to understanding perception and attention (Schneider & Shiffrin, 1977), memory (Hasher & Zacks, 1979), language (Fischler, 1998), and higher order thinking skills such as reasoning (Stanovich, 1999).

Practice and Automaticity

Typically, a process or set of processes used in a particular skill, such as typing, becomes automatic only after extensive practice. Shiffrin and

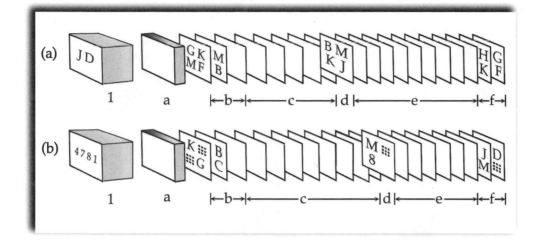

Figure 4.7. A visual search task for studying automatic and consciously controlled processing. SOURCE: Schneider and Shiffrin (1977).

Schneider (1977) investigated the development of automaticity in a search task that has been investigated extensively by cognitive psychologists. The participants viewed a series of frames on a computer screen containing letters and digits. Their task entailed visually searching each frame for a target item while ignoring distractor items. The participants memorized letter or number items at the beginning of each series. Figure 4.7 shows two sample sequences for positive trials that contained a target. In panel (a), the memory set consisted of two target items, the letters J and D. After memorizing the targets, a sequence of frames rapidly appeared on the screen, with one of the target items (J) occurring toward the middle of the sequence on positive trials. Besides target items, the frames contained either distractor items or nonmeaningful masks (dot patterns). The number of items in the memory set and the number in each frame of the sequence varied. The observers pressed a button as quickly as possible on detecting a target. On negative trials, in which targets did not appear, the observers pressed a different button at the end of the sequence.

Schneider and Shiffrin (1977) examined two types of sequences, called varied mapping and consistent mapping. With varied mapping, the letters or numbers that served as targets on one sequence of frames could turn up as distractors on another sequence. In the letter-letter trials shown in panel (a) the observer looked for J and D and ignored the destractor letters (e.g., GK). Then, on a latter sequence, the observer might be looking for B that earlier

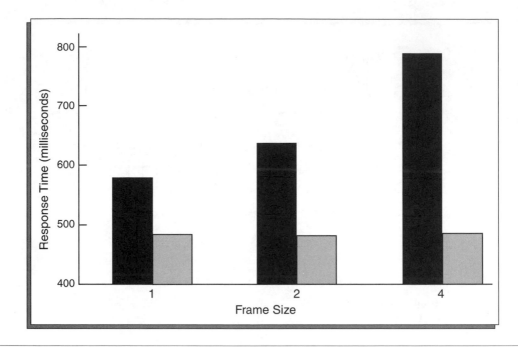

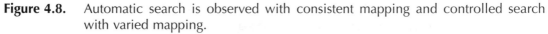

Figure 4.8. Automatic search is observed with consistent mapping and controlled search with varied mapping.

SOURCE: Adapted from Schneider and Shiffrin (1977).

had been a distractor. Thus, to identify the targets accurately, the observer must carefully search each frame of the visual display and compare the items with the memory set on that trial. With consistent mapping, the memory set items (say, the numbers) never appeared as anything other than targets. The distractors were not used in the memory set throughout the experiment in number-letter trials as seen in panel (b).

The participants practiced the search task for 10 hours beforehand and received further practice during the experiments. Schneider and Shiffrin (1977) manipulated the number of items in the memory set (1, 2, or 4) and the number in each frame of the sequence (1, 2, or 4). Shown in Figure 4.8 are the results for memory set size 4 on positive trials, when the target was present, as a function of the number of items in each frame. Whereas the time needed to detect the target increased substantially with frame size in the varied mapping condition, it remained at a low constant value for consistent mapping. Varied mapping produced an effortful, controlled search process. The observer had to consciously and deliberately match each item detected in a frame against each item held in short-term memory to decide whether a target appeared. By sharp contrast, the response times were fast and did not increase at all as frame size increased with consistent mapping, indicating an effortless automatic search process.

Spelke, Hirst, and Neisser (1976) reported that with extensive practice, even tasks that theoretically demand high levels of attentional capacity can be performed without interfering with each other. They trained two individuals to read short stories while simultaneously writing down words dictated by the experimenter. Spelke et al. managed to train their participants to take dictation of short sentences, which should require highly effortful semantic processing, while simultaneously reading. They found that after massive practice, people could accurately transcribe while reading with full comprehension. The authors suggested that neither automaticity nor rapid alternation of attention accounted for the results. They contended that people split attention and simultaneously attended to both reading and dictation. Perhaps so, but it seems equally plausible that at least some of the component processes in reading, taking dictation, or both became automatized. The remaining component processes, then, could have been consciously controlled by a rapid alternation of attention.

Logan (1988) provided one explanation of how changes in the way a task is performed through practice lead to automaticity. Specifically, if a task can be restructured so that performance depends on retrieval from long-term memory, then automaticity occurs. Taking our example from earlier in the chapter, if you multiply 6×6, you do not need to carry out the algorithm because you can retrieve the answer, 36, from a memorized multiplication table stored in your long-term memory. The process is fast, effortless, and (most important here) different in nature from the alternative. If you must multiply 18×32, the only route available is to calculate the answer unless perhaps you calculated the same problem just a few minutes before. Thus, as we learn to do a task automatically, it may be that the underlying processes change qualitatively by relying more on direct retrieval from memory.

Genetics and Maturation

Certain processes may be so basic for human learning and survival that they are genetically programmed to operate through maturation and interaction with the environment. Motor skills exemplify processes that achieve automaticity through genetic programming in addition to practice. Learning to crawl, walk, and run is not simply a matter of practice. At birth, there is a reflex to move the arms and legs in a crawling movement. This reflex typically disappears after about 3 or 4 months, with the ability to crawl appearing later, at about 7 months (Gallahue, 1989). Whereas some species are programmed to walk moments after birth to ensure their survival, our species adopts a more leisurely pace, with the infant wholly dependent on the mother and father for survival. The effortlessness and automaticity that we see in the motor skills of an older child running while at play is only partly due to practice.

Basic cognitive processes may also be genetically programmed or hard-wired in the nervous system (Flavell, Miller, & Miller, 1993). These should appear early in development and require relatively little learning to become fully operational. Moreover, individual differences in the functioning of these processes should be minimal if they are species-specific processes. Age, culture, intelligence, educational attainment, and other factors that strongly influence consciously controlled processes ought to be unimportant for innate automatic processes.

Hasher and Zacks (1979, 1984) proposed that humans innately and automatically process the frequency of occurrence of environmental features and events. They reported evidence that young children, as well as adults, keep track of stimulus frequencies, suggesting that the process undergoes little if any cognitive development. Individual differences in frequency processing also are minimal. Numerous studies have challenged the conclusion that frequency processing is entirely automatic. At times, the intention to keep track of frequency helps performance, and heavy concurrent demands on attention can hurt performance. Even so, the evidence strongly supports the conclusion that frequency processing operates automatically and innately, albeit less than optimally at times (Sanders, Gonzalez, Murphy, Liddle, & Vitina, 1987).

● VISUAL ATTENTION

Besides the work on controlled versus automatic processing, researchers set about to map the cognitive processes and associated neural structures involved in visual attention in detail. The focus of attention in vision is sometimes likened to a spotlight, with ignored stimuli falling outside the beam (Posner, 1980). In selective attention, the diameter of the spotlight is highly focused on a central stimulus and adjacent stimuli are ignored. In divided attention, the beam is diffuse so that not only the central stimulus but also adjacent stimuli receive some processing. Experiments have asked an observer to focus attention on a centrally presented target letter and then examined the influence of flanker letters (Murphy & Eriksen, 1987). The logic of these experiments borrows from the Stroop effect. If the adjacent letters are associated with a wrong response or a different response from the target, then reaction time to the target slows down, just like in the Stroop effect.

Alternatively, the response to the target is faster if the adjacent letters are associated with the same response. Murphy and Eriksen (1987) found that if the observer knew exactly where to focus attention, then the spotlight beam was concentrated. Any letter more than about one letter away from target had no impact on response time. By contrast, if a target could occur anywhere, then the spotlight was more diffuse. Adjacent letters often affected response times in this case.

Neural Basis of Selection

Recall that neurons in the occipital cortex act as feature detectors tuned to respond maximally to highly specific visual features such as a line at a particular orientation. Moreover, the line must stimulate a specific area in the retina of the eye, which defines the receptive field for the neuron in question. A group of cells in the retina—the receptive field—all map onto a specific neuron in the cortex that is "looking for" the feature to which it is tuned. Animal studies done on one of the areas in the visual cortex, called V4, reveal what seems to be the operation of an attentional spotlight narrowing in on relevant stimuli while ignoring others.

For example, the size of a receptive field apparently contracts so as to include a stimulus relevant to the task at hand while excluding an irrelevant stimulus. This occurs when both stimuli fall within the range of the original receptive field (Moran & Desimone, 1985). Furthermore, when the task requires a finer discrimination between, say, the orientation of two lines, the response of a neuron to a specific orientation becomes still more specific or more finely tuned (Spitzer, Desimone, & Moran, 1988). Thus, as Kinchla (1992) noted, "The contraction of receptive fields and the sharpening of tuning curves would seem to serve a selective or 'attentional' function" (p. 734).

The control of these changes in receptive fields lies in the thalamus, a structure deep in the diencephalon that serves as a crossroad for a very large number of sensory pathways. Positron emission tomography (PET) scans with humans have revealed increased blood flow—implying increased neural activity—in a portion of the thalamus called the pulvinar thalamic nucleus when observers receive instructions to ignore an irrelevant but clearly visible stimulus (LaBerge & Buchsbaum, 1990). Equally telling is the clinical evidence with patients suffering damage to the pulvinar thalamic nucleus. Lesions in this area are associated with difficulties in directing visual attention (Rafal & Posner, 1987).

Posner and Peterson (1990) concluded from the relevant evidence that different areas turn the attentional spotlight off from its current focus and move it to a new focal point. The pulvinar thalamic nucleus, in their view, reads out the information available in the new focus of attention, and other regions control disengaging and shifting attention to a new location. A break-down in the overall system of disengaging, moving, and reading out the new focus of attention may cause a disorder called **spatial neglect.** This disorder is characterized by a failure to attend to all areas of the visual field. Individuals with damage to the right hemisphere will neglect objects or events occurring in the left visual field. Although there is nothing wrong with their visual per-ception, they fail to attend to objects on their left. Spatial neglect can be seen in patients who read only the words on the right side of a paragraph pre-sented to them or in those who draw only the right half of a picture they were asked to copy (McCarthy & Warrington, 1990). These patients seem to have trouble in voluntarily shifting the attentional spotlight to the neglected side (Posner, Cohen, & Rafal, 1982).

Executive Control

A final attentional circuit is involved in the executive control of mental processes. **Executive control** refers to a supervisory attentional system that inhibits inappropriate mental representations or responses and activates appropriate ones. Imagine leaving a parking lot to drive home in the evening. If your usual routine is to drive straight home, then executive control is needed to intervene and activate the thought of going first to, say, the grocery store. The automatic response of driving home must be inhibited or else it will control behavior. Norman and Shallice (1986) argued that executive con-trol is always needed when (a) planning or making decisions, (b) correcting errors, (c) the required response is novel or not well-learned, (d) conditions are cognitively demanding or dangerous, and (e) an automatic response must be inhibited and overcome.

The Stroop task provides an excellent way to study this control because there is a strong conflict between the automatic but incorrect response of reading the word name and the correct response of reading the color name. When participants perform the Stroop task in conditions that permit PET scans to be taken, a region in the frontal lobe is activated. The **anterior cin-gulate gyrus**, positioned deep in the frontal lobe, acts as a supervisory atten-tional system, inhibiting the automatic response and selecting the correct response. In reviewing the literature, Posner and DiGirolamo (1998) docu-mented that several studies have shown increases in blood flow using PET in the regions of the anterior cingulate gyrus and the left frontal lobe in tests where there was a response conflict in a Stroop task (see Figure 4.9). The supervisory attentional system of executive control, together with short-term

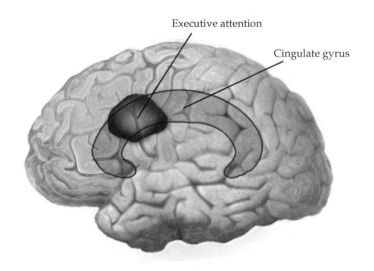

Executive attention

Cingulate gyrus

Figure 4.9. The cingulate gyrus, positioned deep in the frontal lobe, serves an executive attentional function of inhibiting automatic incorrect responses.

memory, plays a crucial role in all complex cognitive tasks, as is discussed in Chapter 5.

The disordered perception and thought of schizophrenia appears to be in part related to a breakdown in the normal processes of selective attention (David, 1993; Place & Gilmore, 1980). This possibly stems from a disorder in the inhibitory capacities of the prefrontal cortex (Cohen, Barch, Carter, & Servan-Schreiber, 1999). Without the ability to inhibit irrelevant information, schizophrenics experience problems in maintaining a representation of the context of their environment and their immediate task. If memories and hallucinations intrude at will, then the thought process disintegrates. A coherent stream of relevant task-related thoughts cannot be maintained if the inhibitory functions that normally enable such coherence break down.

Executive control refers to a supervisory attentional system that inhibits inappropriate mental representations or responses and activates appropriate ones. It is important in planning, decision making, and other complex cognitive tasks.

Perceptual Binding

Another important line of work suggests that attention is necessary for object recognition (Treisman & Gelade, 1980). **Feature integration theory** posits that automatic preattentive processing of features must be followed by controlled attentional processing to bind the features into a whole object. An observer first scans a visual field preattentively, allowing the simultaneous parallel recognition of basic stimulus dimensions such as color and shape.

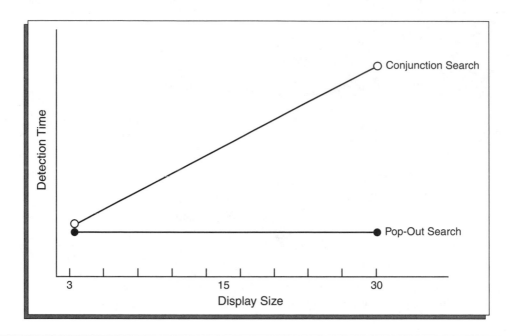

Figure 4.10. Detection time for automatic pop-out search and controlled conjunction search. SOURCE: Adapted from Treisman and Gelade (1980).

A further stage of processing requiring focused attention is then needed to integrate the specific stimulus features into a unitary object. To test their theory, Treisman and Gelade (1980) required observers to detect a target that differed from distractor items in terms of one dimension such as color.

Following the logic of the set size effects discussed earlier, Treisman and her colleagues predicted that the number of distractor items should be irrelevant to speed of detection if the observer could automatically recognize all stimulus features in parallel. For example, finding a red X in a display with nothing but blue Xs and blue Os should be automatic (see the display at the top of Color Plate 4 in the section of color plates). As expected, the results showed that observers could detect such targets just as quickly in a display with 30 items as in a display with only 3 items (Treisman & Gelade, 1980; Treisman & Sato, 1990). This was referred to as a pop-out search because the target popped out at the observer (see Figure 4.10). When they required the observer to search for a unique conjunction of color and form, Treisman and her colleagues expected that focal attention would be needed to integrate the two features. For example, finding a red X in a display that includes red Os and blue Xs demands focused attention (see the display at the bottom of Color Plate 4). For a conjunctive search, she expected and found a strong set size effect; the more distractors, the longer it took to find the target.

Attention, then, can be thought of as the glue that binds together stimulus properties into the perception of a single object. As discussed earlier, different regions of the brain are responsible for processing the shape of an object (temporal lobe) versus its location (parietal lobe). Similarly, color, motion, and depth are distributed in different regions (Livingston & Hubel, 1987). The **binding problem** refers to how the features that are distributed in multiple brain regions are integrated to result in the perception of a single object. As you look at this book, you see an object at a specific location, color, and distance. Your perception is unified even though the mental representation of the book is known to be distributed.

Although the binding problem is not yet fully solved, one important part of the puzzle is that binding requires attention. A peculiar implication follows from this. If attention is not paid to an object, then it apparently is not perceived, although its features are processed. Consider the experiment shown in Figure 4.11, reported by Mack and Rock (1998). The participant fixates on the cross-hair in the center but covertly attends to the large cross to the left. The mask that follows results in backward masking of all the information so as to prevent the use of sensory memory to mentally scan for other objects. On critical trials in the experiment, the fixation spot contains a small object such as the diamond shown here. Note that this shape falls directly on foveal vision for 200 milliseconds, far more time than is normally needed to perceive an object when attention is paid to it. But remember that attention has been covertly shifted to the large cross, disconnecting it from the point of fixation. In this circumstance, between 60% and 80% of the observers failed to perceive the diamond. When asked "Did you see anything on this trial that had not been there on previous trials?" an astonishing large percentage of participants reported that they had not. The same result occurred whether the shape was a diamond, a circle, or a square and whether it was solid black or outlined.

Mack and Rock called their discovery **inattentional blindness.** A superthreshold stimulus that is directly fixated for 200 milliseconds, a long leisurely glance when attention is (as usual) locked onto the fixation point, is simply not seen. Inattentional blindness provides a compelling, but disturbing, demonstration that attention is necessary for binding together features. Without attention and the binding that it supports, perception fails.

A similar phenomenon occurs when a series of stimuli are presented in rapid succession and the observer must attend to and report a target item (Shapiro, 1994). It turns out that any stimuli occurring within about 100 to 600 milliseconds after the target is heeded and reported are not attended and therefore not seen. For example, suppose that 500 milliseconds separates the presentation of a series of letters, as shown in Figure 4.12. If

The binding problem refers to how the features that are distributed in multiple brain regions are integrated to result in the perception of a single object. Attention may be what binds the features together prior to conscious perception.

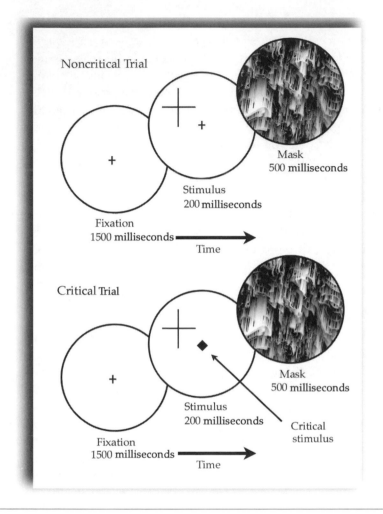

Figure 4.11. Noncritical and critical trials in a task used to study inattentional blindness.
SOURCE: Mack and Rock (1998).

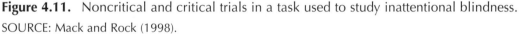

Inattentional blindness
and attentional blink
are failures to perceive
an object that is not
attended.

observers are instructed beforehand to detect the letter T, then they are likely
to miss the letter E because it occurs too close in time to the letter T. It is as
if they blink their eyes, but in reality the only blink is purely attentional. Their
eyes are open, and all letters are registered by the visual system. They fail to
report the letter E and fail to recognize it as having occurred. The interval of
time after the target is presented when other stimuli in the series are not perceived is called **attentional blink.**

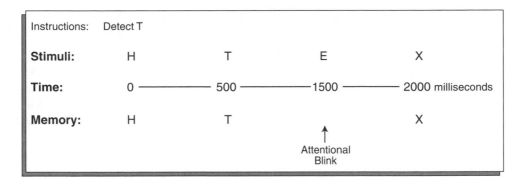

Figure 4.12. A task used to study attentional blink.

SOURCE: Adapted from Shapiro (1994).

Subliminal Perception

Thus, stimuli that are not attended appear to be processed to a degree, but not in a manner that allows their perception. The term **subliminal perception** refers to perception without attention. Based on the facts just reviewed, the term is misleading. Although unattended stimuli are processed, they are not perceived as whole stimuli and so have little if any impact on the ability to recall or recognize the information. By hiding a message in a visual advertisement or by presenting the message for only a few milliseconds in a motion picture, advertisers had hoped to influence future purchasing behavior without the awareness of consumers. Subliminal messages have also been aurally presented and masked by high levels of noise or hidden by being played backward. The latter technique in particular has spurred public outcry, as seen in a rancorous debate in the California legislature over the subliminal influence of rock music on its listeners.

The facts indicate that if a message is not perceived and not remembered, then its impact is unlikely to be significant as compared with one that is both perceived and remembered. Vokey and Read (1985) tested listeners' ability to identify the meanings of backward statements. Each statement fit one of five categories: nursery rhymes, Christian, satanic, pornographic, or advertising. The listeners simply had to identify the correct category, giving them a 20% chance of being correct through random guessing. The listeners performed at about this chance level (19%), indicating that they had not analyzed the meanings of the backward statements. Holender (1986) reviewed many similar negative findings.

Because the subliminal stimuli are not perceived, it is no wonder that they cannot be recalled or recognized. But because their features are processed preattentively, it might also be expected that carefully chosen tests can reveal such processing (Merikle & Reingold, 1992). For example, researchers have found that subliminally presented information slightly alters our future emotional responses to the material even though it cannot be explicitly remembered (Seamon, Marsh, & Brody, 1984; Kunst-Wilson & Zajonc, 1980). People are more inclined to like a stimulus if it has been presented in a subliminal manner previously. Coren (1984) concluded that subliminal advertising operates solely at this level of emotional response. The meaning of the message need not be understood nor remembered explicitly for such emotional changes.

More than 200 studies have documented that subliminal repetitions enhance our degree of emotional comfort with the stimulus, but the mechanism responsible for the effect is still uncertain. Recently, Monahan, Murphy, and Zajonc (2000) suggested that the mere exposure effect improves one's general mood by reducing alertness and tension. They argued that the effect is not dependent on a sense of familiarity with repeated stimuli and can generalize to both related stimuli and even unrelated novel stimuli. If this explanation proves to be correct, then the emotional changes caused by repeated subliminal exposure are diffuse in their effects.

SUMMARY

1. Attention refers to the selection of certain stimuli for processing to the exclusion of others. It also refers to the concentration of mental resources on a particular process. Two broad classes of theories have developed to explain attention. Filter theories address the selective nature of attention, whereas capacity theories address the allocation of resources to specific mental processes. Filter theories postulate a bottleneck in the flow of information from initial sensory processing to registration in conscious awareness. Capacity theories recognize that one or more bottlenecks exist but add the assumption that mental processes compete for limited resources as well.

2. Early selection theory places a bottleneck or filter immediately after sensory memory. Pattern recognition of attended material proceeds, while unattended material fades rapidly from sensory memory because it fails to pass the selective filter. Attenuation theory also places the bottleneck after sensory registration, but it assumes that the filter merely lessens or attenuates the signal strength of unattended material. If the threshold for pattern recognition for a given stimulus, such as one's name, is sufficiently low, then even the weak unattended signals might undergo pattern recognition. Late

selection theory places the filter after all pattern recognition of attended and unattended stimuli has taken place. This view holds that all stimuli are fully analyzed for their meaning. Yet the filter excludes all but the attended stimuli from entering conscious awareness and memory systems.

3. Single capacity theory assumes that mental processes compete for a general pool of attentional resources. Two tasks can also interfere with each other if they both demand a high level of general resources. The general pool is always limited, although the exact amount of available capacity fluctuates with arousal and other factors. The percentage of available capacity used by a process defines the degree of mental effort involved. Multiple capacity theory assumes that pools of resources can be defined in terms of several independent dimensions. Auditory versus visual resources is one such dimension, while verbal versus spatial resources is another. If two tasks both demand, say, verbal capacity, then performance suffers. If one draws on verbal capacity while the other taps spatial capacity, then dual task performance can proceed without interference. Multiple capacity theory, therefore, integrates the insights of filter theories and single capacity theory to provide a comprehensive and detailed description of attention.

4. Automatic processes require little if any mental effort. Moreover, they occur without intentional control; even when an individual attempts to stop an automatic process from operation, it unfolds anyway, as demonstrated by the Stroop effect. Finally, automatic processes operate outside the scope of conscious awareness. Processes develop automaticity either through genetic programming or as the result of extensive practice. Learning proficiency at a skill often entails developing automaticity of underlying processes through practice. Controlled processes contrast with automatic processes on each point. They demand extensive mental effort, they require intentional control to operate, and they enter conscious awareness.

5. The processes and neural basis of visual attention is beginning to be understood. The focus of controlled processing in vision can be likened to a spotlight. The beam of spotlight varies in size, being more diffuse when attentional demands are light and contracting to a narrow beam when demands are heavy. The pulvinar thalamic nucleus appears to serve the function of filtering irrelevant stimuli by controlling how sharply tuned a neuron in the neocortex is to a specific stimulus feature and by altering the size of a neuron's receptive field from the receptor cells in the eye. Other neural circuits appear to turn off the attentional spotlight in one location, move it to a new location, and serve as an executive control system, focusing on relevant mental representations and inhibiting irrelevant ones. A breakdown in the overall system of disengaging, moving, and reading out the new focus of attention may cause a disorder called spatial neglect. This disorder is characterized by a failure to attend to all areas of the visual field.

6. According to the feature integration theory, attention is necessary for visual pattern recognition. Feature detectors operate preattentively or automatically, allowing the identification of shape, color, and other single properties. The identification of a conjunction of two properties, such as color and shape, requires attention. Therefore, attention is the glue that binds together features into a whole object. Evidence shows that with the absence of attention, conscious perception of an object fails to occur, even when the object is fixated directly by the eyes. Inattentional blindness and attentional blink are examples of this failure to perceive in the absence of attention. Another phenomenon called blindsight shows that processing of a visual object in the occipital cortex is necessary for it to enter visual consciousness. Nonetheless, the location of the object can still be guessed correctly despite the individual's blindness in sense of conscious perception.

● KEY TERMS

selective attention

divided attention

shadowing

early selection

attenuation

priming

mental effort

Stroop effect

automatic processes

controlled processes

spatial neglect

executive control

anterior cingulate gyrus

feature integration theory

binding problem

inattentional blindness

attentional blink

subliminal perception

CHAPTER 5

MEMORY

The topic of this chapter has been studied intensely by psychologists since the pioneering work of Hermann Ebbinghaus more than a century ago (Ebbinghaus, 1885). The intense interest in memory is hardly mysterious. The lives of individuals have meaning only because of memory. Our immediate and distant past defines who we are, what we believe, what we can do, and what we feel. Try to imagine what your life would be like if you lost all memory. Imagine no recollection of where you were born, where you grew up, what you did in school, where you work, whom you live with, what you look like, and even what you thought or did just moments ago. The loss of perception or attention would be tragic, but one would still possess a sense of identity so long as memory remained intact. The loss of memory, by contrast, would rob one's very life and personhood.

How is it possible to remember where you lived 5 years ago, what you were doing 5 days ago, or what you were thinking 5 seconds ago? The central story of memory research has been in revealing the complexities of these commonplace achievements of recollection. As will be seen here, there are several kinds of memory stores that underlie our conscious experience of the past. This chapter begins by defining the three basic processes of memory: encoding, storage, and retrieval. Then, the three-store model of memory is introduced, beginning with a presentation of sensory memory. Next, the distinction between short-term and long-term memory is considered, followed by criticisms of the distinction. Then, the extension of the short-term store into a more complex construct called working memory is addressed. Finally, the architecture of long-term memory is detailed.

● ENCODING, STORAGE, AND RETRIEVAL

Memory involves three basic processes. Encoding concerns perceiving, recognizing, and further processing an object or event so that it can be remembered later. The way information is encoded makes a substantial difference in how well it is remembered, as will be seen. It is entirely possible that an event is forgotten because it was not well-encoded in the first place. Encoding must be followed by the successful storage of the information in long-term memory. An object or event might be encoded and held for a brief period of time in short-term memory. For it to be remembered over a long period of time, however, requires storage in long-term memory. The failure to transfer information from short-term memory to permanent storage in long-term memory is another way memory can fail. Finally, retrieval concerns searching long-term memory and finding the event that has been encoded and stored. An event might be available if it is encoded properly and stored successfully in long-term memory. Yet if this event cannot be retrieved successfully, then it is inaccessible to consciousness.

What can you remember about your life when you were a baby? Although long-term memory can retain information for decades, our earliest experiences in life are virtually always forgotten. The inability to recall events from the first 2 or 3 years of life is called infantile amnesia (Howe & Courage, 1993; Spear, 1979). The reason for such amnesia is still unclear. One view is that the events of infancy are permanently stored but irretrievable. An alternative view is that these events were never encoded and stored adequately in the first place.

Freud (1900/1953) championed the first view. Repression of early, anxiety-provoking experiences was a defense mechanism to protect the ego in psychoanalytic theory. Freud used free association to unlock early memories. Another technique for doing so is hypnotic age regression, in which an individual presumably assumes the personality held at an earlier age (Nash, 1987). Repression is not the only explanation for retrieval failure, however. Perhaps the events are coded by the infant in a way that is not linked to the retrieval cues used by an adult. For example, an infant would encode the world without using language to label objects and events. As an adult, attempts to search memory would commonly be organized around linguistic labels for concepts.

Other theorists question the permanence of early childhood memories (Kail, 1984; Loftus & Loftus, 1980). Maybe we cannot retrieve them simply because they do not exist. One reason for this impermanence is that the attentional and perceptual systems of the infant might not have been sufficiently developed to encode the events properly in the first place. Another possibility is that they were encoded and could be retrieved for a brief period of time, but then the events decayed from memory.

Research on the phenomenon has demonstrated that even 2-year-olds can recall events that happened 3 or even 6 months in the past (Fivush, Gray, & Fromhoff, 1987). Moreover, Perris, Myers, and Clifton (1990) reported that 2½-year-old children could recall a single experience in a psychology laboratory that occurred when they were 6½ months old! That attests either to the remarkable memory of young children or to the bizarreness of psychology laboratories.

Yet Howe and Courage (1993) pointed out that the nature of these recollections by preschoolers is very fragmentary. These theorists contended that until children develop a concept of the self, which takes place at about the age of 18 months, they cannot possibly organize memories autobiographically. Shortly thereafter, at about the age of 22 months, children acquire the pronouns "I" and "you." Language acquisition provides an enormously powerful tool for organizing memory as an autobiographical narrative (Nelson, 1990). The source of infantile amnesia most likely lies either in the initial absence of a self-concept or in the absence of language needed to support memory for experiences.

It has been known for centuries that drugs can cause forgetting. Alcohol is by far the most widely used drug with this feature. Halcion and benzodiazepines such as Valium and Xanax are prescription drugs that also can disrupt memory. Alcohol and benzodiazepines dramatically reduce the encoding and storage of information. The details about the context of events are lost (Curran, 2000). As will be described in more detail in Chapter 6, these drugs powerfully affect one's ability to reconstruct the time and the place of a particular event from the past. The event experienced during intoxication may later seem vaguely familiar but it is difficult to remember it fully in context. Intoxication disrupts event coding and storage.

SENSORY MEMORY •

As introduced in Chapter 1, Atkinson and Shiffrin (1968) proposed that human memory is not unitary. According to the three-store model, it is necessary to distinguish among sensory, short-term, and long-term stores that differ in their capacity and duration of storage. Sensory memory refers

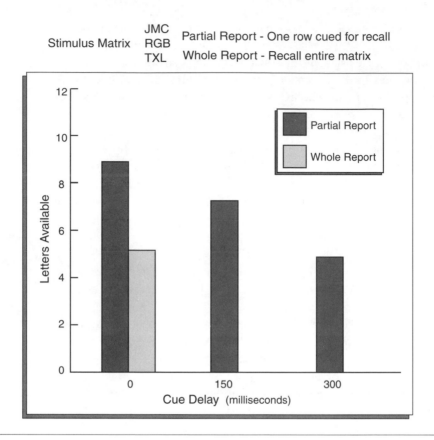

Stimulus Matrix

JMC
RGB
TXL

Partial Report - One row cued for recall
Whole Report - Recall entire matrix

Figure 5.1. Partial report task used to study the capacity and duration of iconic memory.
SOURCE: Adapted from Sperling (1960).

to the brief persistence of stimuli following transduction. Its function is to permit stimuli to be perceived, recognized, and entered into short-term memory. Without sensory memory, events in the environment would be forgotten as soon as they registered in the nervous system.

In vision, this brief persistence is called **iconic memory** and was investigated by Sperling (1960). An observer saw an array of nine letters presented for only 50 milliseconds using a device called a tachistoscope. A sample array is shown in Figure 5.1 along with the results of the experiment. When immediately asked to recall as many letters as possible, the typical participant managed to report four or five. This Sperling called the whole report condition. He suspected, however, that all of the letters persisted briefly in iconic storage. But once the letters were located in space, their shapes were specified, and their names were recognized, some letters were lost. In terms of the three-store model, the letters may have been briefly available in iconic memory, but verbally reporting the letters required their conscious recognition and representation in short-term memory. By the time the observer named four or five, the others had long faded from sensory storage and were no longer available for processing.

To test his hypothesis, Sperling (1960) arranged a partial report condition, in which the observer had to report only the letters from a single row but did not know in advance which row. A high-pitched tone occurred after the 50-millisecond presentation to indicate that only the letters J-M-C needed to be reported. Similarly, a medium-pitched tone cued the middle row, and a low-pitched tone cued the bottom row. Sperling reasoned that if the observer could report all three letters from a single row without knowing in advance which row would be cued, then the true number of letters available in iconic memory equaled three times the number given under partial report. Sperling then delayed the onset of partial report cue systematically from 0 to 1 second to examine how quickly the iconic storage was lost. As seen in Figure 5.1, with an immediate cue, the observer recalled on average about two and a half letters, implying that nearly all nine letters persisted in iconic storage. But within about 200 to 300 milliseconds, the estimated number of letters available dropped to four or five—no different from the number obtained in the whole report condition.

Sperling's work indicated that iconic memory has a large capacity—greater than what can be reported at once—and a duration of only about 250 milliseconds. Several later experiments by others suggest that the iconic store holds most if not all sensations registered by the retina for a brief period of time (e.g., Averbach & Coriell, 1961).

Visual sensory memory is called iconic memory; it has a large capacity but a brief duration of about 250 milliseconds.

The contents of iconic memory normally decay rapidly, but in a rare exceptional case of eidetic imagery, more commonly known as photographic memory, these details persist for longer durations. Some college students find that they can remember images of textbook pages they have studied intensively, such that on tests they can retrieve seemingly accurate images of particular pages. Neisser (1981) found that such strong visual imagery skills are more common in children and are usually lost by the end of adolescence. However, a stringent test for eidetic imagery requires the ability to superimpose one pictorial image on another to form a third novel picture.

The only clear case of eidetic imagery ever documented was that of Elizabeth, an artist who used powerful visual imagery skills to project, as a hallucination, a picture onto a blank canvas in her work. She was tested in the laboratory for this ability by viewing two random dot patterns, one presented to each eye (Stromeyer & Psotka, 1970). When viewed separately, the 10,000 dots in a pattern looked random, signifying nothing. When viewed stereoscopically (i.e., with the unique patterns to the left and right eye presented simultaneously), they merged to form a recognizable object such as the letter T. The researchers presented Elizabeth with a 10,000-dot pattern for 1 minute to her right eye. Following a 10-second rest, she viewed with her left eye the accompanying 10,000-dot pattern and, when asked to superimpose the two, immediately reported seeing the letter T coming at her. She then looked at both patterns through a stereoscope and confirmed that her eidetic image of the T appeared exactly as it should. Note that this outcome implies the ability to retain in memory the precise location of 10,000 random dots! Further tests showed that she could retain the right eye image for up to 24 hours before superimposing on it the left eye pattern.

The auditory system also stores sensations briefly in a component dubbed **echoic memory** by Neisser (1967). Experiments parallel to Sperling's partial report study have been conducted to test the capacity and duration of echoic storage (Darwin, Turvey, & Crowder, 1972; Moray, Bates, & Barnett, 1965). Using stereo headphones, Darwin et al. (1972) presented three separate sequences of letters to an individual: one to the left ear, one to the right ear, and one dichotically (to both ears) that is perceived in the center of the head. Using the same comparison of whole report (report all sequences) versus partial report (report the left, right, or center sequence only), the researchers concluded that more items were stored than could be reported, just as in the case of iconic memory. However, the duration of echoic memory seemed to be much longer, on the order of 2 seconds rather than 250 milliseconds, judging from the effects of delaying the partial report cue.

Many subsequent studies have addressed this discrepancy. In reviewing this work, Cowan (1988) concluded that the studies on echoic memory have actually tapped into two phases of storage. The first one is clearly sensory in nature and persists for about 250 milliseconds, comparable to the duration of iconic sensory memory (e.g., Massaro, 1970). The second phase lasts much longer, at least 3 or 4 seconds (Crowder, 1982a). Auditory representations persisting for several seconds have been not only perceived but also recognized and named. Hence, the long phase observed in these studies is actually a result of storage in short-term memory (Penney, 1989).

Auditory sensory memory is called echoic memory; its duration is brief, but aural stimuli such as speech are also stored for longer periods of time in short-term memory.

● SHORT-TERM VERSUS LONG-TERM MEMORY

All of us have experienced looking up a novel telephone number in the directory and then repeating it silently until we reach for the telephone and dial the number successfully. Without silent rehearsal, the meaningless sequence of digits is easily lost from memory if we wait too long to dial or are interrupted. Subjectively, the number seems available only temporarily in a short-term store. Our experience is quite different from the automatic, well-learned recall of our own telephone number. Unlike the fragile short-term memory, our own number seems locked permanently in a long-term store from which it can be retrieved with ease. Other numbers less often used, such as that of

Box 5.1

A DEMONSTRATION OF THE FREE RECALL METHOD OF VERBAL LEARNING AND MEMORY

Read each word aloud at a rate of about one per second. Cover up each word as you read so as to avoid rereading any items. Alternatively, you can ask a friend to read these words aloud to you. After reading or hearing the words, close the book and try to recall as many words as you can. Do not be concerned about the order of recall. You can write them down in whatever order you like.

1. brick
2. truck
3. stove
4. apple
5. door
6. book
7. ladder
8. rifle
9. pencil
10. lamp
11. goat
12. cabbage
13. baseball
14. tree
15. window

a friend not called for years, can sometimes also be retrieved from a seemingly permanent form of memory, but only with great effort.

Introspection along these lines has suggested a distinction between short-term and long-term memory from the time of James's *Principles of Psychology* in 1890. James referred to immediate memory of events currently attended to as primary memory and all other memory as secondary. Atkinson and Shiffrin (1968) referred to these as short-term and long-term memory in their three-store model. A classic way to study the distinction between these two kinds of memory stores involves hearing or reading a list of words and then trying to recall them without any restrictions on the order of output. You can try this free recall task by reading aloud each word given in Box 5.1.

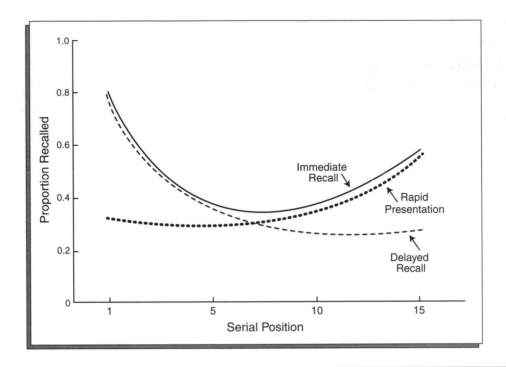

Figure 5.2. Serial position effects and the distinction between short-term and long-term memory.

After doing so, close the book and try to write down as many of the words as you can remember in whatever order you like. Next, check how many words you correctly recalled. In particular, make a note of how many of initial items 1 to 5 you recalled. Next, look at the middle of the list items, numbered 6 to 10. Finally, how many of the final list items 11 to 15 did you recall?

Serial Position Effects

The typical outcome of this free recall procedure is known as the **serial position effect** and is illustrated in Figure 5.2 with the curve labeled "immediate recall." The initial words on the list are recalled reasonably well, a phenomenon called the **primacy effect.** If you recalled most or all of the initial items on the list, then you showed a primacy effect. The words in the middle of the list are typically forgotten. Finally, the words at the end of the list are also remembered well; in fact, these are the words most likely to be recalled first. Were these the items you tended to write down first? Did you recall most or all of them? The high level of recall and early output is aptly labeled the **recency effect.** These effects have been known about for more than a century (Nipher, 1878).

The serial position effect can readily be accounted for in terms of the Atkinson and Shiffrin model and related mathematical models (Murdock, 1974). Once a word was recognized, it passed from sensory memory to short-term memory. If it remained in short-term memory and was rehearsed, then the word was transferred to the long-term store. By assuming a limited capacity to the short-term store, the initial items on the list remained in the short-term store longer than did the later items. Once the capacity of the store was exceeded, a new word entered only by displacing a previous word. So, the initial list items remained in short-term memory long enough to be transferred via rehearsal to long-term memory. Thus, the primacy effect arises from the retrieval of information from long-term memory. The recency effect, on the other hand, reflects retrieval from the short-term store. The final words on the list still reside in the short-term store and can be retrieved so long as recall is immediate; in other words, they did not need to be rehearsed. Although the serial position effect is open to alternative interpretations (Crowder, 1993; Greene, 1986), it remains as a source of support for distinguishing between short-term and long-term stores (Healy & McNamara, 1996).

Also shown in Figure 5.2 are two dissociations that further support the distinction. The recency effect can be eliminated without affecting the primacy effect by delaying recall for 30 seconds (Glanzer & Cunitz, 1966). It is important to prevent participants from rehearsing the list during this delay by giving them an attention-demanding task to perform, namely counting backward by sevens from a number (e.g., 93, 86, 79, 72, 65, . . .). The delay eliminates the use of short-term memory but leaves intact recall from long-term memory. By contrast, speeding the rate of presenting the items, so that they remain in short-term memory for a shorter amount of time and are less likely to be rehearsed, eliminates the primacy effect while sparing the recency effect (Atkinson & Shiffrin, 1968).

The process responsible for the transfer of items from the short-term to the long-term store is presumably rehearsal, for example, repeating the words silently. To establish a direct link between rehearsal and the primacy effect, Rundus (1971) asked people to say aloud any words from the list that they wished during a 5-second interval between each word presentation. Rundus found that the initial items on the list received far more rehearsals than did later items. People tended to repeat aloud the first words many times, but then as the short-term store filled to capacity, they had more words competing for rehearsal than could be handled. Thus, Rundus established a compelling explanation of the primacy effect in terms of rehearsal.

Free recall of a list of words reveals a serial position effect. The final items in the list are recalled first and well—the recency effect. The initial items in the list are also recalled well—the primacy effect. The three-store model attributes the recency effect to the short-term store and attributes the primacy effect to the long-term store.

Neurological Dissociations

Another reason for distinguishing short-term memory from long-term memory came from the study of amnesia, specifically **anterograde amnesia.** This refers to difficulty in remembering events that occur after the onset of amnesia. **Retrograde amnesia,** on the other hand, refers to the loss of memory of events that occurred prior to the onset of the illness.

Anterograde Amnesia. In a famous case, a patient known by his initials "H. M." suffered from untreatable epilepsy. He finally found relief from violent seizures following the bilateral surgical removal of the frontal portions of the medial temporal lobe, including the hippocampus. Illustrated at the left of Figure 5.3 is a normal hippocampus in the left and right medial temporal lobes. At the right of the figure, bilateral lesions of the hippocampus are shown, similar to those produced in the anterior region of H. M.'s medial temporal lobe. Although the operation was a success in treating the epilepsy, H. M. suffered severe anterograde amnesia as a consequence.

Milner (1966) described H. M.'s memory loss in the following words:

> He could no longer recognize the hospital staff, apart from Dr. Scoville himself, whom he had known for many years; he did not remember and could not relearn the way to the bathroom, and he seemed to retain nothing of the day-to-day happenings in the hospital. . . . A year later, H. M. had not yet learned the new address, nor could he be trusted to find his home. . . . He is unable to learn where objects are usually kept. (p. 113)

Anterograde amnesia is forgetting events that occurred after brain trauma. It appears to reflect a disruption in the transfer of events to long-term memory during learning. Retrograde amnesia is forgetting events that preceded the trauma and reflects forgetting from long-term memory.

Milner and her colleagues used several tests to document in detail the nature of H. M.'s loss of memory. They found that he showed profound deficits in learning and remembering both verbal material such as word lists and nonverbal material such as faces and sequences of lights. Specifically, Milner concluded that such anterograde amnesia reflected a failure to transfer information from short-term into long-term memory. Other cases of anterograde amnesia confirm this conclusion. Amnesia patients show a strong recency effect in recalling a list of words, much like the normal control participants (Baddeley & Warrington, 1970). Short-term memory per se is fine. However, the patients showed no primacy effect at all, as would be expected if their problem centered on difficulties in transferring new events into long-term memory.

Besides the evidence from H. M., it is known that bilateral damage from a stroke to the CA1 field of the hippocampus prevents the learning of new events information (Zola-Morgan, Squire, & Amaral, 1986). Additional evidence comes from the magnetic resonance imaging (MRI) data on the living brains of four

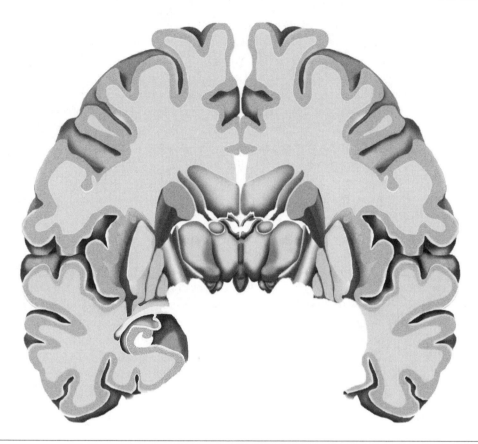

Figure 5.3. The loss of the hippocampus in H. M. is illustrated at the right of the figure. At the left of the figure, the normal position of the hippocampal formation is shown for comparison. In H. M., the loss was bilateral, affecting both the right and left medial temporal lobes.

patients with severe anterograde amnesia that show a smaller than normal hippocampus in all four patients (Squire, Amaral, & Press, 1990). The images have revealed a smaller than normal hippocampus in all four. Deficits in new learning are also found when the hippocampal region of monkeys is lesioned experimentally (Mishkin, 1978; Zola & Squire, 2000). Finally, functional MRI (fMRI) studies have shown that the medial temporal lobes, including the hippocampus, are bilaterally activated when normal participants encode novel pictures into long-term memory. This activation is illustrated in Color Plate 5 in the section of color plates from a study reported by Martin, Wiggs, and Weisberg (1997).

Squire (1992a) theorized that the hippocampus binds together the various places in the neocortex that process different features of a new event such as the shape, color, and location of a visual object. In primates, these areas of the neocortex project to the hippocampus. Thus, the hippocampus and related structures in the medial temporal lobe are positioned to integrate the features of an event, each of which is processed and stored in different regions throughout the neocortex. The binding action of the hippocampus is necessary, according to Squire's theory, to remember objects that are no longer in the focus of attention. For example, in perceiving a visual object, shape, color, and location are identified by the object recognition pathway in the temporal lobe and the location pathway in the parietal lobes reviewed earlier. Over a short-term period, the simultaneous and coordinated activity in these neocortical regions suffice to keep the object in mind. But if one's attention shifts from the object to a new visual scene or to an internal train of thought, then the object can be retrieved only because the hippocampus had bound together the right shape, color, and location. A cue, such as the object's shape, could then be processed by the hippocampus to reactivate all of the relevant neocortical sites and retrieve the whole object from memory. Just as it is necessary to bind the features in perception (as discussed in Chapter 4), it is also necessary to bind the features in memory once the object has left the focus of attention. The hippocampus seems to provide an index of where in the neocortex one can find all of the features that together comprise a memory.

How long is the hippocampus needed for the purpose of keeping track of the features that, bound together, make a memory? If the binding and other learning processes, such as rehearsal, are successful, then the hippocampus no longer seems needed for indexing the event. These processes, then, function to consolidate the event representation in long-term memory, which may take many days or weeks to complete. At this later stage of learning, the event can in theory be retrieved from long-term memory without using the indexing functions of the hippocampus. Thus, the role of the hippocampus in retrieving events may be time limited. Activation of the hippocampus ought to be necessary in retrieving a recently learned event that has not yet been fully consolidated in neocortical areas (McClelland, McNaughten, & O'Reilly, 1995).

Retrograde Amnesia. Strong evidence that the hippocampal role in learning and retrieving events is temporary comes from studies of retrograde amnesia in patients with hippocampal damage. Not only do hippocampal lesions cause anterograde amnesia that disrupts new learning, but they also cause loss of events that occurred prior to the accidents or strokes that caused the lesions. By studying how far back in the past patients' retrograde amnesia extends, one can determine for how long the hippocampus stays involved with the retrieval of learned events. The temporal gradient of amnesia for past events is shown for different groups of participants in Figure 5.4, compiled by Squire, Haist, and Shimamura (1989). The recall of public events that had occurred from 1950 to 1985 was tested.

> The hippocampus and related structures in the medial temporal lobe bind together the features of an event represented in regions distributed throughout the neocortex. Binding the features in memory is necessary to remember the event when it is no longer in the focus of attention.

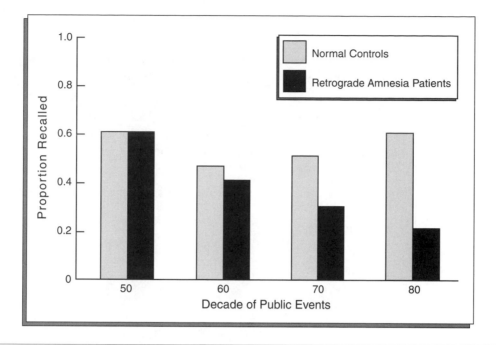

Figure 5.4. Recall of past public events in retrograde amnesic patients.
SOURCE: Adapted from Squire, Haist, and Shimamura (1989).

As can be seen, amnesic patients recalled just as many public events from the 1950s as did normal controls. However, the amnesic patients did progressively worse than the controls for the events from the 1960s, 1970s, and 1980s that occurred closer and closer to the times of when they suffered hippocampal lesions. Presumably, the consolidation process had not yet been completed for these events, and so they were lost to retrograde amnesia.

Impaired Short-Term Memory. So far, the discussion of neuropsychological evidence has focused on problems that arise in storing and consolidating new events in long-term memory. Other evidence on the separation of short-term and long-term memory comes from cases with impaired immediate recall. Warrington and Shallice (1972) first documented what seems to be a defect in short-term memory per se in the patient "K. F." The normal span of short-term memory is about seven items. However, K. F. and others like him show a dramatically smaller short-term memory, particularly when auditory rather than visual presentation is used. K. F. could correctly repeat a single letter even after a 60-second delay. But a mere two letters spoken to him were rapidly forgotten. Three letters showed still greater loss over time, even for those presented visually.

Evidence from patients suffering from anterograde amnesia, retrograde amnesia, and reduced short-term memory capacity supports the distinction between short-term and long-term memory.

Box 5.2

A DIGIT SPAN TEST DEMONSTRATING THE LIMITED CAPACITY OF SHORT-TERM MEMORY

Cover the digit sets given below with a piece of paper and then uncover one set at a time. Read the set quickly, look away, and then try to recall it correctly by writing the numbers in the correct order on another sheet of paper.

6842

59317

274319

4952876

52968471

629479876

123456789

Capacity

Long-term memory is nothing if not spacious. A lifetime of memories can readily be stored, and there are no known limits to how much one can experience, learn, and remember. By sharp contrast, short-term memory is notorious for its limits in storage capacity (Miller, 1956). This can be easily seen in a test of the span of short-term memory for digits, as illustrated in Box 5.2. How many digits were you able to recall correctly in the right order? For most individuals, five or six items can be recalled fairly easily, but eight or nine digits burden short-term memory. In fact, relatively few people accurately recall a nine-digit series, as required by the next to last digit set. But what about the final set? Although it also contains nine items, all nine are easily remembered.

Miller (1956) recognized that the capacity limitation of short-term memory is a very real biological constraint. However, Miller further recognized that a nonbiological cultural process can overcome this limitation. He called the process **chunking.** It is easy to remember the final set of digits because they comprise a single chunk: the ascending order of single-digit numbers. Meaningful patterns of information, often those grounded in the cultural tool of language, allow a person to remember far more than seven individual items. By grouping meaningful information together, we form a coherent chunk of information.

Although the digit span results suggest a capacity limitation of seven chunks, other results place the capacity of short-term memory at only three to five chunks (Broadbent, 1975; Schneider & Detweiler, 1987). The precise capacity of short-term memory varies depending on the task used to make the estimate and the materials used in the task (Cavanagh, 1972). Also, the higher estimates of capacity are distorted by contributions from rehearsal and long-term memory, on the one hand, and sensory memory, on the other (Cowan, 2000). When these factors are controlled effectively, it becomes clear that pure short-term memory capacity is limited to about four chunks.

Duration

As noted earlier, you can retain a telephone number long enough to dial it by rehearsing the number silently. But what if someone interrupts the rehearsal or another task at hand distracts you from dialing? How long will the digits of the telephone number persevere? The answer appears to be about 20 seconds. Depending on the specific task and materials used to assess the duration, estimates range from as brief as 10 seconds to as long as 30 seconds (Cowan, 1988). The classic method is called the Brown-Peterson procedure after the pioneering research by Brown (1958) and Peterson and Peterson (1959).

In this task, an individual listens to a series of three random consonants—a trigram—followed by the presentation of a three-digit number. As a distracting activity, the person counts backward by threes, speaking aloud to the pace of a metronome that clicks every half second. The counting continues for various unpredictable intervals ranging from 3 to 18 seconds; immediate recall without the intervening distraction also is tested at times. Forgetting over this brief interval can be closely approximated by a power function (see Figure 5.5) in which the rate of forgetting levels off as time increases. This is the classic forgetting curve that obtains regardless of whether the retention interval is 20 seconds, 20 weeks, or 20 years (Rubin & Wenzel, 1996). Thus, information in short-term memory is forgotten over a relatively brief time interval, even when it consists of only three chunks below the capacity limit.

The duration of long-term memory must be measured in terms of years, not seconds. Once material is stored in long-term memory, it may well persist for a lifetime. Because of the difficulties in measuring such durations, a precise estimate cannot be given. We do know that the duration of long-term memory is at least 50 years from the remarkable studies by Bahrick and his colleagues (Bahrick, 1983, 1984; Bahrick, Bahrick, & Wittlinger, 1975). Memory for information acquired in high school or college was assessed

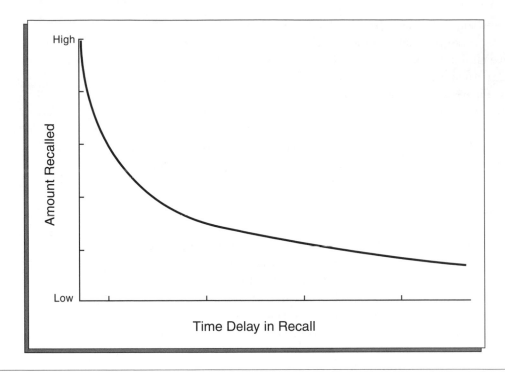

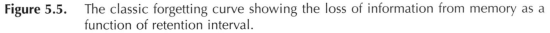

Figure 5.5. The classic forgetting curve showing the loss of information from memory as a function of retention interval.

SOURCE: Peterson and Peterson (1959).

The capacity of short-term memory is limited to about four chunks of information, and its duration is less than 30 seconds. The capacity limits of long-term memory are unknown, and its duration is measured in decades.

many years after graduation. For example, the names and faces of classmates, foreign language vocabulary, and locations of buildings on a college campus were checked. Although much of the information was forgotten, Bahrick (1983) found clear evidence of apparently permanent storage even 50 years after graduation. For example, after 46 years, students could recall the names of campus buildings and correctly place them on a map of the campus.

Conway, Cohen, and Stanhope (1991) measured what students remembered about their cognitive psychology class over a period of about 10 years. They tested their participants for the names of researchers and for concepts acquired by the students. Conway et al. controlled for the differences in the degree of original learning of the material by taking into account participants' grades received in the course. Accurate recognition of both names and concepts declined quickly over the first 40 months or so but then stabilized. It remained well above chance even 125 months later. It should not come as a surprise to any student that free recall of the same information showed more forgetting. Recognition is typically easier than recall. Still, even on the recall measure, Conway et al. found retention of about a third of the material after 10 years (see Figure 5.6).

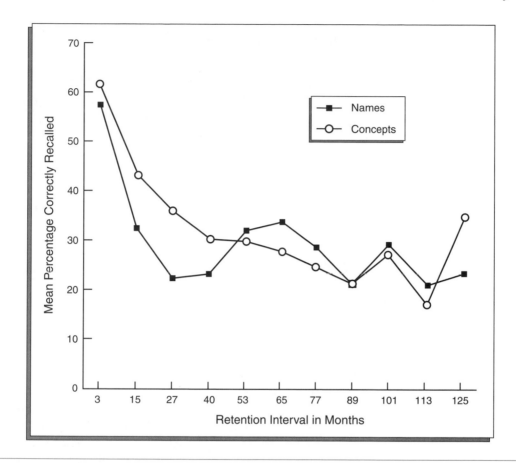

Figure 5.6. Long-term retention of facts about cognitive psychology.
SOURCE: Conway, Cohen, and Stanhope (1991).

Other Distinguishing Criteria

The capacity and duration differences among sensory, short-term, and long-term memory are summarized in Figure 5.7. Besides these basic distinctions among memory stores, efforts were made to identify other differences such as the codes used to store information, the causes of forgetting, and the means of retrieval. As first noted by Craik and Lockhart (1972), these criteria failed to dissociate the three stores. For example, it turned out that short-term and long-term memory rely on visual, acoustic, and semantic codes. Because of such similarities, Craik and Lockhart argued against a structural view of memory and in favor of a process view. Specifically, they suggested that memory representations are linked to the perceptual and

Differences in Memory Stores

	Sensory	Short-Term	Long-Term
Duration	250 milliseconds	20 seconds	years
Capacity	large	4 chunks	very large

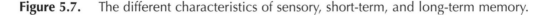

Figure 5.7. The different characteristics of sensory, short-term, and long-term memory.

higher order cognitive processes that are involved during encoding and storing events. As we will see in Chapter 6, their focus on encoding processes strongly influenced the direction of research over the past 30 years.

Coding. Sperling (1960) proposed that the format of iconic storage was precategorical. That is, only preliminary pattern recognition processes had operated on the information, allowing one to locate items in space but not to name them or identify them as members of a category. Sperling argued this position on the basis of studies that included a matrix with half letters and half numbers. The observer failed to show any advantage with a partial report cue to name, say, only the letters, whereas the location cue of the top, middle, or bottom row resulted in nearly perfect recall. However, Merikle (1980) later showed that the haphazard arrangement of the letters and numbers forced the observer to process them one at a time. By carefully arranging the format and spacing of the display, Merikle demonstrated that categorical distinction between letters and numbers could be used to a degree. Thus, location and other physical features are processed faster than the semantic category to which a stimulus belongs, but it is hard to draw a firm line between iconic and short-term memory on the basis of the coding format. A similar difficulty exists for echoic memory (Penney, 1975, 1989).

In fact, even long-term memory uses sensory codes. Paivio (1971, 1983) marshaled an extensive body of evidence showing that people remember material best when they encode into long-term memory both visual images and the verbal labels for semantic categories. As is discussed further in Chapter 6, if you were to learn the list presented in Box 5.1 by both forming an image of each item in your mind's eye and attending to the names, then your overall level of recall would improve.

Initially, short-term memory appeared to be based on a sensory code, specifically the acoustic or articulatory code involved in vocalizing names. Intrusion errors in immediate recall typically reflected confusions in stimuli that sound alike or that are enunciated in similar ways (Conrad, 1964). For example, people often incorrectly recalled the letter B in tests of short-term memory when the correct item was V. Confusion based on a visual code of how letters looked—their orthographic similarity—rarely occurred. The letters F and E differ by only a single distinctive feature in visual coding, yet Conrad's participants failed to confuse them. The high rate of intrusion errors in short-term memory for stimuli that are pronounced alike is called the **phonemic similarity effect.** The acoustic alphabet (e.g., "Alpha," "Bravo," "Charlie," . . . "Victor") used by the military and others avoids such acoustic errors by assigning a name for each letter that is unique in terms of the acoustic-articulatory code.

> The phonemic similarity effect refers to the high rate of intrusion errors in short-term memory for stimuli that are pronounced alike.

Thus, in processing verbal material for later recall, people clearly use an acoustic-articulatory code. But it became clear from later research that short-term memory is not limited to this type of sensory code. Visual codes are used in short-term memory when people hold mental images in the mind's eye for several seconds (Brooks, 1968; Penney, 1975, 1989). Semantic codes are also used in storing material in short-term memory (Wickens, 1972). To see the logic behind this conclusion, consider an experiment by Wickens, Dalezman, and Eggemeier (1976).

Wickens et al. (1976) presented three words on each trial, followed by backward counting to prevent their rehearsal. Each triad of words came from the same semantic category (types of fruit) on the first three trials. On the fourth trial, the researchers shifted the category in the experimental condition to either vegetables, flowers, meats, or professions. The control condition received another triad of fruits. The results are shown in Figure 5.8. Recall decreased systematically on the first three trials as it became more and more difficult to remember which specific fruits had been presented on a particular trial. Then, on the fourth trial, there was an improvement in recall for those receiving a new category. Notice that the degree of semantic similarity between fruits and the new categories accounted for the size of the improvement. This is striking evidence that semantic codes are used in short-term memory. The farther apart the categories are in meaning, the greater the release. This outcome shows convincingly that the semantic code of each triad is stored in short-term memory. Similar semantic codes show less improvement on the final trial than do dissimilar codes.

Forgetting. The decrease in correct recall observed on the first three trials in the Wickens et al. (1976) experiment illustrates an important cause of

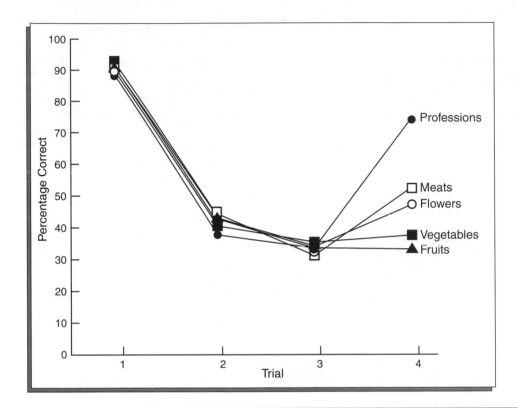

Figure 5.8. Release from proactive interference showing semantic coding in short-term memory.

SOURCE: Wickens, Dalezman, and Eggemeier (1976).

forgetting called interference. **Proactive interference** means that past learning interferes with the ability to learn and remember new information. For example, first learning a list of words (List A) would interfere with learning and recall of a second List B. Imagine an experiment in which we first presented List A, then presented List B, and then tested List B. Proactive interference is defined as poorer recall of List B relative to a condition that first rests, then receives List B, and then is tested on List B. The buildup of proactive interference explains why performance declined in the Wickens et al. experiment until release was obtained by shifting to a novel category on the fourth trial. **Retroactive interference** refers to recent learning interfering with the recall of previous learning. Thus, List A, List B, recall List A does more poorly than List A, rest, recall List A. Learning List B interferes backward in time with the recall of List A.

So, it appears that interference is one source of forgetting in short-term memory. Waugh and Norman (1965) tested a simple alternative explanation of such forgetting, namely that the information decays over time and is no longer available for recall. Participants heard a long sequence of digits followed by a probe digit, which prompted them to recall the digit that had followed the probe earlier in the list. The probe occurred after either one digit or several intervening digits. This allowed an assessment of whether recall declined with increases in the amount of retroactive interference. The digits came at a fast rate in one condition and at a slow rate in another; thus, the time that passed before the probe occurred was longer in the slow rate condition. If decay over time is an important source of forgetting, then recall should be poorer in the slow condition than in the fast condition. Waugh and Norman found that recall decreased with the number of digits intervening before the probe occurred. Thus, interference affected forgetting, yet the rate of presentation had no reliable impact on recall. Decay with time did not seem to be a factor.

Interference is not limited to short-term memory, however. It has long been known that interference is a major source of forgetting in long-term memory (McGeoch, 1942). Theorists during the 1940s and 1950s developed detailed models of how forgetting takes place when wrong responses interfere with right ones. At the same time, findings that followed Waugh and Norman's (1965) work showed that decay in fact does play some part in the forgetting found in short-term memory in addition to interference (Baddeley & Scott, 1971; Reitman, 1974). There is more to forgetting than just decay and interference, as will be seen in Chapter 6, but for now the essential point is that the loss of information from short-term and long-term memory can take place in similar ways.

Consistent with this point, Rubin and Wenzel (1996) examined 210 published data sets that looked at short-term and long-term forgetting with retention intervals of seconds, days, weeks, and months. In all cases, forgetting followed the same function, as illustrated in Figure 5.5. It did not matter whether the time scale was short or long; the course of forgetting looks the same. The only exception was with respect to autobiographical memories—events with personal meaning for the individual—which were retained well even for long periods of time.

Retrieval. Just as short-term and long-term memory are difficult to distinguish on the basis of forgetting, the retrieval processes involved may also overlap. A **serial search** means that the items in memory are somehow ordered and are examined one at a time, starting with the first item and proceeding to the next. A **parallel search,** by contrast, means that all items in memory are examined simultaneously, not serially. Obviously, a parallel search process would result in much more efficient retrieval of information, especially when the amount of information that must be searched is large, as is the case in long-term memory.

If a search is serial, then when does it terminate? A **self-terminating search** refers to one that stops as soon as the item being sought is found. Thus, in a serial self-terminating search for the letter K among the letters D-B-K-X-M ordered in memory, the search would end after examining the third letter. By contrast, an **exhaustive search** refers to one that continues to examine the remaining items in memory even after the target item has been found. In our example, a serial exhaustive search would look at all five letters one at a time. It would not stop at the third position even though the target was found.

The classic study of these retrieval processes in short-term memory came from Sternberg (1966). On each trial, the participant memorized a short list of letters. The number of letters in the memory set varied from one to six, within the capacity of short-term memory. Next, Sternberg presented a probe letter. In the preceding example, the memory set size was five and the letter K was the probe. The person then pushed a "yes" button or a "no" button as rapidly as possible to indicate whether the probe could be found in the memory set. For example, K brings a yes response, whereas L brings a no response.

If all items in memory are searched in parallel, then the set size should not affect retrieval time. Furthermore, a negative trial in which the probe could not be found would be no slower than a positive trial in which the probe matched one of the items. By contrast, if a serial search is used, then reaction time should increase linearly as a function of set size. Each additional letter should add a constant number of milliseconds to the search time. An exhaustive serial search implies that the negative trials and positive trials should take exactly the same amount of time per item; their slopes should be equal. That is, the search does not stop just because a target is found on the positive trials. By contrast, a self-terminating serial search should reveal an advantage—a less steep slope—for the positive trials because the search stops as soon as the target is found.

Sternberg's (1966) results indicated that retrieval from short-term memory involves a serial exhaustive search (see Figure 5.9). A linear equation is fit to these data with a y axis intercept of 397 milliseconds and a slope of 38 milliseconds. The search time increased linearly with set size, and both positive and negative trials showed identical search times per item. This outcome is counterintuitive in that a self-terminating search seems more logical. Why bother searching all items in memory even after the target has been found?

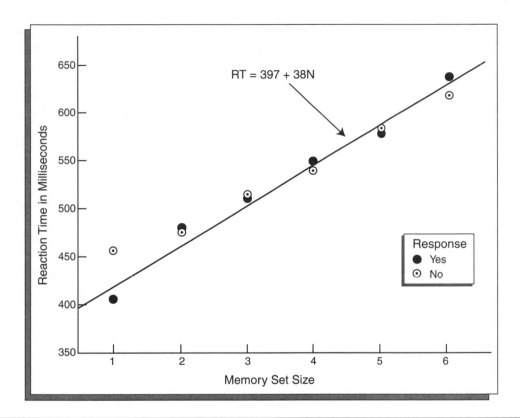

Figure 5.9. Evidence for a serial exhaustive search of short-term memory.

SOURCE: Sternberg (1966).
NOTE: RT = reaction time.

The answer may be related to the extremely rapid rate at which we search our short-term memory. The slope of the function is only 38 milliseconds, which is the extra time needed to examine each additional letter in the memory set.

The story is not this simple, however. The research spawned by Sternberg's (1966) results eventually led to the conclusion that a parallel search probably best characterizes short-term memory (Greene, 1992). Retrieval from long-term memory is also often parallel. It is impossible to explain the rapid speed with which humans are able to retrieve events, facts, and conceptual knowledge if every item in memory is searched in a serial manner. Even a self-terminating search does not help much given the vast amount of information stored in long-term memory. At the same time, searches in long-term memory may proceed in a serial manner. For example, which letter comes five letters after K in the English alphabet? To arrive at the answer probably involves searching forward from K to L, M, N, and O, not directly retrieving P. Thus, it is not possible to distinguish between short-term and long-term memory on the basis of retrieval processes.

Conclusion

The three-store model has fueled major advances in our understanding of human memory. Despite significant challenges to the model, its core assertion that sensory, short-term, and long-term stores can be distinguished in terms of storage capacity and duration still stands and accounts for an impressive range of evidence (Estes, 1988; Healy & McNamara, 1996). Today, the focus of memory scholars is on (a) how short-term memory is put to work in learning, comprehending, and other cognitive tasks and on (b) how long-term memory is organized into separate systems. These points are addressed in the next section and in Chapter 6.

● WORKING MEMORY

The short-term store can explain how people are able to retain a set of events or facts over a time span of several seconds. However, the concept did not seem adequate to explain the kind of retention of information that is needed in more complex cognitive tasks. For example, in reading this or any other book, it helps to remember the meaning of a previous sentence so as to comprehend the meaning of the next sentence. In carrying on a conversation, you need to hold in mind the assertions just made by your partner so as to formulate a response. Everyday cognitive tasks, such as reading and conversing, involve a train of thought; information from the recent past must be remembered to advance to the next thought in the sequence. Individual differences in reading ability were not strongly correlated with measurements of how many digits an individual could retain (Daneman & Carpenter, 1980).

A system more complex than the short-term store was required to adequately explain performance in tasks that required a sustained train of thought. **Working memory** refers to the system for temporarily maintaining mental representations that are relevant to the performance of a cognitive task in an activated state. The term *working memory* stresses that the system is needed to accomplish cognitive work. The span of working memory is measured in a dual task situation demanding that attention be paid to more than remembering a list of words. For example, in the reading span test, participants must read and understand a series of sentences in addition to remembering the last word of each sentence (Daneman & Carpenter, 1980). In the operations span test, participants must perform a series of mental arithmetic problems in addition to remembering the words paired with each problem (Engle, Cantor, & Carullo, 1992). Unlike digit span, these tests of working memory capacity require actively processing task-relevant information at the same time that material is held in short-term storage. Attention is divided between two task requirements in these tasks. Working memory span successfully predicts individual differences in performance in a wide range of complex cognitive tasks, including reading, writing, reasoning, and problem solving (Engle, Tuholski, Conway, & Andrew, 1999).

Multiple Components

A common theme of many models of working memory is that multiple components are involved (Shah & Miyake, 1999). The seminal multicomponent model was suggested by Baddeley (1986). As shown in Figure 5.10, the model assumes that there are two short-term stores that specialize in the retention of verbal information, on the one hand, and visual or spatial information, on the other. Baddeley called these components the phonological loop and a visual-spatial sketch pad. The phonological loop is further fractionated into a passive memory store and a rehearsal loop that refreshes the activation of items held in the store. The phonological loop, then, allows one to maintain verbal information over time by repeating it covertly—silently articulating the letters or words. The visual-spatial sketch pad maintains representations used in visual imagery. It permits one to rehearse information by visualizing it or to imagine a problem and then seek a solution to it in the mind's eye.

The third component is the central executive. This is the attentional component whose function is to control the use of the two memory stores (Baddeley & Logie, 1999). The supervisory attentional system described in Chapter 4 serves here to control and regulate the memory stores in carrying out complex mental tasks. Verbal, visual, and spatial representations are needed to read, for instance, and the memory stores holding these must be coordinated. In everyday thought tasks and in tasks for measuring working memory capacity, attention must be focused on different stimuli and switched at appropriate moments. Relevant information must also be retrieved from long-term memory and brought into the focus of attention as one reads, writes, or solves problems. The central executive, then, is itself a complex component (Baddeley, 1996).

Working memory refers to the system for temporarily maintaining mental representations that are relevant to the performance of a cognitive task in an activated state.

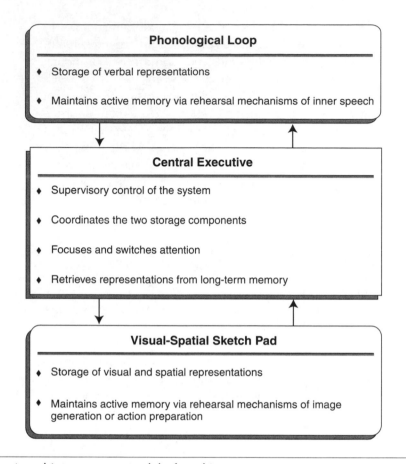

Figure 5.10. A multicomponent model of working memory.

SOURCE: Adapted from Baddeley (1986).

Neurological Dissociations

The fact that verbal working memory stores phonological representations explains why errors are common when similar sounding items are retained over short periods of time, the phonemic similarity effect discussed earlier (Baddeley, 1986). Furthermore, Martin, Shelton, and Yaffee (1994) reported on two brain-injured patients who had poor memory spans. One failed to remember phonological information, presumably because of damage to the phonological store of verbal working memory, and had trouble in repeating sentences. The other failed to remember semantic information and had trouble in comprehending sentences. The observed dissociations indicate that there are separate phonological and semantic components of working memory.

If the rehearsal component of the phonological loop were damaged, then performance on a short-term memory task ought to suffer as a consequence. It turns out that there are a variety of motor output problems known as apraxia or dyspraxia. One kind of dyspraxia involves an impairment in the capacity to program speech output, including the inner speech needed for silently rehearsing information in the phonological loop. This indeed causes errors in verbal memory performance, as predicted by the Baddeley model (Waters, Rochon, & Caplan, 1992). Other studies have identified patients who fail on a test that measures spatial working memory ability but who do fine on a test of visual or object working memory relative to normal controls (Della Sala, Gray, Baddeley, Allamano, & Wilson, 2000). A double dissociation has been demonstrated on these tests. That is, separate patients show the reverse pattern, failing the test of visual working memory and succeeding on the spatial test.

Neuroimaging has recently demonstrated that different regions of the brain are involved in the multiple components of working memory. From a large literature based on animal testing, it is known that the prefrontal cortex is a necessary neural substrate for working memory (Goldman-Rakic, 1995). The neuroimaging findings confirm this point and further show some other regions involved. These studies use the method of subtraction to isolate the processes involved in maintaining different kinds of information in working memory such as verbal, spatial, and visual object representations. For example, in the verbal condition, participants try to retain a set of four letters in memory and are presented with a test probe that either was or was not in the set. Working memory for locations in space and for the shape of objects was also assessed.

The data are summarized in Figure 5.11 by first showing the sites in the left and right hemispheres that showed the greatest PET activation in the spatial versus verbal conditions. The verbal condition activated regions in a region associated with Broca's area and motor areas in the frontal cortex associated with speech production and the covert rehearsal loop. A region in the left posterior parietal lobe was also activated, presumably as a result of storing the phonological representation that was refreshed via rehearsal. By contrast, the spatial condition activated regions in the right parietal and frontal cortex.

As shown in the middle row of Figure 5.11, the results have further shown that maintaining visual objects in working memory activates still different cortical regions in the left hemisphere (Smith & Jonides, 1997). In other words, the visual and spatial components of working memory can be dissociated as well. One component stores visual objects, and another stores their spatial location, a result that is consistent with the separate "what" versus "where" pathways of perceptual analysis discussed earlier.

Working memory includes a verbal component for storing phonological representations and a rehearsal loop for maintaining these representations. It further includes components for maintaining visual objects and their spatial locations and an executive component for controlling access to the stores.

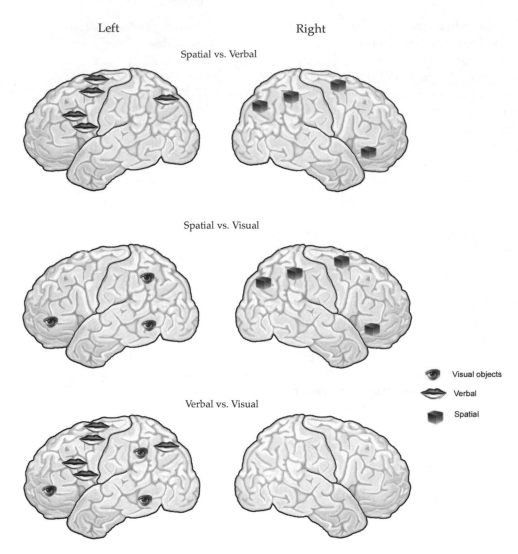

Figure 5.11. Dissociating verbal and spatial working memory with positron emission tomography (PET) data.

SOURCE: Adapted from Smith and Jonides (1997).

Relative to our ability to learn and retrieve events stored in long-term memory years ago, the transient nature of working memory may seem unimpressive. But as Goldman-Rakic (1995) explained, it is no less important than long-term memory:

The brain's working memory function, i.e., the ability to bring to mind events in the absence of direct stimulation, may be its inherently most flexible mechanism and its evolutionarily most significant achievement. At the most elementary level, our basic conceptual ability to appreciate that an object exists when out of view depends on the capacity to keep events in mind beyond the direct experience of those events. For some organisms, including most humans under certain conditions, "out of sight" is equivalent to "out of mind." However, working memory is generally available to provide the temporal and spatial continuity between our past experience and present actions. Working memory has been invoked in all forms of cognitive and linguistic processing and is fundamental to both the comprehension and construction of sentences. It is essential to the operations of mental arithmetic, to playing chess, to playing the piano particularly without music, to delivering speech extemporaneously, and finally, to fantasizing and planning ahead. (p. 483)

SUMMARY

1. The three-store model of memory distinguishes among sensory, short-term, and long-term stores. This highly influential model sought to identify unique characteristics with each store. The efforts proved to be successful with regard to capacity and duration but less so with regard to coding, forgetting, and retrieval. The capacity of short-term memory is limited to about four chunks of information, and its duration is less than 30 seconds. The capacity limits of long-term memory are unknown, and its duration is measured in decades.

2. The hippocampus plays a critical role in storing events in long-term memory. The hippocampus, a structure in the medial temporal lobe of the brain, binds together neural activity from locations distributed across the neocortex during learning. Until an event is consolidated in long-term memory, the hippocampus is needed to index the locations of the distributed memory representation. Damage to the hippocampus causes severe anterograde amnesia, in which recent new events cannot be stored in long-term memory.

3. Free recall of a list of words reveals a serial position effect. The last items in the list are recalled first and well—the recency effect. The initial items in the list are also recalled well—the primacy effect. The three-store model attributes the recency effect to the short-term store and attributes the primacy effect to the long-term store. The model also accounts for evidence from patients suffering from anterograde and retrograde amnesia and from reduced short-term memory capacity.

4. Working memory refers to the system for temporarily maintaining mental representations that are relevant to the performance of a cognitive task in an activated state. It involves short-term memory stores plus

attentional control over processing in a cognitive task. Baddeley's influential model postulated two stores: one for verbal information, called the phonological loop, and one for nonverbal information, called the visual-spatial sketch pad. The central executive controls processing in these short-term stores. Neuroimaging research has demonstrated that the phonological store and rehearsal loop are supported by regions of the left hemisphere. Visual working memory and spatial working memory are supported by separate regions in the left and right hemispheres.

● KEY TERMS

iconic memory
echoic memory
serial position effect
primacy effect
recency effect
anterograde amnesia
retrograde amnesia
chunking

phonemic similarity effect
proactive interference
retroactive interference
serial search
parallel search
self-terminating search
exhaustive search
working memory

PART III

LEARNING, KNOWING, AND REMEMBERING

As already seen, memory is a complex system involving multiple processes and stores. Long-term memory is now examined in detail. To begin Part III, the different systems of long-term memory are presented. Next comes a discussion of how new events are learned or transferred from temporary storage in working memory to long-term memory. Encoding and storing an event is only one aspect of effective memory. It is also necessary to retrieve the event at the proper time. Forgetting specific events or episodes in life may be related to either a breakdown in the encoding process or a failure to retrieve the information when needed. Distortions of memory are another significant failure of the system. It is possible to reconstruct an event from the past incorrectly and yet not be aware that one's memory is in error. Episodic memory is but a part of all that is stored in long-term memory, however. The representation and use of general knowledge about the world in semantic memory is also considered. Abstract human thought is possible only because of the conceptual representations that are the building blocks of semantic memory. The final chapter in Part III addresses how concepts and procedural skills are learned in the first place. Expertise is the result of extensive learning, and its characteristics are discussed.

CHAPTER 6

EPISODIC MEMORY

So far in this book, long-term memory itself has been described as if it were unitary. In the coming chapters, multiple systems of long-term memory are differentiated and described. Consider for a moment everything you need to know so as to be able to drive a car. You need to know what a car looks like, what a steering wheel does, and what the functions are of the two or three pedals on the floor, among other things. You need to know the rules of the road, the meaning of traffic signs, and the purpose of the solid and dashed lines on the streets. You further need several perceptual, motor, and cognitive skills to start the vehicle, put it in gear, steer, brake, and navigate your way to a destination. How does remembering any of this impressive array of knowledge depend on being able to recall the events that took place around you 5 minutes ago? It turns out that long-term memory for such knowledge can be preserved even when an individual suffers severe anterograde amnesia and can no longer remember recent events. Long-term memory itself seems to be partitioned into different systems that can function or fail independently of one another.

The experiments discussed in distinguishing short-term from long-term memory were concerned with remembering specific events. This is called episodic memory and will be the focus of the current chapter once it is differentiated from other kinds of long-term memory. The chapter considers how new events are learned, that is, how they are encoded and stored in episodic memory. Much is known about the operations that support the learning of new events. Next, the processes involved in retrieving or failing to retrieve events from long-term memory are discussed, Finally, the manner in which retrieval cues enable the recollection of past episodes is addressed. Forgetting occurs when the available retrieval cues fail to activate available, but inaccessible, event representations.

● TYPES OF LONG-TERM MEMORY

Just as working memory involves more than one component, long-term memory does not appear to be unitary. Scholars disagree at this point over the criteria that must be satisfied to conclude that there are multiple systems of long-term memory. Mathematical models, and related computer simulations, begin with the assumption that the fewer systems of memory, the better. Not only is a single long-term store a more parsimonious explanation of memory phenomena, but it surely is easier to model with the necessary precision of mathematics (Hintzman, 1990). The danger with the mathematical perspective is in overlooking the messy nature of biological organisms in the search for an elegant computer simulation.

From the perspective of evolutionary biology, fewer and better need not coincide at all. Different systems evolve precisely because they afford successful adaptations to the challenges posed by the environment. Just as with other characteristics of an organism, a novel system of memory shown by a subpopulation of a species will come to dominate if it aids, in some fashion, survival and reproduction. A separate memory system evolves when the functions of existing systems fail to meet the demands of a new environmental challenge (Sherry & Schacter, 1987). The danger with the biological perspective lies in strewing our theories needlessly with a separate memory system for each seemingly separate memory phenomenon. The evidence favoring multiple systems is presented next, followed by some criticisms of how such evidence has been interpreted.

Declarative Versus Nondeclarative Memory

Philosophers have distinguished between declarative and procedural knowledge—knowing what versus knowing how. Knowing the rules and traditions of baseball is not the same as being able to play baseball. Knowing how is often tacit or unconscious, whereas knowing what is explicit or conscious. Memory theorists, in turn, have proposed that long-term memory

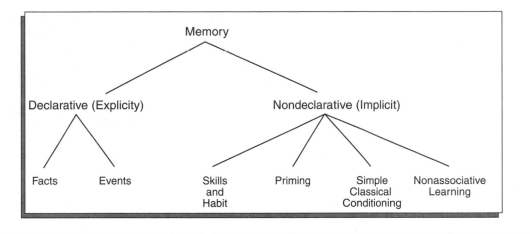

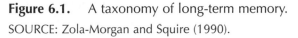

Figure 6.1. A taxonomy of long-term memory.

SOURCE: Zola-Morgan and Squire (1990).

can be divided into major systems: declarative and nondeclarative (e.g., Tulving, 1985; Zola-Morgan & Squire, 1990). **Declarative memory** refers to knowledge of events, facts, and concepts. **Nondeclarative memory** refers to skills and related procedural knowledge.

Squire and his colleagues have identified several kinds of nondeclarative memory. As seen in Figure 6.1, these include skills, priming, dispositions, and nonassociative forms of learning. Motor skills, such as running and typing, are familiar to all. Bear in mind that skills also may be perceptual, such as reading, or cognitive, such as problem solving. Dispositions cover the basic learning of associations through operant and classical conditioning and the nonassociative process of habituation. We habituate when we show less and less of a response to a repetitive ongoing stimulus.

Each kind of nondeclarative memory appears to be supported by a different brain structure (Squire, 1992b). For example, it is well-established that the pathways needed for classical conditioning of skeletal muscles are found in the cerebellum rather than in the hippocampal system used in conscious recollection (Thompson, 2000). Furthermore, there is a rapidly growing body of research using positron emission tomography (PET), functional magnetic resonance imaging (fMRI), and lesion studies that isolates different brain regions for different kinds of nondeclarative memory. Learning sensorimotor skills (e.g., tracing a figure viewed in a mirror), perceptual skills (e.g., reading mirror-imaged text), and cognitive skills (e.g., solving problems) each involves a different neural substrate. Furthermore, the brain regions that mediate classical conditioning are different from those involved in operant conditioning.

Long-term memory is made up of multiple memory systems. A major division in the hierarchy of these systems is the distinction between declarative memory (knowing what) and nondeclarative memory (knowing how).

Implicit Versus Explicit Tests. Explicit or direct tests require the conscious recollection of information, as when a person recognizes or recalls a past event. Implicit or indirect tests require the use of information stored in long-term memory to improve performance, but not its conscious recollection (Richardson-Klavehn & Bjork, 1988; Schacter, 1987). Perceptual priming is a good example of an implicit task that depends on nondeclarative memory. Priming is an increase in the accuracy, probability, or speed of a response to a stimulus as a consequence of prior exposure to the stimulus. In perceptual priming, a prior occurrence of the prime (e.g., chair) improves the chances of later perceiving a very brief exposure of the same word (Jacoby & Dallas, 1981). Repeating the typeface of a visually presented word similarly results in perceptual priming (Schacter & Tulving, 1994). One is faster in recognizing the word "table" if its prior occurrence appeared in lowercase letters (table) than if it appeared in uppercase letters (TABLE). Neuroimaging methods have pointed to regions just outside the primary visual cortex in the occipital lobe as supporting this kind of nondeclarative memory (Buckner, Goodman, et al., 1998).

Tulving and Schacter (1990) argued that dissociations on implicit and explicit tests support the multiple system viewpoint. To illustrate, one variable is the use of normal versus amnesic individuals. Amnesic patients forget recent or past episodic events, yet they still show priming effects right along with normal individuals (Graf, Squire, & Mandler, 1984; Shimamura, 1986). Warrington and Weiskrantz (1970) pioneered the use of a word completion test to reveal normal priming effects in amnesics. They first presented a printed list of words and tested the ability of amnesic and normal individuals to recall and recognize them correctly. They also asked the participants to complete a word fragment (cha___) with the first English word that came to mind. If "chair" appeared on the original study list and the individual completed the fragment as chair, then priming occurred. Whereas recall and recognition failed badly for the amnesic patients, priming on word completion showed no decrement.

Milner (1965) discovered that "H. M." could learn how to trace the outline of a shape while looking in a mirror rather than at the shape. Such motor skill learning remained intact despite the anterograde amnesia for episodic events caused by H. M.'s brain surgery. Learning perceptual skills also may be preserved in amnesic patients (Moscovitch, 1982), as can learning a classically conditioned response (Weiskrantz & Warrington, 1979). By emitting a flash of light just prior to the onset of a puff of air to the eye, both normal and amnesic individuals acquire a conditioned eyeblink response to the presentation of the light alone. Although the amnesic patients retained the conditioned response on a test 24 hours later, they had no conscious recollection of having gone through the conditioning experiment only 10 minutes after it was completed.

Drug-induced dissociations between implicit and explicit memory tests have also been documented. Drugs such as alcohol and scopolamine can produce amnesia for episodes that occurred during the altered state of consciousness. Despite this amnesia, the drugs leave unimpaired performance on implicit tests of procedural nondeclarative memory (Hashtroudi, Parker, DeLisi, Wyatt, & Mutter, 1984; Nissen, Knopman, & Schacter, 1987). Some controversial evidence even suggests that patients show priming effects for words presented to them while under general anesthesia. The words could not be recalled by the patients after the surgery. But when asked to free associate to a cue word, they responded more often with the words presented during anesthesia than did a control group not given the words (Kihlstrom, Schacter, Cork, Hunt, & Bahr, 1990).

Episodic Versus Semantic Memory

As shown in Figure 6.1, declarative memory takes two forms: remembering events and knowing facts and concepts (Tulving, 1972, 1985). **Episodic memory** concerns the recollection of events that took place at specific places and times in the past. **Semantic memory** concerns factual and conceptual knowledge about the world and the words used to symbolize such knowledge. Such memory makes no reference to specific episodes in time and space. Suppose that you spot a bicycle on campus. Recognizing the two-wheeled object as a member of a category illustrates the use of semantic memory; the concept and the word used to refer to the object are activated. If you begin to think about the properties of bicycles in general (e.g., they have two wheels, a seat, and handle bars), then you are still using semantic memory. If, however, you begin to recall the bicycle you received on your sixth birthday, then you are using episodic memory. The specific memories you have of learning to ride it and the accidents you had with it are episodic memories located at places and moments in the past.

The anterograde amnesia case presented earlier in the chapter shows that episodic and semantic memory can be dissociated. H. M. showed a profound loss in storing new episodic memories in long-term memory. However, his general knowledge of the world and his verbal abilities were not at all impaired. As will be seen in Chapter 15, intelligence tests provide a way to assess the factual and conceptual knowledge along with word meanings. H. M. scored very well on an intelligence test, recording an IQ of 112 where 100 is an average score (Milner, 1966).

> Episodic memory is a specifically dated occurrence of an event in a particular context. Semantic memory refers to factual and conceptual knowledge about the world. They are subsets of declarative memory.

A final dissociation comes from a procedure in which participants are asked to make judgments about whether they know an event occurred in the past or whether they remember its occurrence (Rajaram & Roediger, 1997). Remembering means having recollections of personal experiences from the past through mental time travel, that is, taking the self back in time to relive specific episodes. Thus, when you recall the day you graduated from high school, you can mentally travel back in time and recollect particular events, people, and interactions involving you personally. Knowing refers to being aware of facts and concepts in the absence of personally reliving past experiences. Knowing can take the form of a feeling of familiarity about abstract concepts or of being aware that past events happened without the mental time travel of reexperiencing them again. You may, for example, know that a speech was made at commencement exercises, but recollecting the speech, or the face or name of the speaker, might not be possible. Knowing reflects retrieval from semantic memory.

Consider an experiment in which participants are given a list of words and then administered a recognition test. Half of the items on the test are new and half are old. For each item the participants decide is old, they then introspect about the conscious experience associated with this decision and indicate whether they remember the item or simply know that it was on the list. Tulving (1985) introduced this procedure in an effort to measure episodic memory directly with remember judgments and to measure semantic memory with know judgments.

It turns out that remembering and knowing judgments are affected differently by variables that influence memory. For example, if an item is repeated in a list several times in succession, then the number of know responses is high. However, if the repetitions are spaced out so that several items intervene between each repetition, then the number of remember responses is high (Parkin & Russo, 1993). As another example, alcohol (Curran & Hildebrandt, in press) and the antianxiety drugs called benzodiazepines (Bishop & Curran, 1995) reduce the number of remember judgments given to old items on a recognition test. But the drugs have no effect on the know responses. If one assumes that remember judgments reflect episodic memory, whereas know judgments reflect semantic memory, then such dissociations strengthen the case for a separation of episodic and semantic memory (Gardiner & Richardson-Klavehn, 2000).

Criticisms of Multiple Systems

Although there is growing evidence in favor of multiple systems of long-term memory, serious challenges have been raised to the hypothesis.

Different processes operating on a single declarative memory system can also give rise to dissociations (Hintzman, 1990; Jacoby, 1983; Johnson & Hasher, 1987; Roediger, 1984). For example, Roediger and Blaxton (1987) observed that learners often initiate top-down or conceptually driven processes such as focusing on ways of organizing new information. Bottom-up or data-driven processes are forced by the stimuli or data themselves such as whether the modality of presentation was auditory or visual. It may be that implicit tests such as perceptual priming are more affected by data-driven processes, whereas explicit tests depend more on conceptually driven processes. A variable, such as brain injury, could affect only explicit tests because it influences the functioning of conceptually driven processes but not data-driven processes. Perhaps brain-injured amnesic patients demonstrate priming effects in a word completion task because such priming reflects data-driven perceptual processes.

Jacoby (1991) further observed that the implicit tests of memory are not pure measures of nondeclarative memory. It is possible that one recollects having seen a prime earlier in the task, and so part of the facilitation could reflect episodic memory. Nor are explicit tests a pure measure of only episodic memory. For example, on a recognition test, one might call an item old because it seems vaguely familiar rather than remembering it as having actually been on the study list. When an individual intends to recollect an event and experiences a subjective awareness of remembering, consciously controlled processes are at work. Automatic processes of familiarity from past exposure can influence memory without intention or awareness.

To illustrate, Jacoby, Woloshyn, and Kelley (1989) demonstrated that familiarity with a name from a recent past exposure can automatically cause one to categorize the name as famous even though it is unknown. Participants are first read a list of names, either giving it full attention or dividing attention with another task. Next, they are asked to judge whether the names on a second list are famous or not. Some of these names are famous and some are nonfamous. Still others are nonfamous names that were repetitions of names heard in the first part of the experiment. When distracted in the divided attention condition, participants were likely to mistakenly think that repeated non famous names were in fact famous. One brief and relatively unattended exposure was all it took to trigger an automatic influence on memory.

These are important criticisms of the multiple systems position, and more work is needed on (a) how tasks are affected differently by conceptually driven versus data-driven processes and (b) how a single process such as the unconscious influence of familiarity affects both direct and indirect tests. However, it is unclear whether the processing point of view can accommodate all of the data now available (Gabrieli, 1998; Schacter, Wagner, & Buckner, 2000). Although the debate on this issue continues, the terms *semantic declarative memory* and *episodic declarative memory* are used in the remainder of the book and are contrasted with different kinds of nondeclarative memory for ease of exposition.

● ENCODING AND STORING EVENTS

The three-store model assumes that encoding and storing events in long-term memory involves rehearsal. The nature of the rehearsal processes brought into play at encoding is critical, as suggested by Craik and Lockhart (1972). **Maintenance rehearsal** refers to recycling information within short-term or working memory by covertly verbalizing it. **Elaborative rehearsal** refers to linking information in short-term memory with information already stored in long-term memory. Elaborative rehearsal can take many forms. Organizing items into categories, associating items with other known information, and forming visual or auditory images of the items are examples of elaborative rehearsal. For instance, it is easier to remember a list of words if one visualizes the object to which each word refers in addition to encoding the sound of the word itself (Paivio, 1971, 1983). Imagery works better for concrete objects that can readily be visualized (e.g., elephant) as compared with abstract concepts (e.g., gravity).

Mnemonic techniques designed to improve memory generally rely on elaborative encoding in the form of visual images (Bower, 1972; McDaniel & Pressley, 1987). Imagery has been recognized as crucial to memory from the time of the ancient Greeks. Cicero recounted a story about the Greek poet, Simonides, who delivered a long poem at a Roman banquet. On finishing, Simonides left the building just moments before catastrophe struck. The building collapsed, burying everyone in the rubble. According to the legend, Simonides was able to survey the ruins and recall the names of the victims by first imagining where they had been seated.

The mnemonic called the method of loci (places) consists of identifying a sequence of familiar locations and then forming an image of each item to be remembered at each of the locations. Once a clear image is formed, the locations provide a plan for retrieving the items. By imagining a walk to each of the locations in the sequence, the items are remembered (Bower, 1970). A demonstration of the method of loci is presented in Box 6.1.

One reason for the superior recall produced by the method of loci and related techniques is that mental images provide a second code, in addition to the word itself, for the memory system (Paivio, 1971, 1983). Without forming a mental image of the words to be remembered, one is left with only a verbal code. Further investigation of imagery and mnemonics suggests that the imagery makes an event in memory stand out as more distinctive

---

Box 6.1

A DEMONSTRATION OF THE METHOD OF LOCI

The method of loci is a mnemonic technique that uses familiar locations as an aid to memory. To illustrate, first picture a sequence of 10 locations at home or on campus that you know well. Now, try to form an image with each of the following grocery items, placing one item at each location in order. For example, for the first item, you might imagine a banana peel on the front steps of your home. Try to create a distinctive image for each item and location.

Banana

Lettuce

Crackers

Bacon

Milk

Olives

Bread

Hamburger

Tuna

Mustard

Now, close the book and try to recall the items by taking a mental walk to each of the 10 locations. Most people find it much easier to remember the 10 items when using this imaginal technique than when trying to simply rehearse the items repetitively using maintenance rehearsal. Recall from Chapter 5 how difficult it is to retain more than four to seven chunks of information. Yet, most people find it easy to recall all 10 items using the method of loci, a type of elaborative rehearsal.

and, hence, easier to recall (Marschark, Richman, Yuille, & Hunt, 1987; McDaniel & Einstein, 1986). Mnemonics also benefit memory by providing a set of retrieval cues that match the cues encoded with the to-be-remembered material (Bower, 1970). Taking a mental walk with the method of loci is a retrieval plan as well as an encoding plan. Each location visited at the time of retrieval allows one to reconstruct the event originally stored there with relative ease.

Maintenance rehearsal refers to recycling information within short-term or working memory by covertly verbalizing it. Elaborative rehearsal refers to transferring information to long-term memory by linking it with information already stored there.

Craik and Lockhart (1972) made the strong claim that only elaborative rehearsal results in permanent long-term learning because of the necessity to analyze broadly and deeply the features of the stimulus. Because maintenance rehearsal merely recycles items in working memory, it presumably does not result in improved recall. Although early experiments supported this claim (Craik & Watkins, 1973), it became clear through more research that maintenance rehearsal helps memory some, albeit much less than does elaborative rehearsal (Darley & Glass, 1975; Greene, 1987).

Levels of Processing

In Chapter 2, we examined how sensory and semantic features are analyzed during pattern recognition. Data-driven and conceptually driven processes rapidly and accurately identify the objects, events, and symbols of our environment. These perceptual processes operate automatically when attention is devoted to a stimulus and occur to some degree even when the stimulus is unattended. In memory research, the effect of **levels or depths of processing** refers to a memory superiority for events attentively processed at a semantic level as compared with a sensory level.

The usual procedure directs a person to attend carefully to either sensory level features (e.g., Is the word in capital letters? Does the word rhyme with "blue"?) or semantic features (e.g., Does the word fit the sentence "He slipped on his _____"?). In answering these orienting questions about the word "shoe," the focus of attention would be visual, acoustic, or semantic features. These three conditions reflect increasing levels or depths of processing. Recognition or recall of the target words is then tested. The results showed that visual and acoustic encoding is inferior to semantic encoding on memory tests (Craik & Lockhart, 1972). Craik and Tulving (1975) interpreted this level of processing difference in terms of elaborative rehearsal. Semantic encoding produced a more elaborate representation of the target words in memory, which supported superior recall and recognition.

Is there an orienting task that produces maximal elaboration and memory? Some research suggests that processing the information in relation to our own self-concept is superior, a finding called the **self-reference effect.** Rogers, Kuiper, and Kirker (1977) found that when people asked whether a word applied to themselves (e.g., ambitious), later recall rose above that obtained for even the semantic orienting task. The recall results for physical, acoustic, semantic, and self-reference levels of processing are shown in Figure 6.2. Of interest, the same outcome occurs when people make judgments about consumer products shown in advertisements (D'Ydewalle, Delhaye, & Goessens, 1985). Answering the question "Have you ever used

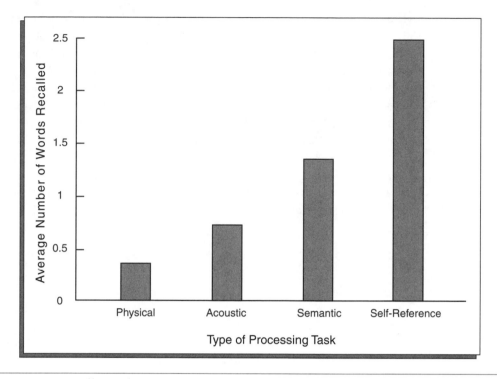

Figure 6.2. Recall as a function of the level of processing.

this product?" supported greater recall of brand names than did a semantic orienting task. Other evidence indicates that the key ingredient in this effect involves relating the information to highly developed representations in long-term memory, providing many links with well-ingrained information (Bellezza, 1986).

Transfer-Appropriate Processing

The principle of **transfer-appropriate processing** holds that test performance hinges on engaging in a process at encoding that is compatible with the demands of the test. For example, different kinds of studying may be called for depending on the nature of the test. Practice at generating and organizing ideas would be highly appropriate as a way to prepare for an essay test, but such preparation might transfer less well to a multiple choice test.

Morris, Bransford, and Franks (1977) found that the typical levels of processing effect can be reversed by picking a test that is appropriate to

Levels or depths of processing refer to a memory superiority for events attentively processed at a semantic level as compared with a sensory level. Processing events semantically in reference to one's own self-concept results in particularly strong memory.

visual or acoustic orienting tasks. They showed that the overlap between encoding and retrieval processes mattered more than the nature of encoding per se. For example, in one condition, participants were tested for recognition of words based on whether they rhymed with a word presented earlier rather than on recognition of the identity of the word as is typical. The authors found that rhyme encoding supported better rhyme recognition than did semantic encoding. Because rhyme encoding is appropriate for the rhyme retrieval test, it transfers better than semantic encoding. The fact remains, however, that recalling or recognizing an event depends critically on its meaning—its semantic features. Because remembering an event requires the retrieval of semantic information, it is semantic encoding that transfers well to standard recall and recognition tests.

Distinctiveness

Plainly, the extent to which one stores information in an elaborate manner predicts how well it will be remembered. But why should elaboration have this effect? One part of the answer is that elaborative rehearsal results in learning the distinctive features of items (Hunt & Einstein, 1981; Hunt & McDaniel, 1993). **Distinctiveness** refers to how the items to be learned are different from each other and other items already stored in memory. A highly distinctive representation is one that can be discriminated easily at the time of retrieval. The more the item stands out in memory, the easier it is to find.

Suppose that you are asked to memorize a list of nonsense syllables and one odd item: a number. People rarely forget the isolated distinctive number, an effect named after its German discoverer, von Restorff, and described in English by Koffka (1935). The power of distinctiveness can be seen in Eysenck's (1979) variation on the levels of processing effect in which he compared sensory versus semantic orienting tasks. His sensory task entailed attending to the sounds of words. In a distinctive encoding condition, Eysenck used unusual pronunciations of the words designed to produce a highly distinctive, albeit sensory, level of processing. Because the unique pronunciations stood out in memory, they were remembered just as well as the words processed with a semantic focus. Typically, semantic encoding produces greater elaboration, which in turn increases the likelihood of storing a distinctive code. Eysenck's finding shows that it is distinctiveness per se that ultimately matters.

Picture Memory. It has long been known that people can recognize with a high degree of accuracy a long series of complex pictures that they have viewed for only a few seconds each. People can discriminate old pictures from new ones nearly perfectly when there are hundreds (Shepard, 1967) or even thousands of pictures (Standing, 1973). The reason seems to be that the pictures used in these studies contained many highly distinctive features, allowing observers to discriminate one from another. However, suppose that you must discriminate a picture of a particular $20 bill from a thousand such pictures. When the pictures all relate to the same schema, there is no distinctiveness and so recognition suffers (Mandler & Ritchey, 1977; Nickerson & Adams, 1979). As will be seen in Chapter 7, schemas are important in retrieval as well as in encoding processes.

Flashbulb Memories. An especially intriguing phenomenon may also shed light on the power of distinctiveness. A **flashbulb memory** is a vivid recollection of some autobiographical event that carries with it strong emotional reactions (Brown & Kulik, 1977; Pillemer, 1984). Depending on your age, you might be able to recall clearly exactly what you were doing, seeing, hearing, and feeling on receiving the news that President Kennedy was assassinated in 1963, that an attempt was made on the life of President Reagan in 1981, that the space shuttle *Challenger* exploded in 1986, or that the World Trade Center was destroyed by a terrorist attack in 2001. As Pillemer (1984) noted, "Images of only a tiny subset of specific episodes—death of a loved one, landing a first job, getting married, hearing about public tragedies—persist over a lifetime, with little subjectively experienced loss of clarity" (p. 64).

Some researchers have challenged whether so-called flashbulb memories are really more accurate than normal memories (e.g., Neisser & Harsch, 1992). Others, however, have confirmed that flashbulb memories can indeed be real for many people so long as the precipitating events had strong personal impacts on them (e.g., Conway et al., 1994).

One explanation for the phenomenon is that a special flashbulb memory system has evolved to capture highly important, emotionally charged events. Brown and Kulik (1977) pondered the adaptive value of such a system for a primitive human who just witnessed an attack on the group leader. A flashbulb recollection of where the attack occurred, who did the attacking, and whether the attack succeeded would offer a survival advantage. On the other hand, the facts can just as easily be explained by distinctiveness without assuming any special mechanism (McCloskey, Wible, & Cohen, 1988). The flashbulb recollection may simply be a highly distinctive event because of its emotionally charged nature. Further research is needed to settle this debate (Schmidt & Bohannon, 1988).

Distinctive memory representations can be discriminated from other related memories. Strong recognition of distinctive pictures and possibly flashbulb memories illustrates the power of distinctiveness in enhancing memory.

Synesthesia. A bizarre demonstration of the power of distinctive encoding came from a famous case study. Over a period of 20 years, Luria (1968) studied the memory abilities of an individual referred to as "S." He tested S.'s memory span for a variety of materials and found it remarkable, seemingly without limit. In Luria's words,

> I gave S. a series of words, then numbers, then letters, reading them to him slowly or presenting them in written form. He read or listened attentively and then repeated the material exactly as it had been presented. I increased the number of elements in each series, giving him as many as thirty, fifty, or even seventy words or numbers, but this, too, presented no problem to him. . . .
>
> The experiment indicated that he could reproduce a series in reverse order—from the end to the beginning—just as simply as from start to finish; that he could readily tell me which word followed another in a series, or reproduce the word which happened to precede the one I'd name. He would pause for a minute, as though searching for the word, but immediately after would be able to answer my question and generally made no mistakes. . . . It was of no consequence to him whether the series I gave him contained meaning words or nonsense syllables, numbers or sounds; whether they were presented orally or in writing. . . . As the experimenter, I soon found myself in a state verging on utter confusion. An increase in the length of the series led to no noticeable increase in difficulty for S., and I simply had to admit that the capacity of his memory *had no distinct limits;* that I had been unable to perform what one would think was the simplest task a psychologist can do: measure the capacity of an individual's memory. (pp. 9-11)

Further testing only compounded Luria's (1968) confusion, for it turned out that the duration of S.'s memory, as well as its capacity, seemed to have no limit. Some tests revealed error-free recall of word lists presented 15 years earlier! Moreover, S. could recall the context in which a list had been presented, describing the place in which Luria had read him the words, the chair in which Luria sat, and even the clothes Luria had worn.

From early childhood, S. experienced synesthesia or cross-talk among sensory modalities such that sounds, for example, were experienced visually as well as aurally. Normal individuals experience mild degrees of synesthesia in that colors are reliably associated with specific pitches of sounds (Marks, 1987). The bright colors of yellow and white elicit high pitches, whereas the dark colors of black and brown echo low pitches. But S. experienced an extreme form in which tones and noises would be apprehended as "puffs" and "splashes" of color. He would perceive the "color" of a speaker's voice, and each speech sound assumed a visual "form" with its own "color" and "taste." Plainly, these images added a unique distinctive code to memory.

Relational Processing

Clearly, then, learning how items to be remembered differ from each other is critical for good memory. **Relational processing** refers to how the items to be learned are related to each other and to other items stored in memory (Hunt & Einstein, 1981; Hunt & McDaniel, 1993). Instead of detecting differences, relational processing looks for similarities. It has long been known that well-organized information is better remembered. A learner must discover the relations among items or, when none is apparent, create his or her own subjective relations.

Category Cues. Tulving and Pearlstone (1966) showed the power of organization in their comparison of free and cued recall. The participants studied a list of 48 words that came from several categories such as tools, fruits, and vehicles. The words occurred in a random order, but the learners noticed the organization of the items nonetheless (see Bousfield, 1953). When asked to recall as many words as possible with no hints or cues (free recall), the participants clustered related items together, for example, apples, oranges, and grapes. More interestingly, if the participants remembered a single item from a category, then they likely remembered most of the others. Conversely, if they forgot an item such as truck, then the other examples of vehicles also were forgotten. In other words, the category served to organize their recall.

But only about a third of the words were remembered in free recall. Tulving and Pearlstone (1966) also provided some participants with the category names as retrieval cues. Remarkably, the cues roughly doubled the number of words successfully recalled. This result for cued recall shows the powerful effect of organization as an aid to retrieval. It also shows that events may be available in memory but inaccessible to recollection without the right retrieval cues. More is said about retrieval cues later in the chapter.

Subjective Organization. The tendency to cluster items from the same semantic category is perhaps not surprising. Yet organization plays a critical role in recall even when a clear basis for it is lacking. Tulving (1962) presented people with lists of unrelated words and tracked their free recall over a series of trials. Over a series of trials of studying the words and attempting to recall them in whatever order the person wished, each participant adopted a consistent pattern of output. That is, each person imposed a **subjective organization** on the words, recalling clusters of items in the same manner trial after trial, even though the clusters themselves were purely idiosyncratic. The more categories people use in organizing the study items, the better they do on both recall tests and delayed recognition tests (Mandler, Pearlstone, & Koopmans, 1969).

Subjective organization refers to the way individuals impose an idiosyncratic organizational scheme on unrelated items to be remembered.

Organization, encoding the relations among events and prior knowledge, benefits both learning and remembering. First, the events may be chunked together during their storage (Mandler, 1979). Just as finding meaningful groupings increases learning on tests of short-term memory, the same effect may be seen in long-term memory. Second, organization provides retrieval cues that are vital to remembering (Tulving & Pearlstone, 1966). The categories imposed by the materials or by the learner serve as highly effective retrieval cues.

● RETRIEVAL PROCESSES

Forgetting may be caused by an inability to retrieve information that is available in memory. Such forgetting may reflect the temporary or even permanent lack of accessibility of information. This could arise because of interference from similar competing information stored in memory or because of a failure to activate the retrieval cues associated with the forgotten information. Contemporary research has focused on the cue-dependent nature of remembering and forgetting. It has emphasized how the context and knowledge related to material in memory play pivotal roles in successful retrieval.

To illustrate, recalling an event from episodic memory, such as one's 10th birthday party, requires retrieval of the time, the place, and the circumstances of stored information. Retrieval can be an active process of reimagining the perceptions, the feelings, and possibly the thoughts about the event and its context. Being provided with a cue, such as a photograph taken at the party, can trigger a chain of recollections that at first seemed lost from memory. The cue activates related knowledge in long-term memory that eventually allows one to retrieve or perhaps reconstruct the needed information. What one knows about birthday parties in general affects both how one's 10th birthday party was encoded and how it will be later retrieved.

Retrieval Mode

Retrieval involves at least two kinds of subprocesses (Moscovitch, 1992). On the one hand, there are the general operations involved in attempting to remember an event, and these are observable regardless of whether the search is successful. The effort to retrieve has been referred to as **retrieval mode.** On the other hand, there are the operations specifically associated with successful recovery of the event.

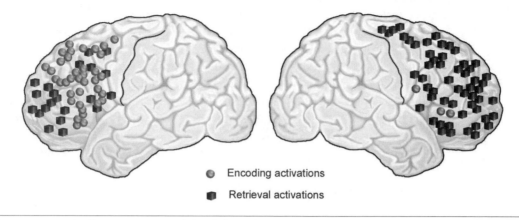

Encoding activations

Retrieval activations

Figure 6.3. Different regions of the left and right prefrontal cortex are involved in episodic encoding and retrieval.

Several studies with positron electrotomography (PET) and functional magnetic resonance imaging (fMRI) have shown that a region in the anterior prefrontal cortex of the right hemisphere is activated when an effort is made to retrieve an event (Buckner, 1996). This is not the only area activated, but it is the best understood to date. For example, as seen in Color Plate 6 in the section of color plates, strong PET activation can be observed in the right hemisphere in temporal regions in addition to prefrontal regions when recollecting about a highly emotional episode from more than a year in the past (Fink et al., 1996). In contrast to the right prefrontal and other regions activated in episodic retrieval, prefrontal regions in the left hemisphere are highly activated during the encoding of events into episodic memory. These activation sites are summarized in Figure 6.3. Tulving and his colleagues proposed the hemispheric encoding/retrieval asymmetry (HERA) model to account for the neuroimaging findings.

It has been difficult to say for certain whether the right prefrontal activation genuinely reflects a retrieval mode as opposed to successful recovery because of limitations in the scanning procedures (Schacter et al., 2000). Scans had to be compared for a group of trials when retrieval was usually successful to a group of trials when forgetting was likely and so the data were noisy. However, new fMRI procedures allow comparisons of scans for individual items on a recognition test. By comparing correct hits on old items (retrieval mode plus retrieval success) versus correct rejections of new items (retrieval mode only), the issue can be resolved. The data from such studies show convincingly similar activation levels in the right anterior prefrontal cortex for both hits and correct rejections (Buckner, Koutstaal, et al., 1998). Thus, the activation observed there is unrelated to retrieval success.

Neuroimaging evidence has identified numerous regions of the brain that appear to be activated when events are successfully retrieved from long-term memory. Different locations are observed depending on whether the events recollected are verbal or nonverbal in nature (Nyberg & Cabeza, 2000). The wide distribution across all lobes of the cortex in both hemispheres is to be expected given that the representation of an event is distributed by its features, as discussed in Chapter 5. The hippocampus is also involved in retrieval for recently learned information. The medial temporal lobe initially stores an event prior to its consolidation in distributed areas throughout the neocortex (McClelland, McNaughten, & O'Reilly, 1995). Finally, certain areas of the prefrontal cortex in both the left and right hemispheres are more active when retrieval succeeds than when it fails (Buckner, 1996). Thus, a variety of prefrontal regions are involved both in the effort to search for an event representation and in its actual retrieval.

Behavioral studies also support the idea that intentional efforts to retrieve are different from the processes of successful retrieval. As pointed out earlier in this chapter, encoding processes do not function well at all when attention is not allocated to them. A comparison of the effects of divided attention on encoding and retrieval has revealed a sharp difference (Craik, Govoni, Naveh-Benjamin, & Anderson, 1996). Dividing at attention encoding greatly reduces recall and recognition performance. The time needed to respond on a secondary task provided a measure of the effort devoted to encoding. The data showed that the effort given to encoding was under conscious control and was lessened in the divided attention condition.

> Retrieval mode refers to the effort to retrieve an event from long-term memory as opposed to its actual retrieval. Activation in the right prefrontal cortex supports retrieval mode, whereas numerous regions are involved in successful retrieval.

By contrast, dividing attention at retrieval had little if any impact on success in recalling and recognizing events. But it caused a major increase in the effort devoted to retrieval, particularly in free recall when the retrieval was most intentional and least automatic. Of great interest, the effort measure did not vary at all with the number of items successfully retrieved. Thus, the effort measure apparently reflected retrieval mode, which is under intentional control as one tries to recollect past events. Success in retrieval, on the other hand, appears automatic and undisturbed by divisions of attention. As Craik et al. (1996) pointed out, their data fit well with the neuroimaging results that discriminate the retrieval mode as a control process carried out in the right prefrontal cortex from the process that actually recovers items from memory.

Encoding Specificity

Tulving (1983) proposed that remembering depends on activating precisely the same cues at retrieval that were originally encoded with the event in question. Tulving's principle of **encoding specificity** asserts that "specific encoding operations performed on what is perceived determines what retrieval cues are effective in producing access to what is stored" (Tulving & Thomson, 1973, p. 369). The interaction between encoding and retrieval conditions is the key to high levels of recall and recognition.

For instance, Light and Carter-Sobell (1970) presented people with a cue and a target word to study such as STRAWBERRY-JAM. Later, they tried to recognize whether the target word (JAM) had appeared during study. If on the test the cue word was switched (TRAFFIC-JAM), they had a harder time recognizing the target than if the retrieval cue matched the encoding cue. Furthermore, when encodings are highly distinctive and retrieval cues are available that match the encoding cues precisely, recall performance can be dazzlingly accurate. Mantyla (1986) obtained better than 90% accuracy in cued recall for a list of 600 words!

Recall of Unrecognizable Events. If one studies a list of words and later tries to remember them on a recognition test versus a recall test, performance is often better on the recognition test (Kintsch, 1970). A cued recall test generally yields better performance than a free recall test in which no retrieval cues are provided. But cued recall still fails to come close to the accuracy typically observed on a recognition test. This makes sense if you think of the word on the recognition test as the perfect retrieval cue; it is an exact copy. Not only is the word familiar, but it allows one to retrieve the context in which the word was originally seen in the experiment (Mandler, 1980).

Suppose that you see someone at a party who looks familiar. Recognition requires not only a judgment about familiarity but also an identification of the context in which you have encountered the person before ("Oh, yes, she was at the grocery store"). This identification is much easier when looking at the person than when given a weakly related cue ("think of shopping") or given no cues at all.

Tulving and Thomson (1973) arranged a situation in which the encoding specificity principle counterintuitively predicts accurate recall of an unrecognizable word. They presented a list of to-be-remembered target words (e.g., BLACK) along with encoding cues that were weak associates of the targets (e.g., TRAIN). After presentation of the list, the participants were given strong semantic associates of the target words (e.g., WHITE) and were asked to think of related words. Not surprisingly, target items (BLACK) were often generated. Next, the participants were asked to examine all of the words they generated and to indicate which if any had originally been presented as targets. Finally, a cued recall test was given in which the encoding context (TRAIN) served as the retrieval cue.

Tulving and Thomson (1973) found that the participants successfully recognized the targets only a quarter of the time. But when given the proper

Box 6.2

A DEMONSTRATION OF THE TIP OF THE TONGUE STATE

Try to name the capitals of the following states in the United States and countries in the European Union. Is there one (or more) for which you believe you know the answer but cannot retrieve it? Can you guess how many syllables are in the name? Can you guess the initial letter of the name?

Maine	Finland
New Hampshire	Belgium
Georgia	Denmark
South Dakota	Italy
Arizona	Germany
Tennessee	United Kingdom
Rhode Island	Luxembourg
Iowa	Portugal
Virginia	Austria
Oregon	Sweden

cue (TRAIN), the participants recalled the targets a stunning two thirds of the time. What is so striking about this is that the retrieval cue is only a weak associate of the target. Yet because it had been encoded with the word initially, it was the ideal cue for recall. This phenomenon of recall of unrecognizable words strongly supports the principle of encoding specificity.

Tip of the Tongue States. Surely, you have seen a familiar face that you could not quite place or perhaps could not retrieve the person's name. People often experience a feeling of knowing or familiarity in which some name, word, date, or other information cannot be retrieved despite a certainty that it is available in memory (see Box 6.2). When such feelings become particularly intense, psychologists refer to the experience as a **tip of the tongue (TOT) state.** Brown and McNeill (1966) studied such TOT states for words by giving people definitions of rare words and asking them to recall the words. Of interest, when people experienced a TOT state, they could correctly identify the number of syllables in the forgotten word more than 60% of the time. Further investigation showed that "TOTs (a) are a nearly universal experience, (b) occur about once a week, (c) increase with age, (d) are frequently elicited by proper names, (e) often enable access to the target word's first letter, (f) are often accompanied by words related to the target, and (g) are resolved during the experience about half of the time" (Brown, 1991, p. 204).

TOT states suggest that information may be available in memory but inaccessible. The forgetting seems to be clearly caused by a failure to find the right retrieval cue. Sometimes, we can successfully recall the forgotten information by stumbling on a thought or perception that triggers the memory. The principle of encoding specificity explains this as another example of cue-dependent forgetting. Numerous other experiments have documented the principle that the specific cues associated with an event during learning provide the key to later recall (e.g., Begg & White, 1985; Jacoby, 1974).

Environmental Context. The context in which learning is experienced ought to serve as a retrieval cue at the time of test, according to the encoding specificity principle. This has been tested by varying the environmental and psychological context in a large number of experiments. Of interest to students, Smith, Glenberg, and Bjork (1978) had people learn a list of words in a particular room and then later try to recall them in the same room or in one very different in appearance. The environmental context affected recall in the direction one would expect. The same room provided the right retrieval cues and supported superior performance. Although the effect was not large, it might pay off to study for an exam in the same room in which you will be tested.

A more compelling demonstration of the importance of reinstating the encoding context was provided by Godden and Baddeley (1975). Scuba divers learned a list of words underwater or on dry land. They were then tested in one of these two contexts, and the results showed a strong crossover interaction, as shown in Figure 6.4. Recall dropped substantially when learning occurred on dry land but then testing was underwater. However, when learning was underwater, performance improved by going underwater again at test relative to testing in a dry environment.

Psychological Context. The emotional state of the individual also may serve as an effective retrieval cue. A **mood congruence effect** may be studied by inducing people into a happy mood or an unhappy mood by thinking about positive or negative life events. Bower (1981) found that the best learning occurs when the material being learned fits with the induced mood. Thus, depressing information is best learned when in a sad mood (Blaney, 1986). **State-dependent learning** is sometimes observed when a person's mood

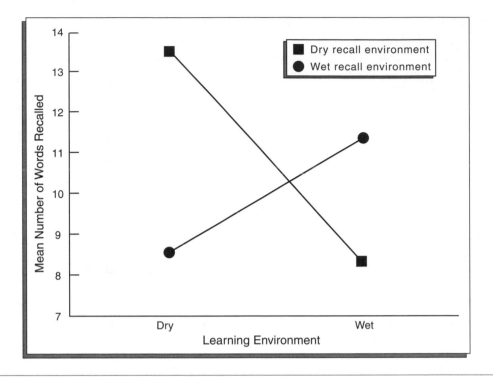

Figure 6.4. Number of words recalled in a dry or wet environment after learning in a dry or wet environment.

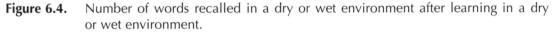

SOURCE: Adapted from Godden and Baddeley (1975).

or state of consciousness (e.g., sober, intoxicated) is directly manipulated during learning and retrieval. That is, recall performance when one's mood at retrieval matches the mood at the time of learning is not reliably better than when the moods do not match.

Several drugs, on the other hand, have shown state dependency effects when dosages are sufficiently large to produce clear signs of intoxication such as slurred speech (Eich, 1980, 1989; Overton, 1971). These include commonly used drugs such as alcohol, amphetamines, barbiturates, and marijuana. Information learned in a sober state is better retained when later recalled in a sober state, whereas information learned in an intoxicated state is better retained when tested while intoxicated. As one would expect from what we know about the importance of cognitive effort and elaboration during study, recall is by far the best during sober learning and sober testing.

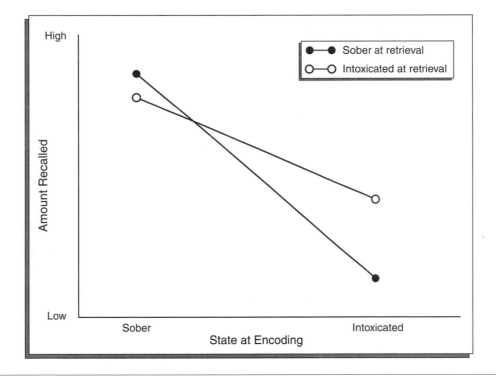

Figure 6.5. Asymmetry in drug-induced state-dependent learning.

However, there is a strong asymmetry in the relationship (Eich, 1989). As illustrated in Figure 6.5, if one is originally sober at study, then retrieving the information at the time of test is relatively easy both when one is sober and when one is intoxicated. At times, intoxication at retrieval can in fact increase the amount remembered (Curran, 2000). By sharp contrast, when the learner is initially intoxicated at study, there is a consistent decline in performance when the retrieval mode is shifted to sobriety.

It should also be noted that intoxication during encoding greatly impairs the degree of learning in the first place. An alert and sober state of mind is required for successful learning (Curran, 2000). It has been known for centuries that drugs can cause forgetting. Alcohol is by far the most widely used drug with this feature, but millions of people also take antidepressants and antianxiety drugs that can cause some memory problems. The elderly are particularly vulnerable because they may combine medications that have psychoactive properties. For example, 10% to 15% of the population over 65 years of age take sleeping pills that can produce brief memory loss. In

Tip of the tongue experiences and state-dependent learning show that the right retrieval cues are critical to successful recall, as predicted by the encoding specificity principle.

> **Box 6.3**
>
> ## ENCODING AND RETRIEVAL PROCEDURES USED IN THE COGNITIVE INTERVIEW METHOD
>
> Try to form a mental image of all the circumstances surrounding the event.
>
> Report everything you can remember about the event. Report even bits and pieces of information that are incomplete.
>
> Recall the event in several sequences rather than just one.
>
> Recall the event from several perspectives rather than just one.

extreme cases, older adults can experience confusion and memory loss that resembles dementia. It is important for physicians to distinguish between true organic dementia and one that is temporarily induced by prescription medications.

Application. The encoding specificity principle has important implications for medical, police, and legal professionals who rely on the recollections of an individual to determine the facts of a case. For example, doctors often try to obtain an accurate clinical picture by interviewing a patient about, say, eating habits. An accurate picture is needed to diagnose eating disorders, such as anorexia and obesity, and to understand the causes of diabetes, high blood pressure, heart disease, allergies, and other conditions. Unfortunately, our current eating habits distort recollections of past habits. If our current habits differ in important respects, then the information about the past is inaccurate (Croyle, Loftus, Klinger, & Smith, 1992).

To improve the accuracy of information obtained by medical, police, and legal professionals, Fisher and Geiselman (1992) developed the Cognitive Interview. The method is illustrated in Box 6.3. It entails asking respondents (a) to mentally picture the personal and environmental context of the event to be remembered; (b) to report all recalled information, including partial information; (c) to recall the specific events in not just one order but several; and (d) to recall the specific events from several different perspectives. Notice that the first aspect of the procedure tries to reinstate the encoding context at the time of recall, in keeping with the encoding specificity principle.

Partial information might serve as a retrieval cue for additional recovery of information, much as happens in the TOT phenomenon. Trying different orders and perspectives helps to avoid the use of a single schema for guiding the reconstruction of events. The Cognitive Interview improves the quality of information obtained in police questionings of eyewitnesses (Geiselman, Fisher, MacKinnon, & Holland, 1986) and in patients' recollections of food consumption (Croyle et al., 1992).

SUMMARY

1. Long-term memory itself is not a unitary store, according to the multiple systems hypothesis regarding the structure of long-term memory. There is a fundamental division in long-term memory between declarative (knowledge of what) and nondeclarative (knowledge of how) systems. Declarative memory is further divided into episodic memory (events that are encoded in terms of specific times and places of occurrence) and semantic memory (general knowledge of facts and concepts). Nondeclarative memory includes skill learning, priming, conditioning, and habituation.

2. Encoding and storage of episodic information in long-term memory varies with the kind of rehearsal given to information stored in short-term memory. Simply recycling information through attention and short-term storage, or what is called maintenance rehearsal, is not highly effective. Repeating a list of words illustrates maintenance rehearsal. Elaborative rehearsal is superior and depends on establishing links between the information held in short-term memory and the information already stored in long-term memory. Forming visual images of the objects referred to by the words in a list illustrates elaborative rehearsal. Mnemonic techniques, such as the method of loci, are kinds of elaborative rehearsal.

3. The level of processing also affects learning success, with deep semantic processing supporting better memory than shallow sensory processing. This probably reflects the importance of establishing a distinctive memory representation that can be easily retrieved in the future. Finally, the organization of newly learned information is necessary for successful recognition and recall.

4. Encoding processes are important, but they cannot be considered apart from retrieval processes. The encoding specificity principle asserts that events are recognized or recalled only when retrieval cues at the time of test match the encoding cues at the time of learning. The retrieval cues allow one to activate the to-be-remembered episode and its context. From this perspective, forgetting represents a failure to access an episode because the retrieval cues are inadequate.

● KEY TERMS

declarative memory

nondeclarative memory

episodic memory

semantic memory

maintenance rehearsal

elaborative rehearsal

levels or depths of processing

self-reference effect

transfer-appropriate processing

distinctiveness

flashbulb memory

relational processing

subjective organization

retrieval mode

encoding specificity

tip of the tongue (TOT) state

mood congruence effect

state-dependent learning

CHAPTER 7

DISTORTIONS OF MEMORY

Each day, one has countless thoughts, fantasies, and recollections about the events of earlier in the day, last week, or years ago. In fantasizing about possible events yet to happen in the future, there is no confusion over whether the mental experience accurately reflects reality. However, in thinking back on events from the past, the possibility of confusing our memory of events with the actual events that transpired is quite real. Where is the line that separates fantasies about the past from accurate recollections? How does one know that an event is not distorted in minor or even major ways? Memory distortion can be more pernicious than forgetting because the rememberer might not be able to tell that the recollection is in error.

As will be seen in this chapter, there are several ways in which encoding, storage, and retrieval processes can lead to inaccurate, distorted episodic memory. The role of organized sets of concepts or schemas in constructing episodic representations at encoding and in reconstructing them at retrieval is also documented in the current chapter. An episodic memory is influenced by the general knowledge of the world stored in semantic memory. The rich warehouse of semantic memory is necessary for the abstract thinking capacities of humans, but it can get in the way of perfectly accurate memories of past events.

● RECONSTRUCTIVE RETRIEVAL

Schemas play a critical role in perception by providing expectations, as discussed in Chapter 3. They play a similar crucial role in memory. The schemas of long-term memory represent everything that we know. These schemas are intricately organized in a complex web of relations. The concepts and facts of semantic memory and the specific autobiographical events of episodic memory are linked in countless ways.

Imagine a scenario of a cat prowling for mice. Where might the cat find mice? In a barn on a farm, of course. Immediately related images might come to mind about farms. You might recall the farm you grew up on, one you visited as a child, or one you saw in a movie last week. In turn, images of cows, pigs, horses, and other farm animals might then come to mind. The thought of a horse would perhaps bring to mind the time you went horseback riding with friends. More images pop into mind as you reflect on each of the friends on the trip. The possibilities of such free association are endless because the schemas of long-term memory are massively interconnected. Virtually any thought, through some chain of associations, can lead to any other thought as a result of such organization.

Much, if not all, of what we learn and retrieve from memory passes through the organizational web. The schemas provide expectations that help us to learn but also at times to miss events that do not fit with these expectations. The schemas help us to remember but also at times to distort memories so as to conform to momentary expectations. The key point here is that schemas enable us to fabricate how past events most likely unfolded. The term **reconstructive retrieval** refers to schema-guided construction of episodic memories that alter and distort encoded memory representations.

The term *reconstructive retrieval* refers to schema-guided construction of episodic memories that alter and distort encoded memory representations.

Many experiments have documented that recall may at times be driven by a schema-based reconstructive process. For instance, Brewer and Treyens (1981) showed how our recollections of places are schema based. After waiting in an experimenter's office for 35 seconds, people were taken to another room and asked to recall the office (see Figure 7.1). Virtually everyone recalled that the office had a chair, a desk, and walls, but only about one of four participants recalled unexpected items such as a skull. Moreover, items that fit preconceptions about a psychologist's office, such as books, were falsely recalled by some participants.

Figure 7.1. Office scene used in a study of reconstructive retrieval.
SOURCE: Brewer and Treyens (1981).

Reconstructing Laboratory Events

The role of schemas in text comprehension and memory is particularly well-researched (Bower, Black, & Turner, 1979; Dooling & Christiansen, 1977; Spiro, 1980). These and numerous related experiments took as their starting point the classic work by Bartlett (1932) on schemas and reconstruction. Particularly well-known are Bartlett's studies in which participants tried to recall a folk tale of North American Indians—the War of the Ghosts. Before discussing the results, try reading the story shown in Box 7.1. Then, after 15 minutes or so, test yourself by trying to write down the story from memory, without going back and rereading it.

Box 7.1

THE "WAR OF THE GHOSTS" STORY USED BY BARTLETT

One night two young men from Egulac went down to the river to hunt seals, and while they were there it became foggy and calm. Then they heard war cries, and they thought, "Maybe this is a war party." They escaped to the shore and hid behind a log. Now canoes came up, and they heard the noise of paddles and saw one canoe coming up to them. There were five men in the canoe, and they said, "What do you think? We wish to take you along. We are going up the river to make war on the people."

One of the young men said, "I have no arrows."

"Arrows are in the canoe," they said.

"I will not go along. I might be killed. My relatives do not know where I have gone. But you," he said, turning to the other, "may go with them."

So one of the young men went, but the other returned home.

And the warriors went on up the river to a town on the other side of Kalama. The people came down to the water, and they began to fight, and many were killed. But the young man heard one of the warriors say, "Quick, let us go home; that Indian has been hit." Now he thought, "Oh, they are ghosts." He did not feel sick, but they said he had been shot.

So the canoes went back to Egulac, and the young man went ashore to his house and made a fire. And he told everybody and said, "Behold, I accompanied the ghosts, and we went to fight. Many of our fellows were killed, and many of those who attacked us were killed. They said I was hit, and I did not feel sick."

He told it all, and then he became quiet. When the sun rose, he fell down. Something black came out of his mouth. His face became contorted. The people jumped up and cried.

He was dead.

SOURCE: Bartlett (1932).

Several features of Bartlett's results indicated that recall took place through an attempt to fabricate or reconstruct the original story. Within 15 minutes of reading the story, people recalled an abstracted summarized version. Three kinds of errors occurred through reconstructive retrieval. **Leveling** refers to a loss of details. The story was leveled to a shorter version. In particular, unfamiliar terms and ideas were omitted. For example, the place called "Kalama" might be forgotten in describing one's journey. Or, the number of men in the canoe might be dropped. Or, the term "Egulac" might be omitted as the home of the two young men in the story.

The reconstruction also resulted in the assimilation of events into a schema. **Assimilation** means that the recollection was rationalized or normalized to fit with preconceived notions. For example, the Indian who had been shot might be described as "hurt" or "wounded" because these terms are more in keeping with our general knowledge. The actual term used (i.e., "sick") might be assimilated to a schema about battles and being shot. Or, one might falsely remember that the two young men were going fishing on the river rather than hunting seals.

Finally, besides losing details and altering them to fit with expectations, some facts in the story were embellished. **Sharpening** refers to remembering details that were not actually stated but that could be inferred from general knowledge. For example, one might remember that "they told him he was hit by an arrow." The story did not actually say anything about an arrow hitting the Indian, but it could be readily inferred from the facts given in the story and from general knowledge about battles among Indians. Remembering that many were wounded in the battle is another example of drawing inferences from a schema. All that was stated is that many were killed; it was not stated directly that some were injured but not killed. The battle schema might again support an inference that not all of the wounds were fatal.

Thus, reconstructive recall causes the loss of some details and the erroneous inclusion of other details. Inferences were drawn based on general knowledge rather than on what was actually stated in the story. Other facts were assimilated into a schema so that they reflected general knowledge rather than the original story. Over hours, weeks, months, and years, repeated attempts to recall the story magnified all of these distortions. Each retelling of the story provided yet another opportunity for a creative reconstruction of a story that bore less and less resemblance to the original narrative.

For comparison purposes, consider the recall of an individual who lacked normal reconstructive processes. Shown in Panel (a) of Box 7.2 is the story as it was recalled by "S.," who, as you may remember from Chapter 6, recalled events verbatim in remarkably accurate detail. Astonishingly, this recall protocol was

Box 7.2

(a) RECALL OF THE "WAR OF THE GHOSTS" BY A MNEMONIST (S.) 1 YEAR AFTER HEARING THE STORY

One day two young men from Egliac went down to the river to hunt seals. While there, it suddenly became very foggy and quiet, and they became scared and rowed ashore and hid behind a log. Soon they heard the sound of paddles in the water and canoes approaching. One of the canoes, with five men in it, paddled ashore, and one of the men said, "What do you think? Let us go up-river and make war against the people."

"I cannot go with you," said one of the young men. "My relatives do not know where I have gone. Besides, I might get killed. But he," said he, turning to the other young man, "will go with you." So one of the young men returned to his village, and the other went up-river with the war party.

"They went to a point beyond Kalama, and the people came down to the river to fight them, and they fought. Soon the young man heard someone say, "This Indian has been wounded." "Maybe they are ghosts," he thought, because he felt perfectly okay. The war party suggested leaving, and they left, and the young man went back to his village.

"There he lit a fire in front of his abode, sat down to await the sunrise, and told his story to the villagers. "I went with a war party to make war with the people. There was fierce fighting, and many were killed, and many were wounded. They said I was wounded, but I did not feel a thing. Maybe they were ghosts."

"He had told it all, and when the sun came up, he gave a little cry. Something black came out of his mouth. He fell over. He was dead.

(b) RECALL BY AN UNDERGRADUATE STUDENT 15 MINUTES AFTER HEARING THE STORY

"Two men went down to the water to fish for seals. It became calm and foggy. They heard noises, so they went to shore and hid behind a log. They heard the sound of paddles and saw a canoe coming closer. The canoe had five men in it, and they asked the two men to come fight with them. The man first said he had no arrows, but the men in the canoe said there were plenty in the canoe. Next he said he could not go because his relatives did not know where he was, but he told the other man he could go. So the other man went with them to fight, and the first man went home. When they got to the village, the people came down to the water to fight. Then the man heard the Indians say to hurry up and leave because he had been shot. He thought they were fighting ghosts, and he told the village he was in the presence of ghosts because they had shot him and he did not feel sick. When he finished his story, he became silent. The next morning, he fell over. Something black came out of his mouth. The people watched him as he died.

SOURCE: Bartlett (1932).

collected 1 year after S. heard the story read to him. In Panel (b) is a typical recall protocol from a college student after a retention interval of only 15 minutes. Examine the story for examples of leveling, assimilation, and sharpening, and notice their conspicuous absence from the recall of S.

Bartlett's pioneering research was strong on theory but weak on methodology. Yet his basic findings stand up under rigorous experimental design and data analysis procedures (Bergman & Roediger, 1999). With instructions to recall the story in a verbatim manner, participants got less than 20% right after a delay of only 15 minutes. As shown in Figure 7.2, the degree of accuracy dropped by half after a week and by half again after 6 months. By contrast, major distortions in elements of the text propositions held constant over these time intervals. The latter included normalizing events to fit a schema (e.g., replacing "canoe" with "boat," replacing "hunting seals" with "fishing") or using a schema to infer a missing detail (e.g., recalling the Indian was hit by an "arrow" even though the story fails to specify this detail).

Reconstructing Autobiographical Events

Much is now also known about the way we reconstruct autobiographical memories of personal as opposed to public events (Conway, 1992). The terrorist attack on the World Trade Center was a public event. You know about the events in New York City on September 11, 2001, because of news accounts without actually having been there to experience them firsthand. The events of your 10th birthday, on the other hand, are known only by you, your parents, and perhaps a few other people. An autobiographical event is one that you personally experienced.

Conway (1992) found that lifetime periods extend over years or even decades and that people remembered autobiographical events in terms such

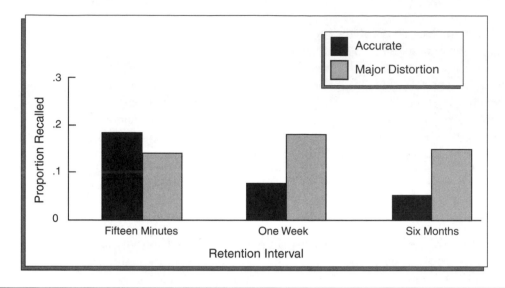

Figure 7.2. Proportions of text propositions recalled of the War of the Ghosts after varying retention intervals.

SOURCE: Adapted from Bergman and Roediger (1999).

as "when I lived in X" or "when I worked for Y." These periods serve to orient us in autobiographical time and provide retrieval cues for more specific recollections. A lifetime period might evoke moods, significant goals, or general themes of the period but not concrete events. The second level is general events or episodes. These are chronologically organized personal experiences that cluster about thematically important landmarks in time. First-time experiences such as falling in love, taking a first job, graduating from high school, and moving away to college serve to remind one of related general events. The third level consists of concrete images or sensory replays of a specific event. In Conway's view, these detailed recollections are always integrated with schema-based representations of general events. What seems like a discrete recollection is in fact tied into higher levels of memory structure.

Recalling one's life inevitably uncovers the significant general events or episodes that define the self. They are recalled not as isolated events but rather as part of a narrative that gives life meaning (Bruner, 1990). Life narratives provide us with a sense of who we are, but that says nothing about their accuracy. In addition to life narratives, people recall flashbulb memories of public events, such as the 1986 *Challenger* explosion, and unique personal experiences (Neisser & Libby, 2000). Personal experiences can be particularly well-remembered. Individuals who experienced the 1989 Loma Prieta earthquake in California provided accounts written a year and a half after the event that were highly similar to those written only a few days after the earthquake (Neisser et al., 1996).

Historians are often faced with the task of weighing autobiographical accounts against other known information (McGlone, 1998). For example, John Adams, late in life at 86 years of age, recalled with remarkable clarity his conversation, 50 years earlier, with Thomas Jefferson over the authorship of the U.S. *Declaration of Independence.* Adams wrote in a letter to Thomas Pickering that Jefferson asked him to draft the declaration and demanded to know why Adams would not do so. "Reasons enough," Adams declared. "Reason first—You are a Virginian, and a Virginian ought to appear at the head of this business. Reason second—I am obnoxious, suspected, and unpopular. You are very much otherwise. Reason third—You can write ten times better than I can." "Well," Jefferson replied, "if you are decided, I will do as well as I can." Jefferson, for his part, denied Adams's story and insisted that a five-member committee of the Second Continental Congress had appointed him to author the most famous document in American history.

The verbatim detail of Adams's account is worrisome, suggesting that it might reflect a schema-based sharpening of details that were in error. In fact, McGlone (1998) noted that Adams had recalled the story differently 20 years earlier in another letter to Pickering. Moreover, in working on his autobiography in 1805, Adams could not recall what he had said. What is more, in his earliest account in 1779, Adams explained to a French diplomat that a committee of five members had appointed Jefferson to draft the document. His first account, closest in time to the actual events, accorded with Jefferson's recollection! Thus, Adams's later fabrication about Jefferson offering the authorship to him illustrates how an event representation becomes integrated with schemas representing general autobiographical knowledge (Conway, 1992). Over the years, Adams's story changed as he entered new periods in his life, with some elements dropping out as novel elements were added.

ENCODING DISTORTIONS ●

In addition to reconstructive retrieval, schemas sometimes constructively distort memory during encoding in multiple ways. The strength and generality of these effects are in dispute (Alba & Hasher, 1983; Mandler, 1984). So, we focus on three that are reasonably well-supported to illustrate constructive effects: selection, interpretation, and integration.

Selection. The selective encoding of information that fits with prior knowledge defines **selection.** This idea was well-illustrated in an experiment by

Bransford and Johnson (1972). They presented people with the following obscure text:

> The procedure is actually quite simple. First you arrange items into different groups. Of course one pile may be sufficient depending on how much there is to do. If you have to go somewhere else due to lack of facilities, that is the next step; otherwise, you are pretty well set. It is important not to overdo things. That is, it is better to do too few things at once than too many. In the short run this may not seem important, but complications can easily arise. A mistake can be expensive as well. At first, the whole procedure will seem complicated. Soon, however, it will become just another facet of life. It is difficult to foresee any end to the necessity for this task in the immediate future, but then, one never can tell. After the procedure is completed, one arranges the materials into different groups again. Then they can be put into their appropriate places. Eventually they will be used once more, and the whole cycle will then have to be repeated. However, that is part of life. (p. 722)

In first reading this, you likely felt what Bartlett (1932) called an "effort after meaning" as various schemas actively struggled to shape the sentences into a comprehensible pattern. Without knowing the title or topic of the text in advance to select the sentences to fit into a preconceived schema, comprehension is poor and so is subsequent recall. The data from Bransford and Johnson's (1972) experiment show this plainly in the first column of Figure 7.3. However, when given the topic of "washing clothes" before reading, both ratings of comprehension and recall scores improved greatly. Notice that receiving the topic after reading failed to help. The schema must be active to select details at the time of learning.

Interpretation. Inferences and suppositions are made to conform new material to activated schemas; these define **interpretation.** Prior knowledge provides a basis for interpreting the meaning of events, and these interpretations become part of memory. Johnson, Bransford, and Solomon's (1973) results illustrate interpretation well. Consider these two versions of a brief passage that were presented to different groups of people:

1. John was trying to fix the birdhouse. He was pounding the nail when his father came out to watch him and to help him do the work.

2. John was trying to fix the birdhouse. He was looking for the nail when his father came out to watch him and to help him do the work.

The two passages were the same but for a minor change. Johnson et al. later gave a recognition test that included the following novel sentence:

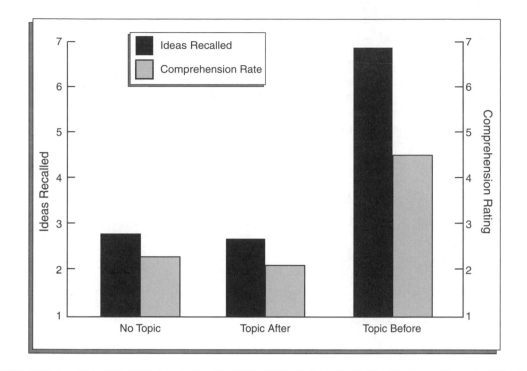

Figure 7.3. Recall and comprehension of the "washing clothes" story.
SOURCE: Adapted from Bransford and Johnson (1972).

3. John was using the hammer to fix the birdhouse when his father came out to watch him and to help him do the work.

The researchers found that the group of individuals who had read Passage 1 were much more likely to say that they had previously seen Passage 3 in the experiment. The false recognition of Passage 3 indicates that these individuals inferred that John was using a hammer, an assumption that fits well with the expectations of schemas activated by the passage.

Integration. The third type of encoding distortion, **integration,** refers to combining features of different events into a unified memory representation. As a result of integration, we remember the main idea or gist of an event rather than the details of its occurrence. Bransford and Franks (1971) investigated integration by presenting people with a long list of sentences. In Figure 7.4, you can read a sample of these sentences. Answer the question after each one to ensure that you comprehended each sentence.

Now take a moment to decide whether the sentences in Figure 7.5 are old sentences that appeared earlier in the list that you read or are new

Instructions: Read each sentence, count to five, answer the question, and go on to the next sentence.

The girl broke the window on the porch.	Broke what?
The tree in the front yard shaded the man who was smoking his pipe.	Where?
The hill was steep.	What was?
The cat, running from the barking dog, jumped on the table.	From what?
The tree was tall.	Was what?
The old car climbed the hill.	What did?
The cat running from the dog jumped on the table.	Where?
The girl who lives next door broke the window on the porch.	Lives where?
The car pulled the trailer.	Did what?
The scared cat was running from the barking dog.	What was?
The girl lives next door.	Who does?
The tree shaded the man who was smoking his pipe.	What did?
The scared cat jumped on the table.	What did?
The girl who lives next door broke the large window.	Broke what?
The man was smoking his pipe.	Who was?
The old car climbed the steep hill.	The what?
The large window was on the porch.	Where?
The tall tree was in the front yard.	What was?
The car pulling the trailer climbed the steep hill.	Did what?
The cat jumped on the table.	Where?
The tall tree in the front yard shaded the man.	Did what?
The car pulling the trailer climbed the hill.	Which car?
The dog was barking.	Was what?
The window was large.	What was?

STOP. Cover the preceding sentences. Now read each sentence in Figure 7.5 and decide whether it is a sentence from the list given above.

Figure 7.4. A memory experiment: Part 1.

SOURCE: Jenkins (1974).

sentences. Check old or new for each one before reading further in the text. After finishing the recognition test, count the number of items that you checked as old sentences.

Typically, people indicate that well more than half of the 30 sentences in Figure 7.4 are old sentences. In fact, none of the test sentences occurred earlier. The test sentences, however, represent plausible sentences based on the schemas that were activated in reading the original sentences. The individual

Instructions: Decide whether each sentence is old or new.

1. The car climbed the hill.   (old ____, new ____)
2. The girl who lives next door broke the window.   (old ____, new ____)
3. The old man who was smoking his pipe climbed the steep hill.   (old ____, new ____)
4. The tree was in the front yard.   (old ____, new ____)
5. The scared cat, running from the barking dog, jumped on the table.   (old ____, new ____)
6. The window was on the porch.   (old ____, new ____)
7. The barking dog jumped on the old car in the front yard.   (old ____, new ____)
8. The tree in the front yard shaded the man.   (old ____, new ____)
9. The cat was running from the dog.   (old ____, new ____)
10. The old car pulled the trailer.   (old ____, new ____)
11. The tall tree in the front yard shaded the old car.   (old ____, new ____)
12. The tall tree shaded the man who was smoking his pipe.   (old ____, new ____)
13. The scared cat was running from the dog.   (old ____, new ____)
14. The old car, pulling the trailer, climbed the hill.   (old ____, new ____)
15. The girl who lives next door broke the large window on the porch.   (old ____, new ____)
16. The tall tree shaded the man.   (old ____, new ____)
17. The cat was running from the barking dog.   (old ____, new ____)
18. The car was old.   (old ____, new ____)
19. The girl broke the large window.   (old ____, new ____)
20. The scared cat ran from the barking dog that jumped on the table.   (old ____, new ____)
21. The scared cat, running from the dog, jumped on the table.   (old ____, new ____)
22. The old car pulling the trailer climbed the steep hill.   (old ____, new ____)
23. The girl broke the large window on the porch.   (old ____, new ____)
24. The scared cat which broke the window on the porch climbed the tree.   (old ____, new ____)
25. The tree shaded the man.   (old ____, new ____)
26. The car climbed the steep hill.   (old ____, new ____)
27. The girl broke the window.   (old ____, new ____)
28. The man who lives next door broke the large window on the porch.   (old ____, new ____)
29. The tall tree in the front yard shaded the man who was smoking the pipe.   (old ____, new ____)
30. The cat was scared.   (old ____, new ____)

STOP. Count the number of sentences judged "old."

Figure 7.5. A memory experiment: Part 2.

SOURCE: Jenkins (1974).

features or ideas of the original sentences become integrated into larger organized ideas. The integration is so compelling that people actually are more confident that they saw a sentence containing all related ideas than they are about having seen sentences containing fewer ideas. This is exactly opposite of what one would expect if we stored the individual sentences in memory verbatim.

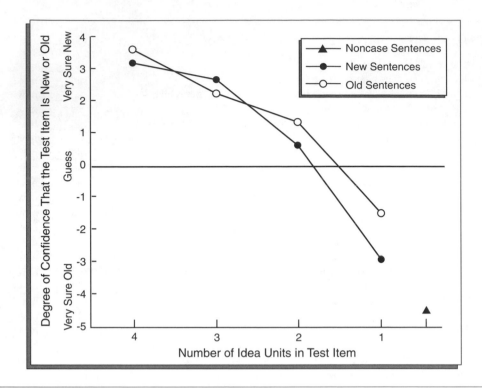

Figure 7.6. Confidence in recognition judgments for both old and new sentences varies with the number of idea units expressed.

SOURCE: Bransford and Franks (1971).

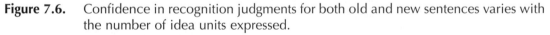

Selection of a subset of event features, interpretation of events to fit preexisting schemas, and integration of features from multiple events are encoding failures that cause memory distortions.

Bransford and Franks's (1971) results are plotted in Figure 7.6. The number of ideas in the test sentence increased from one to four. Noncase sentences were totally novel and unrelated to the schemas activated during reading. They were readily rejected as new sentences. As you can see, the participants falsely recognized new sentences that contained more than one idea, and their confidence increased with each additional idea. The same result occurred for actual old sentences. These results plainly show how integration can distort memory by giving us the gist of the original events.

● SOURCE MONITORING

Why is it that our fantasies, conjured during daydreams, are not later routinely confused as memories of real events? The vivid hallucinatory dreams of rapid eye movement (REM) sleep are still more puzzling. Given that they seem so real at the time, why are dreams not later remembered as having really occurred? One reason is that memory involves source monitoring processes (Johnson, Hastroudi, & Lindsay, 1993). **Source monitoring** refers to evaluative processes that attribute mental experiences to different sources. External sources are perceived events in the environment, whereas internal sources are thoughts, fantasies, and dreams.

> Source monitoring refers to evaluative processes that attribute mental experiences to either external sources (i.e., perceived events) or internal sources (i.e., thoughts, fantasies, and dreams).

Memory Illusions

Discriminating external from internal sources is essential to avoid falling victim to false memories of events that never happened. One of the most disturbing kinds of memory distortion is when one has the illusion of remembering an experience that in fact never happened. Before reading any further, try the demonstration given in Box 7.3. Read the list of words once at a time at a rate of about one each second. Then look away from the list and count backward from 60 at a slow and steady pace. Finally, try to recall as many of the words from the list as you can in any order you like.

In numerous experiments using word lists similar to the one you just recalled, it has proven possible to study an interesting illusion of memory (Deese, 1959; Roediger & McDermott, 1995). Check for yourself the accuracy of your own recall. Were you able to recall words from the beginning of the list, showing the classic primacy effect? What about a recency effect? Were the final few items in the list remembered accurately? Typically, the middle items of the list are not particularly well-recalled. Many participants have trouble remembering "sill," "house," "open," "curtain," and "frame" but have no trouble at all remembering "window." The problem is that window was not in fact an item on the list. Remembering window is an illusion of memory. It illustrates what is called a **false verbal memory,** created as a result of hearing or reading a list of words that are semantically related to the falsely remembered word. The words actually presented in the list are window's top 15 associates in semantic memory—the words that come to mind in free-associating to the target word. People in such experiments may falsely recall the target word as often as half the time, about the same level of accuracy as words actually presented in the middle of the list.

The nonpresented target word (e.g., window) is activated as a result of seeing or hearing close semantic associates. As we will see in Chapter 8, semantic memory is organized according to similarity. A close associate of "window" is likely to activate the representation of window itself. With 15 close associates at work, window is strongly active in memory, creating an illusion of having been actually presented. To avoid false recall, it is necessary

Box 7.3

A MEMORY DEMONSTRATION

Read each word in the following list at a rate of about one word per second. Next, count backward from 60 to 0 at a rate of about one number per second. Finally, without looking again at the list, write down as many of the words as you can remember.

door
glass
pane
shade
ledge
sill
house
open
curtain
frame
view
breeze
sash
screen
shutter

to monitor items generated as potential targets and to distinguish between those with sensory plus semantic activation and those with only semantic activation. Thus, effectively monitoring the source of a memory can prevent the illusion. If one remembered window and then attributed this experience to an internal source (e.g., thinking about window as the other words were read or heard), then the intrusion could be edited from recall. An internal source presumably lacks the sensory features of sound and sight that ought to be available for true memories with external origins.

There is strong evidence that the availability of perceptual details helps people to avoid the illusion. For example, when a picture is visually presented along with each aurally presented word in the list, false recognition of the critical items is substantially reduced (Schacter, Israel, & Racine, 1999). The visual features of the pictures of actually presented words were distinctively different from internally generated intrusions of critical items, allowing participants to tell the two apart. In addition, Smith and Hunt (1998) found that reading the list of words also helps participants to discriminate true memories from false memories of the critical items as compared with hearing the list. As will be discussed in Chapter 12, reading activates representations of both the visual appearance of the words and the sound of words. Thus, participants have two kinds of perceptual details available in memory when reading the list of words. If you failed to experience the memory illusion after reading the list in Box 7.3, then try reading it aloud to a few friends and see whether they experience the illusion from aural presentation.

Despite the strong behavioral evidence that distinctive perceptual details help one to avoid verbal false memories, it has proved difficult to capture these differences in brain activation patterns using neuroimaging methods (Curran, Schacter, Johnson, & Spinks, 2001). One lead is that attentional monitoring failures result in high levels of false memories in patients with lesions in the prefrontal cortex (Melo, Winocur, & Moscovitch, 1999). Recall that the prefrontal cortex is necessary for the executive functions of working memory such as attending to errors and inhibiting inappropriate responses.

Memory distortions can arise from reconstructive retrieval, flawed encoding, and failures to attribute mental experiences to the proper source. These factors are not unrelated, however. If the binding of features together into a cohesive event during encoding is disrupted, then errors in source memory can become more likely (Kroll, Knight, Metcalfe, Wolf, & Tulving, 1996). When researchers gave participants a list of words to study in which certain syllables could be combined differently to make new words, they sometimes observed binding failures. As shown in Figure 7.7, if the first and second syllables of "fiction" and "buckle" are not bound successfully, then the parts might be recombined into a word not actually presented—"fickle." Such a mistake is called a **conjunction error** because two syllables are incorrectly conjoined during recall and not noticed as a novel word. In this case, the conjunction error arises partly because of a failure (a) to encode the words properly and (b) to realize that fickle came from an internal rather than an external source. Kroll et al. (1996) discovered that patients with lesions in the hippocampal regions of the left hemisphere were three to four times as likely to make conjunction errors as were normal controls. Recall that this region is critical in encoding words for long-term storage.

Confabulation

Because cognition is so actively constructive, it is understandable that people can falsely recognize an event or include false intrusions in their

Study	Binding Success	Binding Failure	Recall
decade	decade		decade
fiction		fic___	fickle Conjunction error
island	island		island
meeting	meeting		meeting
buckle		___kle	
police	police		police

Figure 7.7.   Conjunction errors of memory.

otherwise accurate recollections of past events. However, can the constructive nature of cognition also cause one to generate a false past—an autobiographical history that never happened? Providing a narrative account of autobiographical events that never happened is called **confabulation.**

Serious pathological degrees of confabulating a past that never happened are characteristic of a rare psychosis, Korsakoff's syndrome, caused by chronic alcoholism and a variety of other confusional states (Kopelman, 1999). A key feature of Korsakoff's syndrome is severe anterograde amnesia, and poor memory for recent events usually accompanies this condition. Confabulations appear as spontaneous outpourings of recollections that the patient cannot control and cannot monitor as false. Sometimes, confabulations include bizarre events that could not possibly be true, and yet the patient appears perfectly satisfied that the events really happened.

Confabulation is at least in part a breakdown in the ability to attribute fantasies to an internal imagined source and to edit this content so as to prevent false recollections. The spontaneous confabulation seen in neurological patients is indeed associated with prefrontal cortical damage to the executive functions of working memory (Kopelman, 1999). The delusional memories seen in patients suffering from schizophrenia may appear to be similar to confabulations, but they do not arise from lesions in the prefrontal cortex. For example, Kopelman described a garage mechanic who claimed to have been responsible for a well-publicized murder of an aristocrat living in London 8 years earlier. Although completely convinced of the truth of this story, the man had no other signs of memory problems and lived a seemingly normal life until he became preoccupied with the delusional "murder." It was his preoccupation with this false memory that led to his hospitalization and eventual diagnosis of schizophrenia.

EYEWITNESS TESTIMONY ●

Researchers are keenly interested in how constructive processes influence the accuracy of eyewitness testimony. Criminal trials in courts of law often depend on the firsthand testimony of witnesses to crimes. Assuming that a witness is not intentionally lying but rather is trying to provide an accurate account, just how certain can the judge and jury be that the testimony is correct?

Neisser (1981) analyzed the testimony of John Dean regarding meetings Dean had with President Nixon during the Watergate scandal of the early 1970s. Because Nixon had secretly taped conversations with Dean in the Oval Office, there was a transcript (with a few gaps) against which Dean's recollections could be checked. At the time of the congressional hearings at which Dean recounted his conversations with the president, news commentators found Dean's memory quite remarkable given the many details he confidently offered in his testimony. Yet by comparing Dean's sworn testimony to the tape transcripts that the president eventually was forced to turn over to Congress, Neisser could identify the errors in Dean's testimony.

Reconstructive Retrieval. On the whole, Dean did very well in recalling the gist of what Nixon had said. Dean integrated information about different meetings and conversations into broad themes. Yet he also added faulty details. Regarding the September 15 meeting that had taken place 9 months before Dean's testimony, Neisser observed,

> Comparison with the transcript shows that hardly a word of Dean's account is true. Nixon did not say *any* of the things attributed to him here: He didn't ask Dean to sit down, he didn't say [H. R.] Haldeman had kept him posted, . . . he didn't say anything about [G. Gordon] Liddy or the indictments. Nor had Dean himself said the things he later describes himself as saying. (p. 147)

All of these faulty details were reconstructions of what Dean believed he must have heard, said, and done. Schemas most likely sharpened these details as Dean reconstructed the original events for his testimony.

Attorneys in criminal trials are well aware that the testimony of an eyewitness exerts a powerful influence on jurors. The members of a jury typically believe that eyewitness reports are accurate unless for some reason deliberate lying by the witness is suspected. In reality, eyewitnesses can fall victim to distortions of memory because of inaccurate encoding and retrieving of episodes (Loftus, 1979). Errors can and do occur even when witnesses are confident that their testimony is accurate, leading in turn to wrongful convictions. According to some estimates, roughly 8,500 such miscarriages of justice occur each year in the United States alone, with as many as half attributable to incorrect eyewitness testimony (Loftus, 1986).

Besides reconstructive retrieval, efforts to explain these inaccuracies have focused on (a) selective encoding by the witness, (b) attempts to mislead the witness through slanted questioning, and (c) implanted memories. Adult eyewitness testimony is given substantial weight in criminal court proceedings despite the laboratory evidence documenting the potential for error (Ross, Read, & Toglia, 1994; Thompson et al., 1998).

Selective Encoding

The scene of a crime might not be plainly visible because of poor lighting and fleeting glimpses of the perpetrator (Buckhout, 1974). Moreover, eyewitnesses to violent crimes, particularly when they are the victims, may experience tremendous stress that diminishes their ability to encode the events adequately. Even less severe stressors can distort memory through selective encoding. For example, the social anxiety of being the next in line to give a public address can lower subsequent recall of the speech given just before one's own speech (Bond & Omar, 1990). Perhaps you have experienced this while waiting to give a presentation in class. You may remember earlier and later speakers much better than the person just ahead of you.

Not all scholars agree that emotional duress weakens encoding, however. Recall here our earlier discussion of the controversy over flashbulb memories. The literature on eyewitness reports of crimes is similarly open to multiple interpretations. For example, Christianson (1992) concluded that only the peripheral details of a crime tend to get lost under high levels of stress. The central features of the event at times are remembered especially well through effects of selective attention, elaboration, and distinctiveness. Thus, most errors in eyewitness testimony may be caused by factors other than selective encoding.

Memory for facial appearance in particular is often remarkably accurate (Bahrick, Bahrick, & Wittlinger, 1975), possibly because face perception is served by a specialized module, as discussed in Chapter 3. However, recognizing a stranger who has just committed a crime may still fail if the witness attended to, say, the weapon carried by the perpetrator rather than his or her face. The unexpected and rapid nature of the events in a crime may cause selective encoding that interferes with accurate identification (Naka, Itsukushima, & Itoh, 1996).

Errors in eyewitness identification are particularly likely when the police lineup is not properly composed (Wells, 1993). Fillers are individuals whom the police do not regard as suspects in the crime. If the fillers selected do not match the general description of the suspect given by the eyewitness prior to the lineup, then they do not serve as useful control cases. In the most extreme case, suppose that in a six-person lineup the five fillers look nothing at all like the person described by the witness. If an innocent suspect is the only one in the lineup who fits the description, then chances of misidentification are strong. Experiments using staged crimes have shown that misidentifications can exceed 90% when conditions at the time of the crime plus conditions at the time of the lineup conspire against the eyewitness.

The problem of misidentification in lineups is particularly acute when the witness and suspect are of different racial and ethnic backgrounds (Wells & Olson, 2001). For example, Asians recognize other Asians better than they recognize Caucasians, and the reverse relation also holds for Caucasians. One explanation for this finding is that people attend more to the faces of people of their own race than they do to the faces of people of different races (Anthony, Copper, & Mullen, 1992; Chance & Goldstein, 1981).

The Misinformation Effect

Work by Loftus and her colleagues has shown that the questions asked of eyewitnesses after an event can potentially influence their memory. When the questions contain misleading information, they may distort memory, a finding called the **misinformation effect.** For example, Loftus and Palmer (1974) presented people with a film of a traffic accident and then questioned them, as might an investigator or an attorney, about what they had witnessed. One of several questions asked was "How fast were the cars going when they *hit* each other?"

In the various conditions of the experiment, the verb "hit" was replaced by more or less violent words, as shown in Figure 7.8. Later on in the experiment, the participants gave estimates of how fast the cars were traveling when the accident occurred. The results showed that the average speed estimate varied in direct relation to the wording of the question. By using the word "smashed," the interrogator apparently distorted the participants' memory representation of the accident, causing people to give high estimates of vehicle speed.

Moreover, a week later, new questions were posed such as "Did you see broken glass?" In fact, no broken glass appeared in the film, and 80% of the participants correctly answered no to this question. Yet most of those who

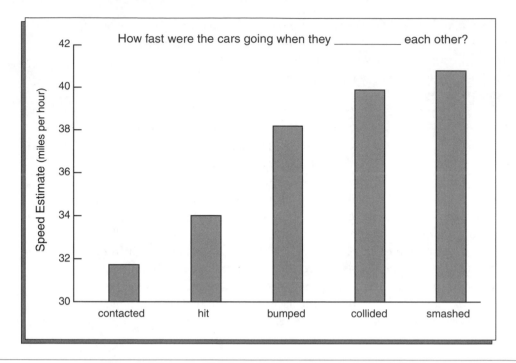

Figure 7.8. Data illustrating the misinformation effect.

SOURCE: Loftus and Palmer (1974).

answered yes were in the condition that had been asked about the cars smashing into each other. As time wore on, the leading question continued to shape the nature of the recollection.

The misinformation effect can be strikingly large. Loftus, Miller, and Burns (1978) showed people a series of slides portraying an accident in which a red car stops at an intersection, turns the corner, and hits a pedestrian. Some participants saw a yield sign at the intersection but were asked either 20 minutes or a week later whether a second car passed the red car "while it was stopped at the stop sign." Loftus et al. administered a recognition test after providing the misleading information that required participants to say which of a pair of slides had been part of the accident series. The key pair showed the red car at either a stop sign or a yield sign. When the misinformation occurred 20 minutes after the accident, the participants incorrectly picked the stop sign about 60% of the time. This rose to 80% when the misleading question occurred after a week.

The misinformation effect refers to distortions in memory created by misleading information introduced through the questions used by an interrogator of a witness.

Implanted Memories

In eyewitness interrogation procedures, it is not uncommon to repeatedly suggest to a suspect that he or she was involved in the crime. Memory implantation refers to an individual creating a false memory in the mind of another person by means of suggestions and questions about the imagined event. Is it possible to implant false memories in the mind of a confused, tired, and fearful suspect? Loftus and Pickrell (1995) discovered that memory implantation is in fact theoretically possible by intermixing true and false information. Adults were told by a close family member about three true events from their past plus one false event that they supposedly had experienced when they were between 4 and 6 years of age (e.g., getting lost in a shopping mall). The researchers found that some of the participants indeed began to recall, from the suggestion alone, that they had been lost in a mall. Indeed, a few provided explicit accounts of how terrifying they found the experience to be. The false recollections in some cases grew more detailed over time. Zaragoza and Mitchell (1996) found that repetitions of the suggestion increased the chances of participants consciously recollecting the false event as actually having occurred. Thus, it is indeed possible to implant a memory, at least in laboratory circumstances, and the effects of repeated exposure to suggestions can be consistent across individuals and persistent over time.

The risk of memory implantation may be especially high for children because of their suggestibility (Ceci & Bruck, 1993, 1995). Laboratory research indicates that preschool-aged children are especially vulnerable to suggestion as compared with older children and adults. But clinical psychologists who specialize in working with abused children contend that such findings do not apply to important actions, particularly those involving a personal bodily experience. It is common for experts in clinical psychology, social work, and psychiatry to testify in court that children do not lie about events as traumatic as bodily abuse and could not be falsely led to believe abuse occurred through suggestion. Whereas young children may be highly suggestible regarding unimportant peripheral events, there is reason to doubt that they are equally suggestible when it comes to sexual abuse.

Ceci, Leichtman, Putnick, and Nightingale (1993), however, reported that a false memory of having been kissed during a bath can indeed be planted in the mind of a young child. In an anatomical doll study, nearly a quarter to a third of 3-year-olds inaccurately answered abuse questions such as "Did he touch your private parts?" and "How many times did he spank you?" (Goodman & Aman, 1990). Such findings may imply that suggestion has led to a false memory, but Ceci and Bruck (1993, 1995) noted that children might also lie for social reasons (e.g., avoiding punishment, game playing, personal gain). Even so, Ceci, Crossman, Gilstrap, and Scullin (1998) reported seven experiments showing that the suggestibility of young children is not constricted to a single domain of unimportant peripheral events. They demonstrated their suggestibility about embarrassing genital touching and painful events from checkups at a pediatrician's office. Ceci et al. concluded that "there is no event domain that is impervious to the deleterious effects of suggestions, especially when they are repeatedly delivered over long retention intervals" (p. 29).

Recovered Memories

The tabloid press frequently reports cases of seemingly sane individuals who recall being abducted by aliens and taken aboard unidentified flying objects (UFOs), living past lives as other persons, being sexually abused during satanic rituals, or witnessing cannibalism of children (Loftus & Ketcham, 1994). From a scientific viewpoint, such reports are difficult to accept as anything other than false because they are so bizarre and implausible. How, then, might they be understood? One reasonable explanation is that such recollections are delusional false memories instilled through sociocultural mechanisms (Spanos, 1996). A **delusional false memory** is one in which an individual with strong beliefs that a bizarre event can occur comes to actually experience a memory of the event. It is not well-understood how a delusional belief originates, but the culture and social circles of the individual play a role, according to Spanos (1996). Suggestions coming from the sensational stories covered in tabloid journalism, bizarre stories reported on television, and statements made by friends, family, and oneself implant a delusional memory, much as occurs under the effects of hypnosis.

Consider stories about encounters with a UFO, for example. Betty Hill was an avid believer in UFOs before the night that she and her husband, Barney, claimed to see a strange light following their car (Klass, 1989). Betty's sister suggested that she and her husband may have been "irradiated" by the light, and soon Betty began to have nightmares in which she and Barney were abducted by aliens who took them on board a UFO, communicated with them telepathically, performed medical tests, and showed Betty a star map. A psychotherapist who treated Betty for her nightmares was able to elicit detailed reports of these events under hypnosis from both her and Barney, who had heard these accounts from his wife numerous times. The psychotherapist concluded that the reports were delusional false memories shared by the couple. Such false memories, then, are likely similar to confabulations but differ in that the individuals do not suffer from lesions in prefrontal cortical regions. The power of their belief system constructs the delusional memories (Koppelman, 1999).

Repression. During the 1990s, numerous allegations of child abuse were reported by the victims as adults, years after the incidents had taken place. These forgotten memories of abuse sometimes surface while an adult is in therapy for severe emotional distress and an inability to cope with daily life (Olio, 1989). A famous case involved Eileen Franklin's recovered memory that her father, George, not only sexually abused her and her sisters but also abused and murdered her best friend 20 years earlier (MacLean, 1993). A clinician testified that Eileen had recovered a repressed memory of the murder. The trauma of the murder had caused Eileen to repress the memory throughout her childhood, according to the testimony in the trial. The defense cited the laboratory evidence that misleading questions and other factors can cause distortions in memory. The jury convicted George Franklin of murder. He served 5 years behind bars before his conviction was reviewed by an appeals court and overturned on the grounds that Eileen's recollections were probably false memories.

Therapists working with individuals who experience recovered memories typically have attributed these individuals' forgetting to repression. **Repression** is a defense mechanism that, in psychoanalytic theory, protects the ego from anxiety by preventing unpleasant memories from entering consciousness. Repression might not be the right mechanism to explain how such powerful memories are forgotten, but some kind of trauma-based amnesia could be at work.

Another possibility suggested by memory researchers and, of interest, by Freud himself is that supposedly lost and then recovered memories of sexual and other abuse are false memories. They may reflect the reconstructive processes of schemas, leading one to recall vividly events that never transpired. We have seen that strong laboratory evidence shows that false memories are possible. As always, however, it is important to evaluate whether such findings are ecologically valid. False memories can indeed occur about a wide variety of everyday events that we hear or read about as well as those we personally experience (Neisser & Libby, 2000). Whether events as traumatic as child abuse can be falsely remembered is less certain. But it is certainly possible that suggestions from therapists and others may serve as misleading information, prompting the reconstruction of false memories.

> Recovered memories may reflect either the retrieval of a previously repressed event or an inaccurately reconstructed false memory.

A vocal debate over these issues has divided the therapeutic community and the academic research community (Lindsay & Read, 1994). Therapists, for their part, have generally maintained that the trauma of rape or other forms of child abuse can indeed produce amnesia for the events. Through the course of psychotherapy, the victim recovers these forgotten events as part of the healing process. Academic researchers, on the other hand, have generally argued that trauma-induced amnesia is rarely if ever the correct explanation. The recollections brought to consciousness are far more likely to be false memories inadvertently induced by the suggestions and practices of the therapist. The therapeutic techniques used to help an individual often include memory work; the individual regresses to an earlier age under hypnosis, receives sexually suggestive questions or dream interpretations from the therapist, or tries to remember childhood events while drugged with sodium amytal. The therapist tries to break through the defense mechanism of repression with these techniques. The client is not consciously trying to suppress thinking about the traumatic event. Rather, the client has no recollection of the event even occurring, although the trauma may be causing him or her anxiety or depression or may be responsible for an eating disorder, a sleep disorder, alcohol or drug abuse, or other significant difficulties. Abuse as a child is horribly traumatic, and so repression as well as conscious efforts to forget about the event are anticipated by the therapist (Olio, 1989).

The problem is that sound empirical evidence that adults can forget traumatic events for years and then recover them accurately is thin (Loftus, 1993; Spanos, 1996). Traumatic memories are notoriously difficult to suppress consciously and are a defining feature of posttraumatic stress syndrome. Victims recall trauma all too easily and frequently, possibly as a way of coping with what has happened to them. In some cases, traumatic memories are stored in a fragmented form that is susceptible to being forgotten (Shimamura, 1997). However, in these circumstances the memory fragments are highly susceptible to distortions and inaccuracies if they are reconstructed later. Thus, the repression and subsequent accurate recovery of sexual abuse is unlikely. This does not mean, however, that it is impossible. Some cases have been substantiated in which prior abuse was apparently forgotten and later recovered (Schooler, Bendiksen, & Ambadar, 1997).

Hypnosis and other techniques of recovered memory therapy have the strong potential of convincingly suggesting events that might never have taken place (Spanos, 1996). Normally, adults can monitor reality so as to draw a clear line between events stemming from memory and those generated in fantasy (Johnson, 1988), but this line can be tragically erased in so-called recovered memory cases by the methods of therapy itself (Loftus, 1993). In some cases, the clients later came to realize that the recollections of sexual abuse uncovered through the practices of therapy were in fact false memories. The lives of everyone involved were shattered by the false accusations.

Trauma-Induced Amnesia. Recovered memory is not the only possible response to a real traumatic experience. According to Yuille and Daylen (1998), the impact of trauma on memory may well be complex, affecting different individuals in different ways. The research to date has focused primarily on how stress narrows attention, affecting the initial encoding of the event. But another possible response is a dissociation of consciousness, producing **trauma-induced amnesia.** This could cause the victim to experience the trauma as if it were happening to someone else or to travel mentally to a different place and time to psychologically avoid the trauma altogether. Dissociation may also affect the storage and retrieval phase by causing amnesia for events that were at one time remembered. Trauma-induced amnesia is rare, but cases have been documented (Schacter & Kihlstrom, 1989).

> Trauma-induced amnesia is a rare kind of dissociated consciousness. The victim experiences the trauma as if it were happening to someone else or psychologically avoids the trauma by mentally traveling to a different place and time.

Conclusions. As illustrated in Figure 7.9, there are several possible causes of recovered memories and different possible responses to traumatic events. As noted in Path A, one may remember the trauma all along or possibly repress the memory for a period of time before it is recovered (Path B). Another possible response to trauma is to forget the event altogether as a result of a dissociation of consciousness at the time of encoding (Path C). As shown in Path D, a recovered memory might also be false, the result of a belief that an event occurred (dotted line) rather than a perception of the event (solid line). Confabulation, misinformation, and memory implantation are possible sources of such false beliefs.

There are two important conclusions to draw from the controversy surrounding recovered memories. First, therapies used in clinical practice must be critically examined to make certain that they do no harm. A technique may promise benefits, but these must always be weighed against its costs. Second, the ecological validity of laboratory studies on false memory must also be critically examined in drawing conclusions. The laboratory research demonstrates that false memories are real and help to explain the experiences of patients in therapy. But this does not mean that trauma-induced amnesia never occurs or that forgotten trauma never resurfaces in or out of therapy. It is difficult, if not impossible, to examine in the laboratory the effects of severe physical or psychological trauma on human memory. The experiences of individuals who have been raped, beaten, shot at, or otherwise traumatized in real life can never in principle be evaluated in laboratory settings for ethical reasons. Field and case studies of assault victims, combat veterans, and concentration camp survivors may offer insights into such effects, but they are never as definitive as well-controlled laboratory experiments.

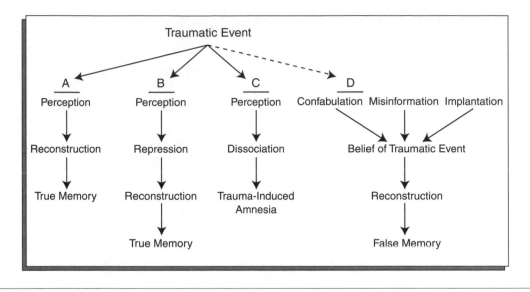

Figure 7.9. Four possible scenarios for the recollection of a traumatic event.

SUMMARY

1. Schemas shape how events are retrieved from long-term memory. A schema is a set of organized concepts that provides expectations about the world. Just as schemas guide human pattern recognition from the top down, conceptually driven processes also guide the reconstruction of events from memory. As a result, details of an event may be dropped from recollection, a process called leveling. Details may also be assimilated or normalized so as to fit the expectations provided by the schema. Finally, a schema-based reconstruction of an event may also sharpen details, elaborating a point by using general knowledge about the world rather than information actually encoded and stored.

2. Schemas also influence what is encoded and stored in episodic memory, causing memory distortions. They establish expectations that result in selection of the features of events that are encoded in the first place. Schemas also constructively guide the encoding of events through a process of interpretation. Inferences are drawn at the time of encoding as well as during reconstructive retrieval. Finally, schemas influence encoding through integration, which means that features of different events are combined into a unified memory representation. As a result of integration, we remember the main idea or gist of events rather than the details of their occurrence.

3. Source monitoring refers to evaluative processes that attribute mental experiences to different sources. External sources are perceived events in the

environment, whereas internal sources are thoughts, fantasies, and dreams. A laboratory demonstration of a memory illusion shows that after a list of words closely associated to a target word is viewed, the target itself is falsely remembered as being on the list. In the illusion, the target word is activated internally but is incorrectly attributed to an external source. Normally, source monitoring processes enable us to easily differentiate between a fantasy and a real memory. These processes break down in Korsakoff's syndrome, which is associated with chronic alcoholism. The patient makes up false memories out of thin air. Confabulations appear as spontaneous outpourings of recollections that the patient cannot control and cannot monitor as false.

4. The constructive and reconstructive properties of human memory have important implications for our legal system. The reliability of eyewitness testimony has been studied extensively. Selective encoding, misleading questions used by interrogators, and the implantation of memories through hypnosis and therapy have been shown to distort recall in laboratory settings. The ecological validity of this research has been challenged. In particular, there is still considerable controversy over whether traumatic events, such as sexual abuse, can produce amnesia for an event that is later recovered. The suggestibility and credibility of young children as witnesses, or of adults who have recovered supposedly repressed memories of sexual abuse, are at the center of this debate.

KEY TERMS ●

reconstructive retrieval
leveling
assimilation
sharpening
selection
interpretation
integration
source monitoring

false verbal memory
conjunction error
confabulation
misinformation effect
delusional false memory
repression
trauma-induced amnesia

CHAPTER 8

SEMANTIC MEMORY

Factual and conceptual knowledge constitutes a key ingredient in speaking and listening, in reading and writing, and in problem solving and thinking. Without an ability to acquire, represent, and use knowledge about the world and its meaningful symbols, high-level forms of human cognition would not be possible. It is through semantic memory that we categorize the world, allowing us to ignore the details and to see a specific object as a general kind. Lakoff (1987) aptly underscored the importance of categorization as follows:

> There is nothing more basic than categorization to our thought, perception, action, and speech. Every time we see something as a *kind* of thing, for example, a tree, we are categorizing. Whenever we reason about *kinds* of things—chairs, nations, illnesses, emotions, any kind of thing at all—we are employing categories. Whenever we intentionally perform any *kind* of action, say something as mundane as writing with a pencil, hammering with a hammer, or ironing clothes, we are using categories. The particular action we perform on that occasion is a *kind* of motor activity. . . . They are never done in exactly the same way . . ., yet . . . we know how to make movements of that kind. Any time we

either produce or understand any utterance of any reasonable length, we are employing dozens if not hundreds of categories: categories of speech sounds, of words, or phrases and clauses, as well as conceptual categories. Without the ability to categorize, we could not function at all, whether in the physical world or in our social and intellectual lives. (pp. 5-6)

In this chapter, the fundamental questions about the representation of knowledge in semantic memory are examined. First, the nature of concepts and how they are mentally represented is considered. Second, the question of whether concrete images are represented differently from abstract conceptual knowledge is weighed. Third, some models of how people use semantic memory to answer simple factual questions are presented.

REPRESENTING CONCEPTS •

Concepts are the general ideas that enable the categorization of unique stimuli as related to one another. The concept of a tree, for example, allows for considerable variations in the individual examples of trees that fit the general idea. A tree concept includes a set of variable dimensions, such as the types of roots, trunks, branches, and leaves, that may be instantiated in a large number of ways. Many unique trees all fit the general concept. The stimuli categorized may be concrete objects or abstract ideas. Mathematical, (e.g., imaginary numbers), philosophical (e.g., free will), and psychological (e.g., depression) concepts are among those that group together highly abstract entities.

Rule-Governed Concepts

The classical approach to categorization assumed that concepts are defined by a set of singly necessary and jointly sufficient features. In other words, the defining features of a concept were governed by a conjunctive rule stating that each and every feature must be present for an object to fit the concept. For example, the concept of a cow could be understood in terms of the features animate, four-legged, hoofed, female, adult, and other distinctive features that set the object apart from, say, a buffalo. **Rule-governed concepts** specify the features and relations that define membership in the class on an all-or-none basis (Bourne, 1970; Bruner, Goodnow, & Austin, 1956). The classical view of categorization regarded all concepts as rule-governed.

Some abstract concepts can be viewed as rule-governed. The definitions of real numbers, gravity, grand larceny, and a touchdown in American football can be specified by mathematicians, physicists, lawyers, or referees, for example. A football carried by the runner so that it crosses the vertical plane above the goal line of the opponent without being dropped is a touchdown. This is not to say that reasonable people cannot argue whether a particular play in question resulted in a touchdown, but rules of football spell out the concept unambiguously. Fans may disagree over the features of the play, but not over the concept itself.

Not all abstract concepts fit the classical view very well, however (Lakoff & Johnson, 1980). For example, what are the defining features of truth or justice? Moreover, it became clear that the objects encountered every day in the environment also do not belong to rule-governed concepts (Rosch & Mervis, 1975; Smith & Medin, 1981).

Object Concepts

Object concepts refer to natural kinds or biological objects and artifacts or human-made objects. They are often organized hierarchically. The hierarchy of subordinate (robin), basic (bird), and superordinate (animal) concepts illustrates this point for natural kinds (Rosch, Mervis, Gray, Johnson, & Boyes-Braem, 1976). A claw-hammer, hammer, and tool illustrate the same point for artifacts.

In contrast to rule-governed concepts, there did not appear to be any set of defining features for object concepts. The philosopher Ludwig Wittgenstein was the first to articulate that some linguistic categories seemed to defy the classical description by lacking defining features. For instance, take the concept of a game. As Lakoff (1987) observed,

> Some games involve mere amusement, like ring-around-the-rosy. Here there is no competition—no winning or losing—though in other games there is. Some games involve luck, like board games where a throw of the dice determines each move. Others, like chess, involve skill. Still others, like gin rummy, involve both. (p. 16)

Games do involve a family resemblance to one another. Each member shares some features in common with other members, but no set of defining features are common to all. Rather, what makes games a category is that the examples show similarities to one another in a wide variety of ways. Object concepts are ill-defined in that it is difficult to decide whether or not a particular poor example falls within the legitimate range of membership.

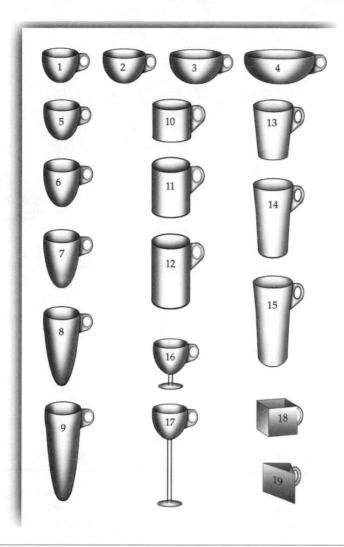

Figure 8.1. The boundary of the object concept of cup is fuzzy.
SOURCE: Labov (1973).

The fuzzy boundary of class membership can be readily seen from the results of Labov (1973), who presented people with the cup-like objects seen in Figure 8.1. Exactly at what point does an object cease to be a cup and become a bowl, a glass, or a mug? For instance, the first four items varied in terms of the ratio of the width of the cup to its depth. In the context of thinking about food, Labov's results showed that the probability of calling the object a bowl increased gradually—not abruptly—as this ratio increased.

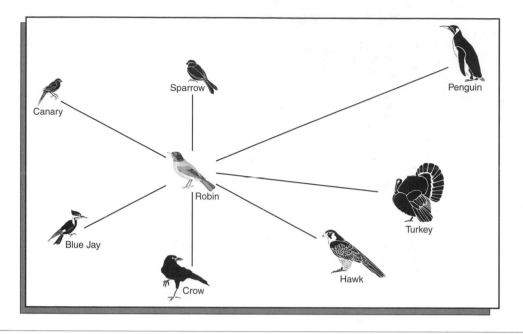

Figure 8.2. Typicality of members in a basic-level category.

Similarly, the probability of calling the object a cup decreased gradually, but for middle ratios both responses often occurred, reflecting the fuzzy boundary of membership. In a neutral context, the cup response became less likely, but people were more reluctant to call Item 3 or 4 a bowl. This difference in judgment with context shows the flexible boundary of object concepts; it shifts depending on which other concepts are active in memory.

An object differs from other members of a concept in terms of its features and the frequency of occurrence of these features in the category (Attneave, 1957). For example, birds differ from one another in terms of size, color, shape of wings, and so on. The range and frequency of occurrence of these features is represented as well, such that one recognizes a turkey as a very large rare bird, whereas a sparrow is more common in terms of its features. The **prototype** is the best or most typical member of a category and serves as an important mental representation of the concept. Moving away from the prototype, there is a gradient of membership. At least for residents of North America, the robin assumes the role of prototype for the bird concept (see Figure 8.2). The turkey lies far out on the gradient from the prototype, whereas the blue jay and sparrow lie closer. The canary or the hawk falls in between these extreme cases.

Table 8.1   Typicality of Members in Superordinate-Level Categories

				Category		
Item	*Furniture*	*Vehicle*	*Fruit*	*Weapon*	*Vegetable*	*Clothing*
1	Chair	Car	Orange	Gun	Peas	Pants
2	Sofa	Truck	Apple	Knife	Carrots	Shirt
3	Table	Bus	Banana	Sword	String beans	Dress
4	Dresser	Motorcycle	Peach	Bomb	Spinach	Skirt
5	Desk	Train	Pear	Hand grenade	Broccoli	Jacket
6	Bed	Trolley car	Apricot	Spear	Asparagus	Coat
7	Bookcase	Bicycle	Plum	Cannon	Corn	Sweater
8	Footstool	Airplane	Grape	Bow and arrow	Cauliflower	Underpants
9	Lamp	Boat	Strawberry	Club	Brussels sprouts	Socks
10	Piano	Tractor	Grapefruit	Tank	Lettuce	Pajamas
11	Cushion	Cart	Pineapple	Tear gas	Beets	Bathing suit
12	Mirror	Wheelchair	Blueberry	Whip	Tomato	Shoes
13	Rug	Tank	Lemon	Ice pick	Lima beans	Vest
14	Radio	Raft	Watermelon	Fists	Eggplant	Tie
15	Stove	Sled	Honeydew	Rocket	Onion	Mittens
16	Clock	Horse	Pomegranate	Poison	Potato	Hat
17	Picture	Blimp	Date	Scissors	Yam	Apron
18	Closet	Skates	Coconut	Words	Mushroom	Purse
19	Vase	Wheelbarrow	Tomato	Foot	Pumpkin	Wristwatch
20	Telephone	Elevator	Olive	Screwdriver	Rice	Necklace

SOURCE: Rosch and Mervis (1975).

Rosch and Mervis (1975) asked people to rapidly list all the features they could think of for a variety of common objects. The objects fit the superordinate categories of furniture (e.g., chair, piano, telephone), vehicle (e.g., car, tractor, elevator), fruit (e.g., orange, grapefruit, olive), weapon (e.g., gun, tank, screwdriver), vegetable (e.g., peas, lettuce, rice), or clothing (e.g., pants, pajamas, necklace). A total of 20 objects per category were used, and they clearly varied in typicality, as can be seen from the examples (see Table 8.1).

The key outcome was that few features applied to all 20 objects. Those few that were common to all failed to distinguish the category from numerous other natural categories (e.g., "You eat it" was listed for all fruits, yet this applies to all foodstuffs). What defined the category was not a small set of defining features but rather a large number of features that applied to some, but not all, instances. Rosch and Mervis (1975) referred to this as the **family resemblance structure** of object concepts. The researchers computed a family resemblance score that reflected the sum of the frequency with which features applied to all instances of the category. They found that this family resemblance score correlated strongly with ratings of typicality. Thus, orange and apple achieve high typicality ratings in the fruit category because they exhibit features that occur frequently among all members of the category. Tomato and olive are given low typicality ratings because their features are not characteristic of most fruits.

The speed with which people categorize an example varies with how close it is to, or how far it is from, the prototype. One can correctly categorize a robin as a bird faster than one can a crow, which in turn can be categorized faster than can a turkey (Rosch, 1975). The order in which children learn the members of a category also depends on their typicality. Highly typical instances are acquired sooner than are atypical instances (Rosch, 1973). The **typicality effect** refers to the gradient of category membership or differences in how well specific instances represent a concept.

> Object concepts have fuzzy boundaries and a gradient of category membership, with some instances more typical than others.

Concepts as Theories. Object concepts are also coherent in that they are integrated with other concepts through theories about how the world is structured. Put differently, a concept is embedded in and consistent with people's background knowledge and folk theories (Keil, 1989; Medin & Ortony, 1989; Murphy & Medin, 1985). For example, a person's knowledge and intuitions about biology dovetail with the concept of a bird. If a person believes that birds breathe, eat, and reproduce, then these abstract theoretical constraints would lead one to reject a robotic manufactured robin as not really being a robin. It may look and act exactly like a robin, but if the person knows it is not an animate object, then it fails to fit the concept.

A concept can be coherent even when there are no obvious perceptual or functional similarities among its instances. For example, what are the similarities that put children, money, photo albums, and pets in the same category? Without considering how the concept is embedded in a person's knowledge about the world, this makes no sense at all. However, in the context of things to take out of the house in case of a fire, individuals are able to list these and other examples without difficulty (Barsalou, 1983). In this case, then, the concept is coherent only by considering, in relation to the nature of fires, the importance of personal property and related world knowledge.

Similarity to perceptual and functional features, then, provides only part of the story of how human categorization works. Deeper, less accessible, theory-based features about the internal structure of natural kinds of objects (e.g., the genetic structure of a dog) constrain our categorizations as well as surface features (Gelman, 1988; Keil, 1989). The representation of a dog in semantic memory includes a theory about the internal structure of the organism. It is this internal structure that really makes a dog a dog. The functional uses of a dog (e.g., hunting) are less relevant to its classification, but functional uses are absolutely critical for artifacts such as a cup (e.g., drinking). Barton and Komatsu (1989) gave participants descriptions of objects that were either natural kinds or artifacts. The researchers changed either the internal molecular structure (e.g., a goat with altered chromosomes, a tire not made of rubber) or the functional features (e.g., a female goat not giving milk, a tire that cannot roll) of the examples to see how these different types of features affected categorizations. They discovered that changes in molecular structure were most important for natural kinds (e.g., a goat with altered chromosomes is not really a goat), whereas the opposite was true for artifacts (e.g., a tire that cannot roll is not really a tire).

Artifacts and natural kinds may be differentiated at a neural level of representation. Patients with associative agnosia can have highly specific losses in their ability to make semantic categorizations. For example, one patient, "J.B.R.," lost the ability to identify the names of objects of living things, such as dogs and horses, but had little trouble with inanimate objects, such as umbrellas and chairs (Warrington & Shallice, 1984). Recall from Chapter 2 that the temporal lobe serves as the termination point for the lateral "what" pathway involved in object recognition. Patients with lesions in different regions of the temporal lobe experience deficits in naming particular categories of objects (Damasio, Grabowski, Tranel, Hichwa, & Damasio, 1996). As shown in Figure 8.3, damage to the anterior region of the temporal cortex causes problems in naming the faces of famous people. Damage to the inferotemporal cortex, along the lower region, is associated with problems in naming animals. Lastly, naming tools was problematic for patients with lesions near the intersection of the temporal, occipital, and parietal lobes.

Schemas

As discussed in earlier chapters, a schema is a cognitive structure that organizes related concepts and integrates past events. We saw that schemas are important in understanding the constructive aspects of perception and memory. Researchers have delineated specific kinds of schemas in developing theories of knowledge representation. For example, **frames** are schemas that represent the physical structure of the environment. Minsky (1977) proposed the term in his theoretical analysis of the perception of a complex visual scene such as a room or the office considered in Chapter 7. Besides perception, frames are used in generating mental maps of the environment and other forms of remembering and imagining. The essence of a frame is a detailed structural description that specifies the concepts and the relations among concepts that define a given physical environment.

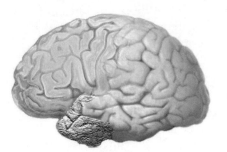

Famous People

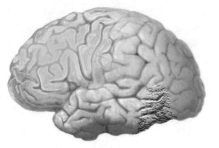

Tools

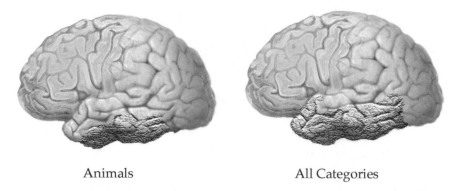

Animals

All Categories

Figure 8.3. Regions in the temporal lobe are associated with representations of specific semantic categories.

Scripts are schemas that represent routine activities (Abelson, 1981; Mandler, 1984). They are usually sequential in nature and often involve social interactions. Schank and Abelson (1977) described the restaurant script to illustrate this class. Each script specifies a theme (eating in a restaurant), typical roles (customer and waiter), entry conditions (hungry customer), and a sequence of scenes and actions within scenes (ordering [which involves getting a menu], reading a menu, etc.). Cantor, Mischel, and Schwartz (1982) studied common social situations and found that they are organized in a stereotypical manner. People can readily describe a prototypical blind date or job interview, for instance.

The sequential nature of many scripts affects their use in perception and memory. Barsalou and Sewell (1985) asked people to recall scenes from a script or examples from an object concept in order of typicality, from the most representative to the least representative. In the case of a script (how to write a letter), recall proceeded at a steady rate, as if the people searched memory in an orderly sequential fashion. By contrast, in the case of an object

Frames and scripts organize conceptual knowledge about the physical environment and routine activities, respectively.

concept (tool), recall started at a rapid rate, as people quickly retrieved prototypical examples, and then slowed progressively.

Meta-representations

So far, semantic memory has been discussed as a system for faithfully representing reality through object representations. However, it is known that during the second year of life, an infant learns to pretend by deliberately distorting reality in play situations. Because the semantic memory system is just beginning its development at this young age, why does the ability to distort reality in mental representations not stand in the way of development? It seems odd from an evolutionary standpoint if the sole goal in cognitive development were to represent reality as accurately as possible. However, another goal appears to be laying the foundation for creative thought, which requires the flexibility to distort reality to see the world in different ways. But how is all of this accomplished?

Leslie (1987) discovered that the development of meta-representations underlie the ability to pretend. A **meta-representation** is a mental representation of another mental representation. Through a meta-representation, one can think about another thought. Primary representations of objects and events in the real world must be accurate and literally correct. Otherwise, primary representations would not help individuals to adapt to their environment. When a toddler pretends that a banana is a telephone, for example, he or she must have a meta-representation that links or equates the primary representations of the two objects. Otherwise, the child's primary representations of a banana and a telephone would be distorted right at the time when the child is coming to learn about different objects and their names in the world. By using a meta-representation, the meanings of banana and telephone are not changed, but the child can still pretend that they are the same object for a period of time. Meta-representations are adaptive because they add a high degree of flexibility and creativity to cognition.

At about the same age, children figure out when others are pretending as well. For example, if a child sees his or her mother pretending that a banana is a telephone, then the child's learning to represent the concept of a telephone could go seriously astray. Unless the child can represent that the mother is using a meta-representation that temporarily links banana and telephone, the child might well come to think of bananas and telephones as literally the same. Instead, the child is learning to mentally represent the mental states of other humans. The child realizes that the mother is only pretending. Understanding that other humans possess mental states is yet another adaptive function.

Premack and Woodruff (1978) coined the term "theory of mind" to refer to the human ability to infer that others, like ourselves, have mental states. Pretending appears to be critical in development of meta-representations and a theory of mind. Even though a theory of mind is beginning to develop at 2 years of age, it requires more pretend play and the development of reasoning ability for it to fully emerge (Leslie, 1987). But by 4 years of age, children can do complex reason using meta-representations. They can, for example, predict the consequences of another person having a false belief. Suppose that Mary hides some candy in a box and then leaves the room (see Figure 8.4). Barbara then moves the candy to a basket without Mary seeing this. Now, where will Mary look for the candy?

Baron-Cohen, Leslie, and Frith (1985) found that young toddlers mistakenly think that Mary, the hider, will know that the candy had been moved from the box to the basket. By 4 years of age, however, the child can appreciate that Mary has a false mental representation of the situation and will look in the box where she left the candy.

These developments in meta-representations may reflect the maturation of an innate theory of mind module (Baron-Cohen, 1995). Failure to develop this module leads to a condition called **mindblindness,** which refers to an inability to understand that other people possess mental representations. Mindblindness is a feature of autism, a kind of mental retardation caused by brain abnormalities present at birth. Autistic children are unable to understand the role that mental states play in predicting another person's behavior or even recognizing that other people are experiencing emotions. Autistic children treat other people as if they were objects—robots without feelings and thoughts. Failures in social communication are a major feature of autism, and they seem to arise because of mindblindness.

● PROPOSITIONS AND IMAGES

The format of knowledge representations may be a concrete, perceptual-like imaginal code or an abstract, verbal-like propositional code.

So far, we have discussed mental representations without concern for their nature. Exactly how is declarative knowledge coded in the mind? What is its format? One possibility is a perceptual format. An **imaginal code** is a concrete means of mental representation that directly conveys perceptual qualities. However, it is also possible that the images we experience in perceiving or imagining are themselves reducible to an abstract, verbal-like format. A **propositional code** is an abstract means of mental representation that is schematic and verbal rather than perceptual. To illustrate, consider the concept of a bird. Shown in Panel (a) of Figure 8.5 is an imaginal representation of a robin, the prototype of the category. The prototype can also be represented as a propositional code, as illustrated in Panel (b).

Mary hides the candy in a box.

Mary goes away.

Barbara moves the candy to the basket.

Where will Mary look for her candy?

Figure 8.4. A task for studying the development of meta-representations and a theory of mind.

Identifying precisely how visual, auditory, and other kinds of images are mentally represented and neurally coded by the brain, however, has been an ongoing and difficult challenge (Kolers, 1983). Some have argued that images are actually based in propositional representations to which one does not have conscious access (Pylyshyn, 1981). On the other hand, some evidence

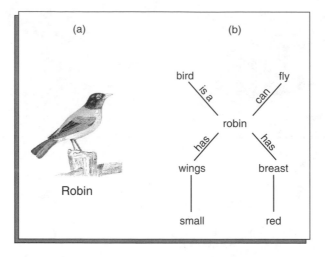

Figure 8.5. An imaginal and a propositional code for the concept of a robin.

clearly suggests that visual images behave like perceptions, not propositions. The key distinction is that visual images possess a spatial or analog quality that cannot in principle be explained in terms of an abstract, propositional, or verbal representation.

The Nature of Images

Shepard and his colleagues pioneered the study of visual images with an extensive series of experiments on mental rotation (Metzler & Shepard, 1974; Shepard & Cooper, 1983; Shepard & Metzler, 1971). The researchers presented people with pictures of three-dimensional objects such as those shown in Figure 8.6. They presented a pair of objects and asked the viewers to decide whether the objects were identical except for their orientation. For example, compare the two objects in Panel (a). Are they the same or different? By mentally rotating the object on the left, you can verify that it in fact matches the object on the right. In Panel (b), a same response is again called for after rotating the figure. However, in Panel (c), the left object can be rotated 360 degrees and it will still not match the right object. Thus, this trial calls for a different response.

Shepard and his colleagues systematically varied the angle of rotation required to determine that the pair of objects is the same. They reasoned that if mental images are like real objects in the mind's eye, then the time required to make a same/different decision ought to increase as a linear function of the angle of rotation. If instead the decision is based on a propositional

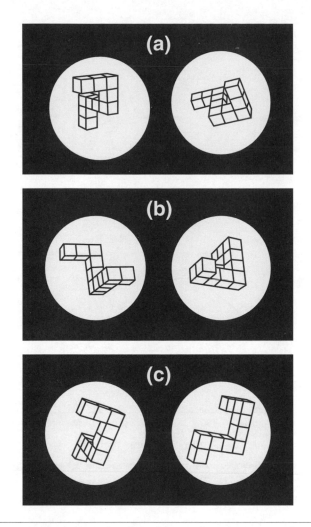

Figure 8.6. Try to mentally rotate the left object of each pair so that it matches the right object.

SOURCE: Shepard and Metzler (1971).

representation of the objects, then a rotation of 180 degrees should be no slower than one of 90 or 45 degrees. In each case, the degrees of rotation would simply be a variable in one of propositional arguments (e.g., left object, clockwise rotation, picture plane, 180 degrees). Their results are illustrated in Figure 8.7 (Shepard & Metzler, 1971). Decision times increased as a linear function of the angle of rotation. Thus, there is a striking resemblance between rotating a real object and rotating a mental representation of that object. The images behave in manner analogous to the real objects.

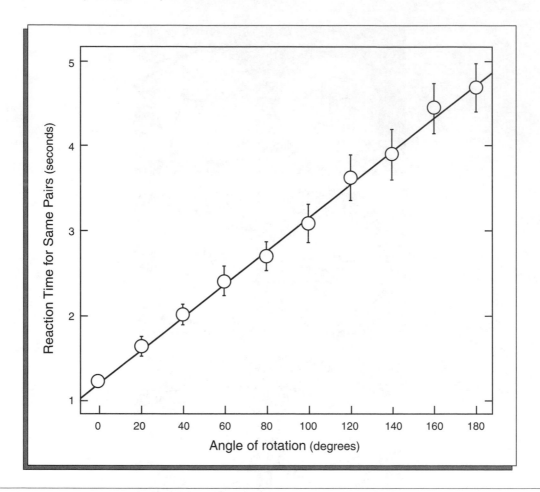

Figure 8.7. Mental rotation time increases with the degrees of rotation required to judge the objects as the same.

SOURCE: Shepard and Metzler (1971).

Analog Properties. Kosslyn (1980, 1981) and his colleagues explored the analog aspect of mental imagery in detail. For example, Kosslyn (1975) showed that the time to scan a mental image depended on "how far" one must scan. Participants memorized a picture of an object, such as a boat, as shown in Figure 8.8. They were then instructed to visualize the object and to scan the mental image to find a feature from a particular starting point. They pressed a button as soon as they "found it" in the image. The results showed that in scanning an image of the boat from the left, it took longer to find the anchor

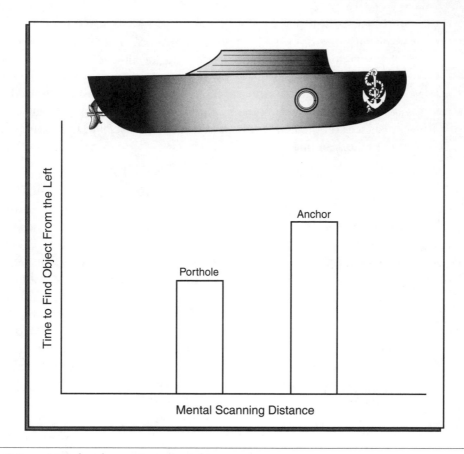

Figure 8.8. A study of scanning mental images.

SOURCE: Adapted from Kosslyn (1973).

than it did to find the porthole. Just as the time to scan the picture would take longer with the greater real distance, the same result applied to the mental scan time as well.

Similarly, small images are harder to scan to find features than are large images. Kosslyn (1975) instructed people to imagine a target animal, such as a rabbit, next to a small animal (a fly) or a large animal (an elephant). Try this yourself. Most people report visualizing a very small image for a rabbit next to an elephant and a much larger image of a rabbit next to a fly. When then asked to search for a property of the target (the rabbit's ears), people take about 200 milliseconds longer when looking at the small image than when looking at the large image. Because the image is an analog of the real rabbit, a small image is harder to see clearly.

Finally, Kosslyn, Ball, and Reiser (1978) asked participants to memorize several locations on a map. Next, they formed a mental image of the map and focused attention on a specific starting location. The experimenters then named a second location and asked the participants to mentally find their way, in a straight-line path, to the new location. The results showed that the time needed to perform this mental scan increased proportionally to the real distances on the map. If the new location was close to the starting location, then the scan time was brief. If it was far away, then more time was needed.

The functional equivalence hypothesis claims that visual imagery uses the same mental representations, processes, and neural structures as does visual perception.

Imagery Versus Perception. All of these studies suggest that visual imagery is functionally the same as visual perception. The **functional equivalence hypothesis** states that visual imagery, while not identical to perception, is mentally represented and functions the same as perception (Finke, 1989). For example, close your eyes and imagine in your mind's eye the room in which you are now seated. Once you have an image of the room, imagine that a close friend enters the room and walks toward you. Your experience is likely to be similar, although not identical, to actually perceiving the room and the movement of your friend walking toward you. The objects and spatial relations among them seem to be represented much the same way as they are in viewing reality. According to this hypothesis, experiencing a change in a mental image ought to be analogous to experiencing a change in perception. The spatial relations of a visual image ought to be analogous to the spatial relations of the real environment.

Recent neuroimaging studies further support the view that imagery uses the same neural machinery as does perception. Positron emission tomography (PET), functional magnetic resonance imaging (fMRI), and event-related potential (ERP) studies indicate that brain activity during imagery is localized in the areas known to be used in vision. For example, when reading a list of concrete nouns (e.g., cat) and forming an image of each object, greater ERP recordings are obtained from the primary visual cortex in the occipital lobe than when just reading the nouns and not forming an image of each object (Farah, Peronnet, Gonon, & Girard, 1988). Lesions in the visual areas not only disrupt sight but also disrupt imagery (Farah, 1988). A patient with bilateral lesions in the ventral occipitotemporal areas known to be involved in face perception had trouble imagining faces well-known to him. For example, when asked to imagine the face of Abraham Lincoln, it appeared to him as a short round face. Finally, Kreiman, Koch, and Fried (2000) directly recorded the activity of single neurons in medial temporal lobes of patients undergoing surgery to correct epilepsy that failed to respond to drug treatments. They identified neurons that showed selective changes in firing rates while viewing a particular object (e.g., a face, a baseball) and again when imagining

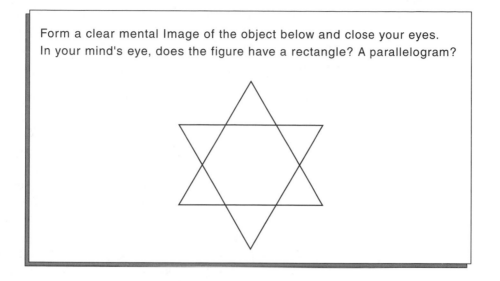

Form a clear mental Image of the object below and close your eyes. In your mind's eye, does the figure have a rectangle? A parallelogram?

Figure 8.9. The Star of David demonstration of the limitations of visual imagery.

the same object. The activity recorded from the regions of the brain known to be involved in declarative memory might have reflected either the retrieval of the object from long-term memory or the maintenance of the image in working memory.

There is an important difference between perception and imagery, however. Images must be maintained in working memory, whereas perceptions are continuously available without relying on memory. Finding a hidden part of an object is much easier when one can perceive the object than when it is mentally imagined (Reed, 1974). Study the object shown in Figure 8.9. Now, form a mental image of the object and, without looking back at the book, try to find a rectangle in the image. Could you find one? What about a parallelogram? Participants in Reed's study were correct in identifying the hidden parallelogram only 14% of the time when they had to rely on a mental image held in working memory. Reed concluded that the object was verbally labeled as the Star of David and stored propositionally in working memory (Star, David) rather than as an image that might be manipulated and searched.

Mental Maps. One common use of imagery is to construct spatial mental models. As Tversky (1991) explained,

> There are many simple, everyday tasks, such as following road directions, using instructions to assemble a bicycle, reading a novel, or helping to solve your child's geometry homework, that seem to entail

constructing a spatial mental model from a description. In order to comprehend *Go straight till the first light, then turn left, go down about three blocks to Oak, and make a right,* it is useful to have a spatial representation. (p. 109)

Mental maps reveal one's beliefs about the environment. Which city is farther west—San Diego, California, or Reno, Nevada? The mental map that most people generate places San Diego farther west (Stevens & Coupe, 1978). After all, California is west of Nevada, so surely San Diego must be far-ther west (see Figure 8.10). In turns out not to be the case. Similarly, most people regard Philadelphia, Pennsylvania, as farther north than Rome, Italy, but this is incorrect as well (Tversky, 1981). Rome is associated with a warm Mediterranean climate and so is assumed to be farther south than it really is.

The distortions in our mental maps reflect our beliefs about how the world is organized. Tversky (1981) argued that these beliefs and associated images are simplified by using two heuristics or rules of thumb. One is the alignment heuristic. The odd shapes of United States and Europe are difficult to imagine exactly, so people tend to align their shapes at the same latitude. Doing so would definitely place Rome at a southern location relative to Philadelphia. But in reality, Europe lies at a more northern latitude relative to the United States.

People also use a rotation heuristic, according to Tversky. This suggests that states or countries that are tilted in reality are visualized as more vertical than they really are. They are rotated to the perpendicular, in other words. This explains the San Diego/Reno confusion. California is imagined in the mind's eye as more or less vertical, forming the western boundary of much of the United States. In fact, California is rotated such that San Diego lies much farther east than most people realize. Reno, sitting on the border of California and Nevada, actually lies slightly west of San Diego. Because of the rotation heuristic, the mental map constructed is at odds with reality.

The Nature of Propositions

Verbal knowledge is coded in terms of abstract representations called propositions. In logic, a proposition refers to the smallest unit of knowledge about which one can sensibly judge it as true or false. "Fred is tall" is a propo-sition; "tall" or "is tall" is not. A proposition is an assertion that may be under-stood and evaluated. It is an abstract representation of the meaning conveyed by language—by all words, phrases, sentences, paragraphs, and whole speeches and documents.

One way to show the elements of a proposition is in a list format (Kintsch, 1974). The list begins with a relation followed by a set of arguments.

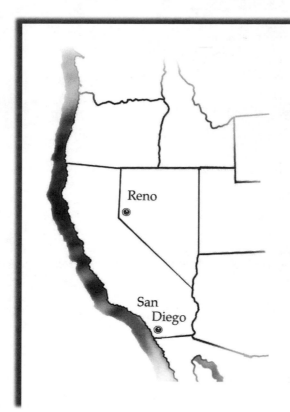

Figure 8.10. Mental maps of the United States versus real maps.

Verbs, adjectives, and other phrases that convey a relationship are listed first. The arguments follow in a specified order; they define the agent of an action (e.g., who does X?), the object of the action (e.g., does X to what?), the time of the action, and other elements of a meaningful assertion.

A proposition is coded as a relation and a set of arguments specifying an assertion that may be true or false.

The propositional code, then, breaks down knowledge into individual factual components and represents how they all are related to each other. Consider a few of the sentences that Bransford and Franks (1971) presented to participants in their experiment concerned with integration in memory encoding. As shown in Figure 8.11, each sentence can be represented by a set of abstract propositions in which each is expressed as a relation and a set of arguments.

Propositions provide an abstract and elemental representation of the meaning of verbal information. They provide the mental code for language. The outcome of Bransford and Franks's (1971) study illustrates this point

1. The jelly was sweet.
   (Sweet, Jelly, Past)

2. The ants in the kitchen ate the jelly.
   (Eat, Ants, Jelly, Past)
   (In, Ants, Kitchen, Past)

3. The ants ate the sweet jelly that
      was on the table.
   (Sweet, Jelly, Past)
   (East, Ants, Jelly, Past)
   (In, Ants, Kitchen, Past)
   (On, Jelly, Table, Past)

Figure 8.11. Propositional representations of the sentences used in an experiment on integration in memory encoding.

well. Recall from Chapter 7 that they tested recognition memory for sentences of the type illustrated in Figure 8.11. People recognized sentences as old if they contained a large number of propositions expressed in the study sentences, even though the specific sentences presented on the test were in fact new. For example, this new sentence "The ants in the kitchen ate the sweet jelly which was on the table" was falsely recognized by nearly all of the participants. It represented the prototype sentence that captured the propositions that occurred frequently in the study sentences.

Latent semantic analysis (LSA) is a mathematical procedure for automatically extracting and representing the meanings of propositions expressed in a text. It allows one to compare two texts in terms of the similarity of their propositions without going through the tedious task of manually determining the propositions of each sentence. It can, for example, represent the propositions of an entire encyclopedia in a computer database. The procedure works by representing the co-occurrence of words and their contexts (Landuaer & Dumais, 1997). For example, the word "model" occurs in numerous contexts in this book. LSA represents the associations between this word and its contexts so as to provide a usage-based meaning of model. It does this for every word it encounters in the text. Words that occur infrequently in the same contexts (e.g., model) are well-defined by their usage, whereas words that occur frequently in many contexts are less so (e.g., the). The net result allows one to compute the similarity in meaning between two words, between a word and a paragraph, or between two paragraphs.

Once LSA has extracted and represented the meaning of a text, it can use this representation for answering questions about it. For example, the mathematical procedure used in LSA was applied to the 4.6 million words that comprise Grolier's *Academic American Encyclopedia.* These words came from 30,473 articles written at a level appropriate for young students. The model's knowledge of word meanings was then tested using the Test of English as a Foreign Language (TOEFL). Each item presents a test word along with four alternatives that are more or less close in meaning. The task is to select the word closest in meaning to the test word. Because LSA can compute the similarity in meaning of two words, it is well-suited for taking this test once it has been trained by "reading" an encyclopedia. In fact, LSA was about as well-prepared as typical applicants to U.S. colleges from non-English-speaking countries who score an average of 64.5% correct on the TOEFL. When LSA was tested, it picked the correct choices 64.4% of the time. By learning the similarity of word meanings from where and how often they occur in an encyclopedia, LSA behaves as if it knows English vocabulary about as well as, say, the foreign graduate teaching assistant you perhaps had in your introductory course in college chemistry, economics, or computer science.

> LSA is a mathematical procedure for extracting and representing the propositions expressed in a text. It allows one to compare two texts in terms of the similarity of their propositional content and to answer questions about a text.

USING SEMANTIC MEMORY ●

How do people use semantic memory to answer simple questions? Is a dog a kind of animal? Is a hammer? How do you retrieve information about these object concepts to give the right answer? Models of the retrieval process have been proposed and tested by manipulating the specific kinds of questions asked and observing how the time to respond correctly was affected. In this final section of the chapter, these models are presented to show how the process of answering even simple questions is difficult to unveil.

Semantic Network Models

The subordinate, basic, and superordinate levels of concepts and their associated features can be organized into a hierarchical structure called a **semantic network model.** Figure 8.12 illustrates a small portion of what you know about the object concept of animals, with Level 0 representing the subordinate level, Level 1 the basic level, and Level 2 the superordinate level. Collins and Quillian (1969) proposed that retrieving information from this network involves working through the various levels as demanded by the

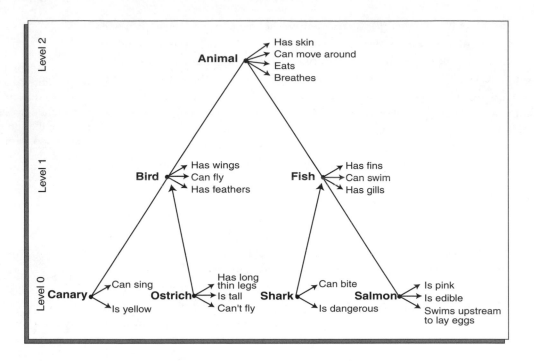

Figure 8.12. A hierarchical network representation of concepts.

SOURCE: Collins and Quillian (1969).

task. For example, to verify that a canary can sing involves entering the network at Level 0 and searching the propositions attached to the canary node. But to verify that a canary can fly requires moving through the network to Level 1. Still more mental travel time is required to answer that a canary has skin, for this feature applies to all animals, a superordinate or Level 2 feature.

Notice that this hierarchical representation of features saves space in long-term memory. It is not necessary, theoretically, to store that a canary can fly and has skin because these facts can be deduced from the hierarchical structure of memory. The **cognitive economy assumption** claims that the features of a concept are represented only once at either the subordinate, basic, or superordinate level of the hierarchy. Although it may take more time to use semantic memory organized in this manner, less storage space is required than if properties were stored redundantly at all levels of the network.

Collins and Quillian (1969) examined how quickly people verified both conceptual feature questions and category questions (see Figure 8.13). Notice that, as predicted, the time needed to answer feature questions increased as a function of feature level. In addition, verifying that a canary is

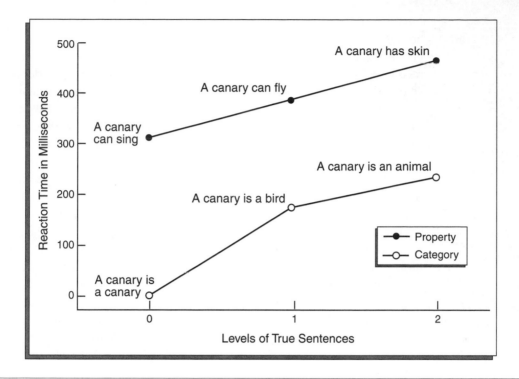

Figure 8.13. Time required to categorize a noun and to verify its properties.
SOURCE: Collins and Quillian (1969).

a canary (an identity judgment) is faster than verifying that a canary is a bird (a basic-level categorization). The most time was needed to verify membership in a superordinate category—that a canary is an animal. Note that nearly one-tenth of second is needed to move from one level to another in answering the category questions. Also note that searching the features associated with a particular level of category requires about 200 milliseconds more.

Collins and Quillian's (1969) proposal that concepts, or the words that name them, can be represented by a massive semantic network has proved to be very useful in designing a novel kind of dictionary. Instead of listing the words alphabetically, *WordNet* represents the semantic relations among words (Miller, 1999). A noun, verb, adjective, and adverb in the language is represented by a **synset,** a set of synonyms for each noun, verb, adjective, or adverb in the language. If a word has more than one meaning, then it appears in more than one synset. *WordNet* contains 122,000 words in 100,000 synsets. The synsets, in turn, are organized in the network by 139,000 pointers representing semantic relations. *WordNet* easily retrieves synonyms and antonyms

WordNet uses a semantic network to represent the meanings of 122,000 English words. Each noun, verb, adverb, and adjective in WordNet is defined by a synset or the set of all synonymous words.

for a given term. This can be very useful in information retrieval systems because it expands the number of possible items to search in a database. Furthermore, the different meanings of a word in different contexts are recognized by *WordNet*. Thus, the term "board" will not be misunderstood when one is intending to search for a "surfboard" versus a "bulletin board."

Subsequent research on Collins and Quillian's (1969) model muddied the waters, however. To begin, Rips, Shoben, and Smith (1973) reported that the hierarchical structure of the network was not consistent. If it were, then one should verify that "A collie is a mammal" faster than "A collie is an animal." The class of mammals is a subset of all animals; therefore, strictly speaking, it ought to be searched faster than the superordinate class. The results did not show this, suggesting that people did not represent clearly a strict hierarchy of class relations.

Furthermore, the assumption of cognitive economy also encountered problems. The associative strength or frequency with which a property occurred proved to be more important than the level of hierarchy. Conrad (1972) reported that strong associations (e.g., an orange is edible) can be quickly answered even though the property of edible ought to require moving to a higher level in the network. Moreover, Conrad failed to find differences where Collins and Quillian (1969) expected them. For instance, the verification time remained the same for these types of statements: "A shark can move," "A fish can move," and "An animal can move." In other words, if one selects a high-level property, theoretically it should take more time to move back down the network to the fish and animal levels (the reverse direction of the Collins and Quillian experiment). The results indicated no difference.

Finally, the typicality effect discussed earlier finds no place in a network model. Why should it be faster to verify that a robin is a bird than to verify that a canary is a bird? Obviously, the specific network model proposed by Collins and Quillian (1969) failed to capture the necessary phenomena. Later attempts came closer (Collins & Loftus, 1975), but at the cost of a lack of precision in their predictions (Chang, 1986).

Typicality effects and violations of the cognitive economy assumption led to the rejection of Collins and Quillian's model of semantic memory.

The Feature Comparison Model

Other researchers took a different tack from network models to account for the typicality effect observed with simple inquiries to semantic memory. Smith, Shoben, and Rips (1974) assumed that people first tried to retrieve the typical or characteristic features of a concept so as to answer a question such as "Is a robin a bird?" Such a list of features works best for the prototype, robin, and is satisfactory for other examples related to the prototype (e.g., canary). However, for cases that are very different from the prototype (e.g., penguin), the characteristic features are not satisfactory. Instead, a second stage is needed in which the defining features of the concept, which go beyond obvious perceptual similarities, must be retrieved. Thus, the sentence "A robin is a bird" will yield a high degree of similarity between the example and the characteristic features and can be answered without further search. By contrast, "A penguin is a bird" requires a two-stage analysis to yield the correct answer. The **feature comparison model,** then, assumes that, first, characteristic features are assessed to answer simple categorization questions and, second (if necessary), defining features are retrieved.

Besides providing an explanation of the typicality effect, the feature comparison model also nicely accounts for another consistent result in the literature, the **category size effect.** Meyer (1970) reported that deciding whether a relation applies for a small category (e.g., all robins are gems) is faster than deciding whether it applies for a large category (e.g., all robins are stones). To respond false to these statements, one must search the categories of gems and stones in long-term memory. Meyer reasoned that the larger the category that must be searched, the more time that is needed to disconfirm the statement. The same result occurred for true categorical statements (e.g., all collies are dogs vs. all collies are animals). Of course, we saw this same outcome in the category-level effect reported by Collins and Quillian (1969).

The feature comparison model explains the category size effect by noting that Stage 2 processing would be needed only for large categories. For instance, to decide that a robin is a bird, the initial comparison of all features would yield a high degree of similarity. An immediate true response would be possible. Yet to decide that a robin is an animal would demand the extra step of comparing defining features alone. Perhaps the unusual violation of the category size effect noted earlier might stem from featural similarity. Recall that people can judge "A dog is an animal" faster than "A dog is a mammal." The overall similarity of dog and animal might be quite high, leading to an immediate response after Stage 1 processing. Because the term "mammal" is less familiar to most people than "animal," a second stage of processing the defining features may be needed.

In sum, the feature comparison model accounts for most of the major results in the literature on semantic memory. However, it too has problems (Chang, 1986). One empirical problem is that false statements involving concepts that are highly similar ought to require Stage 2 processing, thus taking extra time to answer. For example, "All dogs are cats" should take more time to disconfirm than "All animals are birds." The latter statement should be disconfirmed after Stage 1 only. Yet Glass and Holyoak (1975) found that highly similar concepts, such as dogs and cats, are disconfirmed the fastest. Thus, even relatively simple uses of semantic memory are complex to model.

The feature comparison model accounts for typicality effects and the category size effect by postulating a two-stage process of checking, first, defining and characteristic features and, second, characteristic features only.

Nevertheless, feature overlap is clearly a central quality of how questions are answered using semantic memory. The category-based induction task illustrates this point as well as does the task presented earlier. This task can be illustrated by the following statements: "Robins have wings," "Bluebirds have wings," and "How likely is it that all birds have wings?" Osherson, Smith, Wilkie, Lopez, and Shafir (1990) found that this inductive argument is much stronger than one that lessens the degree of feature overlap in the premises such as the following: "Robins have wings," "Ostriches have wings," and "How likely is it that all birds have wings?" The overall similarity of features is one important determinant of how people reason with the concepts of semantic memory.

SUMMARY

1. Object concepts refer to natural kinds or biological objects and artifacts or human-made objects. An object concept categorizes objects and events of significance in the real world. As with any concept, an object concept treats objects that differ as the same if they fall within its defining boundary. With object concepts, this membership boundary is fuzzy or flexible. They are often organized hierarchically. The hierarchy of subordinate (robin), basic (bird), and superordinate (animal) concepts illustrates this point for object concepts. Rule-governed concepts, by contrast, are defined by logical relations among a set of defining features. Their membership boundaries are clear-cut and inflexible. For example, the abstract mathematical concept of an integer is well-defined.

2. All concepts specify the dimensions along which members differ from one another and order the members in terms of a gradient of membership or typicality. The prototype represents the best example of a given concept. Concepts may also be coherent in the sense that they relate in a deep theoretical manner to other concepts or other representations of world knowledge. Concepts may also be organized hierarchically, with the basic level of categorization providing the optimal amount of information about its members. Schemas organize related concepts in meaningful ways. For example, a restaurant script, a kind of schema, organizes everything we know about the routine activities of entering a restaurant, ordering food, paying for the food, and so on.

3. Semantic memory contains factual and conceptual knowledge represented by means of imaginal and propositional codes. Imaginal codes are concrete and perceptual-like, whereas propositional codes are abstract and verbal-like. Each proposition codes for a single limited assertion about the world that can be judged as true or false. Propositional codes, then, break

down knowledge into individual factual components and represent how they all are related to each other. An image behaves in much the same manner as the object it represents. Imagery and perception are functionally equivalent. For example, the time needed to rotate a mental image increases linearly with the angle of rotation, much like the time needed to rotate the object itself. Behavioral and neuroimaging evidence indicates that a dual coding system is used in human semantic memory.

4. Two of the major models of how we retrieve information from semantic memory were presented. Network theory assumes that knowledge is represented hierarchically and that features connected at a superordinate level are not redundantly represented at lower levels. Retrieving a fact involves working through the various levels of the network and searching the relevant nodes for feature information. Feature comparison theory assumes that each concept includes a list of characteristic and defining features. Retrieving a fact first involves a comparison of overall similarity based on both feature types. If similarity is low, then a second stage of comparison is needed based on defining features only. The feature comparison model handles experimental results best, although it too has difficulties in accounting for some findings.

KEY TERMS ●

rule-governed concepts
object concepts
prototype
family resemblance structure
typicality effect
frames
scripts
meta-representation
mindblindness

imaginal code
propositional code
functional equivalence hypothesis
latent semantic analysis (LSA)
semantic network model
cognitive economy assumption
synset
feature comparison model
category size effect

CHAPTER 9

LEARNING CONCEPTS AND SKILLS

As seen at the beginning of Chapter 6 on episodic memory, concepts and procedural skills, as well as specific events, are learned and stored in long-term memory. The issues surrounding the learning of specific events were considered there, and it is now time to extend the discussion to concepts and procedural skills. The problem of understanding concept learning is by itself a major challenge. Consider the explosion of concept learning that characterizes infancy and early childhood. Because words are labels for concepts, this learning can be tracked by examining the growth of vocabulary in young children. Children begin to speak their first words at around 12 months of age. Vocabulary grows at the rate of several new words per day until 6 years of age, by which children know 16,000 or more words (Carey, 1978). For each word, there is an infinite number of possible hypotheses about its meaning and only limited information for deciding which hypothesis is correct. It is astonishing that even a single word is learned given the ambiguities involved, and yet learning proceeds at an astonishingly rapid pace.

In this chapter, the processes used in concept acquisition are discussed first. Next, work on implicit learning of procedural skills is presented. With gains in concepts and skills comes expertise. A body of research has addressed the ways in which experts in a domain differ from novices in their cognitive processing. The chapter concludes with a discussion of these differences.

CONCEPT LEARNING ●

Concept learning begins during infancy and continues throughout the life span. Learning how objects and events are conceptually related is crucially important to intelligent behavior. Developmental psychologists have devised many clever experimental procedures for studying how human concept learning takes place during early childhood. Also, processes of concept learning have been studied by observing how adults acquire novel concepts in the laboratory.

Object Permanence

Perhaps the most fundamental concept acquired is that of **object permanence** or the idea that objects are permanent entities that do not vanish when out of sight. As Piaget (1952) observed, very young infants behave as if an object is not permanent at all but rather comes and goes from the world with its perception. If a doll is placed before a 3-month-old infant, the infant will attend to it and track it with his or her eyes as the doll is moved. However, if the doll is moved out of sight, the infant will make no attempt to search for the doll, either in looking for it visually or searching for it manually. For the 3-month-old, an object out of sight is also out of mind!

Piaget noted that early in infancy, humans fail to grasp the permanence of an object and must learn this concept slowly during the first 1 or 2 years of life. The notion that objects continue to exist in space even when they are imperceptible seems so rudimentary to the adult mind. It is hard to grasp that infants might not have conceptual representation for any object that is not perceived in their immediate environment. In fact, before work of Piaget, it was assumed that the concept of object permanence was genetically predetermined and did not require learning of any kind.

To test an infant's understanding of object permanence, a developmental psychologist might place a toy under Cover A. As already discussed, a young infant will not search for the toy, but certainly by 9 months of age, the child will pull off the cover and happily grab the toy. Piaget and others believed that this initial concept of object permanence was limited, however.

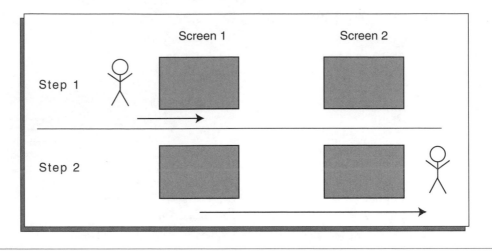

Figure 9.1. Task used to study the learning of object permanence.

SOURCE: Adapted from Moore, Borton, and Darby (1978).

If the researcher very slowly moved the toy from Cover A to Cover B, allowing the infant to see this move take place, a strange thing happened. Instead of now looking under Cover B, the infant often looked under Cover A, found nothing, and abandoned the search. Did this mean that the child really did not have a concept of object permanence?

There is an alternative explanation of what is called the AB error (Flavell, Miller, & Miller, 1993). For example, the child may well have the concept of object permanence established in semantic memory but might not know where the toy went or how to find it. Another more sensitive test supports this interpretation. Two screens were placed in front of an infant with a gap between them, as shown in Figure 9.1. An object such as a doll is first moved horizontally so that it disappears behind the first screen. In the second step, the doll continues to move horizontally. But instead of appearing in the gap, it magically appears at the end of the second screen. Would this magic trick be appreciated by the infant?

If the doll is not represented as permanent, then it should not be disturbing to have it reappear in an unexpected location. However, if it is represented as a permanent object even when out of sight behind the first screen, then the child ought to anticipate its reappearance in the gap. The results showed that the visual tracking of 9-month-old infants is disrupted by the magical reappearance at the end of the second screen (Moore, Borton, & Darby, 1978). They look back and forth and attend to the edges of the first screen, looking there for the object. Infants only 4 or 5 months of age were not bothered at all by this bit of magic because they had not yet learned to represent object permanence. Or so it seemed.

Later research upheld the view that infants under 9 months of age fail to reach for hidden objects and fail to track an object that moves behind a screen that occludes their vision. However, even at a much younger age, they are beginning to form the foundation for representing objects. This can be illustrated with a preferential looking task used by Wynn (1992) with 5-month-old infants. A single toy was placed on a stage and viewed by the infant. Then, a screen was lowered to hide the toy. A second identical toy was next placed on the stage, and it too was then hidden. Now, the test trial was given. In some cases, the screen was raised to reveal one toy, and in other cases, it was raised to reveal two toys. If an infant failed to represent the objects after the screen was lowered, then he or she might be expected to look longer at two toys. Because only one toy was viewed at a time, the presence of two toys ought to be most surprising. However, if the infant represented each toy even when it was out of sight, then the display with only one toy ought to be the most surprising and so the most preferred. The results in fact showed a looking preference for the one toy, demonstrating object permanence.

Mathematical skill can be highly developed in adults, but its origins lie in the concepts learned by infants. The concept of numerosity—how many objects are present—is the foundational concept learned very early in individual cognitive development (Spelke, 2000). It is also found early on in human evolution, as witnessed by the ability of nonhuman primates and other mammals to discriminate differences in the approximate number of objects present (Boysen & Capaldi, 1993).

To illustrate, in Wynn's (1992) experiment, infants not only showed object permanence but also represented the precise number of objects present. Infants were again presented with the task of adding one object to another so that they expected two toys. If the display then showed three toys on the test trial, then they were surprised, as indicated by their looking preference. Five-month-olds revealed the ability to add! As it happens, they can also subtract. When presented with two objects that were then hidden, the experimenter removed one object from behind the screen and showed it to an infant. On the test trial, then, the infant was most surprised if two objects remained on stage. Apparently, the infant had successfully kept track of two objects, subtracted one, and come up with the result that only one should remain.

Infants also learn to compute the approximate number of objects shown to them when large numbers are involved (Xu & Spelke, 2000). Infants are first shown displays with either 8 or 16 dots. After the infant habituates to seeing a particular number of dots, say 8, a test trial is presented with 16 dots. The findings confirmed the hypothesis that infants can discriminate between displays with 8 and 16 dots, but they prefer to look at the novel numerosity. Xu and Spelke (2000) further showed that infants' knowledge is imprecise. They can succeed in making the discrimination when the ratio is 2:1 (e.g., 16 vs. 8, 32 vs. 16) but fail when the ratio is only 3:2 (e.g., 12 vs. 8, 4 vs. 6). Spelke (2000) contended that number concepts (e.g., 5 and 7) and mathematical procedures (e.g., $5 + 7 = 12$) can be learned only because of the core knowledge system of numerosity.

Basic Concepts

Recall that object concepts are organized hierachically. As it happens, the word that refers to the basic level of the hierarchy (e.g., bird) is learned by children before they learn the word for the subordinate (e.g., robin) or superordinate (e.g., animal) level of categorization (Rosch, Mervis, Gray, Johnson, & Boyes-Broem, 1976). This earlier acquisition of the basic level concept can still be detected in adults when they are asked to name the category to which an object belongs. For example, if shown a picture of a robin or a turkey, people can most quickly categorize the object as a bird. The subordinate (robin or turkey) and superordinate (animal) classifications take more time.

It has been argued that basic-level concepts carve the world into groups that provide the optimal amount of information (Murphy & Smith, 1982; Rosch et al., 1976). All examples that fit the same basic-level category share many common features such as the properties found in all birds. This is not true at the superordinate level, where the properties shared by all animals are hard to enumerate. At the same time, the basic level carves the world into far fewer groupings than does the subordinate level. Thus, by first learning and thinking in terms of basic-level categories, one can deal with the environment most adaptively.

It does not seem to be the hierarchy that determines the speed of acquisition. Instead, the frequency with which children are exposed to examples appears critical. It may be that children are typically exposed to many examples of domestic cats and see these contrasted with dogs and birds, for example. Normally, they are not exposed to dogs, cats, tigers, and zebras as members of a superordinate category of mammal and see these contrasted with nonmammals such as fish and birds (Eimas & Quinn, 1994). The importance of this frequency factor has been shown by laboratory studies in which infants 3 to 4 months of age were trained to discriminate members of the mammal category. The infants were shown repeated examples of dogs, cats, tigers, and zebras. With repetition, they habituated to these stimuli, meaning that they paid less and less attention to them. Then, the researchers introduced nonmammal stimuli such as fish and birds. The infants dishabituated to nonmammal category members, meaning that they paid attention to them as novel. By contrast, when novel mammals were presented (e.g., deer, beavers), the infants continued to ignore them. Thus, the infants learned a superordinate mammal category at a very early age simply by being exposed to the right examples often.

LEARNING PROCESSES ●

Automatic and Controlled Processes

Two basic kinds of concept learning processes have been proposed as underlying the findings reviewed thus far. It has long been recognized that processing the frequency of occurrence of stimuli and their features plays a role in concept learning. The study of this dates back to Hull's (1920) investigation of adults learning a novel artificial concept in the laboratory. Participants viewed sets of Chinese characters as shown in Figure 9.2. The concept was defined by a particular feature, called a radical, that was common to all members of a given set. The other features varied across the characters in each set. The learners received multiple lists of each set of characters paired with the name and tried to learn the right name for each character. Hull found that performance gradually improved from list to list, increasing from only about 30% correct on List 1 to about 60% correct on List 6.

Feature Frequency Theory. The interesting outcome in Hull's experiments was that the learners could not consciously identify and verbalize the defining feature—the radical. They found it easier to learn the correct nonsense syllable on later lists but did not know why. Hull interpreted his findings in terms of an unconscious buildup of associative strength of all the features of the Chinese characters and the nonsense syllables with which they were paired. **Feature frequency theory** holds that the gradual accretion of the frequency of occurrence of features discriminates between defining features and irrelevant features. The idea is also called associative strength theory, emphasizing that the learner develops a strong association between the concept and its defining features. Only defining features occur regularly in examples of the concept. In both examples and nonexamples of a given concept,

Name	Radical (concept)	List 1	List 2	List 3	List 4	List 5	List 6
oo							
yer							
ti							
ta							
deg							
ling							

Figure 9.2. Chinese characters used in Hull's classic concept learning experiment.

irrelevant features occur equally often. Thus, over multiple presentations, relevant features stand out as uniquely frequent (Bourne & Restle, 1959).

The inability of Hull's participants to verbalize the defining feature of the concept is consistent with the view that frequency processing is automatic. As discussed in Chapter 3, humans from a very early age can compile the frequency of occurrence of environmental features and events without intention or cognitive effort (Hasher & Zacks, 1979, 1984). Learning can occur through a process of frequency compilation, even though the counting process is not perfectly accurate and certainly is not conscious.

Today, connectionist models provide a clearly defined account of how associative strength or frequency information explains concept learning using the same principles adopted in models of perception, memory, and language (Busemeyer, Byun, Delosh, & McDaniel, 1997). To illustrate, Gluck and Bower (1988) showed how a simple neural network using the delta rule could accurately predict human categorization responses. They presented

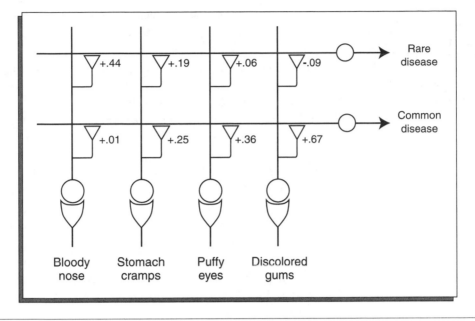

Figure 9.3. A neural network for categorizing diseases based on symptoms.
SOURCE: Anderson (1990).

participants with hundreds of fictitious patients who suffered from some combination of symptoms (bloody nose, stomach cramps, puffy eyes, and discolored gums). The symptom combinations were associated with either a rare disease or a common disease with different probabilities. The neural network is equipped with an output neuron that takes a value from +1 to −1, depending on the probability of the rare disease (see Figure 9.3).

There are four input neurons, one for each symptom, that are active when a particular symptom is present in a patient. The network must learn the strength of synaptic connections among neurons that correctly classifies a patient as having the rare disease or not. The feature frequency or strength information, then, is captured by the synaptic weights that the network settles on during learning (refer to Chapter 2). The weights shown here were able to predict both how humans classified whether a patient had the disease and their ratings of which symptoms were diagnostic. For instance, only bloody nose was rated as predictive of the rare disease, and only it had a synaptic weight in the simulation model.

Associative strength or feature frequency theory contends that a new concept is learned automatically through the slow and gradual accretion of knowledge regarding the frequency of occurrence of features among concept examples.

Hypothesis Testing Theory. The classical alternative to feature frequency theory posits an active learner. **Hypothesis testing theory** assumes that the learner tests hypotheses about the identity of defining features. The defining

Hypothesis testing theory claims that the features and relations that define a new concept are discovered by a controlled process of identifying a hypothesis, testing it, and retaining or resampling it based on feedback.

features of a concept are selectively isolated from among all irrelevant features by a process of elimination based on feedback. All possible features comprise the pool of available hypotheses. The learner samples one or more of the features and then tries to classify examples of the concept based on the current hypothesis. If feedback provided to the learner is positive (meaning that the way the learner classified the examples was correct), then the current hypothesis is retained. If feedback is negative, then the hypothesis is rejected and a new hypothesis is sampled. This is termed the win-stay, lose-shift assumption. A critical feature of hypothesis theory is that learning to classify correctly can occur suddenly and dramatically. If the defining feature is hypothesized, then correct classification follows. Complete learning takes place, then, in a single classification trial.

There is strong evidence that when adults are taught novel concepts in the laboratory, they test hypotheses and can learn in a single trial (Levine, 1966, 1975). In addition, participants can remember information about more than just the hypothesis being tested on a given trial. If a hypothesis is rejected on a trial, they do not mistakenly resample it again on the very next trial. They are able to hold in working memory information about past hypotheses that were already rejected. However, the results of other studies have indicated that learning can still take place even when the winning hypothesis is not remembered from trial to trial (Kellogg, Robbins, & Bourne, 1978). When working memory was tested for storage of stimulus features, responses, feedback, and hypotheses, recognition of the hypothesis provided by the learner on the immediately preceding trial was surprisingly poor. Yet the participant nonetheless learned to categorize the stimuli correctly.

One explanation of these results is that the learners automatically compiled feature frequency information. Because of the many demands placed on working memory in the task, hypothesis testing apparently failed as a useful strategy (Kellogg & Bourne, 1989). Both controlled hypothesis testing and automatic frequency processing seem to play a part in concept learning. This same theme is encountered again later in the section on implicit learning.

Prototype Acquisition

As seen in the last chapter, object concepts are structured around a prototype. How is this structure learned? Numerous studies have shown that when people are shown a series of items from a category, they learn the central tendency of these dimensions (e.g., Posner & Keele, 1968; Reed, 1972). The prototype is defined by the average of each stimulus dimension.

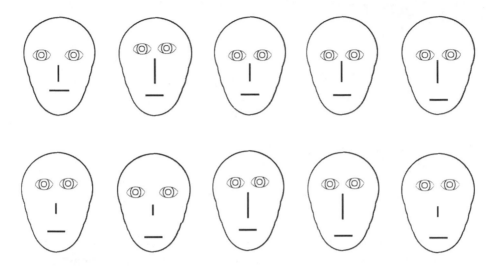

Figure 9.4. Learning an average prototype based on the mean dimension values. Faces in the top row belong to Category 1, and those in the bottom row belong to Category 2.

SOURCE: Reed and Friedman (1973).

Mean Versus Modal Prototypes. For example, Reed (1972) presented participants with the schematic faces shown in Figure 9.4. They were told that the faces on the top row were examples of Category 1 and those on the bottom row illustrated Category 2. After studying these, participants were shown novel faces, as illustrated in Figure 9.5. The middle face is the prototype of Category 1 in that it represents the mean feature values for the dimensions of forehead height, nose length, eye separation, and mouth height. The face on the right is the prototype for Category 2, again displaying the average dimensional values. The face on the left illustrates a face that is a nonprototypical face. The results showed that participants were more likely to correctly classify the prototype faces than any other test faces.

In other experiments, however, the average prototype was defined by the modal or most frequent features rather than by the mean dimension values (Hayes-Roth & Hayes-Roth, 1977). Goldman and Homa (1977) concluded that the most frequent feature values are generally the ones learned by participants but that in special circumstances a mean value is computed. They used features of schematic faces similar to Reed's that were not normally distributed so that the mean and mode were not identical. When there was little variation between features on a dimension (e.g., the smallest nose length was not much different from the largest) and the two categories of faces were hard to discriminate, mean values were learned.

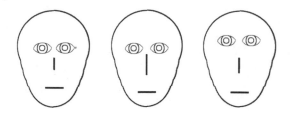

Figure 9.5.   Novel faces illustrating the prototype of Category 1 in the middle and the prototype of Category 2 on the right.

SOURCE: Reed (1972).

Rosch, Simpson, and Miller (1976) argued that these are two fundamentally different processes involved when people learn an average prototype
based on the mean versus the modal value. This may be true, but Neumann
(1977) countered that feature counting could result in a prototype based on
mean values if features are mistakenly perceived at times. The mean value
would receive some extra frequency counts if features only slightly above or
below this value were incorrectly perceived as identical to the mean. Thus,
when the features are difficult to discriminate, errors in perception of the
features could result in a prototype based on means even when the same
feature-counting process is used.

Memory for Specific Instances. Other research has shown that more is
learned about a category than just its central tendency. Specific instances are
also learned and may be used as the basis for categorizing new test items
instead of using a central tendency-based prototype. Storing specific old
instances of concepts and making analogies between new and old instances
is called **nonanalytic concept learning.** Brooks (1978) contrasted this
process with the analytic method of testing hypotheses about the defining
features of concepts. The test item is placed in the same category as the specific instance with which it shares the most features in common. Memory for
specific instances accounts for the finding that items studied during learning
are categorized faster and more accurately than new test instances. Also, test
instances that are similar to a specific old instance are categorized better than
instances that are dissimilar to the prototype (Brooks, 1978; Medin &
Shaeffer, 1978).

Some theorists have challenged the idea that prototypes are abstracted
at all by arguing that the retrieval of specific item information is sufficient by
itself (Hintzman, 1986; Medin & Shaeffer, 1978). However, some neuroimaging evidence speaks against this claim. Making a recognition judgment about

whether a specific instance of a visual concept had been seen before causes increases in activation in the posterior occipital cortex (Reber, Stark, & Squire, 1998). By contrast, making a categorization judgment about prototypical instances causes a decrease in activation in these visual processing regions. Reber et al. (1998) concluded, then, that prototype categorization and specific item retrieval are dissociable processes. Also, behavioral evidence shows that retrieving specific items for use in categorization is likely only when the category contains a relative small number of instances and when testing occurs soon after training (Homa, Sterling, & Trepel, 1981). These conditions support the encoding and retrieval of specific instances. Thus, prototype learning cannot be explained away by assuming that all categorization is done by comparisons with specific old instances. On the other hand, there is little question that the retrieval of specific examples plays a role in human categorization in addition to prototype learning and use (Medin & Ross, 1989).

Nonanalytic processes such as memorizing specific instances can also mediate categorization by comparing new examples to episodic representations of old examples. Neuroimaging evidence suggests that prototype abstraction, on the other hand, results in a fundamentally different representation in long-term memory.

IMPLICIT LEARNING ●

In addition to learning concepts defined by perceptual features and relatively simple relations among them, people can learn complex abstract rules. **Implicit learning** refers to the unconscious acquisition of complex rules that cannot be verbalized (Seger, 1994). Unlike the concept identification task, implicit learning tasks involve many stimulus features that are related in highly complex ways. For example, researchers have studied the acquisition of artificial grammars (e.g., Knowlton, Ramus, & Squire, 1992; Reber, 1967, 1989; Reber & Allen, 1978).

A demonstration of implicit learning of an artificial grammar is the best way to begin. Shown in Figure 9.6 are 20 learning stimuli. First, study and try to memorize as many of the 20 learning stimuli as possible. After studying these carefully, try to identify which of the 30 testing stimuli are grammatical and which are ungrammatical. Provide a response to each one before checking any of your answers against the key, which is given at the end of this chapter. How many of the 30 examples did you identify correctly? More than the 15 expected by chance?

The underlying rules used to generate the grammatical strings are shown in Figure 9.7. Starting with the entry point on the left, a letter string is generated by moving through a series of states. Each move adds a letter to the string. The directed arrows indicate which states can follow a given state. For example, S_4 can lead to either S_3 or S_6 but not to S_5. A recursive move, one with a looped arrow, adds a letter while remaining in the same state.

	Learning Stimuli		Testing Stimuli
1.	PVPXVPS	1.	TSXXTVPS
2.	TSSXXVPS	2.	SVPXTVV
3.	TSXS	3.	PTTVPXVV
4.	PVV	4.	PVPXTTVV
5.	TSSSXXVV	5.	PTTTVPVS
6.	PTVPXVV	6.	PVTVV
7.	TXXVPXVV	7.	TSSXXVSS
8.	PTTVV	8.	TTVV
9.	TSXXTVPS	9.	PTTTTVPS
10.	TXXTVPS	10.	PVV
11.	PTVPS	11.	PTTPS
12.	TXS	12.	TXXTTVPS
13.	TSXXTVV	13.	TSXXTTVV
14.	PVPXTVPS	14.	PVXPVXPX
15.	TXXTTTVV	15.	XXSVT
16.	PTTTVPS	16.	TSSXXTVV
17.	TSSSXS	17.	TXS
18.	TSSXXVV	18.	TXXVX
19.	PVPXVV	19.	PTTTVT
20.	TXTVPS	20.	TSXXVPS
		21.	PTTTVV
		22.	TXV
		23.	PTTVPS
		24.	TXXTTVV
		25.	PSXS
		26.	PTVPPPS
		27.	PTTTTTVV
		28.	TXVPS
		29.	TSSXS
		30.	TSXXPV

Figure 9.6. Demonstration of implicit learning.

Thus, one grammatical letter string is TSXS. Another grammatical string, this time involving two recursions at S_1, is TSSXXVV. TXS is also a grammatical string—the shortest one possible. If you study these rules carefully, you can find five basic string patterns, with loops or recursions indicated in brackets. These are (a) T[S]XS, (b) T[S]XX[[T]VPX], (c) T[S]XX[[T]VPS]VPS, (d) P[[T]VPX]VV, and (e) P[[T]VPX]VPS.

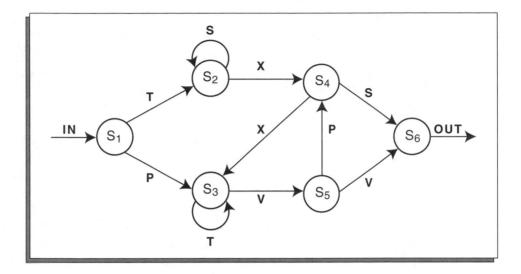

Figure 9.7. Diagram of the artificial grammar used to demonstrate implicit learning.
SOURCE: Reber (1989).

As you can imagine, it would be challenging to try to identify all of the rules involved by means of hypothesis testing. The patterns are sufficiently complex as to make it unlikely that a controlled strategy of testing rules will succeed in identifying the five basic string patterns. Even so, after studying 20 or so examples, people can discriminate grammatical from ungrammatical strings at well above chance levels. Despite their correct categorizations, people are typically unable to verbalize the complete rules of the grammar. One possibility is that they have implicitly learned the rules by adopting a passive unconscious mode of acquisition.

A key feature of implicit learning is that procedural knowledge and declarative knowledge are dissociated. Knowledge of how to categorize the items that are grammatical is different from the ability to represent the rules in a declarative form and then state them using language. Berry and Broadbent (1984) studied the inability to verbalize implicit procedural knowledge using dynamic systems tasks. For example, participants were told to take the role of a manager in a sugar production factory and to regulate the number of employees needed each day to achieve a production goal. They had to manipulate the value of one variable (number of employees), were provided feedback on another variable (sugar produced for the day), and were told to maintain production within a narrow range. The rule governing the relation between the number of employees and production levels was given by this formula: 2(Input) – Previous Result. In other words, participants

> Implicit learning refers to the unconscious acquisition of complex rules that cannot be verbalized. Implicit learning appears to rely on a nondeclarative procedural knowledge representation.

had to learn that the number of employees assigned on a given day, or the input, as well as the resulting production level from the day before, or the previous result, is what determined the new resulting production level. This rule is not obvious, yet over many attempts participants acquired the procedure needed to maintain production within the proscribed range. Nevertheless, they were unable to verbalize the formula itself.

Hayes and Broadbent (1988) accounted for such dissociations by postulating two modes of learning. The S-mode of learning is "selective, effortful, and reportable," whereas the U-mode of learning is the "unselective and passive aggregation of information about the co-occurrence of environmental features and events" (p. 254). Thus, the implicit learning tasks appear to involve similar kinds of processes as those discovered in the concept learning tasks. Hypothesis testing is an example of an S-mode process that allows learners to articulate what they know. Automatic aggregation of the frequency of occurrence of features is an example of a U-mode of learning. Although one might argue that the U-mode of learning is more complex than this implies, the learning of relative frequency information about letters and letter sequences provides a plausible account of unconscious learning and is consistent with the abundant evidence that contingencies are automatically registered (Perruchet, Gallego, & Savy, 1990).

Alternative explanations have been proposed and tested with some success. One straightforward explanation is that the learners successfully tested hypotheses that allowed them to identify some, but not all, of the rules. With an incomplete but adequate set of hypothesized rules that are consciously available, the participants may have been able to discriminate between grammatical and ungrammatical strings at better than chance levels (Dulany, Carlson, & Dewey, 1984; Perruchet & Pacteau, 1992). One difficulty with this explanation is that learners instructed to test hypotheses actually show poorer classification performance than those not so instructed (Reber & Allen, 1978; Reber, Kassin, Lewis, & Cantor, 1980).

Another explanation is that participants compared test strings with a specific grammatical string, one of those initially studied and stored in episodic memory. In accord with nonanalytic concept learning, they may have classified test strings by analogy with specific examples rather than implicitly acquiring the complex rule system (Brooks, 1978; Neal & Hesketh, 1997). One argument against this alternative is that amnesic patients perform as well as normal individuals in learning to distinguish grammatical and ungrammatical strings. Yet amnesic patients could not store and recognize the specific examples presented to them for study (Knowlton et al., 1992).

The debate over whether implicit learning entails automatic unconscious processes is far from settled (Nissen & Bullemer, 1987; Seger, 1994; Whittlesea & Dorken, 1997) despite a variety of findings suggesting learning without conscious awareness and without testing of hypotheses (Curran & Keele, 1993; Lewicki, Czyzewska, & Hoffman, 1988; Stadler, 1993). As Dienes and Berry (1997) noted, however, several implicit learning tasks have shown the same converging pattern of evidence. Participants who deliberately test hypotheses do not learn more, and at times learn less, than those who passively observe or memorize inputs. At the same time, it is hard to argue that implicit learning really reflects the use of episodic memory for specific examples of the rule. Amnesic patients perform seem to just as well as normal controls in each of the tasks after all.

Presumably, amnesic patients can still learn implicitly because the mechanism responsible for keeping track of frequency of occurrence information is still intact. A direct test of this assumption has shown that it is correct (Dopkins, Kovner, & Goldmeier, 1994). Patients with Korsakoff's amnesia successfully processed the frequency of occurrence of examples from a semantic category. They were able to tell whether they had seen more fish or more birds after receiving sentences that included examples such as trout, bass, and canary. However, their explicit recognition of the sentences that included these examples was, as expected, severely impaired relative to that of normal participants.

Least understood at present is how to describe the representation of knowledge learned implicitly. One view is that the associations and frequencies of event features are encoded in a distributed knowledge network, as postulated by connectionist models (Dienes & Berry, 1997; Perruchet & Pacteau, 1992). According to this view, explicit learning through hypothesis testing results in a symbolic representation of the rule that is qualitatively different from a connectionist representation. Explicit learning is easy to articulate because it results in a symbolic representation with verbal labels. Implicit learning, on the other hand, is difficult to articulate because it is represented in a distributed nonsymbolic format. This is not the only possibility, however, and further work is needed to understand the precise nature of implicit knowledge representation (Neal & Hesketh, 1997).

ACQUIRING EXPERTISE •

Experts are individuals who have learned a wealth of factual and conceptual knowledge and have developed the necessary procedural skills to excel in a specific domain of tasks. Novices are intelligent, generally educated individuals who lack a high degree of knowledge about a specific domain. To illustrate, consider a variety of common activities: cooking, driving, running, skating, reading, typing, and solving arithmetic problems. Some depend heavily on perceptual and motor skills (e.g., running, skating), whereas others are primarily cognitive in nature (e.g., reading, arithmetic). Others illustrate blends of perceptual, motor, and cognitive functioning (e.g., driving, typing). Skills, then, should be thought of in broad terms that encompass mental as well as manual tasks. Hammering nails is a skill, but then so too is playing chess.

In each domain, individuals differ in their knowledge and skill level, depending chiefly on their degree of interest, training, and practice. Novices can cook, drive, run, skate, read, type, and do arithmetic. But experts in these domains are exceptionally talented and have devoted considerable portions of their lives to acquiring the requisite knowledge and skills. **Expert-novice differences** refer to the differences in mental representations and cognitive processes associated with domain-specific expertise.

Skills involve procedural nondeclarative memory. However, at the same time that the procedures are learned and practiced, factual and conceptual knowledge about a domain is also acquired. Jobs in the real world—from grocery bagger to heart surgeon—demand a mix of declarative and procedural knowledge. The development of surgical skill, to take an extreme case, takes years of undergraduate and medical school education focusing on factual and conceptual knowledge. Basic skills of medical practice must then be taught, followed by years of specialized training in surgical techniques, diagnosis, and decision making. The skill of a surgeon entails knowledge of facts and concepts; recollections of past cases; the exercise of fine motor, perceptual, and cognitive procedures; and conditioned responses.

There has been a long tradition of studying individuals who have attained remarkably high levels of skill in a specific domain. During the 19th century, the French founder of intelligence testing, Alfred Binet, investigated the phenomenal memory skills of chess masters and of mental calculators who specialized in number memorization. For example, the calculators could memorize a large matrix of numbers after only a brief presentation, far exceeding the usual limitations of short-term memory. Furthermore, they could perform complex arithmetic (e.g., 57,892　63,475) entirely in their heads, without any external aid such as paper and pencil. As if they had a "photographic memory," the calculators reported hearing or seeing the digits as clear auditory or visual images (Ericsson & Chase, 1982). During the electronic age, a century after Binet's work, such an ability is stunning; with ready access to a calculator, performing five-digit multiplication on paper, let alone mentally, is onerous.

A. C. Aitken, a professor of mathematics at the University of Edinburgh, astonished psychologists on tests of his memory and calculation skills (Hunter, 1962, 1964). Presented with a list of 25 words in 1933, Aiken recalled them all, through repeated attempts, 27 years later! He also showed virtually flawless recollection of Bartlett's "War of the Ghosts" tale that he had memorized 27 years earlier. As a mathematician, he quickly understood the equivalencies of numerical expressions. For example, he immediately apprehended that 37×53, $40^2 + 19^2$, and 1,961 are equivalent. Of interest, deliberate practice can enable bright, motivated (and paid) college students to enhance their abilities as mental calculators greatly. Staszewski (1988) reported that after 300 hours of practice on simple (e.g., $7 \times 4,382$) and complex (e.g., $78 \times 41,275$) multiplication, an undergraduate attained the speed and accuracy of a world-class mental calculator.

Cognitive psychologists have studied the development of world-class performers across a broad range of fields, including chess, mathematics, music, dance, tennis, swimming, long-distance running, figure skating, writing, computer programming, scientific discovery, and medical diagnosis. In this section, some fundamental issues about the acquisition of skills are first presented. Then, the literature on expert-novice differences is discussed.

> Expert-novice differences refer to the differences in mental representations and cognitive processes associated with domain-specific expertise.

Skill Acquisition

Phases of Acquisition. Fitts (1964) identified three phases of skill acquisition and argued that each is characterized by qualitative differences in cognitive processing (see Figure 9.8). During the early phase, cognitive processes are used to understand the domain and how a specific task should be performed. For example, by reading and talking with experts, the novice gets acquainted with the demands of the task. During the intermediate stage, specific inputs are associated with appropriate responses. Receiving examples to learn from is critically important during the intermediate stage (VanLehn, 1996). To illustrate, students learning algebra would benefit more from seeing examples of how problems are worked than from working the problems themselves. From the examples received, students learn the important underlying principles. During the intermediate stage, multiple principles must be acquired in this manner. The final phase of skill acquisition involves automating the relevant component processes through practice. It appears that one important change that occurs during the development of automaticity is that mental computations are replaced by direct retrieval. For example, instead of recomputing the answer to a heavily practiced algebra problem, the answer is simply recalled (Logan, 1988).

Procedural Reinstatement. A skill is well-retained for long periods of time when the procedures used to acquire the skill are reinstated at the time of

Phase	Cognitive Processing
Early	Understand the domain and how to perform a specific task
Intermediate	Associate specific stimulus inputs with appropriate response
Final	Automate the relevant component processes

Figure 9.8. Phases of skill acquisition.

test. This is called the **principle of procedural reinstatement.** Two principles of episodic memory are related to this principle. Encoding specificity holds that a cue to retrieve an event from episodic memory is effective only if it was encoded at the time of original learning. Transfer-appropriate processing holds that the value of particular kinds of encoding processes depends on the nature of the test given at the time of retrieval. The procedural reinstatement principle applies these ideas to skill acquisition and retention. In contrast to the ease with which some events may be forgotten from episodic memory, skills can show remarkable durability, at least when the acquisition procedures are reinstated at the time of test. Indeed, durable long-term retention of procedural skills specifically requires the reinstatement at test of the cognitive operations used during acquisition (Healy & Bourne, 1995).

To illustrate, Fendrich, Healy, and Bourne (1991) investigated data entry skills. Participants entered lists of digit sequences with a computer keypad in two acquisition sessions. Then, a third test session was administered a month later. Some of the digit sequences used on the delayed tests were exact repetitions of those used during acquisition (e.g., 1687 ... 28 days later ... 1687). Compared with new sequences, participants were faster at encoding the digits (the time needed to depress the first key after visual presentation of the sequence). Furthermore, they were also faster at executing their responses (measured from the first keystroke to the last). Thus, reinstating the perceptual operations of encoding the digits as well as reinstating the motor operations of key execution speeded reaction time performance.

The skills learned in complex job situations also show strong long-term retention when the procedures acquired during acquisition are reinstated at test. Tank gunnery skills have been studied using a simulation game called the TopGun task. Tank gun turrets are controlled with the hands, and instrument panel displays resemble those of a real M-1 tank. Participants must visually locate targets, lock onto the targets by continuously tracking them, and fire at appropriate ranges. Marmie and Healy (1995) gave participants extensive practice at this task and then waited over a 2-week retention interval before testing participants in exactly the same situation. They found no evidence of forgetting this highly proceduralized skill, and one measure actually improved. Further research showed little forgetting of gunnery skill over delays as long as 22 months, nearly 2 years after acquisition.

Procedural reinstatement shows that skills can be retained extremely well and are not necessarily subject to the forgetting often found with episodic memory. However, there is also a downside to this fact of procedural memory. If the cognitive procedures activated at the time of test do not exactly match those activated at the time of acquisition, then forgetting can and often does occur (Healy & Bourne, 1995). Skills, then, appear to be highly specific and easily disrupted by altering conditions between learning and testing. As will be seen in later chapters on problem solving and other thinking skills, it is extremely difficult to arrange training that generalizes well to novel circumstances.

Deliberate Practice. Ericsson, Krampé, and Tesch-Römer (1993) defined **deliberate practice** as a regimen of effortful activities, typically begun during childhood, that leads to extraordinary performance. Ericsson et al. began with the observation that research designed to uncover genetic reasons for exceptional levels of talent has not succeeded. For example, performance on intelligence tests is known to be affected by heredity, as is detailed later in Chapter 15. Yet intelligence scores cannot accurately predict exceptional levels of performance in many areas, including music and chess. Physical attributes also are in part inherited, yet even in sports one must look beyond genetics alone to understand exceptional performance. Human behavior virtually always arises from the interaction of genetic and environmental factors (Plomin, DeFries, & McClearn, 1990). The amount of time and effort devoted to practice is a critical element of the environment leading to excellence. Advancing to a world-class level of performance requires going beyond the achievements of all others who are equally well-prepared with respect to inborn talents.

Specifically, the practice must be deliberately directed at polished professional performance. First, a person must practice many hours a week, not just the few minutes a day that is typical of many learning a new skill. For example, Ericsson et al. (1993) found that professional violinists, along with the very best violin students, practiced 7 hours per week by 12 years of age. They steadily increased their practice time as they matured, reaching more than 30 hours per week by age 20. Calculating from ages 3 to 20, these individuals averaged more than 10,000 hours of cumulative practice. Talent comes from persistent deliberate practice, a conclusion that may come as a surprise to those readers who thought that outstanding performers came by their skill naturally and easily, through some innate giftedness.

Second, the person must be highly motivated to spend time on the task and to devote high levels of cognitive effort to improvement. As will be seen shortly, performance improves as a mathematical function of the degree of practice. For this practice to be effective, the learner must understand the nature of the task and must receive immediate feedback or knowledge of the results of his or her effort (Bower & Hilgard, 1981).

Third, the individual must discover the best methods or receive direct instruction on them by teachers and coaches. Adopting correct methods or strategies has turned up as essential in cognitive tasks such as mnemonic skill and mental calculation, in motor skills, and in job performance (Ericsson et al., 1993). Teachers and coaches design practice activities that focus on the proven methods. Given the importance of picking up the right methods, it is obviously important for children to have access to teachers, training facilities, and parental support and to have encouragement to study and practice.

> Deliberate practice is a regimen of effortful activities, typically begun during childhood, that leads to extraordinary performance. It requires an extensive commitment of time, strong motivation, and either discovery or instruction in superior methods and strategies.

Preparing for 10 Years. There is a difference between being good at something and being an expert. Achieving a level of expertise that allows one to compete and excel with world-class competition requires many years of deliberate practice. The **ten-year rule** states that even the most talented individuals require a minimum of 10 years of preparation before succeeding at an international level of competition (Lehman & Ericsson, 1998). Most successful individuals at the world-class level prepare substantially longer than 10 years.

For example, Simon and Chase (1973) reported that chess players need about 10 years of intense preparation before they develop their skill sufficiently to compete at an international level. Even the chess prodigy Bobby Fisher needed a preparation period of 9 years (Ericsson et al., 1993). A minimum of 10 years, and more likely 20 years, of practice is needed before an individual composes a truly outstanding musical piece (Hayes, 1981). Perhaps the best-known musical prodigy is Amadeus Mozart. Yet even Mozart fit the rule of no less than 10 years of preparation.

By playing the harpsichord at 4 years of age and composing at age 5, Mozart reached eminence by his 20s, a fortunate occurrence for Western civilization given his early death at age 35. Of all the compositions Mozart produced, about 12% came from the initial 10 years of his career. Compared with later compositions, Mozart's earlier works were not highly regarded by conductors and musical critics. Hayes (1981) discovered that the compositions most often recorded came from his later efforts. Only 4.8% of the recordings came from this early 10-year period, and even that drops to 2.4% when recordings of *The Complete Works of Mozart* are omitted from the analysis. Thus, one of the greatest child prodigies also required a 10-year period of preparation before world-class musical scores came from his pen.

Expert-Novice Differences

As a result of years of preparation and deliberate practice, experts differ from novices in a number of important ways. Most obviously, experts can draw on domain-specific knowledge to solve problems, whereas novices must rely on concepts that are commonly understood in a culture but erroneous. To illustrate, try to solve the physics problems in Figure 9.9 before reading further. The tube, pendulum, and cliff problems tap conceptual knowledge about the mechanics of motion. Without specialized education in physics, and without extensive practice in solving such problems, individuals use their everyday knowledge about how objects behave in motion. **Folk theories** are naive commonsense explanations of scientific phenomena as opposed to theories based on scientific facts. A folk theory of motion is called impetus theory. In the coil problem, individuals assume that the ball acquires an impetus of curvature while in the tube that is maintained after exiting and gradually dissipates over time (McCloskey, 1983).

Indeed, 51% of college students predict that the ball follows a curved trajectory after it exits from the coil. The correct Newtonian answer is a straight trajectory tangent to the curvature of the tube at the point the ball exits. Mistakes are also commonly made in the cliff and pendulum problems. The correct answers are shown in Figure 9.10 along with wrong answers that show more or less similarity to the correct solution. Someone with little experience in physics instruction is likely to give one of the incorrect alternatives. How many did you get correct? Can you describe your reasons for giving the answer that you did?

It is only through intensive instruction at the college level that students succeed in learning the correct scientific concepts in the domain of physics to avoid these errors. Traditional high school physics instruction typically is not sufficient to dislodge the conceptual understanding of folk theories. Providing experiences designed to break down the false folk concepts helps in teaching the correct scientific concepts (Levin, Siegler, Druyan, & Gardosh, 1990).

Students without extensive training in physics are also more affected by the context of the problem (Cooke & Breedin, 1994). For example, novices

Tube

This display shows a thin curved tube. Note that the tube is smooth, even though the graphics may tend to appear rough. In the display, you are looking down on the tube. In other words, the tube is lying flat on a horizontal surface. Therefore, gravity is not a factor. A metal ball is put into one end of the tube, and the ball is shot out the other end of the tube at high speed. Ignore air resistance and any spin the ball may have. Your task is to determine the correct path the ball will follow after emerging from the tube.

Cliff

This display shows the side of a cliff. A metal ball is rolling along the top of the cliff and is traveling 50 mph at the point that it leaves the cliff. Consider the path that the ball will follow as it leaves the cliff, ignoring air resistance.

Pendulum

This display shows a metal ball suspended by a string. The ball and the string move in an arc as a pendulum from Point A to Point B. While the ball is in motion, the string is cut at Point C. Your task is to determine the correct path that the ball will take after the string is cut.

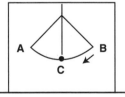

Figure 9.9. Three physics problems.

SOURCE: Cooke and Breedin (1994).

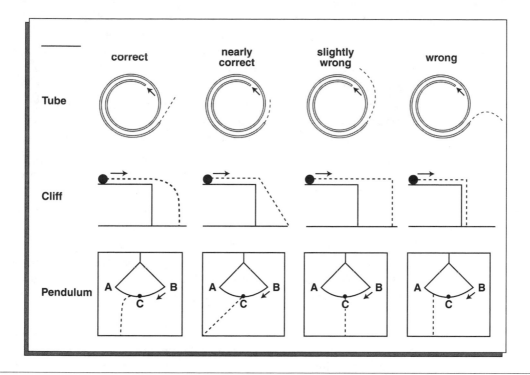

Figure 9.10. Alternative solutions to the tube, cliff, and pendulum problems.
SOURCE: Cooke and Breedin (1994).

are more likely to select the correct answer from the four alternatives shown in Figure 9.10 than to produce the right trajectory by drawing it. For experts, selection and production differ very little. Thus, experts seem to have a clear Newtonian theory in mind that is not affected by the problem context, whereas novices are strongly affected by seeing several options and selecting one. Novices seem to construct an explanation on the fly, using any available source of information that might help with the problem. In addition to drawing on a folk theory of motion, novices use past problems solved and cues from the context of the current problem.

Novices are also more likely to dive immediately into solving the problem with whatever information is at hand (Glaser & Chi, 1988). By contrast, experts think through problems carefully before taking any steps toward solving them. Novices impulsively jump right in, committing themselves to a strategy or plan much too soon. **Metacognition** refers to thinking about thinking in which the object of a cognitive process is another cognitive

Experts in a domain solve problems in a qualitatively different fashion from that of novices. Compared with experts, novices engage in less metacognition and retrieve any relevant source of information, including folk theories that lead to invalid solutions.

process. When experts reflect on different plans and strategies before committing to one, they are engaged in metacognition. Experts also monitor the progress of their plans rather than simply executing them. By thinking about how well a thought process is going, experts engage in still more metacognition.

Memory also functions differently as a result of extensive preparation and practice. Simon and his colleagues estimated that a chess master must store about 50,000 facts regarding specific patterns of pieces and the actions to take when faced with these patterns (Newell & Simon, 1972; Simon & Gilmartin, 1973). Experts do no better on general memory or reasoning tasks, but when asked to remember meaningful configurations of chess pieces from a game, they excelled relative to novices (Chase & Simon, 1973; de Groot, 1965). Specifically, experts could recall and reproduce configurations that were strategically sensible and useful in actually playing chess after viewing the board for only 5 seconds. Whereas novices could reproduce only fewer than 5 pieces, masters could manage more than 20. If the positions on the board were random, then experts could do no better than novices.

For meaningful patterns, experts succeeded by chunking the positions into clusters of four or five pieces. The chunking process, as we have seen, overcomes the limitation of short-term memory. Experts then differ from novices in their ability to encode information mnemonically. **Mnemonic encoding** refers to using the organization of long-term memory to guide the encoding of information into meaningful chunks (Chase & Ericsson, 1982).

In addition, experts are able to retrieve information more effectively than are novices. A **retrieval structure** is a highly specialized means used by experts to gain access to what they know (Chase & Ericsson, 1982). The development of retrieval structures also allows experts to anticipate what they need to remember and to encode the relevant information in a format that ensures later retrieval. Chase and Ericsson (1981, 1982) trained an undergraduate with average intelligence and memory to excel on the digit span test. The training consisted of massive practice—about an hour a day, 2 to 5 days a week, for a duration of 2 years. The student, "S. F.," began with a typical memory span of 7 digits. As shown in Figure 9.11, after about 215 hours of practice, his memory span rose to a remarkable 80 digits!

At the end of each practice session, S. F. tried to recall all of the digits presented during the course of the hour. At first, he recalled little if anything about the digits. But slowly his recall began to increase, paralleling the gains obtained in his memory span. That is, as he learned to become a mnemonic expert, his long-term retention of all digits presented during a session increased to an accuracy of 90% as the short-term span increased to 80 digits.

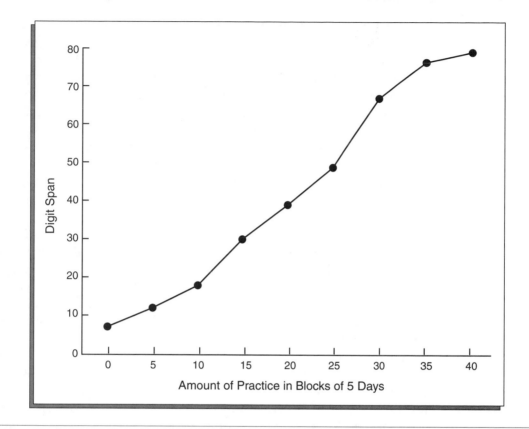

Figure 9.11. Mnemonic practice greatly increases memory span for S. F. Each day in the 5-day block corresponds to an hour of practice. The 43 blocks shown here correspond to about 215 hours of practice.

SOURCE: Chase and Ericsson (1981).

Part of the explanation of his performance is the use of mnemonic encoding. S. F. started by coding the digits phonemically and repeating them silently. With practice, he replaced this relatively ineffective method of main-tenance rehearsal with elaborative rehearsal. Specifically, he began to code the numbers in terms of running times. As a long-distance runner who knew much about the sport, he was able to draw on concepts to chunk the digits.

Here are some excerpts from his verbal protocol describing the chunk-ing process (Chase & Ericsson, 1981). For example, on hearing the digits 3492 as part of a sequence, he labeled it as a running time—either a mile or a 10,000-meter time—after the first two digits. Then, after hearing 9, he recognized the sequence as a near world record in the mile. When S. F. heard another time close to one already encoded, he organized the two times together in memory and then differentiated the sequences, making each code unique. For example, "3492 is 1/10 second faster than, say, 3493" (p. 165). These larger groups of related times invariably were remembered as clusters when recalled at the end of a session, revealing this subjective organization.

The mnemonic coding allowed S. F. to recall seven chunks, with each chunk involving 3 or 4 digits. This permitted accurate recall of 20 or so digits. To achieve a still greater memory span, S. F. devised a special retrieval structure. He started out by separating three chunks from the remaining digits, which he rehearsed by rote. As shown in Figure 9.12, the rehearsal group was retrieved after recalling each of the three chunks. By adding up to 4 digits per chunk plus a rehearsal group of 4 to 6 digits, S. F. attained a digit span up to 18. Next, he devised a hierarchical structure. The first major branch contained four chunks, each with 4 digits. Next, he retrieved the second major branch, which contained four chunks, each with 3 digits. Last came the rehearsal group. This retrieval structure developed with practice, as illustrated in the figure. Further development, with added hierarchical layers, apparently allowed S. F. to handle 80 digits.

Finally, experts can perform a task much faster than can novices, a point that has long been recognized (Chase & Ericsson, 1982). Specifically, the **power law of practice** states that reaction time decreases as a power function of the degree of practice. Within their specific domain, experts perceive, remember, think, and behave faster than do novices. The relation governing performance and practice is a power function (Logan, 1988) that may be described as follows:

$$= RT = a + bN^{-c},$$

where RT is reaction time, a is the asymptote (the minimum value that reaction time may take in the particular task), N is the amount of practice, and b and the exponent c vary from task to task and control the exact shape of the curve.

A stunning range of tasks fits the power law (Logan, 1988). From motor skills such as typing to cognitive skills such as solving geometry problems, one finds the power law. The law is illustrated in Figure 9.13 with data from Neves and Anderson (1981) on learning how to justify proofs in geometry problems. When plotted on a normal scale, the amount of time needed to justify the proofs dropped rapidly with practice initially and then leveled off with higher levels of practice.

The time needed to perform a task decreases as a power function of the degree of practice at the task.

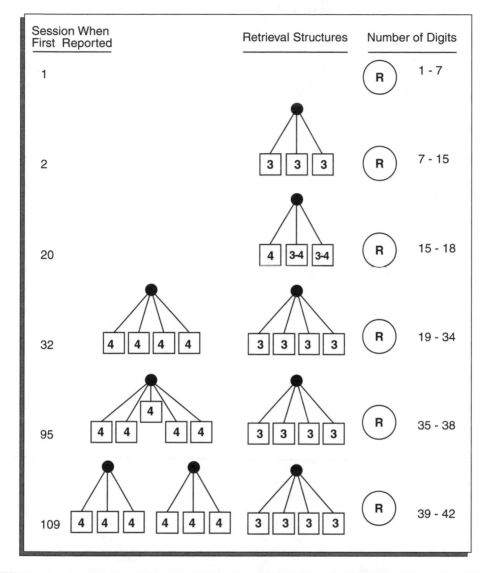

Figure 9.12. The development of S. F.'s retrieval structure. Each square is a digit group; the circled R is the rehearsal group recalled by rote after the digits in the retrieval structures. By Session 109, S. F. recalled 39 to 42 digits using the bottom retrieval structure.

SOURCE: Chase and Ericsson (1981).

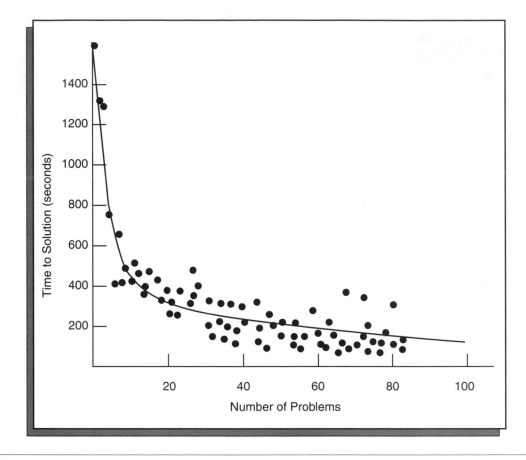

Figure 9.13. Time to solve geometry problems decreased with practice according to a power function.

SOURCE: Neves and Anderson (1981).

SUMMARY

1. Hypothesis testing theory claims that the features and relations that define a new concept are discovered by a controlled process of identifying a hypothesis, testing it, and retaining or resampling it based on feedback. Feature frequency theory contends that a new concept is learned automatically through the slow and gradual accretion of knowledge regarding the frequency of occurrence of features among concept examples. Implicit

learning refers to the unconscious acquisition of complex rules that cannot be verbalized. The processes involved in implicit learning and the resulting representations are not well understood.

2. Skill acquisition proceeds from an early phase of understanding a domain and its tasks, to a middle phase of associating stimulus inputs with appropriate responses, to a final phase of automating the component processes. Reinstating the procedures used during the learning of a skill at the time of test enhances long-term skill retention. Deliberate practice is a regimen of effortful activities, typically begun during childhood, that leads to extraordinary performance. It requires an extensive commitment of time, strong motivation, and either discovery or instruction in superior methods and strategies. It has been estimated that attaining the status of an expert requires a minimum of 10 years of preparation.

3. Experts in a particular domain are skilled at mnemonically encoding information. Experts' organization of long-term memory guides the encoding of information into meaningful chunks. Experts also adopt highly effective strategies for retrieving information of use to them. As we saw earlier, memory depends not only on how well relevant information is encoded but also on how well it is retrieved. The principle of retrieval structure refers to the highly specialized means used by experts to gain access to what they know. Metacognition refers to cognition about cognition or thinking about thinking. Experts in a domain solve problems in a qualitatively different fashion from that of novices. Compared with experts, novices engage in less metacognition and retrieve any relevant source of information, including folk theories that lead to invalid solutions.

4. Experts can perform a task much faster than can novices. Specifically, the power law of practice states that reaction time decreases as a power function of the degree of practice. Within their specific domain, experts perceive, remember, think, and behave faster than do novices. The relation governing performance and practice is a power function (Logan, 1988) that may be described as follows:

$$= RT = a + bN^{-c},$$

where RT is reaction time, a is the asymptote (the minimum value that reaction time may take in the particular task), N is the amount of practice, and b and the exponent c vary from task to task and control the exact shape of the curve.

● KEY TERMS

object permanence

feature frequency theory

hypothesis testing theory

nonanalytic concept learning

implicit learning

expert-novice differences

principle of procedural reinstatement

deliberate practice

ten-year rule

folk theories

metacognition

mnemonic encoding

retrieval structure

power law of practice

Answer key to the implicit learning demonstration in Figure 9.6: Grammatical (g) and ungrammatical (u) strings were as follows for the 30 test stimuli: 1, g; 2, u; 3, g; 4, g; 5, u; 6, u; 7, u; 8, u; 9, g; 10, g; 11, u; 12, g; 13, g; 14, u; 15, u; 16, g; 17, g; 18, u; 19, u; 20, g; 21, g; 22, u; 23, g; 24, g; 25, u; 26, u; 27, g; 28, u; 29, g; 30, u.

PART IV

KNOWING AND USING LANGUAGE

One of the most remarkable and distinguishing features of our species is our use of language. Consider all the ways that you have used language today. From the first "good morning" you spoke or heard, oral communication has been an integral part of your daily activities. From the first glance at the morning newspaper, you have been awash in a sea of written language. The words of this sentence are among the hundreds, if not thousands, you have read today.

Try to imagine your world without language—without the ability to speak, listen, write, and read. Although you could perceive the objects and events surrounding you in the physical world, you could not name them. The power to name, or to refer to this world by means of abstract symbols, opens the door to another universe, one of the intellect. All human endeavors, from the ancient tribal cultures of hunters and gatherers to the recent technological culture of knowledge workers, rest on the foundation of language.

This section opens with a discussion of what is meant by the term *language* and the relation between thought and language. In subsequent chapters, the production and comprehension of language are addressed. Both speech production and the recognition and comprehension of speech have received considerable attention, but for written language reading has been far more investigated than has writing.

CHAPTER 10

LANGUAGE

Human thinking intertwines with language so intricately that some scholars have equated the two. The relation between thought and language will conclude the chapter. To begin, the definition of language requires attention. Just what is this ability of communicating to each other in words? How is it possible to share private thoughts through the public medium of language? In what ways is human language different from the communication systems found in other animals? Language involves stringing together sounds and words in sequences. How are those sequences structured, and are they the same in all human languages found on the planet? In what ways are these sequences determined by innate factors, that is, by our common evolutionary history?

DEFINING LANGUAGE ●

Language is a system of symbols that are used to communicate ideas among two or more individuals. Language uses both mental and external representations. An author communicates with a reader using the symbols of letters and words to get across ideas. In conversation, the speaker and listener exchange mental representations using spoken rather than written symbols. Languages share four rudimentary properties (Clark & Clark, 1977). A language must be learnable by children, it must be able to be spoken and understood readily by adults, it must capture the ideas that people normally communicate, and it must enable communication among groups of people in a social and cultural context.

Language can be used to communicate factual information, but this is not its sole function (Atchison, 1996). Venting emotions, joke telling, and social greeting all are common uses of language that are not aiming to articulate facts. Moreover, some factual knowledge is very difficult to convey with language. For example, try to describe to a friend what a spiral is without resorting to gestures or drawing a diagram. Or, try instructing someone, in words alone, how to tie a square knot. Such visual-spatial knowledge is not easily captured in words.

At the heart of language is the use of symbols to convey meaning. Humans use words, or patterns of sound, to refer to objects, events, beliefs, desires, feelings, and intentions. The words carry meanings. If your friend says he is happy, then you interpret this to mean something about his emotional state. If, instead of speaking, your friend whistles a tune, then his behavior may say something about his emotional state, but it is less meaningful. Your friend might whistle by habit or whistle when he is angry, sad, or happy. Unlike speech, whistling is not specialized to convey a clear meaning. Once humans learn a word, they can retrieve its mental representation, hold it in working memory, and use it in thought. The word itself is represented in addition to the object or event to which it refers.

The words used by humans typically are arbitrary; they lack any connection between the symbols and the meanings they carry and so differ across languages. "Uno," "ein," and "one" are arbitrary sounds referring to the same numerical concept. A single scratch in the dirt or mark on a clay tablet would be a nonarbitrary way of referring to the number one. Ten such marks would nonarbitrarily refer to ten. But the use of nonarbitrary symbols can get very cumbersome. The invention of Arabic numerals for representing numerical quantities vastly simplified the task of representing, say, 432 jars of olive oil or wine.

By putting together strings of words in different orders, one can express a very large number of different meanings. Consider, for example, a 6-word sentence. Suppose that one selected 1 of 10 possible words for the first word of the sentence, another set of 10 possible words for the second word, and so on. The number of unique sentences that could be generated following this procedure would equal 10^6 or 1,000,000 sentences. Because you are not limited to only 6-word sentences or to 10 possible choices, the number of unique sentences that you might utter is infinite in number.

Origins of Language

How did language begin? The answer is unknown and perhaps unknowable, but the question is too tantalizing to ignore. Linguists have reconstructed what they believe early languages were like up to about 10,000 years ago by studying the relationships among the written records of ancient languages, dating back about 5,000 years (Atchison, 1996). However, scholars believe that the origins of language lie much further back in human evolutionary history. Casts made from the skulls of *Homo habilis,* our early ancestor from more than 2 million years ago, reveal what could have been Broca's speech area (Tobias, 1987). However, the unusual shape of the human vocal tract, a necessary requirement for speech, emerged later, perhaps 150,000 to 200,000 years ago, in *Homo sapiens sapiens* (Corballis, 1989; Lieberman, 1984).

A long-debated idea on the origin of language claims that it developed from gestures. However, it appears that language and gestures may well have evolved together (Atchison, 1996). When our ancestors first began to communicate their thoughts to other individuals, they needed a way to refer to specific objects and to relate those objects. It is known that gestures are often synchronized in time with oral statements to convey meaning (Goldin-Meadow, McNeill, & Singleton, 1996). Spoken and gestural outputs are synchronized even in congenitally blind individuals who have never seen anyone gesturing. It could be that gestural and spoken output developed in tandem, with each specialized to communicate particular kinds of information.

Another idea is that language evolved as a consequence of the large brain of humans (Gould & Lewontin, 1979). Language might be an example of taking an existing biological structure and adapting it for a new function. The problem with this view is that language is a very complex function. Adapting an existing structure to handle such a complex new function would seem to be unprecedented. As Atchison (1996) noted, "A type of wading bird uses its wings as a sunshade: there is no evidence of any bird using what was originally a sunshade as wings" (p. 75).

A plausible alternative is that language and a large brain emerged more or less simultaneously (Deacon, 1997). As our hominid ancestors lived together in increasingly larger groups, the degree of social interaction increased. Deception possibly became more important to give one an advantage in getting the food, water, and shelter needed for survival. These kinds of social forces may have selected for a slightly larger brain but at the same time selected for a means of communication. Thus, language and brain size may have fed off each other in evolution. Increasingly sophisticated means of communication demanded increasingly complex brain structures.

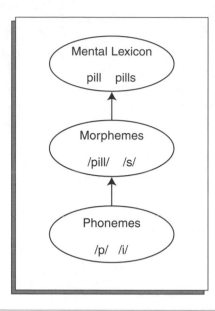

Figure 10.1. Meaningful units of language.

Meaning, Structure, and Use

Semantics. **Semantics** is the study of meaning. A theory of semantics must explain how people mentally represent the meanings of words and sentences. The expression of one's thoughts and their comprehension by listeners or readers obviously depend on these mental representations. As discussed in Chapter 8, sentence meanings can be represented in the form of propositions, that is, abstract codes for the concepts and schemas referred to in a sentence. For example, "The professor praised the industrious student" can be analyzed into two propositions. Each involves a list that starts with a relation followed by one or more arguments:

(praise, professor, student, past)

(industrious, student)

The sounds that we generate in saying a sentence must code meaning in a consistent manner so that listeners can understand our utterances (see Figure 10.1). The coding begins with the phonemes or phonological segments that distinguish one meaningful word from another. As introduced in Chapter 3, pill and kill convey different meanings because they differ in their initial phoneme. As will be seen in Chapter 11, each phoneme is produced by the vocal apparatus in a unique manner. The /p/ of praised and the /b/ of braised are pronounced nearly identically; they differ only in that the vocal cords vibrate for /b/ but not for /p/. This difference, called voicing, is also seen between /s/ and /z/. Say each aloud, and you can feel with your fingers on the Adam's apple the vibration with /z/.

The phonemes of a language are the building blocks of meaningful units, the morphemes. A **morpheme** is a minimal unit of speech used repeatedly in a language to code a specific meaning. A word is a morpheme, such as pill, but so too are prefixes and suffixes, such pre- and -es. Each morpheme signals a distinct meaning. The suffix -ed tells us that the action took place in the past. So, the word *killed* is composed of two morphemes, each of which conveys a specific meaning.

> A morpheme is a minimal unit of speech used repeatedly in a language to code a specific meaning. The word *killed* is composed of two morphemes: kill and -ed.

All the morphemes in a language, taken together, comprise a **mental lexicon** or the dictionary of long-term memory that humans rely on in speaking and listening and in reading and writing. Each morpheme is a lexical entry in this dictionary in the mind. In particular, one is concerned in semantics with content words, that is, the verbs and especially the nouns that refer to natural (e.g., chair) or formal (e.g., the legal definition of marriage) concepts. Function words, such as articles (e.g., the) and prepositions (e.g., by), often serve a grammatical rather than a semantic role. For example, the "by" in "Jill bought groceries by the week" plays the grammatical role of starting a prepositional phrase; the entire phrase could easily be replaced by the adverb "weekly" without a change in meaning. The content words, on the other hand, all contribute to the unique meaning of the sentence.

Syntax. Another landmark of language is its structure. The grammatical rules that specify how words and other morphemes are arranged so as to yield acceptable sentences is defined as **syntax.** Technically, syntax is only part of the study of grammar, the complete set of rules by which people speak and write correctly (including, e.g., punctuation). Here, however, grammar is seen as an abstract set of syntactic rules that describe how the morphemes of a language are sequenced to generate an acceptable sentence. Syntactic rules ensure that speakers and listeners, as well as writers and readers, all are playing the same structural game with language. Because language must follow a linear order—one word after another—either in time (as occurs in speech) or in space (as occurs with text), some convention is needed to order the words and the parts of words (e.g., past tense suffixes).

In English, for instance, a declaration consists of a subject (S) followed by a verb (V) followed by an object (O). Some languages, such as German, follow an S-O-V pattern instead. The grammar of a language specifies the rules that enable one to generate all and only acceptable sentences.

Syntax refers to the rules that specify how words and other morphemes are arranged so as to yield grammatically acceptable sentences.

Nonsentences in the language fail to meet one or more of these rules. If you can speak and understand a language, then you have learned and can use its grammar even if what you know is implicit and not available for conscious articulation. In learning a second language, students sometimes discover, at a conscious level of analysis, grammatical distinctions in their native tongue (e.g., the pluperfect tense).

An implicit knowledge of grammar provides one with linguistic intuitions (Chomsky, 1965). Being able to identify the parts of speech in a sentence—knowing what is the subject as opposed to, say, the verb—is one such intuition. Another is recognizing that two different sentence structures mean the same thing (e.g., "The student passed the exam" and "The exam was passed by the student"). Recognizing syntactic ambiguity, in which multiple structures are possible, is yet another linguistic intuition (e.g., "Visiting relatives can be a pain"). A very basic intuition is recognizing whether a string of words is a grammatical sentence.

To illustrate further the concepts of semantics and syntactics and the idea of linguistic intuitions, consider the three assertions shown in Box 10.1. The first assertion is an English sentence, for it conveys meaning and is syntactically correct. The second assertion is not a sentence because it violates syntactic rules. All of the elements of meaning are there, but they are in the wrong order. The third assertion violates no syntactic rules, yet it fails to make any sense. Your mental representation of the noun "ideas" does not allow them to sleep in any fashion, let alone to dream about a psychologist.

Experiments on comprehension also reveal our sensitivity to grammar. A classic study by Garrett, Bever, and Fodor (1966) illustrates this point. These authors presented listeners with a series of sentences through earphones; they superimposed on the tape-recording of each sentence the sound of a click. The click occurred at various locations relative to the boundaries among

---

Box 10.1

SYNTAX AND SEMANTICS: A DEMONSTRATION

Which of these sentences are grammatical? Which are meaningful?

The psychologist slept fitfully, dreaming new ideas.

Fitfully the slept new, ideas dreaming psychologist.

The new ideas slept fitfully, dreaming a psychologist.

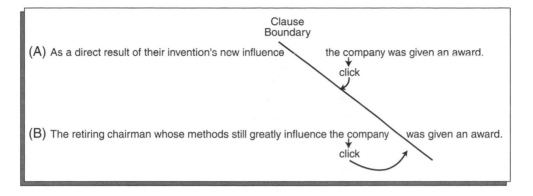

Figure 10.2. The grammatical structure of a sentence influences the perception of a click embedded in the first syllable of the word "company."

the phrases in a given sentence. The listener's task was to identify the location at which he or she heard the click. It turned out that the sound of the click tended to be heard between two syntactic phrases in a sentence even when its actual location occurred earlier or later. Two of the sentences used by Garrett et al. are shown in Figure 10.2. The final words in each sentence ("influence the company was given an award") were tape-recorded once and inserted into the sentences. Thus, the listener heard precisely the same words and pauses, and the click occurred during the first syllable of the word "company." Yet in Sentence A, the word "influence" ends a prepositional phrase and "the" starts the main clause of the sentence. In Sentence B, the word "company" ends a subordinate clause, with "was" being the verb of the main clause. Listeners given Sentence A heard the click occur earlier than did those given Sentence B. Perception of the click "migrated" toward an important syntactic boundary used in comprehending the sentence. This boundary occurred earlier than the click in Sentence A and later than the click in Sentence B.

Pragmatics. The third landmark is the uses or functions of language in social intercourse. Humans may speak or write with themselves as their only audience. But more commonly, the utterances made and texts composed are embedded in a discourse community. Language is intended for and shaped by those who collectively listen, read, comprehend, interpret, and respond to our uses of language. For example, consider the difference in the following two utterances:

It is hot in this room.

Open the window!

The first sentence informs others about how one feels about the room temperature. The second sentence commands someone to let some cool air into the room. But note that in a specific setting, the first sentence might be used to achieve the goal of the second in a polite way. Instead of commanding directly, one can achieve the same effect by merely informing someone standing next to the window.

Pragmatics refers to the manner in which speakers communicate their intentions depending on the social context. A **speech act** refers to a sentence uttered to express a speaker's intention in a way that the listener will recognize (Grice, 1975). There are distinct kinds of speech acts. We inform, command, question, warn, thank, dare, request, and so on. A direct speech act assumes a grammatical form tailored to a particular function. For example, "Open the window" directly commands. An indirect speech act achieves a function by assuming the guise of another type of speech act. For example, one might question ("Can you open the window?"), warn ("If you don't open the window, we'll all pass out"), threaten ("If you don't open the window, I'll shoot!"), declare ("The window really should be open"), inform ("It really is hot in here"), or even thank in a sarcastic tone ("Thanks a lot for opening the window").

Grice (1975) proposed that when two people enter into a conversation, they in essence enter into an implicit contractual agreement called the **cooperative principle.** It means that the participants agree to say things that are appropriate to the conversation and to end the conversation at a mutually agreeable point. One way to understand this contractual agreement is to recall times when people have violated it. Have you ever had someone say something that makes no sense whatsoever in the context of the ongoing conversation or to walk off abruptly to end a conversation without warning? The cooperative principle dictates otherwise. We agree to speak audibly, to use languages that listeners understand, and to follow the rules of those languages.

For example, participants try to be informative by saying what others need to know to understand and not providing unnecessary details, as shown in the following exchange:

Steven: Wilfred is meeting a woman for dinner tonight.
Susan: Does his wife know about it?
Steven: Of course she does. The woman he is meeting is his wife. (Clark & Clark, 1977, p. 122)

Steven misled Susan here by failing to provide enough information in his use of the term "a woman." Susan inferred that the woman in question was someone other than Wilfred's wife.

Pragmatics addresses the various ways in which speakers communicate their intentions depending on the social context. Speech acts serve to inform, command, question, warn, and so on but may do so indirectly rather than directly.

In comprehending the utterances of the current speaker in a conversation, the other participants must frequently make inferences. Grice referred to these as **conversational implicatures.** The following exchange from Grice (1975) illustrates the role that such inferences play in conversation:

Barbara: I am out of gas.
Peter: There is a gas station around the corner.

The syntactic and semantic structure of Peter's sentence simply and briefly conveys propositions about the location of a gas station. Pragmatically, Peter is implying additional propositions, however. He assumes that Barbara will realize he is cooperating with her and so invites her to infer that the gas station is open and has gas available for sale.

Contrasts to Animal Communication

Humans are not unique in using communication or the exchange of information between a sender and a receiver coded in the form of signals understood by both. Pioneering work on communication in the animal kingdom was conducted by von Frisch (1950). The waggle dance of the honeybee directs other members of the hive to distant sources of nectar. The precise nature of the dance communicates the direction and distance from the hive of a source discovered by the dancing bee. Since that time, a stunning array of communication systems have been documented, including the antennae and head gestures of weaver ants, the alarm calls of vervet monkeys, and the complex signaling of dolphins and whales (Griffin, 1984).

One difference between animal communication and human language is the failure of animals to use symbols to represent objects. The dance of the honeybee, for example, conveys information about the environment after coming from a source of nectar. The honeybee dance is not symbolic because it is tied directly to the situation. It is not a separate entity that the bee uses to communicate at a later time when not just returning from or preparing to go to a food source. In humans, words are detached from their referents, and we use them to recall events from the past or to imagine events that have never even happened. The ability to refer to events removed in space and time from the present situation is called **displacement.**

Attempts have been made to teach American Sign Language (ASL) and specially designed languages to chimpanzees, orangutans, and gorillas. Gardner and Gardner (1969, 1975), for example, raised a chimpanzee named Washoe in an environment comparable to one suitable for an American human baby. Those who raised Washoe "spoke" to the chimp using ASL. They trained Washoe to use sign language to ask for what she wanted. Washoe learned more than 130 signs. When shown the picture of an object, she could make the appropriate sign. More important, Washoe occasionally improvised signs or combined them in novel ways. For example, on first seeing a swan, Washoe gave the sign for "water" and the sign for "bird."

Terrace, Petitto, Sanders, and Bever (1979), however, doubted that what Washoe and other apes learned was really language. In particular, they doubted that the apes showed the productivity of human language. **Productivity** refers to the ability to create novel sentences that can be understood by other speakers of the language. Terrace and his colleagues raised Nim Chimsky, a young male chimpanzee. Like Washoe, Nim learned about 130 signs and could use these to request objects or actions that he wanted at the moment. Terrace, however, concluded from careful review of videotapes that Nim's signs were often repetitions of what his human caretaker had just signed. Terrace found little evidence that Nim could combine signs according to syntactic rules. Nim could not generate a simple sentence, in other words.

Other researchers question Terrace's negative conclusion. Even so, no one disagrees that young children with small vocabularies greatly exceed trained apes in their linguistic abilities. A 6-year-old child has a vocabulary on the order of 16,000 words (Carey, 1978). By adulthood, vocabulary is measured in the tens of thousands. Humans can express more ideas than animals for another reason in addition to vocabulary size. As seen earlier, grammar provides a means for producing novel expressions that have never been spoken before. For example, "My dog ordered caviar at the ball game, surprising even the shortstop." It is highly unlikely you have ever heard someone say this sentence. Although some sentences are used repetitively to the point of annoyance (e.g., "Have a nice day"), it is not difficult at all to generate utterly novel sentences.

> Language uses symbols that refer to events displaced in time and space. The mental lexicon and grammar of a language are productive, allowing one to generate an infinite number of novel sentences.

● REPRESENTATIONS OF LANGUAGE

How are the rules of grammar, the mental lexicon, and other constituents of language represented in the mind? Which regions of the brain support these mental representations? Are linguistic representations to some extent prewired through genetic predispositions, or are they entirely learned? To what extent are the cognitive processes that manipulate linguistic representations specific to language, and to what extent are they general processes that operate throughout perception, attention, memory, and thinking? In this section, some preliminary answers to these root questions about the mental representation of language are provided.

Symbolic Versus Connectionist Architectures

Language has been at the center of the debate between advocates of symbolic versus connectionist architectures of the mind. Pinker (1999) argued that symbolic processing models are best suited for explaining the fundamental properties of language because they allow the mind to go beyond similarity. As noted in Chapter 2, similarity lies at the heart of connectionist models. To quote Hinton, McClelland, and Rumelhart (1986),

> If . . . you learn that chimpanzees like onions, you will probably raise your estimate of the probability that gorillas like onions. In a network that uses distributed representations, this kind of generalization is automatic. . . . If you subsequently learn that gibbons and orangutans do not like onions, your estimate of the probability that gorillas like onions will fall, though it may still be higher than it was initially. (pp. 82-83)

However, Pinker observed the following about the use of words and concepts:

> People are not slaves to similarity. We can be told that a whale is not a fish and that Tina Turner is a grandmother, overriding our statistical experience of what fish and grandmothers tend to look like. This suggests an ability to summarize an entire category by a mental variable or symbol, whose meaning comes from the rules it enters into: "a mammal is an animal that suckles," "a grandmother is the mother of a parent." These rules support generalizations that work more like deductions than similarity gradients. For example, we can infer that whales have livers or that Ms. Turner has had at least one baby. (p. 40)

Grammar can be represented by symbolic rules such as sentence = noun phrase + verb phrase + object. No matter which specific nouns and verbs are entered for these variables, the rule still applies. Symbolic rules, then, are like algebraic equations. Any value can be entered into the equation $y = x + 2$, and the rule still holds. To acquire the past tense of regular English verbs, children might test hypotheses about the correct symbolic rule (i.e., past tense = present tense + -ed). The verb "walk" is regular, but the verb "go" is not. Irregular verbs must be learned as exceptions to the rule.

Recall from Chapter 2 that children experience competition for irregular verbs; they do not know whether to say "went" or "goed." In particular, a U-shaped learning pattern takes place in which children begin by correctly producing the past tense of irregular verbs (went) but then decline in performance by making overgeneralization errors (goed). It seems that as they begin to abstract the rule for regular verbs, they mistakenly overgeneralize it to the irregular verbs as well. In the final stage of acquisition, correct performance climbs again as the rule is applied only to regular verbs and not to irregular verbs.

One explanation is that two learning processes are involved. The first involves identifying the symbolic rule, and the second involves learning the exceptions to the rule. The first abstraction process might work by hypothesis testing. Once children hit on the hypothesis that past tense = present tense + -ed, they can correctly use regular verbs (e.g., "I walked," "I danced," "I played"). The second process may involve learning the statistical regularities inherent in language such as which sounds go together to form words in specific sequences. This frequency-based learning process is needed to learn to say "I went" or "I sang." An alternative explanation is that both regular and irregular verbs are learned by tracking statistical regularities and irregularities. The connectionist approach has been tested to see whether a single process can account for learning both kinds of verbs.

Rumelhart and McClelland's Model. Rumelhart and McClelland initially proposed a simple neural network with only an input and output layer to account for the acquisition of English verb tense (see Figure 10.3). The network represented the base form of verbs at the input layer. Each verb's phonological representation was distributed across the input nodes. The output layer represented the past tense phonology of the same verbs. Because the 420 verbs selected were a representative sample of English, most of them were regular verbs (e.g., walk/walked), but irregular verbs of various kinds were also included. For some, the past tense phonology was unrelated to the present tense (e.g., go/went); for others, there were close overlaps in sound (e.g., see/saw, sleep/slept). In fact, a few were phonologically identical (e.g., hit/hit).

Training involved repeated presentations of the present tense and past tense pairs. The weights at the present tense level were adjusted a small amount after each presentation until the appropriate output nodes were activated. After 200 training epochs, the network was able to learn the correct past tense forms of both regular and irregular verbs (Rumelhart & McClelland, 1986). Furthermore, the U-shaped acquisition curve was also approximated by the network (Figure 10.4). Although the network started out doing well with irregular verbs, performance on these declined at about the point that regular verbs were produced correctly 90% of the time. Next, the performance on the irregular verbs slowly began to recover with many more training epochs. Thus, the single learning process embedded in a connectionist architecture seemed, on the surface at least, to be capable of explaining past tense acquisition.

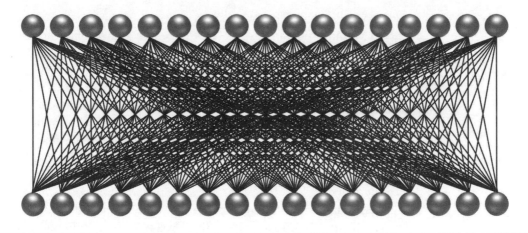

Figure 10.3. A two-layer connectionist model of past tense learning in English.

SOURCE: Rumelhart and McClelland (1986).

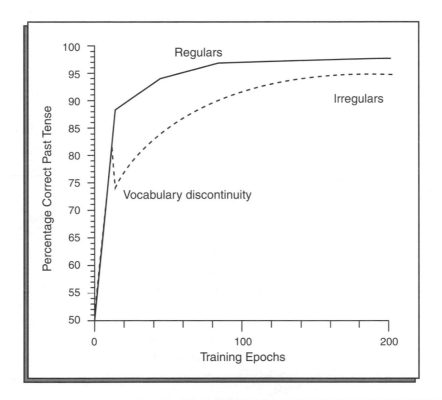

Figure 10.4. Percentages correct in generating regular and irregular verbs as a function of training.

SOURCE: Rumelhart and McClelland (1986).

If the connectionist architecture is complex enough, it can in principle model the U-shaped learning curve without postulating separate learning processes for regular and irregular verbs. The question remains as to whether humans actually use one or two processes to learn inflectional markings and other grammatical features of language.

Pinker and Prince (1988) objected that the simple model shown in Figure 10.3 cannot possibly explain past tense acquisition without cheating by using only certain training patterns. Their reason for this claim is that the two-layer models can solve only problems that are linearly separable such as the inclusive disjunction (OR) problem discussed in Chapter 2. It turns out that the past tense problem is not linearly separable. That is, it resembles the exclusive disjunction (XOR) problem in which very similar input sound patterns must be mapped onto different outputs. Recall that it is necessary to include hidden units to solve these kinds of problems. In response to this criticism, Plunkett and Marchman (1991) added a hidden layer and found that the network could demonstrate the U-shaped learning curve without tailoring the input patterns in any way. So long as both regular and irregular verbs are included in the training set, there will be competition between the two kinds in adjusting the weights. Because of this conflict, overgeneralization errors inevitably will occur.

There is another problem for connectionist models, however. Empirical studies show that some verbs display a strong U-shaped learning curve, whereas others show much weaker curves (Marcus et al., 1992). How can one get a connectionist model to display the U-shaped curve for only some of the English verbs? So far, there is not a good answer to this question, and it may be that any connectionist model that uses back-propagation to adjust its weights will never work (MacWhinney, 1998). These models always produce strong U-shaped curves because they inevitably first learn the irregular verbs so that they are nearly free of errors before overgeneralization errors enter into the picture. Getting weights that will show both strong and weak U-shaped curves is tricky.

Dual Processes in Past Tense Learning. A dual-process model has been empirically supported by neuropsychological evidence (Marslen-Wilson & Tyler, 1997). Aphasic patients sometimes have specific difficulties in comprehending and producing the inflected forms of words. They produce a hesitant "agrammatic speech" in which the appropriate inflections are missing. Although these patients pass tests of their knowledge of word stems (e.g., walk), they fail to understand or produce the regular past tense forms. The -ed inflection is not represented or processed properly. Of interest is whether the lesions in the brain that cause problems with regular verbs also affect irregular verbs. A single connectionist model that explains both regular and irregular verbs ought not spare just irregular verbs when it is "lesioned" by removing nodes.

Marslen-Wilson and Tyler (1997) compared two aphasic patients with normal controls in their speed at making lexical decisions in a priming task. Some target words were preceded by a related prime, as shown in Figure 10.5.

Condition	Test Prime	Control Prime	Target Word
Regular past	jumped	locked	jump
Irregular past	found	shows	find
Semantic	swan	hay	goose
Phonological	gravy	sherry	grave

Figure 10.5. Priming in a lexical decision task: A study of the representation of the past tense in the mental lexicon.

The prime sometimes matched the regular past tense form and sometimes matched the irregular past tense form. Semantically and phonologically related primes were also included. The speed at which target words were correctly called words (remember that some items were nonwords, although these are not shown in the figure) was measured. For normal controls, regular, irregular, and semantic primes speeded reaction time in the lexical decision task, as shown in Figure 10.6. The phonological primes did not produce reliable effects and so are not shown. The aphasic patients "D. E." and "J. G." failed to show priming effects only for the regular verbs. They both had left hemisphere lesions that resulted in their agrammatic speech. Patient "T. S.," by contrast, suffered damage to his right hemisphere. His priming profile differed, with both regular and irregular verbs yielding reliable priming. T. S. showed no semantic priming, however.

Direct evidence that infants can learn abstract algebraic rules has also been reported (Marcus, Vijayan, Rao, & Vishton, 1999). The researchers used the habituation technique of exposing 7-month-old infants to 2 minutes of tape-recorded speech in which "three-word sentences" were presented that fit an "ABA" grammar (e.g., "ga ti ga," "li na li"). After becoming familiar with such ABA sentences, the infants either heard more of the same or were shifted to a test phase. At test, more of the same old ABA sentences were heard, but in addition novel "ABB" sentences (e.g., "ga ti ti," "li na na") were heard. The key question was whether the shift to a novel ABB grammar was noticed by the infants. This was indexed by measuring habituation to a flashing light that accompanied all of the sentences. The infants attended less and less to the light as the ABA sentences were heard repeatedly for 2 minutes. But then, dishabituation—longer gaze times on the flashing light—occurred when ABB sentences were heard. Marcus et al. (1999) ruled out the possibility of

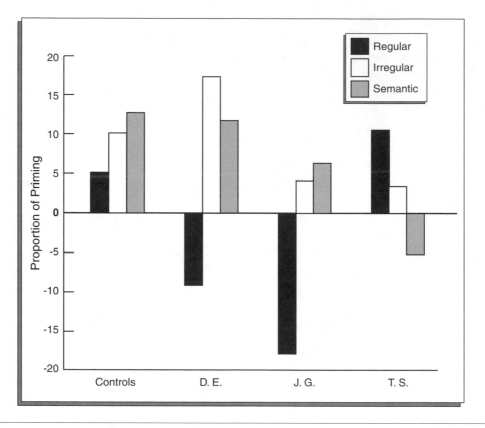

Figure 10.6. Priming effects in normal controls and three patients with acquired aphasia.
SOURCE: Marslen-Wilson and Tyler (1997).

statistical learning alone to explain the dishabituation by changing the specific sounds used on the test. All test sentences used novel sounds for the ABB ("wo fe fe") and ABA ("wo fe wo") grammars. Presumably, a connectionist model could not acquire statistical information about one set of sounds (ga, ti, ti) and apply it to another (wo, fe, fe).

Conclusion. The way in which the past tense and other aspects of grammar are learned and represented is still debated. It is widely agreed that a connectionist model provides an excellent account of how statistical information about language is learned. Still contested is whether a single process is sufficient. The connectionist theorist rejects a second process of abstracting algebraic rules on grounds of parsimony. Occam's razor demands that if connectionism alone is adequate, then the theory should not be complicated with a rule abstraction process. To do so has been compared to Tycho Brahe's efforts to patch up Ptolomy's theory that the earth revolves around the sun (McClelland & Seidenberg, 2000). It could be done by adding a lot of complications, but the Copernican view was more parsimonious. Although dual-process theory is not parsimonious, it may turn out to be correct. Perhaps Occam's razor is not the right tool for dissecting the human mind. Perhaps the course of human evolution has resulted in the development of two distinct processes that contribute in different ways to past tense acquisition. Only further research will determine the truth.

Universal Grammar

The language or languages that you heard and learned to speak as a young child shaped many aspects of your knowledge about language. For example, the word in your mental lexicon that you use to refer to the family pet is dog, chien, or hund depending on whether you acquired English, French, or German. However, other aspects of language are culturally invariant. Linguistic universals are properties that are shared in common by all natural languages found and learned in diverse cultures around the world. For example, at about 3 or 4 months of age, babies all over the planet start babbling, producing sounds that are similar to adult speech but quite meaningless. The babbling peaks between before a child's first birthday, when often the first understandable word will occur (de Villiers & de Villiers, 1978). The first words are invariably composed of a single syllable made up of a consonant and vowel (CV) or two syllables that repeat the same two sounds (CVCV), as in "mama" or "dada," the words all parents want to hear.

Universal grammar refers to the genetically determined knowledge of human language that allows children in all cultures to rapidly acquire the language to which they are exposed. Many aspects of semantics and pragmatics vary across languages and are not universal. However, the syntactic structure of languages may at least in part reflect an innate universal grammar. A language acquisition device (LAD) is the innate mechanism that presumably analyzes the linguistic inputs to which we are exposed and adjusts its parameters to fit that language. Universal grammar and the LAD are thought to reflect an innate cognitive module that is independent of other cognitive systems (Chomsky, 1986; Fodor, 1983). According to this theory, the universal grammar allows certain parameters of variation among languages, and these parameters are set during the acquisition process.

Parameter Setting. For example, during parameter setting, a child exposed to Italian would learn to put a positive setting on the pronoun omission parameter. In Italian, in contrast to English, it is permissible to omit the pronoun before a verb because the inflection on the verb conveys the necessary information about the subject of the sentence. For example, "I love" can be expressed as "Amo." The child exposed to English instead of Italian would learn a negative setting for the parameter of pronoun omission.

To take a different illustration, consider the syntactic order of subject (S), verb (V), and object (O) introduced earlier. A word order parameter in the universal grammar would allow certain combinations and not others. Greenberg (1966) concluded from his examination of natural languages that only four of the six possible orders are used and that one of these (VOS) is quite rare. The common orders are SOV, SVO, and VSO. In theory, the developing infant would come equipped at birth with the implicit knowledge that natural languages never follow the OVS and OSV orders. Children the world over would come prepared to examine whether the language (or languages) to which they are exposed conform to one of the four possible word orders.

Languages also differ in the degree of word order variation allowed. Russian, for example, tolerates more variation in the order of words in a sentence than does English. Pinker (1990) hypothesized that children are programmed to assume that the grammar of their native language demands a fixed order of words. The evidence suggests that early utterances indeed follow a strict ordering, regardless of the language being learned. In the case of English, these early utterances approximate the grammatically correct order. For Russian children, however, their utterances initially fail to show the full scope of possible word orders. It appears that an innate language acquisition device guides children to try out a fixed order first.

Absence of Input. Two kinds of arguments have been advanced in favor of universal grammar from atypical cases in which infants fail to receive language input. First, congenitally deaf children have never heard spoken language; some are not taught standard sign language either. Despite the absence of speech or sign input, such children invent their own gestural language that reflects properties of speech acquired by children with normal hearing (Goldin-Meadow & Mylander, 1990). For example, one-word utterances by normal children occur at about 18 months of age, and these are later followed with two- and three-word utterances. The deaf children similarly invent one-sign gestures at 18 months, followed later by two- and three-sign gestures. Presumably, an innate language acquisition device dictates this common pattern of development.

Second, there may be a critical period during which the LAD is open to input (Lenneberg, 1967). Feral children have been found living with animals, without any contact with a community of speaking humans. If found after

5 years of age, such children are typically unable to learn the phonology of human speech. Without exposure to the phonemes of a particular language, the representations that start out as babbling and eventually develop into speech seem to be lost and unrecoverable after the early years of life. Although less severe, there may be a critical period for learning a second language as well. If you have not learned the phonology of a second language by the time of puberty, then native speakers can detect your foreign accent with ease (Nespor, 1999).

During the 1970s, a child named Genie, who suffered from severe neglect comparable to any "wolf child," was found in Los Angeles (Curtiss, 1977). From about 20 months of age until she was discovered at 13 years of age, her parents isolated her in a small closed and curtained room. Her mother visited her only a few minutes each day to feed her. The child had no exposure to radio or television. Her father beat her for making noise and, along with her brother, barked at her like a dog rather than speaking to her. They believed that she was severely retarded. After her rescue, she was tested for language comprehension, and she had no knowledge of grammar. Because she was past puberty, the critical period hypothesis predicts that Genie should fail to learn once put in a language-rich environment. However, the results were mixed. Genie began producing single words 5 months after her rescue and two-word utterances at 8 months. Her learning of phonology looked very much like normal language acquisition. She started with conso-nant-vowel monosyllables, for example, and worked up to longer words. Her grammatical development was poor, by contrast. Genie never did master syntax. The small number of cases of feral children and the possibility of mental retardation not specific to language prevent drawing strong conclu-sions (McDonald, 1997).

Universal grammar refers to the genetically determined knowledge of human language that allows children in all cultures to rapidly acquire the language to which they are exposed. The evidence is unclear as to whether language is innate.

Neural Systems

Very early in the scientific study of the brain, the localization of language was proposed. In 1861, Broca reported on a patient who had lost his ability to produce meaningful speech but who retained his ability to hear and com-prehend speech (McCarthy & Warrington, 1990). The patient received the nickname "Tan" because he uttered only this sound. Broca observed that the muscles of the vocal apparatus were not at fault, for Tan could eat and drink without difficulty. Broca speculated that Tan suffered from damage to a specific area in his brain that controlled speech, located in the third convo-lution of frontal lobe in the left hemisphere. As it turned out, Tan suffered brain damage in many areas, but we still refer to this part of the brain as

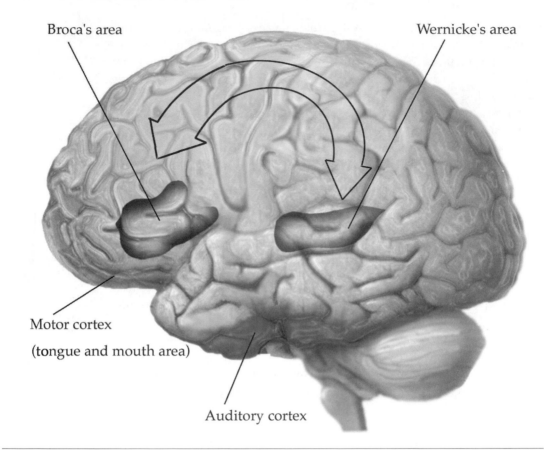

Broca's area

Wernicke's area

Motor cortex
(tongue and mouth area)

Auditory cortex

Figure 10.7. Broca's area and Wernicke's area in the left hemisphere.

Broca's area in honor of his early investigations (see Figure 10.7). **Broca's aphasia** refers to an inability to speak fluently without effort and with correct grammar. Speech is halting and often consists of short sequences of nouns so that the grammatical structure of a sentence is broken. Dronkers, Redfern, and Knight (2000) provided this example of the speech of a Broca's patient in a picture description task: "O, yeah. Det's a boy an' a girl . . . an' . . . a . . . car . . . house . . . ligth po' (pole). Dog an' a . . . boat'N det's a . . . mm . . . a . . . coffee, an' reading" (p. 951). The patient with Broca's aphasia can comprehend single words and short grammatical sentences, however.

In 1874, Wernicke reported on patients who could speak easily (albeit unintelligibly) but who failed to comprehend speech (McCarthy & Warrington, 1990). They tended to pronounce phonemes in a jumble, some times uttering novel words or neologisms. Postmortem examination of one such patient revealed a lesion in the area just behind or posterior to Broca's area. **Wernicke's aphasia** refers to a comprehension dysfunction. Speech is fluent and effortless, although often semantically meaningless. Dronkers et al. (2000) provided the following example of the Wernicke's patient:

Ah, yes, it's, ah . . . several things. It's a girl . . . uncurl . . . on a boat. A dog . . . 'S is another dog . . . uh-oh . . . long's . . . on a boat. The lady, it's a young lady. An' a man. They eatin'. 'S be place there. This . . . a tree! A boat. No, this is a . . . It's a house. Over in here . . . a cake. An it's, it's a lot of water. Ah, all right. I think I mentioned about that boat. (p. 951)

Laterality. Hemispheric dominance or brain lateralization in humans means that one hemisphere controls key motor and cognitive functions. Approximately 90% of people reveal a left dominant hemisphere, meaning that they are right-handed. Recall that the brain shows contralateral control, such that the motor and sensory nerves of the right side of the body are controlled by the left hemisphere of the brain. Right-handedness is found universally across diverse cultures (Corballis, 1989). Moreover, language is localized in the left hemisphere of virtually all right-handed individuals. When right-handed people suffer damage to their left hemisphere, the frequency of aphasia is high (McCarthy & Warrington, 1990). Only rarely does a right-handed individual lose language function from damage to the right hemisphere.

Researchers investigated the localization of language in a remarkable series of studies involving split-brain patients (Gazzaniga, 1970, 1995; Gazzaniga, Bogen, & Sperry, 1965). These individuals suffered horrendous seizures from epilepsy that could not be controlled by the usual therapies. During the 1950s, physicians treating such severe cases successfully controlled the seizures by cutting the connective tissue between hemispheres called the corpus collosum. An epileptic seizure could be likened to an electrical storm; by severing the hemispheric bridge, the surgeons isolated the storm to one hemisphere, lessening its devastation. After recovering from the surgery, these patients behaved quite normally and revealed no cognitive deficits to casual observers. Yet careful testing revealed highly selective deficits.

If a right-handed, split-brain patient was given a common object such as a coin, then the patient's ability to verbalize the name of the object depended on which hand he or she used. If the coin was placed in the patient's right hand, then all information about it would be processed by the left hemisphere. This was because of contralateral control, whereby the left hemisphere controlled the right side of the body and the right hemisphere controlled the left side. Because of the language centers in the left hemisphere, the patient could readily name the object as a coin. But if the coin was placed in the patient's left hand, thereby sending the information to the right hemisphere, then the patient was unable to name the object. When pressed to point to the object just placed in the left hand, the patient could do so—but only by pointing with his or her left hand. This astonishing outcome showed that the right hemisphere indeed knew what the object was but could not name it because language use depended on involving the left hemisphere.

Further experiments verified these observations by taking advantage of the fact that the objects in the left visual field project only to the right visual hemisphere, as discussed in Chapter 3. The split-brain patient sat in front of a display screen and fixated on a central point. A stimulus was flashed briefly (100-200 milliseconds) in the left visual field so that it was received and processed only by the right hemisphere. The patient was unable to name the object, suggesting that language requires processing in the left hemisphere. If asked to pick up the object from among some alternatives behind a screen with the left hand, the patient was usually successful because the right hemisphere successfully recognized the object.

Thus, in right-handed individuals, language critically depends on processing in the dominant left hemisphere. The situation for left-handed individuals is much more complicated, by the way. It appears, from the various tests just noted, that most left-handed individuals show speech functions in both hemispheres. Some left-handers show speech localized in the left hemisphere, and few if any reveal localization in the right hemisphere (McCarthy & Warrington, 1990).

Of great interest, activation is observed in the left hemisphere, including Broca's area, when deaf individuals who learned ASL as their first language observe someone making signs (Neville & Bavelier, 2000). As shown in Color Plate 7 in the section of color plates, the pattern is very similar to that observed in the left hemisphere when hearing individuals read English. Although ASL does not involve speech, it has a complex grammar expressed through hand motions and spatial locations (Poizner, Bellugi, & Klima, 1990). Thus, the functional magnetic resonance imaging (fMRI) results imply that there is a strong biological predisposition for the grammar of a language—whether it involves sounds or visual signs—to be represented in the left hemisphere. The native users of ASL learned English as a second language late in life, after the critical period for grammar acquisition. As can be seen in Color Plate 7, reading English resulted primarily in right rather than left hemisphere activation. This result suggests that the bias for left hemisphere language representation is not expressed when learned after a critical period of development.

Although Broca's and Wernicke's areas in the left hemisphere are rightfully viewed as necessary for language in most humans, it is incorrect to think

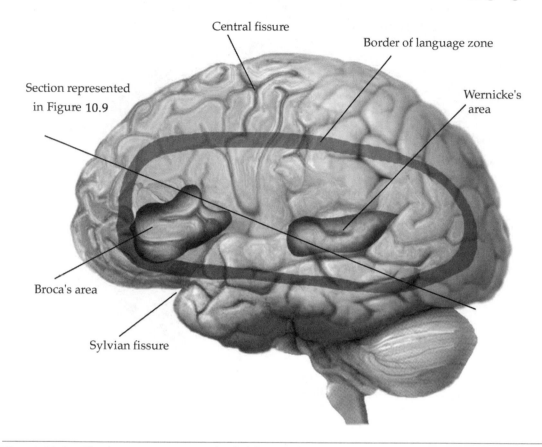

Central fissure

Border of language zone

Section represented
in Figure 10.9

Wernicke's
area

Broca's area

Sylvian fissure

Figure 10.8. The language zone in the left hemisphere.
SOURCE: Adapted from Goodglass (1993).

of language as localized. Many other cortical and subcortical regions are also necessary for comprehension and expression of language, particularly when the reading and writing of visible language is considered in addition to spoken language (Goodglass, 1993). The language zone is pictured in Figure 10.8 from a lateral view of the left hemisphere. It extends beyond Broca's and Wernicke's areas anteriorly into the frontal lobe and posteriorly into the parietal lobe. It includes regions that are both superior and inferior to the Broca's and Wernicke's areas in terms of their vertical location in the left hemisphere. Thus, language is a prime example of how a complex cognitive function involves multiple distributed regions of the brain.

A horizontal section through this zone, illustrated in Figure 10.9, reveals numerous bilateral regions deep within the brain that are also necessary for

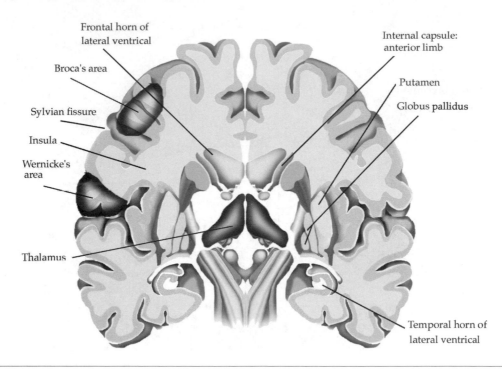

Figure 10.9. Subcortical regions are also involved in language.

SOURCE: Adapted from Goodglass (1993).

language functioning in addition to the lateralized regions identified by Broca and Wernicke. Some support the motor movements involved rather than the higher level linguistic processes (Goodglass, 1993). Thus, language provides an excellent illustration of the point that complex cognitive functions are not strictly localized. Despite the powerful evidence that the areas of Broca and Wernicke are necessary for language, it is incorrect to say that they are sufficient for language.

● THOUGHT AND LANGUAGE

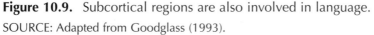

The relation between language and the other cognitive systems underlying thought has long been a central issue in cognitive psychology. Traditionally, there have been three hypotheses on this relation. Thought and language might be identical, language might emerge from or depend on thought, or thought might depend on language (Jenkins, 1969). More recently, the modularity hypothesis, in which language is independent of other cognitive

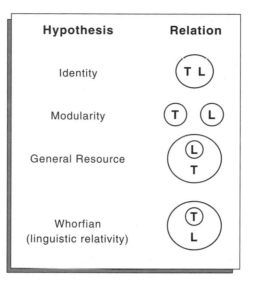

Hypothesis	Relation

Figure 10.10. Possible relations between thought and language.

systems, has been added to the list. There is not yet a consensus on how thought and language are related. With the exception of the identity hypothesis, none of the alternatives can be firmly rejected at this point in time.

The Identity Hypothesis

The identity of thought and language is illustrated symbolically in Figure 10.11 by placing both thought and language in the same set. The **identity hypothesis,** advanced by the behaviorists, equated thought with subvocal speech (Watson, 1924). Numerous experiments set out to identify the muscular movements of the vocal tract that the behaviorists expected whenever a person engaged in thinking. The results were mixed, with subvocal speech observed in some individuals and not in others. Watson (1924) tried to account for the negative results by suggesting that other muscular movements may be just as critical as vocal movements. For example, in lecturing, a professor might make frequent gestures with his or her arms and hands. Perhaps, the professor also might make minute hand and arm movements as well as subvocalizations when thinking in private.

The definitive test of the identity hypothesis was provided by Smith, Brown, Toman, and Goodman (1947). Smith agreed to be paralyzed by the drug curare, losing muscular control. Without access to his muscles, he in theory should have lost his ability to think. But the outcome proved otherwise. Smith found that he could still perceive his surroundings, recall past events, and think under the influence of curare.

The Modularity Hypothesis

At the opposite extreme to the identity hypothesis, perhaps language is unrelated to thought, as shown in Figure 10.11. According to the **modularity hypothesis,** language is independent of thought and is served by a specialized module of language-specific representations and processes.

Recall from Chapter 3 that a module is domain specific in the sense that is specialized for a single kind of input. It also runs automatically given the input, regardless of other concurrent demands on attention. It is cognitively inpenetrable in the sense that the inner workings of the module are not available for conscious introspection; armchair theorizing about how it works may well be wrong. It is informationally encapsulated in the sense that the module operates without receiving information from other cognitive processes or modules. Until the module completes its processing and delivers an output, other information cannot be combined with it at an intermediate stage.

The most striking evidence that language is modular comes from individuals suffering from unique forms of mental retardation (Levy, 1996). William's syndrome is characterized by severe retardation in all cognitive abilities with the exception of language. It is a genetically transmitted disorder that produces "impish" facial features, cardiovascular problems, and low IQ test scores. Despite their impaired intelligence, children with William's syndrome use grammatically complex sentences in their conversations. They score nearly perfectly on difficult tests of language comprehension skills and often show vocabularies that are abnormally large for the children's age. When asked to list names of animals, one such child responded, "weasel, newt, salamander, chihuahua, ibex, yak" (Bellugi, Bihrle, Neville, Doherty, & Jernigan, 1992, p. 11). Their language and social engagement in conversation are somehow spared, while other cognitive functions are not.

Linguistic savants also support the modularity hypothesis. One such savant, Christopher, suffered from autism. Despite an IQ indicative of severe mental retardation, Christopher spoke flawless native English and could converse fluently in 15 other languages. Although his syntactic knowledge of the foreign languages was less than perfect, Christopher acquired fluency with relatively little exposure. Autistic children diagnosed as savants focus their time and attention on a narrow range of activities, which in Christopher's case involved language (Smith & Tsimpli, 1995).

A strong argument against the modularity of language comes from cases of acquired cognitive deficits such as dementia and aphasia (Moscovitch & Umilta, 1990). If the language module is informationally encapsulated, then it should not draw on central systems of memory and attention. If language is really independent of these central resources, then there ought to be individuals who have suffered general intellectual impairment but no language deficit. Such a case is yet to be reported. Also, individuals who acquire aphasia as adults, from strokes or accidents, will often show signs of other kinds of cognitive deficits. Remember that the language zone of the brain is widely distributed and interconnected with the systems of working memory and long-term memory; lesions are rarely limited to one location. Thus, the language and central cognitive systems are too interdependent to satisfy the criterion of informational encapsulation.

The modularity hypothesis takes the position that language is independent of thought and is served by a specialized module of language-specific representations and processes. William's syndrome supports the hypothesis, but acquired aphasias do not.

The General Resource Hypothesis

An alternative view is that language depends on general cognitive resources that underlie nonlinguistic tasks as well. The **general resource hypothesis** regards language as interacting with and built on general cognitive systems. This view is illustrated in Figure 10.11 by showing thought as a subset of general cognitive systems. As Piaget first observed, young infants are engaged in a serious cognitive activity before language begins to unfold with the first spoken words at about 12 months of age. Children as young as 3 to 4 months have acquired the concept of object permanence and can engage in simple reasoning about the properties of physical objects in space (Spelke, 2000).

Indeed, a number of crucial developments seem to provide a platform for language development. For example, there is abundant evidence that the gestural abilities of the infant undergo changes that are related to word production (Bates, Benigni, Bretherton, Camaioni, & Volterra, 1979). The emergence of single words (e.g., mama) from the earlier period of babbling (e.g., mamamamabababa) is predicted in part by (a) specific developments in pointing, giving, and showing; (b) the emergence of gestural naming (e.g., drinking from an empty cup, putting a shoe to one's foot); and (c) the beginnings of being able to imitate gestures.

The Linguistic Relativity Hypothesis

Another possible relation is that thought is shaped by the nature of language rather than vice versa. Language, then, is primary rather than cognition in general. The **linguistic relativity hypothesis** holds that thought depends on the properties of language. This view is also called the Whorfian hypothesis after Benjamin Whorf, an engineer who advanced the idea in the course of studying North American Indian languages as an avocation. The view that language determines thought is illustrated in Figure 10.11 by showing thought as a subset of language.

For example, the mental lexicon and the syntactic structure of a given language might constrain how the native speakers of a language think. Skiers distinguish between the wet slushy qualities of corn snow and the dry fluffy qualities of powder snow, for example. The linguistic relativity hypothesis would hold that skiers perceive and think about the world differently than do people for whom snow is snow. Alternative words in a lexicon affects cognition on this view. Whorf and many other linguists and psychologists have searched for evidence that the way the members of a culture think can be traced to the structure of their language.

An early test of the linguistic relativity hypothesis investigated labels for colors. Languages differ markedly in the words used to identify divisions among the hues of the spectrum (Brown & Lenneberg, 1954). In English, six primary terms are used: purple, blue, green, yellow, orange, and red. In Shona, an African language, this number is reduced to four terms. In another African language, Bassa, only two terms are used, with one referring to the brighter, long-wavelength hues of yellow, orange, and red and the other referring to the darker, shorter wavelengths. Thus, it is interesting to ask whether people perceive the spectrum differently depending on the language they speak.

This hypothesis was tested by assessing the ease with which a native speaker from each of 23 different languages could provide a label for typical versus atypical colors. As it happened, the typical colors were markedly easier to label relative to the atypical colors. For example, the prototype hue for red was easiest to label, whereas a washed out, pinkish red was labeled more slowly. This outcome occurred across all languages tested (Heider, 1972). In addition, members of a Stone Age tribe of New Guinea, the Dani Indians, use a language with only two color terms, yet they behave the same as English speakers in a learning task that depends on color perception. Individuals from both cultures learned arbitrary names to go with different colors that differed in typicality. English speakers made the fewest errors on the prototypical colors—those taken as the best representatives of red, blue, and so on. The Dani did the same, even though their language has no terms for them (Rosch, 1973). The results, then, speak against linguistic relativity.

Bilingual speakers sometimes claim that they think differently depending on the language they are using at the moment and that they dream only in their native tongue (Wierzbicka, 1985). One language can certainly demand more of the listener or speaker than can another. For example, English and Italian differ in that a given word in English may have several meanings (high polysemy), whereas in Italian it has only one or two meanings. In English, "I went out to buy the pot" demands more processing time to understand as the listener sorts out "whether the speaker spends leisure time in gardening or recreational pharmacology" (Hunt & Agnoli, 1991, p. 382). In Italian, "Uscii a comperare il vaso" unambiguously identifies a gardening pot. Italian is also less ambiguous because it relies on inflections rather than word order to assign syntactic roles. A story on the same topic regarding East Germany in 1989 published by similar Italian and American newspapers revealed a startling difference. Two English speakers "agreed that 18 of 33 sentences were potentially ambiguous out of context." Two Italian speakers "found that only 3 of 64 sentences were ambiguous" (p. 384).

Hunt and Agnoli (1991) concluded in favor of the weak version of the Whorfian hypothesis as follows:

> Every utterance in language A has a translation in language B. … The issue is one of cost: Are there statements that are natural in language A that are stateable but unmanageable in language B? The Whorfian hypothesis is properly regarded as a psychological hypothesis about language performance and not as a linguistic hypothesis about language competence. Our review has convinced us that different languages pose different challenges for cognition and provide differential support to cognition. (p. 387)

In conclusion, thought is not fully dependent on language, as suggested by the linguistic relativity hypothesis. In fact, in some ways, language is partly influenced by the nature of our perceptual systems, as predicted by the general resource hypothesis. However, it appears that language can also influence thought, supporting a weak version of the Whorfian hypothesis.

SUMMARY

1. Language is a system of symbols that are used to communicate ideas among two or more individuals. It uses both mental and external representations such as printed text. The symbols of language, such as words, are arbitrary in the sense that they lack any necessary connection with their meaning and they differ from one language to another. A language must be learnable by children, it must be able to be spoken and understood readily by adults, it must capture the ideas that people normally communicate, and

it must enable communication among groups of people in a social and cultural context. All human languages make use of 50 or so speech sounds or phonological segments produced by our vocal apparatus. Each such utterance is a phoneme, defined as a basic speech sound that makes a difference in meaning. A morpheme is a minimal unit of speech used repeatedly in a language to code a specific meaning; it is made up of two or more phonemes such as a word or a suffix.

2. Languages differ in terms of their semantics, syntactics, and pragmatics. Semantics concerns the use of symbols to refer to objects, events, and ideas in the world. The words used in language comprise the lexicon that must be represented mentally in fluent speakers. Syntactics concerns the rules for ordering words to construct meaningful and acceptable sentences in a language. Pragmatics concerns the use of language within social contexts. People command, inform, warn, and otherwise communicate their intentions as direct speech acts (e.g., "Open the window") or as indirect speech acts (e.g., "Dreadfully hot in here, don't you think?"). An implicit agreement, called the cooperative principle, governs conversations ensuring that participants say appropriate things and end the conversation at a mutually agreeable point.

3. Language uses symbols that refer to events displaced in time and space. The mental lexicon and grammar of a language are productive, allowing one to generate an infinite number of novel sentences. It is unclear whether these capacities are best understood in terms of symbolic or connectionist cognitive architectures. Connectionist models based on statistical information may best explain human pattern recognition or memory for irregularities in language, but it has been argued that only symbolic models can explain the learning of grammatical regularities. Whether algebraic-like symbolic rules are learned in past tense acquisition has been intensely investigated, but the evidence is still unresolved. Connectionist theorists argue that both regular and irregular verbs are learned by the same statistical process, whereas others assert that regular verbs are learned by an algebraic process.

4. Universal grammar refers to the genetically determined knowledge of human language that allows children in all cultures to rapidly acquire the language to which they are exposed. Whether language is innate is another hotly debated question that remains unresolved. Language is localized in the left hemisphere of virtually all right-handed individuals. Damage to Broca's area in the left hemisphere causes a language disorder or aphasia. Broca's aphasia refers to an inability to speak fluently without effort and with correct grammar. By contrast, damage to Wernicke's area disrupts language comprehension. Speech is fluent and effortless in Wernicke's aphasia, although it is often semantically meaningless.

5. There are four hypotheses concerning the relation between language and thought, that is, the other nonlinguistic cognitive systems. The identity hypothesis, proposed by behavioral psychologists, viewed thought as equivalent to language. The modularity hypothesis holds that language is a specialized independent module with no relation to nonlinguistic cognition. The general resource hypothesis views nonlinguistic cognitive systems as primary but interactive with language; thus, language is subject to the same constraints as are other nonlinguistic processes. Lastly, the Whorfian or linguistic relativity hypothesis claims that thought is dependent on language rather than the other way around. The structure of a given language ought to constrain the nature of nonlinguistic cognition. Only the identity hypothesis has been firmly ruled out.

KEY TERMS ●

semantics

morpheme

mental lexicon

syntax

pragmatics

speech act

cooperative principle

conversational implicatures

displacement

productivity

universal grammar

Broca's aphasia

Wernicke's aphasia

identity hypothesis

modularity hypothesis

general resource hypothesis

linguistic relativity hypothesis

CHAPTER 11

LANGUAGE PRODUCTION

S peaking is such a familiar skill, its complexity easily escapes us. The mental lexicon of a typical high school graduate includes approximately 45,000 words. This ranges in adults between about 30,000 and 80,000 words (Bock & Garnsey, 1998). Because language is productive, there is essentially an infinite number of unique sentences that can be generated by the grammatical component. To illustrate, if we were to consider English sentences of only 20 words or fewer, then approximately 10^{30} unique sentences can be constructed, a staggering number. In generating frequently used words, functional processing works rapidly and efficiently. The motor system of a speech—a marvel in itself—can readily articulate about four words every second, and the grammatical and phonological components have no trouble in providing the representations needed.

The production of language has not received as much attention from cognitive psychologists as has the comprehension of language. Speaking is, of course, as central to language use as is listening, but researchers have been blocked in studying production because of the difficulties in conducting sound laboratory experiments (Bock, 1996). Similarly, reading has been studied far more intensively in the laboratory than has writing. For comprehension, the word, sentence, or text presented to an individual can be controlled, and the response can be readily measured. By contrast, what the individual might say or write in response to an experimenter's prompt is unpredictable and idiosyncratic.

Rather than experimentation, the natural observation of speech errors or slips of the tongue has largely shaped theories of speech production, and slips of the pen have similarly provided evidence on written spelling. For the reflective thinking processes involved in carefully formulated speech and most writing, observations of pauses in motor behavior and verbal protocols of thinking aloud have been commonly used. Another alternative to experimentation has been the use of neuropsychological case studies that correlate lesions in brain structure with difficulties in speaking and writing.

SPEECH PRODUCTION ●

To speak even a single sentence, one must first plan what to say and how it needs to be said to the listeners at hand. The ideas to be conveyed must be expressed using appropriate words and sentence structure. Even if the speaker has an idea and knows what to say, at times mistakes will occur at the stage of motor output in articulating the specific sounds needed to speak the sentence intended. Speech production has been modeled in terms of first generating a sentence and then articulating it, and these are considered in turn here. Because of extensive practice, a speaker's native tongue is automatic and highly fluent. Humans normally talk at a rate of two to three words per second, but occasional bursts of up to seven words per second spice our production (Bock & Levelt, 1994). This remarkable fluency is taken for granted until one tries to learn a second language. Even in our native language, much can and does go wrong, with the consequence that about half of speaking time is spent hemming and hawing or not saying anything at all. Minor breakdowns or dysfluencies in speech occur on the order of 3 to 12 times per minute (Bock & Garnsey, 1998).

Speech Errors

The errors that occur in everyday speech have been recorded and categorized in an effort to shed light on the cognitive mechanisms underlying production (Stemberger, 1985). Such errors or slips of the tongue were an important window on the unconscious for Sigmund Freud. According to psychodynamic theory, such slips revealed the speaker's unconscious wishes. An English clergyman, William A. Spooner, earned a spot in history for his speech slips rather than his stirring sermons (Clark & Clark, 1977). For example, Spooner chastised a student with "You have hissed all my mystery lectures" and warned his parishioners "Easier for a camel to go through the knee of an idol."

According to cognitive theories, slips of the tongue reflect errors in the language production systems. They are no different from other everyday errors that people make, and they reveal much about everyday mental processes rather than about mysterious unconscious conflicts (Norman, 1981). A Spoonerism, as just illustrated, is in fact a particular type of cognitive error in which two phonetic segments are exchanged in position. Fromkin (1973) identified this and other categories of speech errors. For example, two phonemes might be blended rather than reversed, as when the speaker meant to say "grizzly and ghastly" but came out with "grastly." An error may occur at various levels of language structure. Reversals, for example, may occur at the level of phonetic segments. Instead of saying "Terry and Julia," the speaker erred by saying Derry and Chulia. At the level of syllables, the speaker meant to say "harpsicord" but instead uttered "carpsicord." The phonetic segments were switched across a boundary of one syllable to the next within a single word. As will be seen, the kinds of speech errors that occur can shed light on the underlying processes involved in speech production.

Acquired Aphasia

As introduced in Chapter 10, Broca's aphasia is a loss of speech production caused by lesions to the left frontal cortex. The speech of someone suffering from this disorder may consist of just single words, such as was found in the original case of "Tan," but it might also include short phrases. The output is characterized as telegraphic, but it gets across meaning in a highly abbreviated form, dropping out function words such as articles (e.g., a, the) and prepositions (e.g., of, from). The individual's language production is agrammatic, meaning that the processes that result in syntactically correct sentences do not function properly. This can have consequences for language comprehension as well as production. For example, consider this test sentence: "The dog was chased by the cat. Who chased whom?" A patient with Broca's aphasia might incorrectly respond as follows: "Dog chased cat."

Wernicke's aphasia, by contrast, is characterized by fluent-sounding language production, but the speech is meaningless. The sentences fit grammatical patterns, and the words are pronounced correctly, but it comes out as nonsensical statements, often at a very rapid rate. Instead of being agrammatic, the speech of a Wernicke's aphasic is nonsemantic. This can be seen in specific semantic errors that are made such as saying "television" when the individual means "telephone." In very severe cases, the words that are said are neologisms—made up words—that happen to fit the phonological rules of the language the patient speaks (e.g., "telebision"). The patient seems unaware of his or her errors. There is a pseudogrammatical correctness to the sentences because they have nouns, verbs, and inflections, but they come out as meaningless jargon. The same rambling jargon occurs when the patient writes instead of speaks. Auditory comprehension of sentences is profoundly poor in Wernicke's aphasia. Even the comprehension of common object names is deficient. For this reason, Wernicke's aphasia is usually characterized as a comprehension disorder, in contrast to Broca's aphasia.

The study of these and other kinds of aphasia have helped to guide the development of models of speech production. Just as slips of the tongue provide clues as to the cognitive processes involved in production, the study of how language functioning breaks down as a result of brain lesions offers another avenue. It turns out that there are numerous highly specific kinds of aphasia that may result from breakdowns in only one aspect of language use (Goodglass, 1993). For example, pure word deafness is a rare condition in which speech comprehension fails but in which speaking, writing, and (interestingly) reading all are intact. It appears that the comprehension problems arise from a difficulty in perceiving speech sounds at an elementary level of phonemes. As another example, pure agraphia is a rare disorder of writing in which speech production and comprehension, as well as reading, are spared. The patient is unable to write letters or words, even though the motor system works fine for, say, drawing.

Acquired aphasia in bilinguals is intriguing. A bilingual may recover only one of the languages over time, although in some cases both recover in parallel. Based on a review of the relevant published case studies of bi- and multilingual aphasics, Fabbro (1999) concluded that 40% of patients recover all languages, 32% recover their mother tongue, and the remaining 28% recover a second language. The fact that in parallel recovery is most common strongly suggests that the neural representations of the first and second languages are in close proximity in the brain. It is not surprising that the mother tongue would be recovered but not languages acquired later in life. Surely, one's first language would be best learned and most frequently used. But then why do nearly a third of the cases show recovery of the second language rather than the first?

Fabbro (1999) suggested that the second language may be most frequently used in reading and writing. Also, the second language may become heavily used in particular situations. When confronted with particular topics or tasks, the patient may automatically respond in the second language.

Slips of the tongue in everyday speech and the study of acquired aphasia—language disorders caused by brain injuries—provide insight into the processes underlying speech production.

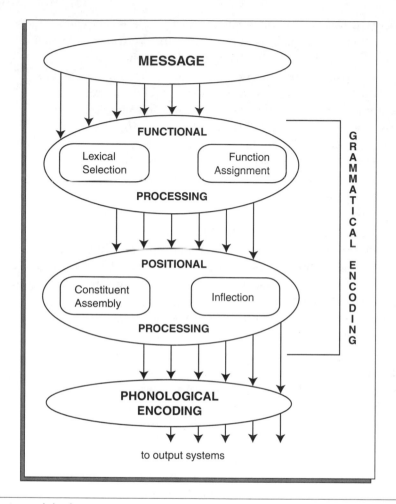

Figure 11.1. A model of sentence generation.

SOURCE: Bock and Levelt (1994).

Finally, the language spoken in the hospital where the patient recovers may play a role. Perhaps the immediate environment plays a role in helping along the recovery and elicits a lesser used, but now more appropriate, second language.

● SENTENCE GENERATION

A detailed process model of how we formulate a sentence was proposed by Bock and Levelt (1994). This is illustrated in Figure 11.1. The message component refers to the conceptual planning that precedes grammatical encoding. A speaker must know the general nature of discourse so as to proceed (Clark & Clark, 1977). Storytelling calls forth one set of expectations on the part of listeners, whereas giving instructions, persuading, making small talk, and swearing to a solemn pledge call forth quite different expectations. The sentences and phrases that are generated must add to the development of the discourse chosen by speakers and the social situation in which they find themselves speaking.

Grammatical encoding refers to the selection of the lexical entries to be used from among those in the speaker's vocabulary and to the assembly of a syntactic framework. The grammatical component produces a representation of the sentence in terms of the words, inflections of nouns as plural or verbs as in the past tense, and the order in which the words will be uttered. All this must be processed before the phonological component begins assigning the specific sounds that will be articulated by the vocal motor output systems. **Phonological encoding** refers to the assembly of sound forms and the intonation to be executed during articulation. Thus, the message, grammatical, and phonological components formulate a single sentence prior to the speaker's lips ever moving. The arrows in Figure 11.1 reflect the progression of time. Although the message component begins and the phonological component ends the process, the components operate in parallel, allowing their overlap in time. Output from a component cascades to the next before all processing is complete. Put differently, the production of a sentence takes place incrementally so as not to conceptualize the entire message before work begins downstream in the production system.

Production is also monitored as each component cranks out representations (Levelt, 1989). If one assumes that monitoring one's own speech is analogous to listening to and monitoring the accuracy of someone else talking, then some time must pass before errors are detected and production is interrupted so that a repair might be made. Suppose that it takes 150 to 200 milliseconds to analyze a speech segment about to be spoken and that it takes 200 to 250 milliseconds to articulate it. This leaves little if any time to catch an error before it is uttered in full—at most only 100 milliseconds. Levelt (1989) further hypothesized that interruptions occur as long as 200 milliseconds after the error is detected, usually without respect to phrase, word, or even syllable boundaries.

Evidence on the timing of repairs in spontaneous speech certainly supports the idea that monitoring takes place at multiple levels. Yet Levelt's (1989) interruption proposal appears to be incorrect (Blackmer & Mitton, 1991). Nearly a fifth of the repairs observed by Blackmer and Mitton (1991) occurred immediately on the occurrence of the error. Such 0-millisecond cutoff-to-repair times imply that "an error segment and its replacement could not have been conceptualized and formulated as a single unit, and yet the replacement can follow the error without a break" (p. 189). Both the production and the monitoring of the sentence seem to occur in incremental steps, with the correction of errors taking place all along the way.

Types of Lexical Representations

As shown in Figure 11.2, contemporary theories of language production usually assume that the mental lexicon contains two kinds of entries: lemmas and lexemes. A **lemma** is an abstract representation of a word that specifies its semantic and grammatical features. For example, the goat in English and *la chèvre* in French each specifies identical semantic information, namely, the concept of a four-legged furry creature that humans domesticate for its milk to make cheese. The goat lemma in each of these languages also must specify its grammatical uses. For example, the lemma indicates that goat is a noun. In French, the lemma must specify that chèvre is a feminine noun, meaning that it takes one grammatical form of the definite article (la) rather than another (le). Gender is a grammatical category that often has little if anything to do with the meaning of the noun. Merely by convention, *mouton* is masculine, whereas *chèvre* is feminine, for example. Words for abstract concepts, as well as words naming concrete objects, have a gender that affects how they must be grammatically encoded. Many other languages, including German, Italian, and Spanish, also specify the gender of a noun in the mental representation called a lemma.

A lemma is an abstract representation of a word's semantic and grammatical features for use in grammatical encoding of a sentence. A lexeme is a representation of the phonological structure of a word for use in phonological encoding of the same sentence.

The second kind of lexical entry in the mental lexicon provides information about the sound structure of the word to be spoken. A **lexeme** is a representation of the phonological structure of a word. For example, the lexeme for goat provides the phonology for its pronunciation in, say, English. The lexemes for goat and sheep are completely different, despite the fact that the corresponding lemma specifies identical semantic information and similar grammatical information. A person who spoke English and French would need to activate not only the right lemma to express a particular idea but also the lexeme appropriate for the language in use at the moment.

The tip of the tongue (TOT) phenomenon introduced in Chapter 6 is handy for testing the theory that the mental lexicon includes separate lemma and lexeme representations. As shown in Figure 11.3, the lemma specifies the semantic and syntactic features needed for grammatical encoding. The lexeme provides the phonological features needed for phonological coding. If these are separate representations, then there ought to be cases in which an individual correctly retrieves the lemma but not the lexeme. For example, during a TOT state, one may retrieve the initial consonant or vowel of the

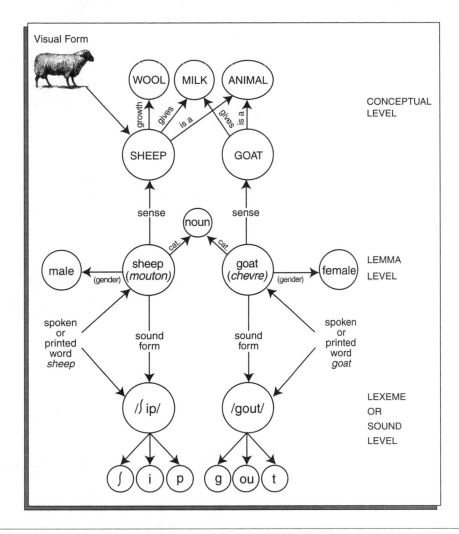

Figure 11.2. The mental lexicon includes conceptual or semantic, lemma, and lexeme representations.

SOURCE: Bock and Levelt (1994).

target word and the number of syllables it has (Brown & McNeill, 1966). These are examples of the phonological features of the lexeme representation. But at times, none of these phonological features is recalled. Of interest is whether in these circumstances the individual can retrieve the gender of the noun, a feature provided only by the lemma.

Vigliocco, Antonini, and Garrett (1997) tested native speakers of Italian by asking them to generate the words that fit a series of dictionary-type

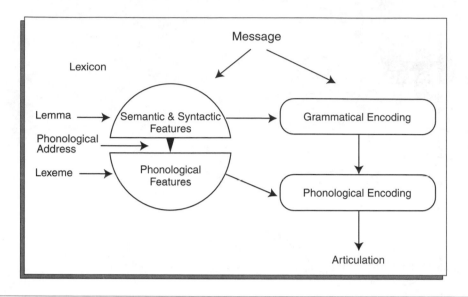

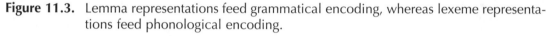

Figure 11.3. Lemma representations feed grammatical encoding, whereas lexeme representations feed phonological encoding.

SOURCE: Vigliocco, Antonini, and Garrett (1997).

definitions. Every time they failed to come up with the right word, a series of questions was administered to evaluate the TOT state. For example, could they guess the number of syllables, any of the letters, or the gender? After participants responded to several questions, the researchers presented the target word to affirm that it was in fact the word the participants were searching for but could not find. These cases were called positive TOTs, and they occurred often enough to allow conclusions to be drawn. The key point here is that the correct gender of the word could be identified 80% of the time (chance was 50%). Even for cases in which no other information about the sound structure of the word was recalled, the average was still 80% correct on gender. The lemma that codes grammatical gender was recognizable even when the lexeme could not be retrieved.

Stages of Grammatical Encoding

Grammatical encoding entails two stages: functional processing and positional processing. During functional processing, the lemmas are first selected for use in the sentence to convey the concepts that the speaker has in mind. Choosing the wrong lexical concept is a common type of speech error. For example, suppose that you were telling a funny story about what

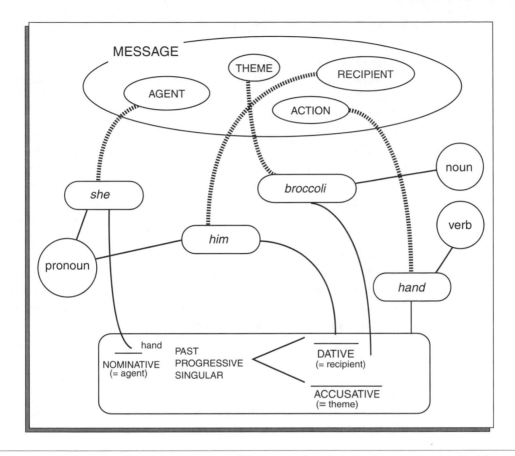

Figure 11.4. Functional processing selects lemmas and assigns each to a grammatical function or case role.

SOURCE: Bock and Levelt (1994).

happened at dinner last night and meant to say "She was handing him some broccoli." If instead the sentence came out as "She was handing him some cauliflower," then the substitution error would not be the right word, but its lemma still preserved the right grammatical category. Broccoli, like cauliflower, is a noun instead of a verb, adjective, adverb, or preposition. A large collection of speech production errors shows that 99.7% of lexical substitutions belong to the same grammatical class (Stemberger, 1985).

The second step of functional processing is to assign each lemma to a grammatical function such as the agent or subject of the sentence (nominative case), the main verb, or the direct object of the verb (accusative case). The products of functional processing are illustrated in Figure 11.4. The feminine pronoun lemma (she) must be assigned to the role of the subject of the sentence, whereas the male pronoun lemma (he) plays the role of the indirect object of the verb (dative case). If an error in function assignment took place with these roles reversed, then the sentence would come out wrong in meaning but fully grammatical ("He was handing her some broccoli"). Notice that this is not just an exchange of words from what was intended ("Him was handing she some broccoli").

Positional processing determines the order in which the words selected for use in the sentence will be uttered. Although the grammatical function of a word is already specified, word order is still up in the air at the close of functional processing in theory. As illustrated in Figure 11.5, positional processing assigns the output of functional processing to a phrase structure tree. The constituent assembly step is familiar from our discussion of syntax in Chapter 10. The order of word production is determined by the phrase structure of the sentence to be uttered. For example, in the sentence "She was handing him some broccoli," the structure begins with the subject of the sentence followed by a verb. The verb, in turn, can be broken into the auxillary verb (was) and the main verb (hand). The second step in positional processing is to attach the inflections that are needed to make certain that the sentence is grammatical. For example, the -ing inflection must be added to the main verb in the present case. An error during inflectional processing might cause you to say "She was hand himming some broccoli." It turns out that inflections such as -ing are much more likely to be shifted in position than are the final sounds of other words such as the -id in morbid (Stemberger, 1985). This means that a piece of grammatical information, and not just a piece of sound structure, has been misplaced.

> During functional processing, the lemmas are first selected to convey particular concepts, and then each is assigned a grammatical function. Next, positional processing assigns the output of functional processing to a phrase structure tree.

Phonological Encoding

Phonology is the study of the speech sounds that are uttered in a particular language. Phonologists try to characterize a language in terms of how sounds are added, dropped, or altered in the production of words and sentences. Some sound contrasts are relevant to meaning, and some are not. For instance, in English the initial sound of vase and base is used to signal a difference in meaning. However, in Spanish /v/ and /b/ are not differentiated. Or, consider the difference in English between the /p/ sound in pill versus spill. In the first case, /p/ is aspirated; that is, a slight puff of air accompanies its articulation. In the second case, /p/ is unaspirated; that is, it is pronounced the same in other respects but for the puff of air. Phonetics is the study of how speech sounds are produced in terms of their articulatory features such as aspiration. Thus, the /p/ in pill is phonetically different from the /p/ in spill. However, the /p/ is the same phoneme in both words. It is a sound that the English language uses to mark differences in meaning. If a speaker

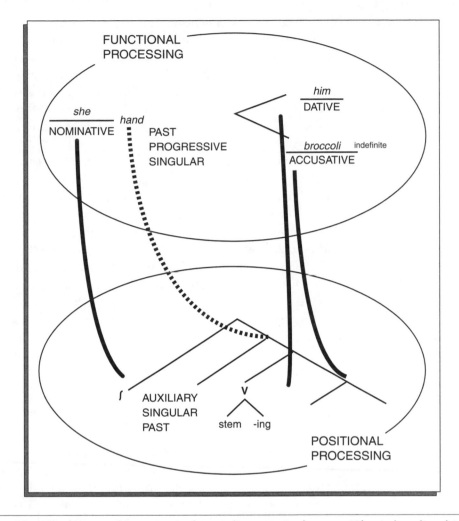

Figure 11.5. The events of grammatical encoding required to say "She is handing him some broccoli."

SOURCE: Bock and Levelt (1994).

pronounced pill with an aspirated /p/ by mistake, the listener would still recognize the meaning of the word. However, the meaning of the word changes when a new phoneme such as /m/ is used. Pill and mill are different in meaning, and this difference is signaled by the different initial phoneme.

The phonological component of sentence formulation, therefore, specifies the sounds representing the exact words of the sentence to be articulated. The abstract representation generated during phonological encoding provides the last step needed before articulation. The phonological representation serves as input to the articulatory program that actually controls the muscles of the vocal tract. One way to see the importance of phonological encoding is to compare the speech of adults with that of children (Gerken, 1994). Whereas an adult says fish, a child might say /fis/. The /s/ sound is substituted for the adult /sh/ sound. Or, the child might drop the initial /f/, mistakenly saying /ish/. These are examples of segmental phonological encoding in which specific small segments of sound are specified.

Phonological encoding also must specify larger sound structures that go beyond a single unit, what is called suprasegmental phonology. For example, in asking a question, one raises the pitch at the end of the sentence. This rise in intonation as the sentence ends is an example of suprasegmental phonology. Another example is the way we use pauses. When an adult speaks to a child instead of to another adult, the pauses and pitches used are exaggerated considerably. The adult talks slow, pauses at syntactic boundaries, and uses higher pitches and large variations in pitch. These changes in suprasegmental phonology along with simplified vocabulary are called "motherese" or "parentese." Although motherese is used by many cultures in speaking to infants and children, the reasons for its use are not fully understood (Gerken, 1994). Perhaps the parent consciously uses it to draw the child's attention or help the child learn, but it is also often used in addressing pets, for example.

> Phonological encoding specifies the sounds representing the exact words of the sentence to be articulated.

Articulation

Phonetics is the study of how speech sounds are actually produced. Each phonetic segment in English, for example, is uttered by shaping the mouth, placing the tongue, shaping the lips, vibrating the vocal cords, and constricting or stopping the flow of air through the vocal tract in a particular way. There are 46 phonemes in the English language. They are categorized as consonants, vowels, and dipthongs, the latter of which involve gliding from the position for one vowel to that for another. Recall that a phoneme makes a difference in meaning. "I till" is not the same as "I bill" by virtue of one phoneme.

Consonants and vowels differ fundamentally in their production. Consonants require constricting the mouth so that the air rushes through only partially or not at all. Vowels require opening the mouth in a particular fashion and then allowing the vocal cords to vibrate and the air to move through the mouth unimpeded. Here, the consonants are used to illustrate the principles involved.

English consonants differ along three dimensions: place of articulation, manner of articulation, and voicing (Glucksberg & Danks, 1975). **Place of**

Table 11.1 Dimensions of Articulation for English Consonants

		Place of Articulation					
Manner of Articulation	*Bilabial*	*Labiodental*	*Dental*	*Alveola*	*Palatal*	*Velar*	*Glottal*
Stops	Voiceless	*p*at				*t*ack		*c*at
	Voiced	*b*at				*d*ig		*g*et
Fricatives	Voiceless		*f*at	*th*in	*s*at	fi*sh*	*h*at
	Voiced		*v*at	*th*en	*z*ap	a*z*ure	
Affricatives	Voiceless					*ch*urch	
	Voiced					*j*udge	
Nasals		*m*at			*n*at		si*ng*
Liquids					*l*ate	*r*ate	
Glides		*w*in				*y*et	

SOURCE: Glucksberg and Danks (1975).

articulation refers to the position in the mouth where there is a constriction of air flow. Bilabial consonants are those uttered with the two lips together. With labiodental consonants, the bottom lip is positioned against the upper front teeth. With dental consonants, the tongue is against the teeth. With alveolar consonants, the tongue is against the alveolar ridge of the gums, a structure just behind the upper front teeth. With platal consonants, the tongue is against the hard plate in the roof of the mouth, a structure just behind the alveolar ridge. Moving back farther, with velar consonants, the tongue is against the soft palate or velum in the rear of the mouth. Finally, glottal consonants involve a constriction of air flow in the glottis, which is the opening between the vocal cords in the larynx, the muscles and cartilage that initiate the air flow of speech. The **manner of articulation,** or the way sound is emitted, divides into six features. Stops involve a complete closure at the place of articulation. Fricatives involve a constriction but not a complete closure. Affricatives involve a two-step sequence of complete closure, followed by a rushing of air through a constriction like a fricative. Nasals involve a complete closure of the mouth so that air rushes through the nose. Liquids and glides differ in how the tongue is shaped.

Illustrated in Table 11.1 are the articulation dimensions for English consonants. The italicized letters of each entry identify the consonant. For example, /m/ as in mat and /n/ as in nat both are nasal consonants, but they differ in terms of the place of articulation. Try uttering these consonants while holding your nose closed, and you will hear the distortion that results, for example, as compared with /p/ as in pat and /k/ as in cat.

The **voicing** dimension distinguishes between consonants that allow the vocal cords to vibrate (voiced) and those that do not (unvoiced). Table 11.1

shows pairs of consonants that differ only on this dimension. For example, /s/ as in sat and /z/ as in zap both are fricatives, and the manner of articulation is alveolar. However, /s/ is unvoiced, whereas /z/ is voiced. That is, /z/ involves the vibration of vocal cords, whereas /s/ does not. Place your fingers on the Adam's apple of the throat, and you can feel the difference. For some pairs, the difference is really a matter of the precise moment when voicing or vocal cord vibration begins. In pronouncing /b/ versus /p/, the closed lips are released, meaning that the point of articulation is bilabial. But in pronouncing the syllable "ba," the vocal cords begin to vibrate as soon as the lips release, whereas with the "pa," a delay of 60 milliseconds occurs (Clark & Clark, 1977). This delay is called **voice onset time.**

English consonants vary in terms of their place of articulation, manner of articulation, and voicing. An articulatory program directs the detailed motor commands to the speech muscles.

The **articulatory program** is the set of instructions for executing output by the vocal muscles. It represents the phonetic segments, stresses, and intonation patterns that must be executed in sequence. Keep in mind that the sound of a sentence can vary its meaning through variations in stresses and intonation. The sentence "You won the award" can be uttered in many different ways, for example. It could express congratulations, disbelief, or envy depending on how the sentence is programmed and articulated. Try these yourself; can you vary your expression so as to communicate these different meanings?

Interaction Among Levels

Shown in Box 11.1 is a series of word pairs that you should read silently to yourself. When you get to the question marks, read aloud the immediately preceding word pair. Give this a try before going any further in the text.

The word pairs were selected to prime your speech production system to commit a Spoonerism. It is called the phonological bias technique, and for this list of words it increases the chances that you will mistakenly say "barn door" instead of "darn bore." Suppose that the last pair of words in the list were "deal back." In this case, the Spoonerism primed would be "beal dack," both of which are not real words. Baars, Motley, and MacKay (1975) found that this type of error is much less likely to occur (10%) than are cases in which the speech error involves real words (30%). The fact that speech errors are more frequent when they result in words than when they result in nonwords is known as the **lexical bias effect.**

The lexical bias effect poses a problem for the model of speech production outlined previously. All of the other errors discussed up to this point support two generalizations (Dell, 1988). First, errors are confined to a specific component of production. Suppose that a speaker means to say "I'll go shut up the barn door" but mistakenly comes up with "I'll go shut up the

Box 11.1

ILLUSTRATION OF THE LEXICAL BIAS EFFECT

Read each of the following word pairs silently to yourself at a rate of about one per second. When you get to the series of question marks, say aloud the last pair you read as quickly as possible.

seed	reap
same	rope
lamb	toy
big	dumb
bust	dog
bet	dart
darn	bore
? ? ? ? ? ? ?	

darn bore." In this case, the error occurs at the level of phonological encoding. A single phoneme /d/ was exchanged with /b/. Such errors tend to occur when the exchanged phonemes sound alike and occupy the same phonological segment (here, they are the initial sound of the word and the syllable). A second conclusion is that the errors produced by a component of sentence production still follow the linguistic rules. Take, for example, the phonological error of saying "thollow hud" instead of "hollow thud." What is interesting about the nonword "thollow" is that it is pronounceable and follows the phonological rules of English. Take, as another example, a lexical substitution error during grammatical encoding such as "I'm sending a mother to my letter." This is a syntactically correct syntax, although it fails to convey the intended meaning.

Bock and Levelt's (1994) model accounts for both generalizations. The production system is organized into components, and the scope of errors is restricted by the rules that apply within each component. Furthermore, the model assumes that the flow of information is always in a forward direction. Each level in the overall system is affected only by the information represented at the level just above it. To illustrate, lexical selection can affect the choice of grammatical decisions. Stemberger (1985) recorded a speaker who said "Most cities are true of that" when the intended sentence was "That is true of most cities." Notice that the subject (cities) and verb (are) agreed in number (plural). The speaker did not say "Most cities is true of that." Thus,

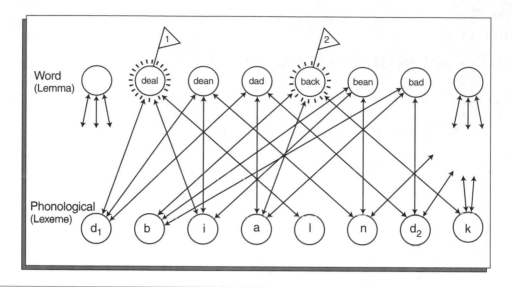

Figure 11.6. A connectionist model accounting for the interaction among phonological (lexeme) or word (lemma) levels of representation.

SOURCE: Adapted from Dell (1988).

once the error in lexical selection took place, the remaining aspects of grammatical encoding accommodated the mistake.

Now, back to the lexical bias effect. Why would the phonological substitution error be more likely when it involves true words (barn door) than when it involves nonwords (beal dack)? Lexical biases have been observed in spontaneous speech, so it is not just a peculiarity of the laboratory. Dell, Schwartz, Marin, Saffran, and Gagnon (1997) explained the phenomenon by assuming that information from later levels of speech production can feed back on earlier levels, contrary to the Bock and Levelt model. Dell (1988) used a connectionist architecture to describe the speech production system rather than the symbolic processing architecture we saw earlier in Bock and Levelt's model. The connectionist model assumes that there are levels of nodes representing semantic, syntactic, word (lemma), and phonological (lexeme) information. Shown in Figure 11.6 are the word and phonological levels needed to explain the lexical bias effect. In production, there are top-down connections between the word node selected for production and the phonemes. Study the links and observe how the words related to a target (e.g., dean) share some but not all phonemes with the target. For example, dean and bean share the middle and end phonemes, whereas dean and dad share only the initial phonemes. According to the model, these links are bi-directional, so that there are bottom-up links from /d₁/ to deal, dean, and dad, for example. Activation can spread in both directions, not only forward from a word to a phoneme but also backward from a phoneme to a word.

Intending to say "dean bad" but coming up with "bean dad" is three times more likely than intending to say "deal back" but coming up with "beal dack." The bottom-up flow of activation from the /i/ and /n/ of the correct word "dean" joins together with the activation from the /b/ of "bad." The error word "bean" captures the backward flow of activation from the phonemes about to be uttered and causes the network to slip to the wrong word. The error word "beal" has no word level node. The backward flow of information has nowhere else to go but to the right word in this situation. As a result, the probability of "dean" mistakenly becoming "bean" is far greater than that of "deal" becoming "beal."

> The symbolic architecture of Bock and Levelt's model assumes no interaction between grammatical encoding and phonological encoding. The lexical bias effect demonstrates that such interaction in fact can occur.

WRITING ●

As a species, humans have been speaking far longer than we have been writing. Casts made of the skulls of *Homo habilis,* our early ancestor from more than 2 million years ago, reveal what could have been Broca's speech area (Tobias, 1987). However, the unusual shape of the human vocal tract, a necessary requirement for speech, emerged later—perhaps 150,000 to 200,000 years ago—in *Homo sapiens sapiens* (Corballis, 1989; Lieberman, 1984). By contrast, the very earliest evidence that we have of humans using written symbols comes from the walls of caves in Europe dating back a mere 25,000 years. And these pictures were not writing as we know it today; the symbols were iconographs in which the objects referred to were directly depicted.

Only later did the symbols come to stand for an idea, that is, to represent something in a nonliteral fashion. Ideographs are symbols that refer in this more abstract way and are the basis of some modern language systems. For example, each of the thousands of Chinese ideographs refers to a particular concept. Schmandt-Besserat (1988) theorized that the origins of **ideographic writing** stem from a token system developed in Sumeria (the region of modern Iran and Iraq) about 10,000 years ago to track jars of oil, grain, and other inventory. Our ancestral accountants were perhaps the first to see the need to keep written records. The Sumerian markings evolved into what is called a pictographic system for representing the many ideas needed in daily communication. From this system came the Sumerian cuneiform script about 5,000 years ago, and the well-known hieroglyphics of the Egyptians came soon after.

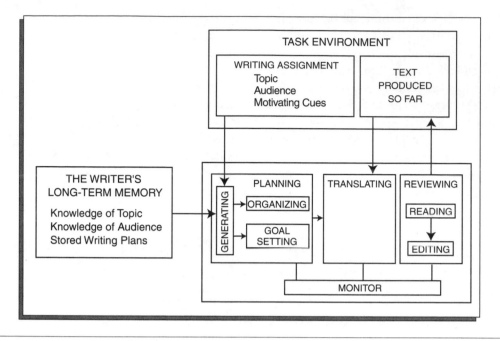

Figure 11.7. A model of the formulation of written text.

Most of the world languages today employ alphabets, a form of **phonetic writing** that first appeared a mere 3,500 years ago in the Sinai desert (Logan, 1986). A small number of letters (22-40 depending on the language) represent the sounds that carry meaning. By combining these letters, the writer can efficiently represent all of the words possible in a language. The invention of an alphabet represented the final step in the evolution of written communication, one that serves us as well during the age of computers as it did during the age of clay tablets. With the tool of the alphabet, modern humans carved out the cultural and intellectual life that we enjoy today.

Writing Processes

Just as in speech production, models of writing must distinguish between planning the conceptual content of the text and fashioning the words, phrases, sentences, and paragraphs used to express those ideas. A highly influential model of text formulation proposed by Hayes and Flower (1980) captured this distinction. As shown in Figure 11.7, the Hayes and Flower model postulated three basic writing processes. **Planning** refers to generating ideas, organizing ideas, and setting goals to achieve during writing such as trying to achieve the right voice or tone for a particular audience. Planning can be seen as invoking the reasoning, decision making, problem solving, and other high-level thinking aspects of writing. Planning involves the retrieval, creation, and manipulation of conceptual representations.

Translating (generating) refers to the linguistic operations needed to generate coherently linked sentences from the planned conceptual content. It involves putting ideas into words. The writer generates sentences using the same language production components as those proposed by Bock and Levelt (1994) for speech production. Furthermore, a written text is often better organized and more coherent than speech (McCutchen, 1984). It is not enough to produce a grammatically correct sentence in which the parts are linked. It also is necessary to link together the sentences of a paragraph, for example, by showing the reader in explicit ways how they relate to the topic sentence. Similarly, paragraphs must relate to one another so as to form a globally coherent text.

Because the transcription of words into written characters typically closely follows language generation, translating can be viewed as including the motor execution phase of text production (Berninger & Swanson, 1994). However, it is important to remember that the formulation of a text may occur without any behavioral output. Writers often devote considerable time to text formulation, including translating ideas into tentative language, during prewriting. Witte (1987) described such mental language as pre-text or "'the last cheap gas' before writers commit themselves to extended written text" (p. 398). Motor execution, then, is distinct from text formulation.

Planning and translating are interlocked but different processes. Text formulation process results in representations that fall along a continuum ranging from nonverbal imagery to textlike mental representations that show some of the formal constraints of written prose (Hayes & Flower, 1980). The products that are more like text have benefited from translating as well as planning. Text formulation proceeds incrementally from often vague ideas to clear, well-written text. It is only through language generation or translating that sentences, coherent paragraphs, and whole texts are produced.

Reviewing refers to reading the text being produced and evaluating and editing it. This can occur during the formulation of text as well as during the monitoring of written output. In reviewing, the writer must step back from the text produced so far and take the potential reader's point of view. If the meaning of the text does not match what the writer had intended, then further planning and sentence generation are needed.

A core finding is that planning, translating, and reviewing do not occur in a linear sequence (Hayes & Flower, 1980; Levye Randall, 1996). Instead the fundamental processes are highly recursive during all phases of text development. In initially drafting a document and in revising previous drafts,

Planning ideas, translating ideas into words and sentences, and reviewing ideas and the text already produced are three basic cognitive processes in writing. These processes can occur repeatedly during the prewriting, drafting, and revision stages of text production.

planning, translating, and reviewing call on each other in complex cycles to develop the content, structure, and expression of the text. As noted earlier, writers even may plan and mentally translate pre-text. The review of pre-text and conceptual representations may occur before a single plan or sentence is externalized. In studies where only one draft is written, however, one finds that planning dominates early on and reviewing dominates later. Yet even in this restricted case, all three processes nonetheless occur through the time spent writing (Kellogg, 1988; Levy & Ransdell, 1996).

Multiple Representations in Working Memory

Written communication is often difficult because writers need to build, maintain, and evaluate three mental structures in working memory during text production (Traxler & Gernsbacher, 1992). They need to build a conceptual structure of what they want to communicate. In addition, they need a representation of what they have written (i.e., the ideas that their texts actually communicated as opposed to what they intended). Finally, they need to be sensitive to how their readers will actually interpret the texts. This last structure is the hardest to build because it requires taking the perspective of another person.

Traxler and Gernsbacher (1992) found that giving the writers feedback on how well their readers had interpreted their texts helps them considerably. Not only did the feedback help writers to improve their original texts (in revisions), but the writers who received feedback on one text later produced more comprehensible novel texts on a different topic. In a second series of experiments, the authors gave writers experience at "being in their readers' shoes" (Traxler & Gernsbacher, 1993). By reading other participants' texts, writers gained their readers' perspective, and the perspective-taking treatment again improved writers' ability to write more comprehensible texts.

Flower and Hayes (1980) also concluded that writers are trying to meet several simultaneous demands and constraints by examining think-aloud protocols. Consider their description of writing based on the thoughts that writers verbalize as they compose:

We know that when people write, they draw upon a variety of mental operations such as making plans, retrieving ideas from memory, drawing inferences, creating concepts, developing an image of the reader, testing what they've written against that image, and so on. To produce any given utterance (which is to be simultaneously correct, effective, felicitous, and true), the writer must integrate a great number of skills and meet a number of demands—more or less all at once. . . . Viewed this way, a writer in the act is a thinker on full-time cognitive overload. (p. 33)

In young writers and at times in adults, planning suffers because writers forget the ideas recently generated and so repeat them. Sentence generation also suffers because the number of linguistic units that may be coordinated is too small due to limitations in working memory capacity (McCutchen, 1996). Just the motor execution processes of writing heavily demand attention in young children. They have not yet automatized handwriting or typing, making the motor transcription of generated sentences enough of a challenge. As a result, young children have little attention left over for the higher order thinking operations required by writing (Fayol, 1998).

The attentional or executive functions of working memory in particular are strained because of the multiple processes that must be juggled concurrently. Remarkably high levels of attentional engagement have been observed in an essay composition task using secondary task reaction times as an indicator of momentary effort. Responding to the tone requires that attention be focused on the tone while writing is ongoing and that a response be scheduled in the motor output system. These are examples of executive functions (Smith & Jonides, 1997). By looking at increases in reaction time above a control situation in which the tones are detected while not writing, the degree of cognitive effort can be evaluated. As shown in Figure 11.8, the attentional demands of writing processes were markedly greater than those observed during learning, reading, and problem-solving tasks (specifically, chess play). In fact, the writing processes demanded as much effort as that observed with experts playing the middle stages of a chess game (Kellogg, 1994). It is not surprising, then, that so many students find writing to be a difficult task.

Given the extraordinary mental effort required by writing, it is also not surprising that writing assignments are a source of anxiety for many college students. Freedman (1983) surveyed college students and reported that 45% found writing to be painful, 61% found it to be difficult, and 41% lacked confidence in their ability to write. About 10% of college students experience writer's block, characterized by intense anxiety and the inability to complete the task. Rose (1984) observed that such blocked writers adopted maladaptive planning strategies that prevented success. For example, one blocked writer stretched prewriting activities over several days, right up to within hours of the deadline for the paper. The student then had a complex plan for the paper, but with so little time left, it was impossible to translate the plan into a draft.

College students are not alone in experiencing writing apprehension and blocking. Karl Marx took 18 years, producing copious notes and plans, in

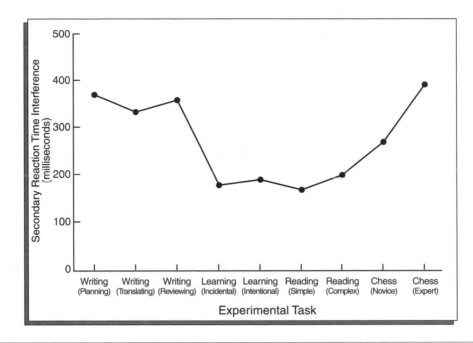

Figure 11.8. Attentional demands on working memory during planning, translating, and reviewing.

SOURCE: Adapted from Kellogg (1994).

writing Volume 1 of *Das Kapital.* The remaining two volumes had to be completed by his friend, Friedrich Engels, after Marx died working on them for another 16 years (Myers, 1991). Van Brooks described the agony that plagued him as a professional writer in his *Opinions of Oliver Allston,* as quoted by John-Steiner (1985):

> In thirty years of writing, I have not gained an ounce of confidence. I begin each new book . . . with a sense of impotence, chaos, and desperation that cannot be overstated. I always feel that I am foredoomed to failure. Every day I begin my work with the same old feeling that I am on trial for my life and will probably not be acquitted. (p. 77)

One way in which adult writers cope with the high-level demands of writing is by slowing the rate of motor transcription (Fayol, 1998). Another way is by designing plans that reduce the number of demands made on attention at any one moment (Hayes & Flower, 1980). For example, by creating an outline in advance of composing a short essay, writers can funnel attention to the process of generating sentences (Kellogg, 1988). By focusing attention on sentence generation to a greater degree than is possible without outlining in advance, the writers produced a superior essay as a consequence of outlining.

Knowledge-Transforming

Bereiter and Scardamalia (1987) noted that writers must solve two different kinds of problems. **Content problems** concern the matter of what to say. Everything that writers know about the events, facts, theories, arguments, and so on related to their topic bears on their ability to solve these problems. The term *problem space,* which we encounter frequently in Chapter 12, refers to a mental representation of the possible steps that might be taken in reaching the solution to a particular problem. **Rhetorical problems** concern the matter of how to say what needs to be said. Within the rhetorical problem space, writers struggle with the difficult issues of constructing text that is clear, persuasive, interesting, and so on. All that writers know about discourse bears on their ability to solve these problems of rhetoric.

Bereiter and Scardamalia (1987) discovered that children plan very differently than do adult writers. When given an assignment, children establish as a goal the retrieval of an idea from memory. Once they have an idea, they immediately translate it into a sentence. That done, they go back to search long-term memory again looking for another idea about which to write a sentence. Children repeat this "think and then say" approach until they cannot think of anything more to say. Bereiter and Scardamalia referred to this as **knowledge-telling**.

For mature writers, knowledge-telling is only one component of the overall process. As described earlier, mature writers juggle many constraints at once. In so doing, they engage in repeated cycles of interaction with the notes, outlines, and text that they have produced so far. By perceiving what they put down on paper or on a computer screen, writers change what they think about the topic at hand or how they think the text should be written. Their content knowledge and discourse knowledge are actively transformed as a result of sampling from the environment at hand. Mature writers engage in cycles of **knowledge-transforming** as well as knowledge-telling.

Verbal protocols reveal a much richer record of planning for adult writers than for children (Bereiter & Scardamalia, 1987). The number of words in thinking-aloud protocols about equals the number of words in the essays produced by children in Grades 4 and 6. The writers say little more than they actually put down on paper. Adults, on the other hand, verbalize nearly four times as many words while thinking aloud than they write as they struggle with the content and rhetorical problems of the task.

Children's writing is restricted to knowledge-telling in which an idea is retrieved from memory and put into words. Mature writers also engage in knowledge-transforming when they reflect on the text already written and alter ideas in long-term memory.

Spelling

The mechanics of writing also imposes demands not found in speech. The letters needed to spell each word must be specified only in writing. **Orthography** refers to the mapping of sounds onto written symbols. The minimal unit that carries meaning in written language is called a **grapheme,** which is the letter or letters used to spell a phoneme. It is the unit corresponding to a phoneme in speech. Unless a person is asked to spell a word orally—as in a spelling bee—the output of speech is at the phonemic and word levels. However, in written output, the graphemes must be specified, and these may differ from the phonology of the word. Homophones provide a case in point. They are pairs of words that sound the same but are spelled differently and carry different meanings (e.g., sale vs. sail). Another illustration is that the phoneme /s/ can take the graphemic form of either /s/ or /c/. "Precede" and "presage" both contain the same phoneme but different graphemes.

The spelling process is perhaps the most extensively investigated component of writing (Badecker, Hillis, & Caramazza, 1990; Caramazza, 1991; Ellis, 1982; Shallice, 1988). Two distinct sources of knowledge are brought to bear in spelling. One is knowledge of the orthographic appearance of a whole word. Through reading, people gain lexical-orthographic knowledge. The other source is an extensive set of rules about how phonology maps onto orthography. There are two separate routes for specifying the graphemes (Caramazza, 1991). In the first route, the word to be spelled activates an entry in an orthographic lexicon that directly specifies the graphemes required to spell the word. In the second route, the word is first coded in terms of sound structures by activating a representation in a phonological lexicon. Next, these representations are converted from phonemes to graphemes, as shown in Figure 11.9. Evidence for the separate routes comes from agraphia, a disorder of producing written language (Beauvois & Dérouesné, 1981; Ellis, 1982; Shallice, 1988).

Goodman and Caramazza (1986), for example, studied a patient with acquired dysgraphia, a normal individual who became agraphic following a stroke or other trauma that damages the brain. Their patient, "J. G.," spelled nonwords as well as anyone by drawing on knowledge of the rules that map phonology to orthography. In the case of nonwords, the only route is through phonological rules. But when asked to spell real words, J. G. often spelled them incorrectly. The nature of the errors were quite reasonable from the standpoint of phonological rules. For example, J. G. spelled "known" as "none." The second route for spelling that draws on the orthography of words stored in the mental lexicon was apparently lost for J. G.

Spelling involves the computation of graphemes either from an orthographic lexicon or from a phonological lexicon via conversion of phonemes to graphemes.

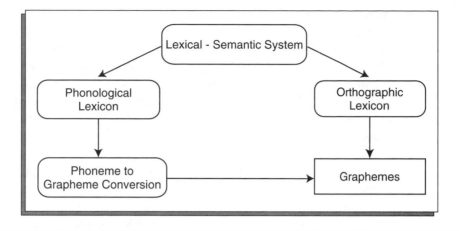

Figure 11.9. A dual-route model of spelling.

SOURCE: Adapted from Caramazza (1991).

SUMMARY

1. The production of language has not received as much attention from cognitive psychologists as has the comprehension of language, primarily because of the difficulties involved in conducting sound laboratory experiments. Rather than experimentation, the natural observation of speech errors or slips of the tongue has largely shaped theories of speech production, and slips of the pen have similarly provided evidence on written spelling. Neuropsychological case studies of acquired aphasia have also been useful in understanding production. Humans can talk at a rate of two to three words per second, sometimes even faster. Minor breakdowns or dysfluencies in speech are common. One kind of speech error, called a Spoonerism, involves exchanges in the position of phonemes (e.g., "You have hissed all my mystery lectures"). Aphasia acquired from brain injuries causes much more severe problems. For example, the speech of a Broca's aphasic is halting, effortful, missing words, and ungrammatical. The speech of a Wernicke's aphasic, by contrast, is highly fluent but meaningless, often containing unintended words (e.g., saying television instead of telephone) or made up words (e.g., telebision).

2. Sentence generation begins with planning the conceptual content of the message. It is not necessary to activate all of the semantic representations needed for a particular utterance prior to the initiation of grammatical encoding, the next step in saying something. Speech processes overlap one another in time. Grammatical encoding refers to the selection of the lexical

entries (i.e., lemmas) from the mental lexicon to be used from among those in the speaker's vocabulary and to the assembly of a syntactic frame. Grammatical encoding produces a representation of the sentence in terms of the words, inflections of nouns as plural or verbs as in the past tense, and the order in which the words will be uttered. Phonological encoding refers to the assembly of sound forms and the intonation to be executed during articulation; lexemes represent this information. Thus, the message, grammatical, and phonological components formulate a single sentence prior to the speaker's lips ever moving. The articulatory program is the set of instructions for executing vocal output. It represents the phonetic segments, stresses, and intonation patterns that must be executed in sequence. Thus, the utterance of a single sentence is a complex cognitive process. Given the speed with which we speak, it is not surprising that errors sometimes occur.

3. Each phonetic segment in English is uttered by shaping the mouth, placing the tongue, shaping the lips, vibrating the vocal cords, and constricting or stopping the flow of air through the vocal tract in a particular way. There are 46 phonemes in the English language that comprise the words used to convey meaning in a sentence. English consonants differ along three dimensions: place of articulation, manner of articulation, and voicing. Place of articulation refers to the position in the mouth where there is a constriction of air flow. The manner of articulation is the way a sound is emitted. For example, stops involve a complete closure at the place of articulation. The voicing dimension distinguishes between consonants that allow the vocal cords to vibrate (voiced) and those that do not (unvoiced). Voiced consonants also vary in terms of the voice onset time, that is, the number of milliseconds that elapse between the beginning of articulation and the onset of vibration.

4. The formulation of written discourse often involves reflective, high-level thinking and memory processes as well as language production. Planning refers to generating ideas, organizing ideas, and setting goals to achieve during writing such as trying to achieve the right voice or tone for a particular audience. Translating refers to the semantic, syntactic, and pragmatic operations involved in putting ideas into words and sentences. Planning and translating can occur in sequence in the form of inner speech long before words are committed to paper in a draft of the text. The writer generates sentences using in part the same language production components as those used in speech. An important difference is that the motor output system—handwriting or typing—is slower than the vocal system. Reviewing refers to reading the text being produced and evaluating and editing it. In reviewing, the writer must step back from the text produced so far and take the potential reader's point of view. If the meaning of the text

does not match what the writer had intended, then further planning and sentence generation are needed. Planning, translating, and reviewing do not necessarily occur in sequence. Instead, the fundamental processes are highly recursive at all phases of text development, from prewriting to a final polished draft. Writing places heavy demands on the various components of working memory. Written spelling alone is complex, involving the computation of graphemes either from an orthographic lexicon or from a phonological lexicon via conversion of phonemes to graphemes.

KEY TERMS ●

grammatical encoding

phonological encoding

lemma

lexeme

phonetics

place of articulation

manner of articulation

voicing

voice onset time

articulatory program

lexical bias effect

ideographic writing

phonetic writing

planning

translating (generating)

reviewing

content problems

rhetorical problems

knowledge-telling

knowledge-transforming

orthography

grapheme

CHAPTER **12**

LANGUAGE COMPREHENSION

T he comprehension of oral and written language has been studied at multiple levels of analysis. The basic unit for the psycholinguist is the word. How a single word—whether heard or read—is recognized has been a fundamental problem in the field of language research. Word recognition must be understood as a memory problem as well as a perceptual problem. Comprehension also involves high-level thought processes that allow one to understand the meaning of another person's speech or a written text. Much of what one extracts from language is not explicitly said by a speaker or an author. Comprehension requires bringing knowledge about the world that is left unsaid or implicit to the process, as happens when inferences are drawn. In this chapter, the processes involved in word recognition are addressed first. Next, the comprehension of a single sentence is studied. Beginning at the sentence level, one must build mental structures that represent the meaning of many words. Finally, the comprehension of multiple sentences that together comprise a coherent text or discourse is addressed. The real-world knowledge of semantic memory becomes especially critical in filling in the gaps of discourse as, say, a reader goes beyond the printed words to grasp the author's meaning.

WORD RECOGNITION ●

So far, the problem of speech recognition has been treated primarily as a perceptual problem of identifying words that are run together in spoken sentences and phonemes that are coarticulated. However, there is also a memory retrieval problem that must be addressed. Assuming that people know anywhere from 30,000 to 80,000 words, how is it that they retrieve the right representation so quickly? The same memory retrieval problem occurs in reading printed characters, where many of the perceptual problems of identifying the word units are solved. Unlike spoken phonemes, printed graphemes are standardized, the words are segmented by spaces, and the sentences are segmented by punctuation. To see how the right word is retrieved from the mental lexicon, we consider some experiments and models of visual word recognition.

Data-Driven and Conceptually Driven Processes

As introduced in Chapter 3, data-driven processes work to recognize visual patterns from the bottom up. In the case of words, there are three distinct domains of features that must be identified (e.g., Graesser, Hoffman, & Clark, 1980; Perfetti, 1985; Stanovich, Cunningham, & Feeman, 1984). For example, consider the features associated with the word "bird." In hearing a spoken word, the sounds are identified as phonological features. These are the phonemes used by the speaker in pronouncing bird. Orthographic features refer to the letters used to spell a word in a visual format (see Figure 12.1). In reading a word, the individual letters and the visual shape of the word as a whole are processed as orthographic features. The graphemes used to represent visually the phonemes of a language must be identified. As shown in Figure 12.1, the identification of graphemes can also activate phonological features. This can happen not only in reading a word aloud but also in reading it silently. The identification of the phonological and/or orthographic features drives the bottom-up identification of the lexical-semantic features—the meaning of the word. As seen in Chapter 10, words or morphemes are verbal labels for underlying concepts. Morphemes and the concepts to which they refer constitute the lexical-semantic domain.

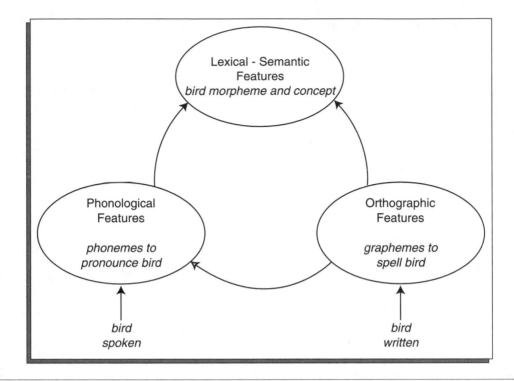

Figure 12.1. Domains of features activated in the comprehension of spoken and written words.

A positron emission tomography (PET) study has shown that specialized areas in the left hemisphere respond to words and pseudowords, both of which look like words in that they follow the orthographic rules of English (Petersen, Fox, Snyder, & Raichle, 1990). As shown in Color Plate 8 in the section of colored plates and the associated table, false fonts and letter strings activate the visual cortex just as do words and pseudowords. All four kinds of stimuli involve a low-level analysis of visual features taken on by the visual cortex at the rear of the brain in both hemispheres. But only the words and pseudowords prompt an analysis by a specialized system in the left hemisphere that analyzes the visual form of words as such. Reading well demands that one handle words effectively and efficiently.

Equally convincing evidence has stressed the role of top-down or conceptually driven processes, as seen in the word superiority effect and other findings discussed in Chapter 3. By using world knowledge and the context in which a word is encountered, it is possible to form hypotheses and make good guesses regarding their identity (Palmer, MacLeod, Hunt, & Davidson, 1985; Thorndike, 1973-1974). In fact, context enables one to identify words even when the critical data are missing, as seen in the following sentence: Rexmaxkaxly xt ix poxsixle xo rxplxce xvexy txirx lextex of x sextexce xitx an x, anx yox stxll xan xanxge xo rxad xt—wixh sxme xifxicxltx (Anderson, 1990; Lindsay & Norman, 1977).

When words do not fit the expectations of conceptually driven processes, there is extra effort required in analyzing the data from the bottom up. This added effort can be detected by monitoring brain waves during sentence comprehension in an event-related potential (ERP) that occurs as a negative voltage change that reaches its peak amplitude 400 milliseconds after the unexpected word appears (Kutas & Hillyard, 1980, 1984). The ERP is labeled an N400. Kutas and Hillyard (1980) presented readers with a set of mundane sentences that occasionally included an anomalous or low-probability word. For example, compare these two sentences:

He likes ice cream and sugar in his *socks*.

He likes ice cream and sugar in his *tea*.

Recording from a region in the parietal lobe, Kutas and Hillyard observed a significant negative component voltage 400 milliseconds after the last word of the first sentence but not the second sentence. In the context of these sentences, the word "socks" is semantically anomalous, whereas "tea" is predictable from conceptually driven processes.

In addition, a large N400 component occurs following the first word of the sentence (He), and smaller ones occur after each succeeding word (Kutas, Van Petten, & Besson, 1988). Notice that the first word of a sentence, as well as the unexpected final word of "socks," must be processed from the bottom up and fit into a mental structure for the sentence. The N400, then, is sensitive to the meaning of the word and is triggered when its meaning is unpredictable. The largest N400 is obtained for semantically unpredictable words, regardless of whether it comes in the middle or at the end of the sentence.

Differences in how well children are able to use both data-driven and conceptually driven processes separate good readers from poor readers (Levy & Hinchley, 1990). Among children in Grades 3 to 6, the younger and poorer readers at a given age shared several common characteristics. They were less sensitive to differences in the phonological features of words, and they were slower in sight word recognition. Furthermore, poorer readers were unable to retain as many words in working memory at one time to establish context as were good readers. Good readers showed markedly higher recall for a well-formed story than for a randomly scrambled presentation of the same sentences. Poor readers also did worse on the scrambled story than one that fit together as coherent discourse. Thus, poor readers were unable to use the global structure of text to good advantage.

Word Frequency

The **word frequency effect** is the most basic result to account for in word recognition. High-frequency words are recognized faster and more accurately than are low-frequency words, regardless of whether they are heard or read. Numerous models of spoken word recognition have been proposed to account for this basic finding. For example, Forster and Bednall (1976) initially proposed that the search of the mental lexicon is serial and self-terminating. The search process began with high-frequency words, which would account for the faster recognition times observed in experiments. This provides a simple parsimonious explanation of the word frequency effect. Alternatively, the search might be done in parallel. If high-frequency words had lower thresholds for being activated than did low-frequency words, then a parallel search model could also explain the word frequency effect (Morton, 1969). Today, theorists (including Forster) agree that the speed of recognition is so fast—often on the order of 200 milliseconds—and the size of the mental lexicon is so large that only models with parallel search are plausible (Lively, Pisoni, & Goldiner, 1994).

The strength of the word frequency effect in reading depends on the kind of word in question. In English orthography, words that follow spelling-to-sound rules are called regular words. The graphemes used to spell a word can be read in a rule-like manner to generate the right pronunciation of the word. For example, the grapheme /f/ always corresponds with the sound /f/ in English. So, fish, fat, and fried all are examples of regular words, meaning that they follow predictable patterns. There is only one exception to this pattern, and that is the word "of." The spelling-to-sound correspondence of other words is unpredictable in English. These nonregular or exception words must be pronounced in ways that violate the patterns found in regular words. For example, "pint" is not pronounced like "lint" with a /p/. Similarly, "have" is not pronounced like "gave" with an initial /h/. As another example, different graphemes map onto a single phoneme in speech. The /ph/ in "phoneme" and "grapheme" ought to be spelled with an /f/ if English were perfectly predictable in its spelling. Languages that have highly consistent spelling to sound regularities, such as Spanish, Italian, and Serbo-Croatian, are said to have transparent orthographies. Languages such as English, or even worse Hebrew, are said to have deep orthographies.

As it happens, the word frequency effect is larger for exception words than for regular words. This is illustrated in Figure 12.2 with results from

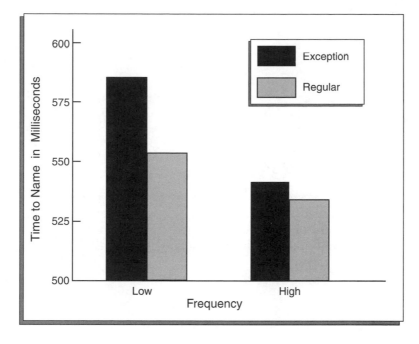

Figure 12.2. The word frequency effect for regular and exception words.

Seidenberg (1985). Words were presented in a sequence, and the time to name each one was recorded. Low-frequency words took longer to name than did high-frequency words, but as can be seen, this difference was more pronounced for the exception words. Notice in particular that if the words were high in frequency, it made little difference whether they were regular or exception words. But for low-frequency words, the exception words took a relatively long time to name. How can models of word recognition explain this pattern of results?

The word frequency effect refers to the faster, more accurate recognition of high-frequency words as compared with low-frequency words. This effect is larger for words with regular spelling than for exception words.

Connectionist Models

One explanation is based on Seidenberg and McClelland's (1989) connectionist model of word recognition (see Figure 12.3). The model uses 400 input units to code the orthographic features of the test word. The output layer consists of 460 phonological units that specify how the word is

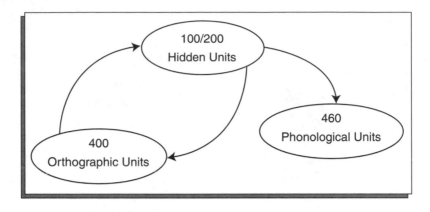

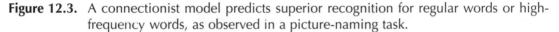

Figure 12.3. A connectionist model predicts superior recognition for regular words or high-frequency words, as observed in a picture-naming task.

SOURCE: Seidenberg and McClelland (1989).

pronounced. A hidden layer, consisting of between 100 and 200 units, provides feedback to the input layer using back-propagation as described in Chapter 2. The model is trained by providing it with a string of letters that are processed in terms of orthography, and a phonological output string is produced. The weights connecting the input and output are adjusted to reduce the difference between the correct pronunciation and the model's output. Seidenberg and McClelland trained their network on more than 2,800 words that were picked to reflect their natural frequency of occurrence in English, with most common words and only a few rare words. The network learned to incorporate the patterns that characterized the more common words in English. After training, the network was able to produce the correct pronunciations of new test words so long as they were regular words or high-frequency exception words. The pattern of errors made by the model corresponded reasonably well with the reaction time data from the naming task. A connectionist model, then, provides a plausible explanation of word recognition.

Dual-Route Models

An alternative explanation is based on a dual-route model of word recognition (Coltheart, Curtis, Atkins, & Haller, 1993). Recall from Chapter 11 that in written language production, there are two routes by which the spelling of a word can be computed. One is from the orthographic output lexicon or the

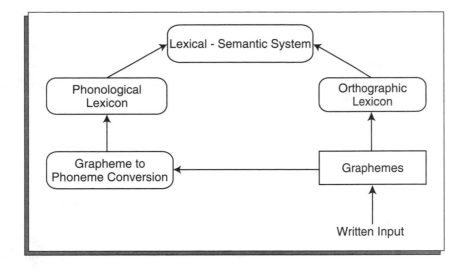

Figure 12.4. A dual-route model of word recognition.

SOURCE: Adapted from Caramazza (1991).

lexical route, and the other is from an assembled route in which the phonemes are converted into graphemes following the rules of English. As shown in Figure 12.4, the same two pathways can be identified on the input or comprehension side as well as on the output or production side.

In the assembled route, a reader would determine how to pronounce the word by converting each grapheme into a phoneme. In the lexical route, the reader would match the orthography of the whole word to a representation in the mental lexicon. Because it takes time to apply the grapheme-to-phoneme conversion process, the dual-route model assumes that the lexical route is the faster for high-frequency words. By the time a high-frequency word is assembled, the party is over. For example, "have" is correctly pronounced by the lexical route long before the incorrect assembled pronunciation that rhymes with "gave" appears on the scene. A low-frequency word, on the other hand, is not quickly found via the lexical route. The assembled output for "pint" arrives soon enough to interfere with the retrieval of the correct pronunciation. So, for low-frequency words, the exception words take considerably longer to recognize than do the regular words.

The dual-route model is based on a symbolic architecture rather than on a distributed connectionist architecture. Each word in the mental lexicon is represented by a symbol in the lexical route. In the assembled route, symbols for each grapheme and rules specifying their conversion to phonological symbols are represented. The issue of word recognition, similar to the acquisition of past tense, has been a contested area in the battle between theorists advocating symbolic architecture and those advocating connectionist architecture. It is still uncertain in the case of word recognition which camp provides the best explanation for all the relevant results. However, there is one finding on dyslexia that the dual-route model handles easier than the connectionist model discussed so far.

Dyslexia

As introduced in Chapter 3, dyslexia is the term used to describe difficulties in reading and spelling that either are present from birth or result from a developmental failure during the learning process. Reading disorders can also result from brain injury and are grouped together as a kind of aphasia known as acquired dyslexia. Some patients can read words only when the words can be sounded out using the assembled route of grapheme-to-phoneme conversion. These patients, called **surface dyslexics,** fail to read exception words correctly because they do not follow the conversion rules. For example, a word such as "busy" might be read as "buzzy." They can read nonwords (e.g., dar) by applying the conversion rules of graphemes to phonemes. Surface dyslexics misread exception words (e.g., lace, yacht, ache, and sew) because they inappropriately try to apply the conversion rule (e.g., reading lace as lake). Another variant ignores phonology altogether, reading entirely by sight vocabulary. For these patients, called **phonological dyslexics,** words cannot be sounded out, but words can be read as whole units if they are familiar enough to be retrieved as lexical entries. Phonological dyslexics cannot read low-frequency rare words. Such patients also cannot read nonwords because they have no lexical entry, and these patients are unable to convert spelling to sound. Exception words are not a problem so long as they are familiar and can be retrieved via the lexical path.

The dual route model predicts these two types of acquired dyslexia. But by adding new layers to the connectionist model, Plaut, McClelland, Seidenberg, and Patterson (1996) contended that surface and phonological dyslexics both can be modeled using the same architecture. So, as in the case of past tense learning, symbolic and connectionist models can provide competing explanations for the same observations. It is not yet clear which point of view provides the best explanation of the observations on human language. Connectionist models use similarity-based activation and frequency-sensitive adjustment of weights for the links between units of a distributed representation to explain phenomena. Exceptions in spelling and irregular verbs are processed by the same network. Dual-route models, on the other hand,

Surface dyslexics fail to read exception words correctly because they rely on the conversion of graphemes to phonemes. Phonological dyslexics ignore phonology and read entirely by sight vocabulary; as a result, they cannot read unfamiliar words.

assume that exception words in spelling and irregular verbs involve direct retrieval, a distinctly different process from the application of spelling or past tense rules.

SENTENCE COMPREHENSION •

Recognizing the words of a sentence is only a start toward comprehension. To understand a sentence and the relation between one sentence and the next, it is necessary to build mental structures that represent meaning. The structures built by a listener or reader at the local levels of words and sentences are considered first. Then, the final section of the chapter extends this approach to see how larger units of language, called discourse, are comprehended. As will be seen in the current discussion, there are two central problems in sentence and discourse comprehension. The first is the problem of inference or the ability of humans to "read between the lines" and infer meanings that are not explicitly stated. The second is the problem of identifying the intended meaning of a sentence when words with more than one literal meaning are used or when words are used in nonliteral ways such as in metaphors.

Comprehension as Structure Building

Gernsbacher (1990) captured a central theme in stating,

The goal of comprehension is to build a coherent mental representation or "structure" of the information being comprehended. Several component processes are involved. First, comprehenders lay foundations for their mental structures. Next, comprehenders develop their mental structures by mapping on information when that incoming information coheres with the previous information. However, if the incoming information is less than coherent, comprehenders engage in another cognitive process: They shift to initiate a new substructure. So, most representations comprise several branching substructures. (pp. 1-2)

Words and sentences activate representations stored in long-term memory, bringing necessary information into the limited-capacity system of working memory. Mental structures are then developed moment by moment as a listener hears further speech or a reader scans more text. The building blocks of the mental structures are memory nodes activated by incoming words and sentences. Once the foundation nodes are laid, later incoming stimuli are mapped to these. The more coherent the incoming discourse, the more likely this mapping will prove to be successful. On the other hand, relatively incoherent discourse will probably activate a different set of nodes altogether, resulting in a new substructure.

As in building any structure, the laying of a foundation is critical, according to Gernsbacher (1990). The time and effort needed to develop mental structures that incorporate the meaning of the text provide useful information about the process. For example, the first sentence of a paragraph takes longer to read than do later sentences because the reader uses it to lay the foundation for a mental structure (Cirilo, 1981; Cirilo & Foss, 1980). This result occurs even when the topic sentence comes later in the paragraph (Kieras, 1978). So, the extra time reflects foundation building, not just the time needed to process the most important or informative sentence. Once memory nodes are activated, they send signals to affect the activation of other memory nodes in the structure. The activation levels of memory nodes are enhanced when the information they represent is needed for further structure building. If, by contrast, these nodes are no longer needed, then their activation levels are suppressed.

The materials with which we build mental structures include more than the actual words appearing in print or uttered in spoken discourse. People presuppose, infer, and interpret far beyond a literal reading of the text. As seen in Chapter 7, memory can be distorted by inferences drawn during the reconstruction of an event. Similarly, comprehension is shaped by the assumptions made by listeners and readers as they process the incoming words and sentences. If a fact is presupposed or inferred in the course of processing a sentence, then it is likely to become part of the mental structure built by the comprehender. In a court of law, for instance, a prosecuting attorney might fire this loaded question at the defendant: "And when, Mr. DeSade, did you stop beating your wife?" The members of the jury might well presuppose that Mr. DeSade in fact abused his wife as part of building a mental structure to represent the attorney's question. In this section, studies of how people go beyond the words as literally stated to comprehend the meaning of a sentence are discussed.

Suppositions

It may be that simply denying an assertion causes listeners or readers to presuppose that the assertion is true. If Mr. DeSade's defense attorney objects to the question just mentioned ("I object, Your Honor; my client is not a wife-beater!"), then the jury may once again presuppose that indeed the defendant is a wife-beater. Research indicates that in comprehending a

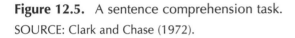

Figure 12.5. A sentence comprehension task.
SOURCE: Clark and Chase (1972).

negative sentence, a reader first presupposes a positive proposition and then denies it (Clark & Chase, 1972).

Clark and Chase (1972) presented readers with a picture like that shown in Figure 12.5 and one of four sentences:

1. The star is above the plus. (true affirmative)

2. The plus is above the star. (false affirmative)

3. The plus is not above the star. (true negative)

4. The star is not above the plus. (false negative)

As you can see from Figure 12.5, Sentences 1 and 3 are true statements, whereas Sentences 2 and 4 are false statements. Clark and Chase argued that the negative sentences (Sentences 3 and 4) required the reader to engage in more processing than did the affirmative assertions of Sentences 1 and 2. Specifically, they argued that the negatives entail both the supposition that the star is above the plus and the assertion that this supposition is false. To expose the additional effort required by the reader, Clark and Chase measured the time required to verify each type of sentence.

If the negative sentences require the reader to presuppose the positive assertion, then the time needed to comprehend this assertion must be factored into total verification time. From the observed times for each of the four sentences, Clark and Chase (1972) estimated that comprehension of the simple assertion (the star is above the plus) takes slightly more than 1,450 milliseconds. All four sentences required this amount of time. The researchers further estimated that the time needed to deny the assertion adds roughly another 300 milliseconds. Only Sentences 3 and 4 needed this extra time.

Not only do more complex sentences require additional processing time than simple sentences, they also activate a greater volume of neural tissue. Just, Carpenter, Keller, Eddy, and Thulborn (1996) presented people with sentences of different complexities and recorded brain activation using functional magnetic resonance imaging (fMRI). The simplest sentence to comprehend was written in active voice and conjoined two clauses without embedding a relative clause. An example of an active conjoined sentence is "The reporter attacked the senator and admitted the error." A somewhat more complex sentence can be constructed from these same words by embedding a relative clause after the subject of the sentence, which interrupts the main clause. An example of an subject relative clause sentence is "The reporter who attacked the senator admitted the error." Finally, in the most complex sentence, the first noun serves as both the subject of the sentence and the object of the relative clause. An example of an object relative clause sentence is "The reporter who the senator attacked admitted the error." Although this type is grammatical, it is very complex in structure. After reading each sentence, the participants answered a question to measure whether comprehension was successful (e.g., "The reporter attacked the senator, true or false?").

The results of the Just et al. (1996) study showed an increase in processing time and the probability of making an error in answering the comprehension question as the sentences increased in grammatical complexity. In addition, activation levels in Wernicke's area in the left hemisphere showed a systematic increase across the three kinds of sentences. Of interest, the activation levels were substantially lower in this same brain region in the opposite right hemisphere, but even there a reliable increase was obtained as the sentences became more difficult to understand. Furthermore, a similar pattern of results was found for Broca's region. Just et al. noted that the role of Broca's area in comprehension is unknown but that it may generate articulatory codes for the words of the sentence or may assist with syntactic processing.

Inferences

The memory research from Chapter 6 showed that people falsely remember inferences (e.g., Johnson, Bransford, & Solomon, 1973). If you read the sentence "Bobby pounded in the nail until the board was safely secured," then you might well recall later that Bobby did some work with a hammer. McKoon and Ratcliff (1980, 1981) provided evidence that readers sometimes draw such inferences during the act of comprehension.

Anaphoric Reference. **Anaphora** is the use of a word to substitute for a preceding word or phrase. The idea may be illustrated with these sentences (adapted from Gernsbacher, 1990, pp. 108-109):

1. *William* went for a walk in Verona, frustrated with his play about star-crossed lovers. *William* meandered through Dante's square, when the balcony scene came to him suddenly.

2. *William* went for a walk in Verona, frustrated with his play about star-crossed lovers. *The bard* meandered through Dante's square, when the balcony scene came to him suddenly.

3. *William* went for a walk in Verona, frustrated with his play about star-crossed lovers. *He* meandered through Dante's square, when the balcony scene came to him suddenly.

Writers frequently use anaphora to establish referential coherence, especially anaphoric pronouns as illustrated by Example 3. Of the 50 most common words that appear in print in the English language, nearly one third are pronouns (Kucera & Francis, 1967).

Anaphoric reference reveals the dynamics of mental representations being activated and suppressed during comprehension. Consider this use of anaphora: "Ann predicted that Pam would lose the track race, but she came in first very easily." Gernsbacher (1990) contended that activation of words in the mental lexicon takes place during inference making. She theorized that readers not only enhance the activation of referents (Pam) but also suppress the activation of nonreferents (Ann). The results of an elegant experiment revealed these separate effects (Gernsbacher, 1989).

Shown in Table 12.1 are examples of the two-clause sentences that Gernsbacher presented on a computer screen. While reading each sentence, a test name appeared at the top of the screen either 150 milliseconds before or 150 milliseconds after the anaphoric reference. In the first example, the anaphora was explicit (Pam), whereas in the second example, a less explicit pronoun occurred (she). The test name was either the referent name (Pam) or the nonreferent name (Ann). The reader had to decide as quickly as possible whether the test name had appeared before in the sentence. Presumably, the more activated the name was in working memory, the faster the person could respond.

The results are shown in Figure 12.6 (from Experiment 2 of Gernsbacher, 1989). The readers actively suppressed the nonreferent name after the occurrence of the explicit anaphora. They needed about 100 milliseconds more

Table 12.1   Sentences Used in an Experiment on the Activation of Referents and the Suppression of Nonreferents

Sentence	Test Name	
Ann predicted that Pam would lose the track race,[2] but **Pam**[2] came in first very easily.	**Pam** Referent name	**Ann** Nonreferent name
Ann predicted that Pam would lose the track race,[2] but **she**[2] came in first very easily.	**Pam** Referent pronoun	**Ann** Nonreferent pronoun
Bill handed John some tickets to a concert,[2] but **Bill**[2] took the tickets back immediately.	**Bill** Referent name	**John** Nonreferent name
Bill handed John some tickets to a concert,[2] but **he**[2] took the tickets back immediately.	**Bill** Referent pronoun	**John** Nonreferent pronoun

SOURCE: Gernsbacher (1989, Experiment 2).
NOTE: The superscript 2 refers to where in the sentences the test names were presented, either before or after anaphora.

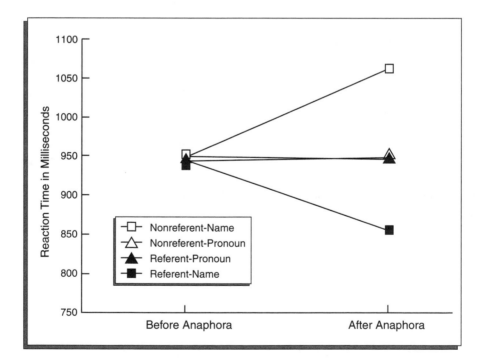

Figure 12.6. Explicit anaphora triggers enhancement and suppression during sentence comprehension.

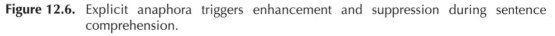

SOURCE: Gernsbacher (1989).

time to respond than when given the same test name just before the anaphora. By contrast, they responded about 100 milliseconds faster to the referent name just after, as compared with just before, the explicit anaphora.

Notice that when pronouns were used instead of names, the activation level of both referents and nonreferents remained stable. This outcome means two things. First, the referent name (Pam) and nonreferent name (Ann) both were equally active in working memory because they occurred in the first clause of the sentence; this can be seen in the equivalent reaction times in the before anaphora condition. Second, activation is neither suppressed nor enhanced if the situation poses ambiguity. Because a pronoun could refer to more than one antecedent, readers hold the activation levels steady in building their mental structures.

Given-New Strategy. Clark (1977) theorized that readers (and listeners) employ the **given-new strategy.** This strategy is based on the assumption that writers cooperate with readers to help make their meanings understood, just as speakers do in conversations. Specifically, writers clearly mark information that the readers already understand, that is, the given information that provides a shared basis for communication between writers and readers. Writers also mark what they are now making an assertion about, that is, the new information that they want readers to grasp.

Returning to the Example 1 of anaphora provided earlier, the reader determines what is being asserted as new information in the second sentence (someone meandered) and what is old information (the person in question is William). The reader next identifies a unique antecedent for the given information in working memory. The new information can then be fit into a new structure that links the predicates of both sentences to the same person.

Haviland and Clark (1974) found that the time needed to read and comprehend a sentence varied with the explicitness of the anaphora. This would be expected if readers used the given-new strategy and experienced more or less difficulty in identifying a unique antecedent for the given information. The term "The bard" identifies the antecedent only by applying one's knowledge of English literature and the writings of William Shakespeare. The pronoun "He" could, in a longer text, match more than one antecedent, so the reference in Example 3 is the least explicit. Thus, in Example 1, a unique referent is specified by repeating the name verbatim. In Examples 2 and 3, the reader must infer a link that is not explicitly given. Haviland and Clark aptly called these **bridging inferences** because the reader must build a bridge between two ideas to grasp their relation.

Polysemy. So far, comprehension has been discussed as if each word in a sentence could mean only one thing. **Polysemy** is the property of language that

Suppositions and inferences permit the reader to build mental structures that are not explicitly mentioned in the text by using real-world knowledge.

The given-new strategy in reading assumes that writers mark information already understood and information meant to be a new assertion.

a single word can have more than one meaning. The hardest inference considered yet is an ambiguous pronoun such as she, he, or it. But even here the reader presumably knows that the pronoun is supposed to refer back to a particular concept that has been given earlier in the text. Language is much richer than these cases because words can be polysemous, that is, interpreted in multiple ways. When a reader encounters words with more than one interpretation, how do cognitive processes arrive at the right meanings? Homonyms and metaphors illustrate the problem that polysemy poses for comprehension.

When one first reads a word, information provided by that word activates potential meanings. Constraints provided by the other words in the sentence and the way the words are arranged in the syntactic structure then alter the activation of those meanings. Eventually, one meaning becomes most strongly activated, and it is then built into the developing structure of the whole text (Kintsch, 1988). Besides a buildup of activation, suppression also plays a role. For example, suppose that the reader comes across a homonym, such as bug or watch, that can be interpreted in multiple ways. The preceding words might bias the interpretation (e.g., spiders, roaches), or the syntax might accomplish the same purpose (e.g., "I like the watch" vs. "I like to watch"). But what becomes of the other meaning? One possibility is that it simply decays with time (Anderson, 1983).

Gernsbacher and Faust (1991) discovered that the mechanism of suppression eliminates the unintended meaning sooner than predicted by decay alone. Using procedures similar to those described earlier, they assessed the activation of multiple meanings at different points in time after the word was read. When only one meaning of a homophone is supported by the context (e.g., Pam was diagnosed by a quack), the inappropriate meaning (i.e., the sound of a duck) was no longer active after 350 milliseconds. But when the context failed to bias a specific meaning (e.g., Pam was annoyed by the quack), both meanings remained activated for up to 850 milliseconds. Thus, it is likely that an active suppression of the inappropriate meanings takes place when the context steers the interpretation process away from those meanings.

Metaphor lies at the heart of language. Our frequent use of metaphor—"time flies"—makes this point most sharply. Metaphors are ambiguous because the intended meaning is quite different from the literal meaning. For example, in the initial two sentences of this paragraph, was a beating heart in sight or were any points literally sharpened? A word is given a novel insightful meaning by linking it in a nonliteral fashion with another word in metaphor. Much of the pleasure that we take in reading, say, a novel, lies in the author's ability to conjure interesting meanings and images from the way language is used. Language, spoken as well as written, just would not be the same without metaphor. But how in the act of comprehension does one know to interpret words figuratively rather than literally? What becomes of the literal meaning in the act of grasping metaphors?

It is possible that readers first try a literal interpretation and then look for nonliteral meanings. Alternatively, they may use the context of the metaphor wisely and immediately capture the nonliteral interpretation. Experiments have shown that with the proper context, the nonliteral meaning of a metaphor is grasped without first trying the literal interpretation (Glucksberg, Gildea, & Bookin, 1982; Inhoff, Lima, & Carroll, 1984). For example, Inhoff et al. (1984) measured how long readers spent looking at and trying to comprehend a sentence with a metaphorical interpretation such as the meaning of "choked" in the following sentence:

1. The directors mercifully choked smaller companies.
   For some readers, this sentence was preceded by an appropriate metaphoric context such as the following:

2. The company used murderous tactics.
   For others, the sentence was preceded by a context designed to encourage a literal reading of the term "choked" such as the following:

3. The company used competitive tactics.

Inhoff et al. found that readers spent less time in comprehending the metaphoric Sentence 1 when it was preceded by Sentence 2 than when it was preceded by Sentence 3. The metaphoric context of Sentence 2 primed activation of a nonliteral interpretation of choked.

> Words in a text must be actively interpreted because they can have more than one meaning. In comprehending metaphors, for example, the nonliteral meaning—not the literal meaning—must be activated.

DISCOURSE COMPREHENSION ●

Structures develop at multiple levels—words, sentences, and discourse. During the 1970s and 1980s, memory researchers began to address how people remembered sentences and stories rather than lists of words, the traditional task of verbal learning. Both European and North American scholars scrutinized the ways in which sentences hang together to constitute stories, conversations, expositions, and other types of discourse (e.g., Kintsch & van Dijk, 1978; Meyer, 1975; Thorndyke, 1977). By the late 1980s, the terms comprehension, psycholinguistics, referential coherence, story grammars, macropropositions, mental models, and causal relations surfaced in hundreds if not thousands of journal articles (Foss, 1988).

One result of the research effort was to clarify the definition of discourse. When does a collection of sentences constitute true discourse versus just a bunch of sentences? The answer, according to Johnson-Laird (1983), is when the references in each sentence are locally coherent with one another and when the sentences can be fit into a global framework of causes and effects. We first consider the issue of referential coherence and then examine alternative frameworks for structuring casual relations.

Referential Coherence

When the words and phrases of one sentence in a paragraph refer unambiguously to those of other sentences in the paragraph, the sentences possess **referential coherence.** Johnson-Laird (1983) offered the following three collections of sentences to illustrate this property of true discourse:

(1) It was the Christmas party at Heighton that was one of the turning-points in Perkins' life. The duchess had sent him a three-page wire in the hyperbolical style of her class, conveying a vague impression that she and the Duke had arranged to commit suicide together if Perkins didn't "chuck" any previous engagement he had made. And Perkins had felt in a slipshod sort of way—for at least at that period he was incapable of ordered thought—he might as well be at Heighton as anywhere. . . . (from *Perkins and Mankind* by Max Beerbohm)

(2) Scripps O'Neil had two wives. To tip or not to tip? Dawn crept over the Downs like a sinister white animal, followed by the snarling cries of a wind eating its way between the black boughs of the thorns. When I had reached my eighteenth year I was recalled by my parents to my paternal roof in Wales.

(3) The field buys a tiny rain. The rain hops. It burns the noisy sky in some throbbing belt. It buries some yellow wind under it. The throbbing belt freezes some person on it. The belt dies of it. It freezes the ridiculous field. (pp. 356-357)

A paragraph is referentially coherent when the words and phrases of one sentence refer unambiguously to those of the other sentences.

Which do you judge to be true discourse? Which is the least qualified for the title? The difference between Examples (1) and (2) is easy to detect. The sentences in Example (1) hang together, whereas those in Example (2) plainly do not. But what about the sentences in Example (3), which Johnson-Laird generated using a computer program? Although each sentence is nonsensical, the paragraph seems structured. The pronouns of one sentence seem to refer back to a previous sentence. Nouns are repeated from one sentence to the next. Words related in meaning—here words describing weather—are laced throughout. These are among the cohesive ties that a writer uses in creating true discourse (Halliday & Hasan, 1976).

Global Frameworks

The nonsensical sentences generated using the computer in Example (3) illustrate that there is more to referential coherence than local cohesion between one word and the next within and between adjacent sentences. An organizing topic, theme, or global structure is also needed. Theme is absent in the following paragraph from Johnson-Laird (1983), even though each sentence makes sense on its own and the local links between sentences are interpretable:

> My daughter works in a library in London. London is the home of a good museum of natural history. The museum is organized on the basis of cladistic theory. This theory concerns the classification of living things. Living things evolved from inanimate matter. (p. 379)

Theorists disagree on the best way to represent the global structure that characterizes true discourse. But they agree that texts are structured beyond the local level of individual micropropositions and that readers use global structures to comprehend and remember texts.

Schemas and Macropropositions. Kintsch and van Dijk (1978) suggested that schemas for different types of discourse guide the construction of a global framework. The individual propositions expressed by the sentences of a text were described by Kintsch and van Dijk as **micropropositions.** They contrasted these with **macropropositions,** defined as the schema-based generalizations that summarize the main ideas or gist of the story. Telling a story, arguing a case, or recalling an episode from memory each would presumably invoke a different schema. The pertinent schema would establish certain goals for the reader and sort through which micropropositions are relevant to these goals. The schema would also generalize the form of the relevant propositions so as to make it useful as a summary of the main ideas or gist of the text. The net result is a summary of the text—a macrostructure— that guides comprehension and memory. Thus, as shown in Figure 12.7, reading involves more than establishing referential coherence by finding overlapping arguments in micropropositions.

A related theoretical position is Graesser's (1981) schema-pointer-plus-tag model. In reading a text, memory traces are built by setting pointers to what a person knows about general world knowledge and by adding tags for

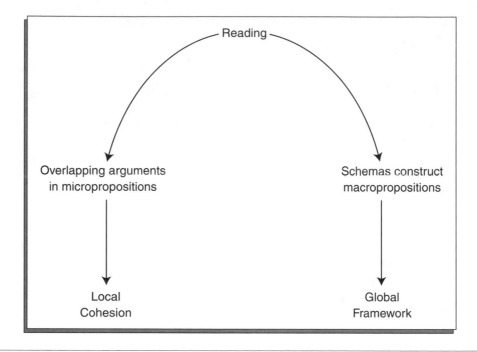

Figure 12.7. Reading requires establishing local cohesion and a global framework.

Global frameworks complete comprehension by using knowledge of the world to organize the text.

specific examples and facts. To comprehend and remember a fairy tale, such as "Little Red Riding Hood," the reader would set pointers to schemas about the woods, grandmother's house, and so on. Tags would differentiate between typical events (e.g., the journey through the woods was long) and highly atypical events (grandmother's teeth were very large).

Story Grammars. Another approach stems from a long tradition in the humanities of characterizing the nature of narratives (Stanzel, 1984). Just what is a story? The answer to this question plainly has relevance to psychological theories of reading, at least with regard to fairy tales, short stories, novels, and other narrative genres (Mandler, 1984; Mandler & Johnson, 1977; Thorndyke, 1977).

A **story grammar** is a set of rules that allows one to generate the acceptable story. Thorndyke (1977) proposed the rules shown in Table 12.2. The first rule states that a story consists of a setting, a theme, a plot, and a resolution. Each of these elements is in turn defined by other rules in the grammar. For instance, characters, a location, and a time comprise the setting. A theme consists of a goal plus an optional episode (as indicated by the

Table 12.2   Story Grammar Providing a Global Framework for Narratives

Rule Number	*Rule*									
1	Story	→	Setting	+	Theme	+	Plot	+	Resolution
2	Setting	→	Characters	+	Location	+	Time		
3	Theme	→	(Event)*	+	Goal				
4	Plot	→	Episode*						
5	Episode	→	Subgoal	+	Attempt*	+	Outcome		
6	Attempt	→	Event*						
			Episode						
7	Outcome	→	Event*						
		→	State						
8	Resolution	→	Event						
			State						
9	Subgoal | Goal |	→	Desired State						
10	Characters | Location | Time |	→	State						

SOURCE: Thorndyke (1977).
NOTE: See text for details.

parentheses). An episode consists of a subgoal, one or more attempts at tackling the subgoal, and an outcome. An asterisk denotes that an attempt may be repeated. The essential idea is that a story can be understood by relying on such a grammar; it specifies all of the essential elements and their relations. So, for example, the story of the "Three Little Pigs" can be understood as a series of episodes: the wolf blowing down the house of straw and the house of sticks, and then failing with the house of bricks. The resolution entails the three pigs safely huddled in the brick house as the wolf slides down the chimney to meet his demise in a pot of boiling water.

Readers in theory use a story grammar to comprehend and remember narrative text in terms of its global structure. Evidence favoring this theory comes from studies of text recall. For example, Mandler and Johnson (1977) found that recall suffers when an ill-formed story is missing elements that are called for by a story grammar. In well-formed stories, readers recalled 88% of the ideas represented by the major elements of the grammar as compared with only 66% in fractured stories. The order in which readers recalled ideas corresponded nearly perfectly with the order predicted by the story grammar; a mere 2% were recalled out of order. By contrast, Mandler and Johnson analyzed the story in terms of its grammatical phrases (e.g., verb phrases) and looked for inversions of these in the recall data. They found seven times as many inversions of these phrases as they did for nodes of the story grammar.

Causal Relations. Other studies of story recall have shown convincingly that particular events are better remembered than others (Nezworski, Stein, & Trabasso, 1981; Omanson, 1982; Stein & Glenn, 1979). Virtually all of the key facts about the protagonist in a story are well-remembered. The time and place in which the story unfolds around the protagonist, the goals in the plot with special attention given to the major conflict between the protagonist and antagonist, and the consequences of actions taken to reach the major goal all are readily recalled. Both children and adults reveal this pattern. Intriguingly, children from diverse cultures around the world recall stories in much the same way (Mandler, Scribner, Cole, & DeForest, 1980).

These and other facts have led some theorists to propose another form of global structure based on the causal relations among events. One approach orders the events of a story into a chain of causes and effects. Events that can be fit into the sequence are recalled, whereas all others are pruned or dropped from the memory structure (Black & Bower, 1979; Schank, 1975). Another approach recognizes that certain key events may cause multiple effects; a network can capture the multiple causal connections of these critical events unlike a linear causal chain (Trabasso & van den Broek, 1985).

Trabasso and his colleagues have found that the story grammar, causal chain, and causal network approaches generate similar predictions. The events surrounding the protagonist assume important roles regardless of which of these formalizations of the stories are used. However, by applying the correlational method called multiple regression, it is possible to separate the influence of the position in a causal chain from the influence of the position in a causal network, for example, or the impact of being a key node in a story grammar from the impact of being a key node in a causal network. The outcome of their research suggests that network models best account for the recall data (Trabasso & van den Broek, 1985).

The central point to be made is that the reader actively constructs a global representation by figuring out the causal connections among events. With the story grammar approach, one gets the impression that the reader need only sort out the events according to the slots of the grammar. The process seems automatic, much like sorting the constituents of a sentence according to a phrase grammar. The value of underscoring the active construction of global text structures was recognized by Kintsch (1988) in his updated propositional model.

Mental Models. The final approach to global structure forcefully advances the theme of the reader actively constructing a representation of the relations among events in a story. Johnson-Laird (1983) proposed a comprehensive theory of cognition that distinguished among procedures, propositions, and models. The models do the work of higher order cognitive processes such as comprehension. Analyzing the propositions of a text is only the beginning of comprehension, according to Johnson-Laird. The reader must also construct a mental model that contains tokens or symbols for each of the elements of the text. The mental model provides a global structure for the text, specifying what is happening to whom and why. Foss (1988) pointed out the close similarity between mental models and the causal fields that Trabasso and his colleagues discussed in their work.

Why do models go beyond propositions? First, Johnson-Laird (1983) pointed out that only a model can unambiguously represent the extension or referent of an idea expressed in a text. A writer might employ diverse propositions to refer to the same entity. For example, the "great white whale," the "denizen of the deep," or even the "diabolical demon" each might refer to the same beast. Only by building a mental model that includes the sea, the ship, the captain, the whale, and so on can the reader keep these co-referential propositions straight.

Second, Johnson-Laird (1983) observed that establishing referential coherence among propositions is insufficient for comprehension. Recall the earlier paragraph about his daughter in London; it lacked a global structure despite its referential coherence. In fact, such coherence may lead to serious misunderstandings on the part of the reader. Take this other example from Johnson-Laird:

> Roland's wife died in 1928. He married again in 1940. His wife now lives in Spain. (p. 380)

Here is a case in which the wife implicitly introduced in the second sentence and referred to in the third is most assuredly not the same woman of the first sentence. Yet there is nothing in the propositions themselves that makes this clear. The reader must build a global structure—a mental model—populated by two women, only one of whom is enjoying the warmth of Spain.

Models of Reading

A detailed model of the processes involved in establishing referential coherence starts with the segregation of individual propositions (Kintsch & van Dijk, 1978; van Dijk & Kintsch, 1983). The propositions that are directly taken from the sentences of the text define the **textbase.** Included in the textbase are propositions that define the microstructure of the text, the local structures of meaning, on a sentence-by-sentence basis. By contrast, the global structure of the text—the macrostructure—is represented as a hierarchy of major headings and minor headings. It is like an outline or a tree diagram that summarizes the text and conveys its essential gist. Unlike propositions in the microstructure, a macroproposition need not be explicitly stated in the text. For example, in a medical text discussing the right atrium, right ventricle, left atrium, and left ventricle, the reader might form a general macroproposition: chamber of heart.

To establish referential coherence, the reader must compare the predicate or arguments of propositions. If the predicate or arguments in two micropropositions overlap with each other, then the reader can link the two as a way of establishing referential coherence. In our earlier example, the repetition of "William" in both sentences of Example 1 would readily provide the basis for such overlap. In the case of Example 3, the reader would need to make a bridging inference to relate "he" back to William. The need to make such inferences makes comprehension more difficult for the reader. The basic assumption made by Kintsch and van Dijk is that referential coherence corresponds to overlap in the arguments of the propositions contained in a text.

Kintsch and van Dijk assumed that the number of propositions that may be active in working memory varies across readers. They assumed a capacity of four propositions on average. Because new propositions continually enter working memory as readers proceed with a text, old propositions must be bumped from working memory to make room. In deciding what to retain at a given point in time, the reader uses a **leading edge strategy,** according to Kintsch and van Dijk. The reader keeps the most recent proposition, and those that overlap with it in terms of their arguments, up to the capacity limit of his or her working memory. So long as this strategy retains the propositions in working memory that must be matched, referential coherence can be established. When matching fails, the reader then searches long-term memory either to reinstate a proposition processed earlier or to make an inference.

The Kintsch and van Dijk model successfully accounts for the degree of difficulty experienced in comprehending texts. The more densely a text is packed with propositions, and the more often it demands bridging inferences among propositions separated in time since input, the harder it is to read (Kintsch, 1974). The number of times that previously processed propositions must be reinstated in working memory and the number of inferences that must be made when reinstatement fails are especially predictive of comprehension difficulties (Miller & Kintsch, 1980). Furthermore, the model explains which propositions will be remembered well later. The longer a proposition is held active in working memory, the more likely it will be encoded successfully into long-term memory (Kintsch & Keenan, 1973).

There is more to reading than building a textbase, however. The reader also adds propositions that represent real-world knowledge held in long-term memory. The concepts and schemas of semantic memory provide the

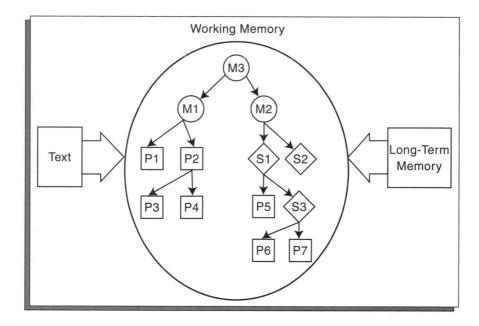

Figure 12.8. The text itself supports the construction of textbase propositions (P), whereas the propositions of the situation model (S) are built from schemas activated in long-term memory. Macropropositions (M) provide the gist or a summary of both the textbase and the situation model.

reader with a personal interpretation of the text. Propositions contributed from the reader's long-term memory, rather than from the text itself, constitute the **situation model.** The reader's elaborations of the text and interpretations drawn from personal knowledge form part of the microstructure of the text and are also important in organizing the text at the level of its macrostructure. For example, the diagram in Figure 12.8 illustrates a case in which a macroproposition (M1) is related solely to propositions derived directly from the text (P1, P2, P3, and P4). However, the reader imposed two propositions (S1 and S2) in a top-down manner from long-term memory as details that flesh out the summary macroproposition labeled M2. The reader obviously knew more about, or cared more about, the material under M2 and was able to build a microstructure reflecting both the textbase and the situation model.

Notice that in building a situation model, a reader may refashion the meaning of a text in ways not at all intended by the author and at either a local or global level. A poor reader, for example, could end up with a poorly developed textbase representation and a situation model that fails to capture what the author was trying to communicate. Thus, a reader jumps beyond the literal words on the page words in building a situation model as well as in making inferences to construct a textbase.

Fixations. The interaction of perceptual processes and working memory as reading unfolds in real time has been investigated (Just & Carpenter, 1980, 1992). Each fixation of the eyes on a word or on part of a word provides a discrete input to the visual system. The duration of most fixations ranges from 200 to 350 milliseconds, with great variability (Pollatsek & Rayner, 1989). A rapid eye movement, called a saccade, jumps the focus of foveal vision to a new point in between these fixations. In reading a book, a saccadic eye movement typically would advance (or at times regress) foveal vision about 5 to 9 character spaces within 15 to 40 milliseconds. The reader in essence gains a series of snapshots of information about the text as the eyes jump across and down the page. The span of each snapshot appears to be biased to the right of the fixation point. The reader extracts information from 4 characters to the left of the point of the fixation point and up to 15 characters to the right (McConkie & Rayner, 1975). Although the reader gains no information during a saccade, he or she is unaware of this end of the movement itself.

Reading typically involves fixating about 80% of the content words (nouns, verbs, and modifiers) and 20% of the function. High-frequency words are fixated in less time than are low-frequency words, indicating that the lexical or semantic properties of the language control eye movements. High-frequency words are often only a few letters in length, but even with word length held constant, the greater the frequency, the shorter the fixation required. Words that are frequent, short, and predictable in the context of the text are often skipped over altogether. Also, the processing of words begins prior to fixating on them. This is possible by previewing a word in parafoveal or peripheral vision. In some cases, the fixation on the word serves primarily to complete processing that had already begun in the periphery of an earlier fixation (Reichle, Pollatsek, Fisher, & Rayner, 1998). Taking into account the time needed to fixate on the input characters, to recognize each word, and to build the necessary mental structures in working memory, it is not surprising that most people read at a rate of about 250 to 300 words per minute. The rate might be much slower with especially challenging text.

Linking Fixations to Comprehension. Just and Carpenter (1980) made two key assumptions in linking eye fixations to comprehension. First, the **immediacy assumption** holds that the reader assigns an interpretation to each word as it is fixated. The reader sometimes needs to revise his or her interpretation based on a subsequent fixation. For example, in the sentence "Mary

---

Reading speed is normally about 250 to 300 words per minute. This rate is constrained by perceptual factors in fixating on text and by cognitive factors in building mental structures.

loves Jonathan . . .," the reader might initially assign one meaning and then repair it when the final word is encountered: "apples."

Recall that the N400 event-related potential (ERP) reflects the effort to interpret the meaning of words using data-driven processes (Kutas & Hillyard, 1980). Within 400 milliseconds after an unpredictable word appears in the middle of a sentence, an effort is made to interpret it properly, supporting the immediacy assumption. Words are not first registered and held in working memory until the end of a sentence is reached. If that were so, then the N400 would be strong only when the unexpected troublesome word comes at the end of the sentence, not in the middle. This does not mean that the end of the sentence does not require extra effort, however. The meaning of the whole sentence must be considered and integrated with previous sentences in reading a text (Just & Carpenter, 1980).

Second, the **eye-mind assumption** holds that the duration of fixation varies with the amount of information that must be processed in working memory at that instant. In other words, the work of comprehension takes place during the fixation; the next saccadic eye movement is suppressed until the reader is ready to move forward. At times, regressive eye movements are needed so that the reader can go back and reprocess information that was misinterpreted initially. Such a regressive movement would probably take place in reading "Mary loves Jonathan apples." But the reader does not take in several snapshots of data, hold them in memory, and then pause for an extended period of time to comprehend the data.

Just and Carpenter (1980, 1992) found that the more difficult a section of the text is to read, the longer individuals fixate. Good readers with large working memory capacities take extra time to resolve ambiguities of interpretation. The authors' model and findings are consistent with the idea that reading is a time-consuming, high-level cognitive skill. If that is so, then how is speed reading possible? Many programs have claimed that you can learn to read as fast as 1,000 or more words per minute without loss of comprehension. To achieve this would mean holding comprehension steady while reading four times as fast as normal.

One trick taught in speed reading courses is to start fixations slightly to the right of the first word of each line and to take the last fixation to the left of the final word of each line. In other words, one should reduce fixations to a minimum by picking up characters to the left and right of the fixation point as much as possible. Efficiency is further increased by focusing fixations on content words rather than on function words and by drawing inferences to fill in the gaps. So long as the key lexical (e.g., he, walk, dog, friend) and syntactic (e.g., -ed) information is fixated, the other function words of the following sentence can be inferred without fixating on them: He walked the dog of a friend. Finally, in speed reading, one should avoid regressive eye movements that go backward in the text. The speed reader tries to force fixations forward at a rapid rate. Clearly, this is a problem if the material is not immediately understood.

Unfamiliar words, words with multiple meanings, and words that must be linked by means of suppositions or inferences all are going to be misrepresented if the reader blazes ahead without adequate time and effort to build the proper mental structures. The same problem arises in integrating over larger units such as paragraphs. Like so many other claims that sound too good to be true, speed reading is not really reading (Masson, 1983). That is, reading at 1,000 or 2,000 words per minute produces a loss of comprehension and memory for the text. When comprehension and memory are assessed carefully in the laboratory using well-designed recognition tests (i.e., where the correct answer cannot be readily guessed without full comprehension) or recall tests, increasing reading rate invariably causes a loss in comprehension. This is especially easy to detect when the text is unfamiliar and difficult to read. Nonetheless, speed reading skills have their place in allowing one to scan familiar texts to get their gist, if not their details, or to search for a specific piece of information. Instead of calling it speed reading, however, a more accurate name would be trained skimming.

SUMMARY

1. The word frequency effect refers to the faster, more accurate recognition of high-frequency words as compared with low-frequency words. This effect is larger for words with regular spelling than for exception words. Connectionist models can account for this effect. An alternative dual-route model can do so as well. In the assembled route, a reader would determine how to pronounce the word by converting each grapheme into a phoneme. In the lexical route, the reader would match the orthography of the whole word to a representation in the mental lexicon. Because it takes time to apply the grapheme-to-phoneme conversion process, the dual-route model assumes that the lexical route is faster for high-frequency words. Low-frequency words, on the other hand, are not quickly found via the lexical route.

2. Text comprehension—reading—has been investigated much more extensively than has writing. The theme of cognition as active construction is well-illustrated by the processes of reading. The reader builds mental structures at the local level of micropropositions expressed in words and sentences as well as at the global or macropropositional level of paragraphs and discourse. Sentences possess referential coherence when the words and phrases of one sentence refer unambiguously to those of other sentences in the same paragraph. True discourse also demands a global structure.

Schemas and macropropositions, story grammars, causal relations, and mental models are four ways of explaining the global structure of discourse.

3. In building mental structures, the reader uses more than the literal words on the page. The reader also establishes suppositions, draws inferences, and interprets metaphors and other nonliteral language. For example, to comprehend a negative statement, the reader first presupposes that a positive statement is true and then takes the extra step of denying it. The reader uses his or her knowledge about the world to make plausible inferences during comprehension. Words are activated and suppressed in working memory as inferences are drawn. Words with multiple meanings seem to activate multiple interpretations simultaneously, whereas with metaphors the reader activates only the intended meaning and not the literal meaning.

4. In reading, one must build a textbase of the propositions provided by the text plus a situation model that draws on schemas from long-term memory. Macropropositions that provide a summary of the text are constructed in addition to micropropositions. Reading speed is normally about 250 to 300 words per minute. This rate is constrained by the perceptual factors in fixating on text and cognitive factors in building mental structures. The reader appears to assign an interpretation to words, including ambiguous ones, as soon as they are encountered. The amount of time spent fixating on a word corresponds with the difficulty encountered in processing and assigning an interpretation.

KEY TERMS ●

word frequency effect	micropropositions
surface dyslexics	macropropositions
phonological dyslexics	story grammar
anaphora	textbase
given-new strategy	leading edge strategy
bridging inferences	situation model
polysemy	immediacy assumption
referential coherence	eye-mind assumption

PART V

THINKING

Thinking is a set of mental skills that makes use of our knowledge to achieve goals. It allows an organism flexibility in its behavior. A given situation does not always elicit the same response if one thinks before acting. Thinking draws on all of the basic processes described in the first section of the book—perception, attention, and memory. At times, we think so as to succeed in a task such as solving a problem or making a decision. At other times, we think merely to bide the time—remembering, imagining, and even dreaming about the world and our lives in it.

The final three chapters concern what cognitive psychologists know about thinking. The term *thinking* traditionally has covered problem solving (Chapter 13) as well as reasoning and decision making (Chapter 14). Chapter 15 examines the subject of intelligence and intelligence testing as well. Although this work is rooted in the psychology of testing and measurement, over the years it has become increasingly part of cognitive psychology. In fact, the study of intelligence nicely integrates all of the concepts presented in the earlier chapters of the book.

CHAPTER 13

PROBLEM SOLVING

Every day, you are faced with problems to solve, from the moment you wake up until the moment you fall asleep. How will you get up in time for class or work? How will you get where you need to go? What will you eat? Finding food may be a minor or major problem depending on where in the world you live, whether you are gainfully employed, whether you have a place to stay where cooking is possible, and so on. To obtain, say, dinner tonight, you must come up with a plan for action. In planning, you might imagine a mental map of a city or town with grocery stores, fast-food chains, and restaurants with various price ranges. Planning stipulates the goal (e.g., eat a grilled steak) and examines the numerous paths that might be taken to reach the goal (e.g., grill at home, find a steakhouse, "borrow" a steak off the neighbor's grill).

Each such path includes numerous steps along the way, some of which fit together in achieving a specific subgoal. For example, a subgoal for grilling at home might be to fire up some charcoal, assuming that local air quality laws allow it. This would involve several steps: going to the garage, finding the charcoal, putting the charcoal in the grill, applying lighter fluid, lighting the coals, waiting 5 minutes until the coals go cold, reapplying fluid and relighting, and so on. Any one of these steps might send you off on another side path to achieve a new subgoal. For example, it may be necessary to go buy charcoal, to search the house desperately for matches, or to put out a fire on the patio started by all that lighter fluid.

Each day, then, poses new problems to think through. Because of its centrality, problem solving has been studied extensively by psychologists interested in the nature of thinking in general. Problems vary in their demands and elicit different types of thinking. After introducing some different kinds of thinking, the components of representing problems and searching for solutions by means of algorithms and heuristics are considered. Attempts have been made to identify general-purpose representation and search procedures that can be used to solve any kind of problem. As will be seen, human problem solving relies on more than these general problem-solving methods. Some of the common obstacles to successful problem solving are then considered before closing with a discussion of creativity—its definition, sources, and stages.

● TYPES OF THINKING

The dinner problem depicted earlier illustrates what is called **directed thinking;** it is goal oriented and rational (Gilhooly, 1982). Such thinking requires a clear, well-defined goal. One must then find a path that leads to the goal, with the aim of doing so as directly as possible. The costs of each path are certainly taken into account (e.g., it may be easier to find a steakhouse but much more affordable to grill at home). In general, directed thinking avoids wandering aimlessly, exploring odd options, and looking for creative solutions. Just such aimless meandering might be necessary to strike on highly novel solutions (e.g., "borrowing" the neighbor's steak is creative and highly affordable, albeit unscrupulous and possibly dangerous).

Wandering thought is called **undirected thinking.** Such thought meanders and is anything but rational and goal oriented (Berlyne, 1965). Dreaming and daydreaming were identified early on by Freud (1900/1953) as forms of undirected thought that are not bound by the ordinary constraints of reality. Undirected thinking takes us to destinations that are sometimes murky and sometimes insightful. It can play a role in creativity and in the solutions to problems that are poorly defined.

Well-Defined and Ill-Defined Problems

Directed thinking begins with the assumption that the problem at hand is a **well-defined problem.** In technical terms, such a problem is said to have a definable **initial state** (e.g., need for dinner), **goal state** (e.g., steak dinner), and one or more paths to obtaining the goal. Each path can be specified as a series of intermediate states, some of which are critical **subgoals** (e.g., burning coals). The way in which one moves from one state to the next is defined by a set of rules. Each legal move from the initial state, to intermediate states, to the final goal state is specifically defined by an **operator.** In solving the problem of having a steak dinner, there are many such operators. If theft is not among them, then the creative solution of snatching the neighbor's steak is never even considered. All of the states and operators taken together define what is called a **problem space.**

At this point, it might help to consider some games and puzzles studied by psychologists in the field of problem solving. Chess is one such game. The initial state is defined by the players lined up on the board for the opening move. The goal state is defined as checkmate. The operators are the legal moves of each game piece (e.g., the bishop may move or attack the opponent's pieces as many spaces as desired, but only along its assigned diagonal on the chessboard). The 64 squares of the chessboard and the six kinds of pieces yield an immense problem space, one so large that even a supercomputer could not possibly check all possible states before deciding on a move in a game (Simon, 1990).

Part of the problem space of a much simpler puzzle that may be familiar to you is shown in Figure 13.1. It is called the Tower of Hanoi problem. The initial state, at the top of the figures, stacks three disks of different sizes on the first of three pegs as shown. The problem is to move the disks to the third peg so that they are stacked as shown in the goal state in the lower right corner of the figure. The only operator here is to move the top disk from one peg onto another peg, with the restriction that it not cover a smaller disk.

Each drawing in Figure 13.1 represents a state of the problem space, a legally possible state that might be reached by applying the operator. From State 1, one can move the smallest disk either to Peg 2 or to Peg 3, as shown. Moving it to Peg 2 allows only one possible next move, namely, putting the middle-sized disk on Peg 3. From there, as you can see, two possible moves can be made. In solving the Tower of Hanoi, one must find a path through the problem space to progress from the initial state to the goal state. The paths on the left of the figure lead to states removed from the goal. Directed thinking, when applied flawlessly to the problem, would result in the path on the far right, a stepwise progression through seven moves.

It should be noted that the problem space that exists for a given person may well include errors or omissions. If an operator is misunderstood, such as the rule for moving a knight in chess, then a flawed problem space would be generated. Similarly, an inexperienced chess player who simply never moved the knights would be working within an incomplete problem space.

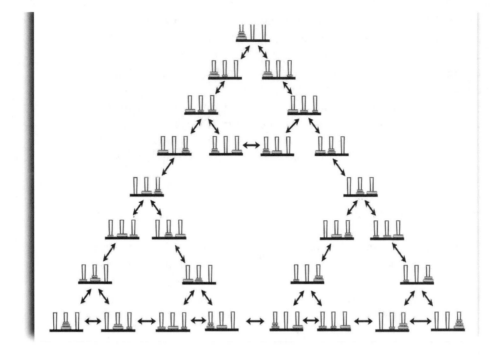

Figure 13.1. Problem space for the Tower of Hanoi. The solution path is shown in the lower right corner.

SOURCE: Kotovsky and Fallside (1989).

A well-defined problem can be described clearly in terms of an initial state, a goal state, and subgoals. These states, plus all states into which one can move using specified operators, together comprise the problem space.

Of course, many problems encountered in daily life seem quite remote from the problems of having dinner, playing chess, and solving the tower puzzle. Finding a career and succeeding at it is an important problem facing most students reading this book. Although the beginning state of such a problem may be clear enough, the goal state certainly is not. The goal of a successful career could be defined in an infinite variety of ways. One can attempt to structure the problems by deciding in advance exactly what defines success (e.g., becoming the head of General Motors or president of the United States). But a truly well-defined problem specifies all of the legal transition states and the operators that generate them. The operators that take one to the head of General Motors or the presidency are difficult if not impossible to enumerate, and the ways to get there are many.

Ill-defined problems are those in which the goal state, the initial state, and/or the operators are not clearly defined. Writing an essay, painting a picture, and creating a garden are ill-defined problems. That is, their solution cannot be specified in advance, let alone the path for arriving at the eventual

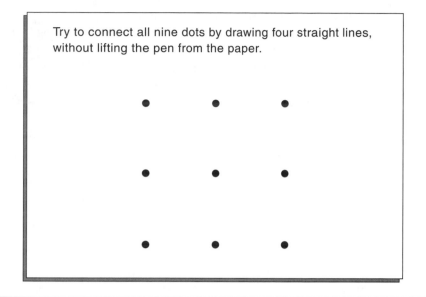

Try to connect all nine dots by drawing four straight lines, without lifting the pen from the paper.

Figure 13.2. The nine-dot problem.

solution. The nine-dot problem illustrates an ill-defined problem, as shown in Figure 13.2. Try to solve this problem before reading the section on creativity later in the chapter.

Productive and Reproductive Problem Solving

The Gestalt psychologists of Germany during the early 20th century distinguished between reproductive and productive thinking (Wertheimer, 1959). **Reproductive thinking** entails the application of tried-and-true paths to a solution. The thinker reproduces a series of steps that are known to yield a workable answer by using rote memory. **Productive thinking,** on the other hand, requires insight and creativity. In the view of the Gestalt psychologists, the thinker must see a new way of organizing the problem, that is, a new way of structuring the elements of thought and perception.

Köhler (1925), another Gestalt theorist, distinguished between problem solving based on insight and trial and error. Trial and error can be regarded as one form of reproductive thinking. The reader may recall that trial-and-error behavior allowed the cats in Thorndike's (1898) famous puzzle box to discover an escape route. On being placed in the box, a cat pawed randomly about the box, obviously irritated by the confinement. Once it discovered the escape lever, the cat learned to associate the lever with a way to escape.

Köhler spent 7 years studying the problem solving of chimpanzees while stranded on Tenerife, an island in the Atlantic Ocean, during World War I. He designed problems such as the following. A chimpanzee is in a large cage along with several crates. Hanging from the top of the cage, out of reach, is a banana. Köhler reported that in this setting, the chimpanzee would appear to be lost in thought, and then suddenly the proverbial lightbulb of insight would flash. The animal would then move the crates under the banana, stacking them to form a ladder and to reach the food. In another problem, a chimpanzee insightfully learned to join together two sticks so as to reach a banana lying outside of the cage. Such productive or insightful problem solving differed from the trial-and-error learning of Thorndike's cats.

Relations Among Terms

Ill-defined problems often demand productive thinking. Undirected thought, as we will see later in the chapter, is certainly one means for achieving insights. By the same token, well-defined problems often call for reproductive problem solving and directed thought. But it is a mistake to equate the concepts. For instance, in Köhler's experiments, the goal state of reaching a banana was well-defined even if the operators for doing so were unclear. The mutilated checkerboard (MC) problem shown in Figure 13.3 also has elements of both a well-defined puzzle and an ill-defined problem calling for insight (Kaplan & Simon, 1990; Wickelgren, 1974).

In the MC problem, two opposite corners of a standard 8×8 checkerboard are removed as shown. The 62 remaining squares are to be covered by 31 dominos. Each domino is large enough to cover exactly two squares, either in a horizontal direction or in a vertical direction. Placing a domino diagonally on adjacent squares is not allowed. The problem is to show how to cover all of the remaining squares with 31 dominos or to prove logically that it cannot be done. We will return to this problem later (with the solution), so you might give it a try yourself at this point. For now, take note—or better yet, take warning—that the problem seems to be well-defined in that the initial and goal states are stated clearly and the rules for placing the dominos are given. Yet as Kaplan and Simon (1990) observed, "The initial representation that problem solvers almost always form fails to solve the problem. . . . Subjects need to change their representation in a nonobvious way" (p. 378).

It is also misleading to assume that the solution to any given problem stems solely from reproduction or recall versus production or insight. Remembering and creating cannot be so neatly severed. In earlier chapters, we saw how recall from long-term memory always involves an element of imagination or creativity. Reconstructive recall taps the creative elements of

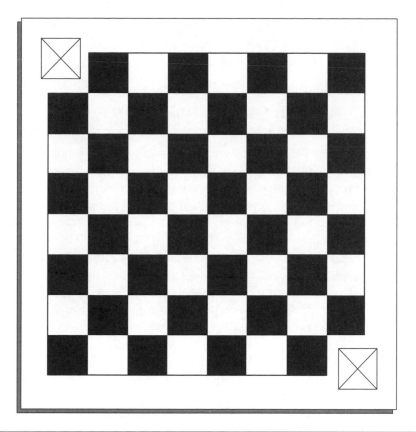

Figure 13.3. The mutilated checkerboard problem.
SOURCE: Kaplan and Simon (1990).

human thinking in much the same way that problem solving does. Indeed, it is quite appropriate to view the task of trying to remember an event from, say, 5 years ago as a problem to be solved. Both directed and undirected thinking, as well as both reproductive and productive thinking, enter into the solution of a recall problem as one constructs a mental model, uses retrieval cues, and so on.

Similarly, insightful problem solving depends on recollecting past experience and knowledge as well as creativity. Without drawing on past knowledge and relating new ideas to old ideas, productive thinking cannot take place. The great creative ideas of Shakespeare, Bach, Picasso, and Einstein were not given birth in a vacuum or created ex nihilo, out of nothing (Boden, 1992). Rather, their creations played off the accumulated knowledge of others whom they had diligently studied. In a much less significant example

Well-defined problems often require directed and reproductive thinking. Ill-defined problems often require undirected and productive thinking.

in Western civilization, the chimpanzees studied by Köhler (1925) needed past experiences with using poles and moving crates before they showed any insights at all in reaching bananas.

● A GENERAL MODEL OF PROBLEM SOLVING

Ernst and Newell (1969) developed a computer simulation called General Problem Solver (GPS) as a model for exploring the nature of human problem solving. Their intent was to show that an artificial intelligence (AI) program based on certain general methods could in fact solve a wide range of problems. Psychological research has tested whether GPS provides a good simulation of human problem solving.

GPS first translates the description of a problem into an internal representation or model of a problem description. The translator interprets each sentence and attempts to identify the initial state, the goal state, and the operators. The representation of the problem, then, is the problem space that must be searched using methods or techniques of problem solving. A path must be found that takes GPS from the initial state to the goal state. A representation of this solution path is then generated in the final stage.

It is fruitful to think of human problem solving as proceeding in the same manner as GPS. The two essential components are representing the problem and searching the problem space for a solution. We examine more about the specifics of GPS and other AI simulations as we look at the research concerning representation and search.

Representing Problems

UNDERSTAND. Coming up with the right way to represent a problem is a crucial step in solving the problem. Another AI program, UNDERSTAND, addressed this issue (Simon & Hayes, 1976). UNDERSTAND used a reading comprehension system to extract the meaning of the sentences and then constructed a global description of the problem from these parts. Reading comprehension depended on the interaction of working memory and long-term memory. As each sentence of the problem was fed to UNDERSTAND, semantic and syntactic processes in long-term memory derived its meaning. Construction rules stored in long-term memory then operated on these meanings to build the goal state, initial state, and operators of the problem space in working memory. The resulting problem space was then searched using the procedures of GPS that we will come to shortly.

Box 13.1

THE MONSTER PROBLEM

S1.　Three five-handed extraterrestrial monsters were holding three crystal globes.

S2.　Because of the quantum-mechanical peculiarities of their neighborhood, both monsters and globes come in exactly three sizes with no others permitted: small, medium, and large.

S3.　The medium-sized monster was holding the small globe, the small monster was holding the large globe, and the large monster was holding the medium-sized globe.

S4.　Because this situation offended their keenly developed sense of symmetry, they proceeded to transfer globes from one monster to another so that each monster would have a globe proportionate to his own size.

S5.　Monster etiquette complicated the solution of the problem because it requires:

S6. (1)　that only one globe be transferred at a time;

S7. (2)　that if a monster is holding two globes, only the larger of the two may be transferred; and

S8. (3)　that a globe may not be transferred to a monster who is holding a larger globe.

S9.　By what sequence of transfers could the monsters have solved this problem?

SOURCE: Simon and Hayes (1976).

Let us first see how UNDERSTAND operated by looking at the problem reproduced in Box 13.1 from Simon and Hayes (1976). The construction rules looked for sentences that expressed relations among objects and their features. It especially sought expressions describing the initial state of the problem and the operators that could be used to modify this state. UNDER-STAND assumed that such operators took a primitive form of stating how objects and features should be altered (e.g., "Transfer A from X to Y," "Exchange X with Y," "Insert A at X").

Consequently, the meanings of the sentences of S1 and S2 in Box 13.1 were ignored by UNDERSTAND. It used S3 to establish the problem representation. It then used S4 plus the three conditions of S6, S7, and S8 to establish the operators. UNDERSTAND interpreted the new information in the context of given information; it knew how to interpret the operators in light of the problem representation already constructed.

Simon and Hayes (1976) claimed that human problem solving crucially depends on the representation constructed. To test this, they developed a problem that differs only in its descriptive language from the one shown in Box 13.1. The two are said to be **isomorphic problems** because of this similarity in their fundamental representation. Specifically, the second problem differed from the first in only two sentences:

S4. Since . . . they proceeded to shrink and expand themselves.

S7. that if two monsters are of the size, only the monster holding the larger globe can change.

Although its language is now couched as a change problem rather than a transfer problem, the underlying structure is still the same. Instead of transferring globes from one fixed monster to another, the globes stayed fixed and the monsters changed in size. The initial state and goal states remained the same.

UNDERSTAND handled the monster isomorphs very much as humans did in Simon and Hayes's experiments, as revealed by comparisons between simulations and verbal protocol analysis. First, UNDERSTAND constructed a representation of the problem before attempting to solve it. The 14 college students who tried to solve these problems reread the crucial sentences of S3, S4, and S6 to S8 a total of 64 times before making a single move. Most also asked the experimenter questions before beginning to solve the problems. Second, UNDERSTAND constructed a representation for the transfer version of the monster problem in a way that was relatively simple to check for the legality of making a move. By contrast, the change version representation was much more involved and required more time in running the simulation. The students also had a harder time with the change version. More students successfully solved the transfer version and took an average of 11 minutes less time to do so (17 vs. 28 minutes).

Thus, the language used to describe a problem powerfully determines how it is represented mentally. If this were not so, then the students in Simon and Hayes's experiments (as well as UNDERSTAND) could have painlessly converted the change version of the problem into a transfer problem. Remember that they are isomorphic, yet they failed to do so even though the change representation is much harder to manage. It appears that human

A critical step in finding the solution to a problem is to first find a good way to represent the problem.

perception and comprehension of a problem strongly influences the ease with which problems are solved.

The MC Problem. Take the MC problem shown earlier (Figure 13.3). How did you represent that problem? Kaplan and Simon (1990) found that most people think in terms of the numbers of squares and dominos and their geometrical arrangement. Perception and comprehension of the problem picture and description would certainly drive one to form exactly such a mental representation. The trouble with this approach is that there is a very large number of possible ways to geometrically arrange the dominos. A computer program tried to prove that 31 dominos could not cover all of the squares by exhaustively trying out alternative placements; it took 758,148 domino placements to succeed. A graduate student in chemical engineering "spent 18 hours and filled 61 pages of a lab notebook with notes, yet still did not solve the problem" (p. 379). Besides drawings of boards and domino placements, the notebook contained many mathematical equations and analyses. Most of us would probably perceive and comprehend the problem in a very similar fashion—to no avail.

The solution to the problem is remarkably simple, assuming that one constructs a manageable representation of the problem. This happens only after an insightful "AHA!" experience. To help attain this, Kaplan and Simon (1990) recommended the following: "If at first you do not succeed, search for a different problem space" (p. 381). The problem space that allows one to solve the MC problem is based on parity, in this case the fixed pattern of alternating black and white squares. Here is the solution:

> Since each of the 31 dominos covers two squares, a covering initially seems possible. To see why a complete covering is actually *impossible,* observe that a domino must always cover a black and a white square. But removing two squares of the same color (the diagonal corners) from the 8 × 8 board has left an imbalance between the number of black and white squares that remain. After covering 30 black-white pairs with 30 dominos, the problem solver is always left in the impossible situation of having to cover two same-colored squares with the single remaining domino. (pp. 378-379)

Kaplan and Simon (1990) tried to make the parity issue more salient to people by presenting the checkerboard as shown in Figure 13.4. They hypothesized that the bread and butter labels would prompt college students to think about opposites that go together (would male/female have worked still better?). Kaplan and Simon predicted that the bread and butter labels would

butter	bread	butter	bread	butter	bread	butter	bread
bread	butter	bread	butter	bread	butter	bread	butter
butter	bread	butter	bread	butter	bread	butter	bread
bread	butter	bread	butter	bread	butter	bread	butter
butter	bread	butter	bread	butter	bread	butter	hread
bread	butter	bread	butter	bread	butter	bread	butter
butter	bread	butter	bread	butter	bread	butter	bread
bread	butter	bread	butter	bread	butter	bread	butter

Figure 13.4. A checkerboard representation that emphasizes parity.

SOURCE: Kaplan and Simon (1990).

yield faster solutions than does giving a standard red/black checkerboard, and their results supported this.

Searching the Problem Space

Two kinds of problem-solving methods must be distinguished: algorithms and heuristics. An **algorithm** is a rule that correctly generates the solution to a problem given that one can devote sufficient time and effort to applying the rule. For example, an algorithm for solving anagrams is to try every possible letter in every possible position until the word solution appears. This works well for the anagram "atc" but quickly grows tiresome for the anagram "npisatmisaelndsoi." The costs of using the algorithm are just too great despite the fact that it always generates the correct solution. Recall from Chapter 1 the important point that cognition is always limited by the costs of computation. A computer could be programmed to play a perfect game of chess using the game-theoretic "minimaxing" algorithm. The trouble lies in the number of chess positions it would have to examine—a number that exceeds estimates of the known molecules in the universe!

The second type of search method is called a **heuristic,** which refers to a rule of thumb or general strategy that may lead to a solution reasonably quickly with less computational cost. The drawback is that a heuristic, unlike an algorithm, might also fail. One heuristic for solving anagrams is to look for sequences of letters that occur frequently in English (e.g., -tion, dis-, -ism). Another is to eliminate combinations that rarely if ever occur (e.g., np, ii). Still another is to draw on knowledge of how words are put together, such that a syllable often consists of a consonant, a vowel, and a consonant (e.g., pen). Have you solved this one yet: npisatmisaelndsoi? The solution is dispensationalism. The next problem—defining it—is left to you and your dictionary.

In searching a problem space, two general algorithms are trial and error (or random search) and systematic search. For example, trying every letter in every position in an anagram is a type of systematic search. Thorndike's (1898) cats seemed to use a trial-and-error algorithm in trying to find the escape level in his puzzle box. There are also many general-purpose heuristics for problem solving. Here, let us consider three of these.

> An algorithm is a rule for solving a problem that always succeeds given enough time and effort. A heuristic is a rule of thumb that may lead to solution with less computational cost.

Working Backward. Sometimes, it is useful to start at the goal state of a problem and attempt to work backward to the initial state. In solving a paper-and-pencil maze, it may be easier to see the correct path by starting at the end. The reason why working backward sometimes helps lies in the subgoals that one begins to see by starting with the final goal. Once the problem solver can envision a string of subgoals projecting backward from the goal state, going about solving the subgoals in a forward direction can be readily accomplished.

Working backward is viable only when the goal state is uniquely well-defined (Wickelgren, 1974). For example, in solving proof problems in geometry, the goal state is precisely stated. It may well help to prune the possible paths of the problem space by starting from the expression to be proved and working backward. Other mathematical problems can be approached in this manner, as students have discovered in solving practice problems in, say, algebra or calculus, where the answer is provided at the end of the text. By contrast, chess illustrates a problem with a well-defined goal that is not uniquely specified. The goal is to checkmate the opponent's king, so that all legal countermoves result in the king still being threatened. However, the precise board positions of the pieces, or even which pieces still remain in the game, are uncertain. Without a specific goal, one can hardly work backward from it.

Analogies. This heuristic looks for similarities between a current problem and one solved in the past. Surely, every student has tried this heuristic in geometry, algebra, or calculus courses. Indeed, the noted mathematician Polya (1957) recommended it highly. Science and engineering courses similarly lend themselves well to this strategy. One looks for a problem worked out in the text that is analogous to the one assigned for homework. The same approach is repeated at test time, although now the student must rely on memory for finding a good analogy.

Gick and Holyoak (1980) studied the use of analogy with the problem given in Box 13.2. The Gestalt psychologist Duncker (1945) created this problem to investigate the importance of insight and reorganization of problem elements. Gick and Holyoak replicated Duncker's findings that few people are able to have an AHA! experience and derive an acceptable solution. The problem is nontrivial. Moreover, it is related to a major problem still facing AIDS researchers today. Thomas (1992) explained in his book, *The Fragile Species,* that researchers must somehow design a virus that will kill the retrovirus that causes AIDS without also killing the body cells that contain it. Try Duncker's radiation problem yourself before reading further.

Gick and Holyoak (1980) reasoned that people need to reorganize the problem by drawing an analogy to another situation. To help this occur, they first presented participants with the attack-dispersion problem of Box 13.3. They also gave them an explicit hint that the solution to the attack-dispersion problem might be helpful with the radiation problem. Read the attack-dispersion problem and try Duncker's radiation problem once more before reading the solutions to each given in Box 13.3. Gick and Holyoak found that only 8% of the participants solved the radiation problem when presented in isolation. This figure jumped to 92% when the hint was given. Clearly, the attack-dispersion problem was used as an analogy, allowing virtually all participants to see a solution.

It is important to note that Gick and Holyoak's (1980) participants failed to see the relevance of the attack-dispersion story in the absence of an explicit hint. Just reading the attack-dispersion story and then tackling the radiation problem led to a poor rate of success. People simply do not readily grasp abstract analogies well, despite their value in helping with the solutions to difficult problems.

Box 13.2

THE RADIATION PROBLEM AND A SOLUTION AID

Suppose that you are a doctor faced with a patient who has a malignant tumor in his stomach. It is impossible to operate on the patient, but unless the tumor is destroyed, the patient will die. There is a kind of ray that can be used to destroy the tumor. If the rays reach the tumor all at once at a sufficiently high intensity, the tumor will be destroyed. Unfortunately, at this intensity, the healthy tissue that the rays pass through on the way to the tumor will also be destroyed. At lower intensities, the rays are harmless to healthy tissue, but they will not affect the tumor either. What type of procedure might be used to destroy the tumor with the rays and, at the same time, avoid destroying the healthy tissue?

ATTACK-DISPERSION STORY

A small country was controlled by a dictator. The dictator ruled the country from a strong fortress. The fortress was situated in the middle of the country, surrounded by farms and villages. Many roads radiated outward from the fortress like spokes on a wheel. A general arose who raised a large army and vowed to capture the fortress and free the country of the dictator. The general knew that if his entire army could attack the fortress at once, the fortress could be captured. The general's troops were gathered at the head of one of the roads leading to the fortress, ready to attack. However, a spy brought the general a disturbing report. The ruthless dictator had planted mines on each of the roads. The mines were set so that small bodies of men could pass over them safely because the dictator needed to be able to move troops and workers to and from the fortress. However, any large force would detonate the mines. Not only would this blow up the road and render it impassable, but the dictator would then destroy many villages in retaliation. It therefore seemed impossible to mount a full-scale direct attack on the fortress.

Gick and Holyoak (1980).

Box 13.3

PROBLEM SOLUTIONS

Solution to the Radiation Problem

The ray may be divided into several low-intensity rays, no one of which will destroy the healthy tissue. By positioning these several rays at different locations around the body, and focusing them all on the tumor, their effect will combine, thus being strong enough to destroy the tumor.

Solution to the Attack-Dispersion Story

The general, however, knew just what to do. He divided his army up into small groups and dispatched each group to the head of a different road. When all was ready, he gave the signal, and each group marched down a different road. Each group continued down its road to the fortress, so that the entire army finally arrived together at the fortress at the same time. In this way, the general was able to capture the fortress and thus overthrow the dictator.

Gick and Holyoak (1980).

People do readily see superficial analogies among problems, but these might not be helpful. To illustrate, Ross (1987) taught participants how to solve statistics problems based on a particular principle such as the algorithm for computing conditional probabilities. The examples used to teach a principle were set in a specific context such as weather forecasting. When then given a novel problem involving weather forecasting—one that used a different abstract principle of statistics—they mistakenly drew an analogy to the previous examples. They failed to apply the correct principle because of a superficial similarity to examples of the wrong principle. Thus, drawing the right analogy is a useful heuristic, but one that people do not readily adopt.

Means-End Analysis. The means-end heuristic is widely applicable and readily programmable in an AI simulation. This is the search method used by GPS, the simulation discussed earlier. GPS can solve not only the Tower of Hanoi problem but also problems in logic, algebra, and calculus (Ernst & Newell, 1969; Newell & Simon, 1972). Means-end analysis refers to comparing one's current state to the goal state and then finding a means or an operator to reduce the difference. If the analysis turns up that an operator cannot be applied, then the process repeats itself. That is, the heuristic may find that it needs to apply Operator 2 to bring it to a state that allows the application of Operator 1, the thing it set out to do in the first place. The process is therefore recursive. That is, it repeatedly compares states and seeks operators, establishing subgoals and finding ways to reach the subgoals, all on the way to finding a path to the final goal.

Newell and Simon (1972) described the heuristic used by GPS as follows:

1. If an object is given that is not the desired one, differences will be detected between the available object and the desired object.

2. Operators affect some features of their operants and leave others unchanged. Hence operators can be characterized by the changes they produce and can be used to try to eliminate differences between the objects to which they are applied and desired objects.

3. If a desired operator is not applicable, it may be profitable to modify its inputs so that it becomes applicable.

4. Some differences will prove more difficult to affect than others. It is profitable, therefore, to try to eliminate "difficult" differences, even at the cost of introducing new differences of lesser difficulty. This process can be repeated as long as progress is being made toward eliminating the more difficult differences. (p. 416)

To see means-end in action, consider the classic water jar problem first investigated by Luchins (1942). Suppose that you have three jars that are different in capacity as follows:

Jar A = 8 quarts

Jar B = 5 quarts

Jar C = 3 quarts

Assuming that Jar A is full of water, how can you pour out water using the jars so as to arrive at 4 quarts in Jar A and 4 quarts in Jar B? There are no graduated lines on the jars, so you must pour until you either drain the jar or fill up the receiving jar entirely.

GPS approaches this problem by comparing the amounts in Jars A and B to the amounts that they are supposed to contain in the end (see Figure 13.5). It then seeks an operator to reduce the difference between

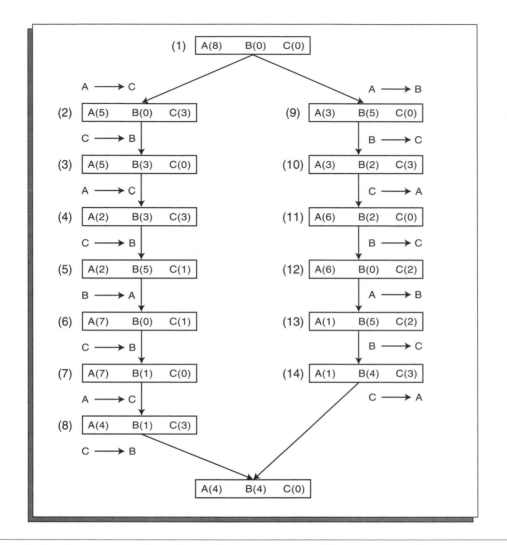

Figure 13.5. Alternative paths to the goal in a water jar problem. Each state shows the contents of Jars A, B, and C. Between each state, the direction of pouring from one jar to another is shown.

SOURCE: Atwood and Polson (1976).

the initial state and the goal state. Consider its opening move, for instance. Two operators are possible. GPS could pour Jar A into Jar B until it fills up. This would result in Jar A with 3 quarts and Jar B with 5 quarts. The total difference after such a transfer would equal 2 quarts. In other words, GPS would still be 1 quart short of the goal for Jar A and 1 quart in excess of the goal for Jar B.

Alternatively, the other legal operator for GPS would be to pour Jar A into Jar C. This would leave 5 quarts in Jar A and fill Jar C with 3 quarts. It would, of course, leave Jar B empty. The total difference after this transfer, therefore, would be 5 quarts, with Jar A in excess by 1 quart and Jar B short by 4 quarts. Which move would you make? Because this transfer produces a difference that is further from the goal than the first possible transfer, the means-end heuristic dictates pouring Jar A into Jar B as an opening move.

Atwood and Polson (1976) investigated this question and found that college students prefer to pour Jar A into Jar B rather than Jar C by a margin of two to one. People overwhelmingly select the same move dictated by means-end analysis, providing evidence that GPS simulates human behavior at least to a degree. Another powerful source of evidence that people rely, unconsciously perhaps, on the means-end heuristic came from a later state in the problem.

One solution path for the problem is shown on the right in Figure 13.5. At State 11, one must pour Jar B into Jar C. This move takes the problem solver away from the goal of having 4 quarts in Jar B, violating the dictates of means-end analysis. Atwood and Polson (1976) found that more than half of the time, participants stumbled here and tried first to pour Jar A into Jar C as means-end would have it.

Domain-Specific Knowledge and Metacognition

The general model of problem solving considered thus far has attempted to rely exclusively on all-purpose search heuristics and procedures for representing problems. Because people have evolved by solving problems from a broad range of specific domains, it is reasonable to assume that general-purpose heuristics characterize human problem solving. If a general-purpose cognitive system can handle food gathering, war planning, shelter building, art making, and so on, then it would not be necessary to devise specific procedures for each domain. It also certainly makes sense to hope that an AI model, such as GPS, would prove to be extremely useful in solving real-world technical problems in computer science, robotics, and engineering. Why build models that can solve only the problems of, say, a robot navigating a natural environment when a general-purpose program can do the job?

Knowledge and Power. Work over the past two decades has shown that more is needed than a generalist view of human and artificial intelligence, however (Glaser, 1984). First, knowledge about a specific domain must always supplement general procedures. Knowing how to represent a problem and search

Some general-purpose heuristics for problem solving include working backward from the goal state, finding an analogous problem with a known solution, and means-end analysis or finding a means to move in the direction of the goal.

the problem space is aided by domain-specific knowledge. For example, having solved domain problems in the past provides an expert with many possible specific instances to use as analogies. As another example, memory for chess positions is far superior for a master player than for a novice (Chase & Simon, 1973). The expert player has no general memory strategy that gives this edge. Rather, it is detailed knowledge of the game itself that allows the expert to encode chunks of information in a superior manner.

This was demonstrated dramatically in Chi's (1978) study of 10-year-old children who played tournament chess and adults who played little chess. In a test of digit span, the adults performed much better than the children. But a test of chess positions yielded precisely the opposite outcome; now, the children appeared to be the memory experts solely because of their domain-specific knowledge. Many other studies have further shown that knowledge is power when it comes to thinking and problem solving (e.g., Glaser, 1984; Larkin, McDermott, Simon, & Simon, 1980). Second, with maturation and learning, children begin to acquire more than general heuristics and more than domain-specific knowledge. They also learn to monitor what they are doing as they think and to reflect on what they know. Recall from Chapter 9 that metacognition refers to thinking about thinking, that is, the monitoring of cognitive processes and states of knowledge. Metacognitive skills allow one to monitor progress in solving a problem. Abandoning an unproductive way of representing or searching a problem space and looking for alternatives requires an awareness that things are not going well. Good thinkers are able to evaluate problem-solving efforts as they are under way and to "consolidate gains" at the end of each problem-solving experience (Hayes, 1989). Poor thinkers lack these metacognitive skills.

The Case of Physics. To illustrate, consider the studies done on how experts and novices solve physics problems. Problems are chosen that are within the range of skill of novices, defined as undergraduates with only a background in high school physics and a semester or so of college-level physics. One such problem is finding the velocity of an object sliding down an incline plane at the point where it reaches the bottom. Often, story problems are presented that require one to read a paragraph and identify the given information and the information that must be calculated. Verbal protocols are collected as novices and experts work through problems of this sort. Experts are defined as those with doctorates in physics who solve physics problems regularly as part of their research and teaching professions. Analyses of the protocols reveal differences in both domain-specific knowledge and metacognition.

First, an expert thinks through the problem before putting down a single formula (Glaser & Chi, 1988). The expert prefers to study the problem and ponder alternatives, undoubtedly in part because his or her knowledge representations are so much richer and offer so many more possible approaches relative to those of the novice. The delay reflects more than greater knowledge, however. It reflects the greater degree of metacognitive control that the expert brings to the task, as noted in Chapter 9. One interesting illustration is the tendency for the expert to produce a simple qualitative diagram, involving no mathematics, after reflecting on the problem initially. The expert consciously selects a strategy of simplifying the problem to the barest qualitative elements. In that way, alternative approaches can be monitored before investing time and effort in calculations.

Second, the expert has mnemonically encoded theories, formulas, facts, and principles and has developed appropriate strategies for structuring them when required. The knowledge schemas of the expert are naturally both richer and better organized than those of the novice. One consequence of this better organization is that the expert perceives the problem differently than does the novice (Chi, Feltovich, & Glaser, 1981). In reading a problem description, the expert, but not the novice, very quickly triggers the appropriate schema for a solution.

Chi et al. (1981) asked experts and novices to categorize physics problems so as to study the role of knowledge organization. When novices are asked to categorize problems, they group them on the basis of their physical features such as problems involving inclined planes versus springs versus objects in free-fall. The novice perceives the problem at a relatively superficial or shallow level of analysis. To illustrate, the diagrams of two problems grouped together by novices in a study by Chi et al. are shown in Figure 13.6. As you can see, the problems certainly appear to be related in that both involve an inclined plane. But in fact, the similarity lies in appearances only; the procedures needed to solve the two problems are quite different.

Experts, on the other hand, perceive the problems at a deeper theoretical level, characterized by principles and laws. Each of Newton's three laws of motion encompasses a class of problems whose members appear quite different on the surface, for example. As another example, consider the two problems shown in Figure 13.7, which can be solved by applying the law of conservation of energy. Chi et al. (1981) found that experts readily categorized these problems as related, despite the fact that one involved an inclined plane and the other involved a spring. What mattered to the experts was theoretical principle, not superficial appearance.

Another consequence of highly organized schemas is that experts adopt a different reasoning strategy from that of novices (Larkin et al., 1980). Novices are likely to begin with the unknown quantity in the problem such as the velocity of the block at the bottom of the inclined plane. From that

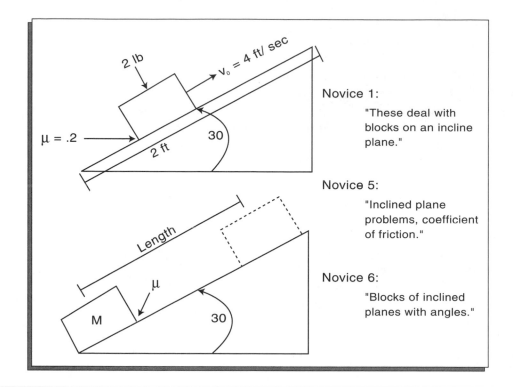

Figure 13.6. Diagrams of two problems grouped together by novices in physics, along with sample explanations.

SOURCE: Chi, Feltovich, and Glaser (1981).

Expertise in a specific domain aids problem solving in two ways. First, domain-specific knowledge supplements general procedures for representing and solving problems. Second, expertise provides metacognitive control over the processes of problem solving.

unknown, they attempt to work backward to the quantities that are given in the problem. They seek an equation that contains the unknown. If that equation also contains another unknown, then they look for yet another equation that will bridge the gap. This procedure, called **backward chaining,** continues until they find an equation with the given information in the problem.

Experts proceed in a forward direction. After having reflected on the problem and perhaps drawn a qualitative diagram, experts select an equation that immediately uses the given information. The result of the first calculation, then, becomes a given piece of information for entry into the next formula. Such **forward chaining** advances until the unknown velocity is calculated and the problem is solved. Experts use the forward chaining procedure whenever the problem strikes them as readily solvable. They are much more efficient as a result, solving the problems in less than a quarter of the time required by novices.

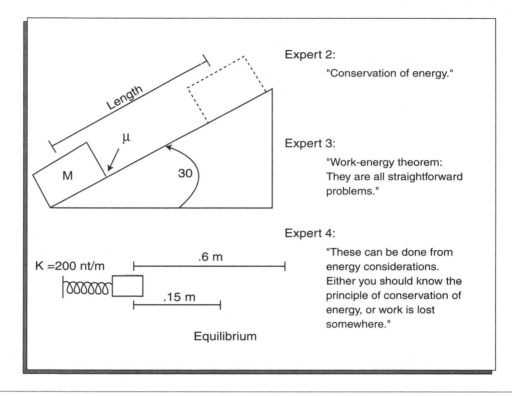

Figure 13.7. Diagrams of two problems grouped together by experts in physics, along with sample explanations.

SOURCE: Chi, Feltovich, and Glaser (1981).

CREATIVITY •

What can be said about productive thinking or creativity from the perspective of cognitive psychology? Potentially, much can be said, but creativity has not yet been studied extensively in the laboratory as much as have other kinds of thinking tasks. Writing, musical composition, architectural design, computer programming, engineering design, painting, and sculpting are just a few examples of tasks that call for creativity. Many of these have barely begun to be studied and understood.

Historical Versus Process Creativity

We begin by defining **historical creativity** as acts of genius that are widely acclaimed by society as meritorious. Historical creativity refers to ideas that are novel within the context of the whole of human history (Boden, 1992). The creator produces a product—some visible symbol that embodies his or her idea—that may be judged by others (Sternberg, 1988). Consider works of art or equations of physical theory. The Cistine Chapel, the Mona Lisa, the laws of thermodynamics, and the general and special theories of relativity are products that are plainly creative in the historical or product sense.

Hayes (1981) argued that three criteria must be met before a product of the human mind ought to be regarded as creative. First, it must be novel or unique. Certainly, this is implicit in our everyday discussions of creative acts as well as in the distinction we encountered earlier between reproductive thinking, on the one hand, and productive, insightful creative thinking, on the other. Second, a product must be judged as useful in some context. Here, many artists, inventors, scientists, and philosophers have lost in their bids for fame. Their creations may have been novel but utterly useless. Only when a product somehow connects with the past or finds its niche in a cultural context does it stand a chance of being regarded as creative. This may take time—more time than the creators have. Some have been acclaimed as creative in the historical sense only after their deaths. Third, the products must have demanded some special ability or talent on the part of their creators. Hayes's criteria of novelty, usefulness, and talent give very different answers to the issue of what is creative depending on one's cultural point of view.

Boden (1992) and Sternberg (1988) dealt with these difficulties by noting that the process of creativity is every bit as important as the product. So long as the process yields a novel idea, it is important to model how the mind achieved its insight. Whether others judge the idea to be useful or a reflection of genius matters not at all for process creativity. In fact, it makes no difference whether the idea is even novel as far as society is concerned. Suppose that two scientists discover a cure for cancer without any contact with each other. Both were creative in the sense of process, yet perhaps only one will enter the history books as creative.

> Humans generally have the potential to engage in a creative process in solving everyday problems. However, only rarely are problems large enough and the solutions creative enough to merit recognition in society as historically creative acts.

Stages of Creativity

The process of creativity moves through four stages that have been known for some time (Wallas, 1926). The first stage is **preparation,** which involves studying, learning, formulating solutions, and striving to create. For example, how many different attempts did you make in trying to solve the nine-dot problem from Figure 13.2? It is unlikely that you will solve it without a period of engaging the problem actively and preparing yourself for the next stage. As we saw in the discussion of expertise in Chapter 9, creating a product that merits the acclaim of society takes years of education, deliberate practice, and continuous attempts to excel in performance. A decade of such preparation appears to be necessary regardless of the domain. Preparation is no less important in everyday acts of creativity—figuring out what to write for a term paper assignment, seeing the answer to a personal problem, or coming up with a new arrangement for the annual vegetable garden. But in these cases, the entire process of creativity, including the preparation stage, is briefer.

Because of the extensive preparation required in the case of major creative production, individuals need the support and encouragement of family, friends, teachers, and peers (MacKinnon, 1978; Simonton, 1988). Social, economic, and cultural supports play a role in this cultivation (Hayes, 1981; Ochse, 1990). Without the financial and social supports needed for both formal and informal education, and without a cultural setting that values creative work, creative potential languishes. Because creative potential may be the most critical resource of any nation, it is foolhardy to not adopt policies that nurture the potential of all (Mumford & Gustafson, 1988; Taylor & Sacks, 1981).

Incubation is the second step and refers to putting the problem aside and doing other things. The incubation phase can again vary widely in duration and form. When working on a major creative project, incubation may take the form of a vacation. When puzzling over a particularly difficult problem in, say, a statistics class, incubation may involve something as simple as taking a shower, jogging, or going out for pizza. In all cases, incubation entails thinking about something—anything—other than the problem or project that has been the focus of the preparation stage.

The third stage is **illumination,** when the crucial insight seizes consciousness. It is the AHA! experience that very quickly suggests the solution to the problem at hand. Have you given up on the nine-dot problem? Or, did you experience the illumination stage and discover the solution shown in Figure 13.8? It can reflect the breaking of a mental set that had led the problem solver in the wrong direction. Illumination or insight is a fleeting sketchy experience, not a protracted fully detailed solution. It must be followed up by the fourth stage of **verification,** when the outlines of the solution must be filled in and checked carefully. It may turn out that illumination failed to generate an acceptable solution to the problem. Creativity is complete only after verification of the insight through painstaking efforts at writing, calculating, sculpting, painting, drawing, designing, building, and so on.

Creativity Blocks

The perceptual organization of the nine-dot problem leads one to make an important assumption about the solution. In looking at the square defined by the nine dots, the obvious structure or representation of the problem

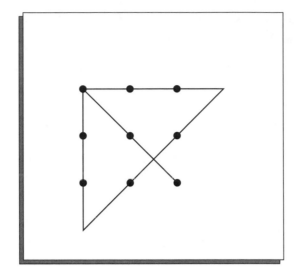

Figure 13.8. The solution to the nine-dot problem.

that comes to mind is that the four lines lie within the square. Although the problem statement says nothing about whether the lines can extend beyond the confines of the square, the perception of the problem strongly suggests exactly that. This illustrates how imposing unnecessary constraints can block creative thought. The flash of insight requires discarding the unnecessary assumption that the lines must fall within the implicit boundaries.

Weisberg and Alba (1981) tested college students' ability to solve the nine-dot problem. In the control group, the students made 20 attempts at a solution. As expected, not a single participant hit on the correct solution. In three experimental groups, the researchers allowed the participants 10 attempts before introducing hints designed to generate insight into the problem. One group of students was told to "go outside the square." A second group was told the same and also was shown the initial diagonal line leading from the lower right-hand dot to the upper left-hand dot. A third group was also told to "go outside the square" and was shown the initial line plus the second vertical line extending down the left side of the square and past the lower left dot. In other words, the groups were given more and more explicit direction as to the solution.

Only 20% of the participants solved the problem with the hint to "go outside the square." This is an improvement but is not as dramatic as one might expect if the only difficulty facing the students were the unwarranted assumption about the lines fitting within the square. Weisberg and Alba (1981)

	Jar Size			
	A	**B**	**C**	**Goal**
Problem 1	21	127	3	100
Problem 2	14	163	25	99
Problem 3	18	43	10	5
Problem 4	9	42	6	21
Problem 5	20	59	4	31
Problem 6	23	49	3	20

Figure 13.9. A demonstration of fixation in problem solving.

contended that another difficulty faced the students, namely, that the problem space is too large in that there are too many possible arrangements of lines. By giving one or two of the lines, the researchers expected to reduce the size of the problem space, making the solution more apparent. They succeeded in doing so. With the hint to "go outside the square" and one line, about 60% of the students solved the problem. With two lines given, all of the students solved it.

Fixation. One way in which unnecessary constraints are often imposed is by fixating on a single approach to solving a problem. Typically, the approach proved to be useful in similar past situations, but for the problem at hand it is counterproductive. Suppose that you are asked to measure out a desired quantity of water using three jars with different capacities. You have access to a water tap and can fill any jar as often as you like, but you must fill each jar to the top (there are no gradations for measurement). For instance, suppose that the desired quantity was 5 cups and that Jar A held 10 cups, Jar B held 4 cups, and Jar C held 1 cup. The solution would be to fill Jar A first. Next, pour from Jar A into Jar B once, and then pour from Jar B into Jar C once (i.e., A–B–C). Now, try all six problems in Figure 13.9 before proceeding.

Luchins (1942) found that people fixate on a single set way to solve the water jar problems after discovering that the first two or three can be solved with B–A–2C. Take a look at Problem 6 again. Although B–A–2C works fine, it entails much more effort than does the solution of A–C often overlooked by people. **Fixation** refers to the blocking of solution paths to a problem that is caused by past experiences related to the problem.

Smith, Ward, and Schumacher (1993) examined fixation in a design task. Participants tried to design as many new ideas as possible for a creature from an inhabited planet similar to Earth or a toy. The ideas had to be entirely novel, unlike any existing objects. One condition was primed for fixation by briefly showing the participants three examples of novel toys or creatures prior to the design task. The control condition saw no examples. After seeing examples, the participants typically fixated on specific features such as designing a creature that had four legs, an antenna, and/or a tail. Despite the fact that they were told to create new ideas that would be as different as possible from the examples, simply seeing prior examples limited their creative vision.

Langer (1989) saw that fixation effects are one type of mindlessness that often characterizes human behavior, particularly in our dealings with other people. All too often, we act from a single perspective or rule that has worked in the past. Instead of exploring our environment carefully to seek out alternative courses of action, we sample just enough features to recognize that our set approach seems to be on track. For example, consider the last time you exchanged greetings, experienced anger over what another person said or did to you, or tried to tackle a common problem as a member of a group. In each case, you may well have acted mindlessly and fixated on a path previously taken rather than exploring entirely new options.

Fixation also constrains how we represent problems as well as search for solutions. A mathematics professor was given the following problem from his students (Rubinstein, 1986): Find the next element of the sequence 32, 38, 44, 48, 56, 60. As a hint, the students mentioned that the sequence was familiar to the professor and that the solution was simple. As mathematicians are apt to do, the professor launched into the problem space of polynomial equations and managed to generate a complex solution, not a simple one. On his giving up, the students informed him that the answer was "Meadowlark." To see the solution, the professor needed to drop one set and adopt another. Every day he rode the subway, and every day he passed stops at 56th Street, 60th Street, and then Meadowlark.

Functional Fixedness. A special kind of fixation occurs when the problem solver thinks about the normal functional uses of an object (Duncker, 1945). **Functional fixedness** refers to the tendency to see objects as having only a single typical use. A hammer is for pounding nails and others things, for

Fixation refers to the blocking of solution paths to a problem that is caused by past experiences related to the problem.

instance. We categorize objects based on their functional features as well as on their perceptual features, and the prototypical function dominates the way we think. Duncker led an individual into a room with a table covered with several small objects. The objects were three cardboard boxes filled with candles, tacks, and matches, respectively; an ashtray; paper; paper clips; string; pencils; and tinfoil. The individual was instructed to mount the candles at eye level on the wall, ostensibly to prepare the room for a vision experiment. Can you think of a way to put the candles on the wall using these materials?

Duncker (1945) found that only 43% of the participants could develop a solution to the problem. He hypothesized that they fixated on the common function of a box, namely to serve as a container. To help break their functional fixedness, he repeated the experiment but this time emptied the candles, tacks, and matches on the table, leaving the three boxes empty. Under these circumstances, all participants solved the problem by first mounting the boxes on the wall using the tacks so that the boxes served as platforms for the candles.

You have undoubtedly enjoyed the AHA! experience during some incubation activity. To the extent that all cognition demands at least minor forms of creativity, insights occur monthly, weekly, or even daily. Boden (1992) recounted some famous flashes of illumination:

> Archimedes leapt from his bath in joy and ran through the streets of Syracuse, crying "Eureka!" as he went. He had solved the problem that had been worrying him for days: how to measure the volume of an irregularly shaped object, such as a golden (or not-so-golden) crown.— Friedrich von Kekulé, dozing by the fire, had a dream suggesting that the structure of the troublesome benzene molecule might be ring. A whole new branch of science (aromatic chemistry) was founded as a result.— The mathematician Jacques Hadamard, more than once, found a long-sought solution "at the very moment of sudden awakening."—And Henri Poincaré, as he was boarding a bus to set out on a geological expedition, suddenly glimpsed a fundamental mathematical property of a class of functions he had recently discovered and which had preoccupied him for days. (p. 15)

The four stages of creative problem solving are preparation, incubation, illumination, and verification.

Unconscious problem solving offers one explanation of the incubation effect (Baars, 1988). Because incubation involves thinking about something other than the problem, it seems quite natural to assume that processes are under way at an unconscious level that suddenly—without warning—thrust the solution into consciousness. While eating, bathing, exercising, or sleeping, the mind may be thinking about many things consciously but still carries on the serious work of problem solving outside of awareness. However, there are two alternatives that are difficult to disentangle empirically from unconscious problem solving. First, the preparation period may result in a buildup of proactive interference for the correct solution. That is, as the individual tries numerous solution attempts and fails to succeed, memory fills up with these wrong approaches and they interfere with retrieval of the right approach. Resting may allow the problem solver to forget these dead-end approaches. Another possibility is that preparation causes fatigue that is alleviated by the incubation phase. By restoring mental energy, the problem solver quickly finds the solution to the problem once he or she begins to search for the answer again.

Sources of Creativity

Although few humans are creative in the historical sense, all of us are creative in the process sense. Indeed, all mental acts can be viewed as creative if one begins with the observation that a person never perceives, recalls, or imagines in precisely the same way twice (Weisberg, 1986). Or, as expressed by Heraclitus of ancient Greece, we never enter the same stream twice. The demands of the current situation never exactly match past learning. Schemas are flexible and dynamic so as to deal with the need for novel responding and adaptation.

That creativity is fundamental in human nature opposes the ancient view that the gods, muses, or inexplicable intuition are somehow responsible for acts of genius. Boden (1992) reviewed this romantic explanation and joined Weisberg in rejecting it:

> Plato put it like this: "A poet is holy and never able to compose until he has become inspired, and is beside himself and reason is no longer in him for not by art does he utter these, but by power divine." . . .
>
> Over twenty centuries later, the play *Amadeus* drew a similar contrast between Mozart and his contemporary, Salieri. Mozart was shown as coarse, vulgar, lazy, and undisciplined in every aspect of his life, but apparently informed by a divine spark when composing. The London critic Bernard Levin, in his column in *The Times,* explicitly drew the conclusion that Mozart (like all other great artists) was, literally, divinely inspired. (p. 5)

As Boden went on to argue, the romantic view fails to even try to explain creativity. It merely sweeps it away under the rug of intuition or into the attic of the muses. As a scientific explanation, it gets us nowhere.

The alternative view assumes that the work on problem solving discussed earlier can tell us much about the process of creativity. It assumes that the problem representations, search heuristics, and diverse forms of knowledge that creators bring to their tasks all are vitally important. Regardless of whether the problem is ill-defined or well-defined, the processes discussed throughout this chapter shed light on creativity (Boden, 1992; Weisberg, 1986). Waiting for one's muse is no longer the heuristic of choice.

Creative Production

Thomas Edison still holds the record for the most patents awarded to a single person by the U.S. Patent Office: 1,093. As Simonton (1997) pointed out, not all of these patents turned out to be useful, and Edison experienced many costly mistakes. In fact, the developmental costs of one of his useless devices exceeded Edison's profits for the electric light bulb. However, as with other recognized historical geniuses such as Albert Einstein, Charles Darwin, Sigmund Freud, Pablo Picasso, and Johann Sebastian Bach, Edison turned out massive volumes of work. Picasso, for instance, created more than 20,000 paintings, drawings, and pieces of sculpture in his lifetime. Thus, creative people create a lot—not a particularly surprising outcome, but one that must be taken into account by theories of creativity.

Simonton (1997) suggested that creative production is Darwinian in nature. First, ideas are conceptually combined to generate a large number of variations. Second, there is a variation-selection process in which most ideas are winnowed out as uninteresting. The high productivity rates of historical geniuses, then, are part of the secret of their success. If their rates of conceptualizing new variations of ideas had been any lower, the winnowing process would have eliminated too many ideas. Thus, a Darwinian view of creativity necessarily assumes that the one or two good ideas a person might have cannot be identified without first generating a large number of bad ideas.

The variation-selection process can be viewed as purely random. A creative problem solver in a given field undoubtedly uses heuristics for identifying problems, representing the problem space, and searching the problem space. However, for historically important creative acts, the problem solver's past experience may well no longer provide any useful guidance. Thus, a nondirected random search of the problem space becomes the only workable option, according to this model.

The variation-selection process operates on both an individual and a social level. For example, the problem solver first selects the ideas that must undergo the verification step of demonstrating that an insight is in fact a solution. Proven solutions must then be selected for further development, whether they involve publication, seeking a patent, or putting a product into production. Selection at a social level then takes over the work of the creator. Some articles submitted to journals are accepted for publication through a peer review process, whereas others are rejected. Some patents are developed by industry into marketable products, whereas others are left on the shelf. The marketplace further selects those products that it is willing to buy and those that it tosses aside as uninteresting or at least not commercially viable. Because the selection process operates at so many levels, it is difficult for the creator to foresee which solutions will prove to be successful and which will be a waste of time.

SUMMARY

1. People think by manipulating mental representations of the world. Through the use of such representations, people can plan courses of action and simulate their effects prior to taking action. The study of problem solving has shed light on how people go about this. Often in solving a problem, one builds a model of the environment with a clear, well-defined goal in mind. One then tries to find a path that leads straight to the goal with little diversion. Such problem solving illustrates directed thinking. Undirected thinking refers to dreaming, daydreaming, and other forms of thought that meander without concern for attaining a goal. Undirected thinking is neither rational nor goal oriented.

2. A well-defined problem is characterized by an initial state, a goal state, and a set of operators. Each legal move from the initial state, to intermediate states, to the goal state is defined by an operator. All of the states and operators taken together define the problem space. To solve a well-defined problem, one must select a sequence of operators that follow a path through the problem space to the goal. An ill-defined problem is missing a clear initial state, goal state, and/or known operators. An ill-defined problem often calls for insight and creativity, what the Gestalt psychologists called productive thinking. Yet even some well-defined problems demand creative insights for solutions.

3. A general model of problem solving entails first representing the problem and then searching the problem space for a path to the goal. Finding a good representation of the problem space is critical and often demands as much insight as does the search process itself. Algorithms are rules for searching the problem space that are guaranteed to succeed, although often at prohibitive costs in time and effort. Heuristics are rules of thumb that may or may not lead to success, but they carry less costs than do algorithms. The General Problem Solver is one of several artificial intelligence programs that simulate aspects of human problem solving. It is based on the premise that a general search heuristic called means-end analysis is powerful enough to solve a wide range of problems. Today, it is recognized that an adequate simulation of human problem solving must address the effects of domain-specific knowledge and metacognition as well as general heuristics.

4. Gestalt psychologists recognized that both perception and problem solving require the proper organization of elements. They identified two common obstacles to successful problem solving. Fixation refers to the tendency to set the mind into a routine approach to problem solving. Thinkers who adopt an automatic or mindless approach to problems often overlook ways of representing and searching the problem space that are ideal. Functional fixedness refers to the tendency to see objects as having only a single typical use. Thinkers prematurely categorize the elements of a problem in accordance with their typical use, thus overlooking novel and useful alternatives.

5. Historical creativity refers to ideas that are novel within the context of cultural history. Few people are recognized as historically creative, yet all of us engage in cognitive processes that are creative, even if our creative products are not judged as novel, useful, or extraordinary. The stages of creativity begin with preparation or working with a problem for an extended period of time. Incubation, or putting the problem aside, is the next stage. The third stage is illumination or coming up with a crucial insight that leads to the solution of the problem. The fourth stage is verification or when the insight is implemented and tested. Creativity appears to follow a Darwinian process. First, ideas are conceptually combined to generate a large number of variations. Second, there is a variation-selection process in which most ideas are winnowed out as uninteresting. The high productivity rates of historical geniuses, then, are part of the secret of their success. They had good ideas as a consequence of having many ideas in the first place.

● KEY TERMS

directed thinking

undirected thinking

well-defined problem

initial state

goal state

subgoals

operator

problem space

ill-defined problems

reproductive thinking

productive thinking

isomorphic problems

algorithm

heuristic

backward chaining

forward chaining

historical creativity

preparation

incubation

illumination

verification

fixation

functional fixedness

CHAPTER 14

REASONING AND
DECISION MAKING

The ability to reason is a hallmark of the human mind. Both ancient and modern philosophers have identified reasoning and language as the pedestals that lift our species above all others. The studies of primates appearing to learn some aspects of language, to some scholars, shook the language pedestal. The pedestal of reasoning and its partner, decision making, are studied here. First, reasoning as it has been defined by philosophers is presented. The surprising news is not that other species are just as capable of reasoning as are humans. Rather, the evidence suggests that people themselves are poor at reasoning, at least when the task is defined in its classical sense. The same can be said about human decision-making abilities when judged against the decision theories of mathematicians. These findings, too, have generated shock waves, transforming the modern view of human thinking.

A description of the syllogistic reasoning task comes first in the chapter. *All men are mortal. Socrates was a man. Therefore, Socrates was mortal.* From a major and minor premise, the reasoner must evaluate the conclusion. The rules for doing so correctly are defined by the formal system called the predicate or functional calculus. This comes from a branch of philosophy called symbolic logic. Perhaps you have received instruction on the proper way to evaluate syllogisms in a logic course. The aim here is to consider some psychological reasons as to why such material may have been a real challenge to learn. Next, conditional reasoning is considered. *If P, then Q. P is true. Therefore, Q must also be true.* The conditional rule is its own quagmire, as far as human cognition is concerned. It turns out that people have a very difficult time in determining how to deduce the proper conclusions. Finally, decision making is considered in light of the normative models of mathematics, on the one hand, and the realities of human cognition, on the other. As with reasoning, it is seen that people make decisions in ways that do not fit with the optimal ways prescribed by mathematics.

● SYLLOGISTIC REASONING

Syllogistic reasoning involves evaluating whether a conclusion necessarily follows deductively from two premises that are assumed to be true. The two premises are referred to as the major and minor premise. Their truth is taken as certain, regardless of whether the statements make any sense in the real world. For example, consider these three syllogisms:

Syllogism 1:

Major premise: All men are animals.

Minor premise: Some animals are aggressive.

Conclusion: Some men are aggressive.

Syllogism 2:

Major premise: All men are animals.

Minor premise: Some animals are female.

Conclusion: Some men are female.

Syllogism 3:

Major premise: All A are B.

Minor premise: Some B are C.

Conclusion: Some A are C.

Do you accept the conclusion of Syllogism 1 as valid? Most readers would. After all, it is not difficult to think of at least a few men who certainly appear to be aggressive. The syllogism does not even require that you conclude that all men are aggressive, a conclusion that more than a few readers might also happily accept.

But then, what to do with Syllogism 2? At least if one puts aside sex change operations, the conclusion does not ring true. The semantics of the conclusion are all wrong. Yet if you examine the first pair of syllogisms, you will see that their form is identical. This point can be driven home by Syllogism 3. Do you accept the conclusion as more valid in this case than in Syllogism 2? Syllogism 1?

The task that philosophers set before us is to ignore the semantics or the meaning of the premises altogether. The premises are simply assumed to be true for the sake of the argument. The preceding examples, then, are really the same syllogism. Because their syntax or structure is identical, their conclusions must be evaluated identically. Either the conclusion is valid in all three, or it is invalid in all three.

The meaningfulness of the premises matters not a wit. One could just as well have said the following. *All men are elephants. Some elephants are plants. Therefore, some men are plants.* The only matter at hand is whether the conclusion must logically follow from the premises. A **valid deductive conclusion** is a conclusion that is necessarily true given that the premises are true. Before reading further, arrive at your evaluation of the validity of our example syllogism(s).

> A valid deductive conclusion necessarily follows from the major and minor premises of a syllogism.

Syllogistic Forms

Presented in Table 14.1 are some of the common syllogistic forms along with the valid conclusions, if any, that follow from the major and minor premises. The conclusion of "Can't say" indicates an invalid syllogism; no conclusion *necessarily* follows from the premises. The first on the list corresponds to the famous "All men are mortal" routine, and as you can see, it is correct to conclude that Socrates was indeed a man. That is, the conclusion must be true given the premises. The next on the list corresponds to our example, and it might surprise you to learn that no valid conclusion follows from these premises. If you missed this, then you are in good company. Only about 10% of college students who have not been trained in logic correctly identify valid and invalid conclusions without error (Dominowski, 1977).

In Figure 14.1, the four types of premises encountered in deductive reasoning are shown. The Euler circles provide a convenient representation of their meanings based on class or set relationships. The universal affirmative—"All A are B"—has two possible interpretations, as shown. Either the

Table 14.1   Examples of Valid and Invalid Syllogisms

Number	Premises	Conclusion
1.	All A are B	
	All B are C	All A are C
2.	All A are B	
	Some B are C	Can't say
3.	No A are B	
	All C are B	No A are C
4.	Some B are not A	
	All B are C	Can't say
5.	All A are B	
	No C are B	No A are C
6.	No B are A	
	Some B are not C	Can't say
7.	Some A are B	
	All B are C	Some A are C
8.	All B are A	
	All C are B	Some A are C
9.	No A are B	
	No B are C	Can't say
10.	Some A are B	
	Some B are C	Can't say
11.	Some A are not B	
	All B are C	Can't say
12.	Some B are A	
	No B are C	Some A are not C
13.	All B are A	
	All B are C	Some A are C
14.	Some A are not B	
	Some B are not C	Can't say
15.	Some B are A	
	Some C are not B	Can't say
16.	All A are B	
	All C are B	Can't say
17.	No B are A	
	Some B are C	Can't say
18.	Some B are not A	
	Some C are B	Can't say
19.	All B are A	
	No B are C	Some A are not C
20.	All A are B	
	No B are C	No A are C

SOURCE: Healy et al. (1995).

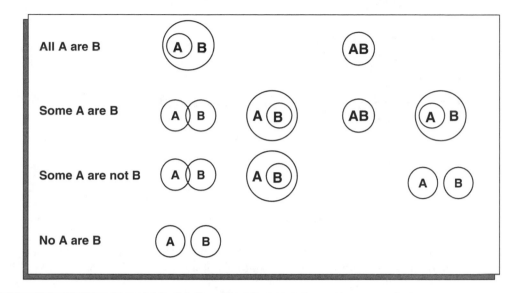

Figure 14.1. Euler circles represent the premises of a categorical syllogism in terms of set relations.

reference classes or sets of A and B are identical or A refers to a subset of B. The universal negative—no A are B—is the only premise that affords a single interpretation! Study the particular affirmative (some A are B) and the particular negative (some A are not B) premises for a moment to understand why they allow each of the meanings shown.

Evaluating the conclusion according to the predicate calculus requires three steps. First, one must accurately consider all possible interpretations of the premises and the conclusion. Second, one must consider all possible combinations of meanings of the major and minor premises. That is, one must consider all pairs of meanings that are allowed by the first step. Third, one must determine whether all possible meanings of the conclusion are consistent with all possible combinations of the premises. If a single interpretation of the conclusion does not follow from a single possible combination of meanings, then no valid conclusion may be drawn. To put this in the form of a question: Is it possible to find one combination of premises that does not fit with one interpretation of the conclusion? If that is so, then the conclusion is invalid. These steps are illustrated in Figure 14.2 for the example syllogism used earlier.

As you can see in Figure 14.2, there are two possible meanings of "All A are B" and four possible meanings of "Some B are C," giving several possible

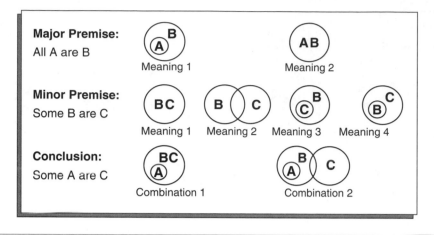

Figure 14.2. All possible meanings of the major and minor premises, followed by two of the eight possible combinations of meanings of these premises. Combination 2 is at odds with the conclusion "Some A are C."

combinations. Consider two of these combinations by combining the first meaning of the major premise with the first two meanings of the minor premise. Combination 1 joins Meaning 1 for the major premise ("All A are B") and Meaning 1 for the minor premise ("Some B are C"). Combination 2 joins Meaning 1 for the major premise and Meaning 2 for the minor premise. Note how the relation between B and C expressed in the minor premise is substituted for the set labeled B in the major premise.

For Combination 1, note that this conclusion follows: *The set labeled A falls within the set labeled BC.* For Combination 2, however, the conclusion is at odds with the diagram: *The set labeled A fails to intersect with the set labeled C.* There is, then, at least one interpretation of the conclusion at odds with at least one combination of the premises. The conclusion is invalid as a consequence. Try working out the other six combinations of the meanings of the major and minor premises and see how many support the conclusion "Some A are C."

Common Errors

Ceraso and Provitera (1971) found that people correctly identify a valid conclusion (e.g., Cases 1, 3, 5, 7, and 8 in Table 14.1) about three quarters of the time. Bear in mind that there are a total of 64 different syllogisms obtained by varying the type of premises and the order in which the premises are given. Only a sample of these are shown in Table 14.1. Of the total 64, only 19 allow a valid conclusion to be drawn.

People do much worse for the 45 invalid syllogisms, those for which no valid conclusion follows. People often agree that a conclusion is valid when one really cannot say for certain. For instance, Syllogism 3 in our example often elicited a response of valid. Ceraso and Provitera (1971) used letters in their syllogisms to remove the possibility that people would evaluate the meaningfulness of the conclusion. Even so, the participants correctly identified invalid conclusions only about a third of the time.

Not only do people perform poorly overall on the invalid syllogisms, but the pattern of errors obtained is quite consistent (Dickstein, 1978). When the major premise contains a universal affirmative (all) statement and the minor premise is a particular affirmative (some) statement, people overwhelmingly regard a conclusion containing the word "some" as valid. They do the same thing if the major premise is also a particular affirmative (some) statement. By contrast, when the major and minor premises both are universal negative statements, people often accept a conclusion that contains the word "no." As you can see from Case 9 in Table 14.1, this is an error.

Cognitive Constraints

An explanation proposed early on by Woodworth and Sells (1935), the **atmosphere hypothesis,** presumed that people do not even attempt to evaluate the conclusion logically. The atmosphere hypothesis was restated by Begg and Denny (1969) in this way. First, if one or more of the premises is negative (either universal or particular), then the conclusion is generally accepted as negative. Second, if one or more of the premises is a particular or "some" statement, then a particular or some conclusion is accepted. Although this explanation accounts for part of the errors, it misses the mark on others. Moreover, the hypothesis provides no account of why intelligent college students would blindly follow these heuristics instead of trying to reason correctly (Dickstein, 1978).

Working Memory. One reason may be the limitations of working memory. College students, as with the rest of the population, may forget or fail to represent in the first place some possible combinations of premises. Johnson-Laird and Steedman (1978) reported that reasoners try to simplify the combinations of premises by avoiding those that call for class inclusion or subset relations. Go back to Figure 14.2 and note that some premise meanings involve a class inclusion relation (e.g., A is a subset of B). These often will be overlooked in generating combinations of meanings of the major and minor premises. By contrast, simple combinations of meanings (e.g., A, B, and C all referring to the same class) are picked up readily. Similarly, people consider only some of the premise combinations when evaluating the conclusion. If a conclusion fits some but not all of the combinations, then it may well be accepted as valid (Dickstein, 1978).

Illicit Conversion. Another cognitive constraint is the misinterpretation of premises. **Illicit conversion** refers to people converting "All A are B" into "All B are A," taking the converse of the premise as true in addition to the premise itself. So, in the case of "Some A are B," people illicitly convert it into "Some A are not B" (Ceraso & Provitera, 1971; Revlis, 1975). Unlike the atmosphere hypothesis, this hypothesis gives people credit for trying to reason correctly but faults them for starting off on the wrong foot by misinterpreting the premises. Ceraso and Provitera (1971) showed the importance of illicit conversions with their findings that errors decrease when efforts are made to stop such conversions. The researchers expanded the premises to prevent misinterpretations ("All A are B, but there are some B that are not A").

> Incorrect interpretations of premises, such as illicit conversion, and failures to consider all possible combinations of premises explain many of the errors that people make in identifying valid conclusions.

Meaning and Knowledge. Because meaning is so critical for memory and thought, people try to make abstract reasoning problems concrete and easier to manipulate in working memory (Gentner & Stevens, 1983; Johnson-Laird, 1983; Johnson-Laird & Bara, 1984). It is possible to eliminate illicit conversions by stating the premises in meaningful ways, for example (Revlis, 1975). When told that all men are animals, you would not likely infer that all animals are men. Yet exactly this happens when the meaning is stripped from the premise by saying "All A are B." Euler circles and Venn diagrams, taught in logic classes, are examples of external representations that concretize the problem, helping one to see the solution. The format of the external representation makes a difference, however, and some do not especially help (Lee & Oakhill, 1984).

Belief bias refers to people accepting any and all conclusions that happen to fit with their system of beliefs (Henle, 1962). Beliefs and meaning, and not the predicate calculus and other abstract systems invented by philosophers, lie at the core of human thinking. College students in North America reject valid conclusions if they do not correspond to what the students know to be true about the world. The supremacy of meaningful beliefs appears to be universal. In fact, non-Western cultures not exposed to formal schooling find the concept of validity hard to grasp (Cole & Scribner, 1974; Luria, 1976).

Luria (1976) asked illiterate farmers from Central Asia to reason deductively, giving them syllogisms of the following sort: "In the Far North, where there is snow, all bears are white. Novaya Zemlya is in the Far North. What color are the bears there." The responses were of this sort: "I don't know; I've seen a black bear, I've never seen any others. ... Each locality has its own animals; if it's white, they will be white; if it's yellow, they will be yellow;" or "How should I know?" (pp. 109-110).

Luria (1976) found that the farmers simply ignored or forgot premises that contradicted their own knowledge and failed to interpret universal statements (e.g., "In the Far North, ... all bears are white") as really universal. They regarded such statements as the view of a particular person. In short, they regarded the reasoning task not as an abstract game but rather as a question rooted in their own or someone else's real-life experience.

Cole and Scribner (1974) found much the same in their work with the Kpelle tribes of Liberia. These people reasoned from their own personal knowledge. They refused to draw conclusions based on premises provided by an experimenter as hypothetical. If pressured by the experimenter to state a conclusion, they justified their answers from personal knowledge, not from drawing valid conclusions from the premises. This may be seen in the following exchange:

> Experimenter (local Kpelle man): At one time spider went to a feast. He was told to answer this question before he could eat any of the food. The question is: Spider and black deer always eat together. Spider is eating. Is black deer eating?
>
> Subject (village elder): Were they in the bush together?
> Experimenter: Yes.
> Subject: Were they eating together?
> Experimenter: Spider and black deer always eat together. Spider is eating. Is black deer eating?
> Subject: But I was not there. How can I answer such a question?
> Experimenter: Can't you answer it? Even if you were not there, you can answer it. [*Repeats question*]
> Subject: Oh, oh, black deer is eating.
> Experimenter: What is your reason for saying that black deer is eating?
> Subject: The reason is that black deer always walks about all day eating green leaves in the bush. Then he rests for a while and gets up again to eat. (p. 162)

Belief bias is especially powerful when reasoners ignore the premises altogether and focus on the conclusion (Evans, Barston, & Pollard, 1983). In this case, they accept a believable conclusion (e.g., "Some good ice skaters are not professional hockey players") and reject an unbelievable one ("Some professional hockey players are not good ice skaters"). Using verbal

Belief bias causes errors in deductive reasoning. Any conclusion consistent with personal belief is incorrectly assumed to be valid.

protocols, Evans et al. (1983) found that some individuals study the premises and try to reason from them. For these individuals, a serious conflict arises when the conclusion is valid but unbelievable. Politicians put belief bias to good use. If a politician can stand for a position that most people believe in, then the premises and logic leading to supporting the position receive less scrutiny.

● CONDITIONAL REASONING

As noted in discussing concept identification, the conditional rule is expressed as an if-then statement. Conditional reasoning refers to the type of deductive reasoning seen in the following examples:

Deduction 1:

If the barometer falls today, then it will storm.

The barometer is falling.

Therefore, it will storm.

Deduction 2:

If P, then Q.

P is true.

Therefore, Q is true.

As in the earlier example of syllogistic deduction, these two deductions convey the same form of conditional reasoning. Given that the first part of the conditional rule is true, then the conclusion reached in each case must be true. It follows as a valid deduction. The abstract form of Deduction 2 removes the meaning from the task and disrupts the typical approach of building a model from concrete experience.

Valid and Invalid Conditional Reasoning

Logicians allow two ways to deduce a valid conclusion from the conditional rule. The first is called modus ponens or affirming the antecedent. Deductions 1 and 2 illustrate affirming the antecedent. P is called the antecedent, and Q is called the consequent. **Affirming the antecedent** means that the second premise asserts that P is true. Given that P is true, then Q must also be true. According to the rule as stated, it can never happen that Q is false if P is true. But what if the premise asserts that the consequent Q is not true. Suppose that you walk outside and see that the weather is balmy. Armed with this knowledge, you could apply the second valid form of conditional reasoning called modus tollens or **denying the consequent.** Given that Q is false (it is not storming), then P must also be false. According to the conditional rule, it can never happen that P is true if Q is false.

A moment's reflection on the conditional rule may reveal the other two types of reasoning that might be tried. Logicians recognize that these can lead to faulty conclusions. The first is **denying the antecedent.** Suppose that you check your barometer and see that it is rising. Your evidence effectively denies the antecedent, not P. Does it follow from this that it will not storm (not Q)? Well, maybe, but not with any certainty. Does it mean that it will storm (Q)? Again, one cannot tell. The if-then rule describes what we must find to be true *given* that the antecedent is confirmed as true. If the antecedent should turn out to be false, then all bets are off. According to the conditional rule as stated, accurate predictions about the weather can be made only *if* the antecedent is true.

The other faulty form of reasoning is **affirming the consequent.** Suppose that you venture outside and find a major storm brewing. Does this tell you with certainty that the barometer is falling? Such a conclusion is certainly possible. But once again, the conditional rule allows us to make predictions about the weather only *given* that the barometer actually is falling. It does *not* make predictions about the barometer *given* that it is storming. In other words the conditional rule does not claim that it will storm *if and only if* the barometer is falling (although a meteorologist would undoubtedly prefer this wording).

Common Errors

As with syllogistic reasoning, people commit systematic errors in conditional reasoning tasks (Markus & Rips, 1979; Rips & Marcus, 1977). The eight possible forms of the conditional syllogism are shown in Table 14.2. College students were asked whether the conclusion followed from the premises *always, sometimes,* or *never.* The correct responses are marked with a superscript. Note that the always and never responses are appropriate when one can affirm the antecedent or deny the consequent, the two valid forms of reasoning. The sometimes response is called for in all other cases.

People perform perfectly in applying modus ponens or affirmation of the antecedent (the first two cases in Table 14.2). But errors occur in all other cases. Most striking about these results is the high proportion of errors connected with modus tollens or denial of the consequent. As the last two cases

Table 14.2 Percentages of *Always, Sometimes,* and *Never* Evaluations of the Eight Forms of the Conditional Syllogism ("If P, then Q")

Minor Premise and Conclusion	Evaluation Response		
	Always	*Sometimes*	*Never*
1. P is true			
Therefore, Q	100*	0	0
2. P is true			
Therefore not Q	0	0	100*
3. P is false			
Therefore, Q	5	79*	16
4. P is false			
Therefore, not Q	21	77*	2
5. Q is true			
Therefore, P	23	77*	0
6. Q is true			
Therefore, not P	4	82*	14
7. Q is false			
Therefore, P	0	23	77*
8. Q is false			
Therefore, not P	57*	39	4

SOURCE: Adapted from Rips and Marcus (1977).
NOTE: The correct response is indicated by an asterisk (*).

in the figure show, about a fourth to a third of the time, people incorrectly give the sometimes response. They seem to be unaware that denying the consequent is just as valid as affirming the antecedent.

Failure to deny the consequent is a persistent error in human reasoning. Even after taking a college-level course in logic that covered the issue, performance remained abysmal. In fact, students who had taken the course did no better in applying the logic of denying the consequent to this task than did students who had no formal training (Cheng, Holyoak, Nisbett, & Oliver, 1986).

> Affirming the antecedent and denying the consequent are valid forms of conditional reasoning. Denying the antecedent and affirming the consequent are not.

Cognitive Constraints

Wason and Johnson-Laird (1972) undertook a series of experiments to understand further the errors made in conditional reasoning. They provided participants with four cards, as shown in Figure 14.3. Each card had a letter

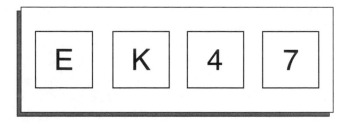

Figure 14.3. The four-card selection task of conditional reasoning.

on one side and a number on the other side. They further gave participants this conditional statement:

> If a card has a vowel on one side, then it has an even number on the other side.

The participants' task was to decide which card or cards had to be turned over to prove that the conditional rule was true. They were to avoid turning over cards unnecessarily.

The results of such experiments showed that nearly half of the time, participants decided to turn over both E and 4. According to the use of modus ponens or affirming the antecedent, the E card had to be turned over. But the 4 card was an error. Affirming the consequent does not allow one to say for certain whether there will be a vowel or a consonant on the reverse side. By sharp contrast, a mere 4% of the participants decided to turn over E and 7. The 7 card denies the consequent. By applying modus tollens, they could disprove the rule by discovering a vowel on the reverse side. Yet hardly anyone thought to do so in this task.

Meaning and Knowledge. One possibility is that people misrepresent the task as a biconditional rule rather than a conditional rule. They may interpret the statement "If P, then Q" to mean "If and only if P, then Q" (Taplin & Staudenmeyer, 1973). This could explain why they so frequently select the 4 card along with the E card in the four-card problem, because in a biconditional rule one would find an even number if and only if the reverse side contained a vowel. It makes perfect sense, therefore, to turn over the 4. Our everyday experience and meaningful uses of language lead us to make such interpretations. Suppose that I say, "If you mow the lawn, then I will give you $10." This promise strongly suggests that if you do not mow the lawn, then I am not about to part with my $10 (Geis & Zwicky, 1971).

On the surface, the failure to apply modus tollens can be taken as evidence that human behavior is not rational. But in the real world, people must take their relevant beliefs and infer something that helps them to achieve a specific goal. For example, if it looks cloudy and also looks like rain outside, then people have no trouble in inferring that they should grab an umbrella. Evans and Over (1996) pointed out that violating modus tollens says more about the arbitrary premises of a task lacking ecological validity than it does about irrationality. There is no personal belief at stake in deciding whether a card with a vowel on one side must have an even number on the other side.

In fact, if prior beliefs of personal relevance are brought into the laboratory task, then the outcome changes. If a task activates a schema or model rooted in practical experience, then modus tollens is easy to apply (Cheng & Holyoak, 1985). For instance, suppose that you again have four cards and that each card has the age of a person on one side (16 or 22 years of age) and the person's drink on the other side (soft drink or beer). How would you test the following rule? "If the person is drinking beer, then he or she is over 21 years of age." As in the other card task, you should turn over as many cards as are necessary to determine whether the conditional syllogism applied. In this situation, you could perhaps draw an analogy to a specific situation encountered in the past. Griggs and Cox (1982) found that college students correctly selected the "drinking beer" and "16 years of age" cards three fourths of the time. That is about 18 times the correct response rate found in the Wason and Johnson-Laird (1972) experiments with the vowel and digit rule!

The beer-drinking problem may be familiar and meaningful because humans are genetically prepared to check for social cheaters who do not follow the rules (Cosmides & Tooby, 1992). When the four-card problem is recast as a problem of catching cheaters, it becomes trivial. Implicit social contracts state that one should not receive benefits (beer in this case) if one does not meet the criteria (being 21 years of age). Cosmides and Tooby (1992) suggested that a heuristic for cheater detection may have evolved because it enables individuals in a group to reciprocate benefits. Our ancestors were good at helping those who they expected would help them in return. Detecting those who wanted something for nothing was adaptive, and the genes underlying this cognitive mechanism may have become part of the human genome.

Perhaps, but the central point to stress is that knowing the task domain well enough to retrieve the meaning of the concepts involved is critical to effective reasoning. The same point can be made with analogical reasoning rather than conditional reasoning. Suppose that you are given the following test:

A cloud is like a sponge because:

a. Both can hold water.

b. Both can give off water.

In abstract conditional reasoning problems unrelated to everyday experience, people fail to use denial of the consequent effectively and incorrectly use affirming the consequent. Reasoning about a concrete lifelike situation reduces these errors.

    c. Both are soft.

    d. Both are fluffy.

The answers given in Responses a and b reflect a relational focus. If you gave one of these answers, then you mapped some relationship between the functional meaning of cloud and sponge. To do that, you needed to see how what you know about the domain of clouds can be mapped onto the domain of sponges. Gentner and Stevens (1983) found that adults given this kind of test provided a relational response nearly every time (89%). However, children ages 4 or 5 years and 7 or 8 years provide relational responses only 61% and 69% of the time, respectively. Notice that Responses c and d merely describe perceptual features of the object and overlook their meaningful functions. Because adults know enough about clouds and sponges, they can go beyond mere appearances in their reasoning.

Confirmation Bias. Another factor in the failure to apply modus tollens is the tendency to seek confirming evidence. Evidence that disconfirms our beliefs may well be actively avoided. Confirmation bias can be seen in the card problem and many other tasks (Klayman & Ha, 1987; Krauth, 1982). For example, in attitude change experiments, people pay more attention to evidence that confirms their beliefs than to evidence that undermines them (Petty & Cacioppo, 1981). Humans are, it seems, less a thinking species than a believing one.

    A striking example of confirmation bias was studied by Wason (1968) in an inductive reasoning task. Unlike the deductive tasks of syllogistic and conditional reasoning, induction requires going beyond the premises to form a general rule. It is useful to think of an inductive conclusion as a belief that one has about the world. The subjective probability or strength of this belief changes as new evidence is accumulated (Rips, 1990). In some cases new evidence causes one to doubt an earlier formed belief, whereas in other cases the belief becomes further entrenched as fact. The belief may be wrong, but this will be discovered only by seeking and finding disconfirming evidence.

    Wason (1968) studied inductive reasoning by first telling participants that they were to discover a general rule that predicts the elements of a sequence. Furthermore, participants learned that 2, 4, and 6 fit the rule. To discover the rule, the participants proposed additional elements, and the experimenter would tell them whether their series fit the rule also. An obvious hypothesis, and one often adopted immediately by the participants, was the rule that the numbers must increase in magnitude by two. Armed with such a hypothesis, people set about to test it by suggesting numerous series of numbers that increase by two. For example, they might offer 8, 10, 12, 14, and 16, and the experimenter informed them that it fit the rule. Next, they might offer 5, 7, 9, 11, 13, 15, and 17, and again the experimenter confirmed their hypothesis. With each confirmation, the participants gained greater confidence that the rule was correct and promptly generated another confirming sequence. Some participants became visibly upset when they vocalized their rules and the experimenter told them that they were wrong!

The rule that Wason had in mind was any series of numbers that increased in magnitude. Thus, 1, 2, and 3 would also have received a nod from the experimenter. The interesting result of Wason's experiment is in how few participants thought to propose series that falsified their hypotheses. Typically, all they sought was confirming evidence.

> Humans often seek evidence that confirms their hypotheses and beliefs. This confirmation bias can lead to false conclusions.

● DECISION MAKING

In fields of human endeavor such as economics, politics, law, science, and medicine, people make decisions. Decision theory is the branch of mathematics concerned with how to go about the process optimally (Rubenstein, 1975). All decision makers are faced with alternative courses of action. Depending on the states of the environment in which these actions are carried out, there may be one of several outcomes. Utilities are the values or gains that the decision maker gets with each outcome. Generally, we assume that the objective is to maximize the utilities that are expected.

Shown in Table 14.3 are the courses of action, states of nature, and outcomes for a farmer who must decide what to plant. Rubinstein (1975) explained the model developed by the farmer this way:

> The states of nature (such as rainfall, levels of temperature, winds, etc.) which are relevant to the success of his crops could be described to various degrees of detail. The simplification to three states—Perfect, Fair, and Bad—constitutes a high level of abstraction. . . . The array of numbers . . . is called a payoff matrix and represents the degree of satisfaction or utility that the farmer believes he will derive. For example, he derives 4 units of utility when he plants crop B and the state of nature is Fair, and he derives no utility when the state of nature is Bad. . . . Normally, you would think of money (say, profit in dollars) as the measure of success in such an enterprise. (pp. 312-313)

Types of Decisions

Some decisions are made under conditions of certainty. That is, we know that particular courses of action will result in particular outcomes for

Table 14.3   A Decision Payoff Matrix

	State of Nature		
Course of Action	*Perfect*	*Fair*	*Bad*
Plant Crop A	10	1	−2
Plant Crop B	8	4	0
Plant Crop C	3	3	3

SOURCE: Rubinstein (1975).

decisions under certainty. If the farmer knew for certain that the weather this year was going to be bad, then he would know exactly how to proceed to maximize his profits. **Decisions under risk** refer to cases in which each state of nature is likely to occur with a known probability (e.g., 10% chance of Perfect, 80% chance of Fair, and 10% chance of Bad). **Decisions under uncertainty** refer to cases in which the probabilities of states of nature are unknown.

Decision making under uncertainty is the most complicated and realistic situation. To proceed effectively, the farmer must arrive at a subjective probability of the various states of nature. Based on past experience, advice from meteorologists, and perhaps a glance at the *Farmer's Almanac,* the farmer assigns probabilities and then determines the best course of action. Suppose that the farmer reasoned that the chances of Perfect, Fair, and Bad weather were 15%, 60%, and 25%, respectively. He could then compute the expected value of utility for each course of action as follows:

Crop A: .15(10) + .60(1) + .25(−2) = 1.6

Crop B: .15(8) + .60(4) + .25(0) = 3.6

Crop C: .15(3) + .60(3) + .25(3) = 3.0

If the farmer is accurate in his probability estimates, then Crop B should go in the ground to maximize profits.

Decisions under uncertainty are difficult because one must estimate the probability that a particular situation will occur.

Subjective Utility

Do people behave in accordance with expected utility theory? If not, what are the mental processes that lead them to deviate with the normative model? Let us take a simpler example than the crop case and see how people behave relative to expected utility theory. Suppose that you are given a choice between two different bets. You can gamble that you will win $8 with

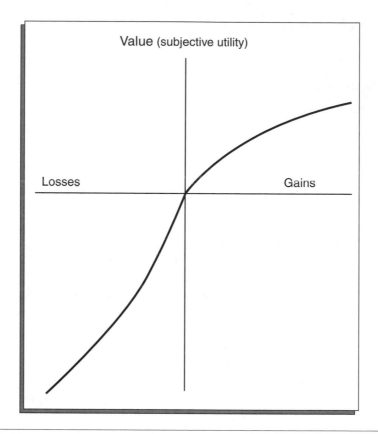

Figure 14.4. Subjective utility is a curvilinear function of losses/gains.

SOURCE: Kahneman and Tversky (1984).

a probability of 1/3 or gamble that you will win $3 with a probability of 5/6. Which bet do you prefer to take?

From a normative point of view, the expected utility of the first choice is $8 × 1/3 = $2.67. The situation is slightly worse for the second choice: $3 × 5/6 = $2.50. So, expected utility theory predicts that most people will choose the first bet, but in fact they do exactly the opposite (Kahneman & Tversky, 1984). Their behavior results from their calculations of subjective utility, which turns out not to be related in a linear way to the actual value of money. Shown in Figure 14.4 is the curvilinear relationship between subjective utility and the magnitude of money lost and money gained.

Notice that the function is concave in the region of gains, meaning that further increases in gains do not result in a linear increase in subjective utility. There is a point of diminishing returns in the subjective utility one gains from further gains in money. On the loss side, the function is convex, meaning that further increases in losses do not result in linear decreases in subjective utility. Put simply, after losing a great deal of money, the loss in subjective utility levels off slightly. Good thing, or else we would feel the sting of loss past the point of being bearable! Finally, notice that the curve is steeper in the loss region than in the gain region. This results in people being risk averse. They really hate to lose because subjective utility drops faster with losses than it rises with gains in money.

In the gambling example, the subjective utility of an $8 gain is not more than twice as great as a $3 gain. If one assumes that the subjective utility of a $3 gain is *U,* then the utility of an $8 gain might only be *2U.* The expected value of the first gamble, then, is $1/3 \times 2U = .67U$ as compared with $5/6 \times U = .83U$. Because now the expected utility is greater for the second gamble, it is not surprising that most people prefer it.

The utility curve shown in Figure 14.4 can cause people to make decisions that are hard to see as rational. A **framing effect** refers to making a different decision depending on where people perceive themselves to be in relation to the curvilinear subjective utility function. To illustrate, Kahneman and Tversky (1984) compared two hypothetical shopping situations. Suppose that you are looking for a $15 item at one store and learn that another store is selling the same item for $10? Do you take the time and effort to save $5? Most people will because the loss side of the utility curve is steep, so it matters subjectively whether one loses $15 rather than only $10. But now suppose that the item you seek costs $125. Would you go to another store to buy it for $120? Fewer people would, even though in both situations the greater loss is exactly $5. Because the subjective utility curve is convex in the loss region, your subjective sense of loss is scarcely different for $125 as compared with $120.

> Subjective utility shows a curvilinear relation to losses and gains. It is convex in the region of losses and concave in the region of gains. People are risk averse because subjective utility drops faster with losses than it rises with gains in money.

Gambling and investing require individuals to consider the subjective utility curve. Odean (1998) studied the behavior of investors on Wall Street and discovered that they tend to shift their point of reference shortly after buying a stock. The subjective utility curve has a zero point—the point of reference from which gains or losses are judged. Where they set this point of reference is critical in deciding whether they regard a stock as too risky to hold or too risky to sell. In particular, shifting expectations about future returns in a downward direction after buying the stock causes investors to sell their winning stocks too soon and to hold their losing stocks too long.

For example, investors must decide whether the market price for a stock is too high. If an investor believes that the stock will rise in value, then the market price he or she paid is worth the risk. If the stock in fact grows in value and the investor uses the purchase price as the point of reference, then the stock price will be the concave gains side of the utility curve. However, if after buying the stock the investor lowers his or her expectations of future growth, then the purchase price will fall on the loss side. Even though the stock rose in value, it would now fall on the steep risk-averse portion of the utility curve. As a consequence, even a winning stock will look too risky, and the investors will sell it off too soon.

What if the stock decreased in value instead of gained? The shift downward in expectations insidiously makes the investor too complacent. Instead of the loss falling on the steep slope of the loss side of the function, it places the loss farther out on the convex part of the curve. It is here that the investor becomes less worried about losing money and more willing to accept risks to win money. Ironically, then, the investor is far too willing to hang onto a stock that is already costing him or her money. Based on an analysis of 10,000 accounts at a large brokerage house, Odean (1998) discovered that investors tend to hold losing investments too long and to sell winning investments too soon. A shift in their reference point to lower expectations for the stocks after they were purchased seemed to best account for their behavior.

Probability Heuristics

Reasoning under uncertainty requires an assessment of probability, so decisions are necessarily affected by how well people judge subjective probability. Are people good or poor intuitive statisticians? An extensive literature exists on this issue. The research aimed at these questions has told us a great deal about the nature of human thinking. But the answers are still not entirely clear. For example, one can marshal evidence that people are good intuitive statisticians (Peterson & Beach, 1967) and other evidence that they are poor at judging probabilities (Kahneman & Tversky, 1982a). Let us turn to some of the key findings and controversies.

To begin, it is well-established that people can keep track of the relative frequency of events. As discussed previously, frequency of occurrence is automatically compiled when events are encoded into long-term memory. So, it is not surprising that when people are asked to estimate the probability of a particular event, they come reasonably close. It turns out that subjective probability deviates from actual probability in a highly systematic way. High-probability events tend to be underestimated, whereas low-probability events are overestimated (Kahneman & Tversky, 1984). Notice that very low-probability events are seen as subjectively more likely than they actually are and receive greater weight in decisions than they deserve (Figure 14.5). This is why the insurance industry can charge the premiums they do. The chances

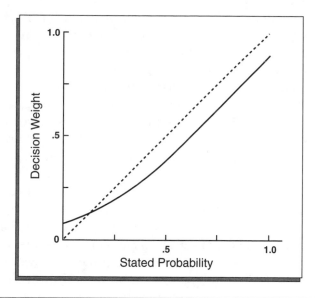

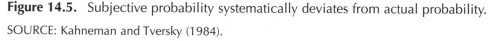

Figure 14.5. Subjective probability systematically deviates from actual probability.

SOURCE: Kahneman and Tversky (1984).

of an earthquake destroying your home are low (depending, of course, on exactly where your home is located). But the subjective probability assigned by the homeowner is often higher than the actual probability, which justifies paying a premium for the protection.

During the 1970s and 1980s, a wide range of cognitive biases and normative fallacies were discovered in tasks calling for decisions under uncertainty. Just as studies of deductive reasoning used a formal normative system to judge how well people performed, human judgments under uncertainty were contrasted with those predicted by statistical theories. Kahneman and Tversky (1973) pioneered these investigations and arrived at the following conclusion in an influential review of the early literature:

> In making predictions and judgments under uncertainty, people do not appear to follow the calculus of chance or the statistical theory of prediction. Instead, they rely on a limited number of heuristics which sometimes yield reasonable judgments and sometimes lead to severe and systematic errors. (p. 237)

Representativeness. To illustrate the first important heuristic, consider these two alternative outcomes from tossing a coin six times. Imagine an outcome in which heads turns up the first three times, followed by three tails

(HHHTTT). An alternative outcome might be HTTHTH. Is the probability of one of these sequences higher than that of the other? Kahneman and Tversky (1972) found that in this and many related tasks, people generally say that the second, random-appearing outcome is more likely.

For those who have had some training in statistics (and can remember and use it effectively), the correct answer is apparent. Both outcomes are equally likely. Each toss of the coin is independent of the others. On any given toss, heads or tails has an equal chance of occurring. The total number of possible sequences is 2^6 or 64. The probability of all heads is 1/64, just as is the probability of any other possible sequence.

Kahneman and Tversky explained that people use a **representative-ness heuristic.** This means that events that are representative or typical of a class are assigned a high probability of occurrence. If an event is highly similar to most of the others in a population or class of events, then it is considered representative. Because most of the 64 sequences of coin tosses will necessarily have several alternations of heads and tails, the HHHTTT outcome strikes us as highly unrepresentative and therefore highly unlikely. Also, if an event is highly similar to the process that generates it, then it is considered representative. When tossing a coin is a random process, we expect random-looking outcomes, not "rigged" ones. Never mind that the probability of all heads is just as likely as any other particular outcome.

Over a large sample of, say, 1,000 coin tosses, the likelihood of heads is .50, the same as that of tails. But for a small sample, such as 6 tosses, a sequence of even six heads in a row does not imply that a rigged or biased coin is being used. Yet sample size is not heeded (Bar-Hillel, 1980; Kahneman & Tverksy, 1972). According to the **law of small numbers,** people mistakenly expect even small samples to look random and to mirror the probabilities obtained with large samples (Tversky & Kahneman, 1971).

The gambler's fallacy results from the mistaken belief that small sample sizes mirror the probabilities obtained with large sample sizes.

Gamblers fall prey to this use of the representativeness heuristic. The **gambler's fallacy** refers to the mistaken belief that future tosses of a coin, drops of the ball in roulette, or rolls of the dice in craps are not independent of past events. If you see seven rolled on the dice five times in a row, then you probably are likely to bet against another seven coming up again on the next roll. People expect events to even out in the short run because they know that events even out in the long run.

Take another quite different illustration of the representativeness heuristic. Kahneman and Tversky (1982a) asked college students to read character sketches and then to make judgments about them such as the one shown in Box 14.1.

Given the description, would you say it is more likely that Linda is a bank teller or that she is a bank teller and a feminist? Overwhelmingly, the students

---

Box 14.1

THE BANK TELLER PROBLEM

Linda is 31 years old, single, outspoken, and very bright. She majored in philosophy. As a student, she was deeply concerned with issues of discrimination and social justice, and she also participated in anti-nuclear demonstrations.

Now, rank order these assertions from the most probable to the least probable:

a. Linda is a teacher in an elementary school.

b. Linda works in a bookstore and takes yoga classes.

c. Linda is active in the feminist movement.

d. Linda is psychiatric social worker.

e. Linda is a member of the League of Women Voters.

f. Linda is a bank teller.

g. Linda is an insurance salesperson.

h. Linda is a bank teller and is active in the feminist movement.

SOURCE: Kahneman and Tversky (1982a).

---

selected the latter description, a finding that has been replicated many times. However, because bank tellers include both feminists and nonfeminists, it must be the case that the bank teller statement is more likely. The conjunctive rule of probability theory informs us that the probability of a conjunction of two events (A and B) cannot be greater than the probability of A or the probability of B. The tendency to judge the conjunction as more likely is called the **conjunctive fallacy.** Of course, the character description sounds more representative of feminists than of bank tellers, leading us into the snare of the conjunctive fallacy.

Availability. The second heuristic used to estimate probabilities is based on the ease with which relevant examples come to mind. In deciding whether to buy the stock of a company, you might recall what you heard on television in a business newscast. If a stock shows a major run-up in price or the company attracts positive attention from the media for reasons other than the stock, then it will be featured on talk shows about the market and written about in the financial news. As a consequence, the stock's availability in the minds of investors takes a major hike upward. It will command attention and channel investors to do more research on it rather than on other equally good opportunities that fail to capture media attention (Odean, 1998). The **availability heuristic** suggests that if relevant examples can readily be retrieved from memory, then the class of events must occur with a high probability.

What proportion of nurses are men? What proportion of car mechanics are women? Unless you happened to know several male nurses or female mechanics, both questions would generate low-probability estimates. Tversky and Kahneman (1973) experimentally examined how the ease of recall influences our beliefs about the world. They composed four lists of people, with each list consisting of 19 names of women and 20 names of men. For half of the lists, only the men's names were famous (e.g., Richard Nixon), and for the other half, only the women's names were famous (e.g., Elizabeth Taylor). The researchers studied two conditions: recall and estimate. After hearing the lists read to them, the college students in the recall condition wrote down as many names as they could remember. In the estimate condition, they judged whether the lists contained more names of men or of women.

The results, not surprisingly, showed that the famous names were easier to recall than the other names on the lists. The key result, however, was that the ease of recalling the names had a direct impact on the probability estimates. Specifically, for the lists that included famous females, the students judged that the lists contained more female names. The opposite pattern occurred for the lists with the famous males.

The availability heuristic can distort our understanding of real health risks because of the bombardment of health information from printed news, the Internet, radio, and television. If a story receives heavy coverage by the media, then it is likely to be available for later recall. The degree of risk publicized may be minuscule when compared with the major hazards we face—hazards that receive far less attention and therefore are less available. Because of the availability heuristic, our perceptions of risk may be in error. People may well worry themselves sick over the wrong risks.

Slovic, Fischhoff, and Lichtenstein (1982) reported on their research in the area of risk perception. People estimate that accidents cause as many deaths as do diseases. In fact, diseases, many of which receive little publicity, cause 16 times as many deaths as do accidents. People also judge death by homicide to be as frequent as death by stroke when in fact the latter is 11 times more frequent. Frequencies of death from botulism and tornadoes

---

Box 14.2

THE AIRPORT DRIVE PROBLEM

Mr. Crane and Mr. Tees were scheduled to leave the airport on different flights at the same time. They traveled from town in the same limousine, were caught in a traffic jam, and arrived at the airport 30 minutes after the scheduled departure time of their flights. Mr. Crane is told that his flight left on time. Mr. Tees is told that his flight was delayed and just left 5 minutes ago. Who is more upset, Mr. Crane or Mr. Tees?

SOURCE: Kahneman and Tversky (1982b).

---

are wildly overestimated. The most underestimated causes of death are those for smallpox vaccinations, diabetes, and stomach cancer, according to Slovic et al.

In one study, the researchers examined newspaper accounts of death over a period of several months to see whether the availability heuristic could account for the observed distortions in risk assessment. As expected, they found that relatively common causes of death, such as diabetes, emphysema, and various types of cancer, were hardly ever reported on by the press. By stark contrast, homicides, car accidents, tornadoes, fires, drownings, and other violent causes of death were reported often. Homicides in particular received the heaviest coverage relative to their actual frequency of occurrence. Such findings pose serious challenges to public safety and health programs. People must first know what the real risks are if they are to take sensible steps to avoid them.

Simulation. The problem provided in Box 14.2 illustrates a third heuristic for making probability judgments (Kahneman & Tversky, 1982b). Before reading further, read through the situation and make a choice as to which individual ought to be most upset. The investigators noted that both gentlemen are in the same trouble: Both suffered through a traffic jam and both missed their flights. Objectively, both should be equally upset. By chance, then, half of the time people ought to say Mr. Tees, and the other half ought to say Mr. Crane. In contrast to this objective prediction, virtually all of the individuals to whom Kahneman and Tversky (1982b) posed this question responded "Mr. Tees." Why pity Mr. Tees more?

Kahneman and Tversky (1982b) proposed that people call on their knowledge representations or scripts for traveling to the airport. They then simulate the trip themselves and readily imagine alternative scenarios in which Mr. Tees could have made his flight. If only the driver had gone a bit faster, if only Mr. Tees had left 5 minutes earlier, if only . . ., then things would have worked out differently. But only for Mr. Tees. Mr. Crane missed his flight—plain and simple.

The **simulation heuristic** involves the construction of a mental model of a situation and then "running the model" so as to predict the course of events. Whereas ease of recall underlies the availability heuristic, ease of construction or imagination underlies the simulation heuristic. As our farmer plans what to plant, he may well imagine possible scenarios and try to assess which is the best course. If it is too difficult to imagine perfect weather, then the farmer could well assign a distorted low estimate of probability for this state of nature.

The availability and simulation heuristics help us to understand a common phenomenon both in everyday life and in the psychology laboratory (e.g., Fischhoff, 1975, 1977; Hell, Gigerenzer, Gauggel, Mall, & Muller, 1988; Hock & Lowenstein, 1989). Namely, once Event X happens, it is easy to believe that Event X was inevitably going to happen. **Hindsight bias** refers to the fact that people confidently judge that they knew an event would occur after it had occurred. Before an event took place, a person might not be able to arrive at a solid prediction. But once history runs its course, the person is highly likely to say, "I knew it all along."

For instance, Fischhoff (1975) presented people with historical information about a battle between two armies. Based on this pre-battle information, the participants gave before-the-fact judgments about whether one of the armies would win or whether there would be a stalemate. For example, they assigned a probability that Army A would win at, say, 25%. After-the-fact judgments came from participants who were given the same pre-battle information but who then had also been told how the battle really turned out. Now that they knew Army A actually won, they thought that the pre-battle information warranted a more confident prediction, say, 50%. On average, participants gave the highest probability estimates of a particular army winning based on the pre-battle information when making after-the-fact judgments. The same information warranted stronger predictions given the clear vision of hindsight.

Hindsight effects are to be expected if people rely on ease of recall (the availability heuristic) and ease of imagining (the simulation heuristic). Once the critical information about the outcome is known, people cannot put it aside. Indeed, it dominates our recollections and imaginations about the situation at hand, distorting our confidence in our judgments.

Representativeness, availability, and simulation are powerful heuristics that affect our ability to make decisions in fully rational ways.

Probability or Frequency

The most fundamental question is whether people can mentally represent probabilities at all. It could be that we process the absolute frequency of events. Probability requires more than this; it requires a representation of relative frequencies. Probability ranges from 0 to 1. It is calculated by knowing the absolute frequency of an event and then dividing it by the maximum number that could have been obtained. In sorting through a deck of cards, you will encounter 13 spades. The probability of picking a spade is 13/52 or .25. Which number is processed and stored in human information processing: absolute frequency or relative frequency?

Estes (1976) examined whether absolute or relative frequency prevails using tasks such as the one shown in Box 14.3. The test pits absolute frequency against probability or relative frequency. Candidate B has won more polls than Candidate A in terms of absolute frequency—9 versus 5. But the probability of Candidate A winning a poll is .83 (5/6), whereas for Candidate B the probability is only .50 (9/18). Estes reported that participants generally selected the candidate with the highest absolute frequency of wins, not the candidate with the highest probability. People apparently can make decisions on the basis of probability only when there are about the same number of opportunities for both events. In other words, if both candidates had appeared in 18 polls, then participants would select Candidate B, not Candidate A. Of course, in this case the use of frequency information would make it appear that people could use probabilities effectively.

Numerous other lines of investigation point to the conclusion that people process the frequency with which events occur in the environment. Estes's (1976) polling results are by no means the only task that favors frequency over probability. The evidence from an astonishing range of tests confirm the view that frequencies of occurrence, and not probabilities, are represented in long-term memory (Gigerenzer, Hoffrage, & Kleinbölting, 1991). Earlier, we reviewed evidence that storing the frequency of events occurs automatically and that the use of such frequency information has important influences on learning and memory.

> People process and use absolute frequency information, rather than probability or relative frequency information, in making decisions.

Automatic Versus Controlled Processes

A two-process theory can explain a number of important features of human reasoning (Evans & Over, 1996; Sloman, 1996). This theory posits analytic processes that are used to maximize goal satisfaction of the individual. They are effortful controlled processes. They are rational in that they reflect efforts to maximize an individual's utility in the here-and-now.

> **Box 14.3**
>
> ## THE POLITICAL POLL PROBLEM
>
> Here are the results of two opinion polls that compared how popular one political candidate was against an alternative candidate. Candidate A had appeared in 6 polls and won 5 of them. Candidate B, on the other hand, had appeared in 18 pools and won 9 of them. Now, for the first time, Candidates A and B will be tested against each other in the same poll. Which candidate do you expect to win?
>
> SOURCE: Estes (1976).

Heuristics processes, by contrast, are automatic and presumably unrelated to rationality in the sense of maximizing utility in the immediate environment. The heuristic processes that characterize human cognition were presumably adaptive and selected for in our evolutionary history. According to evolutionary psychology, the genetic code related to a cognitive process will become prevalent in a population if it leads to some reproductive advantage.

The bank teller (Linda) problem discussed earlier illustrates the conflict between tacit automatic processes and controlled analytic processes. Irrationality arises when the automatic is not overruled by the controlled. The associative system operates on similarity and temporal contiguity. Because the description of Linda is highly similar to one's prototype of a feminist, this conclusion is compelling regardless of what one knows about probability and conjunctive fallacies. On this view, the conjunctive fallacy will be observed when the controlled process of reason fails to intervene in deciding on a response. Whether this theory can fully explain the regularities and oddities of human reasoning requires further research, but it offers an interesting application of the distinction between automatic and controlled processes.

SUMMARY

1. Syllogistic reasoning involves evaluating whether a conclusion necessarily follows from two premises that are assumed to be true. A valid deductive conclusion is *necessarily* true given that the two premises are

true. People identify valid conclusions about three quarters of the time. But they perform much worse with invalid conclusions, recognizing them as invalid only about a third of the time. The pattern of errors is very consistent. When the major premise contains the word "all" and the minor premise contains the word "some," people regard a conclusion with the word "some" as valid. When both the major and minor premises contain the word "no," people regard a conclusion with the word "no" as valid.

2. One reason for our poor categorical reasoning performance is illicit conversion. People improperly assume that "If all A are B, then all B are A." Another reason is that considering all possible combinations of what the premises mean places enormous demands on working memory. Not surprisingly, people simplify the task by considering only a few combinations and by considering only the combinations that are easily interpreted. In general, people reason in ways that are meaningful by constructing mental models of the task that relates to everyday experience. One compelling example is the phenomenon of belief bias, whereby people accept a conclusion as valid if it fits their system of beliefs about the world, regardless of the given premises.

3. Conditional reasoning involves deducing a valid conclusion from a rule in the form of "If P, then Q." One way to draw a valid conclusion is affirming the antecedent. By showing that P is true, it follows that Q is also true according to the conditional rule. The second valid form of reasoning is denying the consequent. By showing that Q is false, it follows that P is also false. People reason virtually flawlessly when affirming the consequent. There is a strong tendency toward confirmation bias or seeking evidence that confirms a conclusion. However, people rarely seek evidence that disconfirms the conclusion—denial of the consequent. Furthermore, people do not understand that this is a valid form of reasoning.

4. Making decisions under uncertainty implies that the probabilities of various scenarios must be estimated subjectively. One does not know for certain what the utility will be for a particular course of action—unless the task is meaningfully related to everyday experience because it cannot be determined by an objective calculation. In reasoning under uncertainty, people rely on a variety of heuristics for making predictions and judgments. The representativeness heuristic assigns a high probability of occurrence to events that are judged typical of a class. According to the availability heuristic, an event is likely to occur if specific examples of the event can be easily recalled. Similarly, the simulation heuristic assigns a high probability to events that can be easily imagined to occur because they fit the sequence of a routine script. Finally, it appears that people encode the frequencies of events, not their relative frequencies or probabilities.

● KEY TERMS

syllogistic reasoning
valid deductive conclusion
atmosphere hypothesis
illicit conversion
belief bias
affirming the antecedent
denying the consequent
denying the antecedent
affirming the consequent
decisions under certainty

decisions under risk
decisions under uncertainty
framing effect
representativeness heuristic
law of small numbers
gambler's fallacy
conjunctive fallacy
availability heuristic
simulation heuristic
hindsight bias

CHAPTER **15**

INTELLIGENCE

W hose name comes to mind first when you hear the word "genius"? For many, the answer is Albert Einstein. *Time* Magazine named him "Person of the 20th Century," and his image turns up on T-shirts and college dormitory rooms everywhere. As Wang (2000) asked, "How could Einstein have sat down at his desk, pondered the universe, and deduced that space is curved and that time can slow down? What was it about Einstein's brain that made him so brilliant?" (p. 1477).

As it happens, Einstein's brain was preserved by the pathologist who performed the autopsy in 1955. Three decades later, neuroanatomists went to work looking for any unusual features. As reported by Wang (2000), the first comprehensive anatomical study was published 44 years after Einstein's death. It revealed that the parietal lobes, an area important for spatial skills, were wider in Einstein's brain than in others of his age. Moreover, the Sylvian fissure that normally runs through the parietal lobe was largely absent, a structural difference that may have been related to Einstein's ability to process spatial relations given the potentially greater number of connections among neurons in this region. In size, Einstein's brain weighed in at 1230 grams, slightly less than average. There is a long history—entirely unproductive thus far—in trying to demonstrate a relation between brain size and intelligence

(Gould, 1981). Perhaps the study of specific neurological features will prove more productive, as discussed later in this chapter.

No single topic integrates the field of cognitive psychology more than intelligence, if only because the concept is broad enough to include everything discussed thus far in this book. Given the breadth of the concept, defining the term is difficult. Sternberg and Detterman (1986) reviewed contemporary viewpoints on intelligence and uncovered dozens of definitions. This is by no means a modern dilemma. Psychologists have always offered different answers when asked about the nature of intelligence (Eysenck & Kamin, 1981). Some have held research on intelligence as among the finest contributions of psychology as a whole (Eysenck, 1973), whereas others have taken a much dimmer view (Gould, 1981; Kamin, 1974).

Humans are nothing if not intelligent when the term is defined in terms of the ability to adapt to, shape, and select environments for the benefit of survival (Sternberg, 1999). Intelligence involves perception, attention, memory, language, problem solving, reasoning, and decision making. Specific cognitive competencies, such as verbal and mathematical abilities, also involve the full range of cognitive processes considered in this book. Intelligence further raises the fundamental issue of how nature or human experience, on the one hand, and nurture or the human genome, on the other, are linked in cognitive development. To what extent is intelligence limited by genetic predispositions? What roles do education and the technological environment of developed countries play in enhancing intelligence? Are there sex differences in cognitive competencies that are linked to genetic differences?

First, the view that there are individual differences in intelligence that pervasively influence human cognitive functioning is presented. The intelligence quotient (IQ) assumes that a single number derived from a test captures an important, core biological characteristic of human intellectual capacity. Efforts to measure IQ as a biological constraint on human performance are presented first, followed by a discussion of alternative points of view. From the beginning of IQ testing, it has been recognized that the IQ score may be a relatively uninformative composite measure of specific cognitive competencies. An individual might excel in one cognitive task and fail in another. Individual cognitive competencies might be highly variable, just as are differences in athletic, musical, emotional, and social competencies. Criticisms of intelligence as a general ability are taken up before addressing the role of genetic and environmental influences on IQ. Finally, the book closes with an examination of the similarities and differences in intelligence between males and females.

DEFINING INTELLIGENCE ●

During the early moments of psychology's history, Sir Francis Galton proposed that individuals differ in their general intelligence and that these differences were rooted in biology (Galton, 1892). Perception, attention, memory, language, problem solving, reasoning, and thinking all were dependent on the raw power of the brain. On this assumption, Galton expected to find that some individuals would excel in many intellectual tasks, whereas others would tend to do poorly in general. To assess the biological capacity of the nervous system, Galton suggested measuring the speed and accuracy of perception and simple motor responses. Many investigations have followed Galton's lead in looking for the biological roots of intelligence in basic perceptual and motor processes (Eysenck, 1987).

During the early part of the 20th century, the precursor of the intelligence tests still in use today was developed by Alfred Binet in France. Binet (1903) looked to tests of problem solving, learning, and memory—the sorts of skills that people use in school. Instead of examining basic perceptual and motor behaviors, Binet sought to find measures of complex judgmental abilities (Sternberg, 1999). He devised numerous tests of cognitive abilities and administered them to French schoolchildren in an effort to assess their scholastic abilities. American schoolchildren later received these tasks in the form of the well-known Stanford-Binet test of intelligence. For Binet, the tests provided a psychometric profile of the students' strengths and weaknesses. A student might, for example, possess a large vocabulary and strong reading skills but show weaknesses in numerical computation and rote memory.

IQ stands for **intelligence quotient,** which is defined as a person's mental age divided by chronological age and multiplied by 100. The term stems from Binet's suggestion of measuring a child's mental age in terms of the performance expected at a particular chronological age. Thus, if a 10-year-old performs on an IQ test at the level normally observed for a 12-year-old, then the individual's IQ would be $(12/10) \times 100 = 120$. Contemporary IQ tests are calculated so that the average score equals 100, the same value arrived at when mental age and chronological age match. Next, deviations from the mean score are determined. As shown in Figure 15.1, IQ scores fit a normal distribution such that about two thirds of the scores fall between 85 and 115. A score of 130 is achieved by approximately the top 2% of the population. An example of a commonly used IQ test is the Wechsler Adult Intelligence Scale (WAIS) developed by Wechsler (1981).

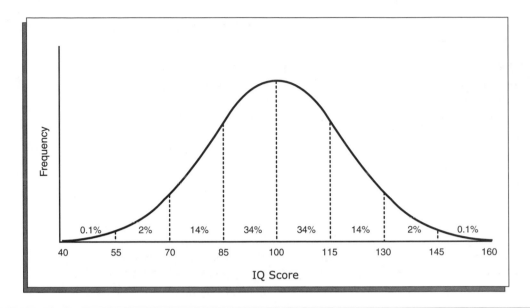

Figure 15.1. Distribution of scores on an intelligence test. The intelligence quotient (IQ) is mental age divided by chronological age multiplied by 100. Thus, the mean of the normal distribution is 100, reflecting an IQ in which mental and chronological age are equivalent.

IQ scores can, depending on the specific test, be used to quantify approximately Galton's conception of general intelligence. To the extent that performance on the subtests correlated strongly with others, it makes sense to ask whether there is an underlying factor that explains the correlations. For example, suppose that one took measures of verbal ability, mathematical ability, spatial ability, reasoning ability, and problem-solving ability (see Figure 15.2) for a group of individuals. Next, correlations could be computed for all possible combinations of these tests. If individuals who scored highly on verbal ability also tended to score highly on each of the other tests, then these correlations would be positive in value. Of course, more complex patterns of correlations might also be found in which only some of the subtests correlate with each other.

The patterns of correlations among the subtests can be analyzed using a statistical technique called factor analysis. It allows one to calculate what is called the first principal component. The larger the first principal component, the larger the correlations among the subtests. Typically, these correlations are moderate in size but statistically reliable. Consequently, an individual who performs well on one subtest is reasonably likely to perform well on many of the other subtests. **General intelligence (g)** refers to the

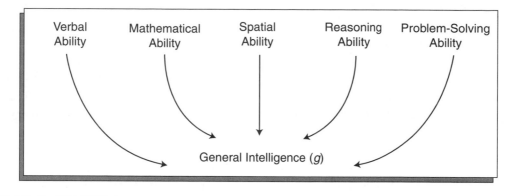

Figure 15.2. Correlations among the subtests of intelligence test reflect an underlying ability called general intelligence (g).

underlying factor that accounts for an individual's performance on an IQ test and in other situations demanding intelligence. An individual's performance on a specific subtest depended on *g* and the domain-specific skills required by the subtests.

Although there was considerable debate about the interpretation of factor analysis, Spearman's *g* proved to be highly influential as the use of IQ tests spread (Gould, 1981). It was promoted by theorists who regarded intelligence as an innate biological capacity of the brain to process information. Just as physical traits such as height are inherited, it was assumed that *g* also was passed from one generation to the next through the human genome.

> General intelligence (g) is viewed as a biologically determined trait that is inherited and can be approximated by a single number: the IQ score.

Biological Measures

Eysenck (1986) argued that IQ test scores, and *g* in particular, depend on the neural efficiency of the brain. Individuals with highly efficient neural systems are presumably those who score well on IQ tests. As an index of neural efficiency, investigators have looked extensively at reaction time. In particular, choice reaction time rather than simple reaction time has been of interest. Simple reaction time taps only the perceptual and motor components, whereas choice reaction time includes a decision component as well. The results from such studies show that individual differences in choice reaction time can correlate negatively with scores on IQ tests. The faster choices are made in the task, the higher the score obtained on the IQ test. The range of the correlation coefficients is on the order of –.30 to –.40 (Jensen, 1987).

Somewhat better results have been reported for another perceptually based reaction time task. Two vertical lines are briefly presented on each trial, followed immediately by a visual mask that disrupts the iconic representation in sensory memory. The participant decides which line is shorter. Inspection time is defined as the minimum exposure duration of the two lines (prior to the mask) needed to get most of the judgments correct (e.g., 90% accuracy). Kranzler and Jensen (1989) found that inspection time correlates negatively with IQ scores, this time as high as –.55.

One advantage of using reaction time and other biological measures of intelligence is that people from different countries speaking different languages might all be tested with a common procedure. Cultural background presumably would not affect such measures. However, reaction time has its limits. Jensen's result showing that high-IQ individuals show only a small increase in choice reaction time as the number of choices are increased looks impressive on the surface. The trouble is that pigeons' choice reaction time shows even less of an increase than is found with high-IQ humans (Vickrey & Neuringer, 2000). If speed of processing information is equivalent to intelligence, then pigeons are apparently smarter than people.

Behavioral reaction times and brain responses to stimuli measured in EEG signals attempt to measure neural processing efficiency and its relation to IQ.

Neurological measures based on EEG recordings have also been studied. For example, an event-related potential (ERP) to an auditory stimulus provides one way to assess the neural efficiency of the brain. Recall that there are different components to an ERP depending on the amount of time that passes before the component peaks in the electroencephalogram (EEG) waves and whether the waves are positive or negative. Some evidence shows that the complexity of the ERP is related positively to IQ in simple perception and reaction time tasks (Hendrickson, 1982; Jensen, 1998). However, our understanding of ERP and other neuroimaging results related to g is still in its infancy and an active area of research (e.g., Matarazzo, 1992).

Working Memory and IQ

Recently, efforts have been made to link the prefrontal cortex in the frontal lobes with certain aspects of intelligence. The prefrontal cortical regions are involved in executive attentional functions in working memory. Damage to the frontal lobes is known to be particularly devastating to performance on tests of general fluid intelligence (Duncan, Burgess, & Emslie, 1995). **Fluid intelligence** refers to the ability to solve novel problems (Cattell, 1963). **Crystallized intelligence,** on the other hand, refers to the breadth and depth of a person's knowledge. Compared with lesions in other regions of the brain, the frontal lobe patients performed markedly worse on tests of their ability to solve novel problems but failed to show impairment in the retrieval of stored concepts and facts. Of interest, then, is why frontal lesions would harm fluid intelligence while sparing crystallized intelligence.

Engle, Tuholski, Laughlin, and Conway (1999) proposed that solving novel problems depends critically on the ability to maintain relevant representations in working memory while suppressing distractions. The more capacity one has for keeping the focus on information that might lead to the solution to a problem, the better. Thus, the authors expected to find that individual differences in working memory capacity—at least when measured in a way that takes into account executive attentional processes—should correlate well with general fluid intelligence. Their results showed that tests of short-term memory ability, such as the digit span test discussed in Chapter 5, are not correlated with general fluid intelligence. However, working memory tests that require the coordination of two independent tasks are good predictors.

For instance, the operation span test requires a person to do a simple arithmetic problem and then store a word in memory. Here is an example:

Is $(8/4) - 1 = 1$? bear

Is $(6 \times 2) - 2 = 10$? beans

Is $(10 \times 2) - 6 = 12$? dad

Recall is then tested for the three words. The number of problems and words is then increased until the individual can no longer accurately remember the words after doing the arithmetic. Individuals with large working memory capacities can coordinate both tasks well and can recall as many as 5 or 6 words by rehearsing words to go beyond the 4-item limit of short-term memory alone. Controlled attention is also needed to focus on the arithmetic problem while maintaining the words in verbal working memory. By examining many similar tests, Engle et al. (1999) estimated that the correlation between capacity differences in the central executive and general fluid intelligence was at least .49.

If Engle et al. (1999) were correct that the central executive plays a critical role in fluid intelligence, then it may be possible to observe activation in the frontal cortex when solving novel problems. Shown in Figure 15.3 are example problems demanding high versus low degrees of general fluid intelligence (see the end of this chapter for the answers). The high fluid intelligence and low fluid intelligence questions were given to individuals to solve while positron emission tomography (PET) images were recorded simultaneously (Duncan et al., 2000). The results are shown in Figure 15.4. There was greater activation in the left lateral prefrontal cortex for the high fluid intelligence problems than for the low fluid intelligence problems. For spatial

The executive functions of working memory that are served by prefrontal cortical regions play a role in general fluid intelligence or the ability to solve new problems.

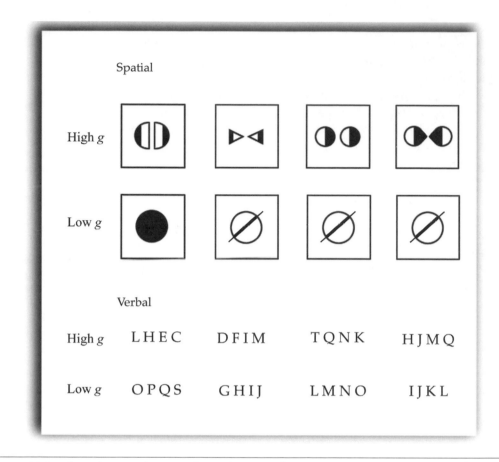

Figure 15.3. Sample questions used in a functional magnetic resonance imaging (fMRI) study that demanded high versus low general fluid intelligence. Select the element that differs from the others in each set of four.

SOURCE: Adapted from Duncan et al. (2000).

problems only, there was also activation in the regions of the left and right hemispheres known to be involved in visual-spatial processing. Thus, evidence is rapidly accumulating that points to the central executive in working memory as critical in at least one important kind of intelligence.

Criticisms of General Intelligence

As the research on general fluid intelligence and working memory illustrates, it is fruitful to look at specific kinds of intelligence rather than *g*. To the

Spatial

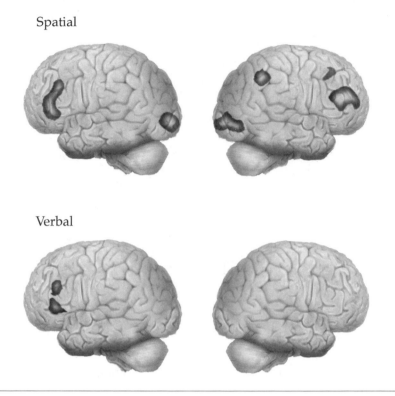

Verbal

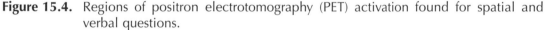

Figure 15.4. Regions of positron electrotomography (PET) activation found for spatial and verbal questions.

SOURCE: Duncan et al. (2000).

extent that all the subtests measured on an IQ test do not correlate well, *g* misses information about performance. The WAIS, for example, provides a verbal IQ and a performance IQ because two clusters of subtests were identified. Measures of reaction time, spatial reasoning ability, and others contribute to the performance score because all of these subtests are highly correlated with each other. A different set of subtests, including vocabulary knowledge and reading comprehension, seem to measure verbal performance. Although a full-scale IQ can be computed by combining the two, the important point is that verbal IQ and performance IQ can vary independently. For example, performance IQ declines steadily past 20 years of age. By contrast, the verbal IQ holds steady well past 60 years of age. These trends are plotted in Figure 15.5 from a study by Kaufman, Reynolds, and McLean (1989).

The standardized tests themselves may also be too constrictive. For example, although IQ captures differences in analytical skills among individuals, it misses differences in creativity, which arguably is just as important in

Contemporary intelligence tests distinguish among separate abilities that develop differently across the life span. Performance IQ decreases with age, whereas verbal IQ remains stable over at least six decades.

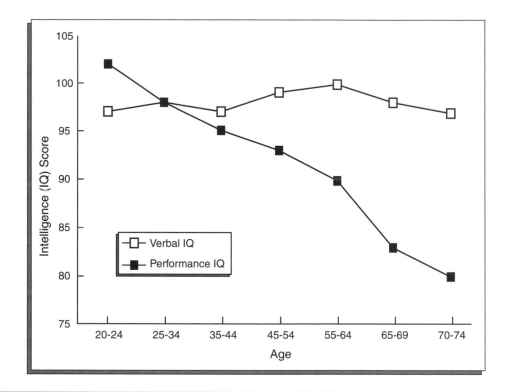

Figure 15.5. Intelligence as measured by the revised Wechsler Adult Intelligence Scale (WAIS-R) as a function of age.

SOURCE: Kaufman, Reynolds, and McLean (1989).

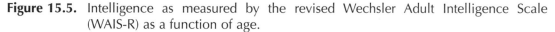

understanding how well people adapt and succeed (Sternberg, 1985). Furthermore, although IQ tests might tell us about intelligence in an academic sense, they do not have anything to say about practical intelligence (Sternberg & Wagner, 1986). An individual might not score high on IQ tests but might be just the person you want to have around when you are, say, lost in a strange city. A "street-smart" individual knows how to get things done in ways that intelligence tests miss. For example, Ceci and Liker (1986) found that the cognitive competencies required in academic settings are not nearly the same as those demanded in nonacademic tasks such as betting on the horses at the race track. Let this serve as a warning to those straight-A students among you who are tempted by gambling.

Gardner (1983) also regarded IQ tests as too narrow to capture the breadth of human intellectual functioning. Although IQ tests can predict academic success well, they are somewhat less successful at predicting job performance outside of school (McClelland, 1973). One observes low to moderate (albeit statistically reliable) correlations between *g* and work performance (Brody, 1996). According to Gardner's (1983) frames of mind theory, a full accounting of human intelligence and its relation to success in everyday tasks would benefit from a broader conception of what counts as intelligence.

Linguistic intelligence, logical-mathematical intelligence, and **spatial intelligence** are well-represented on IQ tests. These refer to verbal ability, mathematical ability, and spatial ability, respectively. But Gardner's frames of mind theory (1983) noted several other domains of intelligence that are ignored on IQ tests. For example, **musical intelligence** refers to individual differences in the ability to perceive pitch, rhythm, and timbre or tonal quality. A good ear for pitch and timbre is important for the development of musical intelligence, but the rhythmic aspect of sensing the emotional aspects of music is equally important. **Bodily-kinesthetic intelligence** refers to individual differences in skilled motor performance. It may be witnessed in the skilled pianist, typist, gymnast, dancer, diver, sculptor, skater, painter, martial artist, and mime, among others. Gardner characterized it as the "ability to use one's body in highly differentiated and skilled ways, for expressive as well as goal directed purposes," and as "the capacity to work skillfully with objects, both those that involve the fine motor movements of one's fingers and hands and those that exploit gross motor movements of the body" (p. 206). **Intrapersonal intelligence** refers to individual differences in the ability to gain access to one's emotions and to draw on these emotions in guiding one's thoughts and behaviors. In Gardner's view, it involves the ability to represent mentally highly complex feelings and contrasts with interpersonal intelligence, which involves reading and representing the intentions and feelings of other individuals. **Interpersonal intelligence,** then, refers to individual differences in the ability to take note of other people's moods, temperaments, motivations, and intentions.

GENETIC AND ENVIRONMENTAL INFLUENCES •

The nature-nurture question refers to the extent to which behavior and cognition depend on the genes inherited from one's parents versus the environment in which one is raised. Behavioral geneticists have long examined the relative contribution of nature versus nurture in determining individual differences in IQ. Psychological pathologies, such as depression, alcoholism, and schizophrenia, are known to run in families. Similarly, to some extent one's performance on an IQ test depends on the genes inherited from parents, grandparents, and so on. At issue is the degree to which genes predispose an individual to develop intellectually. As with any aspect of physical and cognitive development, both genetic information and environmental stimulation are necessary. Possessing genes that predispose one to a high level of cognitive development is not sufficient. An individual with high potential will not likely reach that potential if raised in an impoverished environment without parental interaction during early childhood and without appropriate schooling later.

Heritability

The precise environment and genes of a single individual are not the focus of study, however. Now that a rough draft of human genome has been worked out by geneticists, the search for the set of genes that set the parameters for an individual's intellectual development will no doubt intensify. It is likely that many will be involved. But the focus in behavioral genetics to date has been on answering a different question: To what degree can the individual differences observed on an IQ test be assigned to the genes, on the one hand, and the environment, on the other? **Heritability (h^2)** is the proportion of variance in a population associated with genetic differences among the individuals. For example, if the heritability of IQ is .50, then half of the variability in test scores can be attributed to genetic differences in the population. By definition, then, the other half is the result of differences in the environments experienced by the individuals ($1 - h^2$). It does not mean that the IQ score obtained by one person (e.g., 120) can be split into two pieces, with a score of 60 caused by that individual's specific genes and another 60 caused by the particular environment in which he or she was raised. Heritability, then, is not about specific individuals; rather, it is about individual differences observed in a population.

The best estimate of heritability is obtained by examining the IQ scores of identical twins who were for some reason separated early in life and reared apart in different families and environments. Identical twins are monozygotic, meaning that they developed from a single egg cell. Monozygotic twins have the exact same genes, whereas dizygotic twins share only half of their genes in common. By studying adoptions, it is further possible to compare genetically unrelated children who are raised in the same family with related children separated early in life and raised in different families. A direct estimate of h^2 is provided by the correlation in IQ test scores between monozygotic twins who have been reared apart (see Figure 15.6).

Neisser, Boodoo, et al. (1996) indicated that during childhood the estimates of heritability are between .35 and .45. However, these estimates

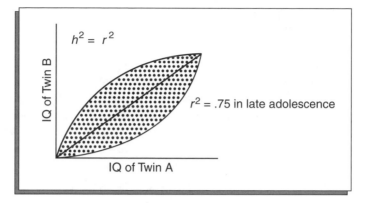

Figure 15.6. Correlation of intelligence quotients (IQs) of monozygotic twins reared apart directly estimates heritability (h^2).

increase with age, and by late adolescence heritability is about .75. This means that during childhood individual differences in IQ scores strongly reflect individual differences in the environments experienced by the children. However, by the time the individuals reach early adulthood, the environment has less of a role in explaining individual differences. Individual differences in the IQ scores of adults primarily reflect genetic differences.

It is a mistake to conclude that the heritability of intelligence observed in adults means that IQ is fixed by the genes. Heritability and immutability are not the same thing (Neisser, Boodoo, et al., 1996). If an environmental change is made, say, in better schools for everyone in the population, then IQ scores would rise for everyone. This change for the better would not alter the heritability of IQ because differences among the individuals would still depend on genetic variability, at least if the testing is done in adults. As Neisser, Boodoo, et al. (1996) noted, improvements in nutrition seem to be causing increases in the average height of human populations, yet height remains a highly heritable trait.

A single gene is not responsible for complex traits such as IQ or *g*. Even several genes each having a deterministic hard-wired effect are not likely to be responsible for the relatively high estimate of h^2. Instead, *g* is likely to be what is called a quantitative trait loci, in which several genes all contribute small effects and do so in a probabilistic way. Such loci create a propensity on average in a population rather than a determined outcome (Plomin, 1997). If a person has the allele, that is, the particular form of a gene associated with high *g* on most of, say, 25 relevant genes, with each having only a very small

Heritability (h^2) is the proportion of variance in a population associated with genetic differences among the individuals. In children, h^2 is estimated at about .40, but as people enter adulthood, more of the IQ differences among individuals reflect genetic differences, with h^2 about .75.

effect, then the probability that the person will attain a high IQ score is relatively good. Chorney et al. (1998) identified a gene for insulin-like growth factor-2 receptor on chromosome 6 (IGF2R gene) and studied it in a high-*g* group of individuals (average IQ = 136) and an average-*g* group (average IQ = 103). The results showed a reliably greater frequency of a particular allele in the high-*g* group (.30) than in the average-*g* group (.16). This allele was also twice as likely to show up in a sample of students who had scored very well on the Scholastic Assessment Test (SAT) (e.g., verbal and math SAT scores of at least 630) as compared with an average control group. However, keep in mind that IGF2R is only one of many genes that have a small effect on *g*. Furthermore, the allele associated with high levels of *g* in the population is not necessary for a particular individual to show a high degree of intelligence. Indeed, it turned up less than half the time in the high-*g* group, making it unethical and useless to screen for this genetic marker as a way of identifying individuals who might benefit from accelerated educational programs.

Environmental Effects

The influence of various factors in the environment $(1-h^2)$ accounts for the largest proportion of the variability in IQ test scores taken by children. The environment refers to all physical and social influences on the developing child such as nutrition, exposure to lead, parents' behavior, educational resources in the home, participation in preschool programs, quality of schools, and cultural and family supports for excelling in intellectual tasks (Neisser, Boodoo, et al., 1996).

To illustrate the importance of parental behavior, consider the development of verbal ability. The extent to which parents talk to their children, for example, correlates with the verbal ability of the children, a difference readily detectable on an IQ test (Hart & Risley, 1995). Failure to talk to young children often means that whatever genetic predispositions there might be for language fail to receive the necessary inputs for normal development. The amount that parents talk with their children in the home is positively correlated with vocabulary size over a wide range of ages. Researchers are quite confident that normal child development requires responsive parents who do not severely deprive, neglect, or abuse their children. However, it is difficult to determine exactly how much parental enrichment is needed for normal development (Scarr & Ricciuti, 1991). There may well be a threshold beyond which additional input from the parents does not cause further gains in IQ.

Preschool programs such as HeadStart have also been shown to lessen the likelihood that children will be held back in school or fail to finish high school (Neisser, Boodoo, et al., 1996). The effects are particularly strong when the program begins during early infancy in providing an enriched environment for cognitive development (Campbell & Ramey, 1994). The effects of schooling in general are also dramatic (Ceci, 1991). Children who attend school regularly show higher IQ scores than do those who attend intermittently. Test performance also drops after summer vacations or other breaks in formal education. Through school, many basic skills are learned such as mathematical and verbal literacy.

The importance of schools in teaching basic skills can be seen in the work of Geary et al. (1997). The mathematical competencies of East Asian students are consistently high relative to students from other parts of world, particularly relative to American students. Geary et al. found that the Chinese students far exceeded the American students at both the 6th- and 12th-grade levels. For example, in a simple subtraction test, the average 6th-grader in the United States performed poorer than 98% of the same-age Chinese students. Taken over all the arithmetic tests, the American 6th- and 12th-graders were at or below 89% of the Chinese students of the same age. There was no difference between the American and Chinese students on an IQ test assessment of *g*. Instead, the difference in mathematical competence arose not from differences in general intelligence but from differences in the schooling received in mathematics. The Chinese students received much more intensive drilling of arithmetic facts and spent more time in working mathematical problems in school. Strikingly, older Americans who were born between 1915 and 1936, and who had schooling comparable to that of the Chinese, in fact performed just as well as the older Chinese.

Because schooling and other environmental factors have improved for people living in technologically advanced societies over the past century, there has been a resultant increase in IQ scores. The average gain has been 3 IQ points per decade since 1940. This environmentally induced gain in IQ is called the Flynn effect after the investigator who first identified it (Flynn, 1987). Intelligence tests are typically restandardized to keep up with these gains and to keep the average score at 100. Thus, someone who gets a 100 on a current IQ test probably would have scored 106 on the test given 20 years ago.

The Flynn effect is shown in Figure 15.7. The scores shown for the different countries cannot be compared directly with each other. In other words, comparisons are only meaningful within a single country over time. For example, in The Netherlands, the scores of 19-year-olds increased by a remarkable 8 points during a single decade, from 1972 to 1982. In 1952, less

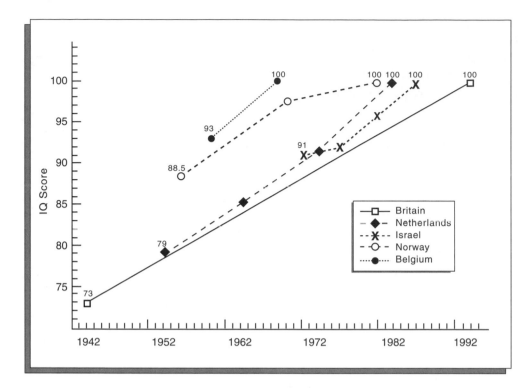

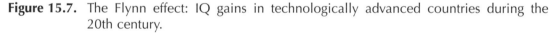

Figure 15.7. The Flynn effect: IQ gains in technologically advanced countries during the 20th century.

SOURCE: Flynn (1998).

than 1% of the Dutch population achieved a score of 140, the cutoff point for genius. By 1982, more than nine times that many met the 140 cutoff or higher.

Flynn contends that the massive gains in IQ in technologically advanced countries has more to do with the IQ tests themselves than with changes in the cultural enrichment of these societies. He believes that the tests merely measure abstract problem-solving abilities rather than real practical intelligence that would make a difference in day-to-day life. The improvements in schooling, for example, could cause gains in test-taking abilities. While this may be part of the answer, it is also possible that we in fact live in a much more complex world today than was experienced by our parents and grandparents (Kohn & Schooler, 1973).

Fewer and fewer people live in isolated rural environments in the United States, for example. First television and more recently the Internet have increased access to information for millions of children (with both good and ill consequences perhaps). Children stay in school longer than ever before in our history. In 1940, a high school education was the ticket needed for entry-level employment in good jobs. Now, it is a college education. Thus, it is not inconceivable that intelligence—in the sense relevant to everyday life and occupational success—has indeed increased in response to an increasingly enriched informational environment.

> The Flynn effect shows that IQ has risen dramatically in technologically advanced countries over the past 50 years.

SEX DIFFERENCES ●

In this final section, our concern is with differences between the sexes in cognitive competencies. Arguments over the differences in abilities of females and males are probably as old as any argument can be. Cognitive psychology has clarified the debate in two ways. First, there is far more similarity in the performances of men and women on cognitive tests than there are differences. Second, the differences that are observed can be readily understood in light of differences in sociocultural factors, biological factors, or both. The differences observed are not a mystery.

Maccoby and Jacklin (1974) wrote a widely read and widely criticized review of gender differences in cognition. They suggested that the genders differ chiefly in three areas: verbal abilities, visual-spatial abilities, and quantitative or mathematical abilities. Before discussing their conclusions and the more recent updates by other investigators, let us digress to examine how the magnitude of gender differences is calibrated.

Meta-analysis

Meta-analysis is a statistical technique for summarizing the results of numerous studies that examine the same question in roughly the same way. By averaging the difference between males and females in, say, verbal ability, one can draw a much stronger conclusion than is possible from a single study or only a handful of studies. Meta-analysis yields an estimate of **effect size,** d, which tells us how large a difference is relative to the variability in the studies. It is defined as the difference in mean scores between males and females in a particular study divided by the standard deviation for the two groups. The larger the value of this ratio, the bigger the effect size. Typically, a d of .20 should be considered a small effect size, .50 a medium effect size, and .80 a large effect size (Cohen, 1969).

In Figure 15.8, three hypothetical differences favoring females over males on a cognitive ability test are shown. The first case at the top is such a

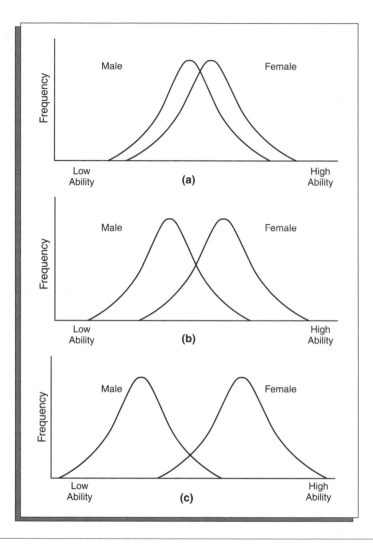

Figure 15.8. Hypothetical frequency distributions illustrating the relative magnitude of gender differences in cognitive ability.

An effect size, *d*, is defined as the difference in mean scores between two groups of individuals (e.g., males vs. females) in a particular study divided by the standard deviation for the two groups.

small effect that it is equivalent to no difference at all. Most males attain the same scores as females. The second case shows a reliable difference. On average, the females attain higher scores than the males. Note that the distributions overlap so much that there are many males who score higher than many of the females. But the mean difference favors the females. In the third case at the bottom, the female advantage is large. Virtually all females score higher than all males. Notice in these three cases, the shapes of the distributions—their variances—are identical. This is not true in all cases. The variability in scores for males is sometimes greater than that for females even when the mean difference is relatively small. That is, the difference between the lowest- and highest-scoring male tends to be greater than the same difference calculated for females (Feingold, 1992).

Verbal Differences

By counting the studies that favor females over males on tests of verbal ability, Maccoby and Jacklin (1974) suggested that females are more competent in this domain. A later review used meta-analysis to soften this conclusion, however. Hyde and Linn (1988) examined 165 studies and concluded that only a subset of verbal tests reveal any gender difference reliably. These tests measured anagram solution, speech production, and general verbal ability—an amalgam of many tests. The verbal score of the SAT, tests of vocabulary, essay writing, and others showed no differences between the sexes. Moreover, the effect sizes for the three that revealed differences were on the order of .20 or .30. In short, men and women shared far more in common in verbal ability than they showed differences. As for differences in variability, Maccoby and Jacklin failed to detect any gender effect. Subsequent research confirmed this conclusion (Feingold, 1992).

As Maccoby and Jacklin (1974) pointed out, when speaking first begins, girls tend to be more articulate, generate longer sentences, and know more words. Their use of grammar tends to be superior to that of boys, and girls spell better than do boys. Fluency tests that require the production of words beginning with specific letters (e.g., rapidly name words beginning with "b") show a female advantage as well. However, the effect size for verbal fluency is small (Kimura, 1999). Taken together, the results show that on tests of verbal ability, females perform slightly better than do males.

Visual-Spatial Differences

Maccoby and Jacklin (1974) argued that, at least from adolescence onward, males outperform females on visual-spatial tests. They viewed this male advantage as remarkably consistent from study to study and from one type of test to another. With respect to variability, it is quite clear that males show far more variability in visual-spatial skills than do females (Feingold, 1992).

Once again, however, subsequent researchers have questioned Maccoby and Jacklin's conclusions with respect to the differences in means. Linn and Petersen (1985), for example, found that the size of the gender difference varied with the precise test used. For example, in the test of spatial perception shown in Figure 15.9, imagine that a container of water is tipped on its side. Which stimulus presented in the figure shows the correct water line of

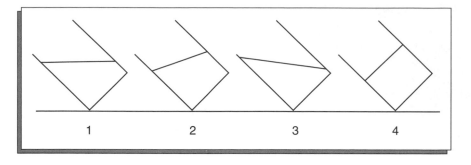

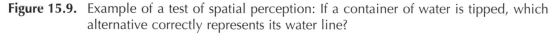

Figure 15.9. Example of a test of spatial perception: If a container of water is tipped, which alternative correctly represents its water line?

SOURCE: Linn and Petersen (1985).

Meta-analyses of the effect sizes in numerous studies indicate that females show an advantage in some verbal tasks, whereas males show an advantage in some spatial tasks.

the container? Children have a difficult time with this test, and so do some adults. However, women tend to give the correct answer (1) nearly as often as do men. The effect size is small to medium on this test of spatial ability ($d = .44$). However, a medium to large effect size was obtained when mental rotation was examined ($d = .73$), using the Shepard and Metzler (1971) geometric figure task discussed in Chapter 8.

Mathematical Differences

Maccoby and Jacklin (1974) observed that boys and girls exhibit very similar mathematical abilities throughout elementary school. But then they begin to diverge during adolescence and early adulthood, with males performing better than females on tests of quantitative ability. Males also show much greater variability than do females at all ages (Feingold, 1992; Maccoby & Jacklin, 1974). The meta-analysis of this work confirmed that males exhibit superior scores on mathematics tests. The small to medium effect size in this case equaled .43 or nearly a half a standard deviation advantage for males (Hyde, 1981).

Hyde (1981) went on to point out the practical meaning of such an effect size. It turns out that an effect size of this magnitude is highly reliable in the statistical sense. But it does not allow one to predict the ability of any given individual with much accuracy. A large number of males score no better than the mean score obtained by females. Remember that males show much greater variability than do females on tests of mathematical and visual-spatial cognition. This can be seen in Figure 15.10. If you had to predict an individual's score on a mathematics test by knowing only the person's gender, you

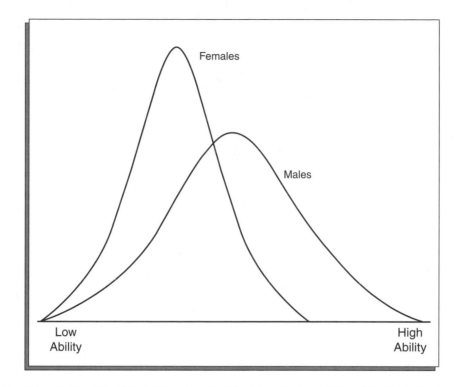

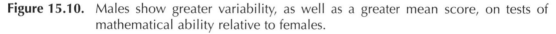

Figure 15.10. Males show greater variability, as well as a greater mean score, on tests of mathematical ability relative to females.

SOURCE: Feingold (1992).

would be able to do so accurately at most 5% of the time. As Feingold (1992) observed, "Boys score only slightly higher than girls on average in mathematics tests but are largely overrepresented among high math scorers" (pp. 62-63).

The small to medium effect size favoring males on mathematics tests does not allow practical accurate predictions about the mathematics potential of a particular boy or girl.

Navigation

Navigation is a competency that can be achieved in more than one way. Moreover, men and women tend to find their way to a location in different ways. When asked to give instructions to a location, women tend to use specific landmarks as referents. Men, by contrast, tend to use directions that specify distances and headings (i.e., north, south, east, west). For example, here are two ways to give directions taken from Kimura (1999, pp. 47-48):

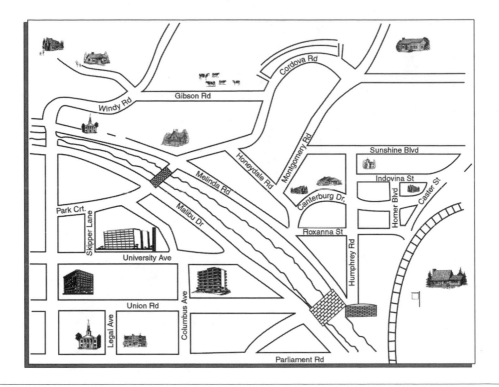

Figure 15.11. Tabletop map used to study sex differences in navigation.
SOURCE: Kimura (1999).

> *Landmarks:* "Go to the United Church and turn left. Turn right when you get to McDonald's, that's Elm Street. You'll see the school at the end of the block."

> *Directions:* "Go north for half a mile, then turn east on Church Street for another half-mile, then north again on Elm Street. The school is at the end of the first block."

Although not all individuals fit the pattern, men tend to give directions, whereas women tend to name landmarks (Ward, Newcombe, & Overton, 1986). Similar differences turn up when participants are asked to learn a new route on a tabletop map such as the one shown in Figure 15.11. Galea and Kimura (1993) traced a route on the map with a stylus that left no permanent marks. The participants observed this and then tried to reproduce the route from memory. Errors were noted, and then the task was repeated until everyone accurately reproduced the route two times in a row. The results showed that men tended to make fewer errors and took fewer trials to master the route. Thus, they learned the route more quickly than did women. When then tested for their recollection of characteristics of the map, men recalled more details about directions and distances, whereas women recalled more details about the landmarks and street names. Males navigate by dead reckoning rather than landmarks.

Do these results remind readers of arguments while driving in an unfamiliar region of the city or countryside? Is it not often the male driver who insists he knows the way but does not have a clue whether the landmark or street he just passed is the right one? Is it not often the woman who prefers to stop and ask for directions? It may be that men and women just differ in their mode of navigation.

Motor Skills

When it comes to throwing a projectile at a target, men do better than women. In one of Kimura's (1999) studies, a dart-throwing task was used. An effect size greater than 1.0 (more than 1 standard deviation) was found that favored men in accuracy. Launching a projectile at a target is a spatial task, but it also involves control of the large muscle groups used on arm movements. The male advantage in targeting shows up early in motor development, well before boys and girls show much difference in muscle size and strength. Even in children as young as 3 years of age, a difference in targeted throwing is observable.

By contrast, women perform better than men at tasks involving control of the small muscles of the hand and especially the fingers. As a consequence, tests of fine motor skills favor females (Kimura, 1999). Of interest, such tests were designed to identify individuals with an aptitude for factory jobs requiring high levels of manual dexterity, and women have always done better on them than have men. Even so, the factory jobs went to men, with the exception of the years during World War II when men were in combat overseas and women were in the factories back home.

Kimura (1999) also found several other tests of manual control on which females do better. Moreover, the differences turn up at ages as young as 3 years. For example, try to copy the finger spacings shown in Figure 15.12. Females, including young girls, can copy these more easily than can males. Kimura attributes the difference to a female advantage in the motor control of distal musculature, the muscles at the most distant points from the center of the body.

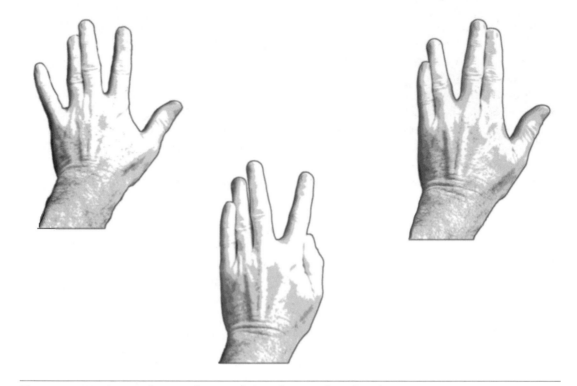

Figure 15.12. A test of manual control that shows a female advantage.

SOURCE: Adapted from Kimura (1999).

Women tend to navigate by landmarks and show good fine motor control, whereas men tend to navigate by dead reckoning and show good targeting skills.

Reasons for Sex Differences

Thus, there is evidence of tendencies for members of one sex to perform better on particular cognitive tests than members of the opposite sex. The most notable feature of the research on sex differences is their relative absence. The frequency distributions for males and females overlap substantially even when a mean difference is detected. Moreover, the differences cannot be used to predict with much accuracy the performance of an individual on a given cognitive test simply by knowing the person's sex. Researchers have nonetheless sought to understand why there are any differences observed at all and why the particular pattern of advantages for females and males occurs. The reasons are not yet known.

Social-Cultural Factors. The differences in socialization and cultural expectations for males and females are conceivably major, and these might explain some sex differences. At least up until the 1970s, boys were typically encouraged to play with balls, blocks, Tinkertoys, and Erector sets as well as to fight with toy guns. By the onset of adolescence, boys were encouraged to take classes in industrial arts, mathematics, and science, and to play sports. The advantages for males on spatial, mathematical, and throwing tests result from their upbringing. Girls, by contrast, were typically encouraged to play with dolls and toy tea sets as well as to play house and talk rather than fight. Girls were steered toward home economics, English, and social studies. Perhaps the female advantages in verbal ability and fine motor skills are related to the socialization practices for girls.

To the extent that socialization practices have changed since the 1970s, one might expect decreases in the effect sizes. In North American and European societies, women are now more actively involved in organized sports, the military, and police departments than they were in the past. Sex differences do appear to be decreasing over time (Feingold, 1988), although it is not clear whether socialization changes are the cause. Furthermore, it is unclear whether the differences in gender roles adopted by boys and girls are exclusively a result of socialization. Biological differences may play a role in the kinds of play in which boys engage, for example (Geary, 1998).

Biological Factors. Here it is important to bear in mind that our brain structure was shaped by evolutionary forces tens of thousands, if not hundreds of thousands, of years ago. Cultural practices during the 20th century are an example of proximate causes of behavior that are closely linked in time. Evolutionary theory deals not with proximate causes but rather with ultimate causes that worked through natural selection over long periods of time long ago (Goldsmith, 1991). Put differently, all of the sociocultural factors described previously may explain part of the gender differences observed in spatial and verbal abilities, but it is still possible that evolutionary causes stemming from much earlier in our history played some role in the differences observed as well. Separating the relative contribution of each is difficult to do. In theory, if you change the sociocultural environment, which takes time and many circumstances falling your way, then the gender differences should disappear. The only differences that remain should, in theory, be those created by natural selection. These do not disappear in a matter of years the way sociocultural differences might.

When *Homo sapiens sapiens* survived in the hunter/gatherer culture of the Upper Paleolithic era of archeological time (60,000 to 40,000 years ago), our ancestors began to build hearths, huts, and organized small villages (Stringer & Gamble, 1993). In similar societies that persisted into the 20th century, there was a division of labor between men and women, which may well have also been true during the Upper Paleolithic era. Kimura (1999) described it this way:

Men were active in manufacturing tools, weapons, and transport devices. They were engaged in scavenging and in hunting small and large game, often traveling far from their home base. They were also responsible for defending the group against predators and enemies. Women contributed by gathering food near the home, preparing food and food-related utensils, making clothing, and caring for the home. The other major difference in men and women was in the care of infants, which was and remains almost exclusively the prerogative of women. There is no society in which men are the chief caregivers to small children. (p. 15)

Natural selection refers to the environment selecting those traits (i.e., the genes that produce them) that enhance survival. If a trait makes it likely that the individual will survive to reproductive age, then the trait will more likely be passed on to offspring. One form of natural selection is called sexual selection. For example, strong visual and spatial skills could readily have helped males to make tools for hunting and to navigate long distances from the rest of the tribe. Men who could not make weapons, spot the game, and find their way home again did not live to have children. Success at all of these tasks put some males at an advantage over other males in competition for females. Those who covered larger territories encountered more females, had more mating opportunities, and probably had more children carrying their genes. At the same time, females may have preferred certain characteristics in their mates over others. If females prefer males large in physical stature over small males, then sexual selection would result in differential reproduction of genes that favor large body size. This could explain why males on average tend to be larger than females (Geary, 1998).

Other selective pressures can be cited because of the division of labor cited earlier during the Upper Paleolithic era. As Kimura (1999) noted,

> Women, in contrast, might be selected for fine motor skills, short-range navigation using landmarks, and efficient perceptual discriminations. The latter would enable them to detect small changes, such as those in a child's face, or slight displacements in the home that might signal an intruder. (p. 15)

Are there differences in male and female brains? One difference has been well-documented. Male brains show greater lateralization than do female brains (Levy & Heller, 1992). **Brain lateralization** refers to the degree to which each hemisphere is specialized for particular cognitive functions. A high degree of lateralization, as found in the male brain, means that language skills are heavily dependent on the left hemisphere and that spatial skills are heavily dependent on the right hemisphere. In females, language skills are

---

Sexual selection is a variant of natural selection in which a trait becomes associated with a given sex. Large body size, good spatial skills, and accurate targeting may have been sexually selected in males.

represented in both hemispheres to a greater extent than in men. If a stroke causes damage to the left hemisphere, then women are more likely to recover language functioning. Also, some of the connecting tissues between the two hemispheres appear to be more developed in females than in males (Kimura, 1999). Overall, then, female brains tend to be more symmetrically developed, whereas male brains are more lateralized, with greater specialization of the right and left hemispheres.

How is the higher degree of brain specialization in males related to the traits that have been hypothesized to be the result of sexual selection? Could the advantage of males in mental rotation, targeting tasks, and navigation over long distances depend on a highly lateralized brain? In females, could verbal fluency, short-term navigation using landmarks, and superior fine motor skills be the result of both hemispheres working well together? The answers to these questions are not yet known. The origin of sex differences and their relation to differences in brain laterality are among the many puzzles for future cognitive psychologists to solve with convincing empirical evidence.

> Female brains tend to be more symmetrically developed, whereas male brains are more lateralized, with greater specialization of the right and left hemispheres. It is not yet known if these brain differences fully explain sex differences in cognition.

SUMMARY

1. IQ stands for intelligence quotient, which is defined as a person's mental age divided by chronological age and multiplied by 100. The term stems from Binet's suggestion of measuring a child's mental age in terms of the performance expected at a particular chronological age. General intelligence (*g*) is viewed as a biologically determined trait that is inherited and can be approximated by a single number, the IQ score. Individual differences in neural functioning were assumed to affect many cognitive abilities, including perception, attention, memory, problem solving, and reasoning. The executive functions of working memory that are served by prefrontal cortical regions play a role in general fluid intelligence or the ability to solve new problems.

2. Binet pioneered psychometric approaches to intelligence, which assumed that cognitive abilities varied independently of one another. Contemporary intelligence tests distinguish separate abilities that develop differently across the life span. Performance IQ decreases with age, whereas verbal IQ remains stable over at least six decades. Other researchers distinguished between practical intelligence and intelligence as measured by IQ tests. Intelligence might involve domain-specific modules in addition to or instead of general intelligence. Linguistic, logical-mathematical, and spatial intelligence have been assessed in various ways on traditional tests of intelligence, but musical, bodily-kinesthetic, intrapersonal, and interpersonal intelligence are other domains that often are ignored on intelligence tests.

3. Heritability (h^2) is the proportion of variance in a population associated with genetic differences among the individuals. In children, h^2 is estimated at about .40, but as people enter adulthood, more of the IQ differences among individuals reflect genetic differences, with h^2 about .75. It is a mistake to conclude that the heritability of intelligence observed in adults means that IQ is fixed by the genes. Heritability and immutability are not the same thing. For example, the Flynn effect shows that IQ has risen dramatically in technologically advanced countries over the past 50 years.

4. Gender differences in cognitive competencies have long been of interest. Meta-analyses of large numbers of studies have shown that females perform better than males on some tests of verbal abilities. The effect size takes into account how large a gender difference is relative to the magnitude of variations among individuals. The gender difference in verbal abilities shows a small effect size. On some tests of visual-spatial ability, males perform better than females. Males also show an advantage on mathematical tests. However, because males show markedly more variability than do females, it is not possible to predict mathematical ability by knowing gender. These and other sex differences could reflect either socialization practices or biological evolution in the form of sexual selection. It is known that male brains show a greater degree of lateralization of functions within a single hemisphere compared with female brains, but it is unclear whether this fact accounts for sex differences in cognition.

● KEY TERMS

intelligence quotient (IQ)
general intelligence (*g*)
fluid intelligence
crystallized intelligence
linguistic intelligence
logical-mathematical intelligence
spatial intelligence

musical intelligence
bodily-kinesthetic intelligence
intrapersonal intelligence
interpersonal intelligence
heritability (h^2)
meta-analysis
effect size
brain lateralization

Answer key to the sample questions in Figure 15.3:
Spatial High *g*- Element 3 because of a symmetry difference.
Spatial Low *g*- Element 1 because it is solid.
Verbal High *g*- Element 3 because its letters are equally spaced in the alphabet.
Verbal Low *g*- Element 1 because its letters are not sequential in the alphabet.

GLOSSARY

Affirming the antecedent: a valid means of conditional reasoning (If P, then Q; P is true).

Affirming the consequent: an invalid means of conditional reasoning (If P, then Q; Q is true).

Algorithm: a rule that correctly generates the solution to a problem given that one can devote sufficient time and effort to applying the rule.

Analytic processing: perceiving the features that comprise the whole stimulus; contrasts with holistic processing.

Anaphora: the use of a word to substitute for a preceding word or phrase.

Anterograde amnesia: a cognitive disorder characterized by an inability to remember events that occur after the onset of the disorder.

Anterior cingulate gyrus: brain region involved in the supervisory attentional system, inhibiting automatic responses and selecting the correct response.

Apperceptive agnosia: a type of object recognition failure in which the difficulty lies in identifying the features of a perceptual category; contrasts with associative agnosia.

Articulatory program: the set of instructions for executing output by the vocal muscles.

Assimilation: a distortion of memory caused by reconstructive retrieval processes in which a recollection is rationalized or normalized to fit with schema-based expectations.

Associative agnosia: a type of object recognition failure in which the difficulty lies in identifying the semantic function of an object despite intact perceptual ability; contrasts with apperceptive agnosia.

Atmosphere hypothesis: presumes that people compare the similarity of the conclusion to the premises in a deductive reasoning task rather than evaluating the conclusion according to the rules of logic.

449

Attentional blink: the interval of time after the target is presented when other stimuli in the series are not perceived.

Attenuation: refers to an attentional filter that lowers the strength of the sensory signal on the unattended channel.

Automatic processes: a kind of cognitive process that is unintentional, unconscious, and effortless; contrasts with controlled processes.

Availability heuristic: a decision heuristic suggesting that if relevant examples can readily be retrieved from memory, then the class of events must occur with a high probability.

Back-propagation of error: a common algorithm or rule for teaching a neural network in which error signals are fed back through the network to adjust connection weights.

Backward chaining: a problem-solving heuristic in which an unknown quantity in a problem is identified, and from that unknown an attempt is made to work backward toward the quantities given in the problem.

Belief bias: refers to people accepting any and all conclusions that happen to fit with their system of beliefs.

Binding problem: refers to how the features that are distributed in multiple brain regions are integrated to result in the perception of a single object.

Blindsight: vision that allows the identification of object locations despite the absence of conscious awareness of the objects, as a result of lesions in the occipital cortex.

Bodily-kinesthetic intelligence: a module in the frames of mind theory of intelligence that refers to skilled motor performance.

Brain lateralization: refers to the degree to which the left or right hemisphere of the brain is specialized for particular cognitive functions.

Brainstem: a structure of the brain consisting of the hindbrain—the medulla and pons—and the midbrain.

Bridging inferences: inferences required to comprehend anaphoric references in which one word (e.g., a pronoun) is substituted for a preceding word (e.g., a noun).

Broca's aphasia: a disorder of language characterized by a lack of fluency and correct grammar in speech.

Categorical perception: the categorization of speech input at the phonemic level.

Category size effect: in answering simple questions using semantic memory, more time is needed to respond when the semantic category is large (e.g., Is a collie an animal?) than when it is small (e.g., Is a collie a dog?).

Cerebellum: a structure of the brain that lies over the brainstem at the rear of the head.

Chunking: relating separate items in a meaningful way so as to form an integrated representation in short-term memory.

Coarticulation: in uttering a word, each time segment of the acoustic signal provides information about the identity of more than one phoneme; phonemes are partly articulated in parallel as well as in series.

Cognitive architecture: the design or organization of the mind's information processing, components, and systems.

Cognitive economy assumption: claims that the features of a concept are represented only once at either the subordinate, basic, or superordinate level of the hierarchy.

Cognitive science: the study of the relationships among and integration of cognitive psychology, biology, anthropology, computer science, linguistics, and philosophy.

Conceptually driven processes: expectations derived from schemas in long-term memory that guide pattern recognition and memory encoding; also called top-down processes; contrasts with data-driven processes.

Confabulation: a memory distortion in which one provides a detailed narrative account of events that never happened.

Conjunction error: a kind of verbal false memory in which a word is falsely remembered because its syllables were encountered in two different words studied earlier.

Conjunctive fallacy: in decision making, the error of judging a conjunction of two events as more likely than the probability of either event alone.

Connectionist models: a class of cognitive architecture based on the assumption that the mind is built like the brain with distributed mental representations, massively interconnected neuron-like units, and parallel processing; contrasts with symbolic models.

Connection weight: in connectionist models, it represents the knowledge state of the network; mathematically, the weight is a multiplier of the output value of the sending node.

Content problems: one type of problem that writers must solve in text production is the matter of what to say; contrasts with rhetorical problems.

Controlled processes: a kind of cognitive process that is intentional, conscious, and demanding of mental effort; contrasts with automatic processes.

Conversational implicatures: inferences made by a participant in a conversation so as to understand the meaning of the speaker.

Cooperative principle: an implicit contractual agreement among the participants in a conversation to cooperate with one another in conveying meaning.

Corpus callosum: the large band of fibers that connects the right and left cerebral hemispheres together deep in the brain.

Crystallized intelligence: refers to the breadth and depth of a person's knowledge; contrasts with fluid intelligence.

Data-driven processes: analysis of incoming data (e.g., edges, lines) held in sensory memory during pattern recognition and memory encoding; also called bottom-up processes; contrasts with conceptually driven processes.

Decisions under certainty: decisions made in which the states of nature that determine the outcome of actions are known with certainty.

Decisions under risk: decisions made in which the states of nature that determine the outcomes of actions occur with known probabilities.

Decisions under uncertainty: decisions made in which the probabilities of the states of nature that determine the outcomes of actions are unknown.

Declarative memory: refers to knowledge of events, facts, and concepts.

Deliberate practice: a regimen of effortful activities often begun during childhood that lead to extraordinary levels of skilled performance.

Delusional false memory: an illusion of memory in which an individual with strong beliefs that a bizarre event can occur comes to actually experience a memory of the event.

Denying the antecedent: an invalid means of conditional reasoning (If P, then Q; P is false).

Denying the consequent: a valid means of conditional reasoning (If P, then Q; Q is false).

Directed thinking: goal-directed, methodical thinking used in solving problems; contrasts with undirected thinking.

Displacement: a quality of language permitting reference to events removed in space and time from the current situation.

Distinctive features: perceptual features that discriminate one stimulus from similar stimuli.

Distinctiveness: refers to how the items to be learned are different from each other and other items already stored in memory; contrasts with relational processing.

Divided attention: the ability to split limited attentional resources among two or more stimuli rather than focusing on a single stimulus; contrasts with selective attention.

Double dissociation: refers to situations in which an independent variable affects Task A but not Task B and in which a different variable affects Task B but not Task A.

Dualism: holds that the mind is an immaterial entity that exists independently of the brain and other bodily organs; contrasts with materialism.

Early selection: refers to an attentional filter that operates after sensory processing but prior to meaningful semantic processing.

Echoic memory: a component in the auditory system that stores sounds for a brief duration.

Ecological validity: the similarity of a laboratory task to real-world tasks, allowing valid generalization from the laboratory finding.

Effect size: the difference in two mean scores in an experiment divided by their standard deviation; describes how large the mean difference is relative to the variability in the data.

Elaborative rehearsal: linking information in short-term memory with information already stored in long-term memory.

Emergent property: implies that the whole is greater than the sum of its parts; according to one version of materialism, the mind cannot be reduced to the brain because mental states are an emergent property of brain states.

Encoding specificity: the specific encoding operations performed on what is perceived determines what retrieval cues are effective in gaining access to the stored representation.

Episodic memory: the recollection of events that took place at specific places and times in the past.

Event-related potential (ERP): an electroencephalogram (EEG) signal that reflects the brain's response to the onset of a specific stimulus.

Executive control: supervisory attentional system that inhibits inappropriate mental representations or responses and activates appropriate ones.

Exhaustive search: a search of memory that continues to examine the remaining items in memory even after the target item has been found.

Expert-novice differences: refers to the differences in mental representations and cognitive processes associated with domain-specific expertise.

Eye-mind assumption: holds that the duration of an eye fixation varies with the amount of information that must be processed in working memory at that instant.

False verbal memory: an illusion of memory in which a target word is falsely remembered following the study of a list of words highly related to the target.

Family resemblance structure: a characteristic of natural object concepts that are defined by a large number of features that apply to some, but not all, category members; contrasts with rule-governed concepts.

Feature comparison model: assumes that semantic memory includes characteristic and defining features of concepts.

Feature frequency theory: holds that the gradual accretion of the frequency of occurrence of features discriminates between defining features and irrelevant features in concept learning; also called associative strength theory.

Feature integration theory: posits that automatic preattentive processing of features must be followed by controlled attentional processing to bind the features into a whole object.

Fixation: refers to the blocking of solution paths to a problem that is caused by past experiences related to the problem.

Flashbulb memory: a vivid recollection of some autobiographical event that carries with it strong emotional reactions.

Fluid intelligence: refers to the ability to solve novel problems; contrasts with crystallized intelligence.

Folk theories: naive commonsense explanations of scientific phenomena as opposed to theories based on scientific facts.

Formants: bands of sound energy at particular frequencies in a speech signal.

Forward chaining: a problem-solving heuristic in which the known quantities in the problem are first identified, and then an attempt is made to work forward toward the unknown quantity.

Frames: schemas that represent the physical structure of the environment.

Framing effect: in decision making, it refers to making a different decision depending on where people perceive themselves to be in relation to the curvilinear subjective utility function.

Frontal lobe: a region of cortex that extends from the anterior of the brain back to the central sulcus and the temporal lobes.

Functional equivalence hypothesis: states that visual imagery, while not identical to perception, is mentally represented and functions the same as perception.

Functional fixedness: an impediment to problem solving, it refers to the tendency to see objects as having only a single typical use.

Functional magnetic resonance imaging (fMRI): a method of neuroimaging that uses a powerful magnetic field to reveal detailed images of neuronal tissue and the metabolic changes associated with activated regions.

Gambler's fallacy: refers to the mistaken belief that future tosses of a coin, drops of the ball in roulette, or rolls of the dice in craps are not independent of past events.

General intelligence (g): refers to the underlying factor that accounts for an individual's performance on an intelligence quotient (IQ) test and in other situations demanding intelligence.

General resource hypothesis: holds that language and thought are shaped by the constraints of general cognitive resources such as memory and attention.

Given-new strategy: a comprehension strategy to first identify the old information known already and then to seek the novel information in a sentence.

Goal state: the solution to a problem, it is the final end state of the problem space and the opposite of the initial state.

Grammatical encoding: refers to the selection of the lexical entries to be used from among those in the speaker's vocabulary and to the assembly of a syntactic framework.

Grapheme: a written symbol that represents a single phoneme.

Heritability (h^2): the proportion of variance in a population associated with genetic differences among the individuals for a given trait.

Heuristic: refers to a rule of thumb or general strategy of problem solving that may lead to a solution quickly with less computational cost.

Hidden layer: in a neural network, it receives information from the input layer and sends forward information to the output layer; it provides a representation that is distinct from the input and output layers.

Hindsight bias: refers to the fact that people confidently judge that they knew an event would occur after it had occurred.

Hippocampus: a structure of the limbic system located in the medial temporal lobe that is involved in the learning and storage of new events in long-term memory.

Historical creativity: acts of genius that are widely acclaimed by society as meritorious and novel within the context of human history.

Holistic processing: perceiving the whole object; contrasts with analytic processing.

Homeostasis: refers to a state of equilibrium of the internal environment of the body.

Hypothalamus: a structure in the diencephalon of the brain and the part of the limbic system that controls the output of the pituitary, the master gland of the endocrine system.

Hypothesis testing theory: assumes that a concept learner actively tests hypotheses about the identity of defining features.

Iconic memory: a component that stores visual features for a brief period of time.

Identity hypothesis: holds that thought is equivalent to language in the form of covert speech.

Ideographic writing: a writing system in which each symbol represents an idea or object directly rather than a particular word or speech sound; contrasts with phonetic writing.

Ill-defined problems: a problem in which the goal state, the initial state, or the operators are not clearly defined; contrasts with well-defined problems.

Illicit conversion: refers to people converting "All A are B" into "All B are A," taking the converse of the premise as true in addition to the premise itself.

Illumination: the third stage of creativity in which insight into the problem solution is obtained.

Imaginal code: a concrete means of mental representation that directly conveys perceptual qualities.

Immediacy assumption: holds that readers assign an interpretation to each word as it is fixated.

Implicit learning: refers to the unconscious acquisition of complex rules that cannot be verbalized.

Inattentional blindness: failure to perceive an unattended object because its features were not bound by attention.

Incubation: the second stage of creativity that refers to putting a problem aside and doing other things.

Informational access: the capacity to become aware of and able to report on mental representations and the processes that operate on them.

Initial state: the beginning of a problem, it is the first state of the problem space and the opposite of the goal state.

Integration: refers to combining features of different events into a unified representation during encoding into long-term memory.

Intelligence quotient: refers to a person's mental age, as measured on a standardized intelligence test, divided by his or her chronological age and then multiplied by 100.

Interpersonal intelligence: a module of the frames of intelligence theory referring to the ability to take note of other people's moods, temperaments, motivations, and intentions.

Interpretation: inferences and suppositions made during memory encoding based on activated schemas in long-term memory.

Intrapersonal intelligence: a module of the frames of intelligence theory referring to the ability to gain access to one's emotions and to draw on these emotions in guiding one's thoughts and behaviors.

Isomorphic problems: problems that appear different on the surface in wording, for example, but share the same problem space at a deep level of analysis.

Knowledge-telling: retrieving an idea from memory and putting it into words during text production.

Knowledge-transforming: altering ideas held in memory during text production as a result of reflecting on the text written thus far.

Latent semantic analysis (LSA): a mathematical procedure for automatically extracting and representing the meanings of propositions expressed in a text.

Law of small numbers: people mistakenly expect even small samples to look random and to mirror the probabilities obtained with large samples.

Leading edge strategy: readers maintain the most recent proposition and those that overlap with it in terms of their arguments in working memory in an effort to establish referential coherence among the sentences of a text.

Lemma: an abstract representation of a word that specifies its semantic and grammatical features.

Leveling: a distortion of memory caused by reconstructive retrieval processes in which details are lost in recollecting an event.

Levels or depths of processing: a memory superiority for events attentively processed at a semantic level as compared to a sensory level.

Lexeme: a representation of the phonological structure of a word.

Lexical bias effect: when the speech production system is primed to commit a Spoonerism by erroneously switching the position of phonetic segments (e.g., mistakenly saying "barn door" when "darn bore" was intended);

the error is more likely when it results in a word than when a nonword is the outcome.

Limbic system: a functional unit of the brain comprised of the cingulate gyrus, fornix, hippocampus, and other related structures.

Linguistic intelligence: a module of verbal knowledge in the frames of mind theory of intelligence.

Linguistic relativity hypothesis: holds that thought is shaped by the properties of language; also called the Whorfian hypothesis.

Logical-mathematical intelligence: a module of mathematical knowledge in the frames of mind theory of intelligence.

Macropropositions: the assertions that represent the gist or a summary of the meaning of a text.

Maintenance rehearsal: recycling information within short-term or working memory by covertly verbalizing it.

Manner of articulation: in uttering English consonants, the way sound is emitted by the vocal tract such as a stop or complete closure versus a fricative or constriction of the air flow.

Materialism: regards mental states as products of the brain and its physiological processes and potentially reducible to brain states; contrasts with dualism.

Mental effort: the proportion of available attentional capacity that is momentarily allocated to a cognitive process.

Mental lexicon: a dictionary of long-term memory that stores the morphemes used in speaking, listening, reading, and writing.

Mental representation: an unobservable internal code for information.

Meta-analysis: a statistical technique for summarizing the results of numerous studies that examine the same question in roughly the same way.

Metacognition: thinking about another thought process.

Meta-representation: a mental representation whose object is another mental representation.

Method of subtraction: used by cognitive psychologists to isolate the properties of a single stage of processing by comparing two tasks that differ only in terms of the stage of interest.

Micropropositions: the individual assertions that represent the meaning of a single sentence.

Mindblindness: refers to an inability to understand that other people possess mental representations.

Misinformation effect: a distortion of memory caused by asking misleading questions about an event encoded in long-term memory.

Mnemonic encoding: refers to using the organization of long-term memory to guide the encoding of information into meaningful chunks.

Modularity hypothesis: holds that language is served by a separate module that is independent of the cognitive resources on which thought depends.

Module: a set of processes that are automatic, fast, encapsulated apart from other cognitive systems, and instantiated in a localized area of the brain.

Mood congruence effect: events encoded during one mood are easiest to retrieve during the same mood; for example, positive life events are easiest to remember when in a happy mood.

Morpheme: a minimal unit of speech used repeatedly in a language to code a specific meaning (e.g., words, suffixes, prefixes).

Musical intelligence: a module in the frames of mind theory referring to the ability to perceive pitch, rhythm, and timbre or tonal quality.

Neocortex: the most recently evolved parts of the cerebral cortex, which is well-developed only in mammals.

Nonanalytic concept learning: storing specific old instances of concepts and making analogies between new and old instances.

Nondeclarative memory: refers to skills and related procedural knowledge.

Object concepts: refer to natural kinds or biological objects and artifacts or human-made objects.

Object permanence: the concept of an object as a permanent entity that does not vanish when out of sight.

Occipital lobe: a region of cortex that lies at the rear base of the brain, just above the cerebellum.

Operator: a legal move in solving a problem; it results in a transition from one state to another within a problem space.

Orthography: the part of grammar that treats the mapping of sounds onto written symbols in spelling words; orthographic features are visual as opposed to the auditory phonological features of a word.

Parallel distributed processing (PDP): connectionist models based on distributed memory representations, massively connected neuron-like units, and parallel processing of information.

Parallel processing: refers to cases in which cognitive operations occur simultaneously in parallel.

Parallel search: means that all items in memory are examined simultaneously, not serially.

Parietal lobe: a region of the cortex that extends toward the rear and sides of the brain beginning at the central sulcus and ending at the occipital lobe and temporal lobe.

Pattern recognition: the step between the transduction and perception of a stimulus in the environment and its categorization as a meaningful object.

Phoneme: speech sound or phonological segment that makes a difference in meaning.

Phonemic similarity effect: the high rate of intrusion errors in short-term memory for stimuli that are pronounced alike.

Phonetics: the study of how speech sounds are actually produced by the vocal apparatus.

Phonetic writing: a writing system in which each symbol represents a distinct speech sound; contrasts with ideographic writing.

Phonological dyslexics: a type of reading disorder in which an individual can read familiar words correctly but has difficulty with unfamiliar words and pseudowords that must be read using grapheme-to-phoneme conversion rules.

Phonological encoding: refers to the assembly of sound forms and the intonation to be executed during articulation.

Place of articulation: in uttering English consonants, it refers to the position in the mouth where there is a constriction of air flow.

Planning: one of three writing processes, it refers to generating ideas, organizing ideas, and setting goals to achieve during writing such as trying to achieve the right voice or tone for a particular audience.

Polysemy: the property of language that a single word can have more than one meaning.

Positron emission tomography (**PET**): a method of neuroimaging that uses radioactively labeled water (hydrogen and oxygen 15) to detect areas of high metabolic activity in the brain.

Power law of practice: states that performance in a task improves as a power function of the amount of practice in doing the task.

Pragmatics: refers to the manner in which speakers communicate their intentions depending on the social context.

Preparation: the first stage of creativity concerned with studying, learning, formulating solutions, and striving to create.

Primacy effect: accurate recall of the initial items studied in a list of items in a memory experiment.

Priming: refers to the presentation of a stimulus biasing how a subsequent stimulus is processed.

Principle of procedural reinstatement: skill is well-retained for long periods of time when the procedures used to acquire the skill are reinstated at the time of test.

Proactive interference: means that past learning interferes with the ability to learn and remember new information.

Problem space: the initial state, goal state, and all possible states in between that may be reached by applying the operators or legal moves in a problem.

Productive thinking: entails insight and creativity in seeking the solution to a problem; contrasts with reproductive thinking.

Productivity: refers to the ability to create novel sentences that can be understood by other speakers of the language.

Proportion of errors: a measure of errors made in a cognitive task.

Propositional code: an abstract means of mental representation that is schematic and verbal rather than perceptual.

Prosopagnosia: a cognitive disorder characterized by a selective inability to recognize faces.

Prototype: the best or most typical member of a category that serves as a summary representation of a concept.

Reaction time: the number of milliseconds to perform a task; it is used to measure the duration of cognitive processes.

Recency effect: accurate recall of the last items presented in a list in a memory experiment.

Reconstructive retrieval: refers to schema-guided construction of episodic memories that alter and distort encoded memory representations.

Referential coherence: when the words and phrases of one sentence in a paragraph refer unambiguously to those of other sentences in the paragraph.

Relational processing: refers to how the items to be learned are related to each other and to other items stored in memory; contrasts with distinctiveness.

Representativeness heuristic: a decision heuristic suggesting that if examples are typical of a class, then they occur with a high probability.

Repression: a defense mechanism that, in psychoanalytic theory, protects the ego from anxiety by preventing unpleasant memories from entering consciousness.

Reproductive thinking: entails the application of tried-and-true paths to the solution of a problem; contrasts with productive thinking.

Retrieval mode: the initial stage of retrieval in which an effortful search is made of long-term memory for the representation of a past event.

Retrieval structure: a highly specialized means of retrieval used by experts in a domain to gain access to what they know.

Retroactive interference: refers to recent learning interfering with the recall of previous learning.

Retrograde amnesia: a cognitive disorder characterized by an inability to remember events that occurred prior to the onset of the disorder.

Reviewing: one of three writing processes, it refers to the reading of the text being produced and evaluating and editing it.

Rhetorical problems: one type of problem that writers must solve in text production is the matter of how to say what needs to be said; contrasts with content problems.

Rule-governed concepts: specify the features and relations that define membership in the class on an all-or-none basis; contrasts with family resemblance structure.

Schema: a mental representation that organizes knowledge about related concepts.

Scripts: schemas that represent routine activities.

Selection: the selective encoding of information that fits with prior knowledge.

Selective attention: the ability to perceive and attend to a particular stimulus of interest while ignoring numerous other stimuli; contrasts with divided attention.

Self-knowledge: awareness of the self as an entity.

Self-reference effect: a level of processing effect whereby encoding processes that relate an item to be learned to self-concepts produces superior memory.

Self-terminating search: refers to a search that stops as soon as the item being sought is found.

Semantic memory: factual and conceptual knowledge about the world and the words used to symbolize such knowledge.

Semantic network model: hierarchical model of semantic memory in which concepts are organized according to subordinate, basic, and superordinate levels and their features.

Semantics: the study of meaning.

Sentience: the basic capacity for raw sensations, feelings, and subjective experience of any kind.

Serial position effect: the outcome when people are asked to recall items presented earlier in a list in any order; the initial and final items of the list are best recalled.

Serial processing: cases in which cognitive operations occur one at a time in a series.

Serial search: means that the items in memory are somehow ordered and are examined one at a time, starting with the first item and proceeding to the next.

Shadowing: the participant repeats aloud the stimuli presented to the attended channel and ignores those in the unattended ignored channel.

Sharpening: a distortion of memory caused by reconstructive retrieval processes in which details are added during the recollection of an event by drawing inferences from general knowledge.

Simulation heuristic: a decision heuristic that involves constructing a mental model of a situation and then "running the model" so as to predict the course of events.

Situation model: a complete mental representation of a text made up of knowledge from long-term memory in addition to the propositions of the textbase.

Source monitoring: refers to evaluative processes that attribute mental experiences to different sources.

Spatial intelligence: a module in the frames of mind theory of intelligence that refers to the ability to reason about the spatial relations of objects.

Spatial neglect: a cognitive disorder of attention in which a portion of the visual field is selectively ignored on a consistent basis despite normal visual abilities.

Speech act: refers to a sentence uttered to express the speaker's intention in a way that the listener will recognize.

Speech spectrogram: the physical acoustic energy of an utterance by plotting frequency in hertz or cycles per second on the y axis and time in milliseconds on the x axis.

Stages of processing: the steps required to form, modify, and use mental representations in a cognitive task.

State-dependent learning: sometimes observed when a person's mood or state of consciousness (e.g., sober, intoxicated) is directly manipulated during learning and retrieval, with matches yielding better recall than mismatches.

Story grammar: a set of rules that allows one to generate an acceptable story.

Stroop effect: has challenged theorists to account for the detailed patterns of errors and delays observed in experiments.

Subgoals: in a problem space, important intermediate states that must be reached between the initial state and the goal state.

Subjective organization: a consistent organizational pattern for recalling unrelated items from long-term memory that is unique to each individual.

Subliminal perception: refers to the unsupported claim that unattended stimuli are perceived as whole objects, although certain features may be processed.

Surface dyslexics: type of reading disorder in which an individual can correctly read regular words and pseudowords but often fails to read irregular words that do not follow grapheme-to-phoneme conversion rules.

Syllogistic reasoning: involves evaluating whether a conclusion necessarily follows deductively from two premises that are assumed to be true.

Symbolic models: a class of cognitive architecture based on the assumption that the mind is built like a digital computer in which mental representations are symbols stored in memory and manipulated according to rules; contrasts with connectionist models.

Synset: a set of synonyms for each noun, verb, adjective, or adverb in the language.

Syntax: the grammatical rules that specify how words and other morphemes are arranged so as to yield acceptable sentences.

Temporal lobe: a region of cortex that lies on the side of the brain, beginning below the lateral fissure; it is bordered by the frontal, parietal, and occipital lobes.

Textbase: a partial mental representation of a text made up of propositions derived directly from its sentences; contrasts with situation model.

Ten-year rule: states that even the most talented individuals require a minimum of 10 years of preparation before succeeding at an international level of competition.

Thalamus: a structure of the diencephalon that is extensively inter-connected with sensory and other regions of the cortex.

Tip of the tongue (TOT) state: a feeling of knowing or familiarity in which some name, word, date, or other information cannot be retrieved despite a certainty that it is available in memory.

Transfer-appropriate processing: holds that test performance depends on the degree to which the processes engaged at encoding are compatible with the demands of the memory test.

Translating (generating): one of three writing processes, it refers to the linguistic operations needed to generate coherently linked sentences from the planned conceptual content.

Trauma-induced amnesia: loss of memory for a traumatic event involving a dissociation of consciousness.

Typicality effect: refers to the gradient of category membership or differ-ences in how well specific instances represent a concept.

Undirected thinking: wandering thought, as in daydreams, that may prompt a creative solution to a problem; contrasts with directed thinking.

Universal grammar: refers to the genetically determined knowledge of human language that allows children in all cultures to rapidly acquire the language to which they are exposed.

Valid deductive conclusion: a conclusion that is necessarily true given that the premises are true in syllogistic reasoning.

Verbal protocols: tape-recordings of people thinking aloud while they carry out a task provide a rich record of conscious processing.

Verification: the fourth stage of creativity when the solution achieved as an insight must be fleshed out and checked carefully.

Voice onset time: the time between the initiation of a voiced phoneme and the moment when the vocal cords begin vibrating.

Voicing: refers to the difference between English consonants that involve vibration of the vocal cords (voiced) and those that do not (unvoiced).

Well-defined problem: a problem in which the initial state, goal state, and operators can be stated clearly; contrasts with ill-defined problems.

Wernicke's aphasia: a disorder of language in which speech comprehen-sion is severely impaired and production is fluent but often meaningless.

Word frequency effect: words that occur frequently in the language are recognized more rapidly than are words that occur infrequently.

Word superiority effect: the counterintuitive finding that a letter is recognized more rapidly when presented in the context of a whole word than when presented as an isolated feature.

Working memory: refers to the system for temporarily maintaining mental representations that are relevant to the performance of a cognitive task in an activated state.

REFERENCES

Abelson, R. P. (1981). Psychological status of the script concept. *American Psychologist, 36,* 715-729.

Alba, J. W., & Hasher, L. (1983). Is memory schematic? *Psychological Bulletin, 93,* 203-231.

Allport, D. A., Antonis, B., & Reynolds, P. (1972). On the division of attention: A disproof of the single channel hypothesis. *Quarterly Journal of Experimental Psychology, 24,* 225-235.

Anderson, J. R. (1983). *The architecture of cognition.* Cambridge, MA: Harvard University Press.

Anderson, J. R. (1990). *Cognitive psychology and its implications* (3rd ed.). New York: Freeman.

Anthony, T., Copper, C., & Mullen, B. (1992). Cross-racial facial identification: A social cognitive integration. *Personality and Social Psychology Bulletin, 18,* 296-301.

Antrobus, J. (1991). Dreaming: Cognitive processes during cortical activation and high afferent thresholds. *Psychological Review, 98,* 96-121.

Atchison, J. (1996). *The seeds of speech: Language origin and evolution.* Cambridge, UK: Cambridge University Press.

Atkinson, R. C., & Shiffrin, R. M. (1968). Human memory: A proposed system and its control processes. In K. W. Spence & J. T. Spence (Eds.), *The psychology of learning and motivation* (Vol. 2, pp. 89-195). Orlando, FL: Academic Press.

Atkinson, R. C., & Shiffrin, R. M. (1971). The control of short-term memory. *Scientific American, 225,* 82-90.

Attneave, F. (1957). Transfer of experience with a class schema to identification of patterns and shapes. *Journal of Experimental Psychology, 54,* 81-88.

Atwood, M. E., & Polson, P. G. (1976). A process model for water jar problems. *Cognitive Psychology, 8,* 191-216.

Averbach, E., & Coriell, A. S. (1961). Short-term memory in vision. *Bell System Technical Journal, 40,* 309-328.

Baars, B. J. (1988). *A cognitive theory of consciousness.* Cambridge, UK: Cambridge University Press.

Baars, B. J., Motley, M. T., & MacKay, D. G. (1975). Output editing for lexical status in artificially elicited slips of the tongue. *Journal of Verbal Learning and Verbal Behavior, 14,* 382-391.

Baddeley, A. D. (1986). *Working memory.* New York: Oxford University Press.

Baddeley, A. D. (1996). Exploring the central executive. *Quarterly Journal of Experimental Psychology, 49A,* 5-28.

Baddeley, A. D., & Logie, R. H. (1999). Working memory: The multiple component model. In A. Miyake & P. Shah (Eds.), *Models of working memory: Mechanisms* *of active maintenance and executive control* (pp. 28-61). Cambridge, UK: Cambridge University Press.

Baddeley, A. D., & Scott, D. (1971). Short-term forgetting in the absence of proactive interference. *Quarterly Journal of Experimental Psychology, 23,* 275-283.

Baddeley, A. D., & Warrington, E. K. (1970). Amnesia and the distinction between long-term and short-term memory. *Journal of Verbal Learning and Verbal Behavior, 9,* 176-189.

Badecker, W., Hillis, A., & Caramazza, A. (1990). Lexical morphology and its role in the writing process: Evidence from a case of acquired dysgraphia. *Cognition, 35,* 205-243.

Bahrick, H. P. (1983). The cognitive map of a city: Fifty years of learning and memory. In G. H. Bower (Ed.), *The psychology of learning and motivation: Advances in research and theory* (Vol. 17, pp. 125-163). New York: Academic Press.

Bahrick, H. P. (1984). Semantic memory content in permastore: Fifty years of memory for Spanish learned in school. *Journal of Experimental Psychology: General, 113,* 1-29.

Bahrick, H. P., Bahrick, P. C., & Wittlinger, R. P. (1975). Fifty years of memories for names and faces: A cross-sectional approach. *Journal of Experimental Psychology: General, 104,* 54-75.

Banaji, M. R., & Crowder, R. G. (1989). The bankruptcy of everyday memory. *American Psychologist, 44,* 1185-1193.

Banks, W. P., & Krajicek, D. (1991). Perception. *Annual Review of Psychology, 42,* 305-331.

Bar-Hillel, M. (1980). What features make samples seem representative? *Journal of Experimental Psychology: Human Perception and Performance, 6,* 578-589.

Baron-Cohen, S. (1995). *Mindblindness: An essay on autism and theory of mind.* Cambridge, MA: MIT Press.

Baron-Cohen, S., Leslie, A. M., & Frith, U. (1985). Does the autistic child have a "theory of mind"? *Cognition, 21,* 37-46.

Barsalou, L. W. (1983). Ad hoc categories. *Memory & Cognition, 11,* 211-227.

Barsalou, L. W., & Sewell, D. R. (1985). Contrasting the representation of scripts and categories. *Journal of Memory and Language, 24,* 646-665.

Bartlett, F. C. (1932). *Remembering: A study in experimental and social psychology.* Cambridge, UK: Cambridge University Press.

Bartlett, J. C., & Searcy, J. (1993). Inversion and configuration of faces. *Cognitive Psychology, 25,* 281-316.

Barton, M. E., & Komatsu, L. K. (1989). Defining features of natural kinds and artifacts. *Journal of Psycholinguistic Research, 18,* 433-447.

Bates, E., Benigni, L., Bretherton, I., Camaioni, L., & Volterra, V. (1979). *The emergence of symbols: Cognition and communication in infancy.* New York: Academic Press.

Beatty, J. (2001). *The human brain: Essentials of behavioral neuroscience.* Thousand Oaks, CA: Sage.

Beauvois, M. F., & Dérouesné, J. (1981). Lexical or orthographic agraphia. *Brain, 104,* 21-49.

Begg, I., & Denny, J. P. (1969). Empirical reconciliation of atmosphere and conversion interpretations of syllogistic reasoning errors. *Journal of Experimental Psychology, 81,* 351-354.

Begg, I., & White, P. (1985). Encoding specificity in interpersonal communication. *Canadian Journal of Psychology, 39,* 70-87.

Bellezza, F. S. (1986). A mnemonic based on arranging words on visual patterns. *Journal of Educational Psychology, 78,* 217-224.

Bellugi, U., Bihrle, A., Neville, H., Doherty, S., & Jernigan, T. (1992). Language, cognition, and brain organization in a neurodevelopmental disorder. In

M. R. Gunnar & C. A. Nelson (Eds.), *Developmental behavioral neuroscience* (Minnesota Symposium on Child Psychology, Vol. 24, pp. 201-232). Hillsdale, NJ: Lawrence Erlbaum.

Bereiter, C., & Scardamalia, M. (1987). *The psychology of written composition.* Hillsdale, NJ: Lawrence Erlbaum.

Bergman, E. T., & Roediger, H. L., III. (1999). Can Bartlett's repeated reproduction experiments be replicated? *Memory & Cognition, 27,* 937-947.

Berlyne, D. E. (1965). *Structure and direction in thinking.* New York: John Wiley.

Berninger, V. W., & Swanson, H. L. (1994). Modifying Hayes and Flower's model of skilled writing to explain beginning and developing writing. In E. C. Butterfield (Ed.), *Children's writing: Toward a process theory of the development of skilled writing* (pp. 57-81). Greenwich, CT: JAI.

Berry, D. C., & Broadbent, D. E. (1984). On the relationship between task performance and associated verbalizable knowledge. *Quarterly Journal of Experimental Psychology: Human Experimental Psychology, 36A,* 209-231.

Bertoncini, J., Bijeljac-Babic, R., Jusczyk, P. W., Kennedy, L. J., & Mehler, J. (1988). An investigation of young infants' perceptual representations of speech sounds. *Journal of Experimental Psychology: General, 117,* 21-33.

Biederman, I. (1985). Human image understanding: Recent research and a theory. *Computer Vision, Graphics, and Image Processing, 32,* 29-73.

Biederman, I. (1987). Recognition-by-components: A theory of human understanding. *Psychological Review, 94,* 115-147.

Biederman, I., Glass, A. L., & Stacy, E. W. (1973). Searching for objects in real world scenes. *Journal of Experimental Psychology, 97,* 22-27.

Biederman, I., & Ju, G. (1988). Surface vs. edge-based determinants of visual recognition. *Cognitive Psychology, 20,* 38-64.

Binet, A. (1903). *L'Etude experimentale de l'intelligence.* Paris: Schleicher, Frencs.

Bishop, K., & Curran, H. V. (1995). Psychopharmacological analysis of implicit and explicit memory: A study with lorazepam and the benzodiazepine antagonist, flumazenil. *Psychopharmacology, 121,* 267-278.

Black, J. B., & Bower, G. H. (1979). Episodes as chunks in narrative memory. *Journal of Verbal Learning and Verbal Behavior, 18,* 187-198.

Blackmer, E. R., & Mitton, J. L. (1991). Theories of monitoring and the timing of repairs in spontaneous speech. *Cognition, 39,* 173-194.

Blakemore, C., & Cooper, G. F. (1970). Development of the brain depends on the visual environment. *Nature, 228,* 477-478.

Blaney, P. H. (1986). Affect and memory: A review. *Psychological Bulletin, 99,* 229-246.

Bock, J. K. (1996). Language production: Methods and methodologies. *Psychonomic Bulletin & Review, 3,* 395-421.

Bock, J. K., & Garnsey, S. M. (1998). Language processing. In W. Bechtel & G. Graham (Eds.), *A companion to cognitive science* (pp. 226-234). Oxford, UK: Blackwell.

Bock, J. K., & Levelt, W. (1994). Language production: Grammatical encoding. In M. A. Gernsbacher (Ed.), *Handbook of psycholinguistics* (pp. 945-984). San Diego: Academic Press.

Boden, M. (1992). *The creative mind: Myths and mechanisms.* New York: Basic Books.

Bond, C. F., & Omar, A. S. (1990). Social anxiety, state dependence, and the next-in-line effect. *Journal of Experimental Social Psychology, 26,* 185-198.

Bourne, L. E., Jr. (1970). Knowing and using concepts. *Psychological Review, 77,* 546-556.

Bourne, L. E., Jr., Dominowski, R. L., Loftus, E. F., & Healy, A. F. (1986). *Cognitive processes* (2nd ed.). Englewood Cliffs, NJ: Prentice Hall.

Bourne, L. E., Jr., & Restle, F. (1959). A mathematical theory of concept identification. *Psychological Review, 66,* 278-296.

Bousfield, W. A. (1953). The occurrence of clustering in the recall of randomly arranged associates. *Journal of General Psychology, 49,* 229-240.

Bower, G. H. (1970). Analysis of a mnemonic device. *American Psychologist, 36,* 129-148.

Bower, G. H. (1972). Mental imagery and associative learning. In L. W. Gregg (Ed.), *Cognition in learning and memory* (pp. 51-88). New York: John Wiley.

Bower, G. H. (1981). Mood and memory. *American Psychologist, 36,* 129-148.

Bower, G. H., Black, J. B., & Turner, T. J. (1979). Scripts in memory for text. *Cognitive Psychology, 11,* 177-220.

Bower, G. H., & Hilgard, E. R. (1981). *Theories of learning* (5th ed.). Englewood Cliffs, NJ: Prentice Hall.

Boysen, S. T., & Capaldi, E. J. (Eds.). (1993). *The development of numerical competence: Animal and human models.* Hillsdale, NJ: Lawrence Erlbaum.

Bransford, J. D., & Franks, J. J. (1971). Abstraction of linguistic ideas. *Cognitive Psychology, 2,* 331-350.

Bransford, J. D., & Johnson, M. K. (1972). Contextual prerequisites for understanding: Some investigations of comprehension and recall. *Journal of Verbal Learning and Verbal Behavior, 11,* 717-726.

Brewer, W. F., & Treyens, J. C. (1981). Role of schemata in memory for places. *Cognitive Psychology, 13,* 207-230.

Broadbent, D. E. (1957). A mechanical model for human attention and immediate memory. *Psychological Review, 64,* 205-215.

Broadbent, D. E. (1958). *Perception and communication.* New York: Pergamon.

Broadbent, D. E. (1975). The magic number seven after fifteen years. In A. Kennedy & A. Wilkes (Eds.), *Studies in long-term memory* (pp. 3-18). London: Wiley.

Brody, N. (1996). Intelligence and public policy. *Psychology, Public Policy, & Law, 2,* 473-485.

Brooks, L. R. (1968). Spatial and verbal components of the act of recall. *Canadian Journal of Psychology, 22,* 349-368.

Brooks, L. R. (1978). Nonanalytic concept formation and memory for instances. In E. Rosch & B. B. Lloyd (Eds.), *Cognition and categorization* (pp. 169-211). Hillsdale, NJ: Lawrence Erlbaum.

Brown, A. S. (1991). A review of the tip-of-the-tongue experience. *Psychological Bulletin, 109,* 204-223.

Brown, J. A. (1958). Some tests of the decay theory of immediate memory. *Quarterly Journal of Experimental Psychology, 10,* 12-21.

Brown, R., & McNeill, D. (1966). The "tip-of-the tongue" phenomenon. *Journal of Verbal Learning and Verbal Behavior, 5,* 325-337.

Brown, R. W., & Kulik, J. (1977). Flashbulb memories. *Cognition, 5,* 73-99.

Brown, R. W., & Lenneberg, E. H. (1954). A study in language and cognition. *Journal of Abnormal and Social Psychology, 49,* 454-462.

Bruner, J. S. (1990). *Acts of meaning.* Cambridge, MA: Harvard University Press.

Bruner, J. S., Goodnow, J. J., & Austin, G. A. (1956). *A study of thinking.* New York: John Wiley.

Buckhout, R. (1974). Eyewitness testimony. *Scientific American, 231,* 23-31.

Buckner, R., Goodman, J., Burock, M., Rotte, M., Loutstaal, W., Schacter, D., Rosen, B., & Dale, A. (1998). Functional-anatomic correlates of object priming in humans revealed by rapid presentation event-related fMRI. *Neuron, 20,* 285-296.

Buckner, R. L. (1996). Beyond HERA: Contributions of specific prefrontal brain areas to long-term memory retrieval. *Psychonomic Bulletin & Review, 3,* 149-158.

Buckner, R. L., Koutstaal, W., Schacter, D. L., Dale, A. M., Rotte, M., & Rosen, B. R. (1998). Functional-anatomic study of episodic retrieval: Selective averaging of event-related fMRI trials to test the retrieval success hypothesis. *NeuroImage, 7,* 151-162.

Buckner, R. L., & Petersen, S. E. (2000). Neuroimaging of functional recovery. In H. S. Levin & J. Grafman (Eds.), *Cerebral organization of function after brain damage* (pp. 318-330). New York: Oxford University Press.

Busemeyer, J. R., Byun, E., Delosh, E. L., & McDaniel, M. A. (1997). Learning functional relations based on experience with input-output pairs by humans and artificial neural networks. In K. Lamberts & D. R. Shanks (Eds.), *Knowledge, concepts, and categories: Studies in cognition* (pp. 408-437). Cambridge, MA: MIT Press.

Campbell, F. A., & Ramey, C. T. (1994). Effects of early intervention on intellectual and academic achievement: A follow-up of children from low income families. *Child Development, 65,* 684-698.

Cantor, N., Mischel, W., & Schwartz, J. C. (1982). A prototype analysis of psychological situations. *Cognitive Psychology, 14,* 45-77.

Caramazza, A. (1991). *Issues in reading, writing, and speaking: A neuropsychological perspective.* Dordrecht, Netherlands: Kluwer.

Caramazza, A. (1992). Is cognitive neuropsychology possible? *Journal of Cognitive Neuroscience, 4,* 80-95.

Carey, S. (1978). The child as word learner. In M. Halle, J. Bresnan, & G. Miller (Eds.), *Linguistic theory and psychological reality* (pp. 264-293). Cambridge, MA: MIT Press.

Cattell, R. B. (1963). Theory of fluid and crystallized intelligence: A critical experiment. *Journal of Educational Psychology, 54,* 1-22.

Cavanagh, J. P. (1972). Relation between the immediate memory span and the memory search rate. *Psychological Review, 79,* 525-530.

Ceci, S. J. (1991). How much does schooling influence general intelligence and its cognitive components? A reassessment of the evidence. *Developmental Psychology, 27,* 703-722.

Ceci, S. J., & Bruck, M. (1993). Suggestibility of the child witness: A historical review and synthesis. *Psychological Bulletin, 113,* 403-439.

Ceci, S. J., & Bruck, M. (1995). *Jeopardy in the coutroom: A scientific analysis of children's testimony.* Washington, DC: American Psychological Association.

Ceci, S. J., Crossman, A. M., Gilstrap, L. L., & Scullin, M. H. (1998). Social and cognitive factors in children's testimony. In C. P. Thompson, D. J. Hermann, D. J. Read, D. Bruce, D. G. Payne, & M. P. Toglia (Eds.), *Eyewitness memory: Theoretical and applied perspectives* (pp. 15-30). Mahwah, NJ: Lawrence Erlbaum.

Ceci, S. J., Leichtman, M., Putnick, M., & Nightingale, N. (1993). Age differences in suggestibility. In D. Cicchetti & S. Toth (Eds.), *Child abuse, child development, and social policy* (pp. 117-137). Norwood, NJ: Ablex.

Ceci, S. J., & Liker, J. K. (1986). A day at the races: A study of IQ, expertise, and cognitive complexity. *Journal of Experimental Psychology: General, 115,* 255-266.

Ceraso, J., & Provitera, A. (1971). Sources of error in syllogistic reasoning. *Cognitive Psychology, 2,* 400-410.

Chance, J. E., & Goldstein, A. G. (1981). Depth of processing in response to own and other-race faces. *Personality and Social Psychology Bulletin, 7,* 475-480.

Chang, T. M. (1986). Semantic memory: Facts and models. *Psychological Bulletin, 99,* 199-220.

Chase, W. G., & Ericsson, K. A. (1981). Skilled memory. In J. R. Anderson (Ed.), *Cognitive skills and their acquisition* (pp. 141-189). Hillsdale, NJ: Lawrence Erlbaum.

Chase, W. G., & Ericsson, K. A. (1982). Skill and working memory. In G. H. Bower (Ed.), *The psychology of learning and motivation* (pp. 1-58). New York: Academic Press.

Chase, W. G., & Simon, H. A. (1973). Perception in chess. *Cognitive Psychology, 4,* 55-81.

Cheesman, I., & Merikle, P. M. (1984). Priming with and without awareness. *Perception and Psychophysics, 36,* 387-395.

Cheng, P. W., & Holyoak, K. J. (1985). Pragmatic reasoning schemas. *Cognitive Psychology, 17,* 391-416.

Cheng, P. W., Holyoak, K. J., Nisbett, R. E., & Oliver, L. M. (1986). Pragmatic versus syntactic approaches to training deductive reasoning. *Cognitive Psychology, 18,* 293-328.

Cherry, C. (1953). Some experiments on the recognition of speech with one and with two ears. *Journal of the Acoustical Society of America, 25,* 975-979.

Chi, M. T. H. (1978). Knowledge structures and memory development. In R. S. Siegler (Ed.), *Children's thinking: What develops?* (pp. 73-96). Hillsdale, NJ: Lawrence Erlbaum.

Chi, M. T. H., Feltovich, P. J., & Glaser, R. (1981). Categorization and representation of physics problems by experts and novices. *Cognitive Science, 5,* 121-152.

Chomsky, N. (1965). *Aspects of the theory of syntax.* Cambridge, MA: MIT Press.

Chomsky, N. (1986). *Knowledge of language: Its nature, origin, and use.* New York: Praeger.

Chorney, M. J., Chorney, K., Seese, N., Owen, M. J., Daniels, J., McGuffin, P., Thompson, L. A., Detterman, D. K., Benbow, C., Lubinski, D., Eley, T., & Plomin, R. (1998). A quantitative trait locus associated with cognitive ability in children. *Psychological Science, 9,* 159-166.

Christianson, S. A. (1992). Emotional stress and eyewitness memory: A critical review. *Psychological Bulletin, 112,* 284-309.

Cirilo, R. K. (1981). Referential coherence and text structure in story comprehension. *Journal of Verbal Learning and Verbal Behavior, 20,* 358-367.

Cirilo, R. K., & Foss, D. J. (1980). Text structure and reading time for sentences. *Journal of Verbal Learning and Verbal Behavior, 19,* 96-109.

Clark, H. H. (1977). Inferences in comprehension. In D. LaBerge & S. J. Samuels (Eds.), *Basic processes in reading: Perception and comprehension* (pp. 243-263). Hillsdale, NJ: Lawrence Erlbaum.

Clark, H. H., & Chase, W. G. (1972). On the process of comparing sentences against pictures. *Cognitive Psychology, 3,* 472-517.

Clark, H. H., & Clark, E. V. (1977). *Psychology and language.* New York: Harcourt Brace Jovanovich.

Cohen, J. (1969). *Statistical power and analysis for the behavioral sciences.* New York: Academic Press.

Cohen, J. D., Barch, D. M., Carter, C., & Servan-Schreiber, D. (1999). Context-processing deficits in schizophrenia: Converging evidence from three theoretically motivated cognitive tasks. *Journal of Abnormal Psychology, 108,* 120-133.

Cole, M., & Scribner, S. (1974). *Culture and thought: A psychological introduction.* New York: John Wiley.

Cole, R. A., & Jakimik, J. (1980). A model of speech perception. In R. A. Cole (Ed.), *Perception and production of fluent speech* (pp. 133-163). Hillsdale, NJ: Lawrence Erlbaum.

Collins, A. M., & Loftus, E. F. (1975). A spreading activation theory of semantic processing. *Psychological Review, 82,* 85-88.

Collins, A. M., & Quillian, M. R. (1969). Retrieval time from semantic memory. *Journal of Verbal Learning and Verbal Behavior, 8,* 240-247.

Coltheart, M., Curtis, P., Atkins, P., & Haller, M. (1993). Models of reading aloud: Dual-route and parallel-distributed processing approaches. *Psychological Review, 100,* 589-608.

Conrad, C. (1972). Cognitive economy in semantic memory. *Journal of Experimental Psychology, 92,* 49-54.

Conrad, R. (1964). Acoustic confusions in immediate memory. *British Journal of Psychology, 55,* 77-84.

Conway, M. A. (1992). A structural model of autobiographical memory. In M. A. Conway, D. C. Rubin, H. Spinnler, & W. A. Wagenaar (Eds.), *Theoretical perspectives on autobiographical memory* (pp. 167-193). Dordrecht, Netherlands: Kluwer.

Conway, M. A., Anderson, S. J., Larsen, S. F., Donnelly, C. M., McDaniel, M. A., McClelland, A. G. R., Rawles, R. E., & Logic, R. H. (1994). The formation of flashbulb memories. *Memory & Cognition, 22,* 326-343.

Conway, M. A., Cohen, G., & Stanhope, N. (1991). On the very long-term retention of knowledge acquired through formal education: Twelve years of cognitive psychology. *Journal of Experimental Psychology: General, 120,* 395-409.

Cooke, N. J., & Breedin, S. D. (1994). Constructing naive theories of motion on the fly. *Memory & Cognition, 22,* 474-494.

Corballis, M. C. (1989). Laterality and human evolution. *Psychological Review, 96,* 492-505.

Coren, S. (1984). Subliminal perception. In R. J. Corsini (Ed.), *Encyclopedia of psychology* (Vol. 3, p. 382). New York: John Wiley.

Cosmides, L., & Tooby, J. (1992). Cognitive adaptations for social exchange. In J. H. Barkow, L. Cosmides, & J. Tooby (Eds.), *The adapted mind: Evolutionary psychology and the generation of culture* (pp. 163-228). New York: Oxford University Press.

Cowan, N. (1988). Evolving conceptions of memory storage, selective attention, and their mutual constraints within the human information-processing system. *Psychological Bulletin, 104,* 163-191.

Cowan, N. (2000). The magical number 4 in short-term memory: Reconsideration of mental storage capacity. *Behavioral and Brain Sciences, 24,* 87-185.

Craik, F. I. M., Govoni, R., Naveh-Benjamin, M., & Anderson, N. C. (1996). The effects of divided attention on encoding and retrieval processes in human memory. *Journal of Experimental Psychology: General, 125,* 159-180.

Craik, F. I. M., & Lockhart, R. S. (1972). Levels of processing: A framework for memory research. *Journal of Verbal Learning and Verbal Behavior, 11,* 671-684.

Craik, F. I. M., & Tulving, E. (1975). Depth of processing and the retention of words in episodic memory. *Journal of Experimental Psychology: General, 104,* 268-294.

Craik, F. I. M., & Watkins, M. J. (1973). The role of rehearsal in short-term memory. *Journal of Verbal Learning and Verbal Behavior, 12,* 599-607.

Crick, F. H. C. (1994). *The astonishing hypothesis: The scientific search for the soul.* New York: Scribner.

Crowder, R. G. (1982). Decay of auditory memory in vowel discrimination. *Journal of Experimental Psychology: Learning, Memory, and Cognition, 8,* 153-162.

Crowder, R. G. (1993). Short-term memory: Where do we stand? *Memory & Cognition, 21,* 142-146.

Croyle, R. T., Loftus, E. G., Klinger, M. R., & Smith, K. D. (1992). Reducing errors in health-related memory: Progress and prospects. In J. R. Schement & B. D. Ruben (Eds.), *Information and behavior,* Vol. 4: *Between communication and information* (pp. 255-268). New Brunswick, NJ: Transaction Publishers.

Curran, H. V. (2000). Psychopharmacological perspectives on memory. In E. Tulving & F. I. M. Craik (Eds.), *The Oxford handbook of memory* (pp. 539-554) New York: Oxford University Press.

Curran, H. V., & Hildebrandt, M. (in press). Dissociative effects of alcohol on recollective experience. *Consciousness & Cognition.*

Curran, T., & Keele, S. W. (1993). Attentional and nonattentional forms of sequence learning. *Journal of Experimental Psychology: Learning, Memory, and Cognition, 19,* 189-202.

Curran, T., Schacter, D. L., Johnson, M. K., & Spinks, R. (2001). Brain potentials reflect behavioral differences in true and false recognition. *Journal of Cognitive Neuroscience, 13,* 201-216.

Curtiss, S. (1977). *Genie: A psycholinguistic study of a modern day "wild child."* New York: Academic Press.

Damasio, A. R. (1999). *The feeling of what happens: Body and emotion in the making of consciousness.* Orlando, FL: Harcourt Brace.

Damasio, H., Grabowski, T. J., Tranel, D., Hichwa, R. D., & Damasio, A. R. (1996). A neural basis for lexical retrieval. *Nature, 380,* 499-505.

Daneman, M., & Carpenter, P. A. (1980). Individual differences in working memory and reading. *Journal of Verbal Learning and Verbal Behavior, 18,* 450-466.

Darley, C. F., & Glass, A. L. (1975). Effects of rehearsal and serial list position on recall. *Journal of Experimental Psychology: Learning, Memory, and Cognition, 104,* 453-458.

Darwin, C. J., Turvey, M. T., & Crowder, R. G. (1972). An auditory analogue of the Sperling partial report procedure: Evidence for brief auditory storage. *Cognitive Psychology, 3,* 255-267.

David, A. S. (1993). Spatial and selective attention in the cerebral hemispheres in depression, mania, and schizophrenia. *Brain & Cognition, 23,* 166-180.

Deacon, T. W. (1997). *The symbolic species: The co-evolution of language and the brain.* New York: Norton.

Deese, J. (1959). On the prediction of occurrence of particular verbal intrusions in immediate recall. *Journal of Experimental Psychology, 58,* 17-22.

de Groot, A. D. (1965). *Thought and choice in chess.* The Hague, Netherlands: Mouton.

Dell, G. S. (1988). The retrieval of phonological forms in production: Tests of predictions from a connectionist model. *Journal of Memory and Language, 27,* 124-142.

Dell, G. S., Schwartz, M. F., Marin, N., Saffran, E. M., & Gagnon, D. A. (1997). Lexical access in normal and aphasic speech. *Psychological Review, 104,* 801-838.

Della Sala, S., Gray, C., Baddeley, A. D., Allamano, N., & Wilson, L. (2000). A means of unwelding visuo-spatial memory. *Neuropsychologia, 20,* 626-646.

Dennett, D. C. (1991). *Consciousness explained.* Boston: Little, Brown.

Deutsch, J. A., & Deutsch, D. (1963). Attention: Some theoretical considerations. *Psychological Review, 70,* 80-90.

de Villiers, J. G., & de Villiers, P. A. (1978). *Language acquisition.* Cambridge, MA: Harvard University Press.

Dickstein, L. S. (1978). Error processes in syllogistic reasoning. *Memory & Cognition, 6,* 537-543.

Dienes, A., & Berry, D. (1997). Implicit learning: Below the subjective threshold. *Psychonomic Bulletin & Review, 4,* 3-23.

Dominowski, R. L. (1977). Reasoning. *Interamerican Journal of Psychology, 11,* 68-77.

Dooling, D. J., & Christiansen, R. E. (1977). Episodic and semantic aspects of memory for prose. *Journal of Experimental Psychology: Human Learning and Memory, 3,* 428-436.

Dopkins, S., Kovner, R., & Goldmeier, E. (1994). Frequency judgments for semantic categories in amnesics and normal controls. *Cortex, 30,* 127-134.

Dronkers, N. F., Redfern, B. B., & Knight, R. T. (2000). The neural architecture of language disorders. In M. S. Gazzaniga (Ed.), *The new cognitive neurosciences* (pp. 949-958). Cambridge, MA: MIT Press.

Dulany, D. E., Carlson, R. A., & Dewey, G. I. (1984). A case of syntactical learning and judgement: How conscious and how abstract? *Journal of Experimental Psychology: General, 113,* 541-555.

Duncan, J., Burgess, P., & Emslie, H. (1995). Fluid intelligence after frontal lobe lesions. *Neuropsychologia, 33,* 261-268.

Duncan, J., Seitz, R. J., Kolodny, J., Bor, D., Herzog, H., Ahmed, A., Newell, F., & Emslie, H. (2000). A neural basis for general intelligence. *Science, 289,* 457-460.

Duncker, K. (1945). On problem-solving. *Psychological Monographs, 58* (Whole No. 270).

D'Ydewalle, G., Delhaye, P., & Goessens, L. (1985). Structural, semantic, and self-reference processing of pictorial advertisements. *Human Learning, 4,* 29-38.

Ebbinghaus, H. (1885). *Uber das Gedächtnis: Intersuchungen zur experimentellen psychologie.* Leipzig, Germany: Duncker & Humboldt. (Translated by H. A. Ruger & C. D. Bussenius, 1913, and reissued by Dover, 1964)

Eccles, J. C. (Ed.). (1966). *Brain and conscious experience.* New York: Springer.

Eccles, J. C. (1994). *How the self controls the brain.* Berlin: Springer-Verlag.

Eich, J. E. (1980). The cue-dependent nature of state-dependent retrieval. *Memory & Cognition, 8,* 157-173.

Eich, J. E. (1989). Theoretical issues in state-dependent memory. In H. L. Roediger, III, & F. I. M. Craik (Eds.), *Varieties of memory and consciousness: Essays in honour of Endel Tulving* (pp. 331-354). Hillsdale, NJ: Lawrence Erlbaum.

Eimas, P. D. (1974). Auditory and linguistic processing of cues for place of articulation by infants. *Perception and Psychophysics, 16,* 531-521.

Eimas, P. D., & Miller, J. L. (1992). Organization in the perception of speech by young infants. *Psychological Science, 3,* 340-344.

Eimas, P. D., Miller, J. L., & Jusczyk, P. W. (1987). On infant speech perception and the acquisition of language. In S. Harnad (Ed.), *Categorical perception* (pp. 161-195). New York: Cambridge University Press.

Eimas, P. D., & Quinn, P. C. (1994). Studies on the formation of perceptually based basic-level categories in young infants. *Child Development, 65,* 903-917.

Ellis, A. W. (Ed.). (1982). *Normality and pathology in cognitive functions.* New York: Academic Press.

Elman, J. L., Bates, E. A., Johnson, M. H., Karmiloff-Smith, A., Parisi, D., & Plunkett, K. (1996). *Rethinking innateness: A connectionist perspective on development.* Cambridge, MA: MIT Press.

Engle, R. W., Cantor, J., & Carullo, J. J. (1992). Individual differences in working memory and comprehension: A test of four hypotheses. *Journal of Experimental Psychology: Learning, Memory, and Cognition, 18,* 972-992.

Engle, R. W., Tuholski, S. W., Laughlin, J. E., & Conway, A. R. A. (1999). Working memory, short-term memory, and general fluid intelligence: A latent variable approach. *Journal of Experimental Psychology: General, 12,* 309-331.

Ericsson, K. A., & Chase, W. G. (1982). Exceptional memory. *American Scientist, 70,* 607-615.

Ericsson, K. A., Krampé, R. T., & Tesch-Römer, C. (1993). The role of deliberate practice in the acquisition of expert performance. *Psychological Review, 100,* 363-406.

Ericsson, K. A., & Simon, H. A. (1980). Verbal reports as data. *Psychological Review, 87,* 215-251.

Ernst, G. W., & Newell, A. (1969). *GPS: A case study in generality and problem solving.* Orlando, FL: Academic Press.

Estes, W. K. (1976). The cognitive side of probability learning. *Psychological Review, 83,* 37-64.

Estes, W. K. (1988). Human learning and memory. In R. C. Atkinson, R. J. Herrnstein, G. Lindsay, & R. D. Luce (Eds.), *Stevens' handbook of experimental psychology* (2nd ed., Vol. 2, pp. 351-415). New York: John Wiley.

Evans, J. St. B. T., Barston, J. L., & Pollard, P. (1983). On the conflict between logic and belief in syllogistic reasoning. *Memory & Cognition, 11,* 295-306.

Evans, J. St. B. T., & Over, D. E. (1996). *Rationality and reasoning.* Hove, UK: Psychology Press.

Evans, L. (1991). *Traffic safety and the driver.* New York: Van Nostrand Reinhold.

Eysenck, H. J. (1973). *The inequality of man.* London: Temple Smith.

Eysenck, H. J. (1979). *The structure and measurement of intelligence.* New York: Springer.

Eysenck, H. J. (1986). Inspection time and intelligence: A historical introduction. *Personality and Individual Differences, 7,* 603-607.

Eysenck, II. J. (1987). Speed of information processing, reaction time, and the theory of intelligence. In P. A. Vernon (Ed.), *Speed of information processing and intelligence* (pp. 21-67). Norwood, NJ: Ablex.

Eysenck, H. J., & Kamin, L. (1981). *The intelligence controversy: H. J. Eysenck vs. Leon Kamin.* New York: John Wiley.

Fabbro, F. (1999). *The neurolinguistics of bilingualism: An introduction.* Hove, UK: Psychology Press.

Farah, M. J. (1988). Is visual imagery really visual? Overlooked evidence from neuropsychology. *Psychological Review, 95,* 307-317.

Farah, M. J. (1990). *Visual agnosia: Disorders of object recognition and what they tell us about normal vision.* Cambridge, MA: MIT Press.

Farah, M. J. (1998). What is "special" about face perception? *Psychological Review, 105,* 482-498.

Farah, M. J., Peronnet, F., Gonon, M. A., & Girard, M. H. (1988). Electrophysiological evidence for a shared representational medium for visual images and visual percepts. *Journal of Experimental Psychology: General, 117,* 248-257.

Fayol, M. (1998). From on-line management problems to strategies in written composition. In M. Torrance & G. C. Jeffery (Eds.), *The cognitive demands of writing: Processing capacity and working memory in text production* (pp. 13-23). Amsterdam: Amsterdam University Press.

Feingold, A. (1988). Cognitive gender differences are disappearing. *American Psychologist, 43,* 95-103.

Feingold, A. (1992). Sex differences in variability in intellectual abilities: A new look at an old controversy. *Review of Educational Research, 62,* 61-84.

Fendrich, D. W., Healy, A. F., & Bourne, L. E. (1991). Long-term repetition effects for motoric and perceptual procedures. *Journal of Experimental Psychology: Learning, Memory, and Cognition, 17,* 137-151.

Fink, G. R., Markowitsch, H. J., Reinkemeier, M., Bruckbauer, J., Kessler, J., & Heiss, W. D. (1996). Cerebral representation of one's own past: Neural networks involved in autobiographical memory. *Journal of Neuroscience, 16,* 4275-4282.

Finke, R. A. (1989). *Principles of mental imagery.* Cambridge, MA: MIT Press.

Fischhoff, B. (1975). Hindsight:foresight: The effect of outcome knowledge on judgment under uncertainty. *Journal of Experimental Psychology: Human Perception and Performance, 1,* 288-299.

Fischhoff, B. (1977). Perceived informativeness of facts. *Journal of Experimental Psychology: Human Perception and Performance, 3,* 349-358.

Fischler, I. (1998). Attention and language. In R. Parasuraman (Ed.), *The attentive brain* (pp. 381-400). Cambridge, MA: MIT Press.

Fisher, R. P., & Geiselman, R. E. (1992). *Memory-enhancing techniques for investigative interviewing: The Cognitive Interview.* Springfield, IL: Charles C Thomas.

Fitts, P. M. (1964). Perceptual-motor skill learning. In A. W. Melton (Ed.), *Categories of human learning* (pp. 243–285). New York: Academic Press.

Fivush, R., Gray, J. T., & Fromhoff, F. A. (1987). Two-year-olds talk about the past. *Cognitive Development, 2,* 393-409.

Flavell, J. H., Miller, P. H., & Miller, S. A. (1993). *Cognitive development* (2nd ed.). Englewood Cliffs, NJ: Prentice Hall.

Flynn, J. R. (1987). Massive IQ gains in 14 countries: What IQ tests really measure. *Psychological Bulletin, 101,* 171-191.

Flynn, J. R. (1998). IQ gains over time: Toward finding the causes. In U. Neisser (Ed.), *The rising curve* (pp. 25-66). Washington, DC: American Psychological Association.

Fodor, J. A. (1983). *The modularity of mind.* Cambridge, MA: MIT Press.

Forster, K. I., & Bednall, E. S. (1976). Terminating and exhaustive search in lexical access. *Memory & Cognition, 4,* 53-61.

Foss, D. J. (1988). Experimental psycholinguistics. *Annual Review of Psychology, 39,* 301-348.

Foss, D. J., & Hakes, D. T. (1978). *Psycholinguistics: An introduction to the psychology of language.* Englewood Cliffs, NJ: Prentice Hall.

Foulke, E., & Sticht, T. (1969). Review of research on the intelligibility and comprehension of accelerated speech. *Psychological Bulletin, 72,* 50-62.

Freedman, S. W. (1983). Student characteristics and essay test writing performance. *Research in the Teaching of College English, 17,* 313-325.

Freud, S. (1953). The interpretation of dreams. In J. Strachey (Ed.), *The standard edition of the complete psychological works of Sigmund Freud* (Vols. 4-5). London: Hogarth. (Original work published 1900)

Friedman, A. (1979). Framing pictures: The role of knowledge in automatized encoding and memory for gist. *Journal of Experimental Psychology: General, 108,* 316-355.

Fromkin, V. A. (Ed.). (1973). *Speech errors as linguistic evidence.* The Hague, Netherlands: Mouton.

Gabrieli, J. D. E. (1998). Cognitive neuroscience of human memory. *Annual Review of Psychology, 49,* 87-115.

Galea, L. A. M., & Kimura, D. (1993). Sex differences in route learning. *Personality and Individual Differences, 14,* 53-65.

Gallahue, D. L. (1989). *Understanding motor development: Infants, children, adolescents* (2nd ed.). Indianapolis, IN: Benchmark Press.

Galton, F. (1892). *Hereditary genius: An enquiry into its laws and consequences.* London: Macmillan.

Gardiner, J. M., & Richardson-Klavehn, A. (2000). Remembering and knowing. In E. Tulving & F. I. M. Craik (Eds.), *The Oxford handbook of memory* (pp. 229-244). New York: Oxford University Press.

Gardner, B. T., & Gardner, R. A. (1975). Evidence for sentence constituents in the early utterances of child and chimpanzee. *Journal of Experimental Psychology: General, 104,* 244-267.

Gardner, H. (1983). *Frames of mind: The theory of multiple intelligences.* New York: Basic Books.

Gardner, R. A., & Gardner, B. T. (1969). Teaching sign language to a chimpanzee. *Science, 165,* 644-672.

Garrett, M., Bever, T., & Fodor, J. (1966). The active use of grammar in speech perception. *Perception & Psychophysics, 1,* 30-32.

Gazzaniga, M. S. (1970). *The bisected brain.* New York: Appleton-Century-Crofts.

Gazzaniga, M. S. (1995). Principles of human brain organization derived from split-brain studies. *Neuron, 14,* 217-228.

Gazzaniga, M. S., Bogen, J. E., & Sperry, R. W. (1965). Observations on visual perception after disconnection of the cerebral hemispheres on man. *Brain, 88,* 221-236.

Gazzaniga, M. S., Ivry, R. B., & Mangun, G. R. (1998). *Cognitive neuroscience: The biology of mind.* New York: Norton.

Geary, D. C. (1998). *Male, female: The evolution of human sex differences.* Washington, DC: American Psychological Association.

Geary, D. C., Hamson, C. O., Chen, G. P., Liu, F., Hoard, M. K., & Salthouse, T. A. (1997). Computational and reasoning abilities in arithmetic: Cross-generational change in China and the United States. *Psychonomic Bulletin & Review, 4,* 425-430.

Geis, M. L., & Zwicky, A. M. (1971). On invited inferences. *Linguistic Inquiry, 2,* 561-566.

Geiselman, R. E., Fisher, R. P., MacKinnon, D. P., & Holland, H. L. (1986). Enhancement of eyewitness memory with the cognitive interview. *American Journal of Psychology, 99,* 385-401.

Gelman, S. A. (1988). The development of induction within natural kind and artifact categories. *Cognitive Psychology, 20,* 65-95.

Gentner, D., & Stevens, A. L. (1983). *Mental models.* Hillsdale, NJ: Lawrence Erlbaum.

Gerken, L. A. (1994). A metrical template account of children's weak syllable omissions from multisyllable words. *Journal of Child Language, 21,* 565-584.

Gernsbacher, M. A. (1989). Mechanisms that improve referential access. *Cognition, 32,* 99-156.

Gernsbacher, M. A. (1990). *Language comprehension as structure building.* Hillsdale, NJ: Lawrence Erlbaum.

Gernsbacher, M. A., & Faust, M. (1991). The role of suppression in sentence comprehension. In G. B. Simpson (Ed.), *Understanding word and sentence* (Advances in Psychology, No. 77, pp. 97-128). Amsterdam: North-Holland.

Gibson, E. J. (1969). *Principles of perceptual learning and development.* New York: Prentice Hall.

Gick, M. L., & Holyoak, K. J. (1980). Analogical problem solving. *Cognitive Psychology, 12,* 306-355.

Gigerenzer, G., Hoffrage, U., & Kleinbölting, H. (1991). Probabilistic mental models: A Brunswikean theory of confidence. *Psychological Review, 98,* 506-528.

Gilhooly, J. J. (1982). *Thinking: Directed, undirected, and creative.* New York: Academic Press.

Glanzer, M., & Cunitz, A. R. (1966). Two storage mechanisms in free recall. *Journal of Verbal Learning and Verbal Behavior, 5,* 351-360.

Glaser, R. (1984). Education and thinking: The role of knowledge. *American Psychologist, 39,* 93-104.

Glaser, R., & Chi, M. T. H. (1988). Overview. In M. T. H. Chi, R. Glaser, & M. J. Farr (Eds.), *The nature of expertise* (pp. xv-xxxvi). Hillsdale, NJ: Lawrence Erlbaum.

Glass, A. L., & Holyoak, K. J. (1975). Alternative concepts of semantic memory. *Cognition, 3,* 313-339.

Gluck, M. A., & Bower, G. H. (1988). From conditioning to category learning: An adaptive network model. *Journal of Experimental Psychology: General, 8,* 37-50.

Glucksberg, S., & Danks, J. H. (1975). *Experimental psycholinguistics: An introduction.* Hillsdale, NJ: Lawrence Erlbaum.

Glucksberg, S., Gildea, P., & Bookin, H. B. (1982). On understanding nonliteral speech: Can people ignore metaphors? *Journal of Verbal Learning and Verbal Behavior, 21,* 85-98.

Godden, D. R., & Baddeley, A. D. (1975). Context-dependent memory in two natural environments: On land and underwater. *British Journal of Psychology, 66,* 325-331.

Goldin-Meadow, S., McNeill, D., & Singleton, J. (1996). Silence is liberating: Removing the handcuffs on grammatical expression in the manual modality. *Psychological Review, 103,* 34-55.

Goldin-Meadow, S., & Mylander, C. (1990). Beyond the input given: The child's role in the acquisition of language. *Language, 66,* 323-355.

Goldman, D., & Homa, D. (1977). Integrative and metric properties of abstracted information as a function of category discriminability, instance variability, and experience. *Journal of Experimental Psychology: Human Learning and Memory, 3,* 375-385.

Goldman-Rakic, P. S. (1995). Cellular basis of working memory. *Neuron, 14,* 477-485.

Goldsmith, T. H. (1991). *The biological roots of human nature: Forging links between evolution and behavior.* New York: Oxford University Press.

Goodglass, H. (1993). *Understanding aphasia.* San Diego: Academic Press.

Goodman, G., & Aman, C. (1990). Children's use of anatomically detailed dolls to recount an event. *Child Development, 61,* 1859-1871.

Goodman, R., & Caramazza, A. (1986). Aspects of the spelling process: Evidence from a case of acquired dysgraphia. *Language and Cognitive Processes, 1,* 263-296.

Gould, S. (1981). *The mismeasure of man.* New York: Norton.

Gould, S. J., & Lewontin, R. C. (1979). The spandrels of San Marco and the Panglossian paradigm: A critique of the adaptionist programme. *Proceedings of the Royal Society of London, 205,* 281-288.

Graesser, A. C. (1981). *Prose comprehension beyond the word.* New York: Springer-Verlag.

Graesser, A. C., Hoffman, N., & Clark, L. F. (1980). Structural components of reading time. *Journal of Verbal Learning and Verbal Behavior, 19,* 135-151.

Graf, P., Squire, L. R., & Mandler, G. (1984). The information that amnesic patients do not forget. *Journal of Experimental Psychology: Learning, Memory, and Cognition, 10,* 164-178.

Greenberg, J. H. (1966). *Language universals.* The Hague, Netherlands: Mouton.

Greene, R. L. (1986). Sources of recency effects in free recall. *Psychological Bulletin, 99,* 221-228.

Greene, R. L. (1987). Effects of maintenance rehearsal on human memory. *Psychological Bulletin, 102,* 403-413.

Greene, R. L. (1992). Unitary and modular approaches to human memory. In D. K. Detterman (Ed.), *Is mind modular or unitary: Current topics in human intelligence* (Vol. 2, pp. 229-250). Norwood, NJ: Ablex.

Grice, H. P. (1975). Logic and conversation. In P. Cole & J. L. Morgan (Eds.), *Syntax and semantics,* Vol. 3: *Speech acts* (pp. 41-48). New York: Seminar Press.

Griffin, D. R. (1984). *Animal thinking.* Cambridge, MA: Harvard University Press.

Griggs, R. A., & Cox, J. R. (1982). The elusive thematic-materials effect in Wason's selection task. *British Journal of Psychology, 73,* 407-420.

Halliday, M. A. K., & Hasan, R. (1976). *Cohesion in English.* London: Longman.

Hart, B., & Risley, T. R. (1995). *Meaningful differences in the everyday experience of young American children.* Baltimore, MD: Paul H. Brookes.

Hasher, L., & Zacks, R. T. (1979). Automatic and effortful processes in memory. *Journal of Experimental Psychology: General, 108,* 356-388.

Hasher, L., & Zacks, R. T. (1984). Automatic processing of fundamental information: The case of frequency of occurrence. *American Psychologist, 39,* 1372-1388.

Hashtroudi, S., Parker, E. S., DeLisi, L. E., Wyatt, R. J., & Mutter, S. A. (1984). Intact retention in acute alcohol amnesia. *Journal of Experimental Psychology: Learning, Memory, and Cognition, 10,* 156-163.

Haviland, S. E., & Clark, H. H. (1974). What's new? Acquiring new information as a process in comprehension. *Journal of Verbal Learning and Verbal Behavior, 13,* 512-521.

Haxby, J. V., Clark, V. P., & Courtney, S. M. (1997). Distributed hierarchical neural systems for visual memory in the human cortex. In B. Hyman, C. Duyckaerts, & Y. Christen (Eds.), *Connections, cognition, and Alzheimer's disease* (pp. 167-180). New York: Springer.

Hayes, J. R. (1981). *The complete problem solver.* Philadelphia: Franklin Institute.

Hayes, J. R. (1989). *The complete problem solver* (2nd ed.). Hillsdale, NJ: Lawrence Erlbaum.

Hayes, J. R., & Flower, L. S. (1980). Identifying the organization of writing processes. In L. W. Gregg & E. R. Steinberg (Eds.), *Cognitive processes in writing* (pp. 3-30). Hillsdale, NJ: Lawrence Erlbaum.

Hayes, N. A., & Broadbent, D. E. (1988). Two modes of learning for interactive tasks. *Cognition, 28,* 249-276.

Hayes-Roth, B., & Hayes-Roth, F. (1977). Concept learning and the recognition and classification of exemplars. *Journal of Verbal Learning and Verbal Behavior, 16,* 321-338.

Healy, A. F., & Bourne, L. E., Jr. (Eds.). (1995). *Learning and memory of knowledge and skills: Durability and specificity.* Thousand Oaks, CA: Sage.

Healy, A. F., & McNamara, D. S. (1996). Verbal learning and memory: Does the modal model still work? *Annual Review of Psychology, 47,* 143-172.

Hebb, D. O. (1949). *The organization of behavior: A neuropsychological theory.* New York: John Wiley.

Heider, E. R. (1972). Universals in color naming and memory. *Journal of Experimental Psychology, 93,* 10-20.

Hell, W., Gigerenzer, G., Gauggel, S., Mall, M., & Muller, M. (1988). Hindsight bias: An interaction of automatic and motivational factors? *Memory & Cognition, 16,* 533-538.

Hendrickson, D. E. (1982). The biological basis of intelligence. In J. J. Eysenck (Ed.), *A model for intelligence* (pp. 151-228). New York: Springer-Verlag.

Henle, M. (1962). On the relation between logic and thinking. *Psychological Review, 69,* 366-378.

Hilgard, E. R. (1980). Consciousness in contemporary psychology. *Annual Review of Psychology, 31,* 1-26.

Hilgard, E. R. (1986). *Divided consciousness: Multiple controls in human thought and action.* New York: John Wiley.

Hinton, G. E., McClelland, J. L., & Rumelhart, D. E. (1986). Distributed representations. In D. E. Rumelhart & J. L. McClelland (Eds.), *Parallel distributed processing.* Cambridge, MA: MIT Press.

Hintzman, D. L. (1986). "Schema abstraction" in a multiple-trace memory model. *Psychological Review, 93,* 411-428.

Hintzman, S. L. (1990). Human learning and memory: Connections and dissociations. *Annual Review of Psychology, 41,* 109-139.

Hoch, S. J., & Lowenstein, G. F. (1989). Outcome feedback: Hindsight and information. *Journal of Experimental Psychology: Learning, Memory, and Cognition, 15,* 605-619.

Holender, D. (1986). Semantic activation without conscious identification in dichotic listening, parafoveal vision, and visual masking: A survey and appraisal. *Behavioral and Brain Sciences, 9,* 1-23.

Homa, D., Sterling, S., & Trepel, L. (1981). Limitations of exemplar-based generalization and the abstraction of categorical information. *Journal of Experimental Psychology: Human Learning and Memory, 7,* 418-439.

Howe, M. L., & Courage, M. L. (1993). On resolving the enigma of infantile amnesia. *Psychological Bulletin, 113,* 305-326.

Hubel, D. H., & Wiesel, T. N. (1959). Receptive fields of single neurones in the cat's striate cortex. *Journal of Physiology, 148,* 574-591.

Hubel, D. H., & Wiesel, T. N. (1963). Receptive fields of cells in the striate cortex of very young, visually inexperienced kittens. *Journal of Neurophysiology, 26,* 994-1002.

Hull, C. L. (1920). Quantitative aspects of the evolution of concepts. *Psychological Monographs, 28*(Whole No. 23).

Hummel, J. E., & Biederman, I. (1992). Dynamic binding in a neural network for shape recognition. *Psychological Review, 99,* 480-517.

Hunt, E. B. (1989). Cognitive science: Definition, status, and questions. *Annual Review of Psychology, 40,* 603-629.

Hunt, E. B., & Agnoli, F. (1991). The Whorfian hypothesis: A cognitive psychology perspective. *Psychological Review, 98,* 377-389.

Hunt, R. R., & Einstein, G. O. (1981). Relational item-specific information in memory. *Journal of Verbal Learning and Verbal Behavior, 19,* 497-514.

Hunt, R. R., & McDaniel, M. A. (1993). The enigma of organization and distinctiveness. *Journal of Memory and Language, 32,* 421-445.

Hunter, I. M. L. (1962). An exceptional talent for calculative thinking. *British Journal of Psychology, 53,* 243-258.

Hunter, I. M. L. (1964). *Memory.* Harmondsworth, UK: Penguin.

Hyde, J. S. (1981). How large are cognitive gender differences? *American Psychologist, 36,* 892-901.

Hyde, J. S., & Linn, M. C. (1988). Gender differences in verbal ability: A meta-analysis. *Psychological Bulletin, 104,* 53-69.

Inhoff, A. W., Lima, S. D., & Carroll, P. J. (1984). Contextual effects on metaphor comprehension in reading. *Memory & Cognition, 12,* 558-567.

Jacoby, L. L. (1974). The role of mental contiguity in memory: Registration and retrieval effects. *Journal of Verbal Learning and Verbal Behavior, 13,* 483-496.

Jacoby, L. L. (1983). Perceptual enhancement: Persistent effects of an experience. *Journal of Experimental Psychology: Learning, Memory, and Cognition, 9,* 21-38.

Jacoby, L. L. (1991). A process dissociation framework: Separating automatic from intentional uses of memory. *Journal of Memory and Language, 30,* 513-514.

Jacoby, L. L., & Dallas, M. (1981). On the relationship between autobiographical memory and perceptual learning. *Journal of Experimental Psychology: General, 110,* 306-340.

Jacoby, L. L., Woloshyn, V., & Kelley, C. M. (1989). Becoming famous without being recognized: Unconscious influences of memory produced by dividing attention. *Journal of Experimental Psychology: General, 118,* 115-125.

James, W. (1890). *The principles of psychology* (Vol. 1). New York: Holt.

Jenkins, J. J. (1969). Language and thought. In J. F. Voss (Ed.), *Approaches to thought* (pp. 211-236). Columbus, OH: Merrill.

Jenkins, J. J. (1974). Remember that old theory of memory? Well, forget it! *American Psychologist, 29,* 785-795.

Jensen, A. R. (1987). Individual differences in the Hick paradigm. In P. A. Vernon (Ed.), *Speed of information processing and intelligence* (pp. 101-175). Norwood, NJ: Ablex.

Jensen, A. R. (1998). *The g factor.* Westport, CT: Praeger.

Johnson, M. K. (1988). Discriminating the origin of information. In T. F. Oltmans & B. A. Maher (Eds.), *Delusional beliefs: Interdisciplinary perspectives* (pp. 34-65). New York: John Wiley.

Johnson, M. K., Bransford, J. D., & Solomon, S. K. (1973). Memory for tacit implications of sentences. *Journal of Experimental Psychology, 98,* 203-205.

Johnson, M. K., & Hasher, L. (1987). Human learning and memory. *Annual Review of Psychology, 38,* 631-668.

Johnson, M. K., Hastroudi, S., & Lindsay, D. S. (1993). Source monitoring. *Psychological Bulletin, 114,* 3-28.

Johnson-Laird, P. N. (1983). *Mental models: Towards a cognitive science of language, inference, and consciousness.* Cambridge, MA: Harvard University Press.

Johnson-Laird, P. N., & Bara, B. G. (1984). Syllogistic inference. *Cognition, 16,* 1-61.

Johnson-Laird, P. N., & Steedman, M. (1978). The psychology of syllogisms. *Cognitive Psychology, 10,* 64-99.

John-Steiner, V. (1985). *Notebooks of the mind: Explorations of thinking.* Albuquerque: University of New Mexico Press.

Johnston, W. A., & Heinz, S. P. (1978). Flexibility and capacity demands of attention. *Journal of Experimental Psychology: General, 107,* 420-435.

Julesz, B. (1986). Stereoscopic vision. *Vision Research, 26,* 1601-1612.

Just, M. A., & Carpenter, P. A. (1980). A theory of reading: From eye fixations to comprehension. *Psychological Review, 87,* 329-354.

Just, M. A., & Carpenter, P. A. (1992). A capacity theory of comprehension: Individual differences in working memory. *Psychological Review, 99,* 122-149.

Just, M. A., Carpenter, P. A., Keller, T. A., Eddy, W. F., & Thulborn, K. R. (1996). Brain activation modulated by sentence comprehension. *Science, 274,* 114-116.

Kahneman, D. (1973). *Attention and effort.* Englewood Cliffs, NJ: Prentice Hall.

Kahneman, D., & Tversky, A. (1972). Subjective probability: A judgment of representativeness. *Cognitive Psychology, 3,* 430-454.

Kahneman, D., & Tversky, A. (1973). On the psychology of prediction. *Psychological Review, 80,* 237-251.

Kahneman, D., & Tversky, A. (1982a). On the study of statistical intuitions. *Cognition, 11,* 123-141.

Kahneman, D., & Tversky, A. (1982b). The simulation heuristic. In D. Kahneman, P. Slovic, & A. Tversky (Eds.), *Judgment under uncertainty: Heuristics and biases* (pp. 201-208). Cambridge, UK: Cambridge University Press.

Kahneman, D., & Tversky, A. (1984). Choices, values, and frames. *American Psychologist, 39,* 341-350.

Kail, R. (1984). *The development of memory in children* (2nd ed.). New York: Freeman.

Kamin, L. (1974). *The science and politics of IQ.* Hillsdale, NJ: Lawrence Erlbaum.

Kaplan, G. A., & Simon, H. A. (1990). In search of insight. *Cognitive Psychology, 22,* 374-419.

Kaufman, A. S., Reynolds, C. R., & McLean, J. E. (1989). Age and WAIS-R intelligence in a national sample of adults in the 20 to 74 year age range: A cross-sectional analysis with educational level controlled. *Intelligence, 13,* 235-253.

Keil, F. C. (1989). *Concepts, kinds, and cognitive development.* Cambridge, MA: MIT Press.

Kellogg, R. T. (1988). Attentional overload and writing performance: Effects of rough draft and outline strategies. *Journal of Experimental Psychology: Learning, Memory, and Cognition, 14,* 355-365.

Kellogg, R. T. (1994). *The psychology of writing.* New York: Oxford University Press.

Kellogg, R. T., & Bourne, L. E., Jr. (1989). Nonanalytic-automatic abstraction of concepts. In J. Sidowski (Ed.), *Conditioning, cognition, and methodology:*

Contemporary issues in experimental psychology. pp. 89-111. Lanham, MD: University Press of America.

Kellogg, R. T., Robbins, D. W., & Bourne, L. E., Jr. (1978). Memory for intratrial events in feature identification. *Journal of Experimental Psychology: Human Learning and Memory, 4,* 256-265.

Kieras, D. E. (1978). Good and bad structure in simple paragraphs: Effects on apparent theme, reading time, and recall. *Journal of Verbal Learning and Verbal Behavior, 17,* 13-28.

Kihlstrom, J. F., Schacter, D. L, Cork, R. C., Hunt, L. A., & Bahr, S. E. (1990). Implicit and explicit memory following surgical anesthesia. *Psychological Science, 1,* 303-306.

Kimura, D. (1999). *Sex and cognition.* Cambridge, MA: MIT Press.

Kinchla, R. A. (1992). Attention. *Annual Review of Psychology, 43,* 711-742.

Kintsch, W. (1970). *Learning, memory, and conceptual processes.* New York: John Wiley.

Kintsch, W. (1974). *The representation of meaning in memory.* Hillsdale, NJ: Lawrence Erlbaum.

Kintsch, W. (1988). The role of knowledge in discourse comprehension: A construction-integration model. *Psychological Review, 95,* 163-182.

Kintsch, W. (1998). *Comprehension: A paradigm for cognition.* Cambridge, UK: Cambridge University Press.

Kintsch, W., & Keenan, J. M. (1973). Reading rate as a function of the number of propositions in the base structure of sentences. *Cognitive Psychology, 5,* 257-274.

Kintsch, W., & van Dijk, T. A. (1978). Toward a model of text comprehension and production. *Psychological Review, 85,* 363-394.

Klass, P. J. (1989). *UFO abductions: A dangerous game.* Buffalo, NY: Prometheus.

Klayman, J., & Ha, Y. W. (1987). Confirmation, disconfirmation, and information in hypothesis testing. *Psychological Review, 94,* 211-228.

Knight, R. T. (1996). Contribution of human hippocampal region to novelty detection. *Nature, 383,* 256-259.

Knowlton, B. J., Ramus, S. J., & Squire, L. R. (1992). Intact artificial grammar learning in amnesia: Dissociation of classification learning and explicit memory for specific instances. *Psychological Science, 3,* 172-179.

Koffka, K. (1935). *Principles of Gestalt psychology.* New York: Harcourt, Brace.

Köhler, W. (1925). *The mentality of apes.* London: Routledge & Kegan Paul.

Kohn, M. L., & Schooler, C. (1973). Occupational experience and psychological functioning: An assessment of reciprocal effects. *American Sociological Review, 38,* 97-118.

Kolers, P. A. (1983). Perception and representation. *Annual Review of Psychology, 34,* 129-166.

Kopelman, M. D. (1999). Varieties of false memory. *Cognitive Neuropsychology, 16,* 197-214.

Kosslyn, S. M. (1973). Scanning visual images: Some structural implications. *Perception and Psychophysics, 14,* 90-94.

Kosslyn, S. M. (1975). Information representation in visual images. *Cognitive Psychology, 7,* 341-370.

Kosslyn, S. M. (1980). *Image and mind.* Cambridge, MA: Harvard University Press.

Kosslyn, S. M. (1981). The medium and the message in mental imagery. *Psychological Review, 88,* 46-66.

Kosslyn, S. M., Ball, T. M., & Reiser, B. J. (1978). Visual images preserve metric spatial information: Evidence from studies of visual scanning. *Journal of Experimental Psychology: Human Perception and Performance, 4,* 47-60.

Kotovsky, K., & Fallside, D. (1989). Representation and transfer in problem solving. In D. Klahr & K. Kotovsky (Eds.), *Complex information processing: The impact of Herbert A. Simon* (pp. 69-108). Hillsdale, NJ: Lawrence Erlbaum.

Kranzler, J., & Jensen, A. R. (1989). Inspection time and intelligence: A meta-analysis. *Intelligence, 13,* 329-347.

Krauth, J. (1982). Formulation and experimental verification of models in propositional reasoning. *Quarterly Journal of Experimental Psychology, 34,* 285-298.

Kreiman, G., Koch, C., & Fried, I. (2000). Imagery neurons in the human brain. *Nature, 408,* 357-361.

Kroll, N. E. A., Knight, R. T., Metcalfe, J., Wolf, E., & Tulving, E. (1996). Cohesion failure as a source of memory illusions. *Journal of Memory and Language, 35,* 176-196.

Kucera, H., & Francis, W. N. (1967). *A computational analysis of present day American English.* Providence, RI: Brown University Press.

Kunst-Wilson, W. R., & Zajonc, R. B. (1980). Affective discrimination of stimuli that cannot be recognized. *Science, 207,* 557-558.

Kutas, M., & Hillyard, S. A. (1980). Reading senseless sentences: Brain potentials reflect semantic incongruity. *Science, 207,* 203-205.

Kutas, M., & Hillyard, S. A. (1984). Brain potentials during reading reflect word expectancy and semantic association. *Nature, 307,* 161-163.

Kutas, M., Van Petten, C., & Besson, M. (1988). Event-related potential asymmetries during the reading of sentences. *Electroencephalography and Clinical Neurophysiology, 69,* 218-233.

LaBerge, D., & Buchsbaum, M. S. (1990). Positron emission tomographic measurements of pulvinar activity during an attention task. *Journal of Neuroscience, 10,* 613-619.

Labov, W. (1973). The boundaries of words and their meanings. In C. J. N. Bailey & R. W. Shuy (Eds.), *New ways of analyzing variations in English* (pp. 340-373). Washington, DC: Georgetown University Press.

Ladefoged, P. (1975). *A course in phonetics.* New York: Harcourt Brace Jovanovich.

Lakoff, G. (1987). *Women, fire, and dangerous things.* Chicago: University of Chicago Press.

Lakoff, G., & Johnson, M. (1980). The metaphorical structure of the human conceptual system. *Cognitive Science, 4,* 195-298.

Landuaer, T. K., & Dumais, S. T. (1997). A solution to Plato's problem: The latent semantic analysis theory of the acquisition, induction, and representation. *Psychological Review, 104,* 211-240.

Langer, E. J. (1989). *Mindfulness.* Reading, MA: Addison-Wesley.

Larkin, J. H., McDermott, J., Simon, D. P., & Simon, H. A. (1980). Expert and novice performance in solving physics problems. *Science, 208,* 1335-1342.

Lee, G., & Oakhill, J. (1984). The effects of externalization on syllogistic reasoning. *Quarterly Journal of Experimental Psychology, 36A,* 519-530.

Lehmann, A. C., & Ericsson, K. A. (1998). Historical developments of expert performance: Public performance of music. In A. Steptoe (Ed.), *Genius and mind: Studies of creativity and temperament* (pp. 67-94). New York: Oxford University Press.

Lenneberg, E. H. (1967). *Biological foundations of language.* New York: John Wiley.

Leslie, A. M. (1987). Pretense and representation: The origins of "theory of mind." *Psychological Review, 94,* 412-426.

Levelt, W. J. M. (1989). *Speaking: From intention to articulation.* Cambridge, MA: MIT Press.

Levin, I., Siegler, R. S., Druyan, S., & Gardosh, R. (1990). Everyday and curriculum-based physics concepts: When does short-term training bring change where years of schooling have failed to do so? *British Journal of Developmental Psychology, 8,* 269-279.

Levine, M. (1966). Hypothesis behavior by humans during discrimination learning. *Journal of Experimental Psychology, 71,* 331-338.

Levine, M. (1975). *A cognitive theory of learning.* Hillsdale, NJ: Lawrence Erlbaum.

Levy, B. A., & Hinchley, J. (1990). Individual and developmental differences in the acquisition of reading skills. In T. H. Carr & B. A. Levy (Eds.), *Reading and its development* (pp. 81-128). San Diego: Academic Press.

Levy, C. M., & Ransdell, S. (1996). Is writing as difficult as it seems? *Memory & Cognition, 23,* 767-779.

Levy, J., & Heller, W. (1992). Gender differences in human neuropsychological function. In A. A. Gerall, H. Moltz, & I. L. Ward (Eds.), *Handbook of behavioral neurobiology* (Vol. 11, pp. 245-274). New York: Plenum.

Levy, Y. (1996). Modularity of language reconsidered. *Brain & Language, 55,* 240-263.

Lewicki, P., Czyzewska, M., & Hoffman, H. (1988). Unconscious acquisition of complex procedural knowledge. *Journal of Experimental Psychology: Learning, Memory, and Cognition, 13,* 523-530.

Liberman, A. M., Cooper, F., Shankweiler, D., & Studdert-Kennedy, M. (1967). Perception of the speech code. *Psychological Review, 74,* 431-459.

Lieberman, P. (1984). *The biology and evolution of language.* Cambridge, MA: Harvard University Press.

Light, L. L., & Carter-Sobell, L. (1970). Effects of changed semantic context on recognition memory. *Journal of Verbal Learning and Verbal Behavior, 9,* 1-11.

Lindsay, D. S., & Read, J. D. (1994). Psychotherapy and memories of childhood sexual abuse: A cognitive perspective. *Applied Cognitive Psychology, 8,* 281-338.

Lindsay, P. H., & Norman, D. A. (1977). *Human information processing: An introduction to psychology* (2nd ed.). New York: Academic Press.

Linn, M. C., & Petersen, A. C. (1985). Emergence and characterization of sex differences in spatial ability: A meta-analysis. *Child Development, 56,* 1479-1498.

Lisker, L. (1986). "Voicing" in English: A catalog of acoustic features signalling lb/ versus/pl in trochees. *Language & Speech, 29,* 3-11.

Lisker, L., & Abramson, A. (1970). The voicing dimension: Some experiments in comparative phonetics. In *Proceedings of Sixth International Congress of Phonetic Sciences, Prague, 1967* (pp. 563-567). Prague, Czechoslovakia: Academia.

Lively, S. E., Pisoni, D. B., & Goldiner, S. D. (1994). Spoken word recognition: Research and theory. In M. A. Gernsbacher (Ed.), *Handbook of psycholinguistics* (pp. 265-301). San Diego: Academic Press.

Livingston, M. S., & Hubel, D. H. (1987). Psychological evidence for separate channels for the perception of form, color, movement, and depth. *Journal of Neuroscience, 7,* 3416-3468.

Loftus, E. F. (1979). *Eyewitness testimony.* Cambridge, MA: Harvard University Press.

Loftus, E. F. (1986). Ten years in the life of an expert witness. *Law and Human Behavior, 10,* 241-263.

Loftus, E. F. (1993). The reality of repressed memories. *American Psychologist, 48,* 518-537.

Loftus, E. F., & Ketcham, K. (1994). *The myth of repressed memory.* New York: St. Martin's.

Loftus, E. F., & Loftus, G. R. (1980). On the permanence of stored information in the human brain. *American Psychologist, 35,* 409-420.

Loftus, E. F., Miller, D. G., & Burns, H. J. (1978). Semantic integration of verbal information into a visual memory. *Journal of Experimental Psychology: Human Learning and Memory, 4,* 19-31.

Loftus, E. F., & Palmer, J. C. (1974). Reconstruction of automobile destruction: An example of the interaction between language and memory. *Journal of Verbal Learning and Verbal Behavior, 13,* 585-589.

Loftus, E. F., & Pickrell, J. E. (1995). The formation of false memories. *Psychiatric Annals, 25,* 720-725.

Logan, G. D. (1988). Toward an instance theory of automatization. *Psychological Review, 95,* 492-527.

Logan, R. K. (1986). *The alphabet effect: The impact of the phonetic alphabet on the development of Western civilization.* New York: William Morrow.

Luchins, A. S. (1942). Mechanization in problem solving. *Psychological Monographs, 54* (Whole No. 248).

Luria, A. R. (1968). *The mind of a mnemonist.* New York: Basic Books.

Luria, A. R. (1976). *Cognitive development: Its cultural and social foundations* (M. Cole, Ed., M. Lopez-Morillas & L. Solotaroff, Trans.). Cambridge, MA: Harvard University Press.

Maccoby, E. E., & Jacklin, C. N. (1974). *The psychology of sex differences.* Stanford, CA: Stanford University Press.

Mack, A., & Rock, I. (1998). *Inattentional blindness.* Cambridge, MA: MIT Press.

MacKay, D. G. (1973). Aspects of the theory of comprehension, memory, and attention. *Quarterly Journal of Experimental Psychology, 25,* 22-40.

MacKinnon, D. W. (1978). *In search of human effectiveness.* New York: Creative Education Foundation.

MacLean, H. N. (1993). *Once upon a time: A true story of memory, murder, and the law.* New York: HarperCollins.

MacLeod, C. M. (1991). Half a century of research on the Stroop effect: An integrative review. *Psychological Bulletin, 109,* 163-203.

MacNeil, J. E., & Warrington, E. K. (1993). Prosopagnosia: A face-specific disorder. *Quarterly Journal of Experimental Psychology, 46,* 1-10.

MacWhinney, B. (1998). Models of the emergence of language. *Annual Review of Psychology, 49,* 199-227.

Maffei, L., & Fiorentini, A. (1973). The visual cortex as a spatial frequency analyzer. *Vision Research, 13,* 1255-1267.

Mandler, G. (1979). Organization and repetition: Organizational principles with special reference to rote learning. In L. G. Nilsson (Ed.), *Perspectives on memory research: Essays in honor of Uppsala University's 500th anniversary* (pp. 293-328). Hillsdale, NJ: Lawrence Erlbaum.

Mandler, G. (1980). Recognizing: The judgment of previous occurrence. *Psychological Review, 87,* 252-271.

Mandler, G., Pearlstone, Z., & Koopmans, H. J. (1969). Effects of organization and semantic similarity on recall and recognition. *Journal of Verbal Learning and Verbal Behavior, 8,* 410-423.

Mandler, J. M. (1984). *Stories, scripts, and scenes: Aspects of schema theory.* Hillsdale, NJ: Lawrence Erlbaum.

Mandler, J. M., & Johnson, N. S. (1977). Remembrance of things parsed: Story structure and recall. *Cognitive Psychology, 9,* 111-151.

Mandler, J. M., & Ritchey, G. H. (1977). Long-term memory for pictures. *Journal of Experimental Psychology; Human Learning and Memory, 3,* 386-396.

Mandler, J. M., Scribner, S., Cole, M., & DeForest, M. (1980). Cross-cultural invariance in story recall. *Child Development, 51,* 19-26.

Mantyla, T. (1986). Optimizing cue effectiveness: Recall of 500 and 600 incidentally learned words. *Journal of Experimental Psychology: Learning, Memory, and Cognition, 12,* 66-71.

Marcel, A. J. (1983). Conscious and unconscious perception: Experiments on visual masking and word recognition. *Cognitive Psychology, 15,* 197-237.

Marcus, G. F., Pinker, S., Ullman, M., Hollander, M., Rosen, T. J., & Xu, F. (1992). Overregularization in language acquisition. *Monographs of the Society for Research in Child Development, 57*(4, Serial No. 228), 1-182.

Marcus, G. F., Vijayan, S., Rao, S. B., & Vishton, P. M. (1999). Rule learning by seven month old infants. *Science, 283,* 77-80.

Marcus, S. L., & Rips, L. J. (1979). Conditional reasoning. *Journal of Verbal Learning and Verbal Behavior, 18,* 199-223.

Marks, L. E. (1987). On cross-modal similarity: Auditory-visual interactions in speeded discrimination. *Journal of Experimental Psychology: Human Perception and Performance, 13,* 384-394.

Marmie, W. R., & Healy, A. F. (1995). The long-term retention of a complex skill. In A. F. Healy & L. E. Bourne (Eds.), *Learning and memory of knowledge and skills: Durability and specificity* (pp. 30-65). Thousand Oaks, CA: Sage.

Marschark, M., Richman, C. L., Yuille, J. C., & Hunt, R. R. (1987). The role of imagery in memory: On shared and distinctive information. *Psychological Bulletin, 102,* 28-41.

Marslen-Wilson, W. D., & Tyler, L. K. (1997). Dissociating types of mental computation. *Nature, 387,* 592-594.

Martin, A., Wiggs, C. L., & Weisberg, J. A. (1997). Modulation of human temporal lobe activity by form, meaning, and experience. *Hippocampus, 7,* 587-593.

Martin, R. C., Shelton, J. R., & Yaffee, L. S. (1994). Language processing and working memory: Neuropsychological evidence for separate phonological and semantic capacities. *Journal of Memory and Language, 33,* 83-111.

Massaro, D. W. (1970). Preperceptual auditory images. *Journal of Experimental Psychology, 85,* 411-417.

Massaro, D. W. (1994). Psychological aspects of speech production. In M. A. Gernsbacher (Ed.), *Handbook of psycholinguistics* (pp. 219-263). San Diego: Academic Press.

Massaro, D. W., & Cowan, N. (1993). Information processing models: Microscopes of the mind. *Annual Review of Psychology, 44,* 383-425.

Masson, M. E. (1983). Conceptual processing of text during skimming and rapid sequential reading. *Memory & Cognition, 11,* 262-274.

Matarazzo, J. D. (1992). Psychological testing and measurement in the 21st century. *American Psychologist, 47,* 1007-1018.

McCarthy, R. A., & Warrington, E. K. (1990). *Cognitive neuropsychology: A clinical introduction.* San Diego: Academic Press.

McClelland, D. C. (1973). Testing for competence rather than for "intelligence." *American Psychologist, 28,* 1-14.

McClelland, J. L., & Elman, J. L. (1986). The TRACE model of speech perception. *Cognitive Psychology, 18,* 1-86.

McClelland, J. L., McNaughton, B. L., & O'Reilly, R. C. (1995). Why there are complementary learning systems in the hippocampus and neocortex: Insights from the successes and failures of connectionist models of learning and memory. *Psychological Review, 102,* 419-457.

McClelland, J. L., & Rumelhart, D. E. (Eds.). (1981). An interactive model of context effects in letter perception: I. An account of basic findings. *Psychological Review, 88,* 375-407.

McClelland, J. L., & Seidenberg, M. S. (2000). Why do kids say goed and brang? *Science, 287,* 47-48.

McCloskey, M. (1983). Naive theories of motion. In D. Gentner & A. L. Stevens (Eds.), *Mental models* (pp. 299-324). Hillsdale, NJ: Lawrence Erlbaum.

McCloskey, M., Wible, C. G., & Cohen, N. J. (1988). Is there a special flashbulb-memory mechanism? *Journal of Experimental Psychology: General, 117,* 171-181.

McConkie, G. W., & Rayner, K. (1975). The effective stimulus during a fixation in reading. *Perception and Psychophysics, 17,* 578-586.

McCulloch, W. S., & Pitts, W. (1943). A logical calculus of the ideas immanent in nervous activity. *Bulletin of Mathematical Biophysics, 5,* 115-133.

McCutchen, D. (1984). Writing as a linguistic problem. *Educational Psychologist, 19,* 226-238.

McCutchen, D. (1996). A capacity theory of writing: Working memory in composition. *Educational Psychology Review, 8,* 299-325.

McDaniel, M., & Pressley, M. (Eds.). (1987). *Imagery and related processes.* New York: Springer-Verlag.

McDaniel, M. A., & Einstein, G. O. (1986). Bizarre imagery as an effective memory aid: The importance of distinctiveness. *Journal of Experimental Psychology: Learning, Memory, and Cognition, 12,* 54-65.

McDonald, J. L. (1997). Language acquisition: The acquisition of linguistic structure in normal and special populations. *Annual Review of Psychology, 48,* 215-241.

McGeoch, J. A. (1942). *The psychology of human learning: An introduction.* New York: Longmans, Green.

McGlone, R. E. (1998). Deciphering memory: John Adams and the authorship of the *Declaration of Independence. Journal of American History, 85,* 411-438.

McKoon, G., & Ratcliff, R. (1980). The comprehension processes and memory structures involved in anaphoric reference. *Journal of Verbal Learning and Verbal Behavior, 19,* 668-682.

McKoon, G., & Ratcliff, R. (1981). The comprehension processes and memory structures involved in instrumental inference. *Journal of Verbal Learning and Verbal Behavior, 20,* 671-682.

Medin, D. L., & Ortony, A. (1989). Psychological essentialism. In S. Vosniadou & A. Ortony (Eds.), *Similarity and analogical reasoning.* New York: Cambridge University Press.

Medin, D. L., & Ross, B. H. (1989). The specific character of thought: Categorization, problem solving, and induction. In R. J. Sternberg (Ed.), *Advances in the psychology of human intelligence* (Vol. 5, pp. 189-223). Hillsdale, NJ: Lawrence Erlbaum.

Medin, D. L., & Shaeffer, M. M. (1978). Context theory of classification. *Psychological Review, 85,* 207-238.

Melo, B., Winocur, G., & Moscovitch, M. (1999). False recall and false recognition: An examination of the effects of selective and combined lesions to the medial temporal lobe/diencephalon and frontal lobe structures. *Cognitive Neuropsychology, 16,* 343-359.

Merikle, P. M. (1980). Selection from visual persistence by perceptual groups and category membership. *Journal of Experimental Psychology: General, 109,* 279-295.

Merikle, P. M., & Reingold, E. M. (1992). Measuring unconscious perceptual processes. In R. F. Bornstein & T. S. Pittman (Eds.), *Perception without awareness: Cognitive, clinical, and social perspectives* (pp. 55-80). New York: Guilford.

Metzler, J., & Shepard, R. N. (1974). Transformational studies of the internal representations of three dimensional objects. In R. L. Solso (Ed.), *Information processing and cognition: The Loyola Symposium* (pp. 147-201). Hillsdale, NJ: Lawrence Erlbaum.

Meyer, B. J. F. (1975). *The organization of prose and its effect on memory.* Amsterdam: North-Holland.

Meyer, D. E. (1970). On the representation and retrieval of stored semantic information. *Cognitive Psychology, 1,* 242-300.

Miller, G. A. (1956). The magical number seven, plus or minus two: Some limits on our capacity for processing information. *Psychological Review, 63,* 81-97.

Miller, G. H. (1999). On knowing a word. *Annual Review of Psychology, 50,* 1-19.

Miller, J. L., & Eimas, P. D. (1983). Studies on the categorization of speech by infants. *Cognition, 13,* 135-165.

Miller, J. R., & Kintsch, W. (1980). Readability and recall of short prose passages: A theoretical analysis. *Journal of Experimental Psychology: Human Learning and Memory, 6,* 335-354.

Milner, B. (1965). Visually-guided maze learning in man: Effects of bilateral hippocampal, bilateral frontal, and unilateral cerebral lesions. *Neuropsychologia, 3,* 317-338.

Milner, B. (1966). Amnesia following operations on the temporal lobes. In C. W. M. Whitney & O. L. Zangwill (Eds.), *Amnesia* (pp. 109-133). London: Butterworth.

Minsky, M. L. (1977). Frame-system theory. In P. N. Johnson-Laird & P. C. Wason (Eds.), *Thinking: Readings in cognitive science* (pp. 355-376). Cambridge, UK: Cambridge University Press.

Mishkin, M. (1978). Memory in monkeys severely impaired by combined but not separate removal of the amygdala and hippocampus. *Nature, 273,* 297-298.

Monahan, J. L., Murphy, S. T., & Zajonc, R. B. (2000). Subliminal mere exposure: Specific, general, and diffuse effects. *Psychological Science, 11,* 462-466.

Moore, M. K., Borton, R., & Darby, B. L. (1978). Visual tracking in young infants: Evidence for object identity or object permanence. *Journal of Experimental Child Psychology, 25,* 183-198.

Moran, J., & Desimone, R. (1985). Selective attention gates visual processing in the extrastriate cortex. *Science, 229,* 782-784.

Moray, N. (1959). Attention in dichotic listening: Affective cues and the influence of instructions. *Quarterly Journal of Experimental Psychology, 11,* 56-60.

Moray, N., Bates, A., & Barnett, T. (1965). Experiments on the four-eared man. *Journal of the Acoustical Society of America, 42,* 196-201.

Morris, C. D., Bransford, J. D., & Franks, J. J. (1977). Levels of processing versus transfer appropriate processing. *Journal of Verbal Learning and Verbal Behavior, 16,* 519-533.

Morton, J. (1969). Interaction of information in word recognition. *Psychological Review, 76,* 165-178.

Moscovitch, M. (1982). Multiple dissociations of function in amnesia. In L. S. Cermak (Ed.), *Human memory and amnesia* (pp. 337-370). Hillsdale, NJ: Lawrence Erlbaum.

Moscovitch, M. (1992). Memory and working-with-memory: A component process model based on modules and central systems. *Journal of Cognitive Neuroscience, 4,* 257-266.

Moscovitch, M., & Umilta, C. (1990). Modularity and neuropsychology: Modules and central processes in attention and memory. In M. F. Schwarz (Ed.), *Modular deficits in Alzheimer-type dementia* (pp. 1-58). Cambridge, MA: MIT Press.

Mumford, M. D., & Gustafson, S. B. (1988). Creativity syndrome: Integration, application, and innovation. *Psychological Bulletin, 103,* 27-43.

Murdock, B. B. (1974). *Human memory: Theory and data.* Hillsdale, NJ: Lawrence Erlbaum.

Murphy, G. L., & Medin, D. L. (1985). The role of theories in conceptual coherence. *Psychological Review, 92,* 289-316.

Murphy, G. L., & Smith, E. E. (1982). Basic level superiority in picture categorization. *Journal of Verbal Learning and Verbal Behavior, 21,* 1-20.

Murphy, T. D., & Eriksen, C. W. (1987). Temporal changes in the distribution of attention in the visual field in response to precues. *Perceptions and Psychophysics, 42,* 576-586.

Murray, J. E., Yong, E., & Rhodes, G. (2000). Revisiting the perception of upside-down faces. *Psychological Science, 11,* 492-496.

Myers, H. F. (1991, November 25). Das Kapital. *The Wall Street Journal,* pp. A1, A10.

Naka, M., Itsukushima, Y., & Itoh, Y. (1996). Eyewitness testimony after three months: A field study on memory for an incident in everyday life. *Japanese Psychological Research, 38,* 14-24.

Nash, M. (1987). What, if anything, is regressed about hypnotic age regression? A review of the empirical literature. *Psychological Bulletin, 102,* 42-52.

Navon, D., & Gopher, D. (1979). On the economy of the human-processing system. *Psychological Review, 86,* 214-255.

Neal, A., & Hesketh, B. (1997). Episodic knowledge and implicit learning. *Psychonomic Bulletin & Review, 4,* 24-37.

Neisser, U. (1963). Decision time without reaction time: Experiments in visual scanning. *American Journal of Psychology, 76,* 376-385.

Neisser, U. (1967). *Cognitive psychology.* New York: Appleton.

Neisser, U. (1976). *Cognition and reality.* San Francisco: Freeman.

Neisser, U. (1981). John Dean's memory: A case study. *Cognition, 9,* 1-22.

Neisser, U., Boodoo, G., Bouchard, T. J., Jr., Boykin, A. W., Brody, N., Ceci, S. J., Halpern, D. F., Loehlin, J. C., Perloff, R., Sternerg, R. J., & Urbina, S. (1996). Intelligence: Knowns and unknowns. *American Psychologist, 51,* 77-101.

Neisser, U., & Harsch, N. (1992). Phantom flashbulbs: False recollections of hearing the news about Challenger. In E. Winograd & U. Neisser (Eds.), *Affect and accuracy in recall: Studies of "flashbulb memories"* (pp. 9-31). Cambridge, UK: Cambridge University Press.

Neisser, U., & Libby, L. K. (2000). Remembering life experiences. In E. Tulving & F. I. M. Craik (Eds.), *The Oxford handbook of memory* (pp. 315-332). New York: Oxford University Press.

Neisser, U., Winograd, E., Bergman, E. T., Schreiber, C. A., Palmer, S. E., & Weldon, M. S. (1996). Remembering the earthquake: Direct experience vs. hearing the news. *Memory, 4,* 337-357.

Nelson, K. (1990). Remembering, forgetting, and childhood amnesia. In R. Fivush & J. A. Hudson (Eds.), *Knowing and remembering in young children* (pp. 301-316). New York: Cambridge University Press.

Nespor, M. (1999). Acquisition of phonology. In R. A. Wilson & F. C. Keil (Eds.), *The MIT encyclopedia of the cognitive sciences.* Cambridge, MA: MIT Press.

Neumann, P. G. (1977). Visual prototype formation with discontinuous representation of dimensions of variability. *Memory & Cognition, 5,* 187-197.

Neves, D. M., & Anderson, J. R. (1981). Knowledge compilation: Mechanisms for the automatization of cognitive skills. In J. R. Anderson (Ed.), *Cognitive skills and their acquisition* (pp. 57-84). Hillsdale, NJ: Lawrence Erlbaum.

Neville, H. J., & Bavelier, D. (2000). Specificity and plasticity in neurocognitive development in humans. In M. S. Gazzaniga (Ed.), *The new cognitive neurosciences* (pp. 83-98). Cambridge, MA: MIT Press.

Newell, A., & Simon, H. A. (1972). *Human problem solving.* Englewood Cliffs, NJ: Prentice Hall.

Nezworski, T., Stein, N. L., & Trabasso, T. (1981). Story structure versus content in children's recall. *Journal of Verbal Learning and Verbal Behavior, 21,* 196-201.

Nickerson, R. S., & Adams, M. J. (1979). Long-term memory for a common object. *Cognitive Psychology, 11,* 287-307.

Nipher, F. E. (1878). On the distribution of errors of numbers written from memory. *Transactions of the Academy of Sciences of St. Louis, 3,* ccx-ccxi.

Nissen, M. J., & Bullemer, P. (1987). Attentional requirements of learning: Evidence from performance measures. *Cognitive Psychology, 19,* 1-32.

Nissen, M. J., Knopman, D., & Schacter, D. L. (1987). Neurochemical dissociation of memory systems, *Neurology, 37,* 789-794.

Norman, D. A. (1968). Toward a theory of memory and attention. *Psychological Review, 75,* 522-536.

Norman, D. A. (1981). Categorization of action slips. *Psychological Review, 88,* 1-15.

Norman, D. A., & Shallice, T. (1986). Attention to action: Willed and automatic control of behaviour. In R. J. Davidson, G. E. Schwarts, & D. Shapiro (Eds.), *Consciousness and self-regulation: Advances in research and theory* (pp. 1-18). New York: Plenum.

Nyberg, L., & Cabeza, R. (2000). Brain imaging of memory. In E. Tulving & F. I. M. Craik (Eds.), *The Oxford handbook of memory* (pp. 501-519). New York: Oxford University Press.

Ochse, R. (1990). *Before the gates of excellence.* New York: Cambridge University Press.

Odean, T. (1998). Are investors reluctant to realize their losses? *Journal of Finance, 53,* 1775-1798.

Olio, K. A. (1989). Memory retrieval in the treatment of adult survivors of sexual abuse. *Transactional Analysis Journal, 19,* 93-100.

Omanson, R. C. (1982). The relation between centrality and story category variation. *Journal of Verbal Learning and Verbal Behavior, 21,* 326-337.

Ornstein, R. E. (1997). *The right mind: Making sense of the hemispheres.* New York: Harcourt Brace.

Osherson, D. N., Smith, E. E., Wilkie, O. , Lopez, A., & Shafir, E. (1990). Category based induction. *Psychological Review, 97,* 185-200.

Overton, D. A. (1971). State-dependent learning produced by alcohol and its relevance to alcoholism. In B. Kissin & H. Begleiter (Eds.), *The biology of alcoholism,* Vol. 2: *Physiology and behavior* (pp. 193-217). New York: Plenum.

Paivio, A. (1971). *Imagery and verbal processes.* New York: Holt, Rinehart & Winston.

Paivio, A. (1983). The empirical case for dual coding. In J. Yuille (Ed.), *Imagery, memory, and cognition: Essays in honor of Allen Paivio* (pp. 307-332). Hillsdale, NJ: Lawrence Erlbaum.

Palmer, J., MacLeod, C. M., Hunt, E., & Davidson, J. E. (1985). Information processing correlated of reading. *Journal of Memory and Language, 24,* 59-88.

Palmer, S. E. (1975). The effects of contextual scenes on the identification of objects. *Memory & Cognition, 3,* 519-526.

Parkin, A. J., & Russo, R. (1993). On the origin of functional differences in recollective experience. *Memory, 1,* 231-237.

Penfield, W. (1959). The interpretive cortex. *Science, 129,* 1719-1725.

Penney, C. G. (1975). Modality effects in short-term verbal memory. *Psychological Bulletin, 82,* 68-84.

Penney, C. G. (1989). Modality effects and the structure of short-term verbal memory. *Memory & Cognition, 17,* 398-422.

Perfetti, C. A. (1985). *Reading ability.* New York: Oxford University Press.

Perris, E. E., Myers, N. A., & Clifton, R. K. (1990). Long-term memory for a single infancy experience. *Child Development, 61,* 1796-1807.

Perruchet, P., Gallego, J., & Savy, I. (1990). A critical reappraisal of the evidence for unconscious abstraction of deterministic rules in complex experimental situations. *Cognitive Psychology, 22,* 493-516.

Perruchet, P., & Pacteau, C. (1992). Synthetic grammar learning: Implicit rule abstraction or fragmentary knowledge? *Journal of Experimental Psychology: General, 119,* 264-275.

Peterson, C. R., & Beach, L. R. (1967). Man as an intuitive statistician. *Psychological Bulletin, 68,* 29-46.

Peterson, L. R., & Peterson, M. J. (1959). Short-term retention of individual verbal items. *Journal of Experimental Psychology, 58,* 193-198.

Petersen, S. E., Fox, P. T., Snyder, A. Z., & Raichle, M. E. (1990). Activation of extrastriate and frontal cortical areas by visual words and word-like stimuli. *Science, 249,* 1041-1044.

Petty, R. E., & Cacioppo, J. T. (1981). *Attitudes and persuasion: Classic and contemporary approaches.* Dubuque, IA: William C. Brown.

Piaget, J. (1952). *The origins of intelligence in children.* New York: International University Press.

Pillemer, D. B. (1984). Flashbulb memories of the assassination attempt on President Reagan. *Cognition, 16,* 63-80.

Pinker, S. (1984). Visual cognition: An introduction. *Cognition, 18,* 1-63.

Pinker, S. (1990). Language acquisition. In D. N. Osherson & H. Lasaik (Eds.), *An invitation to cognitive science,* Vol. 1: *Language* (pp. 199-241). Cambridge MA: MIT Press.

Pinker, S. (1999). *How the mind works.* New York: Norton.

Pinker, S., & Prince, A. (1988). On language and connectionism: An analysis of a parallel distributed processing model of language acquisition. *Cognition, 28,* 73-193.

Place, E. J. S., & Gilmore, G. C. (1980). Perceptual organization in schizophrenia. *Journal of Abnormal Psychology, 89,* 125-144.

Plaut, D. C., McClelland, J. L., Seidenberg, M. S., & Patterson, K. (1996). Understanding normal and impaired word reading and lexical decisions. *Psychological Review, 103,* 56-115.

Plomin, R. (1997). Identifying genes for cognitive abilities and disabilities. In R. J. Sternberg & E. L. Grigorenko (Eds.), *Intelligence: Heredity and environment* (pp. 89-104). New York: Cambridge University Press.

Plomin, R., DeFries, J. C., & McClearn, G. E. (1990). *Behavioral genetics: A primer* (2nd ed.). New York: Freeman.

Plunkett, K., & Marchman, V. (1991). U-shaped learning and frequency effects in a multi-layered perceptron: Implications for child language acquisition. *Cognition, 38,* 43-102.

Poizner, H., Bellugi, U., & Klima, E. S. (1990). Biological foundations of language: Clues from sign language. *Annual Review of Neuroscience, 13,* 283-307.

Pollatsek, A., & Rayner, K. (1989). Reading. In M. I. Posner (Ed.), *The foundations of cognitive science* (pp. 401-436). Cambridge, MA: MIT Press.

Polya, G. (1957). *How to solve it: A new aspect of mathematical method* (2nd ed.). Garden City, NY: Doubleday.

Popper, K. R. (1974). *Conjectures and refutations: The growth of scientific knowledge.* London: Routledge & Kegan Paul.

Popper, K. R., & Eccles, J. C. (1977). *The self and its brain.* Berlin: Springer-Verlag.

Posner, M. I. (1980). Orienting of attention. *Quarterly Journal of Experimental Psychology, 32,* 3-25.

Posner, M. I., Cohen, Y., & Rafal, R. D. (1982). Neural systems control of spatial orienting. *Philosophical Transactions of the Royal Society of London, 298B,* 187-198.

Posner, M. I., & DiGirolamo, G. J. (1998). Executive attention: Conflict, target detection, and cognitive control. In R. Parasuraman (Ed.), *The attentive brain* (pp. 401-424). Cambridge, MA: MIT Press.

Posner, M. I., & Keele, S. W. (1968). On the genesis of abstract ideas. *Journal of Experimental Psychology, 77,* 353-363.

Posner, M. I., & Peterson, S. E. (1990). The attention system of the human brain. *Annual Review of Neuroscience, 13,* 25-42.

Posner, M. I., Peterson, S. E., Fox, P. T., & Raichle, M. E. (1988). Localization of cognitive operations in the brain. *Science, 240,* 1627-1631.

Posner, M. I., & Raichle, M. E. (1994). *Images of mind.* New York: Scientific American Library.

Posner, M. I., & Snyder, C. R. R. (1974). Attention and cognitive control. In R. L. Solso (Ed.), *Information processing and cognition: The Loyola Symposium* (pp. 55-85). Hillsdale, NJ: Lawrence Erlbaum.

Posner, M. I., & Snyder, C. R. R. (1975). Facilitation and inhibition in the processing of signals. In P. M. A. Rabbit & S. Dornic (Eds.), *Attention and performance* (Vol. 5, pp. 669-682). New York: Academic Press.

Premack, D., & Woodruff, G. (1978). Chimpanzee problem solving: A test for comprehension. *Science, 202,* 532-535.

Pylyshyn, Z. W. (1981). The imagery debate: Analogue media versus tacit knowledge. *Psychological Review, 88,* 16-45.

Rafal, R. D., & Posner, M. I. (1987). Deficits in human visual spatial attention following thalamic lesions. *Proceedings of the National Academy of Science USA, 84,* 7349-7353.

Rajaram, S., & Roediger, H. L., III. (1997). Remembering and knowing as states of consciousness during recollection. In J. D. Cohen & J. W. Schooler (Eds.), *Scientific approaches to the questions of consciousness* (pp. 213-240). Hillsdale, NJ: Lawrence Erlbaum.

Reber, A. S. (1967). Implicit learning of artificial grammars. *Journal of Verbal Learning and Verbal Behavior, 6,* 855-863.

Reber, A. S. (1989). Implicit learning and tacit knowledge. *Journal of Experimental Psychology: General, 118,* 219-235.

Reber, A. S., & Allen, R. (1978). Analogical and abstraction strategies in synthetic grammar learning: A functionalist interpretation. *Cognition, 6,* 189-221.

Reber, A. S., Kassin, S. M., Lewis, S., & Cantor, G. (1980). On the relationship between implicit and explicit modes in the learning of complex rule structure. *Journal of Experimental Psychology: Human Learning and Memory, 6,* 492-502.

Reber, P. J., Stark, C. E. L., & Squire, L. R. (1998). Contrasting cortical activity associated with category memory and recognition memory. *Learning & Memory, 5,* 420-428.

Reed, S. K. (1972). Pattern recognition and categorization. *Cognitive Psychology, 3,* 383-407.

Reed, S. K. (1973). *Psychological processes in pattern recognition.* New York: Academic Press.

Reed, S. K. (1974). Structural descriptions and the limitations of visual images. *Memory & Cognition, 2,* 329-336.

Reed, S. K., & Friedman, M. P. (1973). Perceptual versus conceptual categorization. *Memory & Cognition, 1,* 157-163.

Reed, S. K., & Johnson, J. A. (1975). Detection of parts in patterns and images. *Memory & Cognition, 3,* 569-575.

Reicher, G. M. (1969). Perceptual recognition as a function of meaningfulness of stimulus material. *Journal of Experimental Psychology, 81,* 275-280.

Reichle, E. D., Pollatsek, A., Fisher, D. L., & Rayner, K. (1998). Toward a model of eye movement control in reading. *Psychological Review, 105,* 125-157.

Reitman, J. S. (1974). Without surreptious rehearsal, information in short-term memory decays. *Journal of Verbal Learning and Verbal Behavior, 13,* 365-377.

Repp, B. H., & Liberman, A. M. (1987). Phonetic boundaries are flexible. In S. Harnad (Ed.), *Categorical perception: The groundwork of cognition* (pp. 89-112). Cambridge, UK: Cambridge University Press.

Revlis, R. (1975). Two models of syllogistic reasoning: Feature selection and conversion. *Journal of Verbal Learning and Verbal Behavior, 14,* 180-195.

Richardson-Klavehn, A., & Bjork, R. A. (1988). Measures of memory. *Annual Review of Psychology, 39,* 475-543.

Rips, L. J. (1990). Reasoning. *Annual Review of Psychology, 41,* 321-353.

Rips, L. J., & Marcus, S. L. (1977). Supposition and the analysis of conditional sentences. In M. A. Just & P. A. Carpenter (Eds.), *Cognitive processes in comprehension* (pp. 185-220). Hillsdale, NJ: Lawrence Erlbaum.

Rips, L. J., Shoben, E. J., & Smith, E. E. (1973). Semantic distance and the verification of semantic relations. *Journal of Verbal Learning and Verbal Behavior, 12,* 1-20.

Rodriquez, H. S., Porjesz, B., Chorlian, D. B., Polich, J., & Begleiter, H. (1999). Visual P3a in male subjects at high risk for alcoholism. *Biological Psychiatry, 46,* 281-291.

Roediger, H. L. (1984). Does current evidence from dissociation experiments favor the episodic/semantic distinction? *Behavioral and Brain Sciences, 7,* 252-254.

Roediger, H. L. (1991). They read an article? A commentary on the everyday memory controversy. *American Psychologist, 46,* 37-40.

Roediger, H. L., & Blaxton, T. A. (1987). Retrieval modes produce dissociations in memory for surface information. In D. S. Gorfein & R. R. Hoffman (Eds.), *Memory and cognitive processes: The Ebbinghaus Centennial Conference* (pp. 349-379). Hillsdale, NJ: Lawrence Erlbaum.

Roediger, H. L., & McDermott, K. (1995). Creating false memories: Remembering words not presented in lists. *Journal of Experimental Psychology: Learning, Memory, and Cognition, 21,* 300-318.

Rogers, T. B., Kuiper, N. A., & Kirker, W. S. (1977). Self-reference and the encoding of personal information. *Journal of Personality and Social Psychology, 35,* 677-688.

Rosch, E. H. (1973). Natural categories. *Cognitive Psychology, 4,* 328-350.

Rosch, E. H. (1975). Cognitive representations of semantic categories. *Journal of Experimental Psychology: General, 104,* 192-233.

Rosch, E. H., & Mervis, C. B. (1975). Family resemblances: Studies in the internal structure of categories. *Cognitive Psychology, 7,* 573-605.

Rosch, E. H., Mervis, C. B., Gray, W. D., Johnson, D. M., & Boyes-Braem, P. (1976). Basic objects in natural categories. *Cognitive Psychology, 8,* 382-439.

Rosch, E. H., Simpson, S., & Miller, R. (1976). Structural bases of typicality effects. *Journal of Experimental Psychology: Human Perception and Performance, 4,* 491-502.

Rose, M. (1984). *Writer's block: The cognitive dimension.* Carbondale: Southern Illinois University Press.

Ross, B. H. (1987). This is like that: The use of earlier problems and the separation of similarity effects. *Journal of Experimental Psychology: Learning, Memory, and Cognition, 13,* 629-639.

Ross, D. F., Read, J. D., & Toglia, M. P. (1994). *Adult eyewitness testimony: Current trends and developments.* Cambridge, UK: University of Cambridge Press.

Rubin, D. C., & Wenzel, A. E. (1996). One hundred years of forgetting: A quantitative description. *Psychological Review, 103,* 734-760.

Rubinstein, M. F. (1975). *Patterns of problem solving.* Englewood Cliffs, NJ: Prentice Hall.

Rubinstein, M. F. (1986). *Tools for thinking and problem solving.* Englewood Cliffs, NJ: Prentice Hall.

Rumelhart, D. E., & McClelland, J. L. (Eds.). (1986). *Parallel distributed processing; Explorations in the microstructure of cognition* (Vol. 1). Cambridge, MA: MIT Press/Bradford Books.

Rundus, D. (1971). Analysis of rehearsal processes in free recall. *Journal of Experimental Psychology, 89,* 63-77.

Russo, J. E., Johnson, E. J., & Stephens, D. L. (1989). The validity of verbal protocols. *Memory & Cognition, 17,* 759-769.

Sacks, O. (1970). *The man who mistook his wife for a hat and other clinical tales.* New York: HarperCollins.

Salasoo, A., & Pisoni, D. (1985). Interaction of knowledge sources in spoken word identification. *Journal of Memory and Language, 24,* 210-231.

Sanders, R. E., Gonzalez, E. G., Murphy, M. D., Liddle, C. L., & Vitina, J. R. (1987). Frequency of occurrence and the criteria for automatic processing. *Journal of Experimental Psychology: Learning, Memory, and Cognition, 13,* 241-250.

Scarr, S., & Ricciuti, A. (1991). What effects do parents have on their children? In L. Okagaki & R. J. Sternberg (Eds.), *Directors of development: Influences on the development of children's thinking* (pp. 3-23). Hillsdale, NJ: Lawrence Erlbaum.

Schacter, D. L. (1987). Implicit memory: History and current status. *Journal of Experimental Psychology: Learning, Memory, and Cognition, 13,* 501-518.

Schacter, D. L., Israel, L., & Racine, C. (1999). Suppressing false recognition in younger and older adults: The distinctiveness heuristic. *Journal of Memory and Language, 40,* 1-24.

Schacter, D. L., & Kihlstrom, J. F. (1989). Functional amnesia. In F. Boller & J. Grafman (Eds.), *Handbook of neuropsychology* (Vol. 3, pp. 209-231). New York: Elsevier Science.

Schacter, D. L., Reiman, E. , Curran, T., Yun, L. S., Bandy, D., McDermott, K. B., & Roediger, H. L. (1996). Neuroanatomical correlates of veridical and illusory recognition memory: Evidence from positron emission tomography. *Neuron, 17,* 267-274.

Schacter, D. L., & Tulving, E. (1994). What are the memory systems of 1994? In D. L. Schacter & E. Tulving (Eds.), *Memory systems* (pp. 1-38). Cambridge, MA: MIT Press.

Schacter, D. L., Wagner, A. D., & Buckner, R. L. (2000). Memory systems of 1999. In E. Tulving & F. I. M. Craik (Eds.), *The Oxford handbook of memory* (pp. 627-643). New York: Oxford University Press.

Schank, R. C. (1975). The structure of episodes in memory. In D. G. Bobrow & A. Collins (Eds.), *Representation and understanding: Studies in cognitive science* (pp. 237-272). New York: Academic Press.

Schank, R. C., & Abelson, R. (1977). *Scripts, plans, goals, and understanding.* Hillsdale, NJ: Lawrence Erlbaum.

Schiffman, H. R. (2000). *Sensation and perception: An integrated approach* (5th ed.). New York: John Wiley.

Schmandt-Besserat, D. (1988). From accounting to written language. In B. A. Rafoth & D. L. Rubin (Eds.), *The social construction of written communication* (pp. 119-130). Norwood, NJ: Ablex.

Schmidt, S. R., & Bohannon, J. N., III. (1988). In defense of the flashbulb-memory hypothesis: A comment on McCloskey, Wible, and Cohen (1988). *Journal of Experimental Psychology: General, 117,* 332-335.

Schneider, W., & Detweiler, M. (1987). A connectionist/control architecture for working memory. In G. H. Bower (Ed.), *The psychology of learning and motivation* (Vol. 21, pp. 54-119). San Diego: Academic Press.

Schneider, W., & Shiffrin, R. M. (1977). Controlled and automatic human information processing: Detection, search, and attention. *Psychological Review, 84,* 1-66.

Schooler, J. W., Bendiksen, M., & Ambadar, A. (1997). Taking the middle line: Can we accommodate both fabricated and recovered memories of sexual abuse?

In M. A. Conway (Ed.), *Recovered memories and false memories* (pp. 251-292). New York: Oxford University Press.

Scott, A. (1995). *Stairway to the mind.* New York: Springer-Verlag.

Seamon, J. G., Marsh, R. L., & Brody, N. (1984). Critical importance of exposure duration for affective discrimination of stimuli that are not recognized. *Journal of Experimental Psychology: Learning, Memory, and Cognition, 10,* 465-469.

Searcy, J. H., & Bartlett, J. C. (1996). Inversion and processing of component and spatial relational information in faces. *Journal of Experimental Psychology: Human Perception and Performance, 22,* 904-915.

Seger, C. A. (1994). Implicit learning. *Psychological Bulletin, 115,* 163-196.

Seidenberg, M. S. (1985). Constraining models of word recognition. *Cognition, 20,* 169-190.

Seidenberg, M. S., & McClelland, J. L. (1989). A distributed, developmental model of word recognition and naming. *Psychological Review, 96,* 523-568.

Sejnowski, T. J., & Churchland, P. S. (1989). Brain and cognition. In M. I. Posner (Ed.), *Foundations of cognitive science* (pp. 301-356). Cambridge, MA: MIT Press.

Shah, P., & Miyake, A. (1999). Models of working memory: An introduction. In A. Miyake & P. Shah (Eds.), *Models of working memory: Mechanisms of active maintenance and executive control* (pp. 1-27). Cambridge, UK: Cambridge University Press.

Shallice, T. (1988). *From neuropsychology to mental structure.* Cambridge, UK: Cambridge University Press.

Shapiro, K. L. (1994). The attentional blink: The brain's "eyeblink." *Current Directions in Psychological Science, 3,* 86-89.

Shaywitz, B. A., Fletcher, J. M., & Shaywitz, S. E. (1995). Defining and classifying learning disabilities and attention-deficit/hyperactivity disorder. *Journal of Child Neurology, 10*(Suppl. 1), S50-S57.

Shepard, R. N. (1967). Recognition memory for words, sentences, and pictures. *Journal of Verbal Learning and Verbal Behavior, 6,* 156-163.

Shepard, R. N. (1984). Ecological constraints on internal representation: Resonant kinematics of perceiving, imagining, thinking, and dreaming. *Psychological Review, 91,* 417-447.

Shepard, R. N. (1990). *Mind sights.* New York: Freeman.

Shepard, R. N., & Cooper, L. A. (1983). *Mental images and their transformations.* Cambridge, MA: MIT Press.

Shepard, R. N., & Metzler, J. (1971). Mental rotation of three-dimensional objects. *Science, 171,* 701-703.

Sherry, D. F., & Schacter, D. L. (1987). The evolution of multiple memory systems. *Psychological Review, 94,* 439-454.

Shiffrin, R., & Schneider, W. (1977). Controlled and automatic human information processing: II. Perceptual learning, automatic attending, and a general theory. *Psychological Review, 84,* 127-190.

Shimamura, A. P. (1986). Priming effects in amnesia: Evidence for dissociable memory function. *Quarterly Journal of Experimental Psychology, 38A,* 619-644.

Shimamura, A. P. (1997). Neuropsychological factors associated with memory recollection: What can science tell us about reinstated memories? In J. D. Read & D. S. Lindsay (Eds.), *Recollections of trauma: Scientific research and clinical practice* (pp. 253-272). New York: Plenum.

Simon, H. A. (1969). *The sciences of the artificial.* Cambridge, MA: MIT Press.

Simon, H. A. (1990). Invariants of human behavior. *Annual Review of Psychology, 41,* 1-19.

Simon, H. A., & Chase, W. G. (1973). Skill in chess. *American Scientist, 61,* 394-403.

Simon, H. A., & Gilmartin, K. (1973). A simulation of memory for chess positions. *Cognitive Psychology, 5,* 29-46.

Simon, H. A., & Hayes, J. R. (1976). The understanding process: Problem isomorphs. *Cognitive Psychology, 8,* 165-190.

Simonton, D. K. (1988). *Scientific genius: A psychology of science.* Cambridge, UK: Cambridge University Press.

Simonton, D. K. (1997). Creative productivity: A predictive and explanatory model of career trajectories and landmarks. *Psychological Review, 104,* 66-89.

Sloman, S. A. (1996). The empirical case for two systems of reasoning. *Psychological Bulletin, 119,* 3-22.

Slovic, P., Fischhoff, B., & Lichtenstein, S. (1982). Facts versus fears: Understanding perceived risk. In D. Kahneman, P. Slovic, & A. Tversky (Eds.), *Judgment under uncertainty: Heuristics and biases* (pp. 463-489). New York: Cambridge University Press.

Smith, E. E. (1997). Infusing cognitive neuroscience into cognitive psychology. In R. L. Solso (Ed.), *Mind and brain sciences in the 21st century* (pp. 71-90). Cambridge, MA: MIT Press.

Smith, E. E., & Jonides, J. (1997). Working memory: A view from neuroimaging. *Cognitive Psychology, 33,* 5-42.

Smith, E. E., & Medin, D. L. (1981). *Categories and concepts.* Cambridge, MA: Harvard University Press.

Smith, E. E., Shoben, E. J., & Rips, L. J. (1974). Structure and process in semantic memory: A featural model for semantic decisions. *Psychological Review, 81,* 214-241.

Smith, N. V., & Tsimpli, I. M. (1995). *The mind of a savant: Language learning and modularity.* Cambridge, MA: Blackwell.

Smith, R. E., & Hunt, R. R. (1998). Presentation modality affects false memory. *Psychonomic Bulletin & Review, 5,* 710-715.

Smith, S. M., Brown, H. O., Toman, J. E. P., & Goodman, L. S. (1947). The lack of cerebral effects of d-Tubercurarine. *Anesthesiology, 8,* 1-14.

Smith, S. M., Glenberg, A., & Bjork, R. A. (1978). Environmental context and human memory. *Memory & Cognition, 6,* 342-353.

Smith, S. M., Ward, T. B., & Schumacher, J. S. (1993). Constraining effects of examples in a creative generation task. *Memory & Cognition, 21,* 837-845.

Smolensky, P. (1988). On the proper treatment of connectionism. *Behavioral & Brain Sciences, 11,* 1-74.

Spanos, N. P. (1996). *Multiple identities and false memories: A sociocognitive perspective.* Washington, DC: American Psychological Association.

Spear, N. E. (1979). Experimental analysis of infantile amnesia. In J. F. Kihlstrom & F. J. Evans (Eds.), *Functional disorders of memory* (pp. 75-102). Hillsdale, NJ: Lawrence Erlbaum.

Spelke, E., Hirst, W., & Neisser, U. (1976). Skills of divided attention. *Cognition, 4,* 215-230.

Spelke, E. S. (2000). Core knowledge. *American Psychologist, 55,* 1233-1243.

Sperling, G. (1960). The information available in brief visual presentation. *Psychological Monographs, 74*(Whole No. 498).

Sperry, R. W. (1980). Mind/brain interaction: Mentalism, yes—Dualism, no. *Neuroscience, 2,* 195-206.

Spiro, R. J. (1980). Accommodative reconstruction in prose recall. *Journal of Verbal Learning and Verbal Behavior, 19,* 84-95.

Spitzer, H., Desimone, R., & Moran, J. (1988). Increased attention enhances both behavioral and neuronal performance. *Science, 240,* 338-340.

Squire, L. R. (1992). Declarative and nondeclarative memory: Multiple brain systems supporting learning and memory. *Journal of Cognitive Neuroscience, 4,* 232-243.

Squire, L. R., Amaral, D. G., & Press, G. A. (1990). Magnetic resonance measurements of hippocampal formation and mammillary nuclei distinguish medial temporal lobe and diencephalic amnesia. *Journal of Neuroscience, 10,* 3106-3117.

Squire, L. R., Haist, F., & Shimamura, A. P. (1989). The neurology of memory: Quantitative assessment of retrograde amnesia in two groups of amnesic men. *Journal of Neuroscience, 9,* 828-839.

Stadler, M. A. (1993). Implicit serial learning: Questions inspired by Hebb (1961). *Memory & Cognition, 21,* 819-827.

Standing, L. (1973). Learning 10,000 pictures. *Quarterly Journal of Experimental Psychology, 25,* 207-222.

Stanovich, K. E. (1999). *Who is rational: Studies of individual differences in reasoning.* Mahwah, NJ: Lawrence Erlbaum.

Stanovich, K. E., Cunningham, A. E., & Feeman, D. J. (1984). Intelligence, cognitive skills, and early reading progress. *Reading Research Quarterly, 19,* 278-303.

Stanzel, F. K. (1984). *A theory of narrative.* Cambridge, UK: Cambridge University Press.

Staszewski, J. J. (1988). Skilled memory and expert mental calculation. In M. T. H. Chi, R. Glaser, & M. J. Farr (Eds.), *The nature of expertise* (pp. 71-128). Hillsdale, NJ: Lawrence Erlbaum.

Stein, N. L., & Glenn, C. G. (1979). An analysis of story comprehension in elementary school children. In R. O. Freedle (Ed.), *New directions in discourse processing* (pp. 53-120). Hillsdale, NJ: Lawrence Erlbaum.

Stemberger, J. P. (1985). An interactive activation model of language production. In A. Ellis (Ed.), *Progress in the psychology of language* (pp. 143-186). Hillsdale, NJ: Lawrence Erlbaum.

Sternberg, R. J. (1985). *Beyond IQ: A triarchic theory of human intelligence.* New York: Cambridge University Press.

Sternberg, R. J. (1988). *The nature of creativity: Contemporary psychological perspectives.* Cambridge, UK: Cambridge University Press.

Sternberg, R. J. (1999). Intelligence. In R. A. Wilson & F. C. Keil (Eds.), *The MIT encyclopedia of the cognitive sciences* (pp. 409-410). Cambridge, MA: MIT Press.

Sternberg, R. J., & Detterman, D. K. (1986). *What is intelligence? Contemporary viewpoints on its nature and definition.* Norwood, NJ: Ablex.

Sternberg, R. J., & Wagner, R. K. (Eds.). (1986). *Practical Intelligence: Nature and origins of competence in the everyday world.* New York: Cambridge University Press.

Sternberg, S. (1966). High-speed scanning in human memory. *Science, 153,* 652-654.

Sternberg, S. (1969). Memory scanning: Mental processes revealed by reaction time experiments. *American Scientist, 57,* 421-457.

Sternberg, S. (1995). Inferring mental operations from reaction-time data: How we compare objects. In D. Scarborough & S. Sternberg (Eds.), *An invitation to cognitive science,* Vol. 4: *Methods, models, and conceptual issues* (pp. 365-454). Cambridge, MA: MIT Press.

Stevens, A., & Coupe, P. (1978). Distortions in judged spatial relations. *Cognitive Psychology, 10,* 422-437.

Stillings, N. A., Feinstein, M. H., Garfield, J. L., Rissland, E. L., Rosenbaum, D. A., Weisler, S. E., & Baker-Ward, L. (1987). *Cognitive science: An introduction.* Cambridge, MA: MIT Press.

Stringer, C., & Gamble, C. (1993). *In search of the Neanderthals.* New York: Thames & Hudson.

Stromeyer, C. F., & Psotka, J. (1970). The detailed texture of eidetic images. *Nature, 225,* 346-349.

Stroop, J. R. (1935). Studies of interference in serial verbal reactions. *Psychological Monographs, 50,* 38-48.

Sutherland, N. S. (1968). Outlines of a theory of visual pattern recognition in animals and man. *Proceedings of the Royal Society of London, 171,* 297-317.

Taplin, J. E., & Staudenmeyer, H. (1973). Interpretation of abstract conditional sentences in deductive reasoning. *Journal of Verbal Learning and Verbal Behavior, 12,* 530-542.

Taylor, C. W., & Sacks, D. (1981). Facilitating lifetime creative processes: A think piece. *Gifted Child Quarterly, 25,* 116-118.

Terrace, H. S., Petitto, L. A., Sanders, R. J., & Bever, T. G. (1979). Can an ape create a sentence? *Science, 206,* 891-902.

Thomas, L. (1992). *The fragile species.* New York: Maxwell Macmillan International.

Thompson, C. P., Hermann, D. J., Read, D. J., Bruce, D., Payne, D. G., & Toglia, M. P. (Eds.). (1998). *Eyewitness memory: Theoretical and applied perspectives.* Mahwah, NJ: Lawrence Erlbaum.

Thompson, P. G. (1980). Margaret Thatcher: A new illusion. *Perception, 9,* 483-484.

Thompson, R. F. (2000). *The brain: A neuroscience primer* (3rd ed.). New York: Worth.

Thorndike, E. L. (1898). Animal intelligence: An experimental study of associative processes in animals. *Psychological Monographs, 2*(Whole No. 8).

Thorndike, R. L. (1973-1974). Reading as reasoning. *Reading Research Quarterly, 9,* 135-147.

Thorndyke, P. W. (1977). Cognitive structures in comprehension and memory of narrative discourse. *Cognitive Psychology, 9,* 77-110.

Tobias, P. V. (1987). The brain of *Homo habilis*: A new level of organization in cerebral evolution. *Journal of Human Evolution, 16,* 741-761.

Trabasso, T., & van den Broek, P. (1985). Causal thinking and the representation of narrative events. *Journal of Memory and Language, 24,* 612-630.

Traxler, M. J., & Gernsbacher, M. A. (1992). Improving written communication through minimal feedback. *Language and Cognitive Processes, 7,* 1-22.

Traxler, M. J., & Gernsbacher, M. A. (1993). Improving written communication through perspective taking. *Language and Cognitive Processes, 8,* 311-334.

Treisman, A. M. (1960). Contextual cues in encoding listening. *Quarterly Journal of Experimental Psychology, 12,* 242-248.

Treisman, A. M. (1970). Contextual cues in selective listening. *Quarterly Journal of Experimental Psychology, 12,* 242-248.

Treisman, A. M. (1987). Properties, parts, and objects. In K. Boff, L. Kaufman, & J. Thomas (Eds.), *Handbook of perception and performance* (pp. 159-198). New York: John Wiley.

Treisman, A. M., & Gelade, G. (1980). A feature-integration theory of attention. *Cognitive Psychology, 12,* 97-136.

Treisman, A. M., & Sato, S. (1990). Conjunction search revisited. *Journal of Experimental Psychology: Human Perceptual Performance, 16,* 459-478.

Tulving, E. (1962). Subjective organization in free recall of "unrelated" words. *Psychological Review, 69,* 344-354.

Tulving, E. (1983). *Elements of episodic memory.* New York: Oxford University Press.

Tulving, E. (1985). How many memory systems are there? *American Psychologist, 40,* 385-398.

Tulving, E., Mandler, G., & Baumal, R. (1964). Interaction of two sources of information in tachistoscopic word recognition. *Canadian Journal of Psychology, 18,* 62-71.

Tulving, E., & Pearlstone, Z. (1966). Availability versus accessibility of information in memory for words. *Journal of Verbal Learning and Verbal Behavior, 5,* 381-391.

Tulving, E., & Schacter, D. L. (1990). Priming and human memory systems. *Science, 247,* 301-306.

Tulving, E., & Thomson, D. M. (1973). Encoding specificity and retrieval processes in episodic memory. *Psychological Review, 80,* 352-373.

Tversky, A., & Kahneman, D. (1971). Belief in the law of small numbers. *Psychological Bulletin, 76,* 105-110.

Tversky, A., & Kahneman, D. (1973). Availability: A heuristic for judging frequency and probability. *Cognitive Psychology, 5,* 207-232.

Tversky, B. (1981). Distortions in memory for maps. *Cognitive Psychology, 13,* 407-433.

Tversky, B. (1991). Spatial mental models. *Psychology of Learning and Motivation, 27,* 109-145.

Valentine, T. (1988). Upside-down faces: A review of the effect of inversion upon face recognition. *British Journal of Psychology, 79,* 471-491.

van Dijk, T., & Kintsch, W. (1983). *Strategies of discourse comprehension.* New York: Academic Press.

VanLehn, K. (1996). Cognitive skill acquisition. *Annual Review of Psychology, 47,* 513-539.

Vickrey, C., & Neuringer, A. (2000). Pigeon reaction time, Hick's law, and intelligence. *Psychonomic Bulletin & Review, 7,* 284-291.

Vigliocco, G., Antonini, T., & Garrett, M. F. (1997). Grammatical gender is on the tip of Italian tongues. *Psychological Science, 8,* 314-317.

Vokey, J. R., & Read, J. D. (1985). Subliminal messages: Between the devil and the media. *American Psychologist, 40,* 1231-1239.

von Frisch, K. (1950). *Bees: Their vision, chemical senses, and language.* Ithaca, NY: Cornell University Press.

von Neumann, J. (1958). *The computer and the brain.* New Haven, CT: Yale University Press.

Wallas, G. (1926). *The art of thought.* New York: Harcourt Brace.

Wang, S. C. (2000). In search of Einstein's genius. *Science, 289,* 1477.

Ward, S. L., Newcombe, N., & Overton, W. F. (1986). Turn left at the church, or three miles north: A study of direction giving and sex differences. *Environment & Behavior, 18,* 192-213.

Warren, R. M. (1970). Perceptual restoration of missing speech sounds. *Science, 167,* 392-393.

Warrington, E. K. (1985). Agnosia: The impairment of object recognition. In P. J. Vinken, G. W. Bruyn, & H. L. Klawans (Eds.), *Handbook of clinical neurology* (pp. 333-349). New York: Elsevier Science.

Warrington, E. K., & Shallice, T. (1972). Neuropsychological evidence of visual storage in short-term memory tasks. *Quarterly Journal of Experimental Psychology, 24,* 30-40.

Warrington, E. K., & Shallice, T. (1984). Category specific semantic impairments. *Brain, 107,* 829-854.

Warrington, E. K., & Weiskrantz, L. (1970). Amnesia: Consolidation or retrieval? *Nature, 228,* 628-630.

Warrington, K. K. (1982). Neuropsychological studies of object recognition. *Philosophical Transactions of the Royal Society of London, 298B,* 13-33.

Wason, P. C. (1968). On the failure to eliminate hypotheses: A second look. In P. C. Wason & P. N. Johnson-Laird (Eds.), *Thinking and reasoning* (pp. 44-75). New York: Penguin.

Wason, P. C., & Johnson-Laird, P. N. (1972). *Psychology of reasoning: Structure and content.* Cambridge, MA: Harvard University Press.

Waters, G. S., Rochon, E., & Caplan, D. (1992). The role of high-level speech planning in rehearsal: Evidence from patients with apraxia of speech. *Journal of Memory and Language, 31,* 54-73.

Watson, J. B. (1924). *Behaviorism.* New York: Norton.

Waugh, N. C., & Norman, D. A. (1965). Primary memory. *Psychological Review, 72,* 89-104.

Wechsler, D. (1981). The psychometric tradition: Developing the Wechsler Adult Intelligence Scale. *Contemporary Educational Psychology, 6,* 82-85.

Weisberg, R. W. (1986). *Creativity: Genius and other myths.* New York: Freeman.

Weisberg, R. W., & Alba, J. W. (1981). An examination of the alleged role of "fixation" in the solution of several "insight" problems. *Journal of Experimental Psychology: General, 110,* 169-192.

Weiskrantz, L. (1986). *Blindsight: A case study and its implications.* Oxford, UK: Oxford University Press.

Weiskrantz, L., & Warrington, E. K. (1979). Conditioning in amnesic patients. *Neuropsychologia, 17,* 187-194.

Wells, G. L. (1993). What do we know about eyewitness identification? *American Psychologist, 48,* 553-571.

Wells, G. L., & Olson, E. A. (2001). The other-race effect in eyewitness identification: What do we do about it? *Psychology, Public Policy, and Law, 7,* 230-246.

Wertheimer, M. (1959). *Productive thinking.* New York: Harper & Row.

Whittlesea, B. W. A., & Dorken, M. D. (1997). Implicit learning: Indirect, not unconscious. *Psychonomic Bulletin & Review, 4,* 63-67.

Wickelgren, W. A. (1974). *How to solve problems: Elements of a theory of problems and problem solving.* San Francisco: Freeman.

Wickens, C. D. (1980). The structure of attentional resources. In R. Nickerson (Ed.), *Attention and performance* (Vol. 8, pp. 239-257). Hillsdale, NJ: Lawrence Erlbaum.

Wickens, D. D. (1972). Characteristics of word encoding. In A. W. Melton & E. Martin (Eds.), *Coding processes in human memory* (pp. 191-215). New York: Winston.

Wickens, D. D., Dalezman, R. E., & Eggemeier, F. T. (1976). Multiple encoding of word attributes in memory. *Memory & Cognition, 4,* 307-310.

Wierzbicka, A. (1985). The double life of a bilingual. In R. Sussex & J. Zubrzycki (Eds.), *Polish people and culture in Australia* (pp. 187-223). Canberra: Australian National University.

Witte, S. P. (1987). Pre-text and composing. *College Composition and Communication, 38,* 397-425.

Woodworth, R., & Sells, S. (1935). An atmosphere effect in formal syllogistic reasoning. *Journal of Experimental Psychology, 18,* 451-460.

Wynn, K. (1992). Addition and subtraction by human infants. *Nature, 358,* 749-750.

Xu, F., & Spelke, E. S. (2000). Large number discrimination in 6-month-old infants. *Cognition, 74,* B1-B11.

Yarbus, A. L. (1967). *Eye movements and vision* (B. Haigh, Trans.). New York: Plenum.

Yuille, J. C., & Daylen, J. (1998). The impact of traumatic events on eyewitness memory. In C. P. Thompson, D. J. Hermann, D. J. Read, D. Bruce, D. G. Payne, & M. P. Toglia (Eds.), *Eyewitness memory: Theoretical and applied perspectives* (pp. 155-178). Mahwah, NJ: Lawrence Erlbaum.

Zaragoza, M. S., & Mitchell, K. J. (1996). Repeated exposure to suggestion and the creation of false memories. *Psychological Science, 7,* 294-300.

Zola, S. M., & Squire, L. R. (2000). The medial temporal lobe and the hippocampus. In E. Tulving & F. I. M. Craik (Eds.), *The Oxford handbook of memory* (pp. 485-500). Oxford, UK: Oxford University Press.

Zola-Morgan, S., & Squire, L. R. (1990). Neurophysiological investigations of memory and amnesia: Findings from humans and nonhuman primates. In A. Diamond (Ed.), *The development and neural bases of higher cognitive functions* (pp. 434-456). New York: New York Academy of Sciences.

Zola-Morgan, S., Squire, L. R., & Amaral, D. G. (1986). Human amnesia and the medial temporal region: Enduring memory impairment following a bilateral lesion limited to field CA1 of the hippocampus. *Journal of Neuroscience, 6,* 2950-2967.

NAME INDEX

SUBJECT INDEX

SOURCES OF ILLUSTRATIONS

Figure 1.4. Reprinted with permission from McClelland, J. L., & Rumelhart, D. E. (Eds.). (1981). An interactive model of context effects in letter perception: I. An account of basic findings. *Psychological Review, 88*, 375-407.

Figure 1.5. Reprinted with permission from Posner, M. I., & Raichle, M. E. (1994). *Images of mind*. New York: Scientific American Library.

Figure 1.6. Reprinted with permission from Posner, M. I., & Raichle, M. E. (1994). *Images of mind*. New York: Scientific American Library.

Figure 2.9. Reprinted with permission from Posner, M. I., & Raichle, M. E. (1994). *Images of mind*. New York: Scientific American Library.

Figure 3.1. Reprinted with permission from Shepard, R. N. (1990). *Mind sights*. Reprinted with permission of Henry Holt and Company, LLC.

Figure 3.7. From Tulving, Mandler, and Baumel (1964). Reprinted with permission. Copyright © 1964. Canadian Psychological Association.

Figure 3.9. From Biederman, I. (1985). Human image understanding: Recent research and a theory. *Computer Vision, Graphics, and Image Processing, 32*, 29-73. Reprinted with permission from Academic Press.

Figure 3.10. From Biederman, I. (1985). Human image understanding: Recent research and a theory. *Computer Vision, Graphics, and Image Processing, 32*, 29-73. Reprinted with permission from Academic Press.

Figure 3.11. From Biederman, I. (1985). Human image understanding: Recent research and a theory. *Computer Vision, Graphics, and Image Processing, 32*, 29-73. Reprinted with permission from Academic Press.

Figure 3.12. From Bartlett, J. C., & Searcy, J. (1993). Inversion and configuration of faces. *Cognitive Psychology, 25*, 281-316. Reprinted with permission from Academic Press.

Figure 3.13. From Ladefoged, P. (1975). *A course in phonetics*. Reprinted with permission from Harcourt Brace Jovanovich.

Figure 3.14. From Liberman, A. M., Cooper, F., Shankweiler, D., & Studdert-Kennedy, M. (1970). Perception of the speech code. *Psychological Review, 74*, 431-459. Copyright © 1970 by the American Psychological Association. Reprinted with permission.

Figure 3.15. Liberman, A. M., Cooper, F., Shankweiler, D., & Studdert-Kennedy, M. (1970). Perception of the speech code. *Psychological Review, 74*, 431-459. Copyright © 1970 by the American Psychological Association. Reprinted with permission.

Figure 3.16. From Foss, D. J., & Hakes, D. T. (1978). Psycholinguistics: An introduction to the psychology of language. Reprinted with permission from Prentice Hall.

Figure 4.7. From Schneider, W., & Shiffrin, R. M. (1977). Controlled and automatic human information processing: Detection, search and attention. *Psychological Review, 84,* 1-66. Copyright © 1977 by the American Psychological Association. Reprinted with permission.

Figure 4.10. Adapted from Treisman, A. M., & Gelade, G. (1980). A feature-integration theory of attention. *Cognitive Psychology, 12,* 97-136. Reprinted with permission from Academic Press.

Figure 4.11. From Mack, A., & Rock, I. (1998). *Inattentional blindness.* Reprinted with permission from MIT Press.

Figure 5.4. From Squire, L. R., Haist, F., & Shimamura, A. P. (1989). The neurology of memory: Quantitative assessment of retrograde amneisa in two groups of amnesic men. *Journal of Neuroscience, 9,* 828-839.Copyright © 1989 by the Society of Neuroscience.

Figure 5.6. From Conway, M. A., Cohen, G., Stanhope, N. (1991). On the very long-term retention of knowledge acquired through formal education: Twelve years of cognitive psychology. *Journal of Experimental Psychology: General, 120,* 395-409. Copyright © 1991 by the American Psychological Association. Reprinted with permission.

Figure 5.8. From Wickens, D. D., Dalezman, R. E., & Eggemeier, F. T. (1976). Multiple encoding of word attributes in memory. *Memory & Cognition, 4,* 307-310. Reprinted with permission from Psychonomic Society Publications.

Figure 5.9. Reprinted with permission from Sternberg, S. (1966). High-speed scanning in human memory. *Science, 153,* 652-654. Copyright © 1966 from the American Association for the Advancement of Science.

Figure 5.11. From Smith, E. E., & Jonides, J. (1997). Working memory: A view from neuroimaging. *Cognitive Psychology, 33,* 5-42. Reprinted with permission from Academic Press.

Figure 6.1. Reprinted with permission from Squire, L. R., & Zola-Morgan, S. (1991). The medial temporal lobe memory system. *Science, 253,* 1380-1386. Copyright © 1991 by the American Association for the Advancement of Science.

Figure 7.1. From Brewer, W.F., & Treyens, J. C. (1981). Role of schemata in memory for places. *Cognitive Psychology 13,* 207-230. Reprinted with permission from Academic Press.

Box 7.2. From Bartlett, F. C. (1932). *Remembering: A study in experimental and social psychology.* Reprinted with permission from Cambridge University Press.

Figure 7.2. Adapted from Bergman, E. T., & Roediger, H. L., III (1999). Can Bartlett's repeated reproduction experiments be replicated? *Memory & Cognition, 27,* 937-947. Adapted with permission from the Psychonomic Society Publications.

Figure 7.3. From Bransford, J. D., & Johnson, M. K. (1972). Contextual prerequisites for understanding: Some investigations of comprehension and recall. *Journal of Verbal Learning and Verbal Behavior, 11,* 717-726. Reprinted with permission from Academic Press.

Figure 7.4. From Jenkins, J. J. (1974). Remember that old theory of memory? Well, forget it! *American Psychologist, 29,* 785-795. Copyright © by the American Psychological Association. Reprinted with permission.

Figure 7.5. From Jenkins, J. J. (1974). Remember that old theory of memory? Well, forget it! *American Psychologist, 29,* 785-795. Copyright © by the American Psychological Association. Reprinted with permission.

Figure 7.6. From Bransford, J. D., & Franks, J. J. (1971). Abstraction of linguistic ideas. *Cognitive Psychology, 2,* 331-350. Reprinted with permission from Academic Press.

Figure 7.8. From Loftus, E. F., & Palmer, J. C. (1974). Reconstruction of automobile destruction: An example of the interaction between language and memory. *Journal of Verbal Learning and Verbal Behavior, 13,* 585-589.

Figure 8.1. From Labov, W. (1973). The boundaries of words and their meanings. In C. J. N. Bailey & R. W. Shuy (Eds.) *New ways of analyzing variations in English* (pp. 340-373). Reprinted with permission from Georgetown University Press.

Table 8.1. From Rosch, E. H., & Mervis, C. B. (1975). Family resemblances: Studies in the internal structure of categories. *Cognitive Psychology, 7,* 573-605.

Figure 8.6. Reprinted with permission from Shepard and Metzler. Copyright © 1971. American Association for the Advancement of Science.

Figure 8.7. Reprinted with permission from Shepard and Metzler. Copyright © 1971. American Association for the Advancement of Science.

Figure 8.8. From Kosslyn, S. M. (1973). Scanning visual images: Some structural implications. *Perception and Psychophysics, 14,* 90-94. Reprinted with permission from the Psychonomic Society Publications.

Figure 8.12. From Collins, A. M., & Quillian, M. R. (1969). Retrieval time from semantic memory. *Journal of Verbal Learning and Verbal Behavior, 8,* 240-247. Reprinted with permission from Academic Press.

Figure 8.13. From Collins, A. M., & Quillian, M. R. (1969). Retrieval time from semantic memory. *Journal of Verbal Learning and Verbal Behavior, 8,* 240-247. Reprinted with permission from Academic Press.

Figure 9.1. From Moore, M. K., Borton, R., & Darby, B. L. (1978). Visual tracking in young infants: Evidence for object identity or object permanence. *Journal of Experimental Child Psychology, 25,* 183-198. Reprinted with permission from Academic Press.

Figure 9.3. From *Cognitive psychology and its applications* by John R. Anderson © 1980, 1985, 1990, 1995, and 2000 by Worth Publishers. Used with permission.

Figure 9.4. From Reed and Friedman, 1973, *Memory & Cognition, 1,* 157-163. Reprinted with permission from the Psychonomic Society Publications.

Figure 9.5. From Reed, S. K. (1972). Pattern recognition and categorization. *Cognitive Psychology, 3,* 383-407. Reprinted with permission from Academic Press.

Figure 9.7. From Reber, A. S. (1989). Implicit learning and tacit knowledge. *Journal of Experimental Psychology: General, 118,* 219-235. Copyright © 1989 by the American Psychological Association. Reprinted with permission.

Figure 9.9. From Cooke, N. J., & Breedin, S. D. (1994). Constructing naive theories of motion on the fly. *Memory & Cognition, 22,* 474-494. Reprinted with permission from the Psychonomic Society.

Figure 9.10. From Cooke, N. J., & Breedin, S. D. (1994). Constructing naive theories of motion on the fly. *Memory & Cognition, 22,* 474-494. Reprinted with permission from the Psychonomic Society.

Figure 9.11. From Chase, W. G., & Ericsson, K. A. (1981). Skilled memory. In J. R. Anderson (Ed.), *Cognitive skills and their acquisition.* Reprinted with permission from Lawrence Erlbaum.

Figure 9.12. From Chase, W. G., & Ericsson, K. A. (1981). Skilled memory. In J. R. Anderson (Ed.), *Cognitive skills and their acquisition.* Reprinted with permission from Lawrence Erlbaum.

Figure 9.13. From Neves, D. M., & Anderson, J. R. (1981). Knowledge compilation: Mechanisms for the automatization of cognitive skills. In J.R. Anderson (Ed.), *Cognitive skills and their acquisition.* Reprinted with permission from Lawrence Erlbaum.

Figure 10.3. From Rumelhart, D. E., & McClelland, J. L. (Eds.). (1986). *Parallel distributed processing; Explorations in the microstructure of cognition, (Vol. 1).* Reprinted with permission from MIT Press.

Figure 10.4. From Rumelhart, D. E., & McClelland, J. L. (Eds.). (1986). *Parallel distributed processing; Explorations in the microstructure of cognition, (Vol. 1).* Reprinted with permission from MIT Press.

Figure 10.6. From Marslen-Wilson, W. D., & Tyler, L. K. (1997). Dissociating types of mental computation. *Nature, 387,* 592-594. Reprinted with permission from *Nature*, Macmillan Magazines, Limited.

Figure 10.8. From Goodglass, H. (1993). *Understanding aphasia.* Reprinted with permission from Academic Press.

Figure 10.9. From Goodglass, H. (1993). *Understanding aphasia.* Reprinted with permission from Academic Press.

Figure 11.1. From Bock, J. K., & Levelt, W. (1994). Language production: Grammatical encoding. In M.A. Gernsbacher (Ed.), *Handbook of Psycholinguistics* (pp. 945-984). Reprinted with permission from Academic Press.

Figure 11.2. From Bock, J. K., & Levelt, W. (1994). Language production: Grammatical encoding. In M.A. Gernsbacher (Ed.), *Handbook of Psycholinguistics* (pp. 945-984). Reprinted with permission from Academic Press.

Figure 11.3. From Vigliocco, G., Antonini, T., & Garrett, M. F. (1997). Grammatical gender is on the tip of Italian tongues. *Psychological Science, 8,* 314-317. Reprinted with permission from Blackwell Publishers.

Figure 11.4. From Bock, J. K., & Levelt, W. (1994). Language production: Grammatical encoding. In M .A. Gernsbacher (Ed.), *Handbook of Psycholinguistics* (pp. 945-984). Reprinted with permission from Academic Press.

Figure 11.5. From Bock, J. K., & Levelt, W. (1994). Language production: Grammatical encoding. In M.A. Gernsbacher (Ed.), *Handbook of Psycholinguistics* (pp. 945-984). Reprinted with permission from Academic Press.

Table 11.1. From Glucksberg, S., & Danks, J. H. (1975). *Experimental psycholinguistics: An introduction.* Reprinted with permission from Lawrence Erlbaum.

Figure 11.6. From Dell, G. S. (1988). The retrieval of phonological forms in production: Tests of predictions from a connectionist model. *Journal of Memory & Language, 27,* 124-142. Reprinted with permission from Academic Press.

Figure 11.8. From Kellogg, R. T. (1994). *The psychology of writing.* Reprinted with permission from Oxford University Press.

Figure 11.9. From Caramazza, A. (1991). *Issues in reading, writing and speaking: A neuropsychological perspective.* Reprinted with kind permission of Kluwer Academic Publishers.

Figure 12.3. From Seidenberg, M. S. & McClelland, J. L. (1989). A distributed, developmental model of word recognition and naming. *Psychological Review, 96,* 523-568. Copyright © 1989 by the American Psychological Association. Reprinted with permission.

Figure 12.4. From Caramazza, A. (1991). *Issues in reading, writing and speaking: A neuropsychological perspective.* Reprinted with kind permission of Kluwer Academic Publishers.

Figure 12.5. From Clark, H. H., & Chase, W. G. (1972). On the process of comparing sentences against pictures. *Cognitive Psychology, 3,* 472-517. Reprinted with permission from Academic Press.

Table 12.1. From Gernsbacher, M. A. (1989). Mechanisms that improve referential access. *Cognition, 32,* 99-156. Reprinted with permission from Elsevier Science.

Figure 12.6. From Gernsbacher, M. A. (1989). Mechanisms that improve referential access. *Cognition, 32,* 99-156. Reprinted with permission from Elsevier Science.

Table 12.2. From Thorndyke, P. W. (1977). Cognitive structures in comprehension and memory of narrative discourse. *Cognitive Psychology, 9,* 77-110. Reprinted with permission from Academic Press.

Figure 13.1. From Kotovsky, K., & Fallside, D. (1989). Representation and transfer in problem solving. In D. Klahr & N. Kotovsky (Eds.). *Complex information processing: The impact of Herbert A. Simon.* Reprinted with permission from Lawrence Erlbaum.

Figure 13.3. From Kaplan, G. A. & Simon, H. A. (1990). In search of insight. *Cognitive Psychology, 22,* 374-419. Reprinted with permission from Academic Press.

Box 13.1. From Simon, H. A., & Hayes, J. R., (1976). The understanding process: Problem isomorphs. *Cognitive Psychology, 8*, 165-190. Reprinted with permission from Academic Press.

Figure 13.4. From Kaplan, G. A. & Simon, H. A. (1990). In search of insight. *Cognitive Psychology, 22,* 374-419. Reprinted with permission from Academic Press.

Box 13.2. From Gick, M. L, & Holyoak, K. J. (1980). Analogical problem solving. *Cognitive Pychology, 12*, 306-355. Reprinted with permission from Academic Press.

Box 13.3. From Gick, M. L, & Holyoak, K. J. (1980). Analogical problem solving. *Cognitive Pychology, 12*, 306-355. Reprinted with permission from Academic Press.

Figure 13.5. From Atwood, M. E., & Polson, P. G. (1976). A process model for water jar problems. *Cognitive Psychology, 8,* 191-216. Reprinted with permission from Academic Press.

Figure 13.6. From Chi, M. T. H., Feltovich, P. J., & Glaser, R. (1981). Categorization and representation of physics problems by experts and novices. *Cognitive Science, 5*, 121-152. Reprinted with permission of Ablex Publishing.

Figure 13.7. From Chi, M. T. H., Feltovich, P. J., & Glaser, R. (1981). Categorization and representation of physics problems by experts and novices. *Cognitive Science, 5*, 121-152. Reprinted with permission of Ablex Publishing.

Table 14.1. From Bourne, L. E., Jr., Dominowski, R. L., Loftus, E. F., & Healy, A. F. (1986). *Cognitive processes, 2nd ed.* Reprinted by permission of Pearson Education, Inc., Upper Saddle River, NJ.

Table 14.2. Adapted from Rips, L. J., & Marcus, S. L. (1977). Supposition and the analysis of conditional sentences. In M. A. Just & P. A. Carpenter (Eds.). *Cognitive processes in comprehension.* Reprinted with permission from Lawrence Erlbaum.

Table 14.3. From Rubinstein, M. F. (1975). *Patterns of problem solving.* Englewood Cliffs, NJ: Prentice-Hall.

Figure 14.4. From Kahneman, D., & Tversky, A. (1984). Choices, values, and frames. *American Psychologist, 39,* 341-350. Reprinted with permission from the American Psychological Association.

Figure 14.5. From Kahneman, D., & Tversky, A. (1984). Choices, values, and frames. *American Psychologist, 39,* 341-350. Reprinted with permission from the American Psychological Association.

Box 14.1. From Kahneman, D., & Tversky, A. (1982a). On the study of statistical intuitions. *Cognition, 11,* 123-141.

Box 14.2. From Kahneman, D., & Tversky, A. (1982b). The simulation heuristic. In D. Kahneman, P. Slovic, & A. Tversky (Eds.), *Judgment under uncertainty: Heuristics and biases* (pp. 201-208). Cambridge: Cambridge University Press.

Box 14.3. From Estes, W. K. (1976). The cognitive side of probability learning. *Psychological Review, 83,* 37-64. Reprinted with permission from the American Psychological Association.

Figure 15.3. Adapted with permission from Duncan, J., Seitz, R. J., Kolodny, J., Bor, D., Herzog, H., Ahmed, A., Newell, F., & Emslie, H. (2000). A neural basis for general intelligence. *Science, 289,* 457-460. Copyright © 2000 American Association for the Advancement of Science.

Figure 15.4. Reprinted with permission from Duncan, J., Seitz, R. J., Kolodny, J., Bor, D., Herzog, H., Ahmed, A., Newell, F., & Emslie, H. (2000). A neural basis for general intelligence. *Science, 289,* 457-460. Copyright © 2000 American Association for the Advancement of Science.

Figure 15.5. From Kaufman, A. S., Reynolds, C. R., & McLean, J. E. (1989). Age and WAIS-R intelligence in a national sample of adults in the 20 to 74 year age range: A cross-sectional analysis with educational level controlled. *Intelligence, 13*, 235-253. Reprinted with permission from Elsevier Science.

Figure 15.7. From Flynn, J. R. (1998). IQ gains over time: Toward finding the causes. In U. Neisser (Ed.), *The rising curve* (pp. 25-66). Reprinted with permission of the American Psychological Association.

Figure 15.9. From Linn, M. C., & Petersen, A. C. (1985). Emergence and characterization of sex differences in spatial ability: A meta-analysis. *Child Development, 56,* 1479-1498. Reprinted with permission from The Society for Research in Child Development.

Figure 15.11. From Kimura, D. (1999). *Sex and cognition.* Reprinted with permission from MIT Press.

Figure 15.12. From Kimura, D. (1999). *Sex and cognition.* Reprinted with permission from MIT Press.

Color Plate 1. From Peterson, S. E., Fox, P. T., Snyder, A. Z., & Raichle, M. E. (1990). Activation of extrastriate and frontal cortical areas by visual words and word-like stimuli. *Science, 249,* 1041-1044. Reprinted with permission from Elsevier Science.

Color Plate 2. From Haxby, J. V., Clark, V. P., & Courtney, S. M. (1997). Distributed hierarchical neural systems for visual memory in the human cortex. In *Connections, cognition, and Alzheimer's disease.* Reprinted with permission from Springer-Verlag.

Color Plate 5. From Martin, A., Wiggs, C. L., & Weisberg, J. A. (1997). Modulation of human temporal lobe activity by form, meaning, and experience. *Hippocampus, 7,* 587-593. Reprinted with permission of Wiley-Liss, Inc., a subsidiary of John Wiley & Sons, Inc.

Color Plate 6. From Fink, G. R., Markowitsch, H. J., Reinkemeir, M., Bruckbauer, J., Kessler, J., & Heiss, W. D. (1996). A PET-study of autobiographical memory recognition, *Journal of Neuroscience, 16,* 4275-4288. Reprinted with permission from the Society of Neuroscience.

Color Plate 7. From Neville, H. J., & Bavelier, D. (2000). Specificity and plasticity in neurocognitive development in humans. In M. Gazzaniga (Ed.), *The New Cognitive Neurosciences, 2nd edition.* Reprinted with permission from MIT Press.

ABOUT THE AUTHOR

Ronald T. Kellogg is Professor and Chair of the Department of Psychology at Saint Louis University. He holds degrees from the University of Iowa (B.S., psychology) and the University of Colorado (M.A. and Ph.D., experimental psychology). He also attended Stanford University as a National Science Foundation postdoctoral fellow. His past research has examined attention, long-term memory, concept learning, and cognitive processes in writing. His current work concerns the role of working memory in thought and text production and the effects of writing on memory retrieval.